New South Wales

Paul Harding
Michelle Bennett
Andrew Draffen
Sally Webb

LONELY PLANET PUBLICATIONS
Melbourne • Oakland • London • Paris

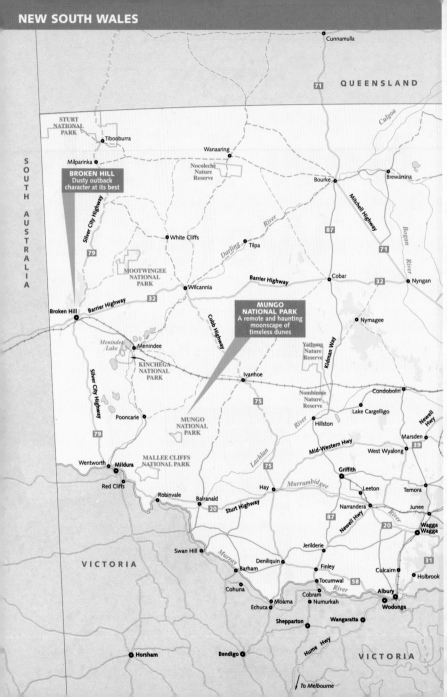

NEW SOUTH WALES

Cunnamulla

QUEENSLAND

Culgoa

STURT
NATIONAL
PARK

Tibooburra

SOUTH AUSTRALIA

Milparinka

Wanaaring

Nocoleche
Nature
Reserve

Bourke

Brewarrina

Mitchell Highway

Bogan River

BROKEN HILL
Dusty outback
character at its best

White Cliffs

Darling River

Tilpa

Silver City Highway

79

MOOTWINGEE
NATIONAL
PARK

Wilcannia

Barrier Highway

Cobar

32

Nyngan

71

Broken Hill

Barrier Highway

32

Cobb Highway

**MUNGO
NATIONAL PARK**
A remote and haunting
moonscape of
timeless dunes

Nymagee

Kidman Way

Menindee Lake

Menindee

KINCHEGA
NATIONAL
PARK

Yathong
Nature
Reserve

Ivanhoe

Nombinnie
Nature
Reserve

Condobolin

Silver City Highway

Pooncarie

MUNGO
NATIONAL
PARK

75

Lake Cargelligo

Hillston

Lachlan River

Marsden

Newell Hwy

39

MALLEE CLIFFS
NATIONAL PARK

Wentworth

Mildura

Mid-Western Hwy

West Wyalong

Red Cliffs

Robinvale

Balranald

20

Hay

Murrumbidgee

Griffith

Leeton

Temora

Sturt Highway

Narrandera

Junee

87

Newell Hwy

River

20

Wagga Wagga

Jerilderie

31

Swan Hill

Murray

Deniliquin

Finley

Culcairn

Holbrook

Barham

Tocumwal

58

River

Albury

Cohuna

Cobram

Numurkah

Wodonga

Echuca

Moama

Shepparton

Wangaratta

VICTORIA

Horsham

Bendigo

Hume Hwy

VICTORIA

To Melbourne

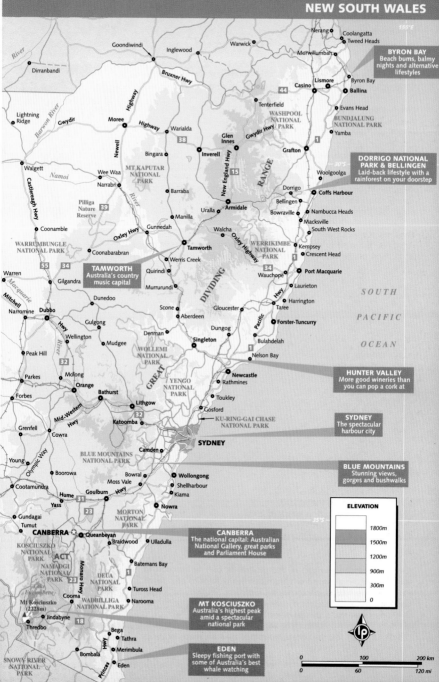

New South Wales
3rd edition – November 2000
First published – October 1994

Published by
Lonely Planet Publications Pty Ltd ABN 36 005 607 983
90 Maribyrnong St, Footscray, Victoria 3011, Australia

Lonely Planet Offices
Australia Locked Bag 1, Footscray, Victoria 3011
USA 150 Linden St, Oakland, CA 94607
UK 10a Spring Place, London NW5 3BH
France 1 rue du Dahomey, 75011 Paris

Photographs
All of the images in this guide are available for licensing from
Lonely Planet Images.
email: lpi@lonelyplanet.com.au

Front cover photograph
Artist Pete Browne has transformed his humble Volkswagon Beetle into
an outback masterpiece – Silverton, New South Wales (Ross Barnett)

ISBN 0 86442 706 9

text & maps © Lonely Planet 2000
photos © photographers as indicated 2000

Printed by The Bookmaker International Ltd
Printed in China

Contents – Text

1

AROUND SYDNEY

HUNTER VALLEY

NORTH COAST

NEW ENGLAND

Contents – Maps

5

SOUTH COAST

AUSTRALIAN CAPITAL TERRITORY

EASTERN ISLANDS

MAP LEGEND   back page

MAP INDEX

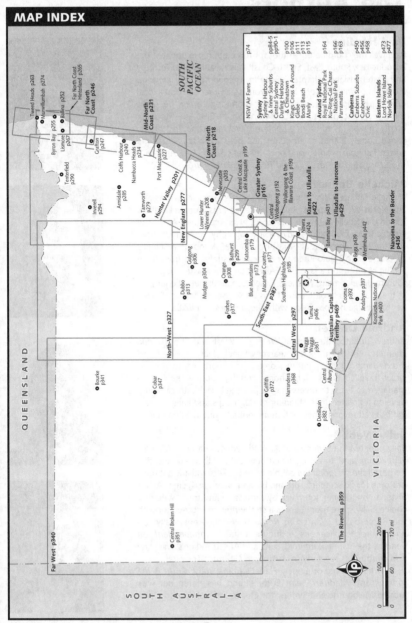

SOUTH PACIFIC OCEAN

NSW Air Fares	p/74

Sydney
Sydney Harbour & Inner Sydney — pp84–5
Central Sydney — pp90–1
Darling Harbour & Chinatown — p100
Kings Cross & Around — p106
Glebe — p111
Bondi Beach — p113
Manly — p115

Around Sydney
Royal National Park — p164
Ku-Ring-Gai Chase National Park — p166
Parramatta — p163

Canberra
Canberra Suburbs — p450
Canberra — p456
Civic — p458

Eastern Islands
Lord Howe Island — p473
Norfolk Island — p477

QUEENSLAND

Tweed Heads p263
Murwillumbah p274
Ballina p252
Byron Bay p255
Lismore p267
Far North Coast p246
Far North Coast Hinterland p265
Mid-North Coast p231
Grafton p247
Tenterfield p290
Coffs Harbour p240
Nambucca Heads p234
Port Macquarie p227
Amidale p285
Imverell p294
Tamworth p279
Hunter Valley p201
New England p277
Lower North Coast p218
Newcastle p203
Central Coast & Lake Macquarie p195
Greater Sydney p161
Central p192
Wollongong & the Illawarra Coast p190
Kiama to Ulladulla p422
Lower Hunter Wineries p208
Nowra p424
Batemans Bay p431
Ulladulla to Narooma p429
Dubbo p313
Gulgong p306
Mudgee p304
Orange p308
Bathurst p299
Katoomba p173
Macarthur Country p171
Blue Mountains p185
Southern Highlands
South-East p387
Bega p439
Merimbula p442
Narooma to the Border p436
North-West p327
Forbes p317
Central West p297
Coona p392
Australian Capital Territory p469
Jindabyne p397
Kosciuszko National Park p400
Bourke p341
Cobar p347
Griffith p372
Narrandera p368
Wagga Wagga p361
Central Albury p416
Tumut p406
Central Broken Hill p351
Deniliquin p382
Far West p340
The Riverina p359

SOUTH AUSTRALIA

VICTORIA

200 km
120 mi
0   100
0   60

The Authors

Paul Harding

Paul was the coordinating author for this edition. He updated the introductory, South-East, South Coast, Australian Capital Territory and Eastern Islands chapters. Born in Melbourne, Paul grew up mostly in country Victoria before working as a reporter on a local newspaper. Upon throwing in that promising career, he spent three years backpacking in Europe and South-East Asia, stopping briefly to work as editor of a London travel magazine. In 1996 he joined Lonely Planet as an editor and now works as a full-time writer. Paul has worked on Lonely Planet's *South-East Asia on a shoestring, India, Australia* and *Read this First: Europe.*

Michelle Bennett

Michelle updated the Hunter Valley, North Coast, New England and North-West chapters. Raised on her parents' farm in Driffield, Victoria, Michelle learnt to milk cows at an early age. At 17 she headed to Melbourne to study social geography. After graduating, she travelled throughout Asia and Europe. A job at a friend's graphic-design studio lured her back to Australia and from there she went on to run a jazz club. After gaining a Masters degree in tourism development, Michelle joined Lonely Planet. She jumped at the chance to update part of this book, especially as it allowed her to indulge her obsession with guesthouses and B&Bs.

Andrew Draffen

Andrew updated the Central West, Far West and The Riverina chapters. Andrew usually researches Lonely Planet's *Brazil* and *Rio de Janeiro* guides, but welcomed the opportunity to visit the lesser-travelled areas of his home country. During the trip he managed to learn to reverse-angle park; get back into camping; develop a greater understanding of slag heaps and lines of lode; get bogged several times; and figure out a Countrylink timetable.

Sally Webb

Sally updated the Sydney and Around Sydney chapters. After 10 years living and travelling in Europe, Sally still called Australia home, so she swapped the cobblestoned streets and ancient ruins of Rome for skyscrapers, surf and harbour views in Sydney. An art historian by training, journalist by profession and travel writer by choice, Sally spent four years as a staff writer and sub-editor with the Rome-based *Wanted in Rome* news magazine. Sally has written for publications including Britain's *Independent on Sunday*, the *Qantas Club* magazine and Ansett Airline's *Vive*. She also contributes regularly to *Australian Gourmet Traveller.*

Sally has worked on Lonely Planet's *Rome, Italy, Corfu & the Ionians* and *Mediterranean Europe*, and has eaten her way around Melbourne and Sydney for *Out to Eat* restaurant guides.

FROM THE AUTHORS

Paul Harding

Thanks to Sue and Steve for showing me how interesting Canberra can be and making my stay such an enjoyable one. As usual, much appreciation goes to the staff at many tourist offices – some can't do enough to help. Particular mention goes to those at Tumut, the Shoalhaven Visitor Centre, Cooma and Yass. To anyone else who proffered information and advice, official or not, thank you.

Thanks also to Jane, Rebecca, Cherry and Anna at Lonely Planet for their help throughout.

Michelle Bennett

Big thanks to Jane Hart (for giving me the gig), and Kath Dolan and the marvellous Mercury department at Lonely Planet. Thanks also to Mr Chicken for his support and many airport pick-ups/drop-offs. And to Cal, Pete and Chico for their wonderful hospitality while I was writing up.

Andrew Draffen

Thanks to all the helpful park rangers, staff in tourist information centres and travellers willing to share information and experiences. Special thanks to my daughter Gabriela for her company on the trip, Claire Minty (Lake Mungo), Teresa Lever (Corowa), Jeff Nicholson (Forbes), Peter and Sally Ware (Hay), Max and Peter (Broken Hill), and the many 'grey nomads' who offered advice and cuppas.

Sally Webb

I am indebted to my sister Anna, who calmly put up with my computer and possessions taking over her previously well-organised home. A big thank you is due to Ali Moore, David Mackey, Emi Weir and Fabrice Le Calvez for their hospitality and friendship, and to Julia Gauci at Tourism NSW for valuable information. Thanks also to Simon Richmond, Matthew Joscelyne, Jo Vintiner and other Sydneysiders by birth or adoption who shared the secrets of their city with me.

This Book

Authors Paul Harding, Michelle Bennett, Andrew Draffen and Sally Webb researched their home territory to update this 3rd edition of *New South Wales*. They built on the efforts of Tom Smallman and David Willett, who were responsible for the 2nd edition, and Jon Murray, who wrote the original book.

FROM THE PUBLISHER

This edition was produced in Lonely Planet's Melbourne office. Cherry Prior coordinated the editing, with help from Anne Mulvaney, Bruce Evans, Kim Hutchins, Jocelyn Harewood and Hilary Ericksen. Anna Judd coordinated the design, layout and mapping, assisted by Jane Hart (design), Kusnandar (mapping and climate charts) and Brett Moore (map checks).

Joanne Newell assisted with indexing, Tim Uden provided layout support, Bruce Cameron wrote the section on travel for people with disabilities, Matt King coordinated the illustrations, Pablo Gastar, Kate Nolan, Trudi Canavan, Martin Harris and Ann Jeffree provided illustrations, Valerie Tellini from Lonely Planet Images organised the photographs, Paul Clifton checked information for gay and lesbian travellers, and Vicki Beale and the design department were responsible for the cover.

Thanks

Many thanks to the travellers who used the last edition and wrote to us with helpful hints, useful advice and interesting anecdotes:

Aimee Said, Alan Weiley, Alistair Kelly, Allison Horsfell, Angeline de Toode, Anne Sissel Aaboen, Annette Ehret, Arthur Schultz, Barry Kavanagh, Beccy Ford, Beryl Gallard, Bethan Smith, Bill & Misao Rogers, Bob Reed, Brad Scholz, Brian Kelly, Camilla Kinchin, Carol McKie, Caroline Grieves, Catherine Lawler, Catherine Wiles, Christine Heard, Cindy Mousseau, Clare White, Colleen McMahon, D Grant, Dag Sjoberg, Damon Pearce, Damon Veitch, Daniel Cole, Danny Byrne, Derek Dupuis, Dirk van der Hoek, Dominique Staehli, Dorothy Bremner, Doug McKenzie, Dr Subhash Jaireth, E G Trowbridge, Edward Oostendorp, Emma Davies, Emma York, Eric Scott, Erik Wilde, Fabian Schulte-Terboven, Fiona & Mike Saint, Fiona K Priestley, Fred Wohlers, Gary Conlan, Gavin Samuels, Glenn Horlick, Hannah Taylor, Hayley Cameron, Helen Proud, Howie Thompson, Ivan & Barbara Stander, Jan Hyde, Jan Wlid, Jane Dunn, Jeanette Pope, Jo Pearce, Joe Hartshorn, John Atwood, John Penlington, Jon Wilson, Josie Amadon-Bedfond, Julie Larkin, June Laux, Karrie Eelhart, Kate Wright, Kathy Friend, Keith Brinkworth, Kerry Gray, Kim Hamblin, Kirsty Hull, Kristi & Jeff Layton, L Hertog, Lauren Archer, Leanne Jones, Les White, Linden News, Lisa Beringer, Lizzy Moon, Lorna Holden, Lyn Murphy, Marcel Hoevenaars, Marga & Theo van der Berg, Margaret Toohey, Marion Juenger, Marius Trippestad Loken, Mark Oçarrigan, Mary Maley, Mary-Anne & Bill Collins, Marylse Veld, Matt Duce, Maurizio Berlini, Maxine McTavish, Megan Grudem, Melanie Bettle, Melodee McCoy-James, Michael Pulman, Michael Ward, Natalie Mundy, Natasha Rowe, Nicola Downey, Paul Boundy, Paul Wagner, Peter Dixon, Peter Matthews, Peter Wise, Phil & Di Roberts, Phil Stiffwick, Prof Dr Andreas Pospischil, R Lewis, Rebecca Alsbury, Richard Palk, Rob Laarman, Ron Schmal, Rosie Fleming, Rowan Rafferty, Roxanne Missingham, Ruth Callan, Sarah Helliar, Sarah Thorne, Steve Langley, Suzanne French, T & T Smallwood, Thomas J LeCompte, Toni Payne, Tony Jenkins, Tony McLeod, Ulf Schlierenhlaemper, Zina McIlraith.

Foreword

ABOUT LONELY PLANET GUIDEBOOKS

The story begins with a classic travel adventure: Tony and Maureen Wheeler's 1972 journey across Europe and Asia to Australia. Useful information about the overland trail did not exist at that time, so Tony and Maureen published the first Lonely Planet guidebook to meet a growing need.

From a kitchen table, then from a tiny office in Melbourne (Australia), Lonely Planet has become the largest independent travel publisher in the world, an international company with offices in Melbourne, Oakland (USA), London (UK) and Paris (France).

Today Lonely Planet guidebooks cover the globe. There is an ever-growing list of books and there's information in a variety of forms and media. Some things haven't changed. The main aim is still to help make it possible for adventurous travellers to get out there – to explore and better understand the world.

At Lonely Planet we believe travellers can make a positive contribution to the countries they visit – if they respect their host communities and spend their money wisely. Since 1986 a percentage of the income from each book has been donated to aid projects and human rights campaigns.

Updates Lonely Planet thoroughly updates each guidebook as often as possible. This usually means there are around two years between editions, although for more unusual or more stable destinations the gap can be longer. Check the imprint page (following the colour map at the beginning of the book) for publication dates.

Between editions up-to-date information is available in two free newsletters – the paper *Planet Talk* and email *Comet* (to subscribe, contact any Lonely Planet office) – and on our Web site at www.lonelyplanet.com. The *Upgrades* section of the Web site covers a number of important and volatile destinations and is regularly updated by Lonely Planet authors. *Scoop* covers news and current affairs relevant to travellers. And, lastly, the *Thorn Tree* bulletin board and *Postcards* section of the site carry unverified, but fascinating, reports from travellers.

Correspondence The process of creating new editions begins with the letters, postcards and emails received from travellers. This correspondence often includes suggestions, criticisms and comments about the current editions. Interesting excerpts are immediately passed on via newsletters and the Web site, and everything goes to our authors to be verified when they're researching on the road. We're keen to get more feedback from organisations or individuals who represent communities visited by travellers.

Lonely Planet gathers information for everyone who's curious about the planet – and especially for those who explore it first-hand. Through guidebooks, phrasebooks, activity guides, maps, literature, newsletters, image library, TV series and Web site we act as an information exchange for a worldwide community of travellers.

Research Authors aim to gather sufficient practical information to enable travellers to make informed choices and to make the mechanics of a journey run smoothly. They also research historical and cultural background to help enrich the travel experience and allow travellers to understand and respond appropriately to cultural and environmental issues.

Authors don't stay in every hotel because that would mean spending a couple of months in each medium-sized city and, no, they don't eat at every restaurant because that would mean stretching belts beyond capacity. They do visit hotels and restaurants to check standards and prices, but feedback based on readers' direct experiences can be very helpful.

Many of our authors work undercover, others aren't so secretive. None of them accept freebies in exchange for positive write-ups. And none of our guidebooks contain any advertising.

Production Authors submit their raw manuscripts and maps to offices in Australia, USA, UK or France. Editors and cartographers – all experienced travellers themselves – then begin the process of assembling the pieces. When the book finally hits the shops, some things are already out of date, we start getting feedback from readers and the process begins again ...

WARNING & REQUEST

Things change – prices go up, schedules change, good places go bad and bad places go bankrupt – nothing stays the same. So, if you find things better or worse, recently opened or long since closed, please tell us and help make the next edition even more accurate and useful. We genuinely value all the feedback we receive. Julie Young coordinates a well travelled team that reads and acknowledges every letter, postcard and email and ensures that every morsel of information finds its way to the appropriate authors, editors and cartographers for verification.

Everyone who writes to us will find their name in the next edition of the appropriate guidebook. They will also receive the latest issue of *Planet Talk*, our quarterly printed newsletter, or *Comet*, our monthly email newsletter. Subscriptions to both newsletters are free. The very best contributions will be rewarded with a free guidebook.

Excerpts from your correspondence may appear in new editions of Lonely Planet guidebooks, the Lonely Planet Web site, *Planet Talk* or *Comet*, so please let us know if you *don't* want your letter published or your name acknowledged.

Send all correspondence to the Lonely Planet office closest to you:

Australia: Locked Bag 1, Footscray, Victoria 3011
USA: 150 Linden St, Oakland, CA 94607
UK: 10A Spring Place, London NW5 3BH
France: 1 rue du Dahomey, 75011 Paris

Or email us at: talk2us@lonelyplanet.com.au

For news, views and updates see our Web site: www.lonelyplanet.com

HOW TO USE A LONELY PLANET GUIDEBOOK

The best way to use a Lonely Planet guidebook is any way you choose. At Lonely Planet we believe the most memorable travel experiences are often those that are unexpected, and the finest discoveries are those you make yourself. Guidebooks are not intended to be used as if they provide a detailed set of infallible instructions!

Contents All Lonely Planet guidebooks follow roughly the same format. The Facts about the Destination chapters or sections give background information ranging from history to weather. Facts for the Visitor gives practical information on issues like visas and health. Getting There & Away gives a brief starting point for re-searching travel to and from the destination. Getting Around gives an overview of the transport options when you arrive.

The peculiar demands of each destination determine how subsequent chapters are broken up, but some things remain constant. We always start with background, then proceed to sights, places to stay, places to eat, entertainment, getting there and away, and getting around information – in that order.

Heading Hierarchy Lonely Planet headings are used in a strict hierarchical structure that can be visualised as a set of Russian dolls. Each heading (and its following text) is encompassed by any preceding heading that is higher on the hierarchical ladder.

Entry Points We do not assume guidebooks will be read from beginning to end, but that people will dip into them. The traditional entry points are the list of contents and the index. In addition, however, some books have a complete list of maps and an index map illustrating map coverage.

There may also be a colour map that shows highlights. These highlights are dealt with in greater detail in the Facts for the Visitor chapter, along with planning questions and suggested itineraries. Each chapter covering a geographical region usually begins with a locator map and another list of highlights. Once you find something of interest in a list of highlights, turn to the index.

Maps Maps play a crucial role in Lonely Planet guidebooks and include a huge amount of information. A legend is printed on the back page. We seek to have complete consistency between maps and text, and to have every important place in the text captured on a map. Map key numbers usually start in the top left corner.

Although inclusion in a guidebook usually implies a recommendation we cannot list every good place. Exclusion does not necessarily imply criticism. In fact there are a number of reasons why we might exclude a place – sometimes it is simply inappropriate to encourage an influx of travellers.

Introduction

Australia's 'original' state, New South Wales (NSW), is also the country's most diverse. Where else can you experience true Australian outback, hike or ski in alpine country, swim or surf along an almost unbroken coastline of superb ocean beaches and party all night in the nation's liveliest city?

The early European history of Australia is also the history of NSW – British explorer Captain James Cook named his 'discovery' New South Wales in 1770 when he sailed up the east coast and landed at Botany Bay. The Aborigines, however, had been leading a peaceful, bountiful existence on the coast and the ranges long before.

For the traveller, Australia's original convict settlement is still the most popular international gateway. Cosmopolitan Sydney, with its beautiful harbour setting and easy-going lifestyle, is one of the world's great cities, showcased by the 2000 Olympic Games. Within easy reach are many beaches and forests, the spectacular Blue Mountains and the wineries of the Hunter Valley.

The coastal route from Sydney to Queensland is deservedly popular and firmly entrenched on the backpacker trail. It passes through resort towns like Byron Bay and an endless string of superb, often deserted beaches, and offers access to the national parks of the Great Dividing Range. Australia's largest ski-fields are in the Kosciuszko National Park, in the south-east of NSW, but this is also a superb place in summer for walking, mountain biking, fishing and horse riding.

The south coast is just as scenic as the north coast but less developed. Stunning

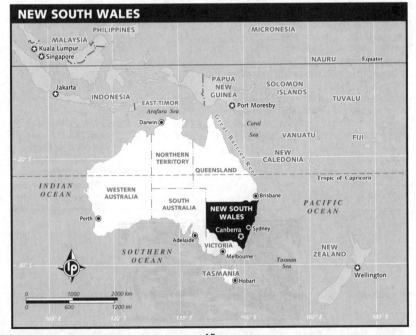

national parks creep right up to the coast here and you'll encounter more tiny bays, secluded beaches, teeming wetlands and forest areas than you could hope to explore on a single visit.

On the Great Dividing Range is a series of high tablelands, including New England, with its spectacular gorges and waterfalls. West of the range you'll meet rural Australia. There are some fine old towns in the rich farmlands of the western slopes and another winery area around Mudgee. Farther west are the vast landscapes of the great plains, merging into the red soil of the baking outback in the north-west. South of the plains is the Riverina with its lazy rivers, fruit-growing areas and red gum forests.

Many national parks have World Heritage status; some are wilderness areas where possibilities for adventure activities abound.

Finally, carved out of an area just north of the Snowy Mountains is the Australian Capital Territory. Here you'll find Australia's capital, Canberra, a fascinating, planned city of parks, gardens and government buildings, with a great cafe and restaurant scene.

From ancient Aboriginal sites to atmospheric country pubs, practically everything that's considered 'typically Australian' can be found in NSW.

Facts about New South Wales

HISTORY
Aboriginal Australia

Aboriginal (which literally means 'indigenous') society in Australia has the longest continuous cultural history in the world, with origins dating to the last ice age. Although mystery shrouds many aspects of Australian prehistory, it seems almost certain that the first humans came here across the sea from South-East Asia. Heavy-boned people whom archaeologists call 'Robust' are believed to have arrived around 70,000 years ago, and more slender 'Gracile' people around 50,000 years ago. Gracile people are the ancestors of Australian Aboriginal people. Archaeological evidence suggests that the descendants of these settlers colonised the entire continent within a few thousand years.

They were the first people in the world to manufacture polished edge-ground stone tools, cremate their dead and engrave and paint representations of themselves and the animals they hunted.

When Europeans arrived in New South Wales (NSW) in the late 18th century there were some 750,000 Aborigines in Australia, speaking a total of 250 regional languages – many of these languages as distinct from each other as English is from Chinese.

Around what is now Sydney there were approximately 3000 Aborigines using three main languages, although there were several dialects and groups. Ku-Ring-Gai was spoken on the North Shore, Dharawal along the coast south of Botany Bay, and Dharug and its dialects were spoken across the plains into the lower Blue Mountains. Some of the largest groups in what is now NSW, such as the Wiradjuri and Kamilaroi, were farther west.

Aboriginal society, based on family groups rather than large political units, couldn't present a united front to the European colonisers, and in the crude realpolitik of the late 18th century, the British assumed that a people that didn't defend its land had no right to that land. Some Aborigines were driven away by force and thousands succumbed to disease. Others left their tribal lands voluntarily to travel to the fringes of settled areas to obtain new commodities such as steel and cloth, and, once there, encountered hitherto unknown substances such as tea, tobacco, alcohol and opium.

At a local level, individuals resisted the encroachment of settlers, but such resistance only temporarily postponed the inevitable.

The Founding of New South Wales

The inhospitable north and west coasts of Australia had been charted in the 1640s by Dutch explorer Abel Tasman, who had named the continent New Holland. It was not until 1770 that Captain James Cook, the British explorer, sailed up the fertile east coast, landing at Botany Bay and naming the area New South Wales.

Following the American Revolution, Britain was no longer able to transport convicts to North America. With jails and prison hulks already overcrowded, it was essential that an alternative be found quickly. In 1779 Joseph Banks, botanist on Cook's 1770 expedition and by then president of the prestigious Royal Society, suggested NSW as a fine site for a colony of thieves, and in 1786 Lord Sydney announced that the king had decided upon Botany Bay as a place for a convict settlement. That the continent was already inhabited was not considered of any significance.

In January 1788 the First Fleet sailed into Botany Bay under the command of Captain Arthur Phillip, who was to be the colony's first governor. Phillip was disappointed with the landscape and ventured north to find a more suitable landfall. In a famous letter to the British Home Secretary Lord Sydney, Phillip advised that he and his crew had found 'the finest harbour in the world'.

The fleet, comprising eight ships carrying about 750 male and female convicts, 400 sailors, four companies of marines and enough livestock and supplies for two years, headed for Sydney Cove.

The early settlement did it hard. The soils around Sydney Cove proved poor and the tools were worse, so the settlers were dependent on their stores and supply ships from England. None came for 2½ years.

Shortly after a supply ship relieved the threat of famine in 1790, the Second Fleet struggled into Sydney Cove, bringing few supplies but another 740 convicts.

For the convicts, NSW was a harsh and horrible place. The reasons for transportation were often minor, and the sentences, of no less than seven years with hard labour, were tantamount to life sentences as there was little hope of returning home. Whippings were common.

Hunger to the point of weakness afflicted most of the convicts, while the need for strong labourers to grow food remained urgent. A farm was established at Parramatta (today's Parramatta Rd basically follows the old cart track), where the soil was more fertile, and gradually the situation improved.

The Early Colony

As crops began to yield, NSW became less dependent on Britain for food. However, there were huge social gulfs in the fledgling colony: Officers and their families were in control and clinging to a modicum of civilised British living; soldiers, free settlers and even emancipated convicts were beginning to eke out a living; yet the majority of the population was in chains, regarded as the dregs of humanity and living in squalor.

Phillip believed NSW wouldn't progress if the colony continued to rely on convict labour. He believed prosperity depended on attracting free settlers, to whom convicts could be assigned as labourers, and on granting land to officers, soldiers and worthy emancipists (convicts who had served their time).

Phillip returned to England in 1792 and his second-in-command, Major Francis Grose, took over. Grose granted land to officers of the NSW Corps. With money, land and cheap labour at their disposal, the officers became exploitative, making huge profits at the expense of the small farmers.

To encourage convicts to work, the officers were given permission to pay them in rum. The officers quickly prospered and were soon able to buy shiploads of goods and resell them at huge profits. The colony was becoming an important port on trade routes, and whaling and sealing were increasing. The officers, who became known as the Rum Corps, met little resistance and grew richer and more arrogant.

A new governor, William Bligh, was appointed to restore order, but the bad temper that had resulted in a mutiny on the *Bounty* again caused his downfall. He suffered another rebellion and was arrested by the Rum Corps. This rebellion, known as the Rum Rebellion, was the final straw for the British government, which in 1809 dispatched Lieutenant Colonel Lachlan Macquarie with his own regiment and orders for the return to London of the NSW Corps.

It was John Macarthur, one of the officers involved in the Rum Rebellion, who saw the country's wool-growing potential and set about breeding a strain of merino sheep that would prosper here. He returned to England for nearly a decade for his part in the rebellion; while he was away his wife, Elizabeth, did much of the work.

Governor Macquarie, having broken the stranglehold of the Rum Corps, set about putting the colony to rights. He instituted a building program, employing talented convict architect Francis Greenway, several of whose buildings remain today (see Macquarie St in the Sydney chapter and Windsor in the Around Sydney chapter). Because hamlets along the flats of the Hawkesbury River were repeatedly flooded, Macquarie established five well-planned towns on higher ground around Windsor (see the Macquarie Towns Area in the Around Sydney chapter). He encouraged explorers to find a route across the Blue Mountains and, when they did, had a road across completed in just six months, then established the town of Bathurst on the plains beyond.

Macquarie also had the idea that convicts who had served their time should have rights as citizens, and he began appointing them to public positions.

The gentry of Sydney Cove wanted nothing to do with ex-cons or their children. Anti-emancipists, including John Macarthur, were outraged at what they saw as a social perversion and began carping about Macquarie's expensive public works programs and creating the impression that the colony was ungovernable. Many wealthier colonists were also annoyed that Macquarie's building programs were using all the available convicts, leaving them no free labour for their farms.

Macquarie, generally agreed to have been the best of the early governors, returned to England under a cloud in 1821. His reign had been a watershed for the colony. When he arrived it was a struggling penal settlement; when he left there was little doubt that a permanent and potentially wealthy colony had been established.

A New People

From the earliest days of NSW, Australian-born colonists saw themselves as different from the upper-crust British officers who ran the colony, and before long the children of convicts became a sizable proportion of the population. They were called Currency Lads and Lasses and considered themselves to be Australians. The power and money in the colony rested with people who had their sights set on making their name or their fortune and returning home. For the free-born, Australia *was* home.

Exploration & Expansion

By 1800 there were two small settlements in Australia – at Sydney and on Norfolk Island. While unknown areas on world maps were shrinking, most of Australia was still one big blank to Europeans. It was even suspected that it might be two large islands and it was hoped that there might be a vast sea in the centre.

George Bass charted the coast south of Sydney almost to the present location of Melbourne during 1797–98, and in the following year, with Matthew Flinders, he sailed around Van Diemen's Land (Tasmania), establishing that it was an island. Flinders went on in 1802 to sail right around Australia – he suggested that the continent should be called Australia rather than New Holland.

The Blue Mountains at first proved an impenetrable barrier, limiting the size of the colony, but in 1813 a path was forced through and the explorers Gregory Blaxland, William Wentworth and William Lawson reached the western plains. Soon after, George Evans led two expeditions across the mountains and found the Macquarie and Lachlan Rivers.

In 1817 a party led by John Oxley set out from the newly founded town of Bathurst down the Lachlan River in search of more good land and perhaps an inland sea. The river petered out into swamps so they headed south-west across arid plains, then turned north, crossing the Lachlan River and reaching the Macquarie River, which they followed upstream to Bathurst. Oxley was unenthusiastic about the country he had found, but if he had persisted through the swamps on the Lachlan, he soon would have reached the Murrumbidgee River.

The following year, Oxley was sent to find the mouth of the Macquarie River, only to find that it too flowed through poor country and ended in great marshes. The party headed east to the coast, crossing some of the best grazing land in the world, found a way across the Great Dividing Range and followed the fertile Hastings Valley to the river mouth, which Oxley named Port Macquarie. This country was much more promising.

In 1819 a route to Bathurst from Cow Pastures (around Camden) was found by Charles Throsby, thereby opening up the southern highlands to graziers, and James Meehan explored a route from the southern highlands to the coast near Jervis Bay, finding still more fertile land.

In 1824 the explorers Hamilton Hume and William Hovell, starting from near present-day Canberra, made the first overland journey southwards, reaching the western shores of Port Phillip Bay. On the way they discovered a large river and named it after Hume, although it was later renamed the Murray by another great explorer, Charles Sturt. By 1830 Sturt had established that the Murrumbidgee and Darling River systems tied in

AJ

Father of the Murray: explorer Charles Sturt, who dispelled the myth of an inland sea

with the Murray, and had followed the Murray to its mouth, finally dispelling the inland sea theory.

By the mid-1830s the general layout of present-day NSW was understood, and settlers eagerly followed the explorers' routes. The settlers often pushed into territory that was outside the defined 'limits of settlement', but the government inevitably expanded those limits.

The colony was increasingly seen as a place in which to make money. The British government and the wealthier colonials began to envisage a rich pastoral colony into which British society could be transplanted.

The increasing number of large landholders began to debate whether convicts (cheap but unreliable) or the free-born (good workers but uppity and expensive) made better farm labourers. A growing minority wanted an end to transportation altogether. This view eventually prevailed and the last ship bringing convicts to NSW arrived in 1848.

When Arthur Phillip arrived in 1788, NSW comprised about half of the continent and Tasmania. The western half of the continent (which became Western Australia

after some shifting of borders) was claimed by Britain in 1829 and Tasmania became a separate colony in 1825. The mainland colonies were progressively carved from NSW – South Australia (SA; 1834), Victoria (1850) and Queensland (1859). From *being* Australia, NSW became one of several Australian colonies.

NSW was granted responsible government in 1855 and two years later all males in the colony were given the vote. Women had to wait until 1902 to be able to vote, but both men and women were given the vote here much earlier than in many other countries – that is, of course, unless you were Aboriginal. Aborigines were finally granted the right to vote in a 1967 referendum.

Gold!

The discovery of gold in the 1850s brought about the most significant changes in the social and economic structure of the colony.

The large quantities of gold found at Ophir (near Orange) in 1851 caused a rush of hopeful miners from Sydney, and for the rest of the century there were rushes throughout NSW and much of Australia. The influx of miners from around the world and the independence of life on the diggings swept away any hope of the Australian colonies remaining strictly controlled pastoral societies.

Although few people made their fortunes on the goldfields, many stayed to settle the country, as farmers, workers and shopkeepers. At the same time, the Industrial Revolution in Britain produced a strong demand for raw materials. With the agricultural and mineral resources of such a vast country, Australia's economic base became secure.

Early 20th Century

During the 1890s, calls for the separate colonies to federate became increasingly strident. Supporters argued that it would improve the economy (which was undergoing a severe depression) by removing intercolonial tariffs. Also, a sense of an Australian identity, spurred by painters and writers, had grown. Sydney was by now a vigorous city of nearly 500,000 people and a great port.

With Federation, which came about on 1 January 1901, NSW became a state of the new Australian nation. But Australia's loyalties and many of its legal ties to Britain remained. When WWI broke out in Europe, Australian troops were sent to fight in the trenches of France and in the Middle East, including at Gallipoli in Turkey.

The site for Canberra, the new national capital, was chosen in 1908 (after much bickering between Sydney and Melbourne), and the Australian Capital Territory (ACT) was created in 1911.

There was great economic expansion in the 1920s, but all this came to a halt with the Great Depression, which hit Australia hard. In 1931 almost a third of breadwinners were unemployed and poverty was widespread.

Sydney's population was approaching one million and conditions in the crowded inner suburbs were desperate. NSW premier Jack Lang attempted to raise money by defaulting on the state's loans from Britain. This made him enormously popular, but he was soon sacked as premier and expelled from the Australian Labor Party (ALP).

By 1932 the economy was starting to recover as a result of rises in wool prices and a rapid revival of manufacturing. With the opening of the Harbour Bridge in that same year, Sydney's building industry picked up again.

'Protection' of Aboriginal People

By the early 1900s, legislation designed to segregate and 'protect' Aboriginal people imposed restrictions on Aborigines' rights to own property and to seek employment. The Aboriginals Ordinance of 1918 authorised the state to remove children from Aboriginal mothers and place them in foster homes or institutional care if it was suspected that the father was non-Aboriginal. This practice continued up until the 1960s, resulting in bitterness that persists to this day. (At the time of writing, a landmark test case is before the Federal Court of Australia. Two members of this 'Stolen Generation' are alleging that their treatment was illegal under the laws of the day and are seeking compensation for pain and suffering.)

WWII & Post-War NSW

When WWII broke out, Australian troops again fought beside the British in Europe, but after the Japanese bombed Pearl Harbor Australia's own national security finally began to take priority. In May 1942 four midget Japanese submarines were destroyed in Sydney Harbour, and a week later a Japanese submarine lobbed shells into the suburbs of Bondi and Rose Bay. Australia's location in Asia suddenly became frighteningly relevant. The Japanese advance was stopped by Australian and US forces in Papua New Guinea, and ultimately it was the USA, not Britain, that helped protect Australia from the Japanese.

In the post-war years, construction boomed again in Sydney and the city rapidly spread west. The new immigration programs brought growth and prosperity.

In 1965 the conservative government committed troops to serve in the Vietnam War, and during those years Sydney's face changed as US GIs flooded into the city for their rest-and-recreation leave. Kings Cross flaunted its sleaziness – and the hippie and peace movements became established.

Assimilation

The process of social change for Aboriginal people was accelerated by WWII. After the war, 'assimilation' of Aboriginal people became the stated aim of the government. To this end, the rights of Aboriginal people were subjugated even further – the government had control over everything, from where Aborigines could live to whom they could marry. Many children were taken from their families and put in white foster homes or missions and people were forcibly moved from their homes to townships. The idea was that they would adapt to European culture, which would in turn aid their economic development. This policy was a dismal failure.

In the 1960s the assimilation policy came under scrutiny, and non-Aboriginal Australians became aware of the inequities. In 1967 non-Aboriginal Australians voted to give Aborigines and Torres Strait Islanders the status of citizens, including the right to vote, and gave the federal government power to legislate for them in all states. The states had to provide Aborigines with the same services as were available to other citizens, and the federal government set up the Department of Aboriginal Affairs to identify and legislate for the special needs of Aboriginal people.

The assimilation policy was dumped in 1972 and its replacement was a policy of self-determination, which for the first time brought Aborigines into the decision-making process.

In 1976 the *Aboriginal Land Rights Act* gave Aborigines in the Northern Territory (NT) indisputable title to all Aboriginal reserves and a means for claiming other crown land. It also provided for mineral royalties to be paid to Aboriginal communities. See the boxed text 'Contemporary Aboriginal Issues' for more on the land rights issue.

The 1970s & Beyond

Support for involvement in Vietnam was far from absolute, and conscripting 18-year-olds to fight a foreign war troubled many Australians. In 1972, for the first time in 20 years, the ALP won office nationally. The government, led by Prime Minister Gough Whitlam, withdrew Australian troops from Vietnam and instituted many reforms, such as free tertiary education and free universal health care.

Labor, however, was hampered by a hostile Senate and talk of mismanagement. On 11 November 1975, the governor general (Queen's representative) dismissed

---

Contemporary Aboriginal Issues

In 1992 the High Court handed down what became known as its Mabo ruling. It was the result of a claim by a Torres Strait Islander, Eddie Mabo, which challenged the established concept of *terra nullius* – the idea that Australia belonged to no-one when Europeans first arrived. The court ruled that Aborigines did once own Australia and that where there was continuous association with the land they had the right to claim it back.

In 1993 the federal government introduced its native-title legislation, which formalised the High Court's Mabo ruling. Then, in 1996, the High Court handed down the Wik decision, which established that pastoral leases don't necessarily extinguish native title. The ruling resulted in some fairly hysterical responses and led to the amended *Native Title Act (1998)*, which reduced Aborigines' rights in favour of the pastoralists.

Another issue that remains unresolved is that of the 'Stolen Generation'. Aboriginal communities are still suffering the psychological, emotional and social consequences of the assimilation policy. Despite recognising the mistakes of the past, Prime Minister John Howard has repeatedly declined to apologise on behalf of previous administrations. However, National Sorry Day, first held on 26 May 1998, recognises the loss and suffering of the Aboriginal people. On 28 May 2000, hundreds of thousands of Australians demonstrated their support for reconciliation by participating in a historic walk across the Sydney Harbour Bridge, as part of Corroboree 2000.

In the meantime, many Aborigines still live in appalling conditions, they're more likely to be jailed than non-Aborigines, Aboriginal deaths in custody remain high and substance abuse is a big problem. However, while most NSW Aborigines live in towns, they remain distinctively Aboriginal. In the Sydney suburb of Glebe, the Tranby Aboriginal Co-operative College is run by and for Aborigines and Redfern has a large, vital Koori population. Across the state you'll find Koori communities whose voices are beginning to be heard in the political process.

Assimilation policies have been discredited, but there are moves by many Koori communities to participate in the Australian economy on their own terms. Small industries producing Aboriginal-designed fashions are appearing, and in a few places in NSW Aboriginal-run tours show the country from the Koori perspective – the cultural centres at Wallaga Lake and Eden on the south coast, Tweed Heads, Armidale and Glen Innes are good examples.

parliament and installed a caretaker government led by Opposition leader Malcolm Fraser. Such action was unprecedented in Australian history and prompted outrage. (See the boxed text 'Federal Politics Since 1901' in the ACT chapter for more on national politics.)

In NSW, long years of conservative rule ended in 1976 with the election of the ALP under Neville Wran. He instituted reforms and presided over the clean-up of a state that had been slipping into corruption. Wran left politics in 1986 and, without his charismatic presence, the ALP lost the next election. Liberal premier Nick Greiner and his successor John Fahey concentrated on balancing the budget. In 1995 the ALP was elected under the leadership of Bob Carr, who went on to a landslide election win in 1999.

After the '80s boom, which saw a lot of development in Sydney, Australia found itself in recession again in the early '90s. However, by the time the century closed – with a spectacular pyrotechnic display over Sydney Harbour – the economy had improved, and the energy and money poured into Sydney for the 2000 Olympics put NSW on a high. In early 2000, unemployment was at 6.5%, the lowest of any state.

GEOGRAPHY

There are four main geographical areas of NSW.

The strip of land between the sea and the Great Dividing Range runs from Tweed Heads on the Queensland border to Cape Howe on the Victorian border. The coast is lined with superb beaches and there are many bays, lakes and meandering estuaries.

The Great Dividing Range runs like a spine along the length of Australia's east coast. In the south of NSW the range rears up to form the Snowy Mountains, with Australia's highest peak, Mt Kosciuszko (2228m). The enormous Kosciuszko National Park protects much of the 'Snowies'. The eastern side of the range tends to form a steep escarpment and is mostly heavily forested. Most of the ancient range's peaks have been worn down to a series of plateaus or tablelands, the largest ones being the

New England tableland, the Blue Mountains, the southern highlands and the Monaro tableland.

The western side of the Great Dividing Range is less steep than the eastern and dwindles into a series of foothills and valleys, which provide some of the most fertile farmland in the country.

The western plains begin about 300km inland, and from here west the state is almost entirely flat. On the western edge of NSW, Broken Hill sits at the end of a long, low range that juts into the state from SA and is rich with minerals. North of the Darling River, which cuts diagonally across the plains, the country takes on the red soil of the outback.

Rivers

There are two types of rivers in NSW. Short, swift and bountiful rivers rise in the Great Dividing Range and flow east to the sea. In the north of the state these eastward-flowing rivers have large coastal deltas and are mighty watercourses.

Also rising in the Great Dividing Range, but meandering westward across the dry plains to reach the sea in SA, are the Darling and the Murray Rivers, and their significant tributaries such as the Lachlan and the Murrumbidgee. These rivers have often changed their sluggish courses, and the Murray-Darling basin takes in nearly all of the state west of the Great Dividing Range. The plains are riddled with creeks, swamps and lakes.

CLIMATE

Australia's seasons are the antithesis of those in Europe and the USA. Summer starts in December, autumn in March, winter in June and spring in September.

The climate in NSW varies depending on the location, but the rule of thumb is that the farther north you go the warmer and more humid it'll be. It's also hotter and drier the farther west you go.

Sydney is blessed with a temperate climate. The temperature rarely falls below 10°C except overnight in winter and, although temperatures can hit 40°C during summer, the average summer maximum is

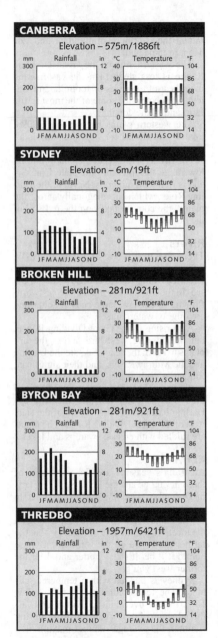

CANBERRA
Elevation – 575m/1886ft

SYDNEY
Elevation – 6m/19ft

BROKEN HILL
Elevation – 281m/921ft

BYRON BAY
Elevation – 281m/921ft

THREDBO
Elevation – 1957m/6421ft

a pleasant 25°C. Average monthly rainfall ranges from 75mm to 130mm.

Canberra is freezing in winter and baking in summer, so spring and autumn are the best times to visit the national capital.

Bourke, in the state's far west, claims NSW's highest recorded temperature, a blistering 51.7°C (125°F) in the shade.

ECOLOGY & ENVIRONMENT

There is an increasing focus on conservation issues, and ecotourism is a valued industry in NSW. Nevertheless, environmental problems remain.

In Sydney there's concern over pollution of harbour and ocean beaches, especially after heavy rainfall, when billions of litres of rubbish and untreated effluent emerge from overflow points. Millions of dollars have been spent installing pollution traps and litter booms to clean storm water.

Noise from aircraft at Sydney's Kingsford-Smith Airport is a major issue for nearby residents. The state government has tried to reduce the level in the worst affected areas by 'spreading' the flight paths.

Outbreaks of toxic blue-green algae have occurred on the upper Hawkesbury River in recent years.

The Snowy Mountains Hydro-electric Scheme was hailed as a marvel of engineering when completed in 1974. Its dams capture the waters of rivers including the Snowy, Murrumbidgee and Murray. The wine-producing and rice- and fruit-growing industries benefited enormously from the secure water supply, but little account was taken of the environmental impact of diverting water for irrigation and electricity. Fish populations in the Snowy River have dwindled and salinisation of the land, caused by tree clearing and irrigation, has grown rapidly. Trees that depended on regular flooding for survival, such as the river red gum, have also declined. Campaigns have been launched to 'Save the Snowy' by allowing more natural flow to revive native fish populations – currently about 99% of the Snowy's original flow is diverted by the hydro-electric system.

On a more positive note, after long-running discussions involving the state government, environmentalists and the logging industry, the 90,000-hectare South East Forests National Park west of Eden was created in 1997. The future of other parts of the southern forest is yet to be decided by the Regional Forest Agreement, which will identify areas to be protected or logged.

For more information on environmental issues contact:

Australian Conservation Foundation (ACF; ☎ 9247 4285), 33 George St, The Rocks.
This is the largest nongovernment organisation involved in protecting the environment.
Web site: www.acfonline.org.au

Australian Trust for Conservation Volunteers (ATCV; ☎ 9564 1244), 18/142 Addison Rd, Marrickville.
The ATCV runs conservation projects around the country, providing transport, food and accommodation for volunteers in return for a contribution to help cover costs. You can organise a stint with the ATCV from overseas, on a package with World Travellers Network (☎ 9264 2477), 14 Wentworth Ave, Sydney.
Web site: www.atcv.com.au

Commonwealth Department of Environment and Heritage
Web site: www.erin.gov.au

Greenpeace
(☎ 9261 4666), 35–39 Liverpool St, Sydney.
Web site: www.greenpeace.org.au

Wilderness Society (☎ 9552 2355), 1st floor, 263 Broadway, Glebe.
The society focuses on protection of wilderness and forests.
Web site: www.wilderness.org.au

In many towns you'll find environment centres run by volunteers. It's always worth dropping in as the people are friendly and can be a good source of information, about both the natural environment of the area and local events.

FLORA

Australia has a huge diversity of plant species – more than Europe and Asia combined.

Australia's distinctive vegetation began to take shape about 55 million years ago when the country broke from the supercontinent of Gondwanaland, drifting from Antarctica to warmer climes. At this time, Australia was completely covered by cool-climate rain-

forest, but due to its geographic isolation and the gradual drying of the continent, rain-forests retreated, plants like eucalypts and wattles (acacias) took over and the grasslands expanded. Eucalypts and wattles were able to adapt to warmer temperatures, the increased natural occurrence of fire and the later use of fire for hunting and other purposes by Aborigines. Now many species actually benefit from fire (or, more correctly, from the smoke from fires).

The eucalypt – often called the gum tree – is everywhere except in the deepest rain-forests and the most arid regions. Of the 700 species of the genus *Eucalyptus,* 95% occur naturally in Australia, the rest in New Guinea, the Philippines and Indonesia.

Gum trees vary in form and height. Species commonly found in NSW include the tall, straight river red gum *(E. camaldulensis);* the stunted, twisted snow gum *(E. pauciflora)* with its colourful trunk striations;

Floral Emblems

All Australian states and territories have a floral emblem. In New South Wales (NSW) it is the waratah *(Telopea speciosissima),* a member of the banksia family. The waratah is a squat shrub with green leaves and crimson flowers. Two species are native to NSW and the first specimens of the waratah were collected in the Blue Mountains in 1793.

The Australian Capital Territory's floral emblem is the royal bluebell *(Wahlenbergia gloriosa),* a protected plant that has violet flowers.

New South Wales' floral emblem, the waratah.

the spotted gum *(E. maculata)* common on the coast; and the scribbly gum *(E. haemastoma)*, which has scribbly insect tracks on its bark. Eucalyptus oil is distilled from certain types of gum trees and used for pharmaceutical and perfumed products.

Around 600 species of wattle are found in Australia. Most species flower during late winter and spring, when the country is ablaze with the bright yellow flowers and the reason for the choice of green and gold as the national colours is obvious. The golden wattle *(A. pycnantha)* is Australia's floral emblem.

Other common natives found in NSW include grevilleas, hakeas, banksias, waratahs *(telopeas)*, bottlebrushes *(callistemons)*, paperbarks *(melaleucas)*, tea trees *(leptospermums)*, boronias, native cypress pines *(callitris)* and she-oaks *(casuarinas)*.

Identifying the state's strange and beautiful plants and trees is rewarding but difficult. Handy guides include the *Field Guide to Native Plants of Australia* (Bay Books), *Key Guide to Australian Trees* (Reed) and *Key Guide to Australian Wildflowers* (Reed).

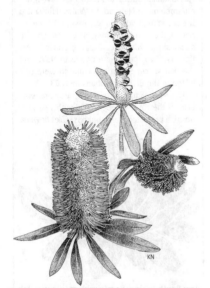

The unusual yet striking seed pod and flowers of the coastal banksia *(Banksia Integrifolia)*.

Endangered Species

Urban expansion north of Sydney is threatening the grevillea caleyi. It can still be seen in Ku-Ring-Gai Chase National Park and along the roadsides near Mona Vale. The native jute, a flowering shrub that can be found on the north coast around Lismore, was virtually extinct but National Parks & Wildlife Service (NPWS) initiatives are contributing to its recovery. Other threatened species in NSW include the flowering shrub Wingecarribee gentian, several other species of grevillea and the Pimelea venosa.

Introduced Plants

The majestic Norfolk Island pine *(Araucaria heterophylla)*, naturally enough a native of Norfolk Island, lines the foreshores of many coastal towns in NSW. There are many other introduced species – most, such as oaks and willows, brought in by homesick settlers to replicate their homeland. One of the most outstanding introduced trees in NSW is the jacaranda. In spring and summer, its vivid mauve or blue flowers bring a splash of colour to many towns around the coast and the ranges.

Some introduced plants have also caused major problems by choking out native flora and pastures. Noxious weeds such as Paterson's curse can be found growing wild in many parts of the state.

FAUNA
Mammals

Native animals you're most likely to see in the wild are wallabies and kangaroos, possums and koalas. However, there's a huge range of small, mainly nocturnal animals going about their business unobserved. Part of the reason for Australia's appalling record on animal extinction is that many species died out before anyone other than the Aborigines knew they existed.

Australia's most distinctive fauna are the marsupials and monotremes. Marsupials such as kangaroos and koalas give birth to partially developed young, which they suckle in a pouch. Monotremes – platypuses and echidnas – lay eggs but also suckle their young.

Kangaroos The extraordinary breeding cycle of the kangaroo is well adapted to Australia's harsh, unpredictable environment.

The young kangaroo, or joey, just millimetres long at birth, claws its way unaided to the mother's pouch where it attaches itself to a nipple that expands inside its mouth. A day or two later the mother mates again, but the new embryo doesn't begin to develop until the first joey has left the pouch permanently.

At this point the mother produces two types of milk – one formula to feed the joey at heel, the other for the baby in her pouch. If environmental conditions are right, the mother then mates again. If food or water is scarce, however, the breeding cycle is interrupted until conditions improve.

As well as many species of wallabies (some endangered), there are two main species of kangaroos in NSW, the grey kangaroo and the majestic red kangaroo, which is common in the far west and can stand 2m tall. Reds have been known to disembowel dogs that bother them.

Possums There's a wide range of possums – they seem to have adapted to all sorts of conditions, including those of the city, where you'll find them in parks, especially around dusk. Some large species are found in suburban roofs and eat cultivated plants and food scraps.

Wombats The wombat is a slow, solid, powerfully built marsupial with a broad head and short, stumpy legs. These fairly placid, easily tamed creatures are legally killed by farmers, who object to the damage done to paddocks by wombats digging large burrows and tunnelling under fences. Like other nocturnal animals, they tend to lumber across roads at night and are difficult to see.

Koalas Distantly related to the wombat, koalas are found along the eastern seaboard. Their cuddly appearance belies an irritable nature, and they'll scratch and bite if sufficiently provoked.

Koalas initially carry their babies in pouches, but later the larger young cling to

MH

Like kangaroos and koalas, wombats raise their young in a pouch.

their mothers' backs. They feed only on the leaves of certain types of eucalypt (found mainly in the forests of the Great Dividing Range) and are particularly sensitive to changes to their habitat.

Platypuses & Echidnas The platypus and the echidna are the only living representatives of the monotremes, the most primitive group of mammals. Both lay eggs, as reptiles do, but have mammary glands and suckle their young.

The amphibious platypus has a duck-like bill, webbed feet and a beaver-like body. Males have poisonous spurs on their hind feet. The platypus is able to sense electric currents in the water and uses this ability to track its prey. Platypuses are shy creatures,

MH

One of only two living examples of egg-laying mammals, the platypus is known to be shy.

The echidna has strong claws, sharp spikes and a sticky tongue, for lapping up ants and termites.

but they occur in many rivers. Bombala, in the state's south-east, is a good place for platypus-spotting.

The echidna is a spiny anteater that hides from predators by digging vertically into the ground and covering itself with dirt, or by rolling itself into a ball and raising its sharp quills.

Dingoes Australia's native dog, the dingo is thought to have arrived in Australia around 6000 years ago. It was domesticated by the Aborigines, but after the Europeans arrived and Aborigines could no longer hunt freely, the dingo again became 'wild'. By preying on sheep (but mainly rabbits, rats and mice) dingoes earned the wrath of graziers. These sensitive, intelligent dogs are legally considered to be vermin. Some are still found in the high country.

Birds
The only bird larger than the Australian emu is the African ostrich, also flightless. The emu is a shaggy-feathered bird with an often curious nature. After the female emu lays the eggs, the male hatches them and raises the young. Emus are common in the Riverina and the far west.

There's an amazing variety of parrots and cockatoos. The common pink and grey galahs are noisy, although the sulphur-crested cockatoos are even louder. Rainbow lorikeets have brilliant colour schemes and in some parks accept a free feed from visitors.

A member of the kingfisher family, the kookaburra is heard as much as it is seen – you can't miss its loud, cackling laugh, usually at dawn and sunset. Kookaburras are common near the coast, particularly in the south-east.

The lyrebird, found in moist forest areas, is famous for its vocal abilities and its beauty. Lyrebirds are highly skilled mimics that copy segments of other birds' songs to create unique hybrid compositions. During the courting season, with his colourful fern-like tail feathers spread like a fan, the male puts on a sensational song-and-dance routine to impress potential partners.

The black-and-white magpie (no relation to the European bird of the same name) has a distinctive and beautiful warbling call. Magpies can be aggressively territorial when nesting (around September). Being 'swooped' by a magpie is unnerving: the bird dives at you silently from behind.

Reptiles
There are many species of snake in NSW, all protected. Many are poisonous, some deadly, but few are aggressive and they'll usually get out of your way before you realise that they're there. See Dangers & Annoyances in the Facts for the Visitor chapter for ways of avoiding being bitten and what to do in the unlikely event that you are.

There's a wide variety of lizards, from tiny skinks to prehistoric-looking goannas which can grow up to 2.5m long, although most species in NSW are much smaller. Goannas can run very fast and when threatened use their big claws to climb the nearest tree – or perhaps the nearest leg!

Bluetongue lizards are slow moving and stumpy. Their even slower and stumpier relations, shinglebacks, are common in the outback.

Animal Rescue
You see a lot of native animals dead by the roadside. You might find injured animals, especially young marsupials, hidden in the pouch. Essentially, baby animals separated

from their mothers will be cold (so wrap them up), stressed (disturb them as little as possible) and dehydrated (but don't give them cow's milk).

Wildlife Information & Rescue (WIRES) is a voluntary organisation that cares for native animals. There are WIRES branches in many places, but for current addresses contact the Sydney head office (☎ 9975 1633, 9975 5567), 5 Darley St, Forestville. Alternatively, a vet will know of local animal welfare organisations such as the Native Animal Network Association (NANA; ☎ 4443 5110) on the south coast.

Endangered Species

Over 700 species of plants and animals are listed as endangered under the *NSW Threatened Species Conservation Act (1995)*. The yellow-footed rock wallaby was thought to be extinct until a group was found in western NSW in the 1960s. National parks were created to protect them and local farmers agreed to protect them on their properties. But the wallabies can't compete with feral goats for food and shelter and their numbers are decreasing. They can still be seen in Mootwingee National Park north-east of Broken Hill.

Since the late 1980s the numbers of Kosciuszko National Park's yellow-and-black corroboree frog have declined rapidly and no-one knows why. In 1997, in an attempt to save the species, 500 eggs were collected and sent to Melbourne for hatching, after which the tadpoles were released back into the park. The mountain pygmy possum, also found in Kosciuszko National Park, is another rare species.

Overfishing, off the southern coast of NSW and elsewhere, has brought the southern bluefin tuna to the edge of extinction. Industrial fishing methods have also reduced the numbers of albatross that feed off the tuna.

Along the north coast around Port Macquarie, urban expansion, traffic and domestic animals are putting enormous pressure on koalas and their habitats.

Introduced Species

The Acclimatisation Society was a bunch of do-gooders in the Victorian era who devoted themselves to 'improving' the countries of the British Empire by introducing plants and animals. On the whole, their work was disastrous.

Exotic animals thriving in NSW include rabbits, cats (big, bad feral versions of the domestic moggie), pigs (now bristly black razorbacks with long tusks) and goats. In the Snowy Mountains and towards the Queensland border you might see wild horses (brumbies). These have all been disastrous for native animals, as predators and as competitors for food and water.

Probably the biggest change to the ecosystem has been caused by sheep. To make

Green & Golden Bell Frog

The first winner in the Sydney Olympics was the green and golden bell frog, a colony of which was discovered in a disused pit in 1992 in what is now Sydney Olympic Park. The frogs, once common on the east coast of New South Wales, are an endangered species: only a few colonies are thought to exist in Australia. Plans to build tennis courts and a multistorey car park on the pit site were shelved. Instead, a series of tunnels and ponds were built at a cost of $400,000 to protect the frogs. The tunnels are intended to allow them to travel safely to nearby Millennium Park.

room for sheep the bush was cleared and the plains planted with exotic grasses. Many small marsupials became extinct. Aborigines were jailed and massacred because they hunted sheep and resisted the theft of their land by graziers.

Sheep were the first hoofed animals to tread NSW's light, fine topsoil. They trod it into a hard-packed mass that couldn't support native flora and was vulnerable to erosion.

NATIONAL PARKS

There are more than 140 national parks in NSW, covering about four million hectares and protecting environments as diverse as the peaks of the Snowy Mountains, the subtropical rainforest of the Border Ranges and the vast arid plains of the outback.

Many parks are World Heritage areas of exceptional beauty and significance. Some parks include designated wilderness areas that offer outstanding remote-area walking. The most recent addition is the 90,000-hectare South-East Forests National Park in the south-east corner of the state.

The NPWS does a good job, and many national parks have visitor centres where you can learn about the area, as well as camp sites and often walking tracks. Where there isn't a visitor centre, visit the nearest NPWS office for information. Bush camping (ie, heading into the bush and camping where you please) is allowed in many national parks, but not all – check before you go.

The NPWS head office is at 43 Bridge St, Hurstville. It has an information line (☎ 9584 6333) open 8.30 am to 4 pm, but the information is pretty general. For information on specific parks, it's better to call the ranger or district office. There's a good Web site at www.npws.nsw.gov.au.

There is, at least theoretically, an entrance fee for vehicles (not walkers) for all national parks: generally around $5 to $7.50 per car ($14 per car *per day* for Kosciuszko National Park). Camping fees are about $5 to $10, and sometimes free for bush camping with limited facilities.

There's a $50 annual pass that gives free entry (but not free camping) to all parks except Kosciuszko. It probably isn't worth buying unless you plan a systematic coverage, but the $60 pass that includes Kosciuszko is definitely worthwhile if you plan to visit Kosciuszko plus a few other parks.

The NPWS is also responsible for some other reserves. State recreation areas often contain bushland, but the quality of the forest might not be as good as in national parks. Many are centred on lakes or large dams where water sports are popular so they can be crowded in summer. There's often commercial accommodation (usually a caravan park), and bush camping is usually not permitted. There are exceptions to this, however.

Nature reserves are generally smaller reserves, usually with day-use facilities, protecting specific ecosystems.

Historic sites protect areas of historical significance, such as the ghost town of Hill End near Bathurst and Aboriginal rock-art sites.

STATE FORESTS

State forests, used for timber harvesting, conservation purposes and public recreation, cover around three million hectares. Bush camping (free) is allowed in most state forests, as are trail bikes, 4WDs, horses and pets. Often there are designated walking trails.

Brochures and maps are available from the State Forests Information Centre (☎ 9871 3377). These forests are administered by State Forests of NSW, which has regional offices and forest centres around the state. The Web site is www.forest.nsw.gov.au.

GOVERNMENT & POLITICS

Australia has a federal system of government, with elements of both the US and Westminster systems. The various state governments have no control over national defence, foreign affairs, immigration, the postal service or income tax, and they're dependent on the federal government for a lot of their funding. The High Court can overrule a state's Supreme Court. Apart from this, state governments are pretty much autonomous, Westminster-style governments, with premiers occupying positions equivalent to that of prime minister. NSW has an upper house (legislative council) and lower house (legislative assembly), both elected.

Australia's head of state is the governor general (Sir William Deane has held office since 1996), and each state has a governor. Governors are technically the British monarch's representative, although they are appointed by the various Australian governments. In NSW, the governor is Gordon Samuels.

Political Parties

There are three main parties. The Liberal Party isn't especially liberal – it's the party of the conservatives and stands for free enterprise, law and order, 'family values' and the like. The Liberals' minority coalition partner is the National Party, which mainly represents country seats.

The Australian Labor Party is a social-democratic party that has been in existence for more than 100 years and grew out of the great shearers' strikes last century. It won the 1999 state election to secure a second term of government. The current NSW premier is Bob Carr.

The only other party of substance is the Australian Democrats, formed, as its first federal leader, Don Chipp, said, to 'keep the bastards honest'.

Independent and Green representatives are also playing an increasingly active and important role in national politics.

ECONOMY

Australia is a relatively affluent industrialised nation, but much of its wealth still comes from agriculture and mining. NSW fits this pattern, with coal exports being the greatest earner of foreign exchange. Other important minerals are gold, silver, copper and lead.

Over 65% of NSW is farmland. The main crops are wheat, barley, oats and rice (about 90% of the rice is exported to Asia). Fruit and timber are important in the south-east, and the Hunter Valley north of Newcastle is the state's principal wine region. Wool and livestock are also significant money earners.

Some of NSW's chief industries are iron, steel, chemicals and textiles.

As in the rest of Australia (and the world), tourism is gaining more importance and the international exposure of the 2000 Olympics was a major boost for NSW.

Most of Australia's foreign trade is conducted in NSW.

POPULATION & PEOPLE

The population of NSW is just over 6.2 million, more than a third of Australia's total. With over four million people living within 100km or so of Sydney, the rest of the state is sparsely populated. More than half the state has less than two people per square kilometre.

NSW's population is diverse. Approximately 20% of people in NSW were born in other countries and many more are children of people who were born in other countries. The Snowy Mountain Hydro-electric Scheme contributed greatly to this melting pot in the 1950s and '60s, when thousands of migrants were brought in from southern and eastern Europe to help with the project.

About 110,000 people in NSW – around 1.8% of the total population – considered themselves to be Aborigines or Torres Strait Islanders in the 1996 census. In south-east Australia, the Aborigines call themselves Kooris.

The Chinese, lured by the promise of the goldfields, have been here since the 19th century, but kept a low profile until after WWII, when mass immigration began. After WWII, many Jewish survivors of the Holocaust came to Australia, along with other European refugees. Subsequent large-scale immigration has drawn people from Italy, Greece, Turkey, Lebanon, the former Yugoslavia, the Pacific and, more recently, from South-East Asia (especially Vietnam).

ARTS
Aboriginal Art

The initial forms of Aboriginal artistic expression were rock carvings, body painting and ground designs, and the earliest engraved designs known to exist date back at least 30,000 years. Art has always been an integral part of Aboriginal life, a connection between past and present, the supernatural and the earthly, people and the land. Aboriginal rock art can by found at many sites in NSW, particularly on the Central Coast.

Earthly art was a reflection of ancestral Dreaming – the 'Creation', when the earth's physical features were formed by the struggles between powerful supernatural ancestors such as the Rainbow Serpent. Not only was the physical layout mapped but codes of behaviour were laid down. Although these laws have been diluted and adapted in the last 200 years, today's ceremonies, rituals and sacred paintings are all based on the Dreamtime.

Aboriginal art has undergone a major revival in the last two decades. There are many galleries featuring the work of Aboriginal artists in Sydney and others in regional areas, such as the excellent Tobwabba gallery in Forster. Modern 'urban Koori art' comes in a wide range of aesthetic forms, often covering political issues or Aboriginal history.

Painting

It's interesting to see what the first European landscape painters made of Australia. The colours seem wrong and the features depicted aren't what would now be regarded as 'typically Australian'. Colonial artists such as Conrad Martens painted Turneresque landscapes of Sydney Harbour in the 1850s that now startle many Sydneysiders.

In the 1880s artists discovered that the Australian landscape had its own moods and that the quality of light in Sydney was radically different from Europe. Major Australian artists, such as Arthur Streeton and Tom Roberts in Melbourne, came to Sydney and established an artist's camp at Little Sirius Cove in Mosman in 1891, which became a focal point for Sydney artists. Their paintings have virtually defined all subsequent reactions to the harbour and its surrounding bushlands. Similarly, Grace Cossington-Smith's paintings of the Harbour Bridge under construction in the 1930s also created enduring images of the city.

At the turn of the century, Sydney Long painted bush scenes peopled with fairies in a strange attempt to mythologise and personify the landscape, something Aborigines

had been doing successfully for thousands of years.

Vigorous and distinctively Australian, the Brushmen of the Bush of Broken Hill, such as Pro Hart and Jack Absalom, produce naive works that are well worth seeing. Broken Hill, a mining town, is, somewhat surprisingly, a major art centre.

Sydney artist Brett Whitely, who died in 1992, was an internationally celebrated *enfant terrible* who painted luscious, colourful canvases. A gallery dedicated to his work is in Surry Hills. Probably Sydney's most famous – and commercially successful – living artist is Ken Done, whose simple, vivid works adorn everything from coasters to T-shirts.

Literature

Two of the first distinctively Australian writers to achieve popular acclaim were Henry Lawson (1867–1922) and AB 'Banjo' Paterson (1864–1941).

Paterson's generally cheerful poems and short stories have to some extent been hijacked by the nostalgia industry, but they're worth reading.

A gloomy alcoholic for much of his life, Lawson nevertheless wrote some extremely funny short stories, such as *The Loaded Dog,* as well as bitter reflections on the Australian way of life, including *The Drover's Wife.*

Less well known, Joseph Furphy (1843–1912) wrote only one book, but one that is arguably among the best ever written in Australia: *Such Is Life.*

Miles Franklin (1879–1954) made a decision early in her life to become a writer rather than a traditional wife and mother. Her best-known book, *My Brilliant Career,* was also her first. She wrote it at the age of 20 and it brought her both widespread fame and criticism. She endowed an annual award for an Australian novel; today the Miles Franklin Award is the most prestigious in the country.

Another well-known writer of the 20th century is Eleanor Dark, who in the 1940s wrote the historical trilogy *The Timeless Land, Storm of Time* and *No Barrier.* These covered the period 1788–1914 and were highly unusual at the time for their sympathetic treatment of Aboriginal culture.

The works of Nobel Prize winner Patrick White include *Voss* (1957), which contrasts the outback with colonial life in Sydney.

Seven Poor Men of Sydney (1934) is a poetic account of a cross section of Sydneysiders by expatriate author Christina Stead. *The Harp in the South* (1948) and *Poor Man's Orange* (1949) are Ruth Park's autobiographical accounts of growing up in Surry Hills. David Ireland's *The Glass Canoe* is an excellent novel exploring urban life in general and pub culture in particular. Frank Moorhouse's *Days of Wine and Rage* (1980) evokes 1970s Sydney. *They're a Weird Mob* (1955) by Nino Culotta (real name John O'Grady) is a humorous tale of an Italian migrant in Sydney. Rosa Cappiello's *Oh Lucky Country* (1984) is a harrowing account of the modern migrant experience.

Less serious but offering an insight into the seamier side of Sydney is the work of crime writer Peter Corris. The genre has produced several other authors, including John Baxter and Marele Day.

Kate Grenville's *Lillian's Story*, loosely based on the life of Sydney eccentric Bea Miles, was made into a film. Other books worth reading are Dorothy Porter's *The Monkey's Mask*, set in the Blue Mountains, Janette Turner Hospital's *The Last Magician*, set in part around Newtown train station, and Justine Ettler's *The River Ophelia*.

Music

In NSW you can hear everything from world-class opera to grungy pub bands. As with the other arts, most Australian music derives from foreign forms but often has a distinctive local twist.

Australian folk music has English, Irish and Scottish roots in much the same way as American folk music. Bush bands, playing fast-paced and high-spirited folk music for dancing, can be anything from performers trotting out standards such as 'Click Go the Shears' to serious musicians who happen to like a rollicking time. Fiddles and banjos feature, plus the indigenous 'lagerphone', a percussion instrument made from a great

many beer-bottle tops nailed to a stick and shaken or banged on the ground. If you have a chance to go to a bush dance, take it! Aboriginal music is a strong influence on contemporary folk music.

Country music, of the US variety, is popular west of the Great Dividing Range, and Tamworth's big festival is the place to be.

The rock music scene is pretty interesting, and although Sydney isn't such a breeding ground for innovative groups as Melbourne is, everyone who's anyone will play in Sydney eventually. Newcastle has a thriving local music scene, which spawned teenage band silverchair.

Recent years have seen a merging of Aboriginal music with rock. This music has probably made the greatest contribution to non-Aboriginal understanding of contemporary Aboriginal culture. Notable Aboriginal rock musicians include the group Yothu Yindi, Archie Roach and Christine Anu. They're uncompromisingly Aboriginal in their outlook.

Theatre & Dance

The prestigious Sydney Theatre Company provides a balanced program of modern, classical, local and foreign drama. The National Institute of Dramatic Art (NIDA) in Sydney is a breeding ground for new talent. The institute stages performances of students' work.

The leading contemporary Australian playwright is Sydney-based David Williamson, whose dissections of Australian middle-class rituals began in 1971 with *The Removalists* and *Don's Party*. Recent Williamson plays include *Money & Friends* and *Sanctuary*, an examination of journalism ethics and political correctness. Other interesting contemporary playwrights include Louis Nowra and Michael Gow.

The Australian Ballet, the national ballet company, is considered one of the finest companies in the world. It tours Australia's major cities, performing classical and modern ballets. It usually presents four ballets a year during its season at the Opera House.

The Sydney Dance Company (SDC) has become the leading contemporary-dance company in Australia, while the internationally acclaimed Bangarra Dance Theatre fuses Aboriginal and modern dance.

Cinema

The country's first cinema was opened in Sydney in 1896, a year after the Lumière brothers opened the world's first cinema in Paris. Maurice Sestier, one of the Lumières' photographers, came to Australia and made the country's first films in the streets of Sydney.

Cinema historians regard the Australian film *Soldiers of the Cross* as the world's first 'real' movie. It was first screened in 1901, cost £600 to make and was shown throughout the USA in 1902. A flourishing industry developed and more than 250 silent feature films were made before the 1930s, when the talkies and Hollywood took over.

In the 1930s, film companies such as Cinesound, based at Bondi Junction in Sydney, sprang up. Cinesound made 17 features between 1931 and 1940, many based on Australian history or literature. *Forty Thousand Horsemen*, directed by Cinesound's great film maker Charles Chauvel, was a highlight of this era. Chauvel is also noted for giving Errol Flynn his first film role.

In 1999 the Fox Studios Australia film and entertainment complex opened. For more information, see the boxed text 'Hollywood on the Harbour' in the Sydney chapter. See also Films in the Facts for the Visitor chapter for a selection of Australian films shot in NSW.

Architecture

Although NSW has some fine Georgian architecture, the Victorian era has left the larger legacy. Any country town worth its salt has an impressive town hall complete with Corinthian columns. Older courthouses are also in neo-Renaissance style, with domes and colonnaded porticos, but those built around the turn of the 19th century have a distinctive, heavy look to them.

Railway stations, post offices and banks are also often worth seeing.

The only private buildings to rival these shrines to government and business are pubs.

Although many country pubs are past their prime (the ubiquitous clubs have stolen their customers), many are still spectacularly grand buildings (on the outside at least), and all dedicated to the thirst of workers.

Around 1900 Australia developed its own style of domestic architecture. Houses of the Federation style, as it is known, were built to make life in a hot climate comfortable, unlike the previous Victorian-era houses, which were basically boxes with verandas tacked on.

California Bungalow and Art Deco became the dominant styles in the 1920s, and there are fine examples of Art Deco apartments still standing in Sydney.

In the 1960s, the so-called Sydney School pioneered a distinctively Australian organic architecture that used over-burnt brick and native landscaping to blend into the local environment, but modern Australian architecture struggles to maintain a distinctive style.

As well as the Sydney Opera House, designed by Jorn Utzon, there are some notable modern buildings, such as the Convention Centre at Darling Harbour and the Sydney Football Stadium (both designed by Philip Cox). The museum in Kempsey is a little gem, designed by Glenn Murcutt.

Art Deco is enjoying a resurgence in popularity, as can be seen in the design of the Coopers & Lybrand building in Sydney.

For information on some grand old buildings contact the National Trust (☎ 9258 0123), Observatory Hill. The Historic Houses Trust of NSW (☎ 9692 8366), 61 Darghan St, Glebe, publishes a useful booklet, *Identifying Australian Houses*.

SOCIETY & CONDUCT
Aboriginal Traditions

The Aborigines have a rich and complex culture, which flourished in Australia for over 40,000 years prior to the arrival of the Europeans.

Aborigines were traditionally tribal people living in extended family groups. Each group had a defined territory, within which were a number of spiritually significant places known as sacred sites. It was the responsibility of the clan, or particular members of it, to maintain and protect the site in the correct way so that ancestral beings were not offended and would continue to look after the clan. Traditional punishments for those who failed in these responsibilities were often severe.

Many Aboriginal communities were seminomadic, while others were sedentary. Where food and water were readily available, as was the case with coastal and southeast areas of NSW, the people tended to remain in a limited area. When they did wander, it was to visit sacred places to carry out rituals or perhaps take advantage of seasonal foods available elsewhere. Along the Riverina, occupying the plains and the outback west of the Great Dividing Range, many Aboriginal groups were spread along the life-giving Murray and Darling Rivers. The traditional role of the men was that of hunter, tool-maker and custodian of male law; women reared the children, gathered and prepared food and were the custodians of female law and ritual.

Environmental Awareness Wisdom and skills obtained over millennia enabled Aborigines to use their environment to the maximum. An intimate knowledge of the behaviour of animals and the correct time to harvest ensured that food shortages were rare. They never hunted or harvested to the point where species were threatened with extinction. Like other hunter-gatherer peoples of the world, the Aborigines were true ecologists.

They burnt undergrowth and dead grass to encourage new growth, which in turn attracted game animals. It also prevented the build-up of combustible material in the forests, making hunting easier and reducing the possibility of major bushfires. Dingoes were domesticated to assist in the hunt and to guard the camp from intruders.

Technology & Trade Similar technology – for example, the boomerang (throwing stick) and spear – was used throughout the continent, but techniques were adapted to the environment and the species being hunted.

Various goods found their way along the long trade routes that crisscrossed the continent. Many of the items traded, such as stone or shell, were rare and had great ritual significance. Boomerangs and ochre were other important trade items. Along the trading networks large numbers of people often met for 'exchange ceremonies', where not only goods but also songs and dance styles were passed on. (Near Brewarrina in north-west NSW you can still see ingenious stone fish traps, which caught fish to feed the huge gatherings there.) In the high country of the Snowy Mountains and the hills around present-day ACT, many tribal groups would come together for the annual Bogong moth harvest, where they would feast on the fat-rich and easily gathered adult moths. This was a time of ceremony and trade.

Ceremony Religion, history, law and art are integrated in complex ceremonies that depict the activities of the ancestral beings, and prescribe codes of behaviour and responsibilities for looking after the land and all living things. The link between the Aborigines and the ancestral beings is totems, and each person has his or her own totem, or Dreaming. These totems take many forms, such as caterpillars, snakes, fish and magpies. Songs explain how the landscape contains these powerful creator ancestors, which can still exert either benign or malevolent influences, tell when and where to hunt or where to find water in drought years, and specify kinship relations and correct marriage partners. For more information see Religion later in this chapter.

Ceremonies are still performed in many parts of Australia. Many of the sacred sites are believed to be dangerous, and entry to them is prohibited under traditional Aboriginal law.

True Blue
Non-Aboriginal Australians have a self-image as a resourceful, self-reliant people at home in the bush, but this has never been strictly correct. That's not to say that the hardy pioneers didn't exist. They did, but

they were objects of bemused admiration for the majority, who lived in towns. 'True blue' Aussie values, such as egalitarianism and willingness to give anyone a 'fair go', are still strong, but while today's multicultural society has seen narrowness and intolerance diminish, there are still plenty of rednecks out there.

The popular myths about hard-riding, hard-drinking Australians obscure the fact that there has always been a strong streak of free thinking. Henry Lawson is well known for his idealisation of mateship in the bush, but fewer people remember that his mother, Louisa, began publishing a feminist magazine, *The Dawn,* in 1888.

RELIGION

Australia is a secular country but almost all religions are represented and given equal official recognition.

A shrinking majority of people in NSW are at least nominally Christian. Most Protestant churches merged to become the Uniting Church, although the Anglican Church of Australia remains separate. The Roman Catholic Church is the largest Christian group (about 30%), with the original Irish adherents boosted by large numbers of Mediterranean immigrants.

Non-Christian minority faiths abound, the main ones being Buddhism, Judaism and Muslim. Islam is the second-largest religion in Australia and Buddhism is one of the fastest growing.

Aboriginal Religion

Aborigines believe that spirit beings, which lived on earth during the Dreamtime before the arrival of humans, created the features of the natural world and were the ancestors of all living things. Despite being supernatural, the ancestors aged and eventually returned to the sleep from which they'd awoken at the dawn of time. Here their spirits remain as eternal forces. Each ancestor's spiritual energy flows along the path it travelled during the Dreamtime and is strongest at the points where it left physical evidence of its activities, such as a tree, hill or claypan. These features are sacred sites.

Aborigines believe that the immortal soul is part of a particular ancestral spirit that returns to the sacred sites of that ancestor after death. It is the individual's obligation to help care for these sites by performing rituals and songs that tell of the ancestor's deeds. By doing this, the order created by that ancestor is maintained.

Aboriginal people believe that to destroy or damage a sacred site threatens not only the living but also the spirit inhabitants of the land. Throughout much of Australia, when pastoralists were breaking the Aboriginal peoples' link to the land, many Aboriginal people sought refuge on missions and became Christian. However, becoming Christian has not, for most Aborigines, meant renouncing their traditional religion. Many senior Aborigines are also devout Christians, and often ministers.

Facts for the Visitor

HIGHLIGHTS
Cities & Towns

Sydney has enough highlights to occupy anyone for a week, and the nearby national parks offer great escapes. Canberra, Australia's capital, is technically not in New South Wales (NSW), but it's only a few hours from Sydney and is an intriguing and underrated city, with plenty of attractions. The outback mining town of Broken Hill, almost at the border with South Australia (SA), is an interesting blend of hard-working rural characters and an influx of artists, all in the middle of nowhere.

The smaller towns are also worth exploring, and they're incredibly diverse. They include Hill End, resembling a ghost town; prosperous old towns like Mudgee; the outback mining settlements of Lightning Ridge and White Cliffs; sleepy riverside centres like Deniliquin; the planned towns of the Murrumbidgee Irrigation Area; fishing ports like Eden, historic towns like Braidwood and Berry; and outback hamlets like Mt Hope or Ivanhoe.

Beaches

The coastline is a string of wonderful beaches, and a visit to Byron Bay in the state's far north is a must. While you're there, check out the alternative lifestyles at Nimbin. Sydney has its share of good surf beaches, including Bondi. The south coast has many interesting bays and beaches that are relatively quiet outside the school holidays. Try Jervis Bay, the beaches south of Batemans Bay, and the Murramarang National Park. North of Sydney, the coastal towns and resorts are much busier. Some good north-coast beaches are around Forster-Tuncurry, Coffs Harbour and Ballina.

If *au naturel* is your thing, there are legal nudist beaches at Watsons Bay, Mosman, Port Stephens, Bermagui and Werrong Beach in Royal National Park. There are numerous other unofficial 'clothing optional' beaches.

National Parks

With such diversity of landscapes, it's hard to say which of NSW's national parks are the best. You can choose between the alpine forests of Kosciuszko, the rainforests of Border Ranges, the eerie outback expanses of Mungo or Sturt, the jagged peaks of Warrumbungle, the spectacular views of the Blue Mountains – or one of the other 140 or so parks! See National Parks in the Facts about New South Wales chapter for more information.

The Great Dividing Range forms a spine running the length of the state, sometimes quite close to the coast. Many of the parks along here are easily accessible and offer great camping and bushwalking opportunities. They include Morton and Budawang in the south, and Barrington Tops and Dorrigo north of Sydney.

Wineries

Wineries are a popular part of travellers' itineraries these days and NSW has one of Australia's great wine regions in the Hunter Valley, north of Sydney. There are more than 50 wineries concentrated in the lower Hunter Valley and others in the upper Hunter. Touring around sampling reds and whites (tastings are usually free) is a great way to spend a couple of days here (just avoid the busy weekends). Mudgee, in the state's central west, has more than 20 wineries, most of them small and locally owned, and Orange is also a prosperous wine region. Murrumbateman, just north of Canberra, is the centre of a cluster of fine cool-climate wineries. Areas to explore in the south include the Riverina (especially around Griffith), and the area around Berry, just north of Nowra.

As well as cellar-door sales and tastings, many wineries have restaurants and some accommodation.

Mountains & Rivers

The Snowy Mountains in Kosciuszko National Park provide a beautiful year-round playground. In winter you can ski and snow-board; in summer you can enjoy some of the state's finest walking. Many people make the early morning climb up Mt Warning, in the far north of the state, to see the first rays of sun visible from the Australian mainland.

Several rivers, including the Murray, rise in the Snowies and they are superb trout-fishing spots. The Murrumbidgee and Darling Rivers course through outback NSW, passing many interesting towns, and there are plenty of good camping spots along the way. A great way to get a feel for the river is to hire a houseboat or take a ride on the *Riverboat Postman* on the Hawkesbury River north of Sydney.

SUGGESTED ITINERARIES

How much of NSW you see will depend largely on how much time you have. The following suggestions may help:

One week You can easily spend a week in Sydney. During the first three or four days explore the sights around Circular Quay, the Rocks, Sydney Harbour Bridge, Darling Harbour, the historic buildings of Macquarie St, and the Botanic Gardens, and take a ferry ride to Manly. In the next few days you could explore Oxford St, the inner suburbs of Paddington and Glebe, and the beachside suburbs of Bondi and Coogee or Balmoral on the North Shore. You might also fit in a day trip to the national parks to the north, to the wineries of the Hunter Valley or to the Blue Mountains. Sometime during the week, take in a performance at the Opera House.

Two weeks In the second week visit the Blue Mountains, where you can go bushwalking for two or three days. Then head south to visit the national capital, Canberra, for a couple of days and onto Kosciuszko National Park for some skiing, bushwalking or boating. Alternatively, head up the coast, with stops in Newcastle, the Hunter Valley, Coffs Harbour (including Nambucca Heads and Dorrigo National Park), Ballina and Byron Bay.

Four weeks Explore the south coast and the excellent nearby national parks. Places worth stopping at include Jervis Bay, Batemans Bay, Morton National Park, Narooma, and Merimbula or Eden. Head west through the Riverina as far as Wentworth (with a side trip to Mildura in Victoria), stopping off at some country towns along the way. Then head north to Broken Hill via the magical Mungo National Park. After two days'

absorbing Broken Hill, you could make a day trip to Mootwingee National Park north of town.

Six weeks In week five head east to visit country towns like Wilcannia, Cobar, Dubbo, Coonabarabran and Tamworth before hitting the coast at Port Macquarie, then continue up to Byron Bay. If you have two or three days left you could head inland to Nimbin and Border Ranges National Park.

PLANNING
When to Go

There's warm weather and clear skies somewhere in NSW at any time of the year. The winter months of June, July and August are the best time to visit the outback and are the only time you'll be able to ski.

Summer in Sydney can be sticky and unpleasant, although it's a great time to cool off at the (crowded) beaches. It's also when the major Sydney festivals are held. Autumn is probably Sydney's best season; the Gay & Lesbian Mardi Gras is held early in March. For details on Sydney's festivals, see the Public Holidays & Special Events section later in this chapter.

The other major consideration is school holidays. Families take to the road en masse at these times, many places are booked out, prices go through the roof and things generally get a bit crazy. The main school holiday period is mid-December (usually straight after Christmas) to late January. The other two-week periods are roughly early to mid-April (Easter), late June to mid-July and late September to early October. If you have the choice, travel outside these times.

What Kind of Trip

Your interests have a large bearing on the kind of trip it'll be, as will the amount of time and money at your disposal. The longer you stay, the more likely you are to step outside the often superficial world of the tourist, and the lower your relative daily expenses will be.

Public transport to many places outside the main cities is limited, so you may want to consider hiring or buying a car (see under Car in the Getting Around chapter for more information). Most attractions can also be visited as part of a guided tour, which is often a good way to get a quick overview of areas you're unfamiliar with.

Travelling alone is fine, provided you follow the normal precautions, and is a great way to meet new people. Travelling in a group (even with one other person) can reduce the cost of accommodation and other expenses, such as car hire.

Maps

The Department of Land & Water Conservation (DLWC) is the main publisher of maps in the state, with a wide range of topographic maps as well as some informative maps designed for tourists. Its series of 1:25,000 maps cover most of the Great Dividing Range and are essential for bushwalking. The DLWC's head office (☎ 9228 6111) is at 23–33 Bridge St, Sydney. For map sales, call ☎ 9228 6360.

The Australian Surveying & Land Information Group (AUSLIG) is the national mapping authority and has credit-card phone sales. Contact AUSLIG (☎ 6201 4300), Maps & Publication Sales, Scrivener Building, Dunlop Court, Bruce ACT 2617.

Shops selling outdoor equipment, and the larger tourist information centres, often carry topographic maps. Most tourist offices can provide a map of their town or area, but the quality varies greatly. Cartoscope (☎ 9929 7431) produces free regional and town maps to most areas in the state. Pick them up at local tourist offices. UBD produces a book with detailed maps of most cities and towns in the state (except Sydney). Lonely Planet has a fold-out, full-colour *Sydney City Map*.

If you plan to do a lot of driving, the National Roads & Motorists Association (NRMA) has a series of regional road maps that show almost every road and track in the state. Its descriptions of road conditions are accurate and up to date. Take a general road map of the whole state as well because the detailed maps show so many alternative routes that it can be difficult to work out which is the most direct. All NRMA offices and some associated garages have at least local maps. They're free to NRMA members, and members of motoring organisations in other states.

The DLWC produces an interesting map: *Aboriginal New South Wales*. It shows which peoples lived where at the time of European settlement and gives a rough guide to sites of Aboriginal significance.

What to Bring

You can buy just about anything along the way, so it's better to pack light and pick up extras as you need them. A travel pack – a combination of backpack and shoulder bag – is a good item for carrying gear.

Bring at least one warm jumper or jacket, even if visiting during the summer. Sydney's rainfall tends to come in drenching downpours, so wet-weather gear and an umbrella are handy.

A sunhat, sunglasses and sunscreen are essential. Lathering zinc cream onto your nose is a socially acceptable way to protect your skin from burning.

If you intend to bushwalk, bring strong, comfortable walking boots. Thongs (rubber sandals) are fine for the beach or a barbecue, but not for sightseeing or bushwalking.

Generally, Australians are casual dressers, although men may be required to wear jackets and ties in Sydney's more expensive hotels and restaurants, and clubs often have mild dress codes that frown upon shorts, sandals or shirts without a collar.

TOURIST OFFICES

Tourism NSW is the state government's tourist promotion body and it runs the Sydney Visitor Centre. For the cost of a local call, you can phone ☎ 13 2077 for recorded information and to have brochures sent to you. It also maintains a good Web site at www.tourism.nsw.gov.au.

Local Tourist Offices

Almost every major town (and many minor ones) has a tourist office with local information not readily available from the larger state organisation. Many are staffed by enthusiastic locals (often they are volunteers) and are excellent sources of information. In smaller towns these often operate from a small local business, such as a craft shop or petrol station.

Australian Tourist Commission

The Australian Tourist Commission (ATC) informs potential overseas visitors about the country and it produces useful booklets and fact sheets. Some 10,000 pages of information can be accessed through its Web site (www.australia.com).

VISAS & DOCUMENTS

Passport

Your most important travel document is your passport, which should remain valid for at least six months after your intended stay. If it's about to expire, renew it before you travel. This may not be easy to do away from your home country.

Applying for or renewing a passport can take from a few days to several months, so don't leave it till the last minute. If you do everything in person, but check what you need to take with you first, the process will probably be quicker.

Visas

All visitors to Australia need a visa. Only New Zealand nationals are exempt, and even they receive a 'special category' visa on arrival.

Visa application forms are available from Australian diplomatic missions overseas, and from travel agents. There are several different types of visas, depending on the reason for your visit. The Department of Immigration and Multicultural Affairs (DIMA) also has a useful Web site at www.immi.gov.au, detailing visa requirements and listing Australian missions overseas.

Tourist Visas Standard tourist visas are issued by Australian consular offices overseas. They are generally valid for a stay of either three or six months. The three-month visas are free if applied for as an Electronic Travel Authority (ETA), otherwise a visa valid for up to six months costs $60. The visa is valid for use within 12 months of the date of issue, and can be used to enter and leave Australia several times within that 12 months.

When you apply for a visa, you need to present your passport and a passport photograph, as well as sign an undertaking that you have an onward or return ticket and 'sufficient funds' for the duration of your stay. The latter is obviously open to interpretation.

You can also apply for a multiple-entry, four-year visa that allows for stays of up to six months on each visit. These cost $60.

Electronic Travel Authority If you require a tourist visa for three months or less you can simply make the application (no form required) through an International Air Transport Association (IATA)-registered travel agent when you buy your ticket. The agent can then issue an ETA (free), which replaces the usual visa stamped in your passport. This system has been operating since 1997 and is open to passport-holders of 31 countries, including Canada, Japan, Singapore, Malaysia, the UK, USA, and most Western European and Scandinavian countries.

Working Visas Young, single visitors from the UK, the Republic of Ireland, Canada, Korea, the Netherlands and Japan may be eligible for a 'working holiday' visa. 'Young' is interpreted as between 18 and 26, although exceptions are made.

This visa allows for a stay of up to 12 months, but the emphasis is on casual employment rather than a full-time job, so you're only supposed to work for three months at a time with a single employer. This visa can only be applied for from outside Australia (preferably but not necessarily in your country of citizenship), and you can't change from a visitor visa to a working-holiday visa. If you leave the country during the period of your visa (to travel or return home), you can apply for an extension to cover the time you were away.

Conditions attached to a working holiday visa include having sufficient funds for a ticket out, and taking out private medical insurance. A fee of about $150 is payable when you apply for the visa.

Visa Extensions The maximum stay is one year, including extensions.

Visa extensions are made through DIMA (☎ 13 1881) offices in Australia and, as the process takes some time, it's best to apply about a month before your visa expires. There's an application fee of $150 – and even if your application is turned down, the DIMA can still keep your money! To qualify for an extension you are required to take out private medical insurance to cover the period of the extension, and have a ticket out of the country.

There's a DIMA office in Sydney at 88 Cumberland St, The Rocks. There are also other offices in Canberra, Newcastle and Wollongong.

Travel Insurance

This not only covers you for medical expenses and luggage theft or loss, but also for cancellations or delays in your travel arrangements under certain circumstances – and everyone should be covered for the worst possible case, such as an accident requiring hospital treatment and a flight home. Cover depends on your insurance and type of ticket, so ask both your insurer and your ticket-issuing agency to explain where you stand. Ticket loss is also (usually) covered by travel insurance. Buy travel insurance as early as possible. If you buy it the week before you fly, you may find, for example, that you're not covered for delays to your flight caused by strikes or industrial action.

Check the fine print: Some policies exclude 'dangerous activities' like scuba diving or motorcycling. If such activities are on your agenda, you don't want that policy. Finally, make sure the policy includes health care and medication in the countries you may visit to/from Australia.

Driving Licence & Permits

Foreign driving licences are valid for the first three months of your visit. If you're staying longer, it's worth obtaining an International Driving Permit (IDP) from your local automobile association before you leave – you'll need a passport photo and a valid licence. IDPs are valid for one year.

Hostel & Student Cards

It's worth bringing a youth hostel membership card (Hostelling International, Youth Hostels Association etc). As well as entitling you to discounts, it's valid for membership of the Youth Hostel Association (YHA) in NSW.

Carrying a student card entitles you to a wide variety of discounts throughout NSW. The most common card is the International Student Identity Card (ISIC), issued by student unions, hostelling organisations and some travel agents such as STA Travel.

Copies

All important documents (passport data page and visa page, credit cards, travel insurance policy, air/bus/train tickets, driving licence etc) should be photocopied before you leave home. Leave one copy with someone at home and keep another with you, separate from the originals.

It's also a good idea to store details of your vital travel documents in Lonely Planet's free online Travel Vault in case you lose the photocopies or can't be bothered with them. Your password-protected Travel Vault is accessible online anywhere in the world – create it at www.ekno.lonely planet.com.

EMBASSIES & CONSULATES
Australian Embassies & Consulates

Australian diplomatic missions overseas include:

Canada (☎ 613-783 7665) Suite 710, 50 O'Connor St, Ottawa
France (☎ 01 40 59 33 00) 4 Rue Jean Rey, Paris 75724
Germany (☎ 030-8800 880) Friedrichstrasse 200, 10117 Berlin
Indonesia (☎ 021-2550 5700) Jalan H R Rasuna Said Kav C 15–16, Jakarta Selatan 12940; *consulate* in Denpasar
Ireland (☎ 01-676 1517) Fitzwilton House, Wilton Terrace, Dublin 2
Japan (☎ 03-5232 4111) 2-1-14 Mita, Minato-ku, Tokyo 108-8361
Netherlands (☎ 070-310 8200) Carnegielaan 4, The Hague 2517KH
New Zealand (☎ 09-303 2429) Union House, 132–138 Quay St, Auckland 1
South Africa (☎ 012-342 3740) 292 Orient St, Arcadia, Pretoria 0083

UK (☎ 020-7379 4334) Australia House, The Strand, London WC2B 4LA; *consulate* in Manchester

USA (☎ 202-797 3000) 1601 Massachusetts Ave NW, Washington DC 20036; *consulate* in Los Angeles.

Embassies & Consulates in Australia

Yarralumla in Canberra is home to most foreign embassies, but many countries maintain consulates in Sydney as well.

Canada
Embassy: (☎ 6273 3844) Commonwealth Ave, Yarralumla
France
Embassy: (☎ 6270 5111) 6 Perth Ave, Yarralumla
Consulate: (☎ 9261 5779) 31 Market St, Sydney
Germany
Embassy: (☎ 6270 1911) 119 Empire Court, Yarralumla
Consulate: (☎ 9328 7733) 13 Trelawney St, Woollahra
Indonesia
Embassy: (☎ 6273 3222) 8 Darwin Ave, Yarralumla
Consulate: (☎ 9344 9933) 236 Maroubra Rd, Maroubra
Ireland
Embassy: (☎ 6273 3022) 20 Arkana St, Yarralumla
Japan
Embassy: (☎ 6273 3244) 112 Empire Circuit, Yarralumla
Consulate: (☎ 9231 3455) 52 Martin Place, Sydney

Malaysia
Embassy: (☎ 6273 1543) 7 Perth Ave, Yarralumla
Consulate: (☎ 9327 7565) 67 Victoria Rd, Bellevue Hill
Netherlands
Embassy: (☎ 6273 3111) 120 Empire Circuit, Yarralumla
Consulate: (☎ 9387 6644) 500 Oxford St, Bondi Junction
New Zealand
Embassy: (☎ 6270 4211) Commonwealth Ave, Yarralumla
Consulate: (☎ 9247 1999) 1 Alfred St, Circular Quay
Papua New Guinea
Embassy: (☎ 6273 3322) 39–41 Forster Crescent, Yarralumla
Consulate: (☎ 9299 6633) 301 George St, Sydney
Singapore
Embassy: (☎ 6273 3944) 17 Forster Crescent, Yarralumla
Thailand
Embassy: (☎ 6273 1149) 111 Empire Circuit, Yarralumla
UK
Embassy: (☎ 6270 6666) Commonwealth Ave, Yarralumla
USA
Embassy: (☎ 6270 5000) 21 Moonah Place, Yarralumla
Consulate: (☎ 9373 9200) 19–29 Martin Place, Sydney

CUSTOMS

When entering Australia you can bring most articles in free of duty, provided that customs is satisfied they're for personal use and

Your Own Embassy

It's important to realise what your own embassy – the embassy of the country of which you are a citizen – can and can't do to help you if you get into trouble. Generally speaking, it won't be much help in emergencies if the trouble you're in is remotely your own fault. Remember that you are bound by the laws of the country you are in. Your embassy will not be sympathetic if you end up in jail after committing a crime locally, even if such actions are legal in your own country.

In genuine emergencies you might get some assistance, but only if other channels have been exhausted. For example, if you need to get home urgently, a free ticket home is exceedingly unlikely – the embassy would expect you to have insurance. If you have all your money and documents stolen, it might assist with getting a new passport, but a loan for onward travel is out of the question.

Some embassies used to keep letters for travellers or have a small reading room with home newspapers, but these days the mail holding service has usually been stopped and even newspapers tend to be out of date.

that you'll be taking them with you when you leave. There's also the usual duty-free per-person quota of 1125ml of alcohol, 250 cigarettes and dutiable goods up to the value of A$400.

Two issues need particular attention. Number one is drugs. Customs has a mania about the stuff and can be extremely efficient when it comes to finding it. Unless you have a real desire to investigate prison conditions in Australia, don't bring any drugs in with you.

Issue two is animal and plant quarantine. You will be asked to declare all goods of animal or vegetable origin and to show them to a quarantine official.

Quarantine authorities are naturally very keen to prevent weeds, pests or diseases getting into the country – Australia has so far managed to escape many of the agricultural pests and diseases that are prevalent in other parts of the world. Fresh food – particularly meat, sausage, fruit and vegetables – is also unpopular with customs, as are flowers.

Weapons and firearms are either prohibited or require a permit and safety testing. Other restricted goods include products (such as ivory) made from protected species, unapproved telecommunications devices and live animals.

When you leave, make sure you don't take any protected flora or fauna with you. Customs comes down hard on animal smugglers.

MONEY
Currency
The unit of currency is the Australian dollar, which is divided into 100 cents. There are $100, $50, $20, $10 and $5 notes, and $2, $1, $0.50, $0.20, $0.10 and $0.05 coins. Shops round prices up (or down) to the nearest $0.05 on your total bill.

Exchange Rates
The Australian dollar fluctuates quite markedly against the US dollar, but seems to stay pretty much in the $0.65/$0.75 range – a disaster for Australians travelling overseas but a real bonus for inbound visitors.

Approximate exchange values are:

country	unit		dollar
Canada	C$1	=	A$1.12
France	1FF	=	A$0.24
Germany	DM1	=	A$0.81
euro	€1	=	A$1.58
Japan	¥100	=	A$1.57
New Zealand	NZ$1	=	A$0.77
UK	UK£1	=	A$2.52
USA	US$1	=	A$1.67

Exchanging Money
You can change foreign currency at any bank or licensed exchange bureau (such as Thomas Cook).

American Express (AmEx), Thomas Cook and other well-known brands of travellers cheques can be changed at most banks. A passport is usually adequate identification.

Buying travellers cheques in Australian dollars is worth looking at. These can be exchanged immediately at banks without incurring commissions and fees.

Fees for changing foreign-currency travellers cheques vary from bank to bank: the National Australia Bank and the Commonwealth Bank charge $5; ANZ $6.50 and Westpac $7 (all per transaction).

ATMs There are Automatic Teller Machines (ATMs) at most banks throughout the state. ATMs can be used day or night and they're linked to the international networks such as Cirrus and Maestro, so you don't need a local bank account to use them.

Credit Cards Visa and MasterCard are widely accepted. Charge cards such as Diners Club and AmEx are not as useful, but many hotels and restaurants take them. Cash advances from credit cards are available at banks, depending on the card.

Having a credit card makes renting a car much simpler. They're favoured over cash and many agencies simply won't rent you a vehicle if you don't have a card.

Local Bank Accounts
Opening an account at an Australian bank isn't easy. A points system operates and you

need to score 100 points before you can have the privilege of letting the bank take your money (and charge you various mysterious fees). Passports, driving licences, birth certificates and other 'major' IDs earn you 40 points; minor ones, such as credit cards, get you 20 points. However, if as a foreign visitor you apply to open an account during your first six weeks in the country, just showing your passport should be enough.

The four major national banks are: ANZ; the Commonwealth Bank; the National Australia Bank; and Westpac. Other banks with a NSW profile are the State Bank of NSW and St George. Post offices act as agencies for the Commonwealth Bank, which can be handy if you're visiting remote areas.

Most travellers opt for an account that includes a cash card that can be used to access money from ATMs. Many businesses, such as petrol stations, supermarkets and convenience stores, are linked to the Electronic Funds Transfer at Point of Sale (EFTPOS) system, which allows you to use your card to pay for services or purchases and withdraw cash directly from your account.

Security
If you're carrying travellers cheques, passport etc, a moneybelt worn under your clothing is a good idea, but keep your daily cash in a purse or wallet for easy access. Most hotels and hostels provide safekeeping, so you can leave your money and other valuables with them.

Costs
With low inflation over the past few years, prices in Australia have remained fairly stable, and a drop in the value of the Australian dollar has meant favourable exchange rates for overseas visitors.

Compared with other Western countries, Australia is cheaper in some ways and more expensive in others. Manufactured goods like clothes tend to be more expensive, but food and wine are both high in quality and low in cost.

Transport isn't expensive in terms of dollars per kilometre, but the distances can be great so fares are correspondingly high.

A New Tax

A Goods & Services Tax (GST) was introduced in Australia on 1 July 2000. This means a 10% tax is added to all manufactured goods (not basic food or primary products) and to services ranging from getting your hair cut to staying in a hotel.

Because the GST replaces wholesale sales tax and several other previously 'hidden' taxes, many items will probably end up being cheaper, but balancing this, many previously untaxed items will be subject to the GST.

For travellers, the GST has a number of ramifications. For a start, accommodation, transport and dining out will be subject to the 10% increase. **Prices quoted in this book do NOT include the GST.** However, prices advertised in Australia will have the tax included.

The good news is that international air travel to and from Australia will be GST-free, as will domestic air travel when purchased outside Australia by nonresidents.

Food on the road is reasonably priced. Even the smallest town has a cafe where you can get a decent hamburger for about $3. Local bowling or ex-servicemen's clubs often have the best-value meals.

If you're travelling on a budget, camping or staying at hostels and using public transport, you could get by on as little as $30 to $40 a day, but it wouldn't leave you much spending money. If you're driving, staying in varying standards of accommodation and enjoying nightlife or outdoor pursuits, expect to spend more like $70 to $80 a day – probably more than that in Sydney. Remember that you'll pay more for accommodation in summer.

All prices in this book are given in Australian dollars unless otherwise specified.

Tipping & Bargaining
Tipping is becoming more common, especially in more upmarket restaurants and cafes, but it isn't yet an entrenched practice in Australia, especially since many restaurants automatically add a service charge. A tip of around 10% is average, but feel free to

vary the amount depending on your satisfaction with the level of service. Taxi drivers don't expect to be tipped, but 'rounding up' the fare to the nearest dollar is common.

A little friendly bargaining is possible at flea markets.

Taxes & Refunds

An extra cost factor is the recently introduced 10% Goods & Services Tax (GST). See the boxed text 'A New Tax' in this section for more information.

If you purchase new or used goods with a total minimum value of $300 from any one supplier within 28 days of departure from Australia, you will be entitled to a refund on any GST paid. Contact the Australian Taxation Office (ATO) inquiry line on ☎ 13 6140 for details.

POST & COMMUNICATIONS
Post

Australia Post (☎ 13 1318) runs the country's mail system. Most post offices open Monday to Friday from 9 am to 5 pm, but you can often get stamps from newsagencies and Australia Post retail outlets on Saturday (9 am to noon) as well. All post offices hold mail (poste restante) for visitors.

It costs $0.45 to send a standard letter or postcard within Australia. International aerogrammes are $0.80 and postcards $1 to anywhere in the world. Airmail letters (up to 50g) cost $1 to Asia and the Pacific region (including New Zealand), and $1.50 to the rest of the world.

Airmail rates for posting parcels are pretty expensive. By airmail a 1/2/5kg parcel to New Zealand costs $15.75/24/39, to the UK $29.50/46/91 and to the USA $25.75/40/76. Economy air (slightly slower) is a bit cheaper. If you send by sea (which takes forever), rates are $17/26/44 for a 1/2/5kg parcel to the UK, Europe and the USA (there's no sea mail service to New Zealand or Asia).

Telephone

Area Codes The area code for most of NSW and the ACT is ☎ 02. The exceptions are Broken Hill, which has the SA ☎ 08 area code, Tweed Heads, with the Queensland

☎ 07 area code, and several towns in the Riverina along the Murray River, with the ☎ 03 Victoria area code. You only need to dial an area code when calling from a region with a different area code.

Local Calls Local calls from public phones cost $0.40 for an unlimited amount of time. You can make local calls from gold or blue coin phones – often found in hotels, shops, bars etc – and from pay-phone booths, which accept coins and phonecards. Local calls from private telephones cost $0.25, although the deregulation of the telecommunications industry in Australia means that some companies are now offering cheaper rates than Telstra (the main carrier).

Long-distance Calls It's also possible to make long-distance (STD) calls from virtually any public phone. Most public phones accept Telstra phonecards, which come in $5, $10, $20 and $50 denominations and are available from retail outlets such as newsagents and pharmacies displaying the phonecard logo. You can also buy prepaid calling cards issued by private companies (such as Primus). These cards require you to dial a toll-free number, then the card number, before making your call. They can be used from any phone.

Some public phones are set up to take bank cash cards or credit cards, and these too are convenient, although you need to keep an eye on how much the call is costing, as it can quickly mount up. The minimum charge for a call on one of these phones is $1.20.

STD calls are cheaper at off-peak times. In ascending order of cost:

Economy From 7 pm Friday to 7 am Monday and 7 pm to 7 am Monday to Friday
Afternoon From 1 to 7 pm Monday to Friday
Day From 7 am to 1 pm Monday to Friday

International Calls From most STD phones you can also make International Subscriber Dialling (ISD) calls.

Dial ☎ 0011 for international access, the country code (eg, 44 for Britain, 1 for the USA, 64 for New Zealand), the city code –

dropping the initial zero if there is one (eg, 20 for London, 212 for New York) – and then the telephone number. Have a phonecard, credit card or plenty of coins handy.

International calls from Australia are among the cheapest you'll find anywhere. A Telstra call from a public phone to the USA or Britain costs $1.60 a minute ($0.80 off-peak). Off-peak is from midnight Friday to midnight Sunday (call ☎ 1222 for more details). International calls from private phones are much cheaper and companies such as Optus, OneTel and Primus offer the cheapest rates of all.

Country Direct is a service that gives travellers in Australia direct access to operators in nearly 50 countries to make collect or credit-card calls. For a full list of the countries hooked into this system, check the *White Pages* telephone book. They include: Canada (☎ 1800 881 150), Germany (☎ 1800 881 490), Ireland (☎ 1800 881 353), Japan (☎ 1800 881 810), New Zealand (☎ 1800 881 640), the UK (☎ 1800 881 440) and the USA (☎ 1800 881 011).

Lonely Planet's eKno communication card is aimed specifically at independent travellers and provides budget international calls, a range of messaging services, free email and travel information, but for local calls you're usually better off with a local phonecard. You can join online at www.ekno .lonelyplanet.com, or by phone from NSW by dialling ☎ 1800 674 100. Once you have joined, to use eKno from NSW dial ☎ 1800 114 478 or ☎ 8208 3000 if you're in Sydney.

Free & Low-Cost Calls Many businesses and some government departments operate a toll-free service, so it's a free call no matter where you're ringing from around the country. These numbers have the prefix 1800. Many companies, such as the airlines, have six-digit numbers beginning with 13, which are charged at the rate of a local call. Numbers beginning with 1300 are also charged at a local call rate. These are often Australia-wide numbers, or they may be applicable to a specific STD district only (such as the state). Unfortunately, there's no way of telling without actually ringing the number.

Mobile Phones Australians have embraced mobile phones with a passion. Calls to (and from) mobile phones are charged at a higher rate than calls to land lines, and are timed – you can recognise them by a four-digit prefix usually beginning with 04. The main mobile networks in Australia are Telstra, Optus and Vodaphone.

Having a mobile phone can be handy, but with the digital network you often won't get a signal outside towns in remote areas – remote being practically anywhere outside Sydney or Canberra! If you have your own phone, you can get on the network reasonably cheaply with a prepaid account (Optus offers one), otherwise you may have to sign on to a lengthy contract.

Fax

All post offices (but few postal agencies) send faxes, and many receive them. To send a fax it costs $4 for the first page and $1 for each subsequent page, or, for overseas faxes, $10 for the first page and $4 for following pages.

It's worth checking if Internet and travellers cafes offer fax services, as they're usually cheaper than post offices. The international code for sending fax messages is ☎ 0015.

Email & Internet Access

Throughout the state you'll find that many public libraries have at least one terminal where you can access the Internet and use email. Charges range from free (which is quite common now but will probably be less so in future) to $5 an hour. The drawback is that you'll probably have to book. In Sydney, there's fierce competition for your Internet dollar, which means that in places like Kings Cross you can get online at an Internet cafe for about $2 an hour. There are also plenty of Internet cafes along the coast, particularly in areas popular with travellers. Youth hostels often have coin-operated Internet terminals. You can open a free Web-based email account, such as Lonely Planet's eKno (www.ekno.lonelyplanet .com), that you can access from any Internet-linked computer.

If you plan to bring your own computer, remember that you might need a universal AC adaptor if the power supply is different from your own country (Australia's is 220–240V), as well as a plug adaptor – often it's easiest to buy these before you leave home.

Also, your PC-card modem may not work in Australia. The safest option is to buy a reputable 'global' modem before you leave home, or buy a local PC-card modem when you arrive. Australia uses the RJ-45 telephone socket and Telstra EXI-160 plugs. For information on travelling with a portable computer, see www.teleadapt.com or www.warrior.com.

There are service providers in Sydney, Canberra and some regional centres if you want to get online locally. They include:

Australia On Line (☎ 1800 621 258)
 Web site: www.ozonline.com.au
On Australia (Microsoft Network; ☎ 02-9934 9000)
OzEmail (☎ 9391 0480)
 Web site: www.ozemail.com.au
Telstra Big Pond (☎ 1800 804 282)
 Web site: www.bigpond.com

CompuServe users who want to access the service locally should call ☎ 1300 307 072 to get the local log-in numbers.

INTERNET RESOURCES

The World Wide Web is a rich resource for travellers. You can research your trip, hunt down bargain air fares, book hotels, check on weather conditions or chat with locals and other travellers about the best places to visit (or avoid!).

There's no better place to start your Web explorations than the Lonely Planet Web site (www.lonelyplanet.com). Here you'll find succinct summaries on travelling to most places on earth, postcards from other travellers and the Thorn Tree bulletin board, where you can ask questions before you go or dispense advice when you get back. You can also find travel news and updates to many of our most popular guidebooks, and the subWWWay section links you to the most useful travel resources elsewhere on

the Web. Other worthwhile Web sites on NSW include:

Visit NSW The official Visit NSW tourism site is as good a place as any to start, with accommodation and sightseeing information, activities and links.
 Web site: www.tourism.nsw.gov.au
NSW Government The NSW Government homepage sounds a bit staid, but it has a lot of useful information and interesting links, including national parks pages.
 Web site: www.nsw.gov.au
National Parks & Wildlife Service (NPWS) This is the NSW government's national parks site.
 Web site: www.npws.nsw.gov.au
Sydney Morning Herald This site features news, sport, classifieds and feature articles.
 Web site: www.smh.com.au
NSW Heritage Council This site has information on the state's heritage projects, archaeology and Aboriginal heritage sites.
 Web site: www.heritage.nsw.gov.au
Historic Houses Trust
 Web site: www.hht.nsw.gov.au

For information on sites relating to Canberra, see the Australian Capital Territory chapter.

BOOKS

Most books are published in different editions by different publishers in different countries. As a result, a book might be a hardcover rarity in one country while it's readily available in paperback in another. Fortunately, bookshops and libraries search by title or author, so your local bookshop or library is best placed to advise you on the availability of the following recommendations.

Lonely Planet

The information in Lonely Planet's *Sydney City Guide* is a more detailed version of the Sydney information in this guidebook. *Out to Eat – Sydney* is an exhaustive guide to restaurants, cafes and other dining establishments in the capital. The *Sydney* condensed guide is a colourful new book that gives you the best of Sydney in a concise format.

Lonely Planet also publishes the *Australia* guide, *Walking in Australia* and *Australian Phrasebook*.

In *Sean & David's Long Drive,* an offbeat road book by Sean Condon (and one of the titles in Lonely Planet's 'Journeys' series), the protagonists visit NSW.

Guidebooks

Burnum Burnum's Aboriginal Australia, subtitled 'a traveller's guide', explores Australia from an Aboriginal point of view.

Gregory's *National Parks of NSW* is a handy guide to the state's national parks, popular nature reserves, state recreation areas and historic sites.

The NRMA publishes star-rated accommodation guides to caravan parks and motel-style accommodation, but they're roughly the size and weight of the Sydney *Yellow Pages* – unsuitable if you're backpacking. *Guide to B&Bs & Rural Retreats in NSW* by Wendy Robinson lists places across the state.

Travel

A great book to read while visiting Sydney is *Sydney* by Jan Morris, one of the best travel writers around.

Aborigines

The Australian Aborigines by Kenneth Maddock provides a good cultural summary. The award-winning *Triumph of the Nomads* by Geoffrey Blainey is also worth reading. For accounts of what's happened to the original Australians since Europeans arrived, read *Aboriginal Australians* by Richard Broome or *A Change of Ownership* by Mildred Kirk.

The Other Side of the Frontier by Henry Reynolds gives a vivid Aboriginal view of the arrival of Europeans in Australia. Reynolds also wrote *With the White People. My Place,* Sally Morgan's prize-winning autobiography, traces her discovery of her Aboriginal heritage. *The Fringe Dwellers* by Nene Gare, describes growing up in a white-dominated society. *The Stolen Children – their Stories* edited by Carmel Bird tells the harrowing stories of Aboriginal children separated from their parents.

History

For a good introduction to Australian history, read *A Short History of Australia* by the late Manning Clark. A single-volume condensation of Clark's definitive (and controversial) six-volume *History of Australia* is also available.

The Fatal Shore, Robert Hughes' best-selling account of the convict era, is a great read. *Finding Australia* by Russel Ward traces the early days from the first Aboriginal arrivals to 1821. Ward's *Concise History of Australia* is a quick introduction.

The Exploration of Australia by Michael Cannon is a fascinating reference book about the gradual European uncovering of the continent. An intriguing combination of history and nature study is Eric Rolls' excellent *A Million Wild Acres.*

Children's Books

Two classics for younger children that are essential reading are Norman Lindsay's *The Magic Pudding* and May Gibbs' *Snugglepot & Cuddlepie.* Lindsay's home, now open as a museum, is near Springwood in the Blue Mountains. There are displays relating to *The Magic Pudding.* Nutcote, May Gibbs' house in North Sydney, is also a museum.

FILMS

Quite a few Australian films have been shot in and around Sydney, and the opening of Fox Studios in 1999 has made it an even more attractive proposition for international films (such as *Mission Impossible 2*).

More interesting are some of the location films shot outside the city. *For the Term of His Natural Life* (1927) used the NSW coast, the Hawkesbury River and Wombeyan Caves, despite being set in a Tasmanian penal colony. *The Chant of Jimmy Blacksmith* (1978), portraying the often violent bigotry against Aboriginals in the early 20th century, was filmed around Armidale, Dorrigo, Dubbo, Mudgee and Port Macquarie. Braidwood was the setting for *The Year My Voice Broke* (1987) and *Ned Kelly* (1969), while *Babe* (starring the cute pig; 1996) used the rural Southern Highlands as a backdrop.

NEWSPAPERS & MAGAZINES

The *Sydney Morning Herald* is one of the country's best newspapers. It's a serious broadsheet, but it captures some of Sydney's larrikinism as well. The other Sydney paper is the *Daily Telegraph*, a tabloid, but much tamer than other products of the Rupert Murdoch stables.

Two national newspapers are available in NSW: the *Australian* and the *Australian Financial Review*. Local newspapers and magazines – from the trashy to the seriously conservative – are also available.

RADIO & TV

The largest broadcaster in the country is the (less and less) government-funded, (so far) commercial-free Australian Broadcasting Corporation (ABC). There are two main services: Radio National, heard just about everywhere, and lighter regional services, generally heard only around major centres. Fine Music is the ABC's classical music station and Triple J is its 'youth' station; neither is available everywhere. Pick up a copy of the free *Travellers Guide to ABC Radio* from ABC shops or radio stations.

Outside Sydney, which has more than 20 radio stations, you'll usually be able to pick up an ABC station, a local commercial station and often a local public station. You might also be able to tune into the foreign-language programs of the Special Broadcasting Service (SBS).

There are five main TV networks in NSW: the ABC, SBS and the three commercial networks, Channels 10, 9 and 7. The ABC and at least one commercial station can be received almost everywhere in the state. SBS is only available in Sydney and several large centres, including Broken Hill and Orange.

PHOTOGRAPHY & VIDEO

A 36-exposure Kodachrome 64 slide film costs around $25 to $28 (including developing), or Fujichrome 100 is about $15 for the film only.

The more-popular colour print films are sold everywhere for about $12 for a roll of 36, but outside Sydney slide or B&W film is harder to find.

There are many camera shops; camera service and developing standards are high.

Protect your film by keeping it cool and having it processed as soon as possible. Other camera and film hazards are dust and humidity. The best results are gained when the light is not too harsh or bright – early in the morning and late in the afternoon, especially in summer.

As in any country, politeness goes a long way when taking photographs: Ask before taking pictures of people. Note that most Aborigines don't like having their photograph taken, even from a distance.

At airports passengers must pass their luggage through x-ray machines. Today's technology doesn't jeopardise lower-speed film, but it's best to carry your film and camera with you and ask the x-ray inspector to check them visually. Don't leave film in your check-in luggage as it receives a higher dose of x-rays.

Overseas visitors thinking of purchasing videos should remember that Australia uses the Phase Alternative Line (PAL) system, which isn't compatible with other standards unless converted.

TIME

NSW uses Eastern Standard Time (as do Queensland, Victoria and Tasmania), which is 10 hours ahead of GMT/UTC (Greenwich Mean Time/Universal Coordinated Time). Note that Broken Hill uses SA Central Time – half an hour behind EST.

Without taking into account daylight-saving time, at noon in Sydney it's: 6 pm the previous day in Los Angeles and 9 pm the previous day in New York, and 2 am the same day in London, 3 am in Rome, 9 am in Bangkok, 2 pm in Auckland.

From the last Sunday in October to the first Sunday in March, NSW is on Eastern Summer Time, one hour ahead of standard time.

ELECTRICITY

Voltage is 220–240V and plugs are flat three-pin, but they are not like British three-pin plugs. Other than in fancy hotels, it's difficult to find converters to take either US flat two-pin plugs or the European round two-pin plugs used with electric shavers or hairdryers. Adaptors for British plugs are found in good hardware shops, chemists and travel agents.

WEIGHTS & MEASURES

Australia uses the metric system. In country areas you'll still hear people using imperial units and when you're receiving directions it's a good idea to make sure that they are talking about kilometres, not miles.

LAUNDRY

Most hostels and cheaper hotels have self-service laundry facilities, while the more expensive hotels will return your clothes washed, dried and neatly folded. Otherwise there are self-service laundrettes or dry-cleaning outlets, many of which open daily. Washing a load costs about $2 and drying it is generally another $2 for 30 minutes. To find a laundrette, look in the *Yellow Pages* under 'Laundries – Self-Service'.

HEALTH

Vaccinations aren't required for entry into Australia unless you've visited an infected country in the preceding 14 days (aircraft refuelling stops don't count).

Medical care in Australia is first class and only moderately expensive. A typical visit to the doctor costs around $35. Health insurance cover is available, but there's usually a waiting period after you sign up before any claims can be made.

There is universal health care in Australia (for Australians and citizens of nations with reciprocal rights) and you can choose your own doctor. Visitors from Finland, Italy, Malta, the Netherlands, New Zealand, Sweden and the UK have reciprocal health rights and can register at any Medicare office.

If you have an immediate health problem, contact the casualty section at the nearest public hospital; in an emergency call an ambulance (☎ 000).

Medical Kit

It's always a good idea to travel with a basic medical kit. Don't forget any medication you're already taking. A small medical kit might include aspirin or paracetamol, anti-histamine, antiseptic, multivitamins, cold and flu tablets, calamine lotion, bandages, Band-aids, scissors and insect repellent.

Health Precautions

The sun is intense in Australia and ultraviolet rays can burn you badly even on an overcast day. Australia has the world's highest incidence of skin cancer, so cover up and wear plenty of sunscreen. The sun is at its fiercest between 11 am and 3 pm, so be especially careful during this period.

Too much sunlight, whether direct or reflected (glare), can damage your eyes. If you're near water, sand or snow, good-quality sunglasses that filter out UV radiation are essential.

Dehydration or salt deficiency can cause heat exhaustion. Take time to acclimatise to high temperatures and drink plenty of water. Wear loose clothing and a broad-brimmed hat. Heat stroke occurs when the body's heat-regulating mechanism breaks down and the body temperature rises dangerously. If you arrive during a hot period, avoid excessive alcohol or strenuous activity.

Salbutamol inhalers (Ventolin) are available without prescription, but you must give your name and address to the chemist.

The contraceptive pill is available by prescription only, so a visit to a doctor is necessary. Condoms are available from chemists, convenience stores and vending machines in hotel toilets.

HIV/AIDS

Human Immunodeficiency Virus (HIV) may develop into Acquired Immune Deficiency Syndrome (AIDS). Exposure to blood, blood products or bodily fluids may put the individual at risk. Transmission is usually through sexual contact and intravenous drug use, but HIV/AIDS can also be spread through infected blood transfusions and by dirty needles – vaccinations, acupuncture, tattooing and ear or nose piercing can be dangerous if the equipment isn't clean. In Australia, although there may be a risk of infection, it's very small. Fear of HIV infection should never preclude treatment for serious medical conditions.

Apart from abstinence, the most effective preventative measure is to use condoms and clean needles. It's impossible to detect the HIV-positive status of an otherwise healthy-looking person without a blood test.

For advice, call the 24-hour AIDS Information Line (☎ 9332 4000, 1800 451 600) or contact the AIDS Council of NSW (☎ 9206 2000, 1800 063 060), PO Box 350, Darlinghurst, NSW 2010.

WOMEN TRAVELLERS

NSW is generally safe for women travellers, although you should avoid walking alone in Sydney late at night. Sexual harassment is uncommon, although the Aussie male culture does have its sexist elements. Don't tolerate any harassment or discrimination. Female hitchhikers should exercise care.

In Sydney some of the major women's organisations (which can direct you to local institutions) are:

Royal Hospital for Women (☎ 9326 5763) 37 Eurimble St, Randwick
Women & Girls Emergency Centre (☎ 9360 5388) 177 Albion St, Surry Hills
Women's Liberation House (☎ 9569 3819) 63 Palace St, Petersham

GAY & LESBIAN TRAVELLERS

Gay and lesbian culture is so strong in Sydney that it's almost mainstream. Oxford St, especially around Taylor Square, is the centre of what is probably the second-largest gay community in the world. The suburb of Newtown is home to Sydney's lesbian scene. Sydney is one of the top three holiday destinations for US gays and lesbians.

The Gay & Lesbian Mardi Gras (see Public Holidays & Special Events later in this chapter) is the biggest annual tourist event in Australia. It culminates in a spectacular parade up Oxford St, watched by more than 650,000 people, and a huge party at the Royal Agricultural Society's Showgrounds.

Despite all this, there's still a strong streak of homophobia among 'dinkum' Aussies, even in Sydney itself, and violence against homosexuals isn't unknown.

For the record, it's legal in NSW for a man to have sex with a man over the age of 18,

and for a woman to have sex with a woman over the age of 16.

The *g'day accommodation guide* gives listings of items of interest to gay travellers. National gay/lesbian magazines include *OutRage, Campaign, Lesbians on the Loose (LOTL), DNA* and the art magazine *Blue*. In Sydney free papers such as *Capital Q Weekly* and the *Sydney Star Observer* have comprehensive listings of gay and lesbian events.

For advice, counselling and referral call the Gay & Lesbian Line (☎ 9207 2800), 4 pm to midnight daily; for information call the 24-hour service (☎ 9207 2822).

SENIOR TRAVELLERS

Australian senior citizens are entitled to some discounts, such as public transport and museum admission fees, provided they show an Australian Pensioners Card. Few of these apply to senior citizens from abroad, though some places may agree to give you a discount if you show your seniors card.

For information on recreational and other activities, contact the Seniors Information Service (☎ 13 1244 NSW only), 6th floor, 93 York St, Sydney. In March there's a seniors week, with exhibitions, concerts, seminars etc.

TRAVEL WITH CHILDREN

Travel with young children requires effort, but it can be done. Try not to overdo things, and consider using some sort of self-catering accommodation as a base. Include children in the planning process; if they've helped to work out where you're going, they'll be more interested when they get there. Include a range of activities – for example, balance a visit to the Art Gallery of NSW with one to the Powerhouse Museum. During school holidays many places put on extra activities for children. Coastal resorts are particularly well suited for kids – even if they tire of the beach there are plenty of playgrounds and theme parks.

In Sydney, look for a copy of *Sydney's Child,* a free monthly paper listing businesses and activities geared to ankle biters.

For more general information see Lonely Planet's *Travel with Children.*

Travel in NSW & ACT for People with Disabilities

People with disabilities can enjoy easy travel in New South Wales (NSW) and the Australian Capital Territory (ACT), with plenty of good transport and accommodation options, accessible attractions and increased information.

Information

The visitors information centres at The Rocks (☎ 9255 1788) and in Canberra (☎ 6205 0666), respectively, provide copies of *Accessing Sydney,* published by the Australian Quadriplegic Association, and *Discover Canberra,* a directory of accessible activities and events.

The National Information & Communication Awareness Network (NICAN; ☎ 1800 806 769, TTY ☎ 6285 3713), PO Box 407, Curtin ACT 2605, is a key information source on recreation, sport, arts and tourism. The Australian Quadriplegic Association (☎ 9661 8855), PO Box 397, Matraville NSW 2036, is also a good resource. Check out its Web site at www.aqa.com.au.

Other useful contacts are:

The Paraplegic and Quadriplegic Association in NSW (☎ 9764 4166, 1800 424 096), which provides some information about accommodation and care.
Web site: www.paraquad-nsw.asn.au
Personal Equipment & Continence Suppliers (PECS; ☎ 9647 1966), a nonprescription medical supplier.
Paraquad Engineering (☎ 9772 3888), which modifies vehicles and installs hand controls etc.
Independent Living Centre (☎ 9808 2233, TTY ☎ 9808 2477), 600 Victoria Rd, Ryde 2112, which provides equipment hire advice.
Web site: www.ilcnsw.asn.au
Deaf Society of NSW (TTY ☎ 9893 8858), Level 4, 169 Macquarie St, Parramatta 2150
Royal Blind Society of NSW (☎ 9334 3333), 4 Mitchell St, Enfield 2136
Multiple Sclerosis Society of NSW (☎ 9287 2929), 447 Kent St, Sydney 2000.

Always contact the council or visitors information centre at your intended destination for a contact at the local access committee, which has up-to-date information about access to facilities and services.

Publications There are several useful publications, other than those already mentioned, for travellers with disabilities: *Easy Access Australia: A Travel Guide to Australia,* PO Box 218, Kew Victoria 3101, has a Web site (www.easyaccessaustralia.com.au) that was due to be up and running by the time this book is published; *Visitors Guide: National Parks in NSW* and *Outdoor Access for Everybody,* put out by the National Parks & Wildlife Service (☎ 1300 361 967), 43 Bridge St, Hurstville 2220; *Access the Best: Blue Mountains,* available from the Blue Mountains Visitors Information Centre; *A Wheely Good Access Guide to Sydney* by Megan Harper, PO Box 1755, Lane Cove NSW 2066; and *Sydney's Then and Now Story: The Historic Houses of Sydney Trust* (☎ 9692 8366), listing access and whether Braille, large-print brochures and audio loops are available for the historic properties that the Trust administers. See also the Web site at www.hht.nsw.gov.au.

Things to See & Do

Most major attractions throughout NSW and the ACT provide excellent access. In Sydney, head for Darling Harbour, where the Maritime Museum, Chinese Garden, Sydney Aquarium, Powerhouse Museum, Cockle Bay Wharf (great food) and Star City Casino have great access. The Bondi Explorer Bus (☎ 13 1500) is easily accessible.

Other Sydney attractions include Centrepoint Tower, the Royal Botanic Gardens, The Rocks, Homebush Bay, Manly and historic Macquarie St.

Travel in NSW & ACT for People with Disabilities

In regional NSW head for the Western Plains Zoo in Dubbo, Country Music Festival in Tamworth, The Water Fall Way from Armidale to Coffs Harbour, fishing at Narooma, wineries in the Hunter Valley, the lighthouse precinct at Cape Byron, and many accessible national parks.

In the ACT, travellers with disabilities will find Parliament House, the Australian War Memorial and the National Gallery are easily accessible, while Civic, Manuka, Watson and Belconnen are good for shopping and are great eating areas.

Organised Tours

NICAN maintains a list of tour operators, as does Information on Disability Equipment Access and Services (IDEAS; ☎ 1800 029 904), which also lists accommodation providers. Try Leisure Options (☎ 1800 801 250); Rambler Tours (☎ 03-9432 3222), for five-star accessible coach tours; Australian Specialised Getaway Disabled Travels (☎ 9456 7770); and Lynwood Tours (☎ 9637 5669).

Places to Stay

Accessing Sydney and *Discover Canberra* are the best sources of accessible accommodation in Sydney and Canberra. NICAN and *Easy Access Australia* provide the best options around NSW for hostels, caravan parks, B&Bs and holiday cottages.

The **Sydney Central YHA** (☎ 9281 9111) provides seven accessible rooms with en suites. The **Hotel Y** (☎ 9264 2451) has two good rooms. The **Rainforest Resort** (☎ 6685 6139) at Byron Bay is fully wheelchair accessible (including the pool and spa). **Clark Bay Farm** (☎ 4476 1640) at Narooma has three fully accessible, self-contained, two-bedroom units (including one high-dependancy unit with ceiling hoist) and pool. Cheap accessible accommodation is scarce in the ACT: **Fenner Hall** (☎ 6279 9101), part of ANU, has three accessible rooms with large en suites but small bedrooms.

Getting There & Away

The Carer Concession Card (contact NICAN), entitling a carer to fly half price, is accepted by Ansett Airlines and Qantas Airways. Sydney and Canberra airports have dedicated parking spaces, drop-off points, accessible toilets, lifts and air bridges.

Countrylink trains (☎ 13 2232, 9379 4850) operate to/from Brisbane, Melbourne, Sydney, Canberra and major regional centres in NSW, and have at least one accessible carriage (two wheelchair spaces and toilet). Long-haul bus travel is not yet an option for the wheelchair traveller.

Getting Around

Sydney's public transport system includes some accessible rail stations and many low-floor buses on innercity routes. Call (☎ 13 1500) for route maps and timetables. Buses aren't an option in Canberra.

Ferries are a great way to view Sydney Harbour, but stick to the terminals at Circular Quay, Manly, Parramatta, Homebush Bay and Darling Harbour, as smaller terminals have steep slippery ramps and even steps. Australian Travel Specialist (☎ 9247 5151) at Circular Quay will book Sydney Ferries, JetCats, Captain Cook Cruises and The Bounty (upper deck only). Some Manly and Parramatta Jet-Cats have accessible toilets.

Sydney's light rail and the elevated monorail are accessible and excellent ways of moving around and seeing the city (☎ 8584 5288).

Accessible taxis can be booked on a national number (☎ 13 1008).

Avis (☎ 13 6333) and Hertz (☎ 13 3039) provide hand-controlled vehicles at no extra cost but advance notice is required.

Budget (☎ 9635 0655) hires out three-wheelchair-capacity vans.

Wheelabout Van Rentals Pty Ltd (☎ 4367 0900), www.wheelabout.com, rents out two-wheelchair-capacity luxury vehicles.

USEFUL ORGANISATIONS

The National Trust of Australia is dedicated to preserving historic buildings; it owns a number of them throughout the country, and some are open to the public. Many other buildings are 'classified' by the National Trust to try to ensure their preservation.

The Trust produces a fine series of city walking-tour guides. These guides are often available free from tourist or trust offices. The Trust has offices in Sydney (☎ 9258 0123) at Observatory Hill, and in the ACT (☎ 6239 5222), 2 Light St, Griffith.

Membership of the Trust is worth considering because it entitles you to free entry to National Trust properties for your year of membership ($52.30 plus a $25 joining fee). Check out the NSW branch Web site at www.nsw.nationaltrust.org.au.

DANGERS & ANNOYANCES
Theft

NSW is a relatively safe place to visit, but you should still take reasonable precautions, especially in Sydney. Don't leave your hotel room or car unlocked; don't leave your money, luggage or valuables unattended or in full view through car windows.

If you're unlucky enough to have something stolen, report the theft to the nearest police station immediately. If your credit cards, cash card or travellers cheques have been taken, notify your bank or the relevant company immediately (most have 24-hour 'lost or stolen' numbers listed under 'Banks' or 'Credit Card Organisations' in the *Yellow Pages*).

Swimming

It seems unnecessary to mention it, but don't ever go swimming if you have been drinking alcohol. Swimming after a heavy meal is also unwise.

The surf lifesaving clubs that line the coast aren't there for show – many people are rescued from the surf each year. If you get into trouble *raise your arm* and keep it raised while treading water or floating. If you've been sensible enough to swim at a patrolled beach (indicated by flags), help will come quickly.

Dumpers – waves that break in shallow water – can cause spinal injuries, but most people who require rescue have been caught in rips. A rip is the 'river' by which water from the surf makes its way back to the sea. Being swept out in a rip can be terrifying, but keep calm. All you need do is stay afloat and raise your arm. Most rips lose momentum quickly.

To rescue yourself from a rip, wait until you seem to have slowed, then swim parallel to the shore for about 30m. By then you should be out of the rip and can swim back in. Never try to swim back to shore against a rip.

You can expect to find rips near the mouths of rivers and lakes, especially after rain, but they can occur anywhere.

In rivers and lakes, watch out for dead trees and never jump or dive in if you're uncertain of the depth.

Sharks & Other Ocean-Going Nasties

Shark attacks are extremely rare – you're much more likely to be involved in a car accident (if that's any comfort). Some major beaches, especially around Sydney, have shark nets to deter sharks from cruising along the beaches and checking out the menu. The more popular beaches also have shark-spotting planes at peak times.

There are various poisonous marine animals, such as stone fish (with poison spines) and deadly blue-ringed octopuses (they're small and hang out in rock pools). If you don't know what it is, don't touch it.

Snakes & Spiders

Snakes are protected. Although there are many venomous snakes, few are aggressive, and unless you stand on one it's unlikely that you'll be bitten. Taipans and tiger snakes, however, will attack if alarmed. Sea snakes can also be dangerous.

To minimise your chances of being bitten, always wear boots, socks and long trousers when walking through undergrowth where snakes may be present. Don't put your hands into holes and crevices, and be careful when collecting firewood.

Sydney's Funnel-Web Spider

The Sydney funnel-web *(Atrax robustus)* is a remarkable spider with a fearsome reputation. Although many people expect that a bite from the funnel-web means certain death, few succumb to this nasty arachnid these days.

Of the several species of funnel-web in New South Wales, only the Sydney funnel-web (found within a radius of about 160km of Sydney) is known to have caused death in humans, and even then only the smaller male spider is considered a real threat – its venom is five times more powerful than that of the scarier-looking female.

The ground-dwelling spider, which is usually black, gets its name from the funnel or tube-like web it spins around a burrow. Unfortunately for Sydney residents, males opt for a nomadic existence away from their burrow when mature, often entering homes during summer or before heavy rain.

KN

Part of the reason for the funnel-web's reputation is its aggressive nature. Rather than scuttle away like many spiders, both the male and female (which measures up to 6cm) will rear up in readiness for an attack if approached, bearing an enormous set of fangs.

If you are bitten, treat as for snake bite and seek immediate medical treatment, preferably with the dead spider for identification – hospitals in and around Sydney carry the funnel-web antivenin. The venom attacks the nervous system and symptoms include intense pain, muscle spasms, weakness, profuse sweating and possibly unconsciousness.

Snake bites don't cause instant death and antivenins are usually available. Keep the victim calm and still, wrap the bitten limb tightly, then attach a splint to immobilise it. Then seek medical help, with the dead snake for identification if possible. Don't attempt to catch the snake if there's even a remote possibility of being bitten again. Tourniquets and sucking out the poison are now comprehensively discredited.

There are a few nasty spiders too, including the funnel-web (see the boxed text 'Sydney's Funnel-Web Spider' in this section), the redback and the white-tail, so it's best not to play with any spider. The funnel-web bite is treated in the same way as snake bite. For redback bites, apply ice and seek medical attention.

Insects

The swarms of bushflies that descend on you in outback areas are unbelievably annoying, but other than driving you demented they do no harm. The flies vanish at sunset, but that's when the mosquitoes come out...

The common bush tick (found in the forest and scrub country along the eastern coast) can be dangerous if left lodged in the skin, as the toxin the tick excretes can cause paralysis and sometimes death. If you're walking in tick-infested areas, check your body, including scalp, for lumps every night. The tick should be doused with methylated spirits or kerosene and levered out, but make sure you remove it intact. Check children and dogs for ticks after a walk in the bush.

Sydney and some of the more humid coastal areas suffer from cockroaches. Sydneysiders seem to get by with a mixture of tolerance and all-out chemical warfare, but if you haven't encountered a giant cockroach before, you're in for a surprise.

Leeches are quite common, and while they will suck your blood, they aren't dangerous. They can usually be removed by the application of salt or methylated spirits.

On the Road

Kangaroos and wandering stock can be a real hazard. A collision with one will badly damage your car and probably kill the animal. Unfortunately, other drivers are more dangerous, especially those who drink. See Hazards in the Getting Around chapter for more information on driving hazards.

Bushfire

In dry, hot weather, bushfires can raze thousands of hectares of eucalypt forests, with the volatile haze of eucalyptus oil exploding into a wall of flames 40m high. If a firestorm develops, the inferno can devour the bush faster than you can drive away from it.

Most fires are started by people. Be *extremely* careful when camping in summer. Apart from a real risk of dying in a fire, the legal penalties for lighting one – accidentally or deliberately – on a Total Fire Ban day are severe. This includes lighting camping stoves fuelled by gas or liquid. *Never* throw a cigarette butt out of a car. Australians don't like 'dobbing' people in to the police, but they make exceptions of those who light fires on Total Fire Ban days.

If there's a fire in the area, leave early – most bushfire deaths occur in the panic of last-minute evacuations.

If you're caught in a fire you must shelter from the intense radiant heat. It melts glass in seconds! Put a wall or at the very least a dampened woollen jumper between you and the flames. In a crisis, stay in your car and park in as clear a space as you can find. Lie on the floor under the dashboard, covering yourself with a woollen blanket if possible. The fire front often passes quickly and it can be safer to head back into the burnt area than to run or drive away.

Bushwalkers should take local advice before setting out. On a Total Fire Ban day, don't go – delay your trip until the weather has changed. Call the Country Fire Authority's recorded message service (☎ 13 1599) for current fire restrictions. If you're out in the bush and you see smoke, even at a great distance, take it seriously. Go to the nearest open space, downhill if possible. A forested ridge is the most dangerous place to be.

EMERGENCIES

In a life-threatening situation dial ☎ 000. This call is free from any phone and the operator will connect you with the police, ambulance or fire brigade. For other crisis and personal-counselling services (eg, sexual assault, poisons information, alcohol or drug problems) check the community information section of the local telephone book.

LEGAL MATTERS

The legal drinking age is 18 and you may need photo identification to prove your age. Stiff fines, jail and other penalties could be incurred if you're caught driving under the influence of alcohol. During festive holidays and special events, random breath-testing stations ('booze buses') are often set up to deter drunk drivers, but you can be stopped by police and asked to take a breath-test at any time. The legal blood-alcohol limit is 0.05%.

Traffic offences (illegal parking, speeding etc) usually incur a fine, for which you're allowed 30 days to pay. Driving at more than 30km/h over the speed limit will result in your licence being suspended. See also Road Rules in the Getting Around chapter.

The importation and use of illegal drugs is prohibited and could result in prison.

If you need legal assistance, contact the Legal Aid Commission of NSW (☎ 9219 5000; helpline ☎ 1800 806 913), 322 Castlereagh St, Sydney.

BUSINESS HOURS

Most offices and businesses open from 9 am to 5 pm, some until 5.30 pm, weekdays. Banking hours are usually from 9.30 am to 4 pm Monday to Thursday, and to 5 pm Friday.

Most shops in the larger towns are open longer hours, to around 9 pm on Thursday and all day Saturday. Sunday trading is becoming more common. On the major highways you'll come across 24-hour petrol stations, often with cafes attached.

Most pubs open at 10 am and close sometime around 11 pm or midnight, later on weekends. Some have 24-hour licences, and popular city pubs often remain open to 1 am.

PUBLIC HOLIDAYS & SPECIAL EVENTS

Public holidays in NSW and the ACT are:

New Year's Day 1 January
Australia Day 26 January
Easter March/April – Good Friday & Easter Monday
Anzac Day 25 April
Queen's Birthday June – second Monday
Bank Holiday August – first Monday (NSW only)
Labour Day October – first Monday
Christmas Day 25 December
Boxing Day 26 December

Most public holidays become long weekends, and if a fixed-date holiday such as New Year's Day falls on a weekend, the following Monday will usually be a holiday. Some country towns have holidays for local festivals, such as show day.

Special events throughout the state include:

January
Australia Day This national holiday, commemorating the arrival of the First Fleet in 1788, is observed on 26 January.
Survival Festival The Aboriginal version of Australia Day, also held on 26 January, is marked by Koori music, dance, and arts and crafts displays in Sydney.
Australasian Country Music Festival Tamworth *is* country music in Australia, and this festival, held on the Australia Day long weekend, is the showcase for the country's top country and western artists.

February/March
Gay & Lesbian Mardi Gras The most colourful event on the Sydney social calendar culminates in a spectacular parade along Oxford St.
Hunter Valley Vintage Festival Wine enthusiasts flock to the Hunter Valley for wine tasting, and grape picking and treading contests.

March
Surfest Australia's longest-running professional surf carnival is held at Newcastle Beach.
Canberra Festival This is a 10-day extravaganza in the national capital.

March/April
Royal Easter Show Livestock contests and rodeos are held in Sydney.
Canberra Festival This festival is held over 10 days in mid-March and ends with a public holiday.

April
Blues Festival This huge event in Byron Bay attracts up to 10,000 visitors.

August
Sydney City to Surf This is Australia's biggest foot race.

September
Mudgee Wine Festival Sample Mudgee's finest wine and welcome in the spring at this yearly festival.

October
Bathurst 1000 Motor-racing enthusiasts flock to Bathurst for the annual 1000km touring-car race on the superb Mt Panorama circuit.

November
Melbourne Cup On the first Tuesday in November, Australia's premier horse race is run in Melbourne. Many country towns in NSW schedule racing events to coincide with it.

December/January
Sydney to Hobart Yacht Race This is one of many summer events.

Agricultural Shows

For a taste of rural life you should visit an agricultural show. Sydney's Royal Easter Show is by far the biggest, but it's a case of the city being given a glimpse of the country. If you would like to take a look at country people kicking up their heels in their own element visit a country show. There are plenty of them.

Field Days

Field days are aimed at farmers, and provide a chance to see the big toys and latest developments in agri-business at close hand, as well as sheepdog trials and other events of general interest. The biggest field days are:

Ag-Quip Field Days Tamworth, mid-August; Gunnedah, August
Henty Machinery Field Days Henty, third week in September
Australian National Field Days Orange, October

There are also small-farm field days, with less emphasis on big machinery and offering a greater chance of meeting alternative

At the Livestock Sales

The graziers wear their best: The standard uniform for men is an Akubra hat (the good one, not the old one), moleskin trousers, boots and a sportscoat; women might be dressed similarly, or in their church-going gear. The sale offers a chance to catch up on district gossip, and tea is drunk amidst the Landcruisers, utes and Fairlanes parked in the shade. Later there might be a few beers at the pub.

Over at the yards, the dogs are working hard, responding to shrill whistles or, if something is going awry, furious yelling. The cattle bellow, the sheep set up a cacophony of baas and clattering hooves, semi-trailers growl in and out with loads of livestock, and there might be a couple of drovers on horseback, cracking whips around a swirling mob of cattle. Up on the boardwalk, the auctioneer's quickfire patter is interspersed with lusty shouts from the bidders, and his clerk knows all the buyers by name. And that all-pervading smell? Big bucks.

lifestylers. A popular small-farm field day is held at Mudgee in mid-July.

Surf Lifesaving Carnivals

The volunteer surf lifesaver is one of Australia's icons, but despite the macho image about a third of lifesavers are female and the proportion is growing. Each summer, surf carnivals are held all along the coast. Check at a local surf lifesaving club for dates, or contact Surf Lifesaving NSW (☎ 9984 7188).

ACTIVITIES

There's virtually no limit to activities on offer in NSW, and many are best enjoyed between the mountains and the sea.

Bushwalking

Opportunities for bushwalking abound in NSW, with a huge variety of standards, lengths and terrains. Almost every national park has either marked walking trails or offers wilderness walking. Near Sydney there are popular walks in the Blue Mountains

and Royal National Parks, with the wilderness areas of Wollemi National Park not far away.

In Kosciuszko National Park you can walk to the summit of Australia's highest peak and branch off on a number of other alpine trails. Longer routes include the three-day **Six Foot Track** to the Jenolan Caves and the 140km **Ensign Barralier Track** from Katoomba to Mittagong. The **Great North Walk** from Sydney to Newcastle can be walked in sections or as a two-week trek. The *Great North Walk Kit* is available from various bushwalking suppliers and NPWS outlets. The **Hume & Hovell Walking Track**, from Yass to near Albury, follows the route of two early explorers and passes through some beautiful high country. It can be walked in sections or as a trek of up to 25 days. The DLWC publishes a guide to the track.

For more information contact the Confederation of Bushwalking Clubs NSW (☎ 9294 6797), check the *Yellow Pages* under 'Clubs – Bushwalking' or visit the Web site www.bushwalking.org.au. Outdoor stockists such as Paddy Pallin and Mountain Designs are also good sources of information. If you want to walk without carrying a pack, contact Great Australian Walks (☎ 9555 7580).

Cycling

There are possibilities for some great rides in NSW, from long rides through the endless western plains to summer mountain biking in the Snowies. See Bicycle in the Getting Around chapter for information.

Bicycle NSW (☎ 9283 5200), Level 2, 209 Castlereagh St, Sydney, publishes a handy book called *Cycling around Sydney*, which details routes and cycle paths in Sydney, the Blue Mountains, Illawarra and the Central Coast. It publishes other booklets on cycling in the state.

Horse Riding

Opportunities for horse riding abound, from hour-long trail rides for beginners, to overnight (or longer) treks. Popular areas for organised horse treks include New England and the high country around the Snowy Mountains.

Touring Wineries

Not exactly an energy-sapping activity, but touring wineries is a popular pastime in NSW, particularly in the Hunter Valley. You can do a self-drive tour (ensuring the driver isn't doing too much tasting) or relax and take a winery tour. See the Highlights section earlier in this chapter for more on wine regions covered in this book.

Skiing

Some excellent downhill and cross-country skiing is available in the Snowy Mountains, with the season running from June to early September. See the Kosciuszko National Park section of the South-East chapter for details.

Rock Climbing & Abseiling

The sheer cliffs of the Blue Mountains are very popular for climbing and abseiling, and beginners' courses are available. See Katoomba in the Around Sydney chapter.

Swimming

A visit to NSW will involve swimming at a beach sooner or later – there are just so many! There are also many lakes and rivers where you can cool off. Also, most towns have an Olympic-sized pool.

Surfing & Windsurfing

With 1900km of coastline, much of it surf beaches, it makes sense to get out there and surf. That isn't as easy as it sounds, though, and boogie-boarding or body-surfing is as far as most visitors get. You can learn to surf in Coffs Harbour and Byron Bay. Surfaris (☎ 1800 634 951) offers excellent surfing trips for all levels of skill up the coast from Sydney to Byron Bay. The five-day trip leaves Sydney every Monday and takes you to remote surfing and camping areas along the coast. Instruction, equipment, camping gear (except a sleeping bag) and meals are included ($385). It also has a three-day tour from Byron Bay (return) for $195, and a Byron to Noosa trip for $210. Check it out at www.surfaris.com.

You can also check surf conditions at several beaches along the coast (including around Sydney) on the Internet at www.wavecam.com.au.

Tracks magazine provides good insights into Aussie surfing, and *Surfing Australia's East Coast* by Aussie surf-star Nat Young is a slim, cheap, comprehensive guide to the best breaks. He's also written the *Surfing & Sailboard Guide to Australia,* which covers the whole country.

There is also plenty of scope for windsurfing, particularly on the beaches around Sydney and farther north. Blownaway Holidays (☎ 9960 5344) organises windsurfing tours out of Sydney.

Diving

There are plenty of places to go diving in Sydney, on the Central Coast and in the waters around Jervis Bay, Ulladulla, Narooma and Merimbula. Outfits like Pro Dive offer four-day Professional Association of Diving Instructors (PADI) dive courses from around $250 ($350 includes all gear and a few extras).

White-Water Rafting

There are some excellent thrills to be had shooting rapids on the upper Murray and Shoalhaven Rivers in the south and the Nymboida River in the north.

Canoeing & Kayaking

Many of the state's waterways are suitable for canoeing, with adventurous runs on the short, swift rivers flowing to the coast and inland from the Great Dividing Range, and long, lazy treks on the meandering inland rivers.

NSW Canoeing (☎ 9660 4597) can help you with general queries and point you towards clubs and hire places. It also has a recorded service (☎ 1902 260 011) telling you river heights throughout the state.

You can rent sea kayaks in Sydney and at towns along the south coast. See under Canoeing & Kayaking in the Sydney chapter for more information.

Hang-Gliding & Paragliding

Hang-gliding is popular near Wollongong and Byron Bay, and you can take tandem flights. Paragliding outfits are found at many beach resorts. At Tumut, in the south-east, you can go up in a powered hang-glider (microlight).

WORK

Finding casual work in NSW isn't difficult if you're in the right place at the right time and are prepared to work hard, but make sure you have enough funds to cover yourself for your stay rather than relying on employment. If you're visiting from overseas, you can legally work only if you have a working holiday visa.

Sydney is the best place in Australia to find office temp work, labouring jobs or work in the hospitality industry. The best prospects for casual work throughout the state include bar work, waiting on tables, washing dishes, nannying, fruit picking and collecting for charities. Hostels often have information about work in the local area.

Harvests are the main source of casual work in rural areas. The Riverina and the south-east around Batlow are particularly prosperous. Pick up a copy of *Working Holidays in the Riverina* from tourist offices in the area for advice on harvest times and useful contacts.

Grape harvests in the Hunter Valley and around Griffith begin around mid-February and last through March. Other fruit is picked around Griffith from November to March. The apple harvest near Orange and Batlow begins in early March. Cherry picking around Young begins in late spring. Hot work on the cotton harvest is sometimes available near Moree and Bourke in early summer.

To receive wages without being taxed at the maximum rate you need a Tax File Number, issued by the Australian Tax Office. Forms are available from post offices and you must show your passport and visa.

WWOOF

Willing Workers on Organic Farms (WWOOF) has been operating in Australia since 1981 and is well established. The idea is that you do a few hours' work each day on a farm in return for bed and board. Becoming a WWOOFer is a great way to meet people and to travel cheaply. There are more than 900 WWOOF associates in Australia, mostly in Victoria, NSW and Queensland. Since it's voluntary (there's no pay), it can be done by visitors on a tourist visa.

To join WWOOF (☎ 5155 0218) send $30 for one person or $35 for two people travelling together and a photocopy of your driver's licence or passport data page to WWOOF Australia, Mt Murrindal Co-op, Buchan, Victoria 3885, and you'll receive a membership number and a booklet listing WWOOF places in Australia. You can also look up the Australian Web site at www.earthlink.com.au/wwoof.

ACCOMMODATION

NSW is well equipped with places to stay to suit all budgets.

Camping & Caravanning

If you want to get around NSW on the cheap, camping is the way to go, with nightly costs for two from around $12 (twice that in some beachside resorts in summer).

Caravan parks are, as the name suggests, intended more for caravans (trailers) than tents, but most have a lawn area set aside for tents. Apart from bathrooms and laundries there are few communal facilities, but most have barbecues and good parks might have a camp kitchen. In most big towns caravan parks are a long way from the centre, which means that you'll need your own transport if you're doing a lot of camping.

Many caravan parks also have on-site vans that you can rent quite cheaply for the night. Self-contained on-site cabins are also widely available and are more comfortable, often containing an en suite. On-site vans cost $30 to $35 a night, cabins $40 to $55.

There are many coastal areas, national parks and riverside locations throughout the state where camping is permitted. In national parks there is usually a charge (around $10 a night for two people) where there are facilities provided. Elsewhere, such as in state forests, bush camping is usually free but check beforehand. See the National Parks section of the Facts about NSW chapter for more information.

Hostels

Hostels are great places for meeting people and are busy travellers centres. They also offer the cheapest secure roof over your head, especially if you're travelling alone.

Australia has an active YHA, with hostels in many parts of NSW. YHA hostels provide basic accommodation, usually in small dormitories or bunk rooms, though most also provide twin rooms for couples. The nightly charges are reasonable – usually $13 to $19 for a bed in a dorm or $20 to $25 per person in a twin. Nonmembers can stay at YHA hostels but pay $3 extra per night.

All hostels have cooking facilities and 24-hour access, and there's usually a communal area. There are generally laundry facilities and often there are excellent notice boards.

Accommodation can usually be booked directly with the manager or through the YHA Travel Centre (☎ 9261 1111, ✉ yha@ yhansw.org.au), 422 Kent St, Sydney. The annual *YHA Accommodation Guide* tells all, or look up the Web site at www.yha.com.au.

To become a YHA member in Australia costs $30 a year (there's also a $19 joining fee, but if you're an overseas resident joining in Australia you don't pay this). You can join at any YHA hostel.

Youth hostels are part of Hostelling International, so if you're already a member of the YHA in your own country, you're entitled to use Australian hostels.

Sydney also has a large selection of independent backpacker hostels, and there are others scattered around the state – mostly along the coast.

The standards vary enormously: Some are run-down innercity hotels where the owners try to fill empty rooms. A few are former motels, so each unit, typically with four to six beds, will have a fridge, TV and bathroom. Others are in renovated homes, which can be quite cosy. The best in terms of facilities are purpose-built, although sometimes they're simply too big.

Prices at backpackers hostels are in line with YHA hostels – about $15 or $16, sometimes more in Sydney and Byron Bay.

VIP Backpackers Resorts (www.back packers.com.au) is one of the backpacker organisations you can join to receive a discount card ($25, valid for 12 months) and a list of participating hostels (37 in NSW). You also receive useful discounts on other services like transport, so it may be worth considering.

Nomads Backpackers (☎ 1800 819 883) has a dozen or so independent hostels in NSW. See its Web site at www.nomads-backpackers.com.

University Accommodation

University colleges in Sydney and Canberra offer inexpensive accommodation during vacations.

Guesthouses & B&Bs

Choices include everything from converted barns and stables, renovated and rambling old guesthouses and upmarket country homes, to simple bedrooms in family homes. Some are listed in this book, but for a greater selection contact Homestay International (☎ 9948 8384), 21 Bareena Dr, Balgowlah Heights; B&B Australia (☎ 9954 5777), 101 Miller St, North Sydney; or B&B Accommodation Register Australia (☎ 9299 6740), 32 York St, Sydney.

Tariffs typically cost $50 to $100 a double – some places in popular areas charge much more in high season.

Home Hostelling Australia (☎ 07-3392 3126) offers *pension*-style accommodation all over NSW, where you stay in a family home. The name is a bit misleading as it's not really hostelling and many of the places offer B&B. Expect to pay $45 to $50 for a double ($60 to $75 in Sydney). You can see the listings and make bookings on the Internet at www.homehostel.com.

Farmstays

Across the state you'll find properties offering accommodation, and sometimes a program of farm activities. Some are just B&Bs in farmhouses, others are cottages that happen to be on farms. Expect to pay around $300 for a week in a self-contained cottage and from about $50 (sometimes less) for B&B to about $180 per person per night for full board and activities.

Some farmstays are listed in this guide, but for a more complete list contact NSW Farm & Country Holidays (☎ 9999 0388, 1800 803 007), PO Box 772, Crows Nest 2065. It has a brochure with tariffs and can make credit-card bookings.

Pubs, Motels & Hotels

Outside Sydney and a few big towns, hotel accommodation means pub accommodation. Although the grandest buildings in country towns are often the pubs, the standard of accommodation rarely lives up to the architecture. Many pubs prefer not to offer accommodation, but the licensing laws require them to do so.

Pub rooms are usually clean but basic, with not much more than a bed, a wardrobe and sometimes a basin. The bathroom is usually shared. Despite the lack of luxury, it's worth considering staying in pubs rather than motels. Apart from the saving in cost (you'll pay about $20/30 for a single/double), staying at 'the pub' means that you have an entree to the town's social life.

The two essentials in choosing a pub room are to get one that isn't directly above the noisy bar, and to check that the bed is in reasonable condition.

A big plus with pubs is that the breakfasts (sometimes included in the tariff, but increasingly an extra charge) can be enormous.

If you want a more modern place with your own bathroom and other facilities, then you're moving into the motel bracket. Prices vary and (unlike pubs) singles are often not much cheaper than doubles. The reason is quite simple – in the old hotels many of the rooms really are singles, relics of the days when single men travelled the country looking for work. In motels the rooms are almost always doubles.

In most places you'll have no trouble finding a budget motel for around $45 to $55 a double (outside the holiday season); better motels cost around $60 to $70.

The upper end of the hotel spectrum is well represented in Sydney and Canberra. There are many excellent four- and five-star hotels and quite a few lesser places where standards vary.

Rental Accommodation

Restricted mainly to Sydney and Canberra, serviced apartments offer hotel-style convenience (the apartment is cleaned for you and there's a reception desk) with cooking facilities and room to move.

Holiday flats, found mainly in beachside towns, are geared to family holidays, so they fill up at peak times and often have minimum rental periods of a week. Outside peak times you might be able to rent one by the night. Standards and prices vary enormously, but if you have a group they can be affordable and might even be cheaper than hostels outside peak season.

Houseboats

The Hawkesbury River near Sydney, Port Stephens and the nearby Myall Lakes, the Clarence River, the Murray River and the estuaries of the south coast, are some of the waterways where you can hire houseboats. Houseboat hire rates are second only to those of ski lodges in complexity, but basically if you have a few people (say three or four) and hire midweek outside peak times, the cost can be comparable to motels.

FOOD

Fresh, high-quality ingredients make eating in NSW a pleasure. The state grows everything from tropical fruit to cold-climate vegetables and is even a major producer of rice. The beef and lamb are among the best in the world, and the Pacific Ocean supplies superb seafood. Add to this the huge variety of ethnic cuisines and you have the recipe for some memorable meals.

'Modern Australian' food has become a recognisable style – an amalgamation of Mediterranean, South-East Asian and Californian cuisines, with a look and taste that's distinctively Australian. Sydney has a multitude of excellent eateries for all budgets. Canberra is catching up, and in the larger towns, especially on the coast, there's a good range of eating places.

In country areas you might find that steak-and-three-veg is still the main meal on the menu. In some small, remote country towns you might still be served canned vegetables.

Self-Catering

A wide range of produce is sold in supermarkets and in neighbourhood shops. Some seasonal variation in prices and availability occurs, but with produce shipped in from all over Australia you can almost always find what you want at a reasonable price.

Delis sell cheeses, processed meats and other delights such as pickled octopus and many varieties of olives. They also have tempting pastries, salads and takeaways.

For more basic supplies, there are corner stores or milk bars stocking staples such as milk, bread, tinned food and maybe fresh fruit and vegetables.

In many coastal towns, fishing cooperatives sell seafood straight off the boat.

Fast Food

Australia's original takeaway food, the meat pie, is sold everywhere. Other fast foods, available from major chains and local takeaway stores, also abound. At the local takeaway shop it's quite common to get salads, and fish and chips are often fried in vegetable oil, not lard. (Note that 'potato cakes' are called scallops in NSW.)

Hamburgers from local takeaways are usually good. If you're a little hungrier, try a steak sandwich. Many towns also have Asian takeaways.

Pub & Club Food

For a sit-down meal in a country town head for the pub, where you can almost always get counter meals for lunch or dinner. These were once eaten at the bar, but nowadays there are usually tables. The quantities are usually large and prices are low, unless the pub serves meals in the dining room and calls it a bistro. Menus mostly have roasts, steaks, sausages, mixed grills and the like, although seafood and pasta dishes are common. There are usually set times for counter meals, say noon to 1.30 or 2 pm for lunch and 6 to 8.30 pm for dinner (or tea, as it's known).

Almost every town has an ex-servicemen's club (also called an RSL club), which uses profits from poker machines to provide an inexpensive dining room or bistro. Visitors are welcome, though there might be some basic dress restrictions. Bowling clubs and golf clubs are similar.

Cafes & Restaurants

In Sydney, Canberra and the other large centres you'll find plenty of cafes and restaurants offering a galaxy of cuisines, but in country towns you might be restricted to an old-style cafe (often just a takeaway shop with tables) and a Chinese restaurant.

If there are more than a couple of Chinese places you'll often find that they are in hot competition and offer good deals, with $5 lunch specials, for example. Don't expect great cuisine though.

Country motels sometimes have dining rooms, but you're often paying restaurant prices for pub food. This scenario is changing, and any place with the hint of a tourist industry, especially along the coast, is likely to have some good places to eat in a range of styles.

Cooking Yabbies

You can catch yabbies at several farms in New South Wales, and just about every creek and dam in the Riverina yields them, but how do you cook them? Here's a recipe from Premier Yabbies (near Culcairn):

Cool the yabbies in iced water – this should induce a state of hibernation, which is more humane than boiling them awake. Alternatively, put them in the fridge for a couple of hours, then pop them in the freezer for 10 minutes to send them off to sleep.

Boil a large pot of water and add a lemon cut into quarters and half a cup of brown sugar.

Put up to 10 yabbies at a time into the pot of boiling water.

Return the water to the boil and wait for the yabbies to float to the top (about three minutes). Remove, rinse and drain the yabbies.

Now you have to shell and clean them, a knack that's acquired through practice. It's similar to cleaning prawns: Remove the shell and tail, then strip out the vein and the digestive tract.

Enjoy!

DRINKS
Nonalcoholic Drinks
Soft drinks, flavoured milks, juices, cordial, mineral water, tea and coffee are available just about everywhere. Tap water can be drunk, but bottled water is also sold.

Alcoholic Drinks
Australian beer will be fairly familiar to US citizens and is similar to what's known as lager in the UK. It has a higher alcohol content than British or US beers, with around 4.9%, though most breweries now produce light beers, with an alcohol content of between 2% and 3.5%. Aussie beer should be chilled before drinking. Ask for a 'middy' (285ml glass) or a 'schooner' (450ml glass).

Toohey's is the largest brewer in the state, with Reschs maintaining a market, especially in rural areas. The Carlton brewery, an interloper from Victoria, has made big inroads, especially with its Victoria Bitter (VB). Carlton also brews Foster's, perhaps the best known of Australia's export beer brands, but it's rarely seen in NSW.

European wine experts now realise just how good Australian wines can be – exporting wine is a multimillion dollar business. Wines need not be expensive. You're entering the 'pretty good' bracket if you pay over $12 for a bottle, and drinkable wines can be found for much less.

Some restaurants are BYO (Bring Your Own), which means that they're not licensed to sell alcohol but you can bring your own. Some are licensed but also allow BYO (usually bottled wine only). There might be a small 'corkage' charge (typically about $1 per person) if you bring your own.

ENTERTAINMENT
Cinemas
In the big cities there are commercial cinema chains, such as Village, Hoyts and Greater Union, and their cinemas are usually found in centres that have anything from two to 10 screens in the one complex. Smaller towns have just the one cinema and many of these are almost museum pieces in themselves. Seeing a new-release mainstream film is expensive in Sydney (around $12.50), but cheaper in country areas (more like $8). City cinemas often have one day a week when the price is lower – sometimes half-price.

In Sydney and Canberra you'll find art-house and independent cinemas that screen alternative films, classics and cult movies.

Nightclubs
There's no shortage of places to dance the night away, but they're confined to the larger cities and towns. Clubs range from the exclusive 'members only' variety to barn-sized discos where anyone who wants to spend the money is welcomed with open arms. Admission costs from $5 to $12.

Some places have dress standards, but it's generally left to the discretion of the people at the door – if they don't like the look of you, bad luck.

Live Music
Many suburban pubs have live music, and these are often great places for catching bands, either nationally well-known names or up-and-coming performers. Most of Australia's popular bands started out on the pub circuit.

The best way to find out about the local scene is to get to know some locals or travellers who have spent some time in the place. Otherwise, there are often comprehensive listings in newspapers, particularly on Friday. Sydney, Canberra, Newcastle and Wollongong have music scenes worth checking out.

Gambling
Hardly a town in the state is without a horse-racing track or a Totalisator Agency Board (TAB) betting office. You can bet on the horses, the trots (harness racing), the dogs (greyhound racing) and even football. Sydneysiders can also bet on some yacht races. Clubs and many pubs have poker machines. Lottery tickets and scratch cards are sold at newsagents. Canberra has a small casino and Sydney has the gaudy new 24-hour Star City casino in Pyrmont.

SPECTATOR SPORTS
If you're a sports fan, NSW has plenty to offer. Many of the following sports are best

Winter white cloaks the mountains of Kosciuszko National Park

Sydney, as seen from the air over North Sydney

Summer wildflowers bloom in Kosciuszko National Park

seen in Sydney (see the Spectator Sports section in the Sydney chapter for details).

Football

At least four types of football are played in NSW. The season runs from about March to September.

Rugby is the main game and it's rugby league, the 13-a-side, working-class version, that attracts the crowds. The main competition is the National Rugby League (NRL). Most NSW teams are based in Sydney but Canberra and Newcastle each have a side, with the remaining teams based in Melbourne, Auckland and Queensland. The other big rugby league series is the State of Origin clash between NSW and Queensland, which generates a lot of passion.

The more gentlemanly game of 15-a-side rugby union, originally for amateurs, has a less fanatical following, but the Australian rugby union team, the Wallabies, is a world-beater.

Aussie Rules football is a unique, exciting sport – only Gaelic football is anything like it. The Sydney Swans is NSW's only team so far in the Australian Football League (AFL), although the Kangaroos have played some experimental 'home' games in Sydney since 1999. The Swans play home games at the Sydney Cricket Ground (SCG).

Soccer is slowly gaining popularity, thanks in part to the success of the national team (the Socceroos) and the high profile of some Aussies playing for overseas clubs. The national league is only semiprofessional and games attract a relatively small but passionate following. In the past most clubs were ethnically based, but they now appeal to the broader community. NSW clubs include the Canberra Cosmos, Wollongong Wolves and Newcastle Breakers. For information, call Soccer Australia (☎ 9380 6099).

Cricket

The Sydney Cricket Ground hosts international Test and one-day cricket matches. The Sydney Test is always the last of the season, held in early January, and the one-day series usually begins after that. There's also an interstate competition, the poorly attended but high-standard Pura Milk Cup (formerly the Sheffield Shield), and statewide district cricket. The cricket season is from October to March.

Horse Racing

Horse racing is as much a social outing as a serious day of punting, and country race meetings can be great events – particularly as many small towns only host one meeting a year. Events like the Snake Gully Cup in Gundagai (November) attract the entire town.

Other Sports

Basketball has grown phenomenally as a spectator sport since the formation of a national league. Baseball is another US sport slowly becoming more popular. Along the coast there are regular surf lifesaving carnivals and competitions. There's also yacht racing; some good tennis, including the NSW Open; netball; and golf.

SHOPPING

If you want to buy a souvenir of Australia, check to see that it was made here. See also Shopping in the Sydney chapter for more shopping information.

Markets

Most cities and towns in NSW have a regular market, ranging from small local flea markets to huge extravaganzas with entertainment and a fairground atmosphere. The markets tend to vary in character and might sell anything from fresh produce to furniture, clothing, antiques, souvenirs, crafts, herbal remedies and New Age art. Sydney has dozens of interesting weekend markets and Canberra has a few as well.

The 'alternative' markets held in the towns of the far north coast hinterland around Byron Bay are worth catching. Between them there is one every weekend but the biggest is at The Channon (see the North Coast chapter). Other markets worth looking out for are at Berry and Moruya along the south coast.

Aboriginal Art & Craft

Over the last few decades, Aboriginal artists have started using nontraditional materials like canvas and acrylic paints, but these works have quickly gained wide appreciation. The paintings depict traditional Dreamtime stories and ceremonial designs, each with a particular spiritual significance.

The best works are beyond the budget of the average traveller, but among the cheaper artworks on sale are prints, baskets, small carvings and some beautiful screen-printed T-shirts produced by Aboriginal craft cooperatives. There are, however, a large number of commercial rip-offs, so it's worth shopping around and paying a few dollars more for the real thing.

Much of the Aboriginal art available in NSW, especially the traditional styles, comes from other areas of Australia and is sold in Sydney galleries. A couple of places worth visiting in NSW are Gurrigai Aboriginal Arts & Crafts, off the Pacific Hwy between Maclean and Ballina, and Timbey's Aboriginal Arts & Crafts in Huskisson,

Jervis Bay, where decorated didgeridoos and boomerangs are among the artworks.

Opals

The opal is Australia's national gemstone, and opals and opal jewellery are popular souvenirs. They are beautiful stones, but buy wisely and shop around – quality and prices can vary widely from place to place. Lightning Ridge, in the state's north-west, is the opal centre of NSW.

Antiques

Look for early-Australian colonial furniture made from cedar or huon pine; Australian silver jewellery; ceramics – either early factory pieces or studio pieces (especially anything by the Boyd family); glassware such as Carnival glass; and Australiana collectables and bric-a-brac such as old signs, tins, bottles etc. Updated annually, *Carter's Price Guide to Antiques in Australia* is an excellent price reference.

Getting There & Away

AIR

Sydney's busy Kingsford-Smith Airport is serviced by major international airlines and domestic carriers.

International air fares to Australia are generally expensive – it's a long way from anywhere and flights are often heavily booked. Plan well ahead if you're flying to Australia at a busy time of year (Christmas is notoriously difficult) or on a particularly popular route. However, there are a number of deals to ease the pain of ticket prices.

All airports and domestic flights are non-smoking.

Buying Tickets

For a cheap ticket, go to an agent rather than directly to the airline. The airline usually quotes the regular fare, but agents can offer special deals, particularly on competitive routes. Occasionally airlines have one-off specials, so watch newspaper travel ads.

What's available and what it costs depends on the time of year, the route you're flying and your choice of airline. Dirt-cheap fares are often less conveniently scheduled, and go by less convenient routes or with less popular airlines.

Things to consider when choosing a ticket are how long it's valid for and the number of stopovers you want. As a rule of thumb, the cheaper the ticket the fewer stopovers you'll be allowed. The Internet is an excellent place to shop for tickets – if not to buy, at least to get an idea of some of the deals that are around.

Round-the-World Tickets Round-the-World (RTW) tickets are popular and many take you through Australia. The airline RTW tickets are often real bargains. Since Australia is on the other side of the world to Europe and the USA, it can sometimes be cheaper to keep going in the same direction rather than return the way you came.

Official airline RTW tickets are usually put together by two airlines and permit you to fly anywhere you want on their route systems as long as you don't backtrack. Other restrictions (usually) include booking the first sector in advance – cancellation penalties then apply. There may be restrictions on how many stops you're permitted and normally the tickets are valid from 90 days up to a year. Typical prices for RTW tickets with South Pacific stopovers start at around £850 or US$2100.

An alternative RTW ticket is one put together by a travel agent using a combination of discounted airline tickets. A UK agent like Trailfinders can put together interesting London-to-London RTW combinations via Australia for around £800 to £1200.

Circle-Pacific Tickets Circle-Pacific tickets use a combination of airlines to circle the Pacific – combining Australia, New Zealand, the USA and Asia. As with RTW tickets, there are advance-purchase restrictions and limits to how many stopovers you can take. However, these fares are likely to be around 15% cheaper than RTW tickets. The Circle-Pacific route is Los Angeles-Hawaii-Auckland-Sydney-Singapore-Bangkok-Hong Kong-Tokyo-Los Angeles.

Air Passes If you are travelling to New South Wales from elsewhere in Australia, air passes are worth checking out. Qantas Airways offers two types. The Boomerang Pass can be purchased overseas only and involves buying a coupon for each sector, but you must buy a minimum of three coupons to begin with: a single sector (Sydney-Melbourne one way) costs $280, two sectors (Sydney-Perth) is $365. The Qantas Backpackers Pass is a much better deal, provided you are a member of a hostelling organisation such as the Youth Hostel Association (YHA), VIP or Nomads. This pass can be purchased in Australia or overseas, but you must buy a minimum of three coupons (sectors) in the first transaction. Fares vary depending on the journey but Sydney-Melbourne one way

Air Travel Glossary

Cancellation Penalties If you have to cancel or change a discounted ticket, there are often heavy penalties involved; insurance can sometimes be taken out against these penalties. Some airlines impose penalties on regular tickets as well, particularly against 'no-show' passengers.

Courier Fares Businesses often need to send urgent documents or freight securely and quickly. Courier companies hire people to accompany the package through customs and, in return, offer a discount ticket which is sometimes a phenomenal bargain. However, you may have to surrender all your baggage allowance and take only carry-on luggage.

Full Fares Airlines traditionally offer 1st class (coded F), business class (coded J) and economy class (coded Y) tickets. These days there are so many promotional and discounted fares available that few passengers pay full economy fare.

Lost Tickets If you lose your airline ticket an airline will usually treat it like a travellers cheque and, after inquiries, issue you with another one. Legally, however, an airline is entitled to treat it like cash and if you lose it then it's gone forever. Take good care of your tickets.

Onward Tickets An entry requirement for many countries is that you have a ticket out of the country. If you're unsure of your next move, the easiest solution is to buy the cheapest onward ticket to a neighbouring country or a ticket from a reliable airline which can later be refunded if you do not use it.

Open-Jaw Tickets These are return tickets where you fly out to one place but return from another. If available, this can save you backtracking to your arrival point.

Overbooking Since every flight has some passengers who fail to show up, airlines often book more passengers than they have seats. Usually excess passengers make up for the no-shows, but occasionally somebody gets 'bumped' onto the next available flight. Guess who it is most likely to be? The passengers who check in late.

Promotional Fares These are officially discounted fares, available from travel agencies or direct from the airline.

Reconfirmation If you don't reconfirm your flight at least 72 hours prior to departure, the airline may delete your name from the passenger list. Ring to find out if your airline requires reconfirmation.

Restrictions Discounted tickets often have various restrictions on them – such as needing to be paid for in advance and incurring a penalty to be altered. Others are restrictions on the minimum and maximum period you must be away.

Round-the-World Tickets RTW tickets give you a limited period (usually a year) in which to circumnavigate the globe. You can go anywhere the carrying airlines go, as long as you don't backtrack. The number of stopovers or total number of separate flights is decided before you set off and they usually cost a bit more than a basic return flight.

Transferred Tickets Airline tickets cannot be transferred from one person to another. Travellers sometimes try to sell the return half of their ticket, but officials can ask you to prove that you are the person named on the ticket. On an international flight tickets are compared with passports.

Travel Periods Ticket prices vary with the time of year. There is a low (off-peak) season and a high (peak) season, and often a low-shoulder season and a high-shoulder season as well. Usually the fare depends on your outward flight – if you depart in the high season and return in the low season, you pay the high-season fare.

costs only $117, Sydney-Brisbane is $139. You must book your flight at least two days in advance and must stay at least two nights at your destination.

Ansett's Kangaroo Airpass gives you two options: 6000km with a minimum of two and a maximum of three stopovers for $949, or 10,000km with a minimum of three and a maximum of seven stopovers for $1499. Quite a few restrictions apply to these tickets, but they can be good value if you want to see a lot of the country in a short time. Ansett also has a Backpackers Pass similar to that offered by Qantas, and the Ansett Australia Airpass, which can only be purchased overseas, with one sector costing $240 and two sectors $300.

Travellers with Special Needs
If you've broken a leg, are vegetarian or require a special diet, are travelling in a wheelchair, travelling with a baby, terrified of flying, or whatever, let the airline staff know as soon as possible so that they can make the necessary arrangements. Remind them when you reconfirm your booking (at least 72 hours before departure) and again when you check in at the airport.

Airports and airlines can be helpful, but they need advance warning. Most international airports provide escorts from the check-in desk to the aeroplane where needed, and there should be ramps, lifts, accessible toilets and reachable phones. If aircraft toilets are likely to present a problem, travellers should discuss this with the airline and, if necessary, with their doctor, at an early stage.

Guide dogs for the blind often travel in a specially pressurised baggage compartment with other animals, away from their owner. Smaller guide dogs, however, may be admitted to the cabin. All guide dogs are subject to the same quarantine laws as other animals when entering or returning to countries that are free of rabies.

Deaf travellers can ask for airport and inflight announcements to be written down for them.

Children under two years of age travel for 10% of the standard fare (or free on some airlines) as long as they don't occupy a seat. They don't get a baggage allowance either. 'Skycots' should be provided by the airline if requested in advance; these will take a child weighing up to about 10kg. Children aged between two and 12 years of age can usually occupy a seat for half to two-thirds of the full fare, and they also get a baggage allowance. Pushchairs (strollers) can often be taken on board the plane as hand luggage.

Departure Tax
There's a departure tax of $30 payable by everyone leaving Australia, which is incorporated into your air fare. Sydney also has a noise tax of $3.40; again, this is added to your air fare.

The UK
The cheapest tickets in London are provided by 'bucket shops' (discount-ticket agencies), which advertise in magazines and papers like *Time Out* and *TNT*. Most bucket shops are trustworthy and reliable, but the occasional sharp operator appears – check that the agent is bonded to an association such as the Association of British Travel Agents (ABTA) or Air Travel Operators Licence (ATOL).

Trailfinders (☎ 020-7938 3366), 194 Kensington High St, London W8, Usit Campus (☎ 0870-240 1010), 52 Grosvenor Gardens, London, SW1, and STA Travel (☎ 020-7581 4132), 86 Old Brompton Rd, London SW7 and 117 Euston Rd, London NW1 (☎ 020-7465 0484), are good, reliable agents for cheap tickets.

The cheapest flights from London to Sydney are Britannia Airways charter flights for as little as £399 return, but strict conditions apply. Bucket-shop tickets from London to Sydney are around £335/490 one way/return during the low season (March to June). In September and mid-December fares go up by as much as 30%, while the rest of the year they're somewhere in between.

From Australia you can expect to pay from around A$900/1400 one way/return to London and other European capitals, with stops in Asia on the way.

The USA & Canada

There are connections across the Pacific from Los Angeles, San Francisco and Vancouver. These include direct flights, flights via New Zealand, island-hopping routes and circuitous Pacific-rim routes via Asia. Qantas Airways, Air New Zealand and United Airlines fly USA-Australia; Qantas, Air New Zealand and Canadian Airlines International fly Canada-Australia. An interesting option from the east coast is via Japan, with Japan Airlines.

To find good fares to Australia, check the travel ads in the Sunday travel sections of papers like the *Los Angeles Times, San Francisco Chronicle-Examiner, New York Times* or Canada's *Globe & Mail*. The magazine *Travel Unlimited* publishes details of the cheapest air fares and courier possibilities for destinations all over the world from the USA. You can typically get a one-way/return ticket from the west coast for around US$1106/1569 in the low season or US$1365/1847 in the high season (December/January). Fares from the east coast are around US$1439/1800 or US$1698/2071 at peak times. Council Travel and STA Travel are good sources for discount tickets in the USA and have lots of offices around the country; in Canada, Travel CUTS offers a similar service. Fares from Vancouver are similar to US west-coast prices. From Toronto, fares cost around C$2050 return in the low season to C$2600 in the high season.

One-way/return fares from Australia include San Francisco A$1000/1400, New York A$1250/1900 and Vancouver A$1100/1550.

New Zealand

Air New Zealand and Qantas Airways link Auckland, Wellington and Christchurch in New Zealand with Sydney. STA Travel and Flight Centres International are reliable discount-travel agents in New Zealand.

An economy fare from New Zealand to Sydney is around NZ$480/1050 one way/return, although if you purchase three months in advance you can pay half that for the return fare. From Sydney to New Zealand expect to pay from A$450 one way and

between A$500 and A$700 return, depending on the time of year. The competition on this route means you'll find good discounts.

Asia

Ticket discounting is widespread in Asia, particularly in Singapore, Hong Kong, Bangkok and Penang. There are numerous fly-by-nighters on the Asian ticketing scene, so take care. Also, Asian routes fill up fast.

Typical one-way fares to Sydney are S$510 from Singapore. From Australia's east coast, some typical return fares to Singapore, Kuala Lumpur and Bangkok range from A$800 to A$1100, and to Hong Kong from A$900 to A$1300.

You can pick up interesting tickets in Asia to include Australia on the way across the Pacific Ocean. Qantas Airways and Air New Zealand offer discounted trans-Pacific tickets.

Africa

There are direct flights each week between Africa and Australia, but only between Perth and Harare (Zimbabwe) or Johannesburg (South Africa). Qantas Airways, South African Airways and Air Zimbabwe fly these routes. Other airlines that connect southern Africa and Australia include Malaysia Airlines (via Kuala Lumpur) and Air Mauritius (via Mauritius) – both have specials from time to time. Sydney to Harare return costs from A$1750; to Johannesburg it's from about A$1650.

South America

Two routes operate between South America and Australia. The long-running Chile connection involves LanChile's Santiago-Easter Island-Tahiti twice-weekly flight. From Tahiti you fly Qantas Airways or another airline to Australia. One-way fares to Sydney cost around US$1600, plus a raft of taxes. Alternatively, there's a route that skirts the Antarctic Circle, flying from Buenos Aires to Auckland and Sydney, operated twice weekly by Aerolineas Argentinas.

Elsewhere in Australia

There are direct flights to Sydney from all Australian capitals, and options for arriving in Canberra and regional centres. The major domestic carriers are Ansett Australia (☎ 13 1300) and Qantas Airways (☎ 13 1313). Qantas has the subsidiary Eastern Australia Airlines, which flies on several routes in NSW, including to Lord Howe Island (book through Qantas). Smaller airlines include Hazelton, Kendell (for both book through Ansett) and Impulse (☎ 13 1381), which often flies in partnership with the major carriers, so you can usually book through Qantas or Ansett as well. Impulse recently began interstate flights, and Virgin has announced it will soon enter the domestic market.

You don't have to reconfirm domestic flights, but if you want to check flight details, the numbers to call are ☎ 13 1515 (Ansett) and ☎ 13 1223 (Qantas). Also check their Web sites at www.ansett.com.au and www.qantas.com.au.

We quote full economy fares, but most airlines offer discounts. For example, Melbourne-Sydney return is $576 full fare, $329 with a seven-day advance purchase, $269 with a 14-day advance and $239 with a 21-day advance. Recent advertised specials were $189 return and $139 one way.

Full-time university or other higher education students get 25% off the regular economy fare on production of student ID or an ISIC card, but you can usually find fares discounted by more than that.

Nonresident international travellers can get up to 40% discount on internal Qantas flights, and 25% on Ansett flights simply by presenting their international ticket when booking. The discount applies only to the full economy fare, so in many cases it will be cheaper to take advantage of other discounts.

Interstate Distances

Travelling interstate from Sydney is a major journey. The nearest state capital is Melbourne, 870km away by the shortest highway route. To Brisbane it's almost 1000km, to Adelaide at least 1400km, Darwin 4000km, and Perth 4100km. Sydney to Darwin via Adelaide is 4450km, and it's nearly 5000km via Townsville.

LAND
Bus

There are several interstate bus companies operating into and out of NSW on major routes. Students, YHA members and other backpacker card holders get discounts of at least 10% with many long-distance companies. On straight point-to-point tickets there are varying stopover deals. Some companies give one free stopover on express routes, others charge a small fee, which might be waived if you book through certain agents.

Greyhound Pioneer Australia (☎ 13 2030) operates the only truly national bus network and McCafferty's (☎ 13 1499) is the next largest. Premier Motor Service (☎ 13 3410), a Nowra-based company, has regular services along the coastal highway from Sydney to Melbourne and Brisbane. There are quite a few other companies running less extensive routes. You can access timetables of major companies and make bookings on the Internet: Check out Greyhound Pioneer (www.greyhound.com.au); Premier (www .premierms.com.au); and McCafferty's (www.mccaffertys.com.au).

If you're heading from Sydney to Melbourne or Brisbane and want to make a few stops on the way, the set route passes offered by Greyhound Pioneer and Premier are a good option – see the Bus Passes section following.

Melbourne It's 12 to 13 hours by the most direct route, the Hume Hwy, to Melbourne. Firefly Express (☎ 9211 1644) charges $50 one way, but often has cheaper deals. Greyhound Pioneer charges $50 for its standard service and $60 for the express service (11½ hours). Greyhound Pioneer and Premier Motor Service both offer the prettier but longer (about 18 hours) Princes Hwy coastal route for $60 – Premier has cheaper sector fares along the way.

Brisbane It takes about 16 hours to get to Brisbane via the Pacific Hwy and the standard fare is $71 ($69 with Premier). You often need to book in advance and some buses don't stop in all the main towns en route.

Fares (and travel times) between Sydney and destinations in northern NSW include Port Macquarie $50 (seven hours), Coffs Harbour $57 (9½ hours) and Byron Bay $69 (13 hours).

McCafferty's and Greyhound Pioneer also have services on the inland New England Hwy, which take an hour or two longer but cost about the same.

Adelaide Sydney to Adelaide takes 18 to 25 hours and costs around $96. Services run via Canberra, Broken Hill or Melbourne. Travelling Sydney-Melbourne-Adelaide with Firefly is cheaper ($70) than travelling Sydney-Adelaide with other companies. Countrylink's daily Speedlink service involves a train to Albury, then a bus to Adelaide ($130).

West Australia The 52- to 56-hour trip to Perth costs $295; to Alice Springs it's about 42 hours (plus some waiting in Adelaide) and $231; to Darwin (via Mt Isa) it's 67 hours and $376.

Bus Passes If you're planning to do a lot of bus travel, the major companies have a variety of useful passes.

Greyhound's kilometre passes are a flexible way to travel. The 2000km pass costs $215, and they go up from there in increments of 1000km, to 20,000km. A 5000km pass is $440. The Aussie Passes allow you unlimited travel for a set number of days (seven days costs $523, 10 days $672). Both passes are valid for 12 months. If you're heading around Australia or want to make a journey on a set route, the Explorer Passes have 38 route combinations and you have from two to 12 months to use them (depending on the distance), with as many stops as you like (but no backtracking). However, Premier Motor Service has far better deals to Brisbane ($88) and Melbourne ($80).

McCafferty's has the Roamer Pass, which is similar to Greyhound's kilometre pass (but cheaper). The 2000km pass is $190 and the 5000km pass is $395. McCafferty's also has seven set-route passes.

Train

The railway system is less comprehensive than the bus networks, and train services are less frequent and more expensive. However, they're as fast as or faster than buses, are generally more comfortable, and special fares can make the prices competitive. Individual states run their own railway services; in NSW it's Countrylink.

For information and bookings on interstate services call the Central Reservation Centre (☎ 13 2232, 6.30 am to 10 pm daily) or contact a Countrylink Travel Centre.

Fares Fare levels for interstate rail travel are economy, 1st class and sleeping berths, although sleeping berths aren't available on all trains. Depending on availability, a limited number of discounted fares are offered on most trains (check newspapers and with travel agents). These cut 10% to 40% off the standard fares.

On interstate journeys you can make free stopovers – you have two months to complete your trip on a one-way ticket and six months on a return ticket.

Interstate routes, fares and travel times from Sydney are:

Adelaide The *Indian Pacific* goes to Perth via Adelaide on Monday and Thursday ($162/334/480, 26 hours). There's also a daily bus/train connection to Adelaide called Speedlink ($130, about 20 hours).

Brisbane A nightly XPT ($104/145/240, about 12½ hours). This train connects with a bus at Casino for passengers travelling to the far north coast of NSW and Queensland's Gold Coast.

Melbourne A nightly XPT (express) train ($104/145/240 in economy/1st class/sleeper, 10 hours).

Perth The twice-weekly *Indian Pacific* ($424/888/1350, 65 hours). The 1st-class fares include meals and all fares are about 25% more in high season (1 September to 31 October). Reservations can be made with Great Southern Railways (☎ 13 2147, fax 08-8213 4491, ✉ enquiries@gsr.com.au), or look up www.gsr.com.au.

Rail Passes A number of rail passes allow unlimited rail travel either across the country or just in one state. The national passes are only available to international visitors. With the Austrail Pass you can travel anywhere on the Australian rail network for a set number of days, starting from 14 days for $575. The Austrail Flexipass differs in that it allows a set number of travelling days within a six-month period, starting from eight days for $475.

Car & Motorcycle

See the Getting Around chapter for details of road rules, driving conditions and information on buying and renting vehicles.

The main road routes into NSW are the Hume Hwy from Melbourne to Sydney; the Princes Hwy from Melbourne to Sydney via the coast; the Pacific Hwy between Brisbane and Sydney via the coast (passing through or near all the north-coast beach resorts, but not a fun road to drive); and the route from Adelaide to Sydney via Broken Hill and Dubbo (wide open spaces and empty roads – except for kangaroos). The Newell Hwy is a good road from Victoria to Brisbane, crossing much of rural NSW along the way.

SEA

Ask around at yacht clubs and check hostel notice boards for yachts needing crew members. *Sydney Afloat* is a free monthly paper that occasionally has ads for crew. You'll find a copy at most yacht clubs.

Cargo ships are more expensive than flying (although cheaper than a cruise ship), but could be interesting. Try an agent such as the Sydney Sea & Air Centre (☎ 9283 1199).

Warning

The information in this chapter is particularly vulnerable to change: Prices for international travel are volatile, routes are introduced and cancelled, schedules change, special deals come and go, and rules and visa requirements are amended. Airlines and governments seem to take a perverse pleasure in making price structures and regulations as complicated as possible. You should check directly with the airline or a travel agent to make sure you understand how a fare (and ticket you may buy) works. In addition, the travel industry is highly competitive and there are many lurks and perks.

The upshot of this is that you should get opinions, quotes and advice from as many airlines and travel agents as possible before you part with your hard-earned cash. The details given in this chapter should be regarded as pointers and are not a substitute for your own careful, up-to-date research.

Getting Around

AIR

Ansett Australia (☎ 13 1300) and Eastern Australia Airlines (☎ 13 1313), a subsidiary of Qantas Airways, have intrastate flights and there are several other operators such as Impulse (☎ 13 1381), Hazelton and Kendell (for both, contact Ansett). Most flights are between Sydney and major country centres (see the chart for fares), with few flights linking country centres. Short-hop domestic flights in Australia are expensive and it would be difficult to put together a tour of the state by scheduled flights without a lot of backtracking to Sydney.

BUS

Countrylink (☎ 13 2232) runs the most comprehensive bus network in New South Wales (NSW). Major bus companies also serve many towns on their express runs from Sydney to other capitals – see under Bus in the Getting There & Away chapter for more information. However, travelling short distances within NSW on an interstate bus is often expensive, and, because of regulations, interstate buses might not be allowed to take you on some sectors. Also, even though a town may be listed on their schedule, interstate buses may only stop if there has been a confirmed booking.

One good option on the popular coastal route is Premier Motor Service (☎ 13 3410), which has reasonably priced sector fares and a good value Sydney-Brisbane pass allowing unlimited stops ($88). There are also frequent services from Sydney to Canberra with the major bus companies ($28).

From major towns, there's usually a local service to smaller places nearby, but these are rarely frequent.

Backpacker Bus

Oz Experience (☎ 1300 300 028) has an established service along the east coast. It has many passes, valid for six to 12 months, with unlimited stops. A one-day trip to the Blue Mountains from Sydney costs $55; the Sydney-Melbourne route via Canberra and the Barry Way is $195 (minimum four days); the Sydney-Brisbane trip is $130 (minimum four days); and a return trip from Sydney to Byron Bay (minimum 12 days) is $295. Book at least 48 hours in advance and reconfirm your seats, especially in summer, as the buses have been known to be oversubscribed.

TRAIN

The NSW government's Countrylink rail network is the most comprehensive in Australia. The trains, in conjunction with connecting buses, take you quite quickly (if not always frequently) to most sizable towns.

As well as the high-speed XPT (express) trains (some with sleepers), there are nippy Explorer trains. Trains run to Albury (and on to Melbourne), Armidale, Canberra, Broken Hill (and on to Adelaide and Perth), Dubbo, Griffith, Kyogle (and on to Brisbane), Moree and Murwillumbah.

On point-to-point tickets, Countrylink's prices can be comparable to the private bus

NSW AIR FARES

All fares in Australian dollars
One-way economy air fares

Coolangatta
Ballina
317
Coffs Harbour
263
Dubbo
Port Macquarie
232
Broken Hill
184
195   Newcastle
363
92
SYDNEY
163
235   195
CANBERRA
159   Cooma
213
Albury
Merimbula

Countrylink Rail Fares

Countrylink's economy one-way train fares from Sydney include:

destination	distance	fare
Albury	658km	$81
Armidale	574km	$75
Bathurst	231km	$35
Broken Hill	1100km	$110
Byron Bay	874km	$92
Canberra	310km	$45
Coffs Harbour	596km	$75
Dubbo	445km	$62
Goulburn	222km	$31
Griffith	641km	$81
Lithgow	156km	$24
Narrabri	569km	$75
Orange	296km	$42
Parkes	407km	$59
Tamworth	455km	$67
Wagga Wagga	511km	$71

companies and there are sometimes special deals. Stopovers (free) must be booked when you buy the ticket. With a one-way ticket you have to complete the journey within a week. With a return ticket the outward trip must be completed in a week and the return trip within two months.

The NSW Discovery Pass allows you to travel anywhere in the state for one month and costs $249; there's a discount of $50 for YHA members.

Most Countrylink services have to be booked (☎ 13 2232, 9217 8812).

CityRail (☎ 13 1500), the Sydney metropolitan service, runs frequent electric trains south through Wollongong ($7.80 one way) to Bomaderry ($13.40); west through the Blue Mountains to Katoomba ($10) and Lithgow ($15); north to Newcastle ($15.20); and south-west through the Southern Highlands to Goulburn ($22). Some services duplicate Countrylink services, but they're a little slower and much cheaper, especially if you buy a day-return ticket. You can't book seats on CityRail trains. Off-peak return fares are available after 9 am weekdays and all day on weekends.

CAR

Many of the finest features of NSW and the ACT are not readily accessible by public transport. For many visitors this means having to buy or rent a car. Overseas licences are acceptable in Australia, but an International Driving Permit is preferred.

Although the east of NSW is reasonably closely settled (well, compared with the Northern Territory), don't expect to find major roads everywhere you want to go.

You'll certainly find stretches of divided road, particularly on roads out of Sydney, but elsewhere highways are usually only two lanes wide. Between cities, signposting on the main roads is generally OK, but once you enter the maze of rural back roads you'll need a map – the National Roads & Motorists Association (NRMA) has a series of useful regional roadmaps. Street signage in rural towns can be poor.

Tourist offices around the state can supply you with 'tourist drive' brochures, which describe scenic local routes, and include a rough map showing points of interest.

Service stations generally stock diesel, super and unleaded fuel. Liquid petroleum gas (LPG, Autogas) is available in major centres, but harder to find elsewhere. Prices vary from place to place and from price war to price war, but generally they are in the $0.80-plus per litre range. It is usually cheaper in Sydney but in remote areas the price can soar, and some outback service stations are not above exploiting their monopoly position. Distances between fill-ups can be long in the far west, so make sure you have enough fuel.

Road Rules

Australians drive on the left-hand side of the road. An important road rule is 'give way to the right': If an intersection is unmarked (unusual), you must give way to vehicles entering the intersection from your right.

The speed limit is 100km/h except where otherwise indicated. On major roads this is sometimes raised to 110km/h, while the usual limit in towns is 60km/h, sometimes rising to 80km/h on the outskirts and dropping to 40km/h in residential areas and near

The Road to Ruin

Local drivers on little-used rural roads often speed, and they often assume that there's no other traffic. Be wary of oncoming cars at blind corners and other hazards which abound on country roads.

Animals

Animals are common hazards on country roads, and a collision is likely to kill the animal, seriously damage your vehicle and possibly injure or kill you and others. Kangaroos are most active around dawn and dusk, and they travel in groups. If you see one hopping across the road in front of you, slow right down – its friends are probably just behind it. In remote areas many people avoid travelling between 5 pm and 8 am because of the hazards posed by animals.

If an animal appears in front of you, hit the brakes (gently if you're on dirt) and swerve to avoid the animal only if it's safe to do so. Many people have been killed in accidents as a result of swerving to miss an animal.

Other animals with no road sense include cows, sheep and emus. Once again, if you see one you can expect more to be following.

In the country it's fairly common to meet a herd of sheep or cattle being driven along the road. Sometimes you'll have been warned by signs placed on the roadside, but often you'll get no warning. Stop and assess the situation (drovers won't appreciate it if you scatter a herd), then drive through *very* slowly.

Dirt Roads

You don't have to get far off the beaten track to find yourself on dirt roads. The coating of fine dust gives little or no traction if you have to brake or swerve (especially when wet). Most are regularly graded and reasonably smooth, but don't be tempted to speed – it's very easy to lose control.

On dirt roads that are dry, flat, straight, free of animals and traffic, and wide enough to allow for unexpected slewing as you hit potholes and drifted sand, you could, with practice, drive at about 80km/h. Otherwise, treat dirt like ice.

---

schools. Speed cameras and radar guns catch people who exceed these limits.

The blood alcohol limit in NSW is 0.05%, which most people reach after drinking two full-strength beers in an hour (although there is a lot of variation between individuals). These limits are enforced with random breath tests; penalties for exceeding them are heavy, which accounts for the popularity of low-alcohol beer.

Parking in Sydney can be a real nightmare – there are just way too many cars for all those narrow streets. Beware of towaway zones or you may return to find that your car has mysteriously vanished. A lot of cheaper accommodation in Sydney has no parking, so you're left with the choice of paying for commercial parking or constantly shifting your car to avoid fines. Outside Sydney, parking meters are rare and many country towns insist on rear-to-kerb angle parking.

Rental

There are some places where if you haven't got your own wheels you have to choose between a tour and a rented vehicle since there is no public transport and distances are too great for walking or even cycling. Competition is fierce, so rates tend to vary and lots of special deals pop up and disappear again.

The three major companies, Budget (☎ 13 2727, 1300 362 848), Hertz (☎ 13 3030) and Avis (☎ 13 6333), have agents everywhere. Thrifty Car Rental (☎ 1300 367 227) also has a wide network, and there are many local firms. The big operators will often have higher rates than the local firms, but not always. You'll need to calculate insurance, per-

The Road to Ruin

Gates & Grids

Rural roads sometimes run through private property where you might encounter closed gates and cattle grids. The golden rule about gates is: Always leave a gate as you find it (ie, open or closed).

Cattle grids (usually sections of railway tracks or iron pipe laid across a pit) stop stock from wandering. They're usually no hassle to drive across but it always pays to slow down.

Outback Driving

You often don't need a 4WD to tackle the unsealed roads in the state's far west, but you do need to be prepared. Backtracking hundreds of kilometres to pick up a minor part or to arrange a tow is unlikely to be easy or cheap. Joining the National Roads & Motorists Association (NRMA) provides you with some peace of mind.

You need to carry a fair amount of water in case of disaster. Food is less important – the space might be better allocated to an extra spare tyre.

If you run into trouble in the back of beyond, stay with your vehicle. It's much easier to spot a car than a human being from the air. Also, the heat can quickly kill you once you leave the shelter of your car.

The number one rule of outback driving is to seek local advice, preferably from the police. They know the road conditions and can advise you whether your vehicle is suitable for a particular track. Many outback routes are OK for 2WD vehicles, but you might need high clearance to cope with ruts and washouts if the road hasn't been graded since the last rains.

The Department of Land & Water Conservation (DLWC) tourist map *The Outback* is informative, but if you plan to drive on the minor unsealed roads you should supplement it with more detailed maps.

After rain, some outback roads are closed, not necessarily because 4WDs can't get through but because they'll damage the road. Some drivers see this as a challenge but 'bushbashing' (making your own road through the bush) is definitely not on.

For the full story on safe outback travel see Lonely Planet's *Outback Australia*.

---

kilometre rates and all other costs contained in the fine print. The big companies usually allow one-way rentals, although there might be a drop-off charge and other restrictions.

Insurance usually includes an 'excess' – if you have a prang, the excess is the amount you pay before the insurance company takes over. With some of the small companies this can be very high, but most companies offer to lower the excess if you pay an additional amount ($5 or $10 a day). The insurance may not cover you in a single-car accident (eg, if you hit a tree) – check the fine print. Most companies prefer to rent to people over 21, and some require you to be over 25, although there are a few who will rent to 18-year-olds (often with a higher insurance premium or a higher excess).

The major companies have rates for un-limited kilometres in Sydney and some other major centres, but in country areas it's usually restricted to 100km per day plus so many cents per kilometre after that. Straightforward city rentals are all much the same price. It's on special deals, odd rentals or longer periods that you find the differences. Weekend specials – usually three days for the price of two – are usually good value.

Daily rates including insurance are typically: from $50 to $65 a day for a small car (eg, Hyundai Excel); about $65 to $75 a day for a medium car (eg, Nissan Pulsar, Toyota Camry); and $70 to $100 a day for a big car (eg, Holden Commodore, Ford Falcon). Prices drop if you hire for more than a week. Local companies in cities often rent late-model small cars for as little as $35 to $40 per day.

'Rent-a-wreck' companies specialise in renting out older cars, typically from $25 to

$35 a day. If you want to travel around, or close to, the city, they're worth considering.

4WDs Renting a 4WD vehicle is more affordable if a few people get together. Something small like a Suzuki costs around $100 per day; for a Toyota Landcruiser you're looking at around $145, which should include insurance and some free kilometres (typically 100km). Check the insurance conditions, especially the excess, as they can be onerous. It will probably cost an extra $25 a day to have the excess reduced to a sensible level.

Britz Australia (☎ 1800 331 454), 182 O'Riordan St, Mascot, hires out camper vans (from $96 a day, depending on the season) and 4WD camper vans (from $164). This price applies to a minimum of four days hire but includes unlimited kilometres. The price goes up for fancier vehicles, and a collision damage waiver costs $28 per day.

Purchase

If you're buying a second-hand vehicle, reliability is all important.

You can buy through a dealer (you'll probably pay more, but you'll get a guaranteed title and help with paperwork), or privately by checking classified newspaper ads or hostel notice boards. Sydney is the best place to buy a car. Parramatta Rd is lined with used-car lots, and there are other setups geared especially to travellers. The daily Kings Cross Car Market (☎ 9358 5000), on the corner of Ward Ave and Elizabeth Bay Rd, is for private sellers (there's a charge of $35 and your car must have a roadworthy certificate) and is something of a travellers' rendezvous. The Flemington Sunday Car Market (☎ 1900 921 122), near Flemington Station, charges sellers $60.

Several dealers, such as Travellers Auto Barn (☎ 9360 1500), 177 William St, Kings Cross, will sell you a car with an undertaking to buy it back at an agreed price. Always read the small print.

Before you buy it's worth having the car checked by a mechanic. The NRMA (☎ 13 2132) will do this for $125/145 for members/ nonmembers. Many garages do inspections for much less.

For full details of the paperwork required to buy a car, pick up a copy of the Roads & Traffic Authority (RTA) pamphlet *Six Steps to Buying a Secondhand Motor Vehicle,* available at RTA and NRMA offices. Motor

Road Distances (km)

	Albury	Bega	Bourke	Broken Hill	Canberra	Dubbo	Grafton	Mildura	Moree	Newcastle	Port Macquarie	Sydney	Tamworth
Albury	---												
Bega	433	---											
Bourke	863	960	---										
Broken Hill	918	1256	614	---									
Canberra	347	226	734	1102	---								
Dubbo	550	627	368	749	401	---							
Grafton	1200	1064	818	1393	899	650	---						
Mildura	622	966	780	296	812	807	1457	---					
Moree	926	1003	449	1059	777	376	369	1183	---				
Newcastle	734	588	761	1142	423	393	483	1171	501	---			
Port Macquarie	981	828	914	1295	663	612	256	1419	544	247	---		
Sydney	478	431	777	1158	290	409	633	1019	625	157	397	---	
Tamworth	890	835	642	1023	696	340	310	1147	272	280	272	404	---

All distances are approximate and have been calculated over highways and roads, not by the shortest route.

Registry offices also have information. If you're buying privately, it's essential to check that the registration is still valid, that the vehicle isn't stolen or owned by a finance company, and that there are no outstanding fines – the RTA pamphlet tells you how to do this.

Every vehicle registered in NSW has third-party insurance – a Green Slip. This covers you against injuries you might cause, but not damage to other people's property, so it's a good idea to have third-party property insurance. The major insurance companies don't sell third-party property insurance to travellers, but the Kings Cross Car Market (and some dealers) can arrange it, even if you didn't buy the car there.

When the time comes to sell the car, fill in a Notice of Disposal card (available from a Motor Registry office), or you might be liable for fines incurred by the new owner.

National Roads & Motorists Association

The NRMA is the NSW motoring association; it provides emergency breakdown service, literature, excellent maps and detailed guides to accommodation. It has reciprocal arrangements with other state associations and with some organisations overseas (bring proof of membership with you). The NRMA's head office (☎ 13 2132) is at 338 George St, Sydney. There are other offices around the state and most towns have a garage affiliated with the NRMA. It costs $86 to join the NRMA, but members of interstate and some overseas motoring organisations pay only $40.

MOTORCYCLE

Motorcycles are a popular way of getting around. The climate is good for biking much of the year, and many small trails from the road often lead to perfect bush camp sites.

A fuel range of 350km will cover most fuel stops. You'll need a rider's licence – a car licence isn't enough – and a helmet.

Bike rental can be pricey, but running costs are lower than for a car. In Sydney try Bikescape Motorcycle Rentals and Tours (☎ 9699 4722), corner of Abercrombie and Cleveland Sts, Chippendale. Rates start at $60 per day, with gear. Britz Australia (☎ 1800 331 454) also hires out rental.

Buying your own two wheels is quite feasible. Australian newspapers and the local bike press have extensive classified advertisements – $3000 to $4000 gets you something that will take you around the country if you know a bit about bikes. The main drawback is trying to sell the bike again afterwards and, if you're an overseas visitor, getting insurance.

An easier option is a buy-back arrangement with a large motorcycle dealer, although this isn't common and the major disasters that can befall bikes make agreeing on a buy-back price very much a matter for negotiation. Better Bikes (☎ 9718 6668), 605 Canterbury Rd, Belmore, offers buy-back deals and has plenty of bikes in stock.

Take some spares and tools even if you can't use them, because someone else often can. The basics include: a tyre tube (front wheel size, which will fit on the rear but usually not vice versa); puncture repair kit with levers and a pump (or tubeless-tyre repair kit with two or three carbon dioxide cartridges); a tyre valve; the bike's standard toolkit; throttle, clutch and brake cables; tie wire, cloth (gaffer) tape and nylon 'zipties'; a handful of bolts and nuts in the usual emergency sizes (M6 and M8), along with a few self-tapping screws; one or two fuses; a bar of soap for fixing tank leaks (knead to a putty with water and squeeze into the leak); and, most important of all, a workshop manual for your bike.

If you break down, park your bike where it's clearly visible and stay with it.

BICYCLE

NSW is a great place for cycling and it's possible to plan rides of any duration and through almost any terrain. There are thousands of kilometres of good roads carrying so little traffic that the biggest hassle is waving back to the drivers.

Bicycle helmets are compulsory, as are front and rear lights for night riding.

Cycling has always been popular and not only as a sport: Some shearers rode huge

Long-Distance Cycling

Until you get fit you should be careful to eat enough to keep you going – remember that exercise is an appetite suppressant. It's easy to be so depleted of energy that you end up camping under a gumtree just 10km short of a shower and a steak. No matter how fit you are, water is still vital: Dehydration can kill you.

It can get very hot in summer, and you should take things slowly until you're used to the heat. Cycling in 30°C-plus temperatures isn't too bad if you wear a hat and plenty of sunscreen, and drink *lots* of water. Be aware of the blistering 'hot northerlies', the prevailing winds that make a north-bound cyclist's life uncomfortable in summer. In April, when the south-east region's clear autumn weather begins, the 'southerly trades' prevail.

Check with locals if you're heading into remote areas, and notify the police if you're about to do something particularly adventurous. That said, you can't rely too much on local knowledge of road conditions, as most people have no idea of what a heavily loaded touring bike needs. What they think of as a great road may be pedal-deep in sand.

distances between jobs. It's rare to find a reasonably sized town that doesn't have a shop stocking at least basic bike parts.

If you're coming specifically to cycle, it makes sense to bring your own bike. Check with your airline for costs and the degree of dismantling/packing required. Within Australia you can load your bike onto a bus or train to skip the boring bits. Bus companies require you to dismantle your bike, and some don't guarantee that it will travel on the same bus as you. Trains are easier, but supervise the loading and if possible tie your bike upright, otherwise you may find that the guard has stacked crates of Holden spares on your fragile alloy frame.

You can easily rent bikes along the way for a day or longer; youth hostels and sports shops often have bikes for rent.

Much of eastern Australia seems to have been settled on the principle of not having more than a day's horse ride between pubs,

so it's usually possible to get a shower at the end of the day. Most people carry camping equipment, but it's feasible to travel from town to town staying in pubs or on-site vans.

Bicycle NSW (☎ 9283 5200), 209 Castlereagh St, Sydney, has more information and publishes booklets on cycling throughout the state. Bike shops are also good sources of information on routes and suggested rides, or check out Lonely Planet's *Cycling Australia*.

HITCHING

Hitching is never entirely safe in any country, and we don't recommend it. Travellers who decide to hitch should understand that they're taking a small but potentially serious risk. People who do choose to hitch will be safer if they travel in pairs and let someone know where they are planning to go.

The ideal combination for successful hitching is one female and one male. Any more makes things very difficult and two guys hitching together can expect long waits. It's not advisable for women to hitch alone, or even in pairs.

Look for a place where vehicles will be going slowly and where they can stop easily: the ideal location is on the outskirts of a town.

University and hostel notice boards are good places to look for hitching partners. Just as hitchers should be wary when accepting lifts, drivers who pick up travellers should also be aware of the risks.

LOCAL TRANSPORT
Bus & Train

Sydney has a good public transport network run by the State Transport Authority (STA). In Canberra, Wollongong and Newcastle, it's also possible to get around by public transport. Anywhere else it becomes a bit problematic. There are buses in cities such as Wagga Wagga, Nowra and Dubbo, but they're fairly infrequent.

Taxi

Sydney has a lot of taxis, but you won't see many plying for trade on the streets of country towns. That doesn't mean they aren't there – even small towns often have at least one taxi and you can find the number in a local phonebook or at the tourist office. Taxi fares vary through the state, but shouldn't differ much from Sydney.

ORGANISED TOURS

Most tours are connected with a particular activity (eg, bushwalking or horse riding) or area (eg, outback tours from Broken Hill). Major tour companies in Sydney have programs of tours to Canberra, the Blue Mountains, the Hunter Valley and the Hawkesbury River (see Organised Tours in the Sydney chapter). The YHA Travel Centre (☎ 9261 1111) in Sydney is a good source of budget tour information.

A good way of travelling between Sydney and Byron Bay is with Ando's Opal Outback Tours (☎ 9559 2901, 1800 228 828). The five-day trip departs Sydney every Sunday and travels inland via Lightning Ridge. Tours include opal fossicking, gold panning, horse and camel riding, and accommodation is in miners cabins, shearers quarters and outback pubs. The tour gets good feedback from backpackers, and, at $399, it's a bargain.

See Backpacker Bus earlier in this chapter for trips between Sydney and Melbourne and along the coast to Brisbane, which are operated as tours. Pioneering Spirit (☎ 1800 672 422) runs an interesting bus tour from Sydney to Brisbane via the coast for $215, though most travellers jump off at Byron Bay ($195). It leaves Sydney every Friday (October to the end of May) and includes the Hunter Valley and Dorrigo National Park. The fare includes local accommodation and there's a 10% discount for YHA members. Its office is at the Travellers Contact Point in Sydney.

Sydney

postcode 2000 • pop four million

Sydney, Australia's oldest and largest settlement, on one of the most spectacular harbours in the world, is a vibrant, alluring city of many natural attractions, bold colours, skyscrapers and yachts.

The city has come a long way from its convict beginnings, but it still has a rough-and-ready energy that makes it an exciting place to visit. It offers an invigorating blend of the old and the new, the raw and the refined. You can explore The Rocks historic area in the morning, then ride the monorail to ultramodern Darling Harbour in the afternoon. While high culture attracts some to the Opera House, gaudy nightlife attracts others to Kings Cross.

Sydney attracts the majority of Australia's immigrants, and the city's mixture of pragmatic egalitarianism and natural indifference has made it a beacon of pluralism, and one of the world's most tolerant and diverse societies. A potpourri of ethnic groups contribute to the city's cultural life: Chinese newspapers, Lebanese restaurants and Greek Orthodox churches are as much a part of the city as its Anglo-Irish traditions. Evidence of the region's original inhabitants survives in the Aboriginal stencils that can be found in coastal caves, and in the indigenous names of many streets and suburbs.

Sydney is, above all, an outdoor city rich with natural assets. Whether it's yacht racing on the harbour, bushwalking in Sydney Harbour National Park or the Blue Mountains, or body-surfing at Bondi Beach, there's action on tap for everyone.

Sydneysiders tend to be casual, forthright, irreverent and sybaritic. According to outsiders, they're also faddish, mobile-phone-addicted and obsessed with real estate. However, Sydney's corporate culture has always been balanced by the knowledge that the best things in Sydney – the beaches, the mountains, the surf and the much-loved harbour – are free.

HIGHLIGHTS

- Sailing on Sydney Harbour, one of the best ways to view the city
- Enjoying the view from an alfresco cafe or restaurant table at Circular Quay or Campbells Cove in The Rocks
- Strolling through Sydney Harbour National Park
- Seeing a performance at the Sydney Opera House
- Conquering the 'coat hanger' – climbing the Harbour Bridge
- Taking in the excellent displays at the Powerhouse Museum and Art Gallery of NSW
- Partying at the Gay & Lesbian Mardi Gras
- Swimming or lazing at superb harbour and ocean beaches
- Eating a pie at Harry's Cafe de Wheels in Woolloomooloo

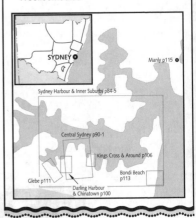

ORIENTATION

The harbour divides Sydney in half, with the Sydney Harbour Bridge and the Harbour Tunnel joining north and south. Central Sydney and most places of interest are south of the harbour. To explore beyond the inner suburbs, a street directory is essential.

City Centre

The central city area is relatively long and narrow, and only George and Pitt Sts (the main commercial and shopping streets) run the 3km from the waterfront at Circular Quay south to Central Station.

The Rocks and Circular Quay, where you'll find the Harbour Bridge and the Opera House respectively, mark the northern boundary of the centre; Central Station is on the southern edge; the inlet of Darling Harbour is the western boundary; and a string of parks borders Elizabeth and Macquarie Sts on the eastern side.

Inner Suburbs

Cafes, restaurants, interesting shops and good pubs are scattered throughout the inner suburbs.

East of the city centre are Kings Cross, Woolloomooloo, Potts Point and Elizabeth Bay. Farther east again are exclusive suburbs such as Double Bay and Vaucluse. South-east of the city centre are the interesting suburbs of Darlinghurst, Surry Hills and Paddington. At the city's eastern extreme are the ocean-front suburbs of Bondi Beach and Coogee.

West of the centre is the radically changing suburb of Pyrmont and to the southwest of here Glebe, a bohemian suburb famous for its eateries. West of Pyrmont is Rozelle and the arty suburb of Balmain.

Kingsford-Smith Airport is in Mascot, which juts into Botany Bay 10km south of the city centre.

North Shore

The suburbs north of the bridge are known collectively as the North Shore. Mainly middle-class enclaves, they lack the vibrancy and diversity of the areas south of the harbour, but there are some excellent views, beaches and pockets of bushland.

Directly across the Harbour Bridge from the city centre is North Sydney, the city's second business district. Military Rd runs east from North Sydney through the harbourside suburbs of Neutral Bay, Cremorne and Mosman. Hunters Hill, west of the bridge, is one of Sydney's most expensive suburbs.

To the north-east, Manly sits on a narrow peninsula near the entrance to Sydney Harbour, fronting both ocean and harbour. A string of ocean beaches runs north from Manly to Palm Beach, another of Sydney's wealthy suburbs. Palm Beach fronts the Pacific Ocean and backs onto Pittwater. On the western side of Pittwater is Ku-Ring-Gai Chase National Park.

Greater Sydney

Westward, Sydney's suburbs stretch for more than 50km, encompassing Parramatta, once a country retreat for the colony's governor, and ending at Penrith at the foot of the Blue Mountains. South-west of the city, there's a similar sprawl of housing developments, swamping old towns such as Campbelltown and Liverpool.

Maps

Lonely Planet's *Sydney City Map* ($7.95) is a comprehensive reference for the city centre and surrounding suburbs, as well as for important tourist sites around the city. It also features a walking tour.

For driving or exploration beyond the city centre, a street directory is indispensable. UBD and Gregory's charge $25 to $35 for their full-sized directories, though there are smaller versions.

For maps of country areas, contact the National Roads & Motorists Association (NRMA; ☎ 13 2132). For topographic maps, visit the Department of Land and Water Conservation (DLWC), 23–33 Bridge St; you can make credit-card telephone orders (☎ 9228 6111). If you're planning to go bush, pick up a copy of Tourism New South Wales' *Best Bush Map* ($4.95). It covers more than 1200 parks and state forests, and lists more than 100 camping sites.

INFORMATION
Tourist Offices

There's a Tourism NSW Travel Centre (☎ 9667 6050) on the international arrivals level at Sydney airport; it's open from 6 am

SYDNEY

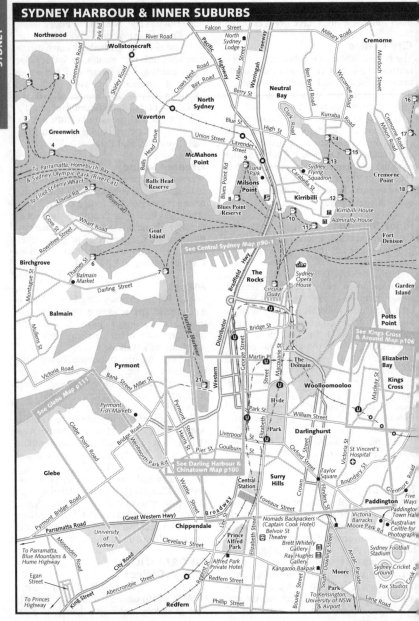

SYDNEY HARBOUR & INNER SUBURBS

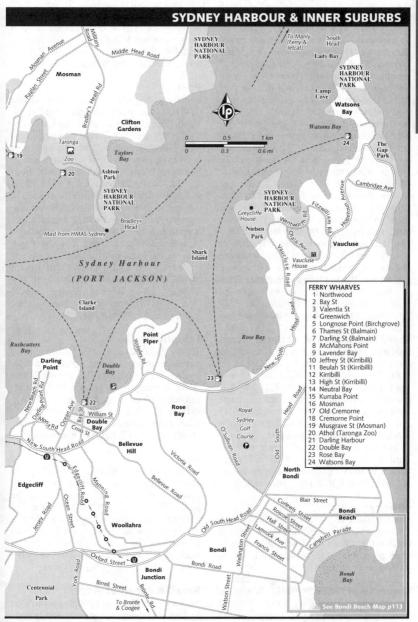

Mosman

Middle Head Road

Mosman Avenue

Raglan Street

Military Road

Bradley's Head Rd

SYDNEY
HARBOUR
NATIONAL
PARK

To Manly
(Ferry &
Jetcat)

South
Head

Lady Bay

SYDNEY
HARBOUR
NATIONAL
PARK

Camp
Cove

Watsons
Bay

Clifton
Gardens

Taronga
Zoo

Taylors
Bay

Ashton
Park

SYDNEY
HARBOUR
NATIONAL
PARK

Bradleys
Head

Mast from HMAS Sydney

Watsons Bay

The
Gap
Park

Cambridge Ave

Hopetoun Avenue

SYDNEY
HARBOUR
NATIONAL
PARK

Greycliffe
House

Nielsen
Park

Fitzwilliam Rd

Wentworth Rd

Ofala Ave

Vaucluse
House

Vaucluse

Shark
Island

New South Head Road

Sydney Harbour
(PORT JACKSON)

Clarke
Island

Rose Bay

Vaucluse Road

Rushcutters
Bay

Point
Piper

Wolseley Rd

Double
Bay

Darling
Point

New Beach Rd

Darling Point Rd

D'Nora Rd

Ocean Ave

Bay St

William St

Cross St

Double
Bay

New South Head Road

Rose
Bay

Rose
Bay

Royal
Sydney
Golf
Course

O'Sullivan Road

North
Bondi

Old South Head Road

Bellevue
Hill

Edgecliff

Jersey Road

Ocean Street

Edgecliff Road

Manning Road

Victoria Road

Bellevue Road

Woollahra

Oxford Street

Bondi
Junction

York Road

Birrell Street

Bronte Rd

To Bronte
& Coogee

Bondi

Bondi Road

Watson Street

Wellington Street

Old South Head Road

Francis Street

Lamrock Ave

Hall Street

Roscoe Street

Curlewis Street

Blair Street

Campbell Parade

Bondi
Beach

Bondi
Bay

See Bondi Beach Map p113

Centennial
Park

0   0.5   1 km
0   0.3   0.6 mi

FERRY WHARVES
1 Northwood
2 Bay St
3 Valentia St
4 Greenwich
5 Longnose Point (Birchgrove)
6 Thames St (Balmain)
7 Darling St (Balmain)
8 McMahons Point
9 Lavender Bay
10 Jeffrey St (Kirribilli)
11 Beulah St (Kirribilli)
12 Kirribilli
13 High St (Kirribilli)
14 Neutral Bay
15 Kurraba Point
16 Mosman
17 Old Cremorne
18 Cremorne Point
19 Musgrave St (Mosman)
20 Athol (Taronga Zoo)
21 Darling Harbour
22 Double Bay
23 Rose Bay
24 Watsons Bay

to midnight daily. As well as being a travel agency and a great source of information on Sydney and NSW, it sells hotel accommodation at vastly discounted rates – hotels use Tourism NSW as a daily 'dumping ground' for otherwise unoccupied rooms. The centre can help you find a room in a four- or perhaps a five-star hotel for a really cheap rate. You could also try the airport's electronic bookings board, near the Travel Centre, for hotel accommodation, or the useful Backpacker Board, which lists 75 hostels in Sydney (you can phone them for free there).

The excellent Sydney Visitors Centre (☎ 9255 1788, 1800 067 676) at 106 George St, The Rocks, is open from 9 am to 6 pm daily; it can book hotel accommodation, and there's a hostel notice board too. There's another visitors centre (☎ 9286 0111) at Darling Harbour, next to the IMAX Theatre.

City Host tourist information kiosks are located at Circular Quay, Town Hall station, and Martin Place. Opening hours are 9 am to 5 pm in winter, 10 am to 6 pm in summer.

In the Sydney Coach Terminal on Eddy Ave (outside Central Station) there's a Travellers Information Service (☎ 9281 9366, 9669 5111), which makes bus and accommodation bookings (not hostels, but there's a hostel notice board) from 6 am to 10 pm.

On Central Station's main concourse is the Travellers Aid Society (☎ 9211 2469). It provides general information and assistance with travel problems, and is open from 6.45 am to 5 pm weekdays and 7 am to noon weekends; hot showers cost $3.

The Countrylink Travel Centre at Wynyard station on York St (☎ 13 2232) can book travel as well as hotel accommodation; it's open from 8.30 am to 5 pm weekdays.

Money

All terminals at the airport have foreign-exchange facilities and ATMs. At Central Station there is an ATM near the suburban train platforms on the lower level, but no exchange facilities.

Thomas Cook has foreign-exchange branches at 175 Pitt St (☎ 9231 2877), in the Queen Victoria Building (QVB; ☎ 9264 1267) and in the Kingsgate shopping centre (☎ 9356 2211), beneath the Coca-Cola sign in Kings Cross. The QVB branch is open daily, the others Monday to Saturday. American Express (☎ 9239 0666), 92 Pitt St, opens weekdays and Saturday morning.

Post

Sydney's original General Post Office (GPO), in the grand Victorian building on Martin Place, has been refurbished as an up-market hotel, restaurant and shopping complex. There is a small post office branch there open from 10 am to 2 pm weekdays and on Saturday. Another post office operates from 130 Pitt St. Poste Restante (☎ 9744 3732) and post office (PO) boxes are located at 310 George St, in the Hunter Connection Building near the Wynyard station entrance; it's open from 8.15 am to 5.30 pm on weekdays.

American Express and Thomas Cook provide mail services for their clients. Alternatively, there's Travellers Contact Point (☎ 9221 8744), Suite 11–15, 7th floor, 428 George St, or Internet Bakpak Travel (☎ 9360 3888), a resource for backpackers, at 3 Orwell St, Kings Cross.

Telephone

Telstra Phone Centre, at 231 Elizabeth St, has coin, phonecard and credit-card telephones. It's open daily. The 24-hour Translating & Interpreting Service (☎ 13 1450) can help with language difficulties. For help in finding a number within Australia, call directory assistance (☎ 1223) or Yellow Pages Direct (☎ 13 1319, business numbers only).

Fax

Faxes can be sent from or received at post offices. Some businesses have fax services, which works out much cheaper than the post office. Kinko's (☎ 9267 4255) at 175 Liverpool St, opposite Hyde Park, charges $1 a page for local faxes and is open 24 hours. You can receive faxes for free at Backpackers World (☎ 9380 2700, fax 9380 2900), 212 Victoria St, Kings Cross.

Email & Internet Access

Internet cafes have been popping up all over Sydney and the resulting price war is good news for travellers. Kings Cross has the highest concentration of Internet cafes, several of which are open 24 hours, and there are plenty in Manly, Bondi, Glebe, Newtown and the southern end of the city. Besides allowing you to access email and surf the Web, many also offer word-processing, fax, scanning and printing services.

Global Gossip is open from 8 am until at least midnight, and has locations all over Sydney, including 770 George St (☎ 9212 1466) and 14 Wentworth Ave (☎ 9263 0400) in the city, 108 Oxford St, Darlinghurst (☎ 9380 4588), and 111 Darlinghurst Rd, Kings Cross (☎ 9326 9777). Backpackers World (see under Fax earlier in this chapter) also has Internet access. For good specials, check out the Kings Internet Cafe (☎ 9356 2311), 41 Darlinghurst Rd, Kings Cross.

Serving both food and coffee, Well Connected (☎ 9566 2655), at 35 Glebe Point Rd, Glebe, is Sydney's longest-running and most comfortable Internet cafe. If you fancy logging on with a beer, there's the pricier Hotel Sweeney (☎ 9267 1116), at 236 Clarence St in the city.

Other places include Newtown Internet Salon (☎ 9519 0010), at 423 King St, and CyberBondi (☎ 9300 0363) 22/33 Campbell Parade, Bondi Beach.

Coin-operated computer stations that look like video-game machines are also popping up, but they're relatively expensive. Most public libraries offer free Internet access, but you need to book ahead. Many hostels are also getting wired up.

Internet Resources

The *Sydney Morning Herald*'s excellent online city guide includes entertainment, the arts, dining, accommodation and shopping options, and can be found at www.city search.com. For transport information head to the State Transit Authority (STA) site at www.sydneytransport.net.au.

Other useful Web sites include Active Sydney (www.active.org.au) for news, views and links for activist events around Sydney, and Izon's Backpacker Journal at www.izon.com, which is full of backpacker-friendly information and useful links.

Travel Agencies

Thomas Cook (☎ 9231 2877), 175 Pitt St, has a travel agency as well as a foreign-exchange desk; it's open from 8.45 am to 5.15 pm weekdays and 10 am to 2 pm Saturday. American Express (☎ 9239 0666), 92 Pitt St, opens from 8.30 am to 5.30 pm weekdays and 9 am to noon Saturday.

A number of travel agents cater for budget travellers. STA Travel has its head office (☎ 9212 1255) at 855 George St, Ultimo, plus branches in Kings Cross and Paddington. Others include Let's Travel Australia (☎ 9358 2295), 175 Victoria St near Kings Cross station, and Eden Travel (☎ 9368 1174), at level 2, 65 York St in the city. Travellers Contact Point (☎ 9221 8744), Suites 11–15, 7th floor, 428 George St, offers assistance with finding accommodation and work, organised tours, luggage storage, postal services and Internet access.

Bookshops

Dymocks and Angus & Robertson are large Sydney chain stores. Dymocks' main branch (☎ 9235 0155), 424–430 George St, is an enormous shop with a huge range of stock and a cafe. You'll find an Angus & Robertson (☎ 9235 1188) in the Imperial Arcade, 168 Pitt St.

The Travel Bookshop (☎ 9261 8200) at 175 Liverpool St, specialising in travel books and maps, opens from 9 am to 6 pm weekdays, 10 am to 5 pm Saturday. The friendly Abbey's Bookshop (☎ 9264 3111), 131 York St, opposite the QVB, carries a wide range of literature, including many foreign-language titles. Green Books (☎ 9261 1919), 92 Liverpool St, has books and posters on environmental issues and indigenous cultures.

Oxford St has a handful of excellent bookshops. The Bookshop Darlinghurst (☎ 9331 1103), 207 Oxford St, near Taylor Square, specialises in gay and lesbian literature. Ariel (☎ 9332 4581), at No 42–44, Paddington, focuses on art and design. Berkelouw (☎ 9360 3200), at No 19 opposite Ariel, has second-hand and antique books, a good travel section and a small cafe.

In Glebe, Gleebooks (☎ 9660 2333), 49 Glebe Point Rd, is worth checking out, as is its other outlet (☎ 9552 2526), at No 191, for second-hand and children's books.

Libraries

The City of Sydney Library has its main branch (☎ 9265 9470) on the 3rd floor at the Town Hall and is open from 8 am to 7 pm weekdays, 10 am to noon Saturday. There's another smaller branch (☎ 9265 9977) farther south in a restored sandstone building at 744 George St, Haymarket. It's open from 8.30 am to 6 pm weekdays, 10 am to 1 pm Saturday. The libraries have public telephones, photocopiers and computers, a collection of CD-ROMs, and Internet access.

Cultural Centres

Among the many foreign cultural centres in Sydney are:

Alliance Française (☎ 9267 1755) 257 Clarence St, city
British Council (☎ 9326 2022) 203 New South Head Rd, Edgecliff
Goethe Institut (☎ 9328 7411) 90 Ocean St, Woollahra
Italian Institute of Culture (☎ 9392 7939) 1 Macquarie Place, city
Japan Cultural Centre (☎ 9954 0111) Level 14, 201 Miller St, North Sydney

Laundry & Left Luggage

There are dozens of convenient laundrettes and dry-cleaning places around town, many of which are open daily.

There is a cloakroom at Central Station (☎ 9379 4395) where you can leave luggage for 24 hours at $1.50 per item, but unless you pay this levy in person on a daily basis, you'll be charged $4.50 a day. The cloakroom opens from 6.30 am to 10.30 pm daily.

There are luggage lockers in the Greyhound Pioneer office on Eddy Ave outside Central Station. They cost $4 to $8 for 24 hours, depending on the size of your bag. Some of the backpacker service specialists in Kings Cross also store luggage.

Medical Services

Several places give vaccinations and advice, but you need to book an appointment.

The Traveller's Medical & Vaccination Centre (☎ 9221 7133), Room 12, 7th floor, 428 George St above Dymocks bookshop, opens from 9 am to 5 pm weekdays and to noon on Saturday.

Kings Cross Travellers Clinic (☎ 9358 3376), Suite 1, 13 Springfield Ave, opens from 9 am to 1 pm and 2 to 6 pm weekdays, 10 am to noon on Saturday.

Many of the city's public hospitals have casualty departments, including St Vincent's Hospital (☎ 9339 1111), on the corner of Victoria and Burton Sts, Darlinghurst, and Sydney Hospital (☎ 9382 7111), Macquarie St, in the city.

Some chemists with longer opening hours are:

Blake's Pharmacy (☎ 9358 6712) 28 Darlinghurst Rd, Kings Cross; open from 8 am to midnight daily.
Darlinghurst Prescription Pharmacy (☎ 9361 5882) 261 Oxford St, Darlinghurst; open from 8 am to 10 pm daily.
Park Chemist (☎ 9552 3372) 321 Glebe Point Rd, Glebe; open from 8 am to 8 pm daily.
Wu's Pharmacy (☎ 9211 1805) 629 George St, city; open from 9 am to 9 pm Monday to Saturday and to 7 pm Sunday.

Emergency

In a life-threatening emergency, dial ☎ 000. This call is free from any phone and the operator will connect you with the police, ambulance or fire brigade.

There are several police stations in the city, including one at 192 Day St (☎ 9265 6499) near Darling Harbour, another at The Rocks on the corner of George and Argyle Sts (☎ 9265 6366), and one in Kings Cross behind the El Alamein Fountain at 1–15a Elizabeth Bay Rd (☎ 8356 0099).

Some other useful emergency numbers include:

Chemist	☎ 9235 0333
Dentist	☎ 9369 7050
Interpreter Service	☎ 13 1450
Life Crisis	☎ 13 1114
Poisons	☎ 13 1126
Rape Crisis Centre	☎ 9819 6565/7842
Salvo Care Line	☎ 9331 6000
Youth Line	☎ 9951 5522

The Wayside Chapel (☎ 9358 6577, 24 hours), 29 Hughes St, Kings Cross, is a crisis centre.

Dangers & Annoyances

Sydney isn't an especially dangerous city, but you should remain alert. The usual big-city rules apply: Never leave cars or rooms unlocked, never leave luggage unattended, never show big wads of money and never get drunk in the company of strangers. Use extra caution in Kings Cross, which attracts drifters from all over Australia and gutter-crawlers from all over Sydney.

Harassment of gays, lesbians and non-Europeans isn't rife, but does happen.

Sydney is generally safe for women travellers, although you should avoid walking alone late at night. Gross sexual harassment is uncommon, but you should be a little wary, especially in pubs.

Some Sydney beaches become polluted after heavy rainfall. Local radio stations give updates on the latest conditions.

SYDNEY HARBOUR

The harbour has moulded and shaped the Sydney psyche since settlement; today it's both a major port and the city's playground. Its waters, beaches, islands and waterside parks offer all the swimming, sailing, picnicking and walking you could wish for.

Officially called Port Jackson, Sydney's extravagantly colourful harbour stretches from the North and South Heads some 20km inland to join the mouth of the Parramatta River.

The best way to view the harbour is to take a cruise or catch a ferry. The Manly ferry offers vistas of the harbour east of the bridge, while the Parramatta RiverCats cover the west. You can also take trips to some of the small islands that are part of Sydney Harbour National Park.

Sydney Harbour National Park

This park protects scattered pockets of bushland and includes several small islands. It offers some great walking tracks, scenic lookouts, Aboriginal carvings, beaches and a handful of historic sites. On the southern shore it incorporates South Head and Nielsen Park; on the North Shore it includes North Head, Dobroyd Head, Middle Head and Ashton Park. Fort Denison, Goat, Clarke and Shark Islands are also part of the park. The National Parks & Wildlife Service (NPWS) information centre (☎ 9247 5033) is at Cadman's Cottage, 110 George Street, The Rocks. It is open 9.30 am to 4.30 pm weekdays, and from 10 am to 4.30 pm weekends.

Islands Previously known as Pinchgut, **Fort Denison** is a small fortified island off Mrs Macquarie's Point. It was originally used as a punishment 'cell' to isolate troublesome convicts, until it was fortified in the mid-19th century during the Crimean War amid fears of a Russian invasion.

The largest island in the bay, **Goat Island**, west of the Harbour Bridge, has been a shipyard, quarantine station and gunpowder depot, and is now a filming location for the popular *Water Rats* TV show.

Fort Denison and Goat Island are heritage sites, so you'll need to join a tour if you want to visit them – contact the NPWS information centre (☎ 9247 5033). At the time of writing, Fort Denison was closed for conservation work.

There's also a *Water Rats* tour ($18/14 adults/concession) at 11.45 am Wednesday, and a 'Gruesome Tales' tour ($22/18, includes supper) on Saturday nights. The latter is not suitable for children!

Clarke Island off Darling Point, **Rodd Island** at Iron Cove and **Shark Island** off Rose Bay make great picnic getaways, but you'll need to hire a water taxi or have access to a boat to reach them. To visit these islands you need a permit ($3 per person), available from Cadman's Cottage.

Walks There's a fine, short walk round **South Head**. It begins at Camp Cove and passes Lady Bay, Inner South Head and **The Gap**, ending at Outer South Head. Bus No 325 from Circular Quay runs past Nielsen Park to Watsons Bay. Ferries run to Watsons Bay on weekends.

On the North Shore, the 4km **Ashton Park track** begins below Taronga Zoo and

SYDNEY

CENTRAL SYDNEY

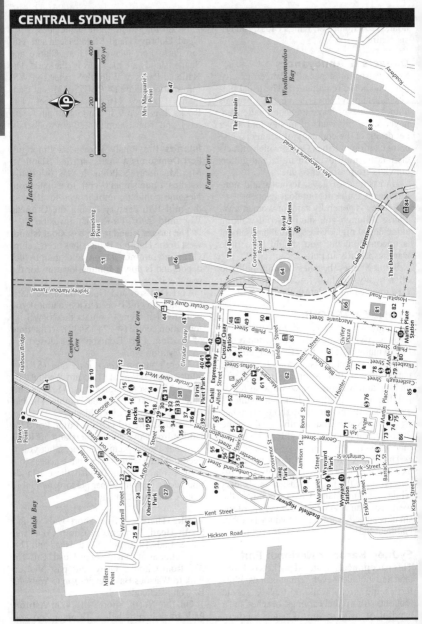

400 m
400 yd
200
200
0
0

CENTRAL SYDNEY

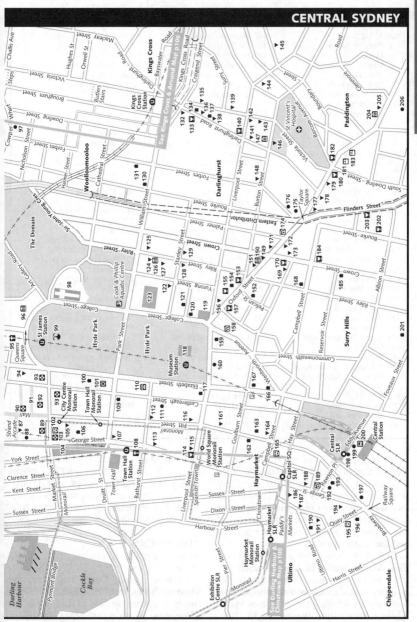

See Kings Cross & Around Map p106

See Darling Harbour & Chinatown Map p100

Challis Ave
Mackay Street
Hughes St.
Orwell St.
Road
145
Road
Steps
Victoria Street
Kings Cross
Glenmore
Brougham Street
Butlers Stairs
Kings Cross Station
144
Road
Road
Street
205
Paddington
204
206
Cowper Wharf
97
Dowling Street
Nicholson Street
Forbes Street
Cathedral Street
Harmer Street
132
133
134
135
136
137
138
139
140
141
142
143
146
147
148
St Vincent's Hospital
182
Barcom Avenue
Victoria Street
183
181
Woolloomooloo
131
130
Darlinghurst
Darlinghurst Road
South Dowling Street
179
180
178
177
176
175
Taylor Square
Flinders Street
203
202
The Domain
Sir John Young Cres.
William Street
Forbes Street
Bourke Street
Liverpool Street
Burton Street
Palmer Street
Eastern Distributor
Bourke Street
174
173
172
171
150
151
149
170
169
168
184
185
Crown Street
Albion Street
Riley Street
Surry Hills
201
Cook & Phillip Aquatic Centre
Art Gallery Road
College Street
96
98
123
124
125
126
127
128
129
Stanley Street
Crown Street
Riley Street
Yurong Street
Stanley Street
155
154
153
152
156
157
158
159
160
Oxford Street
Pelican St.
Commonwealth Street
Wentworth Avenue
Campbell Street
Reservoir Street
Foveaux Street
St James Station
95
99
94
93
92
Queens Square
Hyde Park
Park Street
Hyde Park
College Street
Elizabeth Street
122
121
120
119
118
117
Museum Station
Strand Arcade
Mall
90
91
88
87
89
93
102
103
104
105
106
100
101
110
109
112
111
116
115
114
113
108
107
161
163
164
165
166
167
162
Castlereagh Street
Pitt Street
City Centre Monorail Station
Town Hall Monorail Station
Monorail
World Square Monorail Station
Haymarket
Goulburn Street
Hay Street
Central SLR
Eddy Avenue
199
200
198
Central Station
York Street
Clarence Street
Kent Street
Sussex Street
George Street
Town Hall Station
Druitt St.
Bathurst Street
Liverpool Street
Spanish Town
Sussex Street
Dixon Street
Harbour Street
Town Hall
Market Street
Monorail
Capitol SQ SLR
Rawson Pl
186
187
188
189
190
191
192
193
194
195
196
197
Chinatown
Campbell Street
George St.
Quay Street
Railway Square
Broadway
Central Station
Haymarket SLR
Paddy's Markets
Haymarket Monorail Station
Exhibition Centre SLR
Pier Street
Ultimo Road
Harris Street
Ultimo
Chippendale
Darling Harbour
Cockle Bay
Pyrmont Bridge

CENTRAL SYDNEY

PLACES TO STAY
3 Pier One Parkroyal Sydney Harbour
6 Harbour View Hotel
7 Mercantile Hotel
10 Park Hyatt Hotel
16 Old Sydney Parkroyal
25 Lord Nelson Brewery Hotel
26 Observatory Hotel
34 Harbour Rocks Hotel
35 Stafford
36 Russell Hotel
49 Ritz Carlton
50 Intercontinental
55 Quay West Suites
56 ANA Hotel Sydney
68 Grand Hotel
69 York Apartment Hotel
74 Westin Hotel
77 Sydney City Centre Apartments
100 Sheraton on the Park
106 Sydney Hilton Hotel; Marble Bar; Royal Arcade
109 Park Regis
117 Hyde Park Inn
119 Hyde Park Plaza
120 Sydney Marriot Hotel
121 Sydney Park Inn
130 Tokyo Joe's
131 Forbes Terrace
134 Top Of The Town Hotel
137 L'Otel
152 Oxford Koala Hotel
154 Parkridge Corporate Apartments; The Park All-Suite Hotel
159 Y on the Park
162 CB Private Hotel
163 Hotel Backpack
166 Sydney Central Private Hotel
167 Southern Cross Hotel
168 Cambridge Park Inn
185 Crown Lodge International
190 Aaron's Hotel
193 Sydney Central YHA
196 Country Comfort Hotel
201 Excelsior Hotel

PLACES TO EAT
1 Pier Four (Wharf Theatre)
9 Wolfie's
12 Doyle's at the Quay; Quay
17 G'Day Cafe
28 Clocktower Square Shopping Centre
29 Gum Nut Tea Garden
30 Phillip's Foote
32 Sailor's Thai
37 Rockpool
39 Vault
43 Sydney Cove Oyster Bar; Portobello Caffe
45 Aria
53 Kable's (Regent Hotel)
58 Rocks Teppanyaki
61 Obelisk Cafe
73 Food Emporium
87 Harris Coffee & Tea
94 Bar Coluzzi
105 Arizona
107 Woolworth's
112 Edinburgh Castle Hotel; Pitt St Bistro
113 Planet Hollywood
115 Vender
116 Diethnes Restaurant
122 Beppi's
124 Baraza Cafe
125 The Edge
127 Pacifico
128 Two Chefs
129 Italian Restaurants
132 Michaelangelo's Cafe
135 Bar Coluzzi
136 Govinda's; The Movie Room
138 Le Petit Crème
139 Una's Coffee Lounge
141 Fishface
142 Fez Cafe
143 Fu Manchu
144 Bills 1
145 Buon Ricordo
146 Bandstand Cafe
148 Dov Cafe
149 Thai Panic; Don Don
151 1 Burton
156 Burdekin Hotel
161 Mother Chu's Vegetarian Kitchen
164 Chamberlain Hotel
169 Pablo's Vice
170 Roo Bar
171 Betty's Soup Kitchen; Tandoori Palace
172 Tamana's; North Indian Flavour
173 Maltese Cafe
177 Cafe 191
178 Balkan
179 Kim's
186 House of Guangzhou; Fuji San
187 Emperor's Garden BBQ & Noodles
188 Ru Yuan Vegetarian Restaurant
191 Chinese Noodle Restaurant; Green Zone
194 Malaya on George
205 Fringe Bar & Cafe

ENTERTAINMENT
23 Hero of Waterloo Hotel
44 Dendy Cinema

heads east round Bradleys Head, skirting Taylors Bay to reach Clifton Gardens. Take the Taronga Zoo ferry from Circular Quay to get to Ashton Park. From Taronga you can walk west to **Cremorne Point** via a combination of parks, stairways, streets and bush. You get good views of the harbour and the southern shore.

One of the best walks in the park is the 8km **Manly Scenic Walkway**, which follows the harbour shore from Manly to The Spit Bridge and takes about four hours. Collect a leaflet detailing the walk from Manly Visitors Information Bureau, on the fore-shore at Manly Beach. For more information, call the NPWS (☎ 9977 6229) or Manly Municipal Council (☎ 9976 1500).

Sydney Harbour Ferries publishes a useful pamphlet detailing some picturesque harbourside strolls.

THE ROCKS

Sydney's first non-Aboriginal settlement was made on the rocky spur of land on the western side of Sydney Cove, from which the Harbour Bridge now crosses to the North Shore. It became known as The Rocks because of the prominent sandstone outcrops on

CENTRAL SYDNEY

54 George St Bar
57 Harts Pub
60 The Basement
67 Wentworth Hotel; Legends
80 Wine Banc
102 State Theatre
114 Century Tavern
133 Cauldron
140 Darlo Bar
153 Central Station Records; Q Bar
155 Exchange Hotel; Lizard Lounge
157 DCM
165 Capitol Theatre
180 Beauchamp Hotel
181 Academy Twin Cinema
182 Albury Hotel
183 Verona Cinema
184 Bentley Bar
195 Her Majesty's Theatre
202 Beresford Hotel
203 Flinders Hotel

OTHER

2 Pier One; Harbourside Brasserie
4 South-Eastern Pylon; Harbour Bridge Museum
5 Colonial House Museum
8 Metcalfe Arcade; Arts & Crafts Society of NSW
11 Sydney Opera House
13 Overseas Passenger Terminal
14 Cadman's Cottage; NPWS Office
15 Sydney Visitors Centre
18 Rocks Centre
19 Argyle Centre
20 Bridge Climb; National Aboriginal & Islander Skills Development Association

21 Argyle Cut
22 Garrison Church
24 Argyle Place
27 Sydney Observatory
31 Police
33 Ken Done Gallery
38 Museum of Contemporary Art
40 CountryLink Travel Centre
41 CityRail Information; Tourist Information
42 Ferry Information
46 Government House
47 Mrs Macquarie's Chair
48 Justice & Police Museum
51 Old Customs House; Cafe Sydney
52 Goldfields House; Australian Wine Centre
59 National Trust Centre
62 Lands Department Building
63 Museum of Sydney
64 Conservatorium of Music
65 Boy Charlton Pool
66 State Library of NSW
70 Countrylink Travel Centre
71 Post Office
72 Westpac Bank
75 Post Office
76 American Express
78 Commonwealth Bank
79 Tourist Information Kiosk; Ticketek
81 Parliament House
82 Sydney Hospital; Sydney Eye Hospital
83 Finger Wharf
84 Art Gallery of NSW
85 MLC Centre; Theatre Royal
86 Coles Express
88 Dymock's Bookshop; Traveller's Contact Point;

Traveller's Medical & Vaccination Centre
89 Grace Brothers
90 Skygarden
91 Imperial Arcade
92 Centrepoint; Sydney Tower
93 David Jones
95 St James Church
96 Hyde Park Barracks Museum
97 The Gunnery; Artspace
98 St Mary's Cathedral
99 Archibald Memorial Fountain
101 Great Synagogue
103 Gowings
104 Queen Victoria Building
108 St Andrew's Cathedral
110 Telstra Phone Centre
111 Bicycle NSW
118 Anzac Memorial
123 Australian Museum
126 Watters Gallery
147 Sydney Jewish Museum
150 Aboriginal Art Print Network
158 Global Gossip
160 Travel Bookshop
174 Global Gossip
175 Darlinghurst Courthouse
176 Old Darlinghurst Gaol
189 Global Gossip
192 Thomas Cook Boot & Clothing Company
197 Firefly Express Coaches; Premier Buslines
198 Greyhound Pioneer
199 McCafferty's
200 Sydney Coach Terminal; Central Park Cafe
204 Coo-Ee Aboriginal Art Gallery
206 Victoria Barracks

the hillside. Soon after settlement The Rocks became the centre of the colony's maritime and commercial enterprises. Warehouses and bond stores were built and the area was filled with convicts, officers, freed convicts who had been granted a ticket of leave, whalers and sailors. Brothels and inns soon followed.

In the 1820s and '30s the nouveaux riches built three-storey houses on what is now Lower Fort St (which overlooked the slums), but the area remained notorious until the 20th century. In the 1870s and '80s, The Rocks' infamous pushes (street gangs) haunted the area, snatching purses, holding up pedestri-

ans, feuding and creating havoc. The area fell into decline as modern shipping and storage facilities moved away from Circular Quay. It declined further following an outbreak of bubonic plague in 1900, which led to whole streets being razed. The construction of the Harbour Bridge began two decades later and resulted in further demolition.

Redevelopment began in the 1970s and has turned the area into a sanitised, historical tourist precinct, full of narrow, cobbled streets, fine colonial buildings, converted warehouses, and tearooms. If you ignore the kitsch, it's a delightful place.

SYDNEY

City Views

The most elevated view in Sydney is from **Sydney Tower** (☎ 9231 1000), the 300m needle soaring from the Centrepoint shopping centre, corner of Market and Pitt Sts. The views extend west to the Blue Mountains and east to the ocean, as well as to the streets of inner Sydney below. The tower is open from 9 am to 10.30 pm daily (11.30 pm on Saturday); entry costs $10 ($8 concession). To get to the tower, enter Centrepoint from Market St and take the lift to the podium level.

The **Harbour Bridge** offers excellent views. You can get onto the bridge from a stone staircase off Cumberland St in the Rocks or from near Milsons Point train station on the North Shore. A footpath runs right across. If the view from the footpath isn't enough, you can climb the 200 stairs inside the south-east pylon for panoramic views of the harbour and city. BridgeClimb (☎ 8274 7777) offers a breathtaking 1500m climb to the top of the bridge for $119 during the week, $143 on the weekend (see the boxed text 'Conquering the Coat Hanger').

For a sea-level view of the Opera House, harbour and bridge, walk to **Mrs Macquarie's Point**, at the headland east of the Opera House. The point has been a lookout since at least 1810, when Elizabeth Macquarie, wife of Governor Lachlan Macquarie, had a stone chair hewn into the rock so she could sit and watch ships entering the harbour and keep an eye on hubby's construction projects just across Farm Cove. The seat is still there today.

If you're in the vicinity of Kings Cross, the northern end of **Victoria St** in Potts Point is a good vantage point for views of the cityscape and its best-known icons, especially at night.

To get the best views of all, catch a ferry – the **Manly ferries** are especially good because they traverse the length of the harbour east of the Harbour Bridge. The ferries that travel west of the bridge (such as the Hunters Hill ferry) are also worth catching, both for the experience of cruising under the bridge and to see the narrow waterways humming with workday activity.

Orientation & Information

George St leads into The Rocks from the city centre. It curves under the Harbour Bridge and meets Lower Fort St, which leads south to Observatory Park and north to the waterfront near Pier One. Cumberland St runs parallel to George St and almost all of the area's attractions are crammed into the narrow paths and alleyways between the two.

The Sydney Visitors Centre (☎ 9255 1788, 1800 067 676), 106 George St, is open from 9 am to 5 pm daily. The centre has a good range of publications, souvenirs and maps. The Rocks isn't large, but there are many small streets and hidden corners, so a map is handy.

Things to See & Do

The oldest house in Sydney is **Cadman's Cottage** (1816), 110 George St, close to the visitors centre. It was once the home of the last government coxswain, John Cadman. When the cottage was built it was on the waterfront and the arches to its south housed longboats. The cottage is now an office of the NPWS (☎ 9247 5033), open from 9.30 am to 4.30 pm weekdays, 10 am to 4.30 pm weekends.

Susannah Place, 58–64 Gloucester St, is a terrace of tiny houses dating from 1844. It's one of the few remaining examples of the modest housing that was once standard in the area.

The Rocks has several shopping centres. They include the **Argyle Centre** on Argyle St, which was a bond store between 1826 and 1881 but today houses shops, studios and the Woolshed theatre restaurant; **The Rocks Centre**, also on Argyle St, and the **Metcalfe Arcade** on George St.

The work of Sydney artist Ken Done is on show at the **Ken Done Gallery** (☎ 9247 2740), 1 Hickson Rd, off George St, in a converted warehouse. It's open from 10 am to 5.30 pm daily.

A short walk west along Argyle St through **Argyle Cut**, an old tunnel excavated through the hill by convicts, takes you to the other side of the peninsula and to **Millers Point**, a delightful district of early colonial homes.

At the west end of the cut is **Garrison Church** (1848), the first church in Australia. Nearby are **Argyle Place**, an English-style village green, and the Lord Nelson and Hero of Waterloo hotels, which vie for the title of Sydney's oldest pub.

Farther north, at 53 Lower Fort St, is the **Colonial House Museum** (☎ 9247 6008), a private house with colonial-era furniture and knick-knacks. It's open from 10 am to 4.30 pm daily ($1/0.50 adults/children).

Built in the 1850s, the **Sydney Observatory** (☎ 9217 0485) has a commanding position atop Observatory Hill, overlooking Millers Point and the harbour. There is a small museum with interactive displays and videos. The observatory is open 10 am to 5 pm daily; daytime admission is free. A small planetarium has shows ($2) at 11.30 am and 3.30 pm weekends. The observatory also opens nightly at 6.15 and 8.15 pm for tours, video screenings and telescope viewing. These must be booked and cost $8/3.

The **National Trust Centre** (☎ 9258 0123) houses the SH Ervin Gallery, which has changing exhibitions; it's open from 11 am to 5 pm Tuesday to Friday and from noon on weekends ($6/3 for adults/concession).

The waterfront from Dawes Point to Darling Harbour was Sydney's busiest before container shipping and the construction of new port facilities at Botany Bay. Although Darling Harbour has been redeveloped, there are still many old and crumbling wharves and warehouses around Dawes Point. **Pier One**, at the tip of Dawes Point, has been renovated but is still an under-used shopping and leisure complex. By contrast, **Pier Four** (also known as Wharf Theatre) is home to the Sydney Theatre and Sydney Dance Companies. Tours of the theatre company are held at 10 am Thursday (or by appointment) and cost $5 – bookings are advisable (☎ 9250 1700 or inquire at the box office).

South of The Rocks on Essex St, up towards St Patrick's Church, you'll find the site of the **public gallows**, which were in use until 1804, and Sydney's **first jail**.

The Rocks **Walking Tours** (☎ 9247 6678) offers guided 75-minute walks ($12/8.50; children under 10 free) from the visitors centre at 10.30 am and 12.30 and 2.30 pm on weekdays, and 11.30 am and 2 pm weekends.

SYDNEY HARBOUR BRIDGE

From the northern end of The Rocks, the imposing 'old coat hanger' crosses the harbour at one of its narrowest points, linking the southern and northern shores. Considered ugly by some, it has, however, always been a popular icon. The two halves of the mighty arch were built out from each shore, supported by cranes. Construction started in July 1923. After nine years of work, when the ends of the arches were only centimetres apart and ready to be bolted together, a gale blew up and winds of over 100km/h set them swaying. But the bridge survived and the arch was completed, with the official opening taking place in March 1932.

The bridge cost $20 million, a bargain in modern terms, but it wasn't paid off until 1988. It took nine years to build, and it normally takes 10 years to completely repaint it.

You can climb inside the south-eastern stone pylon that houses the small **Harbour Bridge Museum**. Admission to the pylon is $2/1 for adults/children, and it's open from 10 am to 5 pm daily. The pylons supported the cranes used to build the bridge, but today they're purely decorative.

Cutting 'Red' Tape

The Sydney Harbour Bridge was opened in 1932 – twice.

Before New South Wales (NSW) Premier Jack Lang could cut the ribbon, a Captain de Groot charged up on horseback and cut it with his sword, declaring the bridge open on behalf of 'decent and loyal citizens'. The captain was a member of the New Guard, a mob of right-wing revolutionaries who were outraged that Lang was shepherding NSW through the Depression with 'socialist ideas', such as feeding the poor. After de Groot was led away, Lang opened the bridge on behalf of 'the people of NSW', 750,000 of whom were in attendance.

Conquering the Coat Hanger

'I am afraid of heights', said Lizzie from Dublin. This comment from one of our group didn't augur well for the activity we were about to embark upon – a climb to the top of the Sydney Harbour Bridge, 134m above sea level.

Needless to say, both Lizzie and this writer survived to tell the tale.

The climb – up (and down) 1439 steps – takes three hours, the first hour of which is spent preparing for the ascent.

First we had to sign a safety disclaimer and pass a breath test to ensure that our blood-alcohol reading was below the legal limit. Then we changed into rather fetching grey 'bridge suits', removing watches, hair clips and any loose jewellery – anything, in fact, that could accidentally fall onto the traffic and people below. We were given safety harnesses and instructed on how to use the safety equipment. Next we were given fleeces and raincoats in pouches, which clipped into our harnesses. There were scrunchies for ponytails, cords for glasses and handkerchiefs with elastic loops sewn onto them so they couldn't blow away when blowing your nose. Finally, we practised on a stairway, were assigned radios and earpieces so that we could hear our climb leader, and, like a team of space shuttle astronauts, we marched off on our adventure.

The word 'terrifying' came to mind at times, particularly at the start of the climb, with only a narrow, see-through (albeit sturdy) metal grille preventing us from plunging to the ground, about 50m below. Once we got to the arch of the bridge it was a lot less frightening. From that point on, until we got to the top, the climb was easy and offered an unequalled 360° view of Sydney and its harbour. An enthusiastic round of 'I spy' took place at the top as we spotted landmarks of Sydney while standing atop the greatest landmark of them all.

Adjectives such as 'exhilarating' and 'breathtaking' don't do the climb justice. This is one of Sydney's great experiences. As we descended I couldn't help feeling that I'd conquered the world – not just the coat hanger – and the climb down was a piece of cake.

BridgeClimb (☎ 8274 7777, ✉ admin@bridgeclimb.com) is at 5 Cumberland St, The Rocks. Climbs cost $119 during the week, $143 on the weekend, and include a complimentary group photo. Night climbs ($143 to $165) are also available; advance bookings are advisable for all climbs. Remember to wear rubber-soled shoes, and note that cameras are not allowed, but the climb leader of each group takes photos that you can buy on your return.

Sally Webb

Cars, trains, cyclists, joggers and pedestrians use the bridge. The cycleway is on the western side, the pedestrian walkway on the eastern; stair access is from Cumberland St in The Rocks and near Milsons Point station on the North Shore.

The best way to experience the bridge is on foot; don't expect much of a view from a car or train. Only when driving south will you have to pay the $2 toll. The intrepid can climb to the top of the bridge (see the boxed text 'Conquering the Coat Hanger').

SYDNEY OPERA HOUSE

Australia's most recognisable icon sits dramatically on Bennelong Point on the eastern headland of Circular Quay. The Opera House's soaring shell-like roofs were actually inspired by palm fronds but look a little like white turtles in congress. Started in 1959, the Opera House was officially opened in 1973 after a tumultuous series of personality clashes, technical difficulties and delays (see boxed text 'The Soap Opera House').

The Opera House looks fine from any angle but the view from a ferry coming into Circular Quay is one of the best. It is also well worth the effort to experience a performance or sit at an outdoor cafe and watch harbour life go by. The Opera House (☎ 9250 7777) has four auditoriums, and stages dance, theatre, concerts and films, as

Collaroy Beach at sunset

Fashionable Bondi Beach

Sydney Opera House at dusk

SIMON BRACKEN

Fine viewing from a revolving restaurant

KRZYSZTOF DYDYNSKI

Window shopping Sydney-style!

GREG ELMS

Girls on parade, Mardi Gras

ROSS BARNETT

Alfresco dining at Doyles, Watsons Bay

SIMON BRACKEN

Dinosaur Designs, Oxford Street

The Soap Opera House

The hullabaloo surrounding construction of the Sydney Opera House was an operatic blend of personal vision, long delays, bitter feuding, cost blowouts and narrow-minded politicking.

The New South Wales (NSW) government held an international design competition in 1956, which was won by Danish architect Jorn Utzon with plans for a $7-million building. Construction of Utzon's unique design began in 1959, but the project soon became a nightmare of cost overruns coupled with construction difficulties. After political interference and disagreements with his consultants about construction methods, Utzon quit in disgust in 1966, leaving a consortium of three Australian architects to design a compromised interior. The parsimonious state government financed the eventual $102 million cost in true-blue Aussie fashion – through a series of lotteries. The building was completed in 1973.

After all the brawling and political bickering, the first public performance staged at the Opera House was, appropriately, Prokofiev's *War & Peace*. The preparations were a debacle and a possum appeared on stage during one of the dress rehearsals.

well as opera. It's also home to the Performing Arts Library & Archives, open 9 am to 5 pm weekdays.

There are tours (☎ 9250 7250) of the building, and although the inside isn't as spectacular as the outside, they're worth taking. Tours are held about every half hour between 9 am and 4 pm daily ($12.90/8.90 adults/children and students). There are also intermittent backstage tours ($20.90).

The bimonthly *Opera House Diary* details forthcoming performances and is available free at the Opera House.

The box office (☎ 9250 7777, **e** bookings@soh.nsw.gov.au) is open from 9 am to 8.30 pm Monday to Saturday, and from 2½ hours before Sunday performances.

CIRCULAR QUAY

Circular Quay, built around Sydney Cove, is one of the city's major focal points. Sydney Cove was the landing place of the First Fleet, and the site of the first European settlement. Circular Quay was for many years the shipping centre of Sydney; early photographs and paintings show a forest of masts crowding the skyline. Today it's both a commuting centre and a recreational space.

Circular Quay is the departure point for harbour ferries, the start of many bus routes and a stop on the City Circle railway. It has ferry and bus information booths and a Countrylink Travel Centre (☎ 13 2232).

Circular Quay East runs out beside the Royal Botanic Gardens to Bennelong Point with the Opera House perched on the end. Along Circular Quay West is the small **First Fleet Park**, a good place to rest after you've pounded the pavements; the **Overseas Passenger Terminal**, where liners moor; and the little bay of **Campbells Cove**, backed by the low-rise Park Hyatt Hotel.

Museum of Contemporary Art

The Museum of Contemporary Art (MCA; ☎ 9241 5892), 140 George St fronting Circular Quay West, has a fine collection of international modern and contemporary art, including painting, sculpture, design, film, video and electronic art. It also stages temporary exhibitions of the sublime and the ridiculous. It's open from 10 am to 6 pm Wednesday to Monday (but it closes at 4 pm in winter); admission costs $6/4 for adults/children.

Customs House

Built in 1885, the grand old Customs House (☎ 9247 2285) on Alfred St has been totally revamped, and now houses an impressive arts and cultural centre. The **Djamu Gallery** (☎ 9320 6429) features works by contemporary Aboriginal, Torres Strait Islander and Pacific artists; the **Object Gallery** showcases modern art, craft and design. Upstairs is the **City Exhibition Space**, with a huge scale model of Sydney, and other exhibits documenting the changing face of the city. There are also gallery shops and eateries. It's open from 7 am to 5 pm daily. Entry is free, except for entry to the Djamu Gallery, which costs $8 ($5 YHA, $2 children).

MACQUARIE PLACE & AROUND

Narrow lanes lead south from Circular Quay towards the city centre. On the corner of Loftus and Bridge Sts, under the shady Moreton Bay fig trees in Macquarie Place, are a cannon and anchor from the First Fleet flagship, HMS *Sirius*. Other pieces of colonial memorabilia here include gas lamps, an ornate drinking fountain (1857), a National Trust-classified gentlemen's convenience (not open) and an **obelisk** (1818), indicating road distances in miles to various points in the nascent colony.

The square has a couple of pleasant outdoor cafes and nearby, on Bridge St, is the imposing 19th-century **Lands Department building**, featuring statues of surveyors, explorers and politicians.

The excellent **Museum of Sydney** (☎ 9251 5988), 37 Phillip St, stands on the site of the colony's first and infamously fetid Government House, built in 1788. The museum uses multiple-perspective and installation art to explore Sydney's early history – including the early natural environment, the culture of the indigenous Eora people and convict life. It's open from 9.30 am to 5 pm daily ($6/3 for adults/children).

The **Justice & Police Museum** (☎ 9252 1144), in the old water police station at 8 Phillip St, was designed by colonial architect James Barnet and completed in 1886. It's now set up as a 19th-century police station and court and has various exhibits on criminal activity, once a major industry in The Rocks. You can take part in mock trials. The museum opens from 10 am to 5 pm Sunday; in January it is open Sunday to Thursday ($6/3 adults/concession).

CITY CENTRE

Central Sydney stretches from Circular Quay in the north to Central Station in the south. The business hub is towards the northern end near Circular Quay, but redevelopment at the southern end is gradually shifting the focus of the city.

Martin Place is Sydney's civic centre, if only by default. This grand pedestrian mall extends from Macquarie St to George St and is lined by the monumental buildings of financial institutions and the colonnaded Victorian former GPO. The Commonwealth Bank on the corner of Martin Place and Elizabeth St, and the Westpac on George St, opposite the western end of Martin Place, have impressive old banking chambers.

The street has a couple of fountains, plenty of public seating and an amphitheatre – a popular lunchtime entertainment spot, especially during January's Festival of Sydney, when there's free entertainment daily.

The huge, sumptuous **Queen Victoria Building** (QVB), opposite the Town Hall, takes up an entire block bordered by George, Market, York and Druitt Sts. It houses about 200 shops, cafes and restaurants. It was built in 1898 in the style of a Byzantine palace, to house the city's fruit-and-vegetable market. There are guided tours (☎ 9265 6864) twice daily.

The ornate exterior of the **Town Hall** (1874), on the corner of George and Druitt Sts, is matched by the elaborate chamber room and concert hall inside. The concert hall contains an impressive organ and is a venue for free monthly lunchtime concerts (☎ 9265 9007). Across the open space to the south, **St Andrew's Cathedral** (☎ 9265 1661), built in the same period, is the oldest cathedral in Australia, and has just undergone a major restoration. There are free organ recitals most Fridays.

Opposite the QVB, underneath the Sydney Hilton Hotel and the Royal Arcade, is the **Marble Bar**, an extravagant piece of Victoriana. The bar was built by George Adams, who founded Tattersall's lotteries. When the old Adams Hotel was torn down to build the Sydney Hilton Hotel, the bar was carefully dismantled and reassembled. The city's other ostentatious building is the **State Theatre**, to the north at 49 Market St. It was built as a movie palace during Hollywood's heyday and is now a National Trust-classified building. Except during the Sydney Film Festival in June, it stages only live shows. Tours of the opulent interior (☎ 9373 6660) run Tuesday to Sunday, and cost $12/$8 for adults/children.

On Pitt St, a block south of Martin Place, is the busy **Pitt St Mall**, with shopping arcades and department stores nearby. The lovingly restored **Strand Arcade**, which houses speciality and designer shops, runs west off the mall to George St.

To the south-west are the lively **Chinatown** and the much smaller **Spanish Town**. Chinatown, west of George St between Liverpool and Quay Sts, is a colourful and bustling area, encompassing Dixon St and **Haymarket**, and the restored Paddy's Markets. Spanish Town is along Liverpool St between George and Sussex Sts. A block east, the office, accommodation and shopping complex of **World Square**, currently a big hole in the ground, will at some point become one of Sydney's most impressive skyscrapers.

The dynamism of this part of the city is spreading south to breathe life back into the zone around **Central Station** (1906) and **Railway Square** at the intersection of Broadway, George and Quay Sts on the city centre's southern periphery. At the turn of the 20th century this was Sydney's business district. Running beneath Central Station from Railway Square is a long pedestrian subway, emerging on the east side at Devonshire St in Surry Hills. It's usually crowded with commuters (and buskers), but can be spooky late at night.

DARLING HARBOUR & PYRMONT

Darling Harbour is a huge, purpose-built waterfront leisure complex on the city centre's western edge. Once a thriving dockland area with factories, warehouses and shipyards, it was opened in 1988 but hasn't been the success that was hoped for. However, developments like Darling Walk and the snazzy new wining-and-dining precinct of Cockle Bay Wharf are attracting more visitors.

Although the complex covers a large area it's possible to see it all on foot. If you're bent on seeing everything, consider the Darling Harbour Superticket ($29.95/19.50 adults/children), which gives you a harbour cruise, entry to the Sydney Aquarium and Chinese Garden, a restaurant meal, a monorail ride and a discount on a tour of Sydney Olympic Park. You can buy the Superticket at the aquarium, monorail stations, the Chi-

nese Garden or through Matilda Cruises (☎ 9264 7377); it's valid for one month.

Darling Harbour Visitors Centre (☎ 9286 0111), under the elevated freeway near the IMAX Theatre, opens daily during business hours.

Harbourside

Harbourside (☎ 9281 3999), a large, graceful structure that recently underwent a $50 million refurbishment, is basically a shopping mall. Most shops are open from 10 am to 9 pm daily.

Sydney Aquarium

Sydney Aquarium (☎ 9262 2300), displaying the richness of Australian marine life, consists of three 'oceanariums' moored in the harbour, with sharks, rays and big fish in one, Sydney Harbour marine life and seals in the others. There are also transparent underwater tunnels and informative, well-presented exhibits of freshwater fish and coral gardens.

The aquarium is near the eastern end of Pyrmont Bridge and opens from 9.30 am to 9 pm daily ($15.90/8 or $36.90 for families).

Australian National Maritime Museum

It's hard to miss the maritime museum (☎ 9552 7777) at the western end of Pyrmont Bridge: Its roofs appear to billow like sails. This thematic museum tells the story of Australia's relationship with the sea, from Aboriginal canoes and the First Fleet to surf culture and the America's Cup.

Vessels moored at the wharves include the destroyer HMAS *Vampire*, a Vietnamese refugee boat, the WWII commando boat *Krait* and an 1888 racing cutter. There's an audiovisual display of sailing life, maritime craft demonstrations and entertainment.

The admission price varies depending on how much you want to see. To see the lot – the museum and the moored vessels – costs $9 ($4.50 concession, $19.50 family, children under 15 free). Prices include guided tours, which take place on the hour from 10 am to 3 pm daily. The complex opens from 9.30 am to 5 pm daily.

DARLING HARBOUR & CHINATOWN

PLACES TO STAY
2 Pyrmont Bridge Hotel
5 Hotel Nikko
7 Metro Suites
8 Wynyard Hotel
10 All Seasons
   Premier Menzies
11 Carrington Apartments
13 Forbes Hotel
15 Savoy Apartments
23 Hotel Ibis
24 Novotel Sydney Hotel

25 Woolbrokers Arms
33 Downtown Serviced
   Apartments
39 Waldorf
47 Furama Hotel
49 George Hotel

PLACES TO EAT
6 Slipp-Inn
18 Zenergy
31 Marigold
   Restaurant

35 Sir John Young Hotel;
   Grand Taverna
37 Casa Asturiana
38 Capitan Torres
40 Regal
42 Glasgow Arms Hotel
45 Pumphouse Tavern Brewery
46 Harbour Plaza
48 Sussex Centre
50 Dixon House Food Court
51 Hingara
52 Bodhi

OTHER
1 Star City Casino Complex
3 Australian National
   Maritime Museum
4 Sydney Aquarium
9 Eden Travel
12 NRMA
14 CBD Hotel
16 Halftix
17 Abbey's Bookshop
19 Hotel Sweeney
20 YHA Travel Centre
21 Police
22 Harbourside
26 Motor Vehicle Museum
27 Sydney Convention Centre
28 IMAX Theatre
29 Darling Harbour Visitors Centre
30 Darling Walk; Sega World
32 Paddy Pallin
34 Cinema Complexes
36 City of Sydney RSL
   & Community Club
41 Sydney Exhibition Centre
43 Powerhouse Museum
44 Sydney Entertainment Centre

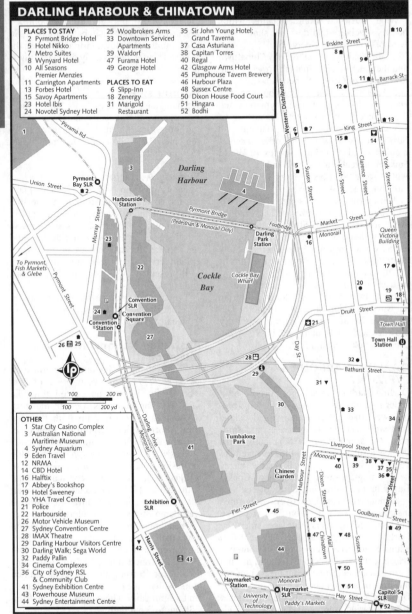

Junior Sydney

Sydney makes entertaining kids easy.

The **harbour** offers fun both on and off the water. If the sun is shining head for the beach – you can't go wrong. Older kids will enjoy exploring spectacular Sydney Harbour National Park, or take a harbour cruise – even a harbour ferry will do the trick. The Aussie Duck amphibian vehicle, which starts off on land before splashing into the harbour at Pyrmont, is good for its novelty value.

Most children are fascinated by underwater life, and the **Sydney Aquarium** in Darling Harbour is one of the world's best. It has enormous tanks featuring sharks, seals and Sydney Harbour marine life. **Taronga Zoo** also has a worldwide reputation and is another popular destination for families – but plan your itinerary carefully on arrival as it is a huge place. There are bird and seal shows and regular talks by animal keepers.

Several of Sydney's best museums have heartily thrown out the 'don't touch' mentality and are now encouraging interaction and participation. The **Powerhouse Museum** is the ultimate museum for children. They can get involved with experiments (such as using energy created by pedalling an exercise bike to power gadgets and toys). Level 2 of the **Australian Museum** is designed with kids in mind and has exhibits on human evolution and biodiversity. The Discover room has microscopes where children (and interested adults) can examine specimens.

Merrylands, in the western suburbs, is the home of Kidseum, the Sydney Children's Museum (☎ 9897 1414). The small science museum takes up a corner of a park, conveniently equipped with an impressive adventure playground and bike track (with traffic signals). The compact museum is a total hands-on experience, and children can fiddle with magnets and prisms and get involved with various experiments. The museum is on the corner of Walpole and Pitt Sts, Merrylands (take the train from Central Station).

Other fun activities include climbing the **Harbour Bridge** pylon or, if the children are over 12, there's the ultimate Harbour Bridge experience, BridgeClimb (see boxed text 'Conquering the Coat Hanger'). The entertaining **Fox Studios** Backlot (see boxed text 'Hollywood on the Harbour') will appeal to all ages.

For more ideas and information, see the Things to See & Do, Activities and Organised Tours sections in this chapter, or seek out the free monthly magazine *Sydney's Child*, available at The Rocks Visitors Information Centre and some newsagents.

Powerhouse Museum

Australia's largest and Sydney's most spectacular museum (☎ 9217 0111), 500 Harris St, is housed in a vast building that was once the power station for Sydney's trams.

The museum covers the decorative arts, design, social history, industry, science and technology. Stamps, Georgian silver candlesticks, the world's first 'black box' flight data recorder, a space suit and an 18th-century manuscript of Handel's *Messiah* are just some of the exhibits. The superbly displayed collections invite interaction, with video and computer activities, experiments and performances. There is a variety of free tours, including a tour of the museum's highlights at 1.30 pm weekdays.

The museum opens from 10 am to 5 pm daily ($8/2 or $18 for families); entry is free on the first Saturday of every month.

IMAX Theatre

The IMAX Theatre (☎ 9281 3300), with its yellow-and-black-chequered facade, rises between two elevated freeways. It shows eye-popping, 45-minute feature films on its giant six-storey screen every hour, 9 am to 10 pm daily, but it's not cheap ($13.95/9.95).

Chinese Garden

The exquisite 10-hectare Chinese Garden (☎ 9281 6863/0111), between Harbour St and Pier St, is the biggest outside China – and it's an oasis of tranquillity. It was designed by landscape architects from NSW's Chinese sister province, Guangdong, to commemorate the 1988 bicentenary of European settlement. The garden has mountains, wilderness, forest and a lake interspersed with pavilions, waterfalls and lush plants.

The garden opens from 9.30 am to sunset daily ($4/2).

Tumbalong Park & Around

The pleasant grassy area in the centre of the Darling Harbour complex is Tumbalong Park. The park has an amphitheatre, which hosts free entertainment most lunch times and weekends.

The **Sydney Convention** and **Sydney Exhibition Centres**, on the western edge of the park, were designed by Australian architect Philip Cox, who also designed the Sydney Aquarium, the Australian National Maritime Museum and the Sydney Football Stadium. The centres' roofs are suspended from steel masts, continuing Darling Harbour's maritime theme.

South of the Chinese Garden, the old pumphouse, which used to supply hydraulic power to Sydney's lifts, is now the **Pumphouse Tavern Brewery**, which brews its own beer. Farther south again, on the edge of Chinatown, is the **Sydney Entertainment Centre**, a venue for rock concerts and sporting events.

Darling Walk, on the eastern side of the park, is a new development containing **Sega World** (☎ 9273 9273), Australia's first indoor theme park. It uses the latest in computer graphics and virtual technologies and there are live stage shows. Beneath Sega World is a complex of cafes, restaurants, shops and a performing-arts space.

A short walk from the Powerhouse Museum, the **Motor Vehicle Museum** (☎ 9552 1210), Level 1, 320 Harris St, has over 175 vehicles on display, from vintage beauties to Morris Minors. It's open from 10 am to 5 pm Wednesday to Sunday and school holidays ($10/5).

Star City Casino Complex

Built near the waterfront in Pyrmont west of the Maritime Museum, the new casino complex offers the usual gaudy assortment of 24-hour gambling rooms, shops and theme bars, as well as two large theatres, a nightclub and a five-star hotel. For information, call ☎ 9657 8393 or 1800 700 700.

Pyrmont Fish Markets

Fish auctions are held weekdays west of Darling Harbour, on the corner of Pyrmont Bridge Rd and Bank St beside the approach roads to Glebe Island Bridge. They begin at 5.30 am and last three to six hours, depending on the catch. The complex includes eateries and several fabulous fish shops.

Call ☎ 9660 1611 for information about tours.

Getting There & Around

The two main pedestrian approaches to Darling Harbour are from Market and Liverpool Sts. The footbridge from Market St leads onto the lovely old Pyrmont Bridge, a pedestrian and monorail-only route that crosses Cockle Bay. It was famous in its day as the first electrically operated swing span bridge in the world.

Town Hall is the closest train station, from where it's a short walk down either Druitt or Market Sts. The monorail (☎ 9552 2288) circles Darling Harbour and links it to the city centre.

Bus No 456 connects Circular Quay with the Powerhouse Museum and the casino. The Sydney Explorer bus stops at five points around Darling Harbour every 20 minutes.

The light-rail (read tram) system runs from Central Station to Darling Harbour and Pyrmont. A one-way fare is $2, return $3.

STA ferries to Darling Harbour and Pyrmont leave Circular Quay's Wharf 5 every 30 minutes from 8 am to 7.30 pm weekdays (until 10 pm weekends), and cost $3.20/1.60 for adults/children per trip. They stop at Darling Harbour's Aquarium wharf, and the Pyrmont Bay wharf near the casino. Matilda Cruises (☎ 9264 7377) operates the Darling Harbour Rocket ferry, which leaves the Harbourmaster's Steps at Circular Quay West every 20 minutes ($3.25/1.60).

The People Mover is an incongruous, trackless, toy-town style minitrain that makes a 20-minute loop around Darling Harbour's sights from 10 am to 5 pm ($2.50/1.50).

For more information, see Getting Around later in this chapter.

MACQUARIE STREET

Sydney's greatest concentration of early public buildings grace Macquarie St, which runs along the eastern edge of the city from Hyde Park to the Opera House. The street is named after Lachlan Macquarie, the first governor to have a vision of the city as something more than a convict colony. In the early 19th century he commissioned convicted forger Francis Greenway to design a series of public buildings.

Hyde Park Barracks Museum & St James Church

These two Greenway gems on Queens Square at the northern end of Hyde Park face each other across Macquarie St. The barracks (1819) were built originally as convict quarters, then became an immigration depot and later a women's asylum. They now house a museum on the history of the building and Sydney's social history. The museum (☎ 9223 8922) opens from 9.30 am to 5 pm daily ($6/3). The church (1819–24) contains traditional stained glass but also the more modern, striking 'creation window' in the Chapel of the Holy Spirit.

Parliament House

Parliament House (1810), used by the Legislative Council of the colony from 1829, is still used by the NSW Parliament. This simple but elegant two-storey, sandstone building, surrounded by verandas, is the world's oldest continually operating parliament building and was originally the northern wing of the Rum Hospital (1816), the southern wing of which later became the Royal Mint (the first to be established outside London). Parliament House is open from 9 am to 4 pm weekdays; admission is free. There are free tours (☎ 9230 2111) at 10 and 11 am and 2 pm on nonsitting weekdays. The public gallery is open on sitting days; question time is at 2.15 pm, Tuesday to Thursday.

Sydney Hospital & Sydney Eye Hospital

Just south of Parliament House is the country's oldest hospital (☎ 9382 7111). Dating from the early 1880s, it was the site of the first Nightingale school, and the home of nursing in Australia. In front of the hospital is the bronze **Little Boar**, a copy of a statue in Florence, with water dripping from its mouth. Rubbing its polished snout – coupled with a donation that goes to the hospital – is said to grant you a wish. There's a pleasant cafe in the hospital courtyard.

State Library of NSW

The State Library of NSW (☎ 9273 1414) is more of a cultural centre than a traditional library. It has one of the best collections of early works on Australia, including Captain Cook's and Joseph Banks' journals, and Captain Bligh's log from the *Bounty*. The library's exhibition galleries open from 9 am to 5 pm weekdays, 11 am to 5 pm weekends.

Conservatorium of Music

The conservatorium (☎ 9351 1222) was built by Greenway as the stables and servants' quarters of Macquarie's planned new government house. However, Macquarie was replaced as governor before the rest of the new house could be finished. Greenway's life ended in poverty because he couldn't recoup the money he had invested in the building.

The building was temporarily closed for renovations at the time of writing but the conservatorium's students continue to fine-tune their jazz, classical music and singing, hosting concerts at venues around the city – including the popular, free 'Lunchbreak' series (1.10 pm Tuesday during term time) at St Andrew's Cathedral next to Town Hall.

ROYAL BOTANIC GARDENS

The Royal Botanic Gardens encompass Farm Cove, the first bay east of Circular Quay. They have a magnificent collection of South Pacific plant life, an old-fashioned formal rose garden and an arid garden with cacti and succulents. The visitors centre (☎ 9231 8125) is open from 9.30 am to 4.30 pm daily.

The gardens were established in 1816 and include the site of the colony's first vegetable patch. There's a fabulous tropical display housed in the interconnecting Arc and Pyramid glasshouses. It's a great place to visit on a cool, grey day. The multistorey Arc has a collection of rampant climbers and trailers from the world's rainforests and is open from 10 am to 4 pm daily ($2 admission). The Pyramid houses the Australian collection, including monsoonal, woodland and tropical rainforest plants. At the time of writing, it had been closed to the public (for safety reasons) for over a year and no reopening date could be given.

The gardens open daily from sunrise to sunset. Informative guided walks (free) leave daily at 10.30 am from the visitors centre.

THE DOMAIN

The Domain is a large, grassy area south and east of Macquarie St that was set aside by Governor Phillip in 1788 for public recreation. Then, it also contained Australia's first farm. It is separated from the Royal Botanic Gardens by the Cahill Expressway, but you can cross the expressway on the Art Gallery Rd bridge. On Sunday afternoons it's the gathering place for impassioned soapbox speakers. Free events are staged here during the Festival of Sydney (in January), as is the popular Carols by Candlelight at Christmas.

ART GALLERY OF NSW

The Art Gallery of NSW (AGNSW; ☎ 9225 1744), in the north-eastern corner of the Domain, dates from 1880, but has modern extensions discreetly moulded into the hillside. Its magnificent collection includes Australian art from the early colonial period to the present, Asian art and European art (from the masters to contemporary artists). The new Yiribana Gallery is the world's largest permanent collection of Aboriginal and Torres Strait Islander art. There is also an excellent program of temporary exhibitions.

The AGNSW is open from 10 am to 5 pm daily, and free guided tours are held at 1 and 2 pm (also 11 am and noon, Tuesday to Friday). Tours of the Yiribana Gallery run at 11 am, Tuesday to Friday, and there's a free Aboriginal dance performance at noon Tuesday to Saturday. Admission is free, but you have to pay to see some of the temporary exhibitions.

Galleries

The Art Gallery of NSW and the Museum of Contemporary Art, at Circular Quay West, shouldn't be missed. Other galleries abound, especially in the inner-eastern suburbs. They have free copies of the *Guide and Map to Art Galleries in Eastern suburbs and the inner city*. The *Sydney Morning Herald* 'Metro' section, published Friday, lists galleries and art exhibitions, but for more detailed information look for the monthly *Art Almanac* ($2) at galleries and newsagents; it covers all of Australia. The many galleries include the following:

Aboriginal Art Print Network (☎ 9332 1722, 68 Oxford St, Darlinghurst) opens 9 am to 6 pm weekdays, 11 am to 5 pm Saturday and noon to 5 pm Sunday. It has limited-edition prints (etchings, lithographs and screen prints) by Aboriginal artists, including Queenie Mackenzie and Rover Thomas.

Artspace (☎ 9368 1411, The Gunnery, 43–51 Cowper Wharf Rdwy, Woolloomooloo) opens 11 am to 6 pm Monday to Saturday. Its public gallery features changing exhibitions of contemporary work, with an emphasis on conceptual art, new media, installations and critical practice.

Australian Centre for Photography (☎ 9331 6253, 257 Oxford St, Paddington) opens 11 am to 6 pm Tuesday to Saturday.

Australian Galleries (☎ 9360 5177, 15 Roylston St, Paddington) opens 10 am to 6 pm Tuesday to Saturday. It exhibits works by contemporary Australian painters and sculptors.

AUSTRALIAN MUSEUM

Established only 40 years after the First Fleet dropped anchor, the Australian Museum (☎ 9320 6000), 6 College St, across from Hyde Park, is a natural-history museum with an excellent Australian wildlife collection. One gallery traces Aboriginal history from the Dreamtime to the present.

Guided 30-minute tours occur on the hour from 10 am to 4 pm. There are plenty of activities to keep children amused. The museum opens from 9.30 am to 5 pm daily ($5/2, $12 for families).

HYDE PARK & AROUND

The pleasant Hyde Park is large enough to offer a break from traffic and crowds but retains a city-centre feel.

At the northern end is the richly symbolic Art Deco **Archibald Memorial Fountain.** Near Liverpool St, at the southern end, is the dignified **Anzac Memorial** (1934), which has a small free exhibition containing photographs and exhibits covering the wars in which Australians have fought. There are tours at 11.30 am and 1.30 pm daily. Pine trees near the memorial were grown from seeds gathered at Gallipoli.

St Mary's Cathedral (1882), across College St from the park's north-eastern corner, took 14 years to build. Even then it wasn't completed, and two spires – to designs by the cathedral's original architect William Wardell – were being built at the time of writing. Though you can hardly tell from the outside, it is one of the world's largest cathedrals. There's a free tour of the cathedral and crypt at noon on Sunday, departing from the College St entrance.

The impressive 1873 **Great Synagogue** (☎ 9267 2477) on Elizabeth St north of Park St has free 45-minute tours at noon on Tuesday and Thursday, leaving from the entrance at 166 Castlereagh St.

You can enter **Museum station** from the south-western corner of Hyde Park. It and the nearby renovated St James station date from the 1920s and were Sydney's first underground stations.

KINGS CROSS & AROUND

The Cross is a bizarre cocktail of strip joints, prostitution, crime and drugs, peppered with a handful of classy restaurants, designer cafes, upmarket hotels and backpacker hostels. It has always been a bit raffish, from its

Galleries

Boomalli Aboriginal Artists Cooperative (☎ 9698 2047, 191 Parramatta Rd, Annandale) opens 10 am to 5 pm Tuesday to Friday. It exhibits works by Aboriginal artists.

Coo-ee Aboriginal Art Gallery (☎ 9332 1544, 98 Oxford St, Paddington) opens 10 am to 6 pm Monday to Saturday, 11 am to 5 pm Sunday. Aboriginal art is on show.

Ray Hughes Gallery (☎ 9698 3200, 270 Devonshire St, Surry Hills) opens 10 am to 6 pm Tuesday to Saturday. It exhibits the work of Australian artists, including landscape painter Peter Cooley, and tribal and indigenous art from the Cook Islands and Africa.

Roslyn Oxley9 Gallery (☎ 9331 1919, Soudan Lane, Paddington) opens 10 am to 6 pm Tuesday to Friday, 11 am to 6 pm Saturday. Contemporary Australian and international artists are featured.

Sherman Galleries (☎ 9331 1112, 16–18 Goodhope St, Paddington; ☎ 9360 5566, 1 Hargrave St, Paddington) opens 11 am to 6 pm Tuesday to Saturday. It features contemporary Australian artists.

Tin Sheds Gallery (☎ 9351 3115, 154 City Rd, University of Sydney) opens daily (from 1 pm on weekends). It features contemporary Australian art.

Wagner Art Gallery (☎ 9360 6069, 39 Gurner St, Paddington) opens 10.30 am to 6 pm Monday to Saturday. It features contemporary Australian art.

Watters Gallery (☎ 9331 2556, 109 Riley St, East Sydney) opens 10 am to 5 pm Tuesday and Saturday, 10 am to 8 pm Wednesday to Friday. The gallery focuses on contemporary painting by established Australian artists.

SYDNEY

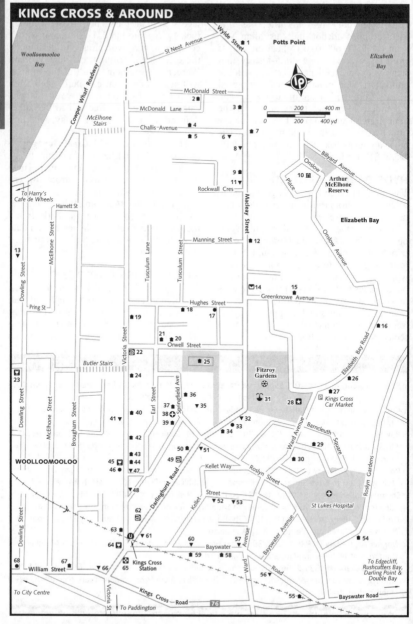

KINGS CROSS & AROUND

KINGS CROSS & AROUND

PLACES TO STAY
1   Oakford Potts Point
2   Rucksack Rest
3   Holiday Lodge Hotel
4   Simpsons of Potts Point
5   Challis Lodge
7   Chateau Sydney Hotel
9   Macleay Lodge
12 De Vere Hotel
15 Manhattan Park Inn
    International
16 Montpelier Private Hotel
18 Nomads The Palms
19 Victoria Court Hotel
20 Sydney Central Backpackers
21 Eva's Backpackers
24 Virgin Backpackers
25 Jolly Swagman Hostel
    (Springfield Mall)
26 The Sebel
27 17 Elizabeth Bay Rd
29 Barncleuth House (Pink
    House) Travellers Hostel
30 Madison's Hotel
34 Kingsview Motel
36 Regent's Court
37 Springfield Lodge

39 Bernly Private Hotel
40 Travellers Rest
42 Original Backpackers
43 Highfield Private Hotel
44 Plane Tree Lodge
50 Maksim Lodge
54 Medina Executive Apart-
    ments
55 Backpackers Headquarters
58 Crescent on Bayswater Hotel
59 Barclay Hotel
63 Holiday Inn
67 O'Malley's Hotel

PLACES TO EAT
6   Spring Cafe
8   The Pig & The Olive
11 Macleay St Bistro
13 Frisco Hotel
32 Bourbon & Beefsteak
35 Pad Thai
41 Star Bar & Grill
47 Roy's
48 Joe's Cafe Deluxe
51 Oporto
52 Dean's Cafe
53 Cafe Iguana

56 Cafe 59
57 Bayswater Brasserie
60 Waterlily Cafe
61 Action Pizza;
    House Kebab
66 Williams on William

OTHER
10 Elizabeth Bay House
14 Post Office
17 Wayside Chapel
22 Internet Bakpak Travel
23 Old Fitzroy Hotel
28 Police
31 El Alamein Fountain
33 Sydney Aussie Rules Social
    Club
38 Kings Cross Travellers
    Clinic
45 Soho Bar
46 Let's Travel Australia
49 Kings Internet Cafe
62 Global Gossip
64 Kings Cross Hotel
65 Kingsgate Shopping Centre;
    Thomas Cook
68 Bayswater Car Rental

early days as a centre of bohemianism to the Vietnam War era, when it became the vice centre of Australia. Today, the Cross retains its risqué aura, with a hint of menace and more than a touch of sleaze. Sometimes the razzle-dazzle has a sideshow appeal; sometimes Darlinghurst Rd can be about as appetising as finding a cockroach in your cornflakes.

However, it's also the travellers headquarters of Sydney, with Australia's greatest concentration of hostels and late-night Internet cafes. Weary travellers can even pull up a milk crate along Darlinghurst Rd for a therapeutic Chinese massage. There are also many good (and increasingly trendy) places to eat, and plenty of entertainment that doesn't involve the sex industry. You don't have to walk far from the neon lights to find gracious old terraces in tree-lined streets.

Darlinghurst Rd is the trashy main drag. It doglegs into Macleay St, which continues into the more salubrious suburb of Potts

Point. Most hostels are on Victoria St, which diverges from Darlinghurst Rd north of William St.

The Cross is a good place to swap information and buy or sell things. Notice boards can be found in hostels, shops and along Victoria St. At Kings Cross Car Market (☎ 9358 5000), on the corner of Ward Ave and Elizabeth Bay Rd, travellers buy and sell vehicles.

The most notable landmark in Kings Cross is the thistle-like **El Alamein Fountain**, in the brick-paved Fitzroy Gardens. The fountain is known locally as 'the elephant douche'. Bunkered down behind the fountain is a fortress-like police station (☎ 9265 6233).

To the north, in the suburb of Elizabeth Bay, is the 1839 **Elizabeth Bay House** (☎ 9358 2344), 7 Onslow Ave. Once known as 'the finest house in the colony', it has been meticulously restored and refurbished with early 19th-century furniture. The house is open Tuesday to Sunday 10 am to 4.30 pm ($6/3/15 for adults/children/families).

On Cowper Wharf Rdwy is **Harry's Cafe de Wheels**, the famous Woolloomooloo pie cart, which has been open since 1945. Nearby is the Finger Wharf, jutting into Woolloomooloo Bay, which has been redeveloped into a residential, shopping, hotel and dining complex. Opposite is the innovative **Artspace** gallery.

East of the Cross is **Rushcutters Bay**, both a small suburb of apartment blocks and a pretty bay backed by a sizable park, and home to the Cruising Yacht Club (CYCA).

Getting There & Away

The simplest way to get to the Cross is on a CityRail eastern-suburbs train from Martin Place, Town Hall or Central. It's the first stop outside the city loop on the line to Bondi Junction.

The STA's Airport Express bus No 350 runs to Kings Cross, as does the private Kingsford-Smith Transport (see the Getting Around section later in this chapter for more information). From Circular Quay, bus Nos 200, 323, 324, 325, 326 and 327, and 333 (a free service), run to Kings Cross; from Railway Square near Central Station take bus No 311.

You can walk from Hyde Park along William St in 15 minutes. A prettier, longer route involves crossing the Domain, descending the hill behind the Art Gallery of NSW, walking past Woolloomooloo's wharf and climbing McElhone Stairs to the northern end of Victoria St.

INNER EAST

The lifeblood of Darlinghurst, Surry Hills and Paddington, **Oxford St** is one of the more exciting places for late-night action, with its strip of shops, cafes, bars and nightclubs. Its flamboyance and spirit are largely attributed to its vibrant, vocal gay community. The Sydney Gay & Lesbian Mardi Gras parade passes this way.

The main section of Oxford St runs from the south-eastern corner of Hyde Park to the north-western corner of Centennial Park. Taylor Square, at the junction of Oxford, Flinders and Bourke Sts, is the hub of social life in the area. (Be warned: Oxford St street numbers restart west of the junction with South Dowling and Victoria Sts, on the Darlinghurst-Paddington border.) South-east of Taylor Square, Darlinghurst Rd and Victoria St run north off Oxford St to Kings Cross, while Oxford St continues on through Paddington and Woollahra, eventually reaching Bondi Junction. Bus Nos 380 and 382 from Circular Quay, and No 378 from Railway Square, run the length of the street.

Darlinghurst

This is the innercity mecca for bright young things who want to be close to the action. It's a vital area of trendy, self-conscious, urban cool that's fast developing a cafe culture. There's no better way to soak up the ambience than to sip coffee while loitering in a few sidewalk cafes. Darlinghurst encompasses the vibrant 'Little Italy' of Stanley St in East Sydney and is wedged between Oxford and William Sts.

Facing Taylor Square is **Darlinghurst Courthouse** (1842) and behind it is the old **Darlinghurst Gaol**, where author Henry Lawson was incarcerated several times for debt. Today it houses East Sydney Technical and Further Education (TAFE) College.

Sydney Jewish Museum (☎ 9360 7999), 148 Darlinghurst Rd on the corner of Burton St, has exhibits on the Holocaust and Australian Jewish history. It's open from 10 am to 4 pm Monday to Thursday and to 2 pm Friday, and 11 am to 5 pm Sunday ($6/3 for adults/children).

Surry Hills

Surry Hills, east of Central Station, is a former working-class neighbourhood that's undergoing gentrification. It's a multicultural area and the centre of Sydney's rag trade and print media. The main attraction is the **Brett Whitely Gallery** (☎ 9225 1881/1744), 2 Raper St. The gallery, in the former studio of this modern Australian painter, contains a selection of his paintings and drawings. It's open from 10 am to 4 pm weekends ($6/4).

Surry Hills is a short walk south of Oxford St. Catch bus Nos 301–304, 390 or 391 from Circular Quay.

Paddington

Paddington, 4km east of the city centre, is an attractive innercity residential area of leafy streets and tightly packed terrace houses. It was built for aspiring artisans in the later years of the Victorian era. During the lemming-like rush to the dreary outer suburbs after WWII, the area became a slum, but underwent restoration during the 1960s. Today it's a fascinating jumble of beautifully restored terraces, trendy shops, restaurants, art galleries, bookshops and interesting people.

You can wander through Paddington's streets and winding laneways any time, although the best time is from around 10 am Saturday when the **Paddington Village Bazaar**, in the grounds of the Uniting Church on the corner of Newcombe and Oxford Sts, is in full swing.

There are free tours of the stately **Victoria Barracks** (☎ 9339 3000), on Oxford St between Oatley and Greens Rds, at 10 am Thursday; the tours include a performance by the military band. The **Army Museum** at the barracks is open between 10 am and 3 pm on Sunday (admission is free).

The **Australian Centre for Photography** (☎ 9331 6253), 257 Oxford St, has regular exhibitions.

The utilitarian **Moore Park**, south of Paddington, has a playing field, a walking, cycling and skating track, a horse trail, a golf driving range and grass skiing. It's also home to the historic **Sydney Cricket Ground** (SCG) and the **Sydney Football Stadium**. Sportspace (☎ 9380 0383) offers behind-the-scenes guided tours of the facilities at 10 am and 1 and 3 pm daily (except on match days); they cost $18/12 for 1½ hours.

The former Royal Agricultural Society (RAS) Showgrounds, also at Moore Park, has been taken over by the new **Fox Studios Australia** film and entertainment complex (☎ 9383 4000). See the boxed text 'Hollywood on the Harbour' for more information.

Centennial Park, Sydney's biggest park, is farther east again. It has running, cycling and horse tracks, barbecue sites, football pitches and more. You can hire bikes and in-line skates from several places on Clovelly Rd, Randwick, near the southern edge of the park, or hire horses (from $30 an hour weekdays) from one of five stables situated around the park – contact the stable manager (☎ 9332 2809).

At the southern edge of the park is **Randwick Racecourse**, and south of there is the

Hollywood on the Harbour

The USA may have Hollywood, but Australia has Sydney, and Sydney has Fox Studios. The state-of-the-art film studios at Driver Ave, Moore Park, in the eastern suburbs, are among the most sophisticated in the world, and boast six vast film and television sound stages.

Since its opening in 1999, several major movies have been produced at Fox Studios, including *Babe: Pig in the City*, *The Matrix*, *Mission Impossible 2* starring Tom Cruise, and Baz Luhrmann's *Moulin Rouge* with Nicole Kidman and Ewan McGregor. Parts of Jane Campion's *Holy Smoke*, starring Kate Winslett and Harvey Keitel, were filmed there, and Episode II and III of the *Star Wars* prequels are in the pipeline.

You'll have to be a major film star or have some pretty good connections to see the studios in action. However, what the regular punter can enjoy is the Fox Studios Backlot – a movie-based theme park with dozens of different attractions and 'experiences'.

You can wander through the sets from *Babe: Pig in the City*, see the world of *The Simpsons*, learn all about movie sound production, tour a star dressing room and see the costumes, make-up and props used in dozens of films. 'The Titanic Experience' is especially popular and is a spectacular display of special effects. 'Lights! Camera! Chaos!' is a musical extravaganza about the crazy world of Flying Fox Films, a film studio run by Australian animals.

Backlot tickets cost $37.95/22.95 for adults/children; family passes are available during school holidays. Booking is recommended; call Foxtix ☎ 1300 369 849. The Fox tickets will allow you free travel on Sydney's buses on the day of your visit. Bus No 339 from Central Station goes directly to Fox Studios.

SYDNEY

University of NSW, on Anzac Parade. Many buses run along Anzac Parade, including No 336 from Circular Quay.

EASTERN SUBURBS

The harbourside suburbs east of Kings Cross are some of Sydney's most expensive. The main road through this area is New South Head Rd, the continuation of William St.

Darling Point, east of Rushcutters Bay, was a popular place for the city's first merchants to build mansions. Inland is the suburb of **Edgecliff**. The wealthy harbourside suburb of **Double Bay** is farther east. Double Bay's main shopping street is Bay St, which runs north off New South Head Rd. It eventually leads to a quiet waterfront park and the ferry wharf. Double Bay is worth a visit. There are plenty of cafes and patisseries that don't necessarily cost a fortune, and you can at least window-shop for designer clothes.

There's a small beach near the ferry wharf and a saltwater pool to the east, near Seven Shillings Beach. The latter is actually part of **Point Piper**, the headland which separates Double Bay from **Rose Bay**. Rose Bay has a pair of longer beaches, visible at low tide, though people rarely swim here. It's also served by ferries. Inland, behind the wharf area, is the Royal Sydney Golf Course.

Rose Bay curves north onto the peninsula that forms the southern side of the entrance to Sydney Harbour. On the harbour side of the peninsula is **Vaucluse**, the most exclusive suburb of all. Vaucluse was a desirable address even in the colony's early days, but it's ironic that **Vaucluse House** (1828), one of its finest mansions, was built by William Wentworth, an outcast from high society because of his democratic leanings.

Vaucluse House (☎ 9337 1957) opens from 10 am to 4.30 pm Tuesday to Sunday; admission is $6/3 for adults/concession. Built in fine grounds in the Gothic Tudor style, it's an imposing, turreted example of 19th-century Australiana. Catch bus No 325 from Circular Quay and get off a couple of stops past **Nielsen Park**, which is part of Sydney Harbour National Park.

Watsons Bay is nestled on the harbour side of the peninsula as it narrows towards South Head. On the ocean side is **The Gap**, a dramatic cliff-top lookout. On the harbour north of Watsons Bay are the small fashionable beaches of **Camp Cove** and **Lady Bay**. At the tip of the peninsula is **South Head**, with great views across the harbour to North Head and Middle Head.

Getting There & Away

The closest suburb to a rail link is Double Bay, which is north-east of the Edgecliff train station on the eastern-suburbs line. Take the New South Head Rd exit from the station.

Ferries run from Circular Quay to Double Bay, Rose Bay and, on weekends, to Watsons Bay. An ordinary water taxi would cost about $50 between four people. Bus Nos 324 and 325 run from Circular Quay to Watsons Bay.

INNER WEST

Once a tough, working-class neighbourhood, **Balmain** attracted artists in the 1960s and renovators in the 1980s. Darling St, Balmain's spine, runs the length of the peninsula and is dotted with bookshops, restaurants, antique shops, bakeries and boutiques. There's a **market** from 8.30 am to 4 pm every Saturday at St Andrew's Congregational Church. It's worth catching the **Hunters Hill ferry** from Circular Quay just for the journey; it stops at Thames St, Darling St and Longnose Point (Birchgrove) wharves. Bus Nos 441, 442, 445 and 446 also come here.

Glebe, south-west of the city centre close to the University of Sydney, has climbed the

Clergyman's Land

The word 'glebe' actually means 'land granted to a clergyman'. This particular glebe was assigned to Reverend Richard Johnson, the first chaplain of the colony. Though Johnson had convict helpers to clear the land and plant oranges and vegetables, most of Glebe stayed bushy and busy with parrots, kangaroos and swamp creatures until well into the 1830s.

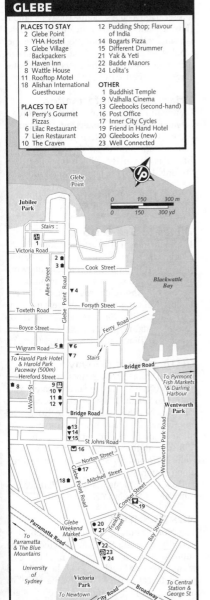

social scale in recent years but still has a bohemian atmosphere. The main thoroughfare, Glebe Point Rd, runs the length of the entire suburb, offering recycled-clothing shops, affordable restaurants and second-hand bookshops. There are several good places to stay and Glebe's proximity to the city makes it an interesting alternative to the Cross.

The **Buddhist Temple**, on Edward St, was built by Chinese immigrants during the 1850s gold rush, and has been fully restored by Sydney's Chinese community. It welcomes visitors, but remember that it's a holy place. At the northern tip of Glebe Point Rd is **Jubilee Park**, with views across the bay to Rozelle and back towards the city.

From the airport you can take the Kingsford-Smith Transport (☎ 9667 3221) bus; from the city and Railway Square, bus Nos 431–434 run along Glebe Point Rd. From Central Station, walk south on George St and Broadway, turning right into Glebe Point Rd after about 1km. The walk will take you 15 minutes.

Rozelle lies across Rozelle Bay from Glebe. The main attraction is the **Sydney Maritime Museum Restoration Site** (☎ 9818 5388), at James Craig Rd, beside the bay. Moored here are several fully restored vessels including the 1874 windjammer *James Craig,* the *Lady Hopetoun,* a VIP yacht built in 1902, and the tugboat *Waratah,* from the same era. Undergoing restoration are the *John Oxley,* a large Scottish pilot boat dating from 1928, and the harbour ferry *Kanangra,* built early this century. The museum runs a 'Fish & Ships' tour of the vessels that includes a 20-minute boat trip across Blackwattle Bay to Pyrmont Fish Markets.

The site opens from 9 am to 4 pm Tuesday, Thursday and Saturday (later in summer); admission is free, but there's a donation box to help with restorations. Take bus No 440 from Circular Quay.

On the southern border of the University of Sydney, **Newtown** is a melting pot of social and sexual subcultures, students and home renovators. King St, its relentlessly urban main drag, is full of funky clothes stores, bookshops, cafes and Thai restaurants. While it's definitely moving up the

SYDNEY

social scale, Newtown comes with a healthy dose of grunge and political activism and harbours several of Sydney's live-music venues. The best way to get there is by train, but bus Nos 422, 423, 426 and 428 from the city run along King St.

Leichhardt, south-west of Glebe, has a city-wide reputation for its Italian eateries, on Norton St. Bus Nos 436–440 run here from the city.

INNER SOUTH

South-west of Central Station, the small suburb of **Chippendale** is a maze of Victorian terraced houses – an unscrubbed version of Paddington. South of Railway Square, near the corner of Lee (George) and Regent Sts, is the quaint neo-Gothic **Mortuary station**, where coffins and mourners once boarded funeral trains bound for Rookwood Cemetery, in what is now the city's western suburbs.

Chippendale borders the east of the University of Sydney, Australia's oldest tertiary institution. **Nicholson Museum** (☎ 9351 2812), at the university, displays Greek, Assyrian, Egyptian and other antiquities. It's open from 8.30 am to 4.30 pm weekdays; admission is free.

Redfern, farther south, is predominantly working class, and relations between the police and the community (especially the large Koori community) are bad at times. However, its proximity to the city is attracting developers and renovators.

The site of the former Eveleigh Locomotive Workshops, at the corner of Garden and Boundary Sts, is home to the National Technology Park and National Innovation Centre. Some buildings contain Victorian steam-powered blacksmithing equipment, used by **Wrought Artworks** (☎ 9319 6190) to manufacture artefacts. The curious can wander in and watch.

BONDI BEACH

Although it's Australia's most famous beach, Bondi Beach isn't as glamorous as the tourist brochures might suggest. It's still largely working class and successive waves of migrants have made it their home. In recent years it has become more fashionable and has received a huge facelift. Today its unique flavour is blended from the mix of old Jewish and Italian communities, dyed-in-the-wool Aussies, New Zealand, Irish and UK expatriates, working travellers and devoted surfers, all bonded by their love for the beach.

Orientation & Information

Campbell Parade, the main beachfront road, is where most shops, hotels and cafes can be found. The corner of Campbell Parade and Hall St is the hub. The main road into Bondi Beach is Bondi Rd, which branches from Oxford St east of the mall in Bondi Junction.

The post office is on the corner of Jacques Ave and Hall St. Hall St also has a small Jewish area where you will find kosher shops.

Things to See & Do

The main reason for visiting Bondi is the beach, where you can swim, surf or just hang out. If the water's too rough for swimming there are sea-water swimming pools. Accessible **Aboriginal rock engravings** are a short walk north of Bondi Beach on the golf course in North Bondi. A cliff-top coastal walking path travels south to the beaches at Tamarama, Bronte and Coogee.

Getting There & Away

Bondi Junction is the terminus of the eastern-suburbs CityRail line, and is the nearest train station to Bondi Beach. From there you can take bus No 380, 382 or 389 to Bondi and Bondi Beach. Alternatively, you can take these buses from Circular Quay or bus No 378 from Railway Square, which continues south to Bronte; bus Nos 378 and 380 run along Oxford St.

Buses stop along Campbell Parade, terminating at Brighton Blvd in North Bondi.

NORTH SHORE

The North Shore is the unofficial but universally recognised name applied to the suburbs north of the harbour. The area's pretty bays and beaches, good shopping and places to eat make it worthwhile to leave the cosmopolitan delights of the southern side to see how wealthier Sydneysiders live.

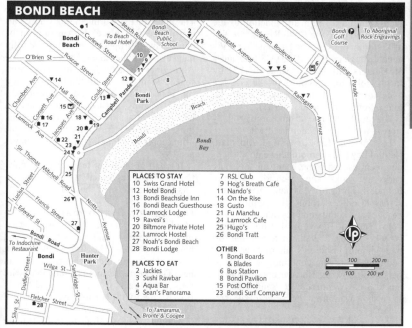

BONDI BEACH

PLACES TO STAY
10 Swiss Grand Hotel
12 Hotel Bondi
13 Bondi Beachside Inn
16 Bondi Beach Guesthouse
17 Lamrock Lodge
19 Ravesi's
20 Biltmore Private Hotel
22 Lamrock Hostel
27 Noah's Bondi Beach
28 Bondi Lodge

PLACES TO EAT
2 Jackies
3 Sushi Rawbar
4 Aqua Bar
5 Sean's Panorama

7 RSL Club
9 Hog's Breath Cafe
11 Nando's
14 On the Rise
18 Gusto
21 Fu Manchu
24 Lamrock Cafe
25 Hugo's
26 Bondi Tratt

OTHER
1 Bondi Boards
& Blades
6 Bus Station
8 Bondi Pavilion
15 Post Office
23 Bondi Surf Company

The Sydney residences of the governor general and the prime minister are on Kirribilli Point, east of the Harbour Bridge. The prime minister stays in **Kirribilli House** (1854) and the governor general in **Admiralty House** (1846).

Luna Park, an amusement park at Milsons Point on the edge of Lavender Bay, was at its peak in the 1930s but now opens sporadically. Still, if you've got kids, you'll have a hard time keeping them away. Check with the tourist offices for the latest.

McMahons Point is a pleasant, sleepy suburb on the next headland west. It's tipped by **Blues Point Reserve**, named after the Jamaican-born Billy Blue, who ferried people across from Dawes Point in the 1830s.

Kirribilli, Lavender Bay and Blues Point are all serviced by ferries from Circular Quay. Otherwise you can walk across the Harbour Bridge or take a North-Shore train to Milsons Point.

North Sydney, north-west of the bridge, is Sydney's second business district. Along Mount St at No 7 is Mary MacKillop Place (☎ 9954 9688), a museum that tells the life story of a girl from the bush who became a nun – and Australia's first saint. The museum is open from 10 am to 4 pm daily ($7.50/3 for adults/children).

A kilometre or so north along the Pacific Hwy from North Sydney is the suburb of Crows Nest, which has a number of good places to eat and the 1880s **Sexton's Cottage Museum** (☎ 9936 8400), in St Thomas' Rest Park at 250 West St. It has displays relating to early life in the area and is open from 1 to 4 pm Thursday and from 2 to 4 pm on the first Sunday of the month (free).

Farther west, **Balls Head Reserve** has great harbour views, and old Aboriginal rock paintings and carvings (although these are hard to discern). Take a train to Waverton, turn left when you leave the station and follow Bay Rd, which becomes Balls Head Dr.

The elegant suburbs of Hunters Hill and Woolwich, on a spit at the junction of the Parramatta and Lane Cove Rivers, are full of Victorian houses. The National Trust **Vienna Cottage** (☎ 9258 0123), 38 Alexandra St, Hunters Hill, built of stone in 1871 by Jacob Hellman, is typical of the era. It's open from 2 to 4 pm on the second and fourth Sunday of the month ($3).

Hunters Hill ferries from Circular Quay stop at Woolwich's Valentia St wharf.

East of the Harbour Bridge, **Mosman**, **Neutral Bay** and **Cremorne** have good shopping centres and some beautiful foreshore parks and walks. The beachside suburb of **Balmoral**, north of Mosman, faces Manly across Middle Harbour. It has three fine beaches and some good restaurants.

In Neutral Bay you'll find **Nutcote** (☎ 9953 4453), 5 Wallaringa Ave, the former home of children's author May Gibbs and now a museum containing exhibits on her life and work. Nutcote opens from 11 am to 3 pm Wednesday to Sunday ($6/3). It's a short walk from the Neutral Bay ferry wharf.

A footpath runs from Bogota Ave through bushy gardens to the end of **Cremorne Point**, south-east of Neutral Bay. This is an excellent spot to picnic or go for a swim, with great views of the harbour.

The 30-hectare **Taronga Zoo** (☎ 9969 2777) has an attractive setting overlooking the harbour. It houses over 4000 critters, including a substantial number of Australian ones.

The zoo is open from 9 am to 5 pm daily ($16/8.50). Ferries to the zoo depart from Circular Quay's Wharf 2 half-hourly from 7.15 am on weekdays, 8.45 am Saturday and 9 am Sunday. The zoo is on a steep hill and it makes good sense to work your way down the hill if you plan to depart by ferry. You can either climb to the top entrance or take the 'Aerial Safari' cable car. A ZooPass ticket, sold at Circular Quay and elsewhere, will cost you $21/10.50 and includes return ferry rides, the bus to the entrance, the cable car and zoo admission. A ZooLink ticket is similar to the ZooPass but also includes train travel.

MANLY

The jewel of the North Shore, Manly was one of the first places in Australia to be named by Europeans – Arthur Phillip named it after the 'manly' physique of the Aborigines he saw here in 1788. Sun-soaked Manly boasts all the trappings of a full-scale holiday resort and a sense of community identity, but isn't afraid to show a bit of tackiness and brashness to attract visitors. It makes a refreshing change from the prim, upper-middle-class harbour enclaves nearby.

It's half an hour by ferry from Circular Quay (15 minutes by JetCat) and the trip offers fantastic views of the city.

Orientation & Information

Manly straddles the narrow peninsula leading to North Head and has both ocean and harbour beaches. The ferry wharf is on Manly Cove, on the harbour side. From here The Corso (the main commercial strip) runs to the ocean, where you'll find Manly Beach, lined with Norfolk pines. Most of The Corso is a pedestrian mall.

Manly Visitors Information Bureau (☎ 9977 1088), open from 10 am to 4 pm daily, is on the foreshore near The Corso. It has useful, free pamphlets on the 8km Manly Scenic Walkway (which follows the shoreline to The Spit Bridge at Middle Harbour and takes about three hours) and sells Manly Heritage Walk booklets ($3.50). There are small lockers where you can leave your things while you go for a swim. There's a bus information booth at the entrance to the wharf.

Daylight Swimming Legal!

While you're enjoying Manly Beach, thank William H Gocher that you're not breaking the law by swimming in daylight. Such immorality was illegal until Gocher, a local newspaper editor, announced in 1902 that he would take a dip in daylight, defying the authorities to arrest him. He had to swim three times before he was arrested, but the subsequent court case led to the legalisation of daylight bathing.

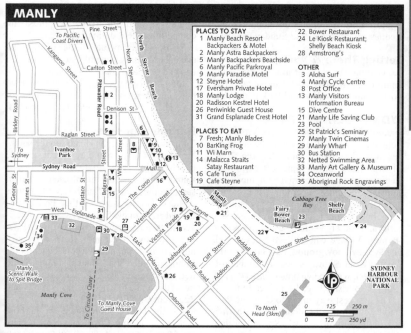

MANLY

PLACES TO STAY
1 Manly Beach Resort
Backpackers & Motel
2 Manly Astra Backpackers
5 Manly Backpackers Beachside
6 Manly Pacific Parkroyal
9 Manly Paradise Motel
12 Steyne Hotel
17 Eversham Private Hotel
18 Manly Lodge
20 Radisson Kestrel Hotel
26 Periwinkle Guest House
31 Grand Esplanade Crest Hotel

PLACES TO EAT
7 Fresh; Manly Blades
10 BarKing Frog
11 Wi Marn
14 Malacca Straits
Satay Restaurant
16 Cafe Tunis
19 Cafe Steyne

22 Bower Restaurant
24 Le Kiosk Restaurant;
Shelly Beach Kiosk
28 Armstrong's

OTHER
3 Aloha Surf
4 Manly Cycle Centre
8 Post Office
13 Manly Visitors
Information Bureau
15 Dive Centre
21 Manly Life Saving Club
23 Pool
25 St Patrick's Seminary
27 Manly Twin Cinemas
29 Manly Wharf
30 Bus Station
32 Netted Swimming Area
33 Manly Art Gallery & Museum
34 Oceanworld
35 Aboriginal Rock Engravings

Things to See & Do

Manly is well endowed with **beaches**: North Steyne Beach north of The Corso; Manly Beach (technically south Steyne Beach); Fairy Bower Beach, around the rocky headland at the southern end of Manly Beach; beautiful Shelly Beach, farther around; Queenscliff Beach, near the steep Queenscliff headland; and, farther along, Freshwater Beach.

There's another stretch of sand on the harbour side at Manly Cove.

Oceanworld (☎ 9949 2644), West Esplanade, is on the headland at the western end of Manly Cove. It has turtle and shark feeding, an eerie underwater perspex tunnel that lets you eyeball the fish (and vice versa) close up, and hourly dangerous snakes shows. The sharks are handfed at noon Monday, Wednesday and Friday. Oceanworld is open from 10 am to 5.30 pm daily ($14.50/7.50; $39 for families, $10 concession).

Manly Art Gallery & Museum (☎ 9949 2435), next to Oceanworld, has exhibitions on beach themes and local history (much the same thing in Manly). It's open from 10 am to 5 pm Tuesday to Sunday; admission is $3 (children free).

North Head

Spectacular North Head, at the Sydney Harbour entrance about 3km south of Manly, offers good views of the ocean, harbour and city skyline. Most of the headland is in the Sydney Harbour National Park; contact the NPWS office (☎ 9977 6522) for information.

The old **Quarantine station** housed disease carriers from 1832 to 1984. The station is run by the NPWS; guided tours are held at 10.40 am weekdays and 1.25 pm weekends ($10/7); bookings required. Proposals to redevelop the site as a hotel and restaurant complex have been fiercely opposed.

The centre of the headland is an off-limits military reserve, but you can visit the

National Artillery Museum (☎ 9976 3855) in North Fort. It's open from noon to 4 pm Wednesday, Saturday and Sunday ($4/2).

Getting There & Away

See Getting Around later in this chapter for details on ferries to Manly. Alternatively, bus No 169 runs from Wynyard Park in the city.

SYDNEY OLYMPIC PARK

Sydney Olympic Park, in the suburb of Homebush Bay, 14km west of the city centre, was the main venue for the 2000 Olympics and Paralympics. It comprises Stadium Australia (the main Olympic stadium), the Sydney Superdome, the Sydney International Aquatic Centre, a baseball stadium, hockey and tennis centres, an archery park and other venues, as well as the Olympic Village where the athletes stayed. The **Sydney Showground**, new home of the Royal Easter Show, is also at Homebush Bay. Check with the visitors centre (☎ 9714 7958) or tourist offices for guided tours.

The quickest way to get to Olympic Park is to catch a train to Lidcombe station, then board the Olympic Park Sprint service, which runs every 10 minutes between 6 am and 11 pm ($3.20 one way). Alternatively, you can catch a train from Central Station to Strathfield, then the No 403 bus to the park. You can also catch a RiverCat from Circular Quay up the Parramatta River to the Olympic Park wharf ($3.40 one way).

BEACHES

Sydney's beaches are some of its greatest assets. They're easily accessible and usually good, although some post warnings that swimming is inadvisable after heavy rains because of storm-water runoff.

There are two types – harbour beaches (sheltered, calm and generally smaller) and ocean beaches (which often have good surf).

Although they get busy on hot summer weekends, Sydney's beaches are never really packed. Swimming is generally safe, but some beaches can be dangerous. At ocean beaches you're only allowed to swim within the 'flagged' areas patrolled by the famed lifesavers. Efforts are made to keep surfers

separate from swimmers. High points of Sydney's beach life are the surf lifesaving competitions held during summer.

Shark patrols operate during summer, and ocean beaches are generally netted – Sydney has had one fatal shark attack since 1937.

Many of Sydney's beaches are 'topless' but some aren't: take your lead from the locals. There are also a couple of nude beaches.

Harbour Beaches

Immediately inside the Heads, on the southern side, is tiny **Lady Bay Beach**, a nude beach, mainly gay. South of Lady Bay is **Camp Cove**, a small but pleasant sliver of sand popular with families and topless bathers. This is where Arthur Phillip first landed in Sydney. South of Camp Cove is **Watsons Bay**, which hosts two of the delightful Doyle's outdoor seafood restaurants. Another popular harbour beach is the family-oriented **Shark Beach**, complete with nets, at Nielsen Park in Vaucluse. These beaches can be reached by bus Nos 324 and 325 from Circular Quay.

On the North Shore there are harbour beaches at **Manly Cove** (suburban beach), **Reef Beach**, **Clontarf** (families), **Chinaman's Beach** (quiet hideaway) and **Balmoral** (popular day trip for North Shore residents). The Manly ferry docks at Manly Cove and Reef Beach is a 2km walk along the Manly Scenic Walkway. For Clontarf, catch bus No 131 or 132 from Wynyard. The other beaches are accessible, with a bit of walking, by catching bus No 175 or 178 from Wynyard Park along Military Rd and crossing The Spit Bridge.

Southern Beaches

South of the Heads there's a string of ocean beaches all the way to Botany Bay.

Bondi Beach, with its crowds and surfies, is Australia's best-known beach (see under Bondi Beach earlier in this chapter). It's a favourite with young visitors to Sydney.

Tamarama, a little south of Bondi, is a pretty cove with strong surf that's popular with Sydney's beautiful people. Take bus No 361 from Bondi Junction or catch a Bondi Beach bus and walk from the bottom of Bondi Rd. Next south is **Bronte**, a broader beach popular with families. Take bus No 378 from the city or Bondi Junction.

The tiny inlet of **Clovelly** is nestled between Bronte and Coogee. It has a breakwater that makes it safe for swimming. Catch bus No 339 from George St in the city or No 329 from Bondi Junction. **Coogee**, a relaxed Bondi Beach, has a wide, sweeping beach and is a good spot to rest up from the rigours of the surf. Take bus No 373 or 374 from Circular Quay, or the 372 from Central Station. **Maroubra** is farther south again; take bus No 376, 377 or 395 from Circular Quay. Botany Bay is better for sailing rather than swimming due to its large shark population.

Northern Beaches

A string of ocean-front suburbs stretches 30km north along the coast from Manly, ending at beautiful, well-heeled Palm Beach and spectacular Barrenjoey Head, at the entrance to Broken Bay. There are plenty of beaches along the way. **Freshwater**, the first north of Manly, attracts a lot of teenagers; then there's **Curl Curl** (families and surfers); **Dee Why** and **Collaroy** (families); and the long sweep of **Narrabeen** (surfers). The most spectacular are **Whale Beach** and **Bilgola**, near Palm Beach, which have dramatic, steep headlands. Several of the northernmost beach suburbs also back onto **Pittwater**, a lovely inlet off Broken Bay and a favoured sailing spot.

Bus Nos 136 and 139 run from Manly to Freshwater and Curl Curl. Bus No L90 from Wynyard Park stops at Collaroy, Narrabeen, Bilgola, Avalon and Whale Beaches, and continues north to Palm Beach. From Manly, take bus No 155 or 157 to Mona Vale and pick up No 190 there.

This route is popular as the first step on the journey to NSW's northern coast and as a weekend excursion to the Central Coast.

PARKS & GARDENS

Sydney has plenty of parks, many with harbour views, making it a wonderful city for a picnic or a stroll.

The **Royal Botanic Gardens**, **The Domain** and **Hyde Park** border the eastern side of the city centre (see under those sections earlier in this chapter). There are also a few smaller

parks in the city centre that provide respite from the cement. **Wynyard Park** is a wedge of Victoriana on York St outside Wynyard station; **Lang Park** is a few blocks north and **First Fleet Park** is north again, at Circular Quay. **Observatory Park**, on the western side of the Bradfield Hwy, is a pleasant place with old trees and good views.

There are two small parks at Elizabeth Bay, north-east of Kings Cross: the delightful **Arthur McElhone Reserve** opposite Elizabeth Bay House, and **Beare Park**, down by the water. The nearest swathe of green to the Cross is **Rushcutters Bay Park**, a pretty waterfront area to the east.

East of Surry Hills and south of Paddington are the adjacent **Moore** and **Centennial** Parks, both large recreational areas.

Many headlands and bays on the North Shore have small parks, including Blues Point, Kirribilli (Careening Cove), Neutral Bay (Anderson Park), Cremorne Point and Mosman (Reid Park). Finding them without a street directory can be difficult.

On the North Shore there's an 8km corridor of bushland called **Garigal National Park** stretching from Bantry Bay on Middle Harbour north to Ku-Ring-Gai Chase National Park at St Ives. **Lane Cove National Park**, between the suburbs of Ryde and Chatswood, is also on the North Shore. Both parks have extensive walking tracks and Lane Cove has lots of picnic areas.

See also Sydney Harbour National Park earlier in this chapter.

ACTIVITIES

The *Sydney Morning Herald*'s Friday 'Metro' guide lists activities. Notice boards at hostels are usually crammed with suggestions and travel agents often have good information on day trips.

Swimming

Sydney's harbour beaches offer sheltered water conducive to swimming. At the ocean beaches swimming is safe if you follow instructions and swim within the flags. There are some notorious but clearly signposted rips even at Sydney's most popular beaches, so don't underestimate the surf just because

Hello Sailor!

The best way to see Sydney is from the water. There are many companies that offer cruises and entertainment on paddle-steamers or motor launches (see Organised Tours in this chapter), but if you've got a few days spare why not learn to sail.

Yachting has been popular on the harbour since the 1830s and the Australian Yacht Club was formed in 1862. Today, Sydney has a plethora of sailing schools, some specialising in small dinghies (great for children) and others in cruising and racing yachts. Most of these offer practical, on-water instruction following Australian Yachting Federation standards. The Competent Crew, Inshore Skipper and Coastal Skipper certificates (for which several theory components, such as seamanship and coastal navigation, and additional sailing hours must also be completed) are recognised worldwide.

East Sail Sailing School (☎ 9327 1166), at d'Albora Marinas, New Beach Rd, Rushcutters Bay, is Australia's biggest sailing school. It runs introductory to racing-level courses; lessons are held daily. The yachts on which you learn are also used for charters, so they have top-notch equipment and are well maintained. The introductory course (four three-hour practical sessions on the water, and a theory session) costs $380. The next course, Competent Crew, costs $350.

East Sail also offers good-value learn-to-sail packages that include night sails, theory courses and races. The Monday evening races for sailing school students and graduates are popular, social and fun. Off-shore weekends, up to Pittwater and the Hawkesbury or down the coast to Woollongong, are offered each month and provide an opportunity to experience ocean sailing and the delights of 'après-sailing', for which a strong liver stands you in better stead than strong sea legs.

Pacific Sailing School (☎ 9326 2399), at the CYCA at Rushcutters Bay, uses smaller boats – Blazers and J24s – for courses from beginners ($435) to advanced level.

On the North Shore, several sailing schools offer instruction from beginner to advanced levels. The Australian Sailing Academy (☎ 9960 3077), The Spit, Mosman, has four-week courses catering for all skill levels, from $360 to $390.

The friendly Sunsail (☎ 9955 6400), 23A King George St, McMahon's Point, runs introductory and Competent Crew courses, each held over two days ($350 each).

Northside Sailing School (☎ 9969 3972), at the southern end of Spit Bridge in Mosman, specialises in dinghy sailing. Two six-hour lessons cost $290, and boat hire is around $50 for two hours. The school offers a range of activities for eight- to 16-year-olds, including five-day sailing camps ($290).

Pittwater and Broken Bay offer some of the world's best cruising, with plenty of sheltered mooring spots. Scotland Island Schooners at Church Point (☎ 9999 2285) has two-day introductory courses for $200 and Competent Crew courses for $400.

Most sailing schools also offer yacht charters and usually give discounts to ex-students who have successfully completed courses with that particular school. Prices vary, but as an indication East Sail charges $325 midweek for a 9.5m (31-foot) yacht for half a day self-skippering. If you want the services of a skipper you'll pay an additional $35 per hour.

Fully skippered and crewed half-day yacht charters cost $850 for a yacht for up to 15 people. If you just want a taste of sailing Sydney and don't have much time, East Sail also offers a Sydney Harbour Sailing Adventure for $60 per person from 10 am to 12.30 pm most days of the week (booking essential).

---

it doesn't look threatening. Efforts are made to keep surfers separate from swimmers.

There are more than 100 public swimming pools in Sydney, including the saltwater Andrew 'Boy' Charlton pool in the Domain on the edge of Woolloomooloo Bay; the Prince Alfred Park pool, near Central Station; the Olympic pool at Sydney Olympic Park; the small pool at Fairy Bower Beach, Manly; and the two oceanside pools at Coogee, one of which, McGiver's Pool, is for women only. Sydney's most central (and one of its best and cleanest) pools is at the Cook & Phillip Centre. The Boy Charlton and Alfred Park pools close during winter.

Surfing

South of the Heads, the best spots are Bondi, Tamarama, Coogee and Maroubra. Cronulla, south of Botany Bay, is also a serious surfing spot. On the North Shore, there are a dozen surf beaches between Manly and Palm Beach; the best are Manly, Curl Curl, Dee Why, North Narrabeen, Mona Vale, Newport Beach, North Avalon and Palm Beach itself.

In Manly, Aloha Surf (☎ 9977 3777), 44 Pittwater Rd, rents out surfboards and boogie boards (including wet suits) for $20/30 for a half/full-day (until 7 pm).

At Bondi Beach you can hire surfboards, body boards and wet suits from Bondi Surf Company (☎ 9365 0870), 72 Campbell Parade, for $20 to $30 for three hours, $40 for the day (passport or credit-card identification required).

In Coogee, Surfworld (☎ 9664 1293) is at 250 Coogee Bay Rd, near the corner of Arden St.

Sailing & Boating

There are plenty of sailing schools in Sydney and an introductory lesson or two is a fun way of getting onto the harbour (see the boxed text 'Hello Sailor!').

Diving

The best shore dives in Sydney are: Gordons Bay Underwater Nature Trail, north of Coogee; Shark Point, Clovelly; and Ship Rock, Cronulla. Popular boat dive sites are Wedding Cake Island, off Coogee; around the Sydney Heads; and off the Royal National Park. In Manly you can make beach dives from Shelly Beach.

Plenty of outfits will take you diving and many run dive courses. Pro Dive has several outlets in and around Sydney, including at 428 George St (☎ 9264 6177) in the city, and 27 Alfreda St, Coogee (☎ 9665 6333). Four-day diving courses cost from $245, boat dives cost $105, and shore dives $55 (gear included). In Manly, the Dive Centre Manly (☎ 9977 4355), 10 Belgrave St, has one-day

courses for $95. It also hires out snorkelling gear ($15) and wet suits ($12). Pacific Coast Divers (☎ 9977 5966), 169 Pittwater Rd, Manly, is similar; snorkelling gear is $10.

Canoeing & Kayaking

The NSW Canoe Association (☎ 9660 4597), Wentworth Park Complex, Ultimo, has information on clubs that provide lessons. Call from 9 am to 5 pm weekdays.

Sydney Kayak Centre (☎ 9969 4590), at the southern end of The Spit Bridge in Mosman, rents out sea kayaks to paddle on Middle Harbour. Single kayaks cost $10 per hour for the first two hours, $5 for subsequent hours. Double kayaks cost twice that.

Natural Wanders (☎ 9899 1001), 45 Wharf Rd, Birchgrove, has weekend kayak tours of the harbour. From Lavender Bay, they head under the Sydney Harbour Bridge to Bradleys Head, stopping in secluded bays, and at Taronga Zoo for brunch. The tour operator can tailor a tour to suit you, and relates the history and architecture of the area. The tour takes four hours and costs $75. No prior experience is necessary.

In-line Skating

The beach promenades at Bondi and Manly are the most favoured spots for skating, but Coogee and Bronte are becoming popular with skaters too.

Manly Blades (☎ 9976 3833) in Manly Beach Plaza, 49 North Steyne, hires out skates for $10 an hour, $15 for two hours, or $20 for the day. It also offers lessons. You can also hire skates at Manly InLine Action (☎ 9976 3831), 93 North Steyne.

Bondi Boards & Blades (☎ 9365 6555), 148 Curlewis St, rents out skates for $10 for the first hour, $5 for subsequent hours. Protective gear is free.

Golf

The most central of Sydney's 40-odd public golf courses is at Moore Park (☎ 9663 3960). It charges $27 for 18 holes on weekends, $24 on weekdays. Other public courses include Bondi (☎ 9130 3170) on Military Rd in North Bondi, and Barnwell Park (☎ 9713 1162) on the corner of William St and Lyons Rd in

SYDNEY

Five Dock. Hudson Park (☎ 9746 5702) is a golf driving range at Homebush Bay.

Horse Riding

There are four outfits offering horse rides in Centennial Park – contact the stable manager (☎ 9332 2809) for details. They're based at the RAS Showgrounds (enter on the corner of Lang and Cook Rds). Prices start from around $30 per hour on weekdays, and bookings are necessary.

Tennis

There are tennis courts for hire all over the city, including the following:

Coogee South Squash & Tennis (☎ 9344 7976) 222 Malabar Rd, Coogee
Jensen's Tennis Centre (☎ 9698 9451) next to Central Station, Broadway, Surry Hills
Miller's Point Tennis Court (☎ 9256 2222) Kent St, The Rocks
Parklands Tennis Centre (☎ 9662 7521) on the corner of Anzac Parade and Lang Rd, Moore Park, Paddington

Jogging

The foreshore from Circular Quay around Farm Cove to Woolloomooloo Bay and the Royal Botanic Gardens and The Domain are popular routes with joggers. North Shore inhabitants often choose to commute to work in the city by running across the Harbour Bridge.

Centennial Park and the promenades at Bondi Beach and Manly are the best jogging spots. The cliff trail between Bondi Beach and Bronte is also good.

ORGANISED TOURS

There is a vast array of city and area coach tours. For details, check the free magazines at hotels, or ask at Australian Travel Specialists (☎ 9555 2700), at Circular Quay's Wharf 5. It's open from 7 am to 9 pm weekdays, 8 am to 9pm weekends.

Australian Pacific (☎ 9247 7222), AAT King's (☎ 1800 334 009), Newmans (☎ 9247 7222), Murrays (☎ 13 2259), Clipper Gray Line (☎ 9241 3983) and Great Sights Tours (☎ 9241 2294) carry most tourists around town. You can join a half-day city or koala-cuddling tour (from around $40 to $50), or a full-day city tour (from around $60 to $70). Many companies also offer tours to the Blue Mountains, Jenolan Caves, Hunter Valley and Canberra etc.

Sydney Aboriginal Discoveries (☎ 9368 7684) offers a variety of interesting tours focused on indigenous culture and history. Outings cost from $25 (concession) to $60, and include a harbour cruise, a camping trip, a walkabout tour, a feast of native Australian foods, and an Aboriginal philosophy meeting (adults only).

The NPWS runs tours of Sydney's historic forts and islands. See the Sydney Harbour National Park section earlier in this chapter.

Blue Thunder Bike Tours (☎ 9977 7721) and Eastcoast Motorcycle Tours (☎ 9555 2700) show you Sydney from the back of a Harley-Davidson. Blue Thunder will take you anywhere from the Blue Mountains to the northern beaches. A one-hour tour of Sydney costs $80; day trips are around $350. Both have set tours or you can plan your own itinerary.

A unique way to see Sydney – both land and harbour – is by the Aussie Duck, an amphibian vessel that does the rounds of the city before plunging into the harbour. Tours (1½ hours) with a light, chatty commentary cost $45/25.

If a bird's-eye view of the city appeals, South Pacific Seaplanes (☎ 9544 0077) runs scenic flights of the harbour, starting from $75 for a 15-minute flight.

Harbour Cruises

A wide range of cruises from Circular Quay offer relatively inexpensive excursions on the harbour. You can book most at Australian Travel Specialists (☎ 9555 2700), at Wharves 6 and 2.

STA ferries offer some good-value cruises, such as the 2½-hour trip that goes as far as Sydney Heads and The Spit Bridge (departs at 1 pm weekdays, 1.30 pm weekends). Tickets cost $19/12. For sparkling views of the city at night, there's a Harbour Lights cruise, departing 8 pm Monday to Saturday ($16.50/10.50). There's also a one-hour morning cruise of the eastern bays, departing at 10 and 11.15 am ($13/8.50). STA cruises depart from Wharf 5, and tickets can be bought from the ferry information office under the Cahill Expressway opposite Wharf 4.

The Sydney Harbour Explorer, run by Captain Cook Cruises (☎ 9206 1111), is a hop-on hop-off service that stops at the Opera House, Watsons Bay, Taronga Zoo, The Rocks and Darling Harbour. Boats run every two hours from 9.30 am to 3.30 pm ($20/12). Captain Cook Cruises has its own booking office at Wharf 6.

East Sail (☎ 9327 1166) at d'Albora Marinas, New Beach Rd, Rushcutters Bay, offers a Sydney Harbour Sailing Adventure for $60 per person from 10 am to 12.30 pm most days of the week (bookings essential). It will organise transport to or from your hotel. Wear white-soled sports shoes.

Sail Venture Cruises (☎ 9262 3595) sails big catamarans around the harbour five times a day. They depart from Darling Harbour's Aquarium wharf and also pick up at Circular Quay's east pontoon. The trip takes about 2½ hours. The options include the coffee cruise for $25/12, buffet lunch cruise for $48/24 or dinner cruise for $90/45.

Sailing cruises are also offered on the *Bounty* (☎ 9247 1789), a replica of the ship lost by the infamous Captain Bligh in the famous mutiny – this one was made for the film starring Mel Gibson. It sails twice daily on weekdays and three times a day on weekends. There is a choice of cruises available. Prices range from $45 for the 1½-hour Sunday-morning-brunch sail, to $80 for the 2½- hour, daily evening dinner cruise. The boat leaves from Campbell's Cove at The Rocks. The *Svanen* (☎ 9698 4456) also sails from here.

There are also tours of harbour islands – see under Sydney Harbour National Park earlier in this chapter.

Walking Tours

Several people offer guided walks in Sydney. Sydney Aboriginal Discoveries (☎ 9368 7684) offers a variety of outings with an indigenous focus, including walkabout tours of city landmarks and sacred places.

Maureen Fry (☎ 9660 7157), 15 Arcadia Rd, Glebe, caters mainly for groups of about eight people but she can take individuals or perhaps fit you in with a group. A two-hour guided walk costs $15.

Bicycle Tours

CTA Cycle Tours (☎ 1800 353 004) runs weekend day tours for $45 ($40 YHA), including gear and ferry transport.

Flights

Palm Beach Seaplanes (☎ 1300 656 787) offers scenic 15-minute flights (departing Rose Bay) over Sydney Harbour, Bondi and Manly for $75 per person. Longer flights, taking in the harbour, northern beaches, Hawkesbury River, Sydney Olympic Park and the Blue Mountains are also available ($150 for a 30-minute flight, $525 for a 90-minute flight).

SPECIAL EVENTS

In addition to the statewide holidays and events, Sydney has some major celebrations of its own.

January

Sydney Festival Wide range of events, from international performing arts to street theatre, in-line skating and huge, free concerts in The Domain.

Great Ferry Boat Race Held on Australia Day (26 January); contested by the city's ferries, which are decorated with balloons and streamers for the race from the Harbour Bridge to Manly and back.

Survival Festival 26 January; Aboriginal Australia Day, marked by Koori music, dance, arts and crafts.

Flickerfest Ten-day international short-film festival, held at Bondi Pavilion. Call ☎ 9211 7133 for details.

January/February

Chinese New Year Celebrated (literally with a bang!) in Chinatown.

February/March

Gay & Lesbian Mardi Gras The Mardi Gras attracts more visitors and generates more tourist dollars than any other event in Australia. The month-long festival includes a sports carnival, the blessing of the Mardi Gras, theatre, an arts festival and *lots* of parties, culminating in an amazing parade (first Saturday in March) and Mardi Gras Party. Tickets to the party normally sell out by mid-January, and are usually only available to Mardi Gras members, though interstate and overseas visitors can get temporary membership. For information, call the Mardi Gras office (☎ 9557 4332, @ reception@mardigras.com.au), 21–23 Erskineville Rd, Erskineville. Online information is available at www.mardigras.com.au.

March/April
Golden Slipper Sydney's major horse race, held at Rosehill.
Royal Easter Show Held at Sydney Showground at Homebush Bay; a 12-day event traditionally beginning with a massive parade of farm animals; has a distinctly agricultural flavour, but has plenty of events to entertain city slickers.
Sydney Cup Major horse race, held at Randwick.

June
Sydney Film Festival At the magnificent State Theatre; subscribe to the whole season or buy tickets to special screenings. Call ☎ 9660 3844 for details.
Sydney Biennale Held in even years; international arts festival at the Art Gallery of NSW and other city venues.
Feast of Sydney Food-and-wine festival celebrated all over the city.

July
National Aboriginal and Torres Strait Islander Week Demonstrations of traditional dances, music and art.

August
City to Surf Run Held on the second Sunday; more than 40,000 runners pound the 14km from Park St in the city to Bondi Beach. All entrants get their name and finishing position published in the *Sydney Morning Herald*; entry forms appear in the *Herald* months before the race, but you can enter on the day (about $20).

September
Royal Botanic Gardens Spring Festival Includes concerts, brass bands, a plant market, and a display of spring flowers in the David Jones city store.
Festival of the Winds Second Sunday; kite-flying festival with a multicultural theme at Bondi Beach; includes competitions for best home-made kites.
Taylor Square Arts Festival A week-long affair.

Rugby League Grand Final Held at Sydney Football Stadium.

October
Manly International Jazz Festival Labour Day long weekend; styles range from traditional and big band to fusion, bop and contemporary.

November
Kings Cross Carnival First weekend; busking competition, food and wine tastings.

December
Carols by Candlelight Pre-Christmas celebration in The Domain.
Sydney to Hobart Yacht Race 26 December; Sydney Harbour is crowded with boats farewelling yachts competing in the race.
New Year's Eve Circular Quay and Darling Harbour are popular places to gather; the city puts on a huge fireworks display.

PLACES TO STAY
There's a huge variety of accommodation available in Sydney, with good options in every price range.

Almost every hotel and hostel lifts its rates or cancels special deals during the busy summer months, and school holidays (and the Mardi Gras) can make accommodation both scarce and pricey. But in winter, when things are slow, it's worth seeking out bargains.

Many larger hotels cater primarily to businesspeople, so their rates may drop on weekends. Some bigger hotels include breakfast and parking in their rates. Mid-range and top-end hotels publish 'rack' (standard) rates, but there are often special deals offered, so ring around.

For longer-term stays, there are places in the 'Flats to Let' and 'Share Accommodation' ads in the *Sydney Morning Herald* on Wednesday and Saturday. Many people find flats to share through other travellers. Hostel notice boards are another good source. Serviced apartments often sleep several people; lower weekly rates can be inexpensive for a group.

Disabled travellers can get information on accommodation options in Sydney from the National Information & Communication Awareness Network (NICAN) and Accessing Sydney (see the boxed text 'Trave

When is a Pub not a Pub?

First-time visitors to Australia may be confused by the distinction between hotels and…well, hotels. There are three kinds.

Until relatively recently any establishment serving alcohol was called a hotel and was legally required to provide accommodation. These hotels are also known as pubs (public houses). Not surprisingly, the accommodation facilities at many were minimal, designed merely to satisfy the licensing authorities. A pub room is usually pretty basic – bathrooms are almost always shared and you probably won't have a phone in the room.

Private hotels are usually boarding houses with similar facilities to pubs, but without a bar. These often have 'private' in their name to distinguish them from a pub.

Hotels in the business of providing accommodation with all the usual facilities, such as room service, are usually rated at three stars or higher.

Sydney has a range of all of these types of hotels. Pubs are generally the cheapest and most spartan, but can be good value, especially in country areas or on the fringes of the city.

17km south of the city, has sites from $29, vans/cabins from $50/70 a double and four-person air-con cabins for $150.

Hostels Sydney has a huge number of hostels. The largest concentration is in Kings Cross, but there are others in Bondi, Coogee, Glebe, Surry Hills and Manly. Facilities vary from dorms with en suite, TV, fridge and cooking facilities to just a bare room with a couple of bunks; many also offer single and/or double accommodation. Youth Hostel Association (YHA) hostels are often better run and cleaner than many backpacker places. Some hostels have set hours for checking in and out, though all have 24-hour access once you've paid.

The average low-season price for a dorm bed is around $20. Many hostels offer reduced weekly rates, and most are acutely aware of the competition, so prices can fluctuate. Hostelling International (HI) and YHA members usually receive discounts, as do members of VIP Backpackers International.

If you're Australian, finding a hostel that will accept you might be tricky if you can't prove you're travelling. Some Sydney hostels ban Australians in order to stop locals using hostels as dosshouses and because of bad experiences with lecherous drunks. Hostels may demand a passport as identification, although in the low season these quibbles sometimes vanish in the quest for a buck. YHA hostels take members of any nationality.

The YHA's Membership & Travel Centre (☎ 9261 1111), 422 Kent St (see Darling Harbour & Chinatown map), can book you into any YHA hostel in Australia, and many others around the world. The centre is also a domestic and international travel agency. It's open from 9 am to 5 pm weekdays (to 6 pm Thursday) and 10 am to 2 pm Saturday.

As well as the backpacker-only hostels, many pubs and boarding houses fill spare rooms with bunks. Some are perfectly OK, but most lack the hostel atmosphere and the essential information grapevine.

in NSW & ACT for People with Disabilities' in the Facts for the Visitor chapter).

From November to February prices at beachside resorts can be as much as 40% higher than low-season rates. The rates quoted here are for the high season.

Places to Stay – Budget
Camping Sydney's caravan parks, most of which also have tent sites, are a fair way out of town. *East's Lane Cove River Caravan Park* (☎ 9888 9133), Plassey Rd, North Ryde, 14km north of Sydney, has van sites from $17 to $20 and cabins for $65 a double.

Sheralee Tourist Caravan Park (☎ 9567 7161, 88 Bryant St, Rockdale), 13km south of the city, has powered sites for $20/120 per night/week and on-site vans for $40/180 a double. Tent sites cost $15 a day for a two-person tent.

Grand Pines Caravan Park (☎ 9529 7329, 289 The Grand Parade, Sans Souci),

City Centre & Woolloomooloo The slick 532-bed *Sydney Central YHA* (☎ 9281 9111,

@ sydcentral@yhansw.org.au), on the corner of Pitt St and Rawson Place, is near Central Station in the renovated, heritage-listed Daking House. It's the largest hostel in the world and has a heated rooftop pool, sauna and licensed cafe. Dorms cost $25 per person ($28 nonmembers) and twins and doubles with/without bathroom cost $70/62. All en suite twin rooms are set up for disabled travellers. Double and twin rooms are for YHA members only. Bookings are advised.

The super-civilised *Y on the Park (☎ 9264 2451, @ y-hotel@zip.com.au, 5–11 Wentworth Ave),* the revamped Young Women's Christian Association (YWCA) hostel, is more a hotel than a hostel. It has an enviable position, opposite Hyde Park and with the city centre and Oxford St a short walk away. The standard is high, with spotless well-furnished rooms and a cafeteria. Single/twin rooms cost $62/85 or $98/120 with attached bathroom. Dorm accommodation costs $26 a night, but the maximum stay is three nights. Both genders can stay.

Convenient to Central Station, the 12-storey *Hotel Backpack (☎ 9571 9049, 412 Pitt St)* has dorm beds for $22 to $25 and double rooms for $65 and $75 (with bathroom). There's a communal kitchen and laundry.

Nearby in Woolloomooloo, *Forbes Terrace (☎ 9358 4327, 153 Forbes St)* is clean and quiet, and has a good courtyard area. It charges $20 for a dorm bed, $60 for twins and doubles. Rooms have TV, fridge and tea- and coffee-making facilities. Clean linen is supplied free.

A newcomer in Woolloomooloo is *Tokyo Joes (☎ 9331 0822, 132 Bourke St).* Dorm beds cost from $15 per night.

Kings Cross & Around There are heaps of hostels in the Cross and there's little to distinguish many of them.

Heading north along Victoria St from Kings Cross station, the first hostel you come to is *Plane Tree Lodge (☎/fax 9356 4551, 174 Victoria St).* It's a fairly average Kings Cross hostel, with a variety of rooms, each with TV and fridge. Rates are $25 in a dorm, $55/60 for an acceptable twin/double.

The Swedish-staffed *Highfield Private Hotel (☎ 9326 9539, 166 Victoria St)* is secure, clean and has a good atmosphere. Rates stay much the same all year, with singles/doubles for $40/60. Dorm beds cost $20 and all rooms have shared bathrooms.

Original Backpackers (☎ 9356 3232, @ info@originalbackpackers.com.au, 162 Victoria St) is the original backpacker hostel in this area and, having expanded, is going strong. The atmosphere is good, it's clean and there are decent-sized common areas, with a courtyard, pool table and jukebox out the back. Dorm beds cost $25 and twins and doubles start at $60.

Travellers Rest (☎ 9380 2044, 156 Victoria St) has comfortable, well-equipped rooms each with a phone, sink and TV; all but singles have a fridge. Some rooms have balconies overlooking Victoria St. Rates vary little year-round: dorm beds cost $18/115 a night/week; doubles cost $45 a night.

Virgin Backpackers (☎ 9357 4733, 144 Victoria St) is the newest hostel in the area. Rooms have TV and fridge, and bathrooms are shared. Dorm beds cost $20 a night; doubles are $50.

The family-owned-and-operated *Eva's Backpackers (☎ 9358 2185, 6–8 Orwell St)* is clean, friendly and well run. The place has a great reputation among backpackers. There's a rooftop barbecue area and a sociable kitchen/dining room. Dorm beds cost $22; doubles or twins $50. It's so popular that it's often full, even in winter.

Farther up Orwell St is the clean and cheery *Sydney Central Backpackers (☎ 9358 6600, @ scb@one.net.au, 16 Orwell St).* Dorm beds/doubles cost $25/60. There's a rooftop garden with views of the Opera House and Harbour Bridge, and a kitchen with free tea and coffee.

Over the road is the busy *Jolly Swagman* hostel *(☎ 9358 6400, 14 Springfield Mall).* It has a good atmosphere, good security and Internet access, and there's someone at the desk 24 hours. Dorms cost $25; doubles are $60. Rooms have fridges and each bed has its own reading light.

Nearby in Hughes St is *Nomads The Palms (☎ 9357 1199, 23 Hughes St),* with a

TV lounge and communal kitchen. It has dorm beds for $24 and double rooms for $59.

The long-established *Rucksack Rest* (☎ *9358 2348, 9 McDonald St*) off Macleay St in Potts Point is quiet, clean and in reasonable condition. The rooms are fairly small but comfortable, and dorms sleep no more than three people. Dorm beds go for $18, single rooms $35, twins and doubles from $42 to $48. If you stay a week, you pay for only six nights.

One of the most popular Kings Cross hostels is *Barncleuth House Travellers Hostel* (☎/*fax 9358 1689, 6 Barncleuth Square*), east of Darlinghurst Rd. It's also called the Pink House Travellers Hostel. It has a courtyard garden and cosy log fires. Dorm beds cost from $25, doubles and twins $60.

The secure, squeaky-clean *Backpackers Headquarters* (☎/*fax 9331 6180, 79 Bayswater Rd*) has beds for $19/20 per night in 10-bed/six-bed dorms. There's one double room for $60. Avoid the noisier rooms facing Kings Cross Rd. The place is often full.

Surry Hills Set in an old house, *Kangaroo Bakpak* (☎ *9319 5915, 665 South Dowling St*) is a relaxed and friendly place that gets consistently good feedback. Dorm beds cost $20 ($100 weekly), and the rooms at the front have balconies. Doubles/twins cost $52. From Central Station, take bus No 372, 393 or 395.

Nomads Backpackers (☎ *9331 6487, Captain Cook Hotel, 162 Flinders St*) has beds in 10-bed dorms for $17 or in four-bed dorms for $22; doubles/twins cost $55. It's on a busy intersection near the Moore Park cricket ground and football stadium, and gets booked out when big games are on.

The *Excelsior Hotel* (☎ *9211 4945, 64 Foveaux St*) is only a few blocks from Central Station. Most rooms offer reasonable pub accommodation (but the bands in the downstairs bar can be a bit raucous), and most dorms have three to six beds. Dorm beds/doubles cost $19/49. VIP cardholders get discounts.

Alfred Park Private Hotel (☎ *9319 4031, 207 Cleveland St*) is also close to Central Station. Occupying two adjacent houses, it has plain but clean rooms of varying sizes and ambience, with a pleasant courtyard, a kitchen and a balcony overlooking the park. Each room has a TV and fridge. Beds in dorms with attached bathrooms cost $30. Singles/twins cost $60/80 ($90 with private bathroom).

Glebe The hostels, restaurants and entertainment options in Glebe make it a good area to stay in.

Located in a large, brick block, the friendly *Glebe Point YHA Hostel* (☎ *9692 8418,* @ *glebe@yhansw.org.au, 262–264 Glebe Point Rd*) has beds in four- and five-bed dorms for $20/23 and clean but bare twin/double rooms for $27 per person (non-YHA members pay an extra $3.) It offers a large range of activities as well as luggage storage.

Two doors down is *Glebe Village Backpackers* (☎ *9660 8133, 256–258 Glebe Point Rd*). Set in a sprawling old house, this is a hostel suited to travellers who place sociability above cleanliness. It's well worn, but people like the lively atmosphere; there's a crowded notice board and plenty of outside seating. Dorm beds cost around $21 ($130 per week); doubles and twins $60 ($360). The cafe downstairs does $5 breakfasts.

Wattle House (☎ *9552 4997, 44 Hereford St*) is a small hostel in a pleasant, old house. It's clean, renovated and has nice extras, such as free linen and doonas. The owners are friendly. This is *not* a hostel for party animals. It has a minimum stay of three nights for advance bookings; rooms are often full. A bunk in a four-bed dorm costs $22; twins/doubles cost $60.

Newtown The YHA operates a summer hostel at *St Andrews College* (☎ *9557 1133*) at the University of Sydney, where dorm beds cost $20 and twins/doubles $24 per person.

Billabong Gardens (☎ *9550 3236, 5–11 Egan St*) is a lovely hostel, built by one of Sydney's original hostel owners. It's clean and quiet. There's a small solar-heated pool surrounded by thriving native plants, and a large professional-looking kitchen. Beds in dorms cost $23 ($135 weekly) with shared bathroom, and twins/doubles cost $60 nightly ($80 with bathroom). The hostel picks up travellers from the airport by arrangement. From Railway Square, catch bus No 422, 423, 426 or 428 up Newtown's King St, and get off at Missenden Rd. Egan St is a few blocks along on the right. By train, go to Newtown station and turn right; Egan St is about four blocks along, on the left.

Bondi Beach Bondi is a popular base for long-term, working travellers.

The long-running **Lamrock Hostel** (☎ 9365 0221, 7 Lamrock Ave), a block back from Campbell Parade, is a well-worn but bright house with dorm beds for $20 ($100 weekly), singles for $140 weekly ($25 a night once you've stayed for a week) and doubles/twins for $40 ($220 weekly). Studio flats sleeping four to five cost $90 per person per week. Just down the street is the popular **Lamrock Lodge** (☎ 9130 5063, 19 Lamrock Ave). Dorm beds cost $26, single rooms are $35 and twins are $60. There is a minimum three-day stay.

Noah's Bondi Beach (☎ 9365 7100, 2 Campbell Parade) is at the southern end of the beach. It's a well-run place in a great location, with worn but clean rooms. Beds in four-/six-bed dorms cost $24/22; double rooms cost $55. Most rooms have TV and fridge, Internet access is available and there's a lounge with pinball machines and a pool table.

Coogee It's farther from the city than Bondi and other traveller centres, but Coogee's relaxed atmosphere and low-season specials make it a popular spot. It's worth ringing hostels before arriving because some have limited office hours.

Surfside Backpackers Coogee (☎ 9315 7888, 186 Arden St) is opposite the beach and main bus stop. The entrance is on Alfreda St. It's a fine hostel, with a five-backpack rating – and it has balconies, some with views of the beach. Dorm rates are $20.

The popular **Coogee Beach Backpackers** (☎ 9315 8000, 94 Beach St) is a short, stiff walk up the hill at the northern end of the beach. It occupies a Federation-era house and a modern block next door. There are good common areas and a deck with great views of the ocean. Dorms cost $20; doubles $48.

The smaller **Indy's** (☎ 9315 7644, 302 Arden St) is on the hill at the southern end in a pleasant, Victorian-era house. Beds in four-bed dorms cost $25/140 nightly/weekly; some rooms on the lower floor are a bit musty, so investigate first. There's a TV room, and rates include breakfast.

North Shore Being an affluent area, there's not a lot of hostel accommodation the North Shore. Manly, with its great ocean and harbour beaches and few city hassles, is the exception, and it's only 30 minutes by ferry (15 minutes by JetCat) from Circular Quay.

The **Manly Beach Resort Backpackers** (☎ 9977 4188, 6 Carlton St) is part of a motel. Backpackers have their own section with a communal kitchen and Internet access. Beds in spacious, clean dorms cost $20. The long-established, pleasant and strictly run **Manly Astra Backpackers** (☎ 9977 2092, 68 Pittwater Rd), nearby, has doubles (no dorms) for $50.

About a block from the beach, **Manly Backpackers Beachside** (☎ 9977 3411, 28 Raglan St) has beds in modern three-bed dorms for $22 and in four- to six-bed dorms for $21. It also has twins/doubles for $50 and doubles with bathrooms for $55.

The **Steyne Hotel** (☎ 9977 4977, 75 The Corso) has bunks in four-bed dorms at a relatively pricey $35 a night, including breakfast. There are good shared kitchen facilities, and bistro-style meals available in the bar downstairs.

Farther out of town, but beautifully positioned right on Collaroy Beach and great for the northern beaches, is the **Sydney Beachouse** (☎ 9981 1177, fax 9981 1114, 4 Collaroy St), a well-equipped, new YHA hostel where dorm beds cost $20 to $21, doubles are $52 and family rooms $94. Extras include free surfing lessons. Take bus No 190, 182 or 184 from Wynyard station.

If you want to get right out of the city, the relaxed beachside suburb of Avalon has the **Avalon Beach Hostel** (☎ 9918 9709, 59

Avalon Parade). It's a sociable place, but it's not particularly clean or quiet. Dorm beds cost $18/20 ($125 weekly); doubles cost $44. Phone in advance because it's often full.

Take bus No L90 from Town Hall or Wynyard Park in the city, or No L88 from Town Hall. Ask for Avalon Beach ($4.60, 1¼ hours).

University Accommodation Many residential colleges accept casual guests. Those listed accept nonstudents, both men and women. Unless otherwise stated, rooms are available during holidays only, mainly the long mid-December to late January break.

Although most places quote meal-inclusive rates, it's often possible to negotiate a lower bed-only rate. Ask about weekly or fortnightly rates which, if available, might also be cheaper.

University of Sydney The University of Sydney is south-west of Chippendale, close to Glebe and Newtown.

International House (☎ 9950 9800, 96 City Rd, Chippendale) has fully serviced single rooms. B&B costs $65. *St Johns College (☎ 9394 5200, 8a Missenden Rd, Camperdown)* has singles (with en suite) available all year. B&B costs $67 ($300 weekly).

Wesley College (☎ 9565 3333) has B&B for $40/46 for students/nonstudents. The *Women's College (☎ 9517 5000, 15 Carillon Ave, Newtown)* has B&B singles for $36 (students and YHA members) or $45.

University of NSW Although this university is farther from the city centre, it's only a short bus ride from the southern ocean beaches and Oxford St. All prices in this section are for singles per night.

International House (☎ 9663 0418, Gate 2, High St, Kensington) offers students full board for $42; for several weeks around Christmas it offers B&B for $30.

New College (☎ 9662 6066), Anzac Parade, Kensington, has B&B accommodation for $50.

Kensington Colleges (☎ 9315 0000, The High St, Randwick) has B&B for $30/40 students/nonstudents.

Guesthouses & Hotels A wide variety of accommodation falls into this category. There are some fine budget hotels and guesthouses, which work out only fractionally more expensive than hostels if you're travelling with friends. A refundable key deposit of $10 is often required.

City Centre The rambling *CB Private Hotel (☎ 9211 5115, 417 Pitt St)* first opened in 1908 and was once the largest residential hotel in the country, with over 200 (mostly single) rooms. It's plain, well run, and reasonably clean, though it has seen a lot of wear and lacks power points. Nightly rates are $39/59 for singles/doubles with shared bathroom; beds in four-bed dorms cost $20 a night.

The *George Hotel (Darling Harbour & Chinatown map; ☎ 9211 1800, 700a George St)* is one of the best innercity budget hotels. It's plain, clean and equipped with cooking and laundry facilities. Rooms with common bathroom cost $39/58, while better doubles cost $80. Weekly rates are available.

The basic *Sydney Central Private Hotel (☎/fax 9212 1005, 75 Wentworth Ave)* is a short walk from Central Station and Oxford St. It has cooking and laundry facilities. Rooms with shared bathroom cost $40/60 ($140/240 weekly); doubles with private bathroom cost $80. The traffic can be noisy.

The Rocks The small *Harbour View Hotel (☎ 9252 3769, 18 Lower Fort St)* is beside a Harbour Bridge approach pylon. There's some noise from trains and even more from the bands in the bar, but with clean singles/doubles for $50/60 (including breakfast) it's pretty good value for the location.

Pyrmont The *Woolbrokers Arms (☎ 9552 4773)*, on the corner of Allen and Pyrmont Sts, is close to Darling Harbour. Motel-style B&B costs $85 a double. Rooms vary in size and all have TV and fridge; bathrooms are separate.

Kings Cross & Around There are some reasonable hotels in the heart of the Cross. The friendly *Bernly Private Hotel (☎ 9358 3122,*

15 Springfield Ave) has uninspiring but acceptable singles/doubles with shared bathroom for $45/55. It also has 'deluxe' en suite rooms with telephones for around $85.

With its pink exterior, *Springfield Lodge* (☎ *9358 3222, 9 Springfield Ave)* is hard to miss. The rooms are average; all have fridge, TV and tea- and coffee-making facilities. Those with shared bathroom cost $45/55 and with attached bathroom $65/75. Bookings are advised.

Montpelier Private Hotel (☎/fax *9358 6960, 39a Elizabeth Bay Rd)* has plain but cheap rooms for $39/49 with shared bathroom, tea- and coffee-making facilities, TV and fridge.

Not as cheap as it once was, but in a good spot nonetheless, is the low-key, well-maintained *Challis Lodge* (☎ *9358 5422, 21–23 Challis Ave, Potts Point)*. In a pair of renovated cavernous terraces not far from the Cross, it has simple but clean rooms for $60/80 (shared bathroom) or $80/100 (attached bathroom).

Around the corner, *Macleay Lodge* (☎ *9368 0660, 71 Macleay St)* has good-value, bright rooms from $40/50 (better rooms on the upper floors cost more). Bathrooms are shared. Nearby, *Holiday Lodge Hotel* (☎ *9356 3955, 55 Macleay St)* has basic motel-style rooms with air-con, TV, phone and fridge for $65/75.

Newtown Despite its worn exterior, *Australian Sunrise Lodge* (☎ *9557 4400, 485 King St)* is clean and pleasant, with reasonable motel-style singles/doubles with TV and fridge for $59/69, or en suite rooms for $89.

Bondi Beach In Bondi Beach, hotel rates vary depending on demand; prices listed here are for the busy summer season.

The renovated *Biltmore Private Hotel* (☎ *9130 4660, 110 Campbell Parade)* has a TV lounge, kitchen and laundry. It charges $20 ($120 weekly) for dorm beds and $35/45 ($190/280 weekly) for singles/doubles.

Occupying three houses two blocks back from the beach is *Bondi Beach Guesthouse* (☎ *9389 8309, 11 Consett Ave)*, with dorm beds for $20 ($120 weekly) and rooms for

$30/50. Most rooms have TV and fridge, and there are laundry facilities and some off-street parking.

Pink *Bondi Lodge* (☎ *9365 2088, 63 Fletcher St)* is a short walk up the hill from the southern end of the beach, but is well placed to get to neighbouring Tamarama. It offers bed, breakfast and dinner for $30 in a dorm or from $60/80 in rooms.

Coogee The *Grand Pacific on the Beach* (☎ *9665 6301)*, at the bottom of Carr St, has seen better days; rooms have a TV, fridge and tea- and coffee-making facilities. Bathrooms are communal, and there's a guests kitchen and laundry. Singles/doubles cost $25/35.

Metro Coogee Beach (☎ *9665 1162, 171 Arden St)*, at the northern end of the beach, has basic but clean accommodation, with dorm beds for $20 and doubles for $55, including breakfast. There's a barbecue area up top.

North Shore With laundry and parking facilities, *St Leonards Mansions* (☎ *9439 6999, 7 Park Rd, St Leonards)* occupies three old houses and has well-equipped, clean singles/doubles for $65/90 ($240/260 weekly). Most rooms have phone, fridge, cooking facilities and en suite; some have balconies with views. From St Leonards station, head west along the Pacific Hwy; Park Rd is the second street on your left.

North Sydney Lodge (☎ *9955 1012, 310 Miller St, North Sydney)* is a pleasant guesthouse opposite St Leonards Park. All rooms ($87) have bathrooms, and rates include breakfast.

The quiet suburb of Kirribilli, north-east of the Harbour Bridge, has several guesthouses. *Tremayne Private Hotel* (☎ *9955 4155, 89 Carabella St)* is a large, clean, quality guesthouse originally built as accommodation for country girls attending school in Sydney. Rooms cost $200/260 per week (shared bathroom) or $300 per week for doubles with en suite bathrooms. Some rooms have bathroom views.

Glenferrie Lodge (☎ *9955 1685, 12a Carabella St)*, to the south, is in a large, old house. It's been refurbished in a fairly chintzy style, but the rooms are clean and each has a fridge. Rooms with shared bathroom cost $60/80 ($330/440 weekly) including a buffet-style breakfast and dinner; there are sometimes discounts.

Neutral Bay Motor Lodge (☎ 9953 4199), on the corner of Kurraba Rd and Hayes St, is near the ferry wharf. It's a quiet, friendly guesthouse with clean, tasteful double rooms with private bathroom for $75.

Manly Popular Manly is particularly susceptible to summer price rises.

The large *Eversham Private Hotel* (☎ 9977 2423, 27–29 Victoria Parade) has been undergoing structural renovations for some time now, but rooms rates have remained constant. Unpromising singles cost $28/123 nightly/weekly. There's a dining room and some deals include meals.

Places to Stay – Mid-Range
This section covers places charging about $80 to $170 for a double. It's a wide price range, and standards vary accordingly.

B&Bs B&B accommodation is a good way of meeting locals and getting inside advice on things to see and do. The B&B Sydneyside (☎ 9449 4430), PO Box 555, Turramurra, NSW 2074, finds accommodation in private homes in Sydney for about $55 to $75 a night for a single; $70 to $110 a double. Hostelling in Homes is an Internet-based agency for backpacker B&Bs in NSW, with rooms for $65 to $85 a double. Check out the Web site at www.homehostel.com.

Hotels & Motels Some mid-range hotels offer top-value facilities at little more than budget prices. Some hotels in this section are pubs that provide slightly above-average accommodation.

City Centre Excellent value for the location, *Wynyard Hotel (Darling Harbour & Chinatown map;* ☎ 9299 1330), on the corner of Clarence and Erskine Sts, is a pleasant pub with singles/doubles with shared bathroom for $85/95. Prices include breakfast and use of laundry facilities. The rooms are plain, but clean and comfortable, and weekly rates are available. There's a rooftop area with views, and a good guest kitchen.

Another innercity pub is the heritage-listed *Grand Hotel* (☎ 9232 3755, 30 Hunter St) where rooms with shared bathrooms cost $80/100; rooms are modest, sizes vary and all have TV, fridge and tea- and coffee-making facilities.

Park Regis (☎ 9267 6511, 27 Park St) is a fairly sparse motel-style place with plain rooms for $150 a night, but it often has specials. It has free parking, and stunning views from the 40th-floor laundry!

The friendly, well-appointed *Hyde Park Inn* (☎ 9264 6001, 271 Elizabeth St) charges $145/160 (including breakfast) for standard rooms, some with kitchenettes.

Aaron's Hotel (☎ 9281 5555, ✉ aarons@ ak.com.au, 37 Ultimo Rd, Haymarket) is near Chinatown and Darling Harbour. It has plain, clean, light rooms with TV and attached bathroom for $130 a double.

Southern Cross Hotel (☎ 9282 0987, ✉ southx@hotmail.com.au), on the corner of Goulburn and Elizabeth Sts, has a rooftop pool and garden, and a piano bar; it's within walking distance of Hyde Park, Oxford St and Darling Harbour. The standard rate is $165 per night, but it often has specials.

The incongruously named *Country Comfort Hotel* (☎ 9212 2544), on the corner of George and Quay Sts, is near Central Station and Darling Harbour and next to Her Majesty's Theatre. It's decorated in pseudo-rural style; rates are $167 per room.

The Rocks The *Lord Nelson Brewery Hotel* (☎ 9251 4044, 19 Kent St, Millers Point) is a swish boutique pub in a sandstone building. Rooms cost $180; all have fax machines.

Right near the bridge, the *Mercantile Hotel* (☎ 9247 3570, 25 George St) is a restored pub with a strong Irish connection. Reasonable singles/doubles cost $70/100 with breakfast and shared bathroom.

Darling Harbour On the western side of Darling Harbour, the *Glasgow Arms Hotel*

(☎ 9211 2354, 527 Harris St), near the Powerhouse Museum, has rooms in a renovated old-style pub. Air-con B&B costs $100/120 single/double with bathroom.

Hotel Ibis (☎ 9563 0888, 70 Murray St), overlooking the harbour, has pleasant if characterless rooms for $165 ($185 with a harbour view).

Kings Cross & Around The friendly *O'Malley's Hotel* (☎ 9357 2211, 228 William St) is an Irish pub with traditionally decorated, air-con singles/doubles from $70/85 with breakfast. The rooms are well furnished; the doubles have bathrooms. The only drawback is the noise – the traffic on William St rarely lets up.

Maksim Lodge (☎ 9356 3399, 37 Darlinghurst Rd) is another friendly place, with rooms for $80/90; all have bathroom, fridge, phone and TV.

The *Barclay Hotel* (☎ 9358 6133, 17 Bayswater Rd) has a range of air-con rooms with TV, telephone and bathroom for $70/80, though some rooms are stuffy.

At the renovated *Kingsview* (☎ 9358 5599, 30 Darlinghurst Rd), in the heart of the Cross, rooms with air-con, TV, telephone and attached bathroom cost $75.

The friendly *Madison's Hotel* (☎ 9357 1155, 6–8 Ward Ave, Elizabeth Bay) is in a converted 1930s building with a modern extension. Rooms cost $99 a night including breakfast. *Crescent on Bayswater* (☎ 9357 7266, 33 Bayswater Rd) is in a huge, modern brick building. A room/suite costs $200/220, which includes breakfast and car parking; there are sometimes special deals.

The hip *L'Otel* (☎ 9360 6868, 114 Darlinghurst Rd) is a stylish boutique hotel with individually designed rooms (some in retro '50s style) popular with soap stars and models. It charges $100 to $160 for a plush room with TV, telephone and attached bathroom, but was being refurbished at the time of writing, so prices might rise.

Top of the Town Hotel (☎ 9361 0911, 227 Victoria St) is near L'Otel, and has a rooftop restaurant and swimming pool. Reasonable doubles with showers cost $105; there's also a slick Internet cafe.

De Vere Hotel (☎ 9358 1211, ✉ info@ devere.com.au, 46 Macleay St) has rooms with TV, telephone and bathroom for $100. At the *Manhattan Park Inn International* (☎ 9358 1288, 8 Greenknowe Ave) the standard rate for doubles is $105. Some rooms have views of Elizabeth Bay.

To the north is *Chateau Sydney Hotel* (☎ 9358 2500, 14 Macleay St), where the rooms have small balconies. Rooms cost $145 (city view) to $165 (harbour view).

Victoria Court Hotel (☎ 9357 3200, ✉ info@victoriacourt.com.au, 122 Victoria St) is a quiet retreat. There's security parking and a pleasant courtyard. Rooms cost $120 to $250, and include continental breakfast. *Holiday Inn* (☎ 9368 4000, ✉ hotel res@hipps.com.au, 203 Victoria St) charges from $155 (with breakfast and parking); the better rooms have harbour views.

The three-star, four-storey *Bayside* (☎ 9327 8511, 85 New South Head Rd) has standard double rooms with bathroom for $110 – but check for specials.

Eastern Suburbs The pleasant, friendly *Savoy Double Bay Hotel* (☎ 9326 1411, ✉ info@savoyhotel.com.au, 41–45 Knox St) is small but in a good location. Doubles cost $135 to $155, including a light breakfast.

To enjoy the harbour in a quiet locale and still be within a short ferry ride of the city, try the harbourside *Watsons Bay Hotel* (☎ 9337 4299, 1 Military Rd, Watsons Bay), which was under renovation at the time of research. Call for prices for very comfortable doubles with bathroom.

Darlinghurst & Surry Hills The 13-storey, three-star *Oxford Koala Hotel* (☎ 9269 0645), on the corner of Oxford and Pelican Sts, has doubles for $130 double, and apartments (sleeping four) for $180.

The *Crown Lodge International* (☎ 9331 2433, ✉ citycrow@bigpond.com, 289 Crown St), a little south of Oxford St, offers basic motel accommodation for $100 a double.

The more upmarket *Cambridge Park Inn* (☎ 9212 1111, 212 Riley St) has a gym, sauna, heated pool and restaurant. Rooms cost $150 to $165, but there are often specials.

Glebe A guesthouse and an upmarket hostel, *Alishan International Guesthouse (☎ 9566 4048, @ kevin@alishan.com.au, 100 Glebe Point Rd)* boasts multilingual staff, good kitchen and laundry facilities and a small garden with a barbecue. Dorm beds cost $25 while singles/doubles with bathroom cost $85/95, and there's a room set up for disabled travellers.

Rooftop Motel (☎ 9660 7777, 146–148 Glebe Point Rd) is a simple motel charging from $90 for en suite rooms – some have lurid green carpet, but it's a friendly place and there's a rooftop pool. Farther north, on the corner of Wigram Rd, *Haven Inn (☎ 9660 6655, 196 Glebe Point Rd)* has decent-sized rooms (for an innercity motel) for $110 ($130 with a city view). There's a heated swimming pool, secure parking and a restaurant.

Bondi Beach The beachfront, peach-coloured, layer-cake is *Hotel Bondi (☎ 9130 3271)*, on the corner of Campbell Parade and Curlewis St. It's an impressive old pile with small single rooms for $45, doubles for $85 (add $20 for a balcony and beach view) and renovated suites from $165.

Bondi Beachside Inn (☎ 9130 5311, 152 Campbell Parade) has small, motel-style rooms for $110. They all have air-con, phone, TV, kitchen and balcony.

The refurbished *Beach Road Hotel (☎ 9130 7247, 71 Beach Rd)* is a large pub two blocks back from the beach. Heavy on the beach-theme decor, it has several bars, a couple of eateries and a nightclub. The clean, bright rooms have air-con, fridge and bathroom, and go for $60/75.

Ravesi's (☎ 9365 4422), on the corner of Campbell Parade and Hall St, is an interesting, three-star hotel with 16 rooms and suites, some with terraces. Rooms cost $105 to $295, depending on the view and degree of luxury. Check for special deals in winter and spring.

Coogee The huge, central *Coogee Bay Hotel (☎ 9665 0000)*, on the corner of Arden St and Coogee Bay Rd, has standard air-con singles/doubles with fridge, TV,

telephone and en suite for $99; quieter, renovated boutique rooms are $170.

Manly In Manly, a beach resort, many places have seasonal and weekend deals.

The *Steyne Hotel (☎ 9977 4977, 75 The Corso)* has OK rooms with shared bathroom from $70/95 for singles/doubles. *Manly Lodge (☎ 9977 8655, 22 Victoria Parade)* is a guesthouse with a holiday atmosphere. Most rooms are small, but have TV, fridge, air-con and attached bathroom; some have spas. Doubles/twins start at $120, including breakfast, and there's a communal sauna, gym, and giant trampoline.

Manly Beach Resort (☎ 9977 4188, 6 Carlton St) is a reasonable motel with good security offering singles/doubles from $95/105 to $105/115, which includes a continental breakfast.

Periwinkle Guest House (☎ 9977 4668, 18–19 East Esplanade) is an elegantly restored Victorian house facing the harbour beach at Manly Cove. Most rooms have bathrooms and all have double beds; room rates start at $120. There's a stylish, cosy kitchen, and laundry facilities are available.

Manly Paradise Motel (☎ 9977 5799, 54 North Steyne) is on the beachfront. It has a rooftop pool and air-con motel rooms with TV, fridge and bathroom for $115, or $125 with a partial ocean view.

Serviced Apartments Serviced apartments – anything from a hotel room with a fridge and a microwave, to a full-size apartment – can be good value, especially for families.

City Centre The *Sydney City Centre Apartments (☎ 9233 6677, 7 Elizabeth St)*, in the heart of the financial district, offers fully equipped bedsit apartments of a reasonable size, complete with washing machine and dryer. Rates are $100 a day (minimum three-day stay).

Near Hyde Park and Oxford St, *Sydney Park Inn (☎ 9360 5988, 2–6 Francis St)*, behind the NSW police headquarters, provides fully equipped air-con studios. Rooms cost $115; some are lighter than others.

Darling Harbour Close to Darling Harbour, **Metro Suites** (☎ 9290 9200, 132 Sussex St and 27–29 King St) has good serviced apartments. The clean, bright rooms sleep four to five people, are split-level and have great views. There's a kitchenette, and a clothes washer and dryer. Apartments cost $155 ($125 per night if you stay a week or more).

The nearby **Savoy Apartments** (☎ 9267 9211, 37–43 King St) are a little more expensive at $165 ($140 per night if you stay a week or more).

Downtown Serviced Apartments (☎ 9261 4333, 336 Sussex St) has a tennis court and swimming pool, plus a rooftop garden with good views of the harbour. The apartments each have two bedrooms, a kitchen and living room and cost $170 for two people (extra person $20).

The **Waldorf** (☎ 9261 5355, 57 Liverpool St) has a rooftop pool, spa, barbecue area and free parking. Rates start at $175.

Kings Cross & Around On the northern continuation of Macleay St, **Oakford Potts Point** (☎ 9358 4544, 1800 657 392, 10 Wylde St) charges $175/225 for one-/two-bedroom apartments and from $103 for studio rooms. Nearby, **Macleay Serviced Apartments** (☎ 9357 7755, fax 9357 7233, 28 Macleay St) has hotel-style rooms with good self-catering facilities for $110 or $130 (harbour view).

In Elizabeth Bay, **17 Elizabeth Bay Rd** (☎ 9358 8999) has well-equipped, serviced one-/two-bedroom apartments for $160/205. Weekly rates are $140/175 per night. **Medina Executive Apartments** (☎ 9356 7400, 68 Roslyn Gardens) has bright, quiet rooms overlooking an atrium from $90 to $120 nightly.

Coogee The brand new **Coogee Sands Apartments** (☎ 9665 8588, 165 Dolphin St) has small viewless studios for $155 and larger apartments with ocean views (sleeping five) for $250.

Places to Stay – Top End
Hotels This section covers accommodation costing from $165 a night. Travel agents in other states or countries can book many of these places and probably have access to special deals and packages.

Airport The **Sydney Airport Hilton** (☎59518 2000, 20 Levey St, Arncliffe) charges around $190 to $300 a room; most rates include breakfast, parking and a shuttle service to and from the airport.

City Centre The **Sydney Hilton Hotel** (☎ 9266 2000, 259 Pitt St) is in the heart of the city. Standard doubles cost $320, but there are cheaper weekend deals for $244, and other specials. The historic Marble Bar is downstairs.

The grand **All Seasons Premier Menzies** (Darling Harbour & Chinatown map; ☎ 9299 1000, 14 Carrington St), across from Wynyard Park, has rooms from $195 with breakfast.

The luxurious **Westin** (☎ 8223 1111, ✉ info@westin.com.au, 1 Martin Place), in the restored GPO building, has modern 'tower' rooms for $275 or magnificent 'heritage' rooms in the historic building from $335 a double.

Several hotels overlook Hyde Park. **Sheraton on the Park** (☎ 9286 6000, 161 Elizabeth St) has a magnificent marble lobby. Good rooms with views of the city/park cost from $275, but there are always specials.

Sydney Marriott Hotel (☎ 9361 8400, 36 College St) has rooms for $199 and suites from $270. Next door, but with the same street number, is **Hyde Park Plaza Hotel** (☎ 9331 6933, fax 9331 6022) where rooms start at $235. Both hotels are close to the nightlife and restaurants of Oxford St.

The Rocks & Circular Quay In a superb location, the charming **Russell Hotel** (☎ 9241 3543, 143a George St) is a small boutique-style hotel with traditionally decorated rooms, pleasant lounge areas and a sunny roof garden. Singles/doubles cost $110 with shared bathroom or from $180 with private bathroom. Suites cost $230.

The **Stafford** (☎ 9251 6711, 75 Harrington St) has plain but comfortable self-contained studios and single-bedroom apartments (some in a row of restored terrace houses) for $210 to $250. **Harbour Rocks Hotel** (☎ 9251 8944, 34–52 Harrington St), diagonally opposite, also occupies restored 19th-century buildings. Rooms start at $195.

From the rooftop pool of the **Old Sydney Parkroyal** (☎ 9252 0524, 55 George St) there are great views of The Rocks, Sydney Harbour Bridge, the harbour and the Opera House. Standard doubles cost $230, but the hotel offers specials.

The lovely, three-storey **Observatory Hotel** (☎ 9256 2222, 89–113 Kent St), on the Millers Point side of the Bradfield Hwy, has plush rooms for $495. The nearby **ANA Hotel Sydney** (☎ 9250 6111, 176 Cumberland St) has 573 stylish rooms starting at $275 and suites (all with harbour views) from $450.

The luxurious **Park Hyatt Hotel** (☎ 9241 1234, 7 Hickson Rd) has one of the best locations in Sydney – on the waterfront at the edge of Campbells Cove, in the shadow of the Harbour Bridge and facing the Opera House. It charges from $600 to $1200.

The **Ritz-Carlton** (☎ 9252 4600, 93 Macquarie St) is in an elegant brick building. Comfortable rooms/suites cost from $289/469. The **Intercontinental** (☎ 9230 0200, fax 9240 1240, 117 Macquarie St) next door, is in a beautiful sandstone building that once housed the state treasury. It's one of the few hotels with an environmental 'mission statement'. Rooms cost from $400 but there are often specials from $210.

The luxurious new **Pier One Parkroyal Sydney Harbour** (☎ 8298 9999, @ hotel@ pierone.parkroyal.com.au), at Walsh Bay beside the Harbour Bridge, has been built in a former naval wharf. It offers hip designer heaven in a heritage casing, and the foyer features a 12 sq metre glass floor over the harbour. Rooms cost $265 to $365.

Darling Harbour The 700-room **Hotel Nikko** (☎ 9299 1231, @ reservations@hotel nikko.com.au, 161 Sussex St) charges $199 to $219 depending on the view, but often has specials.

A hotel with good views of Darling Harbour and the city is the 530-room **Novotel Sydney Hotel** (☎ 9934 0000, 100 Pyrmont St). It has a swimming pool, spa, gym and tennis court; rooms cost from $235 to $430. It's somewhat cut off from the harbour and you need to walk across covered footbridges (over Darling Drive) to get there.

Furama Hotel (☎ 9281 0400, 68 Harbour St), in a renovated 19th-century wool store, is directly opposite Sydney Entertainment Centre. It has a walk-in rate of $135 for standard rooms.

Kings Cross & Around Definitely worth a look if you're after a bit of luxury, **Simpsons of Potts Point** (☎ 9356 2199, 8 Challis Ave) is in a superb old house in a quiet spot a short walk from Kings Cross. Large, well-furnished doubles with bathroom go for $175.

Regent's Court (☎ 9358 1533, 18 Springfield Ave) is a boutique hotel in a converted Art-Deco apartment block close to the Cross. Stylish rooms cost $170 to $185. There's a lovely Italian-style rooftop garden.

The **Sebel** (☎ 9358 3244, 23 Elizabeth Bay Rd) has a reputation for celebrity guests, especially from the music industry. It has some quality touches, including a gym and rooftop heated pool. Rates are $169 to $459, with seasonal specials and good weekend deals.

Double Bay With its gold-and-deep purple decor, **Sir Stamford** (☎ 9363 0100, 22 Cross St) perches above the Cosmopolitan shopping centre. Pleasant rooms cost from $275, though there are usually packages from $189. At the plush **Ritz-Carlton Double Bay** (☎ 9362 4455, 33 Cross St) rooms cost from $235 to $285, suites $385 to $2000. It's popular with the powerful and famous who require discretion.

Bondi Beach & Coogee The top-dollar place to stay in Bondi is the huge, balustraded **Swiss Grand** (☎ 9365 5666), on the corner of Beach Rd and Campbell Parade. Suites cost $209; those with beach views start at $249.

In Coogee, **Holiday Inn** (☎ 9315 7600, 242 Arden St) charges $169/189 for rooms with Coogee/ocean views.

North Shore The *Duxton Hotel (☎ 9955 1111, 11 Alfred St)* is across from Milsons Point station, with easy access to North Sydney and the city. It's a stylish, modern, four-star hotel, oriented to business travellers. Room rates start at $215 (weekdays) or $130 (weekends).

Manly There are two four-star hotels in Manly. The *Manly Pacific Parkroyal (☎ 9977 7666, 55 North Steyne)* has a gym and swimming pool; rooms cost from $190 to $450. *Radisson Kestrel (☎ 9977 8866, 8 South Steyne)* has double rooms with aircon, TV and bathroom from $209 to $399. Both have some rooms with ocean views.

Serviced Apartments In The Rocks, *Quay West Suites (☎ 9240 6000, 98 Gloucester St)* has quality apartments with views of Sydney Harbour or the city starting at $380.

The 11-storey *Carrington Apartments (Darling Harbour & Chinatown map; ☎ 9299 6556, 57–59 York St)* has rooms for $140 to $180. From the 6th-floor swimming pool at *York Apartment Hotel (☎ 9210 5000, 5 York St)* you can see the approaches to Sydney Harbour Bridge. Rates for the York's spacious rooms start at $295, including free parking.

Not far from Hyde Park, *Parkridge Corporate Apartments (☎ 9361 8600, 6–14 Oxford St)* has decent single/double suites for $160/190. There's a minimum stay of three nights.

In Manly, *Grand Esplanade Crest Hotel (☎ 9976 4600, 1800 334 033, 54a West Esplanade)* is directly opposite the ferry terminal; studio apartments cost $180/195 for two/three people.

PLACES TO EAT

With great local produce, innovative chefs, inexpensive prices and bring your own (BYO) alcohol licensing laws, eating out is one of the great delights of Sydney. The city has a huge variety of restaurants and almost everywhere you'll find good places to eat. There are top restaurants, modest Chinese, Indian and Vietnamese restaurants (almost

as cheap as eating at home) and pubs serving counter meals – good for solid, inexpensive fare.

City Centre

There's no shortage of places for a snack or a meal in the city centre on weekdays, but many, especially north of Liverpool St, close in the evenings. They're clustered around train stations, in shopping arcades and tucked away in the food courts at the base of office buildings.

Fast Food In Pitt St Mall there's reasonably priced food in the *Mid City Centre* food court on street level. Mexican, Italian, Thai etc dishes cost $4 to $7. The *Woolworth* supermarket, on the corner of George and Park Sts, has a 2nd-floor cafeteria, open daily, which serves meals like roast lamb or pork from around $5.

For innercity snacks at odd hours, *Coles Express (☎ 9221 3119),* on the corner of King and George Sts, is open from 6 am to midnight daily. There's a patisserie section, fresh fruit and vegetables, and hot meals from $3.95.

The *Y on the Park (5–11 Wentworth Ave)* has a cafeteria serving sandwiches for around $2.80 and hot meals for $7. It's open weekdays from 7.30 am to 7 pm, weekends 8 am to 9 pm.

Cafes There is a range of *cafes* below street level of the QVB, forming an arcade through to Town Hall station. Many remain open after the shops have closed. On the ground floor of the QVB, *Bar Cupola* serves good coffee and Italian-style sandwiches and sweets.

Obelisk, on Macquarie Place, has outdoor tables in a lovely spot just near the obelisk. Gourmet rolls, baguettes and chunky toasted sandwiches cost $6.50, Caesar salad $7.90. *Bar Coluzzi (99 Elizabeth St),* near the Hyde Park fountain, serves good coffee and a range of interesting snacks for $5 to $7.50; cakes and biscuits cost $2.50.

For a quiet cup of tea or coffee away from the city bustle, follow the smell of roasted beans to *Harris Coffee and Tea*, on the ground floor of the elegant Strand Arcade, between Pitt St Mall and George St. It has a wide choice of coffee and teas from around $2.

Farther south, *Zenergy (Darling Harbour & Chinatown map; 69 Druitt St)* is part of a small chain serving wholesome vegetarian fare – cheap and tasty sandwiches, salads and vegie burgers start from around $3.50. Breakfast specials are $2.50 to $3.

Vender (86 Liverpool St) is a small espresso bar with funky lights and a selection of filled pitta breads and salads for $7 to $9. It's near the George St cinemas, is open until 11 pm, and has good hot chocolate.

For palatable fast food near Central Station, there's *Central Park Cafe*, on Eddy Ave, next to the coach terminal in Haymarket. The options range from fresh fruit salads to roasts; focaccia and gourmet sandwiches cost $4.50.

Pubs The *Hotel Sweeney (Darling Harbour & Chinatown map; ☎ 9267 1116)*, on the corner of Clarence and Druitt Sts, has a 2nd floor bistro where you can get $12 meals, or grab a drink and surf the Internet upstairs. Upstairs at the Edinburgh Castle Hotel is the welcoming *Pitt St Bistro (☎ 9264 8616)*, on the corner of Pitt and Bathurst Sts, serving interesting and relatively inexpensive meals (around $11) in pleasant, light surrounds.

South of Pitt St Mall, *Arizona (☎ 9261 1077, 231–247 Pitt St)*, on the 1st floor beside the City Centre monorail stop, is one of a small chain of licensed 'western' bar/restaurants. Heavy on the kitsch decor, it serves Tex-Mex food, including nachos for $10.50. *Chamberlain Hotel (☎ 9211 1929)*, on the corner of Pitt and Campbell Sts, has $6 bar meals.

Restaurants If high altitudes and revolving restaurants don't make you queasy, *Sydney Tower Restaurant (☎ 8223 3800, Level 1, AMP Tower)*, on the corner of Market and Pitt Sts, has main courses from $27.50 for vegetarian dishes, to $42 for lobster. It's open for dinner Tuesday to Saturday. *Level 2 Sydney Tower Restaurant (☎ 8223 3800)* has an all-you-can-eat buffet for $40, offering a selection of meats, seafood and Asian dishes, but little for vegetarians. Children under 12 pay $15. It's open daily for lunch and dinner. Diners aren't charged for the ride to the top of the tower, so you're $10 ahead. Bookings are recommended.

Hip and groovy Sydneysiders have been flocking to the old *GPO (1 Martin Place)* since it was renovated and transformed into a food emporium. For those with deep pockets there are several restaurants to choose from: *Post (☎ 9229 7744)*, a French brasserie–style restaurant; *Sosumi*, a sushi conveyor belt; and *Prime (☎ 9229 7777)*, a traditional steak house. There is also a cafe, *GPO Espresso*, which serves some of Sydney's best coffee, and *GPO Produce*, which sells fine food, from lobsters to cheese and ready-made meals.

Slipp-Inn (Darling Harbour & Chinatown map; ☎ 9299 4777, 111 Sussex St) has a range of eating options. The Thai noodle bar upstairs is open weekdays for lunch (meals cost about $7); the restaurant downstairs has mains for around $24 (open for lunch and dinner Tuesday to Friday); the pizza bar ($12 to $16) opens similar hours.

Diethnes (☎ 9267 8956, 336 Pitt St), north of Liverpool St, is a large, friendly Greek restaurant (downstairs). Lamb specials cost $10.50 to $12.50, delicious haloumi (fried cheese) is $6.

Planet Hollywood (☎ 9267 7827, 600 George St) is as tacky – and popular – as ever. Burgers cost $11.50 to $14.25.

Spanish Town consists of a small group of Spanish restaurants and bars along Liverpool St, between George and Sussex Sts. *Capitan Torres (☎ 9264 5574, 73 Liverpool St)* has a great bar, tapas from around $3, and good seafood for $15 to $20. *Casa Asturiana (☎ 9264 1010, 77 Liverpool St)* specialises in northern-Spanish cooking, and reputedly has the best tapas in Sydney, for $5 to $7. *Grand Taverna (☎ 9267 3608)*, on the corner of Liverpool and George Sts at the Sir John Young Hotel, is another popular Spanish place. Mains like lemon sole and ocean perch cost $15 to $16.

Ru-Yuan Vegetarian Restaurant (☎ 9211 2189, 768 George St) is a clean, airy place serving tasty vegan Chinese food. Sichuan spicy beancurd on rice costs $7.80.

Another vegan Asian restaurant is *Mother Chu's Vegetarian Kitchen* (☎ *9283 2828, 376 Pitt St*), open for dinner daily and lunch weekdays. Noodle dishes cost around $7, main courses (like honey-glazed gluten with walnut and sesame) $9 to $12. Similar is *Bodhi* (*Darling Harbour & Chinatown map; ☎ 9281 9918, 187 Hay St*). The lunch-time yum cha upstairs is legendary, and the take-away downstairs has $2 vegie pies.

The licensed *Malaya on George* (☎ *9211 0946*), on the corner of Valentine and George Sts, is a modern, spacious Malaysian/Chinese eatery. Mains, including vegetarian dishes, cost $12 to $16.

The Rocks

The cafes and restaurants here are aimed mainly at tourists and are usually open late. There are some good deals available, especially in the numerous pubs.

Fast Food, Cafes & Pubs There's a small food hall in the modern *Clocktower Square Shopping Centre*, on the corner of Harrington and Argyle Sts.

Gum Nut Tea Garden (☎ *9247 9591, 28 Harrington St*), near Argyle St, is an old house with a courtyard where you can have coffee, cake and light meals for under $7.

G'Day Cafe (*83 Harrington St*), just north of Argyle St, has breakfast or focaccia for $4. It has a $1.50 surcharge on Sunday.

Harbour View Hotel (☎ *9252 3769, 18 Lower Fort St*) has basic, inexpensive meals; steak sandwiches cost $5. At the *Hero of Waterloo* (☎ *9252 4553, 81 Lower Fort St*) you can get green chicken curry for $10.50. *Lord Nelson Brewery Hotel* (☎ *9251 4044, 19 Kent St*) also does decent pub grub.

Restaurants The informal *Phillip's Foote* (☎ *9241 1485, 101 George St*) is a pub-style eatery with a salad bar and a pleasant outdoor barbecue area where you can cook your own steak or fish ($18).

At the stylish *Sailor's Thai* (☎ *9251 2466, 106 George St*), chicken-and-coconut soup costs $26; there's a noodle bar upstairs.

Rockpool (☎ *9252 1888, 107 George St*) is one of Sydney's best eateries. Chef Neil Perry draws on Asian influences to create sensational dishes. The interior is space-age Art Deco, the service spot-on. Mains include grilled swordfish with artichoke for $38, and the emphasis is on freshly caught seafood – strict vegetarians should look elsewhere.

Vault (☎ *9247 1920, 135 George St*) is in a refurbished Gothic building. Meaty mains (like suckling pig) cost $26 to $34. The wine room has a cheaper menu; artichoke tortellini is $16.

Rocks Teppanyaki (☎ *9250 6000*), on the corner of Essex and Cumberland Sts, is an upmarket Japanese restaurant. King prawns cost $29.

The mellow and lovely *Kable's* (☎ *9238 0000, Regent Hotel, 199 George St*) is one of Australia's best restaurants, and the prices reflect this, but there are lunchtime specials, with two courses and coffee for $42.50.

Restaurants at Pier One on Dawes Point, to the west of the Harbour Bridge, include *Harbour Watch* (☎ *9241 2217*), a seafood place where most mains cost $25. The informal *Harbourside Brasserie* (☎ *9252 3000*) nearby is cheaper, with soup for $8.90 and chicken schnitzel for $16.90. Dramatically situated in a converted warehouse near the Sydney Theatre Company, *Wharf Restaurant* (☎ *9250 1761, Pier 4*), at the Wharf Theatre, is a pleasant, open space with a soaring ceiling and great views. Three courses will cost you about $50.

Circular Quay

Many cafes and restaurants that line the quay, especially on the western side, have good views of the harbour, although you pay for the position. Most are aimed at tourists.

For fuel rather than views, there are lots of cheap stalls on the wharves as you head towards the ferries, although most of what's on offer has a high grease count. A good option for hot days is *Casa Del Gelato* on Wharf 5, which boasts 20 flavours.

Cafes The Museum of Contemporary Art has the stylish *MCA Cafe* (☎ *9241 4253*).

The outside tables have good views of the quay, the food is interesting and the service professional; poached chicken costs $14.50.

On the eastern side of Circular Quay next to Sydney Cove Oyster Bar is *Portobello Caffe* (☎ 9247 8548), which serves pastries and cakes for $3 to $7, and expensive but decent coffee; it has some outdoor tables.

Restaurants Seafood is the speciality at *Doyle's at the Quay* (☎ 9252 3400, *Overseas Passenger Terminal, Circular Quay West*). Most mains, like John Dory fillets, cost around $29. There's a minimum charge of $15 per adult.

More formal than Doyle's, and directly upstairs, is *Quay* (☎ 9251 5600), one of Sydney's most highly regarded seafood restaurants. Starters cost $19 to $36 and most mains (like snapper roulade) are $42 to $52. If you're still solvent, finish with passionfruit souffle ($24).

There's a collection of restaurants with large outdoor areas and great views overlooking the quay farther north in the renovated Campbell's Storehouse complex. They include *Wolfie's* (☎ 9241 5577), which has seafood entrees for $13.90 to $16.90 and Tasmanian salmon for $19.50.

Behind Circular Quay on the top floor of the renovated Customs House is *Cafe Sydney* (☎ 8298 0303, 31 Alfred St), with great views and an outdoor terrace. Starters cost $14 to $18, mains (such as wok-braised bugtails with black mushrooms and bok choy) cost $14 to $29.

Sydney Cove Oyster Bar (☎ 9247 2937), on the eastern side of Circular Quay, offers purely Australian produce, including wine. Oysters cost from $18.50 a dozen; other dishes, like a cheese-and-fruit platter, start from $13. It's open from mid-morning until about 8 pm daily (until 11 pm in summer). There is a surcharge on weekends.

Sleek new arrival *Aria* (☎ 9252 2555, 1 Macquarie St), near the Opera House in the building branded as 'the toaster' at Opera Quays, has made a splash as one of the city's best new dining spots. The views of the Opera House and the Harbour Bridge are great and the food is excellent – but

pricey. Starters cost $25 to $30 and mains (such as baked Atlantic salmon on a pea puree with a poached egg and butter sauce) cost $35 to $40.

There are three restaurants in the Opera House complex. On the western side, *Concourse* (☎ 9250 7300) is on the lower level protected from the breeze. The limited menu includes chargrilled swordfish ($15 to $19). *Harbour* (☎ 9250 7191) serves mostly seafood, with main courses for around $23. Upstairs, maximising the building's stunning architecture, is the chic but accessible *Bennelong Restaurant* (☎ 9250 7578). There's live jazz nightly, a seafood and crustacean bar for fishy snacks, and a cocktail lounge open till around midnight. If you eat before 7.30 pm, a three-course meal costs $39; later on it's $65. Mains cost around $29.

Darling Harbour & Pyrmont

The biggest concentration of eateries is at Cockle Bay Wharf, officially heralded as Sydney's newest dining precinct. Most are fairly slick, and few are cheap. Across the water at Harbourside are a handful of top-notch restaurants and a swag of fast-food outlets.

Fast Food, Cafes & Pubs At Cockle Bay Wharf, *The Health Tree* takeaway has fresh juices, tasty salads for $3 to $7, and vegetable lasagne for $6.50. Opposite is *Schwob's Swiss*, a gourmet sandwich joint; the caviar-and-chive variety costs $6.90.

Most of the fast-food outlets at Harbourside are in the food court on the ground floor. Upstairs is *Festival Cafe*, a large, tourist-style coffee lounge (without views) serving sandwiches and burgers for around $6 to $10. For a quick, portable meal, pop downstairs to *Shakespeare's Pies*, where pies like Thai broccoli and tandoori chicken cost between $2 and $3.80.

You can eat with the locals at the *Glasgow Arms Hotel* (☎ 9211 2354, 527 Harris St), near the Powerhouse Museum. It has a good bistro; burgers cost $10.90.

Restaurants Perched on a leafy rooftop at the northern end of Cockle Bay Wharf is

SYDNEY

Chinta Ria (☎ *9265 3211*), a Malaysian place serving tasty, reasonably priced meals with great style. Most mains are $9 or $10; chicken laksa is $12.

In the Harbourside complex, *Jordon's* (☎ *9281 3711*) and *Jo Jo's* (☎ *9281 3888*) are two of the more expensive restaurants. Both have in-house bars, and excellent views. The more relaxed Jordon's is a seafood restaurant; its 'famous fish and chips' costs $18.50. At Jo Jo's, starters like the antipasto platter cost around $16.50, while a main dish of poached salmon is $25.

Shipley's Restaurant (☎ *9281 0400, 68 Harbour St)*, at the Furama Hotel opposite the Sydney Entertainment Centre, has entrees from $10.95, interesting main dishes (like chicken breast with orange and peach schnapps glaze) for around $20, and a breakfast buffet (from $15.50).

Pyrmont Fish Markets has several places to eat. *Doyle's at the Markets* (☎ *9552 4339)* is a bistro, but also does takeaway. It serves fish of the day with chips for $9.80, and has seating outside.

Chinatown

Chinatown is a dense cluster of mostly Chinese restaurants, cafes, takeaways and shops catering to the Chinese community. There are also Thai, Vietnamese, Japanese and Korean eateries. Officially, Chinatown is confined to the pedestrian mall on Dixon St, but its culinary delights have spilled over into the surrounding streets, especially around Haymarket.

You can break the bank at some outstanding Chinese restaurants, or eat well for next to nothing in a food hall. Weekend yum cha makes such a popular brunch that you may have to queue for it.

Fast Food The best place to start is the downstairs food hall in the pagoda-style *Harbour Plaza*, on the corner of Dixon and Goulburn Sts. There's a wide range of dishes for $4.50 to $6.50. There's a food hall on the top level of the *Sussex Centre*, diagonally across from the Harbour Plaza fronting Dixon St and backing onto Sussex St; and another in the *Dixon House Food Court*, on the corner of Dixon St Mall and Little Hay St.

Cafes Open daily, *Emperor's Garden BBQ & Noodles* (*Central Sydney map; 213 Thomas St)* is a popular cafe-style Chinese eatery specialising in meat and poultry dishes. Pork and rice costs $5.

On the corner of Ultimo Rd and Thomas St is the inexpensive and spotless Japanese cafe *Fuji San* (*Central Sydney map)*. It has a few tables and most meals cost from $5 to $10; it also does takeaway.

Restaurants At the intimate, busy *Chinese Noodle Restaurant* (☎ *9281 9051, ground floor, Prince Centre, Thomas St)*, the noodles are handmade in traditional northern Chinese style, and most meals cost around $6. Next door is the Japanese/Korean *Green Zone* (*Central Sydney map)*, serving beautifully presented food like beef sukiyaki for around $8 to $14.

The crowded Cantonese restaurant *Hingara* (☎ *9212 2169, 82 Dixon St)* does good seafood mains, most in the $10 to $15 range.

The popular *House of Guangzhou* (*Central Sydney map; ☎ 9281 2205, 76 Ultimo Rd)*, occupying two floors, has an aquarium full of beautiful (inedible) fish, and a reputation for good seafood; bookings are essential. Most mains cost around $11 to $19.

The huge *Marigold* restaurant (☎ *9264 6744, 299–305 Sussex St)* serves Cantonese food with great style and wide-ranging prices – broccoli in oyster sauce is $9, scallops $25. Despite its size you need to book.

In the same price bracket, the grand and heavily chandeliered *Regal* (☎ *9261 8988, 347–353 Sussex St)* is another large place popular for Sunday yum cha. Mains start at $16.

Kings Cross & Around

There are plenty of places where you can eat cheaply and watch Kings Cross life go by. Alternatively, check out the fine cafes and restaurants in Potts Point.

Fast Food, Cafes & Pubs Eternally popular with backpackers are the three pizza slices for $1 from *Action Pizza* on Darlinghurst Rd (near the corner of Bayswater Rd).

Oporto (☎ 9368 0257, 3c Roslyn St) is one of a small chain specialising in Portuguese-style chicken. Chicken burgers start at $3.85.

There are inexpensive, no-frills cafes on William St, just off Darlinghurst Rd. You can usually find a full breakfast for under $5. *Williams on William* (☎ 9358 5680, 242 William St) has breakfast specials for $3.90, pasta for $5.

The licensed *Waterlily Cafe* (6 Bayswater Rd) is one of the nicest cafes in the Cross, with a few outside tables and a friendly atmosphere. Thai tuna cakes cost $7 and a full cooked breakfast (with free-range eggs) $6. Another good one is the cute and reasonably priced *Cafe 59* (59 Bayswater Rd), which serves fine coffee, hearty breakfasts and lunches, and an array of nutritious drinks.

The small but comfortable *Joe's Cafe Deluxe* (☎ 9368 1188, 190 Victoria St), near Kings Cross station, has a range of pasta and bagels; a breakfast plate of scrambled eggs, bread, tomatoes and mushrooms costs $9.50. Farther north is *Roy's* (☎ 9357 3579, 176 Victoria St), a slick Italian-style cafe with huge servings. It has some vegetarian dishes and is equally good for a coffee or a meal.

For cheap Thai food, try the tiny *Pad Thai* (15 Llankelly Place), serving soups for $5 and noodles for $7.

Catering to avid carnivores, the increasingly slick *Cafe Iguana* (☎ 9357 2609, 15 Kellet St) has kangaroo, crocodile, and Balmain bugs on the menu; mains cost around $17. The cosily bohemian *Dean's Cafe* (☎ 9368 0953, 5 Kellet St) has toasties for $6.50 and a good selection of drinks. It is open late.

In Woolloomooloo, *Harry's Cafe de Wheels* (Woolloomooloo Finger Wharf) must be one of the few pie carts in the world to be a tourist attraction. It opened in 1945, and stays open 18 hours a day, serving pies and mash galore.

Popular with sailors from the nearby naval base, *Frisco Hotel* (☎ 9357 1800, 46 Dowling St, Woolloomooloo) has a bistro downstairs and an upstairs restaurant with a balcony. Mondays and Tuesdays are 'spag nights', when pasta dishes cost $6.

For great coffee and fresh, tasty fare from around $6, try the diminutive and bustling *Spring Cafe,* Challis Ave, Potts Point. It's always busy, so you may have to improvise with seating.

Restaurants With its splendidly tacky Las Vegas decor and red-tinted lighting, the *Bourbon & Beefsteak* (☎ 9358 1144, 24 Darlinghurst Rd) is a touristy but surreal spot to quell the late-night munchies. It serves breakfast 24 hours – pancakes with maple syrup cost $7.50, bacon and eggs $9.50.

Bayswater Rd has several upmarket eateries. *Bayswater Brasserie* (☎ 9357 2177, 32 Bayswater Rd) is a classy but casual restaurant with excellent service where, if you choose carefully, you needn't spend a fortune. Mains ($12.50 to $27) include cuttlefish in black ink sauce.

Star Bar & Grill (☎ 9356 2911, 155 Victoria St) is a hip restaurant and noodle bar offering delicious Chinese and Malaysian food. Seared scallops cost $14. It's open Tuesday to Saturday for dinner only.

On Macleay St, the long-established BYO *Macleay St Bistro* (☎ 9358 4891, 73a Macleay St) has a Modern Australian menu with mains like oven-baked salmon with papaya salad priced from $13 to $29. It's open nightly for dinner and for lunch Friday to Sunday (no bookings).

The Pig & the Olive (☎ 9357 3745, 71a Macleay St), with its terracotta walls and pig-theme decorations, serves out-of-the-ordinary pizzas (from $12) with inventive toppings.

Darlinghurst & East Sydney

This area has the greatest concentration of cafes and restaurants in Sydney, ranging from the budget to the expensive. In Darlinghurst, most are either on Oxford St or Victoria St. In East Sydney, they're mainly on Stanley St between Riley and Crown Sts and are mostly Italian style.

Fast Food & Cafes The northern end of Victoria St, near Kings Cross, has plenty of eateries. Most are trendy and probably transient, but not the bustling *Bar Coluzzi (322 Victoria St),* which is a caffeine institution. Another stayer is the BYO *Una's Coffee Lounge (☎ 9360 6885, 340 Victoria St),* just south of Surrey St, an Austrian cafe that serves solid, inexpensive fare. Mains cost $8 to $14.

Bills 1 (433 Liverpool St) has a large communal table and a great selection of glossy magazines. It's open for breakfast and lunch; scrambled eggs cost $7.50, sweetcorn fritters with bacon $11.50.

At the busy *Fez Cafe (☎ 9360 9581, 247 Victoria St)* the food has a Middle-Eastern flavour; mains cost $7.50 to $16. It serves good coffee, and breakfast until 3 pm.

The *Bandstand Cafe* in Green Park is squeezed into a renovated bandstand. It serves coffee, cakes and basic light meals; lunches cost around $10 – and you can sit outside.

Le Petit Créme (☎ 9361 4738, 118 Darlinghurst Rd) is a popular French-style cafe, with some alfresco tables. Breakfasts start from $4.50. The small and appealing *Fishface (☎ 9332 4803, 132 Darlinghurst Rd)* serves delicious seafood and fills quickly in the evening. Classy beer-battered fish and chips costs $7.50.

Dov Cafe (☎ 9360 9594, 252 Forbes St), a popular BYO place in an old sandstone building, has delicious Mediterranean and Israeli-inspired food. Tasty cold dishes cost $8, cakes $4.50. It's also open for breakfast.

In East Sydney on Stanley St, the ultra-cheap *No Name* is above the Arch Coffee Lounge; there's no sign outside indicating it's there. Walk past the pool table and pinball machines right to the back, then climb the stairs. Filling spaghetti meals cost $6, a large salad $3. *Bill & Toni's (☎ 9360 4702, 74 Stanley St),* upstairs, is popular with locals. Pasta dishes start at $6.50.

For something more stylish try the licensed, mid-range *Cafe Divino (☎ 9360 9911, 70 Stanley St)* with its white tablecloths, blackboard menu and smartly dressed waiters. Chilli spaghetti costs $12.50. The

BYO *Palati Fini (☎ 9360 9121, 80 Stanley St)* has similar prices and is popular at dinner time. Penne carbonara is $13.

The voluminous *Baraza Cafe (☎ 9380 5197, 91 Riley St)* is a casual place to drop in for spicy cuttlefish laksa ($13.50) or a game of pool.

Restaurants The smart Hare Krishna restaurant *Govinda's (☎ 9380 5155, 112 Darlinghurst Rd)* serves healthy vegetarian food. It offers an all-you-can-gobble smorgasbord ($14.90) from 6 to 10.30 pm. The price includes admission to the cinema upstairs.

Fu Manchu (☎ 9360 9424, 249 Victoria St) is a funky place for a delicious and filling bowl of noodles ($9.50 to $12.50). You sit on red stools at long communal tables.

In East Sydney, long-standing *Beppi's (☎ 9360 4558),* on the corner of Stanley and Yurong Sts, serves traditional Italian fare. Expect to pay about $60 a head for a three-course meal.

Two Chefs (☎ 9331 1559, 115 Riley St) is a small, stylish restaurant with mains for $14.50 to $23.50.

The huge *Pacifico (☎ 9360 3811, upstairs, 95 Riley St),* between Stanley and William Sts, is an airy, upstairs Mexican cantina with enchiladas for $12.50 and guacamole for $8.50. *The Edge (☎ 9360 1372, 60 Riley St),* just opposite, is popular with Sydney foodies. It serves Modern Australian food; mains cost $18 to $24.

Oxford St & Around

Fast Food, Cafes & Pubs You can get fast, good-value North Indian and tandoori meals at *North Indian Flavour (129 Oxford St)* and *Tamana's,* nearby. A special of rice with a choice of three curries costs $3.50.

The area's prime people-watching spot is *Cafe 191 (☎ 9360 4295, Taylor Square).* Have a coffee or try the eclectic menu – Thai green curry costs $12.50.

The groovy, laid-back *Roobar (253 Crown St)* is another fine place to escape the hubbub. It serves open sandwiches ($7) and risotto ($12.50), and offers international calls and Internet access. Behind it is the tiny *Pablo's Vice (257 Crown St)*, on the corner of Goulburn St, which has killer coffees and outdoor perches.

For pasta on the cheap, visit the low-key *Maltese Cafe (310 Crown St)*, where you can fill up for $4 or $5.

If you don't mind the smell of beer, the refurbished *Burdekin Hotel (☎ 9331 3066, 2 Oxford St)*, near Hyde Park, serves pasta meat and vegie burgers for $10 to $15.

Restaurants The reassuringly homely *Betty's Soup Kitchen (☎ 9360 9698, 84 Oxford St)* is a better restaurant than its name might suggest. It has filling soup and damper for $5.50 and lamb stew for $8.80. Nearby is the modish and extremely busy *Thai Panic*, with excellent fresh curries and stir-fries that cost from $7.50 to $9.50.

Off Oxford St, by Oxford Square, *1 Burton (☎ 9331 4745)* is an upmarket Italian restaurant with outdoor tables and a name to match its address. Mains cost $18.50 to $21.

Beside Betty's on the corner of Crown St is the popular *Tandoori Palace (☎ 9331 7072, 86 Oxford St)*, where reasonably priced Indian food is served. Meat and vegetarian mains cost around $9. Farther down, cheerful *Don Don (☎ 9331 3544, 80 Oxford St)* offers delicious Japanese fare in generous portions. Udon soup with tempura is $7.50.

Along Oxford St east of Taylor Square is a clutch of mid-priced restaurants serving cuisine ranging from Cambodian to Californian. The long-established *Balkan (☎ 9360 4970, 209 Oxford St)* is a restaurant specialising in central European food. *Kim's (☎ 9380 5429, 235 Oxford St)* is a small, popular Vietnamese restaurant that has seafood and beef mains for $9 to $13. It's open for dinner daily, except Tuesday.

Surry Hills

Surry Hills is an interesting multicultural dining area. Crown St is its main food thoroughfare but it's a long street and cafes and restaurants occur in clusters. The biggest concentration is between Cleveland and Devonshire Sts, both of which also have a number of eateries.

Cafes The stylish and modern *Bills 2 (☎ 9360 4762, 355 Crown St)* is not quite as expensive as it looks; gourmet filled rolls cost $10.50 and dinner mains $10 to $15.

The vibrant *Rustic Cafe (☎ 9318 1034)*, on the corner of Crown and Devonshire Sts, has a varied menu including yam chips ($6.50) and rump steak ($13.90). There's a bar upstairs with sunny window seats.

The *Universal Deli Cafe (555 Crown St)* has quiche ($4), good sandwiches and coffee, and delicious fresh salads.

Mohr Fish (☎ 9218 1326, 202 Devonshire St) is a small but popular designer fish cafe; seafood mains cost around $17, takeaway fish and chips $7.

La Passion du Fruit, on the corner of Bourke and Devonshire Sts, is an inexpensive, popular cafe, with snacks like focaccia for around $6 and mains for $11. It's closed Sunday. *Johnnies Seafood Cafe*, on Fitzroy St, has grilled fish and chips for $4.80. *Cafe Niki (☎ 9319 7517, 544 Bourke St)* is a pleasant wood-lined cafe with fruit whips for $4, open bagels for $7, and comfortable outside seats.

Restaurants For consistently good food try *Prasit's Northside Thai Take-Away (☎ 9332 1792, 395 Crown St)*, a nifty, box-like Thai restaurant. Banana flower chicken salad is $13.50. A little south is the larger and pricier *Prasit's Northside on Crown (☎ 9319 0748, 413 Crown St)*, with a gorgeous gold-and-purple colour scheme, and mains at around $20. Farther south again, the spacious *Thai Orchid (☎ 9698 2097, 628 Crown St)* looks upmarket, but meat mains are only $9.80. Nearby is the smaller, more intimate *Thai Cotton (☎ 9319 3206, 622 Crown St)*; mains cost $8 to $11.

Lebanese eateries line Cleveland St between Elizabeth and Wilton Sts. *Abdul's (☎ 9698 1275, 565 Elizabeth St)* is basic but relaxed and friendly. Many dishes are under $6; shish kebabs cost $2. Most places charge less than $10 for mains, including *Fatima's (☎ 9698 4895, 296 Cleveland St)* and *Emad's (☎ 9698 2631)* next door.

Turkish pide (sort of a pizza) is popular along Cleveland St, especially at *Erciyes*

(409 Cleveland St), diagonally opposite the junction with Crown St. Almost everything on the menu is $8. *Golden Pide,* on the corner of Bourke and Cleveland Sts, serves pide for $6 or $7 and doner kebabs for $3 or $4.

For inexpensive Indian fare on Cleveland St there are several good options, including the BYO *Tandoori Rasoi* (☎ 9310 2470), on the corner of Bourke Sts. It serves meals such as chicken or vegetarian curry for $7.90, and you can watch your meal being prepared through a window to the kitchen.

The Uruguayan *Casapueblo* (☎ 9319 6377, 650 Bourke St), near the corner of Cleveland St, is one of the few South American restaurants in the city. It's open for dinner Tuesday to Saturday. Deftly spiced mains (like chicken with wine, leeks, beans and rice) cost around $14.50.

Paddington

Oxford St continues east from Darlinghurst through Paddington. Locating restaurants can be tricky, as the street numbers begin again at the junction with South Dowling St.

Fast Food, Cafes & Pubs Vegetarians have many options at *Sloanes* (☎ 9331 6717, 312 Oxford St), a modern little cafe with a courtyard. Mains cost from $7.50 to $12.50.

Centennial Park Cafe, a five-minute walk inside the park from the Centennial Square entrance off Oxford St, is good for those needing a touch of the rural. It's a pleasant, open-sided cafe surrounded by parkland – it serves Modern Australian lunches for around $12 to $17.

Fringe Bar & Cafe (☎ 9360 3554), on the corner of Oxford and Hopewell Sts, is a fashionable place in a renovated pub, offering filled focaccia for $6.50 and sushi for around $7.

At Five Ways (the junction of Glenmore Rd and Goodhope, Heeley and Broughton Sts) there are great views from the iron-laced balcony at *Royal Hotel* (☎ 9331 2604, 237 Glenmore Rd). Lemon risotto with zucchini flowers costs $12.50.

Noted for its fine dining, *Bellevue Hotel* (☎ 9363 2293, 159 Hargrave St) has mains for $17 to $18.

Restaurants There are several good restaurants at Five Ways. The BYO *Creperie Stivell* (☎ 9360 6191, 2b Heeley St) has a pleasant courtyard area and offers crepes, *pannequets* (a type of crepe) and blintzes for $4.90 to $13.90. The simple and beautifully decorated *Eat Thai* (☎ 9361 6640, 229 Glenmore Rd), on the corner of Heeley St, has a lovely atmosphere and a range of stir-fries, including spicy duck and rice noodles ($10.50).

Paddington has several distinguished restaurants, many of them Italian. They include *Darcy's* (☎ 9363 3706, 92 Hargrave St), which serves Italian seafood dishes such as smoked salmon penne; most mains cost $25.

At *Buon Ricordo* (☎ 9360 6729, 108 Boundary St) you can enjoy authentic Italian food for around $60 for three courses. Northern Italian cuisine is on offer at the large *Lucio's* (☎ 9380 5996, 47 Windsor St). Indulgent mains (like quails with bacon) cost $26.

Glebe

Glebe Point Rd was Sydney's original 'eat street' and though it has been left behind by the food innovations sweeping the inner east, it has a laid-back atmosphere and varied, good-value food.

Cafes On the corner of Francis St is the old favourite, *Badde Manors* (☎ 9660 3797, 37 Francis St). It's a relaxed, sometimes chaotic place. Salads cost from $6.50, pasta around $8.50, and there's a great gelati selection. Late breakfasts are popular on weekends.

Despite Glebe's 'students and bohemians' tag, many eateries have edged into higher price brackets, so it's good to see that the popular and relaxed *The Craven,* next to the old Valhalla Cinema, remains a good, inexpensive place for a coffee or meal. Filled focaccia starts at $5 and other dishes are around $10. Most nights it's open till 10.30 pm.

The very comfortable *Well Connected* (☎ 9566 2655, 35 Glebe Point Rd) offers coffee, all-day breakfasts and a good, fresh menu – plus two floors of computer terminals. A little farther down is *Lolita's,* a student hang-out with some good spots to sit and read. Bruschetta costs $4.50, focaccia $6.50.

Many of the eateries along Glebe Point Rd are sugar-rush heaven, and the tiny take-away *Pudding Shop* (☎ 9660 1794, 144b Glebe Point Rd) is a great source of the sweet and sticky. It also has hot pies.

Bogarts Pizza (☎ 9552 4656, 211 Glebe Point Rd), between Bridge and St Johns Rds, is reputed to have the best pizza ($7 to $17) on the strip, and also does pasta.

Restaurants For tapas ($6.80 to $11.80) such as king prawns cooked with chilli and ginger, try *Different Drummer* (☎ 9552 3406, 185 Glebe Point Rd).

Several Asian places offer excellent value for money. The friendly *Lien* (☎ 9660 2079, 331 Glebe Point Rd) serves Thai, Malaysian and Vietnamese food. It has vegetable dishes for $6.80 and seafood for $10.90. The nearby *Lilac Restaurant* (☎ 9660 5172, 333 Glebe Point Rd) serves Chinese, Malaysian and Indonesian food. Beef mains cost from $8.50, lunch specials are $5.80, and there's a good vegetarian selection.

Yak & Yeti (☎ 9552 1220, 41 Glebe Point Rd) is a Nepalese restaurant with vegetable dishes for around $10 and meat dishes for $12 to $16; there's not much elbow room, but the food is tasty.

Flavour of India (☎ 9692 0062, 142a Glebe Point Rd) is next to the Pudding Shop. Starters like chicken tikka cost $6.50 to $9.50. It also has a good vegetarian selection. A few blocks farther along, *Perry's Gourmet Pizzas* (☎ 9660 8440, 381 Glebe Point Rd) is a good pit stop for cheap pizzas.

Balmain

In Sydney's inner west, Balmain has some good eating places. Because much of the trade is local, the service is usually friendly and the standards consistent. Most are on Darling St, a good place to visit at night. You can get here by ferry from Circular Quay or bus Nos 441, 442, 445 and 446.

Near the Darling St wharf in East Balmain, *Pelicans Fine Foods* (81 Darling St) opens for breakfast, fresh-roasted coffee and light meals daily. Next door, *Reveille*

(☎ 9555 8874, 79 Darling St) has an eclectic French–Modern Australian menu and a select clientele. Mains cost around $23; it opens at 7 pm and is closed Sundays.

Sausolito (☎ 9810 9521, 246 Darling St) serves modern Italian and Mediterranean cuisine; focaccia starts at $6.50, pasta is $7.50. Tucked away behind the Institute Arcade is *La Lupa Trattoria* (☎ 9818 1645, 332 Darling St). Mains, mostly chicken or fish, cost $12.50 to $16.50.

In a house set back from the road, *Jiyu No Omise* (☎ 9818 3886, 342 Darling St) is a Japanese restaurant open for dinner. Teriyaki steak is $15.80. Nearby *Cafe Smooth* (☎ 9555 7008, 348 Darling St) is a relaxed cafe-gallery with paintings on the walls, magazines and books to read, and an unusual communal table as its centrepiece. A cooked breakfast costs $10.

Leichhardt

Leichhardt, another interesting culinary centre in Sydney's inner west, is known as Sydney's 'Little Italy'. You'll find most cafes and restaurants on Norton St, which is a short ride from George St on bus No 438 or 440.

Bar Italia (☎ 9560 9981, 169–171 Norton St) is an enormously popular restaurant, cafe and gelataria. Pasta mains cost around $7.50 and bar snacks from $3.50, but one of its biggest draw cards is the delicious gelato (from $3.50). The nearby *Cafe Barzu* (☎ 9550 0144, 121 Norton St) does excellent pizzas for $10 to $15, and has fancy cakes.

On the other side of the road, popular *Portofino* (☎ 9550 0782, 166 Norton St) is a cafe and bar with a large, diverse Italian menu. Pastas cost $12 to $19, seafood starts at $10. The small *Mezzapica* (☎ 9568 2095, 128 Norton St) is also popular.

Newtown

Newtown's long King St has a huge range of eateries, many budget-priced. You'll find plenty of places that serve ethnic cuisine, from African to Vietnamese, offering an interesting introduction to the suburb's community life.

The cheapest place to eat is the *Hare Krishna Centre* near the train station (turn left as you come out), open from 11 am to 3 pm Monday to Saturday. Sydney's Indian fast-food phenomenon is represented by *Tamana's Indian Diner*, which has two places on King St (Nos 196 and 236) offering three curries with rice for $4.90.

At the convivial *Green Iguana Cafe* (☎ 9516 3118, 6 King St) breakfast costs $2.50 to $7, potato-and-coriander soup $5.90. There's a notice board with information on neighbourhood happenings.

The entrance to the eccentric *Mac-Donna's* (☎ 9565 1102, 275 Australia St), just off King St, is decorated with a bizarre 'bead curtain' of strung-up kids' toys. Extravagant vegetarian burgers cost $5.50.

Le Kilimanjaro (☎ 9557 4565, 280 King St) is a bustling African restaurant with a menu full of tempting dishes such as spiced couscous. Mains are $8.50, side dishes $5.

Green Gourmet (☎ 9519 5330, 115 King St) is a roomy, Asian, vegetarian place. Mains start at $10, and there's a $6 lunch buffet.

Old Saigon (☎ 9519 5931, 107 King St) is an interesting Vietnamese restaurant with toy helicopters hanging from the ceiling and a hands-on approach to cuisine: You can cook your own meat at the table (complete with hissing grill) and construct individualised rice-paper rolls. Mains cost about $12.

Back at the Ranch (☎ 9519 7869, 175 King St) is a Tex-Mex restaurant that's especially good value at lunch time when meals are almost half-price. At dinner time, enchiladas and burritos cost $11.90.

Double Bay

This exclusive neighbourhood has some excellent (and expensive) places to eat, many on and around Bay St.

Peron's (☎ 9328 6004, 42 Bay St) is part of the Cosmopolitan shopping centre and serves a range of delicious salads and snacks. The nearby *Courtyard Cafe* (☎ 9326 1602, 37 Bay St) serves good pasta; mushroom gnocchi costs $10.90. One of the city's top Italian restaurants is the spacious but intimate *Botticelli* (☎ 9363 3266, 21 Bay St), where pasta mains cost $15 to $19. It's a good place for a romantic dinner.

Taste of India (☎ 9327 5712, 370 New South Head Rd), near Knox St, is one of the best Indian restaurants in Sydney. A mushroom bhaji is $11.90, mango chicken $13.90.

Bondi Beach & Around

Campbell Parade is one long string of takeaways, cafes and restaurants, many with sea views. Hall St, leading away from the beach, also has some interesting places.

The good-value *Gusto* (☎ 9130 4565, 16 Hall St) is a popular little deli. It has healthy snacks at fairly low prices; chicken-and-cheese melts cost $7. The nearby *On the Rise* (☎ 9365 1278, 39 Hall St) is a bakery-cum-eatery selling muffins, gourmet breads, and filled focaccia for $5.

Beneath the Swiss Grand Hotel, the *Hog's Breath Cafe*, on Campbell Parade, has reasonably priced food and drink; chicken burgers are $9.95. A few doors along, *Nando's* is the place for Portuguese-style barbecued chicken. *Noodle King* (☎ 9130 8822, 126 Campbell Parade) does good, cheap meals; barbecue pork wonton noodle soup or chicken laksa costs $6.50.

There's a strip of trendy cafes/bars at the southern end of the beach. Most of them have outdoor seating, ocean views and Mediterranean-influenced bistro fare. At *Lamrock Cafe* (☎ 9130 6313, 72 Campbell Parade) risotto costs $12.90 and vegetarian burgers $10.50.

In North Bondi, *Sean's Panorama* (☎ 9365 4924, 270 Campbell Parade) and *Aqua Bar* (☎ 9130 6070, 266 Campbell Parade) next door are extremely popular with locals for weekend brunches, and they also offer changing Modern Australian menus.

Also in North Bondi, the *RSL Club* (☎ 9130 3152, 118–120 Ramsgate Ave) has lunch specials for $4.

Sushi Rawbar (☎ 9365 7200), on the corner of Warners and Wairoa Aves, does traditional Japanese food. Excellent sashimi costs $8.80, California rolls cost $7.50 and chicken teriyaki costs $12.80. Directly opposite, the light and airy *Jackies* (☎ 9300 9812) does good Modern Australian cuisine.

At the southern end of the beach, *Fu Manchu* (☎ 9300 0416, 80 Campbell Pa-

rade), younger sibling of the eponymous noodle bar in Darlinghurst, has filling noodle soups with Asian greens for $9.50. There are daily seafood specials, and tables outside. The popular **Bondi Tratt** *(☎ 9365 4303, 34 Campbell Parade)* is good for breakfast; delectable marscapone-and-banana honey pancakes cost $7.50.

Heading upmarket, the stylish **Hugo's** *(☎ 9300 0900, 70 Campbell Parade),* near Lamrock Ave, is a groovy place to show off your designer shades. Lunch mains cost around $16; a full dinner will cost around $50. The Modern Australian food is fabulous and the view even better, but don't sit outside if it's windy.

There are a couple of good restaurants back towards the city. **Indochine** *(☎ 9387 4081, 99 Bondi Rd)* is a popular Vietnamese place, with braised pork for $10.30.

Coogee

There are numerous takeaways on Coogee Bay Rd offering cheap eats, but you're better off hitting the cafes for healthier food, sunnier demeanours and outdoor tables. **Cafe Congo** *(☎ 9665 3101, 208 Arden St),* north of Coogee Bay Rd, is popular, inexpensive and colourful. There's nothing African about the menu, which is mostly Italian with a mix of Mexican. Nachos cost $7, lasagne $8. The nearby **La Casa** is similarly priced, with spaghetti or fish and chips for $9.

There are several bright, pleasant places on Coogee Bay Rd serving standard cafe fare for between $5 and $11, including the beach-theme **Coogee Cafe** *(221 Coogee Bay Rd),* where most lunches cost $8, and the colourful **Globe** *(203 Coogee Bay Rd),* with breakfasts (until 3 pm) from $4 and sandwiches from around $5.

Renato's *(☎ 9665 8975, 237 Coogee Bay Rd)* is a good-value Italian restaurant, which has pasta from $7 to $9. Nearby is **Erciyes 2** *(☎ 9664 1913, 240 Coogee Bay Rd),* which is an offshoot of the popular Erciyes Turkish restaurant in Surry Hills. The food, including kebabs, dips and salads, is tasty and inexpensive, with nothing over $9.

On Dolphin St at the Beach Palace Hotel (1st floor) is the large **Regal Pearl** *(☎ 9665 3308),* an upmarket Chinese restaurant specialising in seafood. Lobster tail goes for $35.

Watsons Bay

The long-established **Doyle's on the Beach** *(☎ 9337 2007, 11 Marine Parade)* is famous for its seafood. Main courses average around $25. Next door, at **Doyle's on the Quay**, which shares the fabulous view, most mains are similarly priced, although indulgent dishes like lobster and smoked salmon salad cost around $43.

Right on the water, **Doyle's Wharf Restaurant** *(☎ 9337 1572),* Watsons Bay Wharf, is open daily for lunch, Wednesday to Saturday for dinner. Lobster straight from the tank is $60. At lunch time on weekdays you can catch Doyle's water taxi from the Harbour Master's Steps on the western side of Circular Quay to Watsons Bay. The taxi costs $6/10 one way/return, and services start at 11.30 am.

On the other side of Robertson Park, in the beautiful old Dunbar House, **Fisherman's Lodge** *(☎ 9337 1226)* is a slightly less expensive option (the Atlantic salmon costs $23.50).

North Shore

Crows Nest, north-west of North Sydney, has many popular eating places. Most are on or near the three-way intersection of the Pacific Hwy, Falcon St and Willoughby Rd.

At **Wood Fire Pizza Company** *(☎ 9439 3113, 308 Pacific Hwy)* the specialty is almost a health food. The pizzas aren't cheap ($12.90 to $16.90) but the quality is good, with exotic toppings like artichokes, brie, snow peas and scallops.

Along Willoughby Rd, the main shopping precinct, places to try include the upstairs **Blue Elephant** *(☎ 9439 3468, 36–38 Willoughby Rd);* it has Sri Lankan food for around $15. **Talay Thai** *(☎ 9906 3535, 88 Willoughby Rd)* has stir-fries for $9 to $12.50 (takeaways are a little cheaper); there are outside tables.

Borderland *(☎ 9436 3918, 97 Willoughby Rd)* is a Mexican restaurant offering lunches like dips for $5.50 and nachos for $5.80;

dinner mains cost $10.90 to $17.50. The crowded but low-key **Ten-Sun** (☎ *9906 2956, 103 Willoughby Rd*), north of Albany St, is a Japanese noodle bar, with meals under $10.

A block west, Alexander St also has some good restaurants, including the large **Rangoon Racquet Club** (☎ *9906 4091, 70 Alexander St*). It doesn't serve Burmese food, but rather, the 'aromatic cuisine of British colonial India'. Elephant boy curry (beef marinated in a spicy sauce) costs $15.50, dhal $8.95.

North Sydney Noodle Market (☎ *0412 335 660*) is a praiseworthy attempt to capture the atmosphere of Asian street-food markets. It's held in the park near the corner of Miller and McLaren Sts in North Sydney from 5.30 pm on Friday from October to Easter. Numerous stalls serve Chinese, Indian, Malaysian, Nepalese and Vietnamese food.

Prasit's Northside Thai (☎ *9957 2271, 77 Mount St*), on the corner of Elizabeth Plaza, is a licensed Thai restaurant with good spiced fish cakes for $9.90, and mains for around $15.50.

For innovative fish and seafood, head to **Just Hooked** (☎ *9460 2223, 236 Military Rd*). Specialities include seafood paella, and simple but delicious fish and chips. Main courses cost $16 to $19.

In the quiet suburb of Balmoral, you'll find good restaurants, most with views across the harbour. Between Raglan St and Botanic Rd are some inexpensive cafes, including **Sam's Espresso Bar**, which has filling sandwiches for $3 to $4, and good cakes. Nearby **Bottom of the Harbour** (*21 East Esplanade*), serves some of the best fish and chips ($5.65) in Sydney.

In the prime location on the foreshore in a beautiful old building is **Bathers' Pavilion** (☎ *9969 5050, 59 The Esplanade*). Innovative chef Serge Dansereau creates gastronomic wonders to match the Moorish interior and the amazing views across the harbour to North Head. Be warned: You pay for what you get. The stylish **Bathers' Pavilion Cafe** (☎ *9969 5050*) is more affordable but still with great food. Pasta costs $15, wood-fired pizza $16 and desserts $12.

Equally well positioned, the swanky **Watermark** (☎ *9968 3433, 2a The Esplanade*), at the junction with Botanic Rd, has views of the marina and across to Manly. Scallop ravioli costs $22.

Manly

You don't have to go any farther than the wharf to eat ($4 to $7); The Corso is also jammed with places, and there are others along North and South Steyne.

On Shelly Beach east of the main beach is **Shelly Beach Kiosk**, where you can get sandwiches for $4.50, and ice creams.

Cafe Steyne (☎ *9977 0116, 14 South Steyne*) serves everything from daiquiris to melts, though an average dish on the large menu is pasta from $6.80 to $12.30. The chic but laid-back Tunisian eatery **Cafe Tunis** (☎ *9976 2805, 30–31 South Steyne*) has good coffee and interesting food. Pitta bread rolls with a choice of fillings cost from $10.50.

BarKing Frog (☎ *9977 6307, 48 North Steyne*) is a fashionable bar and cafe with good coffee, starters such as baked bruschetta for $9.80 and mains from $18.

Fresh (*1/49 North Steyne*) has quick and tasty budget fare, including muesli, fresh juices and giant cheese melts ($3.50).

For a reasonably priced Thai meal, try **Wi Marn** (☎ *9976 2995, 47 North Steyne*), which has starters for $6 and seafood dishes from $13.

Follow the foreshore path east from the main ocean beach to reach the small **Bower Restaurant** (☎ *9977 5451, 7 Marine Parade*), on tiny Fairy Bower beach. It has snacks, coffees and main courses of Modern Australian food ($23). It's BYO and is open for breakfast and lunch daily. Farther around at Shelly Beach is the upmarket **Le Kiosk Restaurant** (☎ *9977 4122, 1 Marine Parade*), serving mostly Asian-influenced seafood. Expect to pay about $55.

For tasty Malay and Thai dishes, **Malacca Straits Satay Restaurant** (☎ *9977 6627, 49 Sydney Rd*) has a good reputation, if a slightly dubious colour scheme. Main courses cost $7 to $13.

There's a seafood buffet at **Manly Pacific Parkroyal** (☎ *9977 7666, 55 North Steyne*, for $31.50 weekdays and $34.50 weekends, and a champagne-and-jazz lunch on Sunday for $26.50.

On Manly Wharf, *Armstrong's* (☎ 9976 3835), at the western end, has a good reputation for Modern Australian food, with the emphasis on seafood. Crisp-skinned salmon with asparagus costs $15.

ENTERTAINMENT

The *Sydney Morning Herald*'s 'Metro' section, published on Fridays, lists most events in town for the week ahead. The free weekly *Sydney City Hub* is a street-smart rag bursting with news on music and arty events. For more specialised music listings pick up one of the free and widely available weekly papers such as *Drum Media*, *Revolver* or *3D World*.

Ticketek (☎ 9266 4800), 195 Elizabeth St, is the city's main booking agency for theatre, concerts, sports and other events. Phone bookings can be made from 7.30 am to 10 pm weekdays, 9 am to 4 pm Saturday, and 9 am to 8 pm Sunday. It also has agencies around town and publishes a bimonthly *Entertainment Guide*.

Halftix (☎ 9966 1622), 201 Sussex St, near Cockle Bay Wharf, sells half-price seats to shows. Tickets are only available for shows that night. Halftix is open daily except Sunday. You can also book through the Web site at www.halftix.com.au.

Performing Arts

The *Sydney Opera House* (☎ 9250 7777) is the performing arts centre of Sydney. Opera Australia, The Australian Ballet, The Sydney Symphony Orchestra, Sydney Philharmonia Choirs, Musica Viva Australia and the Sydney Theatre Company stage regular performances here.

For more information on companies' programs contact: *Australian Ballet* (☎ 9223 9522, Level 15, 115 Pitt St); *Australian Opera* (☎ 9319 1088, 480 Elizabeth St, Surry Hills); *Musica Viva Australia* (☎ 9698 1711, 120 Chalmers St, Surry Hills); *Sydney Dance Company* (☎ 9221 4811, Pier 4, Hickson Rd, Walsh Bay); *Sydney Philharmonia Choirs* (☎ 9251 2024, Pier 4, Hickson Rd, Walsh Bay); or the *Sydney Symphony Orchestra* (☎ 9334 4644, 52 William St, East Sydney).

Theatre Sydney has numerous theatres and a vigorous calendar of productions, ranging from Broadway and West End shows at mainstream theatres to experimental theatre at smaller inner-suburban venues. Most tickets cost from $20 to $50.

Sydney Opera House (☎ 9250 7777) has three main theatres. The *Drama Theatre* regularly puts on plays by the Sydney Theatre Company, and the *Playhouse* offers everything from Aboriginal performances to Shakespeare; the new *Studio* venue hosts contemporary arts and musical events.

The Sydney Theatre Company, the city's top theatre company, has its own venue at the *Wharf Theatre* (☎ 9250 1777, Pier 4, Hickson Rd, Walsh Bay).

The major commercial theatres are: the restored *Capitol Theatre* (☎ 9320 5000, 17 Campbell St, Haymarket); *Her Majesty's Theatre* (☎ 9212 3411, 107 Quay St) near Railway Square; and the *Theatre Royal* (☎ 9320 9191, MLC Centre, King St) in the city centre. A sight in itself is the opulent *State Theatre* (☎ 9373 6655, 49 Market St), between Pitt and George Sts – they don't make them like this any more! These theatres are often the venues chosen for imported big-budget productions.

On the North Shore, the small *Ensemble Theatre* (☎ 9929 0644, 78 McDougall St, Milsons Point) presents mainstream theatre in a great setting on the waterfront.

The *National Institute of Dramatic Art* (NIDA; ☎ 9697 7600, 215 Anzac Parade, Kensington), at the University of NSW, regularly stages excellent productions by its students. At the University of Sydney, the *Footbridge Theatre* (☎ 9692 9955), Parramatta Rd, Glebe, is also worth keeping an eye on.

The *Seymour Theatre Centre* (☎ 9364 9444), on the corner of Cleveland St and City Rd, Chippendale, houses three theatres offering a variety of performances.

The *Belvoir Street Theatre* (☎ 9699 3444, 25 Belvoir St, Surry Hills) and *Stables*

Theatre (☎ 9361 3817, 10 Nimrod St, Kings Cross) feature original, experimental Australian works.

The not-so-new *New Theatre (☎ 9519 3403, 542 King St, Newtown)* produces some cutting-edge drama in addition to traditional pieces.

Aboriginal Performance You can see dance inspired by tradition performed by the renowned *Bangarra Dance Theatre (☎ 9569 4555, 40–76 William St, Leichhardt);* the *Aboriginal Dance Theatre (☎ 9699 2171, 88 Renwick St, Redfern);* and the *National Aboriginal & Islander Skills Development Association (☎ 9252 0199, 3 Cumberland St, The Rocks).*

Cinemas

There's a cluster of mainstream multi-screen cinemas on George St south of Town Hall between Bathurst and Liverpool Sts. New releases at these major cinemas cost a pricey $12.50, but they're cheaper on Tuesday. Films screening are listed in the daily press.

One cinema that shows inexpensive mainstream films is the *Ritz Theatre (☎ 9611 4811, 43 St Paul's St, Randwick).* It charges just $7 ($4 children) for all sessions.

Two cinemas on the North Shore are *Greater Union (☎ 9969 1988, 9 Spit Rd, Mosman)* and the *Manly Twin Cinemas (☎ 9977 0644, 43 East Esplanade, Manly).*

The new *Fox Studios Australia* film and entertainment complex *(☎ 9383 4000, Driver Ave, Moore Park)* has a whopping 16 Hoyts cinemas, four of which show independent and art-house films.

For more unusual fare, try the independent *Dendy (☎ 9247 3800, 2 East Circular Quay),* which shows alternative as well as commercial films. It has other cinemas: at 19 Martin Place on the corner of Castlereagh St (☎ 9233 8166); and 261 King St (☎ 9550 5699) in Newtown (turn right out of the train station). Tickets cost $12 ($7.50 on Monday).

Other cinemas showing foreign and alternative films are: *Academy Twin (☎ 9361 4453, 3a Oxford St); Hayden Orpheum Picture Palace (☎ 9908 4344),* at the junction of Military and Cremorne Rds, Cremorne, a fabulous Art-Deco gem; the upstairs *Verona Cinema (☎ 9360 6099, 17 Oxford St, Paddington); Encore Cinema (☎ 9281 6493, 64 Devonshire St, Surry Hills); Walker Cinema (☎ 9959 4222, 121 Walker St, North Sydney).*

In Darlinghurst south of Kings Cross, the cushioned *Movie Room (☎ 9360 7853, 9380 5155, 112 Darlinghurst Rd),* above Govinda's restaurant, shows mainstream blockbusters, art-house fare and old favourites. Admission is $14.90, but includes an all-you-can-eat smorgasbord at Govinda's. There are screenings nightly at 7.30 and 9.30 pm. Govinda's opens at 6 pm.

The Australian Film Institute (AFI; ☎ 9332 2111) screens interesting new work and classics at the *Sydney Film Centre/ Chauvel Cinemas (☎ 9361 5398),* Paddington Town Hall, Oxford St. The AFI is the best to contact for information.

Centennial Park is the outdoor venue for the excellent twilight *Moonlight Cinema (☎ 1900 933 899, 13 6100 for bookings),* which has screenings during summer.

Pubs & Bars

Pubs and bars are an important part of Sydney's social scene. Many pubs now have the ubiquitous poker machines, most serve food and some have live entertainment. There's often a totally different atmosphere during the week compared with the weekend, when the hordes are out on the town.

City Centre A must for most visitors is the ornate *Marble Bar (☎ 9266 0610, 259 Pitt St),* underneath the Sydney Hilton Hotel. It has live music some nights, including blues and jazz.

Two contrasting pubs face each other on the corners of York and King Sts – the traditional *Forbes Hotel* and the trendy Art-Deco *CBD Hotel.* Both are popular with office and shop workers.

As yet untouched by the renovating squad, *Century Tavern,* on the corner of George and Liverpool Sts, has a downbeat rock and roll charm, and curved glass windows looking down onto the street.

Super stylish and popular with sharply dressed types, the nevertheless cosy *Wine*

Banc (53 Martin Place) is a modern cigar-cum-wine bar tucked away in an old bank vault.

The Rocks & Circular Quay There are some nice old pubs in The Rocks. The *Fortune of War (137 George St)*, behind the Museum of Contemporary Art, claims to hold Sydney's oldest hotel licence – but a couple of other pubs nearby disagree.

Both in Millers Point, *Hero of Waterloo (81 Lower Fort St)* and *Lord Nelson Brewery Hotel (19 Kent St)* are probably Sydney's best-known pubs and two of its busiest. Both vie for the title of 'Sydney's oldest pub'. Hero of Waterloo has music on weekends, including traditional Irish music, and the Lord Nelson brews its own beer.

One of Sydney's best places for Guinness and regular live Irish music is the beautifully green-tiled *Mercantile Hotel (25 George St)*, near the Harbour Bridge.

The more upmarket *Harts Pub*, on the corner of Gloucester and Essex Sts, The Rocks, has live music on Thursday and Friday. The *George St Bar (199 George St)* is another upmarket (but more modern) boozer.

If you're feeling sophisticated, the bar at the smart *Bennelong* restaurant in the Opera House is a good spot to drop in for a cocktail, hear some live jazz, and check out the awesome architecture – dress respectably and you'll be welcome. *Legends* is an upmarket bar on Bligh St under the Wentworth Hotel. A neon sign promises 'free beer tomorrow'.

Darling Harbour & Pyrmont The *Pumphouse Tavern Brewery (17 Little Pier St)*, near the Sydney Entertainment Centre, offers a variety of beers brewed on the premises.

Pyrmont Bridge Hotel (96 Union St) is a typical Sydney pub that's pleasantly unpretentious given its surroundings. The more formal upstairs bar has good city views.

Kings Cross & Around Kings Cross and surrounding areas have plenty of places where you can go for a drink. The huge *Kings Cross Hotel*, near Kings Cross station, is recommended by many travellers as a reasonable place for a night out. More expensive places in the Cross include *Cafe Iguana* and *Dean's Cafe* on Kellet St. Both have front courtyards. *Soho Bar (Piccadilly Hotel, 171 Victoria St)*, has good cocktails.

Old Fitzroy Hotel, on the corner of Cathedral and Dowling Sts, Woolloomooloo, is popular with British backpackers and has good live theatre nights.

Oxford St & Around A number of good pubs line Oxford St. These include the *Burdekin Hotel (2 Oxford St)*, which has a stylish cocktail bar downstairs and a fashionable restaurant upstairs. *Lizard Lounge (Exchange Hotel, 34 Oxford St)* is a casual bar popular with lesbians. Farther east is the discreet but groovy *Q Bar (44 Oxford St)*, a cavernous bar/nightclub-cum-pool hall above Central Station Records.

On the other side of Taylor Square, the *Albury Hotel (6 Oxford St)* in Paddington is a gay pub that often has good entertainment, including drag shows. Other gay pubs in the area include: *Beauchamp Hotel*, on the corner of Oxford and South Dowling Sts; *Flinders Hotel (63 Flinders St);* and *Beresford Hotel (354 Bourke St)*.

Lively pubs for 20-somethings include the *Fringe Bar (106 Oxford St)*, near the Victoria Barracks, and the *Palace Hotel (122 Flinders St)* at the junction with South Dowling St.

The funky *Darlo Bar*, on the corner of Darlinghurst and Liverpool Sts, is a good place for a drink. Occupying its own tiny block, this is surely the narrowest pub in Sydney. It's pretty much a neighbourhood pub, but it's a very interesting neighbourhood. Good food, drinks and cocktails are available, and the service is friendly.

Surry Hills The popular *Cricketers Arms (106 Fitzroy St)* sometimes has DJs. The renovated *Dolphin Hotel (412 Crown St)*, on the corner of Fitzroy St, is good for a quiet drink or a meal in the large restaurant. The *Bentley Bar (320 Crown St)*, on the corner of Campbell St, is another reasonable local.

Glebe The eccentric *Friend in Hand Hotel (58 Cowper St)*, full of old photos and crazy bric-a-brac and with a resident cockatoo, has a reputation as a party pub. It stages events such as crab racing (Wednesday) and poetry slams (Tuesday); there's music on Friday and Sunday.

Another popular Glebe pub is *Harold Park Hotel (115 Wigram Rd)*, which has a sunny courtyard beer garden.

Newtown The trendy *Bank Hotel (324 King St)* has a beer garden and is popular with lesbians, especially on Wednesday. Another pub with a beer garden is *Iron Duke Hotel*, on the corner of Botany and McEvoy Rds; it sometimes has live music on weekends. The busy *Botany View Hotel (597 King St)* serves decent Guinness on tap. *Marlborough Hotel (145 King St)* has live music on weekends and a Wednesday night trivia quiz.

Live Music

There are plenty of pubs, clubs and bars offering live music, and five-star hotels often have famous cabaret artists.

The Basement (☎ 9251 2797, 29 Reiby Place, Circular Quay) has good food, good jazz and sometimes big international names. It's a smoke-free venue. *The Bridge (☎ 9810 1260, 135 Victoria Rd, Rozelle)* has rock, DJs and comedy. Sometimes big Aussie names and overseas acts perform here. The *Cat & Fiddle Hotel (☎ 9810 7931, 456 Darling St, Balmain)* has jazz, blues, pop and rock bands nightly except Monday.

The *Golden Sheaf Hotel (☎ 9327 5877, 429 New South Head Rd, Double Bay)* has a free band on Sunday night and DJs Wednesday to Saturday (lounge, funk and groove). It has good food and is popular with travellers. The *Hopetoun Hotel (☎ 9361 5257, 416 Bourke St, Surry Hills)*, a tiny corner pub, has live independent bands.

The *Lansdowne Hotel (☎ 9211 2325, 2 City Rd, Chippendale)* has live independent, world music, jazz and hip-hop Sunday to Thursday, and DJs Friday and Saturday ($5).

Rose, Shamrock & Thistle Hotel – 'The Three Weeds' (☎ 9810 2244, 193 Evans St), on the corner of Belmore St, Rozelle, has rock, pop, blues and folk bands (sometimes big names) Thursday to Sunday.

Selina's (☎ 9665 0000), at the Coogee Bay Hotel, Coogee Bay Rd, Coogee, has rock (often top Australian and international bands) for which you can pay a fair bit; the main nights are Friday and Saturday, but there are cheaper bands most other nights.

Nightclubs

You'll find beats of almost every description in Sydney. *Cauldron (☎ 9331 1523, 207 Darlinghurst Rd)*, on the corner of Farrel Ave, Darlinghurst, is a long-running, slick basement club popular with the fashion-conscious 'in crowd'. Music ranges from retro to house. *DCM (☎ 9267 7380, 33 Oxford St, Darlinghurst)* is a large, mixed gay-straight disco (Sydney's biggest), with weekend drag shows. Wear your hot pants.

Midnight Shift (☎ 9360 4319, 85–91 Oxford St, Darlinghurst), a gay club on two levels with a big dance floor and great lighting, is popular with dancing queens. Lesbian night is on the third Thursday of each month. *Q Bar (☎ 9360 1375, Level 2, 44 Oxford St)* is a groovy, hard-to-find pool hall-cum-club tucked away above a record shop. It has R&B, house, trip-hop and drum and bass, and is open extra late.

Cave (☎ 9566 4755, Star City Casino, Pyrmont) is a flashy joint. The music is predominantly house and techno. *Home (☎ 9266 0600, Cockle Bay Wharf, Darling Harbour)* is a huge, hip and happening club on three levels, with over-the-top lighting, playing mostly house music. It has international DJs on Saturday and a hefty admission charge ($10 to $25).

Soho Bar (☎ 9358 4221, 171 Victoria St, Potts Point), at the Picadilly Hotel, is four different bars in one; watch the attitude on the door. It has funk, groove and commercial house.

Slipp-Inn (☎ 9299 4777, 111 Sussex St) is a hip joint playing a mishmash of breakbeat, house, garage, drum and bass and hip-hop.

Comedy

The *Comedy Store (☎ 9357 1419, Fox Studios, Driver Avenue, Moore Park)* has shows from 8.30 pm; the box office is open 10 am to 5 pm daily. Relocated from its former Petersham location, the Comedy Store is a plush cabaret-style nightclub with seating for over 250 people. It has launched talents such as Vince Sorrenti, Kitty Flanagan and Rash Ryder.

The *Enmore Theatre (☎ 9550 3666, 130 Enmore Rd, Newtown)* presents stand-up comedians with ethnic backgrounds as diverse as Sydney's. *Wogs out of Work* is one of its success stories. Tickets are $20 to $50.

The *Fringe Bar (☎ 9360 3554, 106 Oxford St, Paddington)* is another venue that often has live comedy acts. Tickets are $4.

RSL & Leagues Clubs

A lot of evening entertainment in Sydney takes place in Returned Services League (RSL) and football leagues clubs. This can include big-name acts – from old crooners to decent Australian rock. The clubs may be 'members only' for locals, but as an interstate or international visitor you would generally be welcome. Ring ahead and ask.

The most lavish club is the *St George Leagues Club (☎ 9587 1022, 124 Princes Hwy, Kogarah)*. More centrally, there are: *City of Sydney RSL & Community Club (☎ 9264 6281, 565 George St);* the *South Sydney Leagues Club (☎ 9319 4156, 263 Chalmers St, Redfern); Balmain Leagues Club (☎ 9555 1650, 138 Victoria Rd, Rozelle);* and the *Sydney Aussie Rules Social Club (☎ 9358 3055, 28 Darlinghurst Rd, Kings Cross)*.

Gambling

Australians love to gamble and Sydney provides plenty of opportunity for punters to be separated from their money. The *Star City Casino* complex is on the waterfront in Pyrmont. It's open 24 hours; for information, call ☎ 1300 300 711. A free shuttle bus connects The Rocks and city centre with the casino, or you can catch the ferry to the Pyrmont Bay wharf, just across the road from the casino.

Sydney has four horse-racing venues: *Canterbury Park (☎ 9930 4000, King St, Canterbury)*, south-west of the city centre; *Rosehill Gardens (☎ 9930 4070, Grand Ave, Rosehill)*, near Parramatta; *Royal Randwick*

(☎ 9663 8400, Alison Rd, Randwick), closest to the city, near Centennial Park; and *Warwick Farm (☎ 9602 6199, Hume Hwy, Rosehill)*, near Liverpool.

Horse racing alternates between these tracks throughout the year. However, it's more colourful and exciting during the spring and autumn carnivals, when major events like the Golden Slipper at Rosehill or the Sydney Cup at Randwick take place.

A little down the social scale are harness-racing meetings at *Harold Park Paceway (☎ 9660 3688, Ross St, Glebe)* and greyhound racing at *Wentworth Park (☎ 9552 1799, Wentworth Park Rd)*, also in Glebe.

Coin-fed gambling machines known as pokies (poker machines) are the most common form of gambling. They're everywhere.

Free Entertainment

On summer weekends there's free music in many parks, especially in The Domain during the Sydney Festival in January. There's often free music at lunch times in Martin Place, at Darling Harbour and (on Tuesdays) at St Andrew's Cathedral next to the Town Hall.

Over the Labour Day long weekend (early October) there are free outdoor jazz concerts at the Manly Jazz Festival. You can be entertained by buskers around the Opera House and Circular Quay, in The Rocks and Kings Cross, and along The Corso in Manly. Alternatively, you can listen to the mad and the erudite venting their obsessions at Speakers Corner in The Domain on Sunday afternoon.

There's a free Aboriginal dance performance at the Art Gallery of NSW at noon Tuesday to Saturday. There's also free entertainment at many of Sydney's weekend flea markets.

Tropfest (☎ 9368 0434) is a one-day short film festival in late February, which screens simultaneously at The Domain and in Darlinghurst's Victoria St (which is blocked off for the occasion).

SPECTATOR SPORTS

You'll find vocal crowds and world-class athletes in action most weekends of the year.

Surf Lifesaving Carnivals

The volunteer surf lifesaver is one of Australia's icons, but despite the macho image, many are female.

You can see lifesavers in action each summer at surf carnivals along the coast. Check at a local surf lifesaving club for dates or contact Surf Life Saving NSW (☎ 9984 7188), PO Box 430, Narrabeen NSW 2101.

Football

The football season runs from March to September.

Rugby League Sydney is one of the world capitals of rugby league. The main competition is run by the National Rugby League (NRL) and includes interstate sides (and a New Zealand team). Games are played at various grounds, but the sell-out finals are played in September at the *Sydney Football Stadium* (☎ 9360 6601) in Moore Park. Tickets to most games cost from $15 to $25.

The Australian Rugby League (ARL) runs the other big rugby league series – the State of Origin, played between NSW and Queensland – and international matches.

Rugby Union Rugby union is a less brutal game than rugby league, and has a less fanatical following, but the Wallabies (the Australian rugby union team) are world-beaters. You can occasionally see them in action against international teams.

Australian Rules The Sydney Swans home ground is the 40,000-seat *Sydney Cricket Ground (SCG;* ☎ 9360 6601) in Moore Park, though the Kangaroos have also played some experimental 'home' games at the SCG since 1999. Tickets cost from $14.60 to $27.

Soccer Games are played at the Sydney Football Stadium and other grounds. For information, contact Soccer Australia (☎ 9380 6099).

Cricket

The *SCG* (☎ 9360 6601), Moore Park, Paddington, is the venue for sparsely attended interstate matches, well-attended Test matches and sell-out World Series Cup (one-day, international) matches. Local district games are also played here. The cricket season runs from October to March.

Tennis

The NSW Open (which is held in the second week of January as a prelude to the Australian Open in Melbourne) has moved to the *NSW Tennis Centre* at Homebush Bay. Ground passes cost $20 per day and reserved seats from $25 to $70.

Indoor games are played at the *Sydney Entertainment Centre* (☎ 9320 4200) near Darling Harbour.

Yachting

On weekends, hundreds of yachts weave around ferries and ships on Sydney Harbour. Many are racing, and the most spectacular are the speedy 18-footers. The racing season runs from mid-September to late March. The oldest and largest 18-footer club is the Sydney Flying Squadron (☎ 9955 8350), 76 McDougall St, on the northern side of Kirribilli Point.

The greatest yachting event on Sydney Harbour is the Boxing Day (26 December) start of the Sydney to Hobart Yacht Race. The harbour is crammed with competitors, media boats and a huge spectator fleet. Special ferries are scheduled by Sydney Ferries to follow the boats; call ☎ 13 1500 in November to find out when tickets go on sale.

Basketball

Australia's basketball league has all the razzmatazz of US pro basketball (and quite a few US players as well), thanks largely to the TV coverage it receives. The season runs from April to November and games are played on weekends at the *Sydney Entertainment Centre* (☎ 9320 4200). The teams in Sydney are the Kings (men) and the Flames (women).

Netball

Netball doesn't have as high a profile as basketball in Australia, even though the Australian team won the World Championships in 1999. The game can be just as exciting to watch; finals matches in particular. Sydney's National Netball League teams (women) are the Sydney Swifts and the Sydney Sandpipers. The netball season runs from April to August and games are played on weekends at the Anne Clark Centre in Lidcombe. For information contact Netball NSW (☎ 9552 6077).

SHOPPING

Shopping centres in the city include the QVB (on George St), the Strand Arcade (between Pitt St Mall and George St), the Royal Arcade (beneath the Sydney Hilton Hotel), and the Imperial Arcade (connecting Pitt St Mall and Castlereagh St).

Next to the Imperial Arcade is the Centrepoint shopping centre, beneath the Sydney Tower, and nearby is the seven-storey Skygarden. Two of the newer shopping centres are Piccadilly, south of Pitt St Mall, and the upmarket Chifley Plaza, on the corner of Elizabeth and Hunter Sts. In The Rocks, there's the Argyle Centre, and at Darling Harbour there's Harbourside.

The biggest shopping centre in North Sydney is Greenwood Plaza, above North Sydney station.

Major department stores are Gowings, on the corner of Market and George Sts; Grace Brothers, 436 George St; and David Jones, on Market St.

The most fashionable shops tend to be on Oxford St; Crown St also has several fashionable shops. Newtown's King St is popular for grunge shopping. If you're looking for bargains, there are several factory outlets and seconds shops in Redfern, clustered around the corner of Regent and Redfern Sts.

Aboriginal Art

A large range of traditional and contemporary Aboriginal art is available from the following:

Aboriginal Art Gallery (☎ 9264 9018) Shop 47, Level 2, QVB, 455 George St, city
Aboriginal Art Shop (☎ 9247 4344) Upper Concourse, Sydney Opera House
Aboriginal & Tribal Art Centre (☎ 9241 5998) 117 George St, The Rocks

Australia's Northern Territory & Outback Centre (☎ 9283 7477) Shop 28, 1/25 Harbour St, Darling Walk, Darling Harbour
Boomalli Aboriginal Artists Co-operative (☎ 9698 2047) 191 Parramatta Rd, Annandale
Coo-ee Aboriginal Emporium & Art Gallery (☎ 9332 1544) 98 Oxford St, Paddington
Gavala Art Shop & Cultural Centre (☎ 9212 7232) Harbourside, Darling Harbour
Hogarth Galleries Aboriginal Art Centre (☎ 9360 6839) 7 Walker Lane, Paddington

Australiana

Arts, crafts, T-shirts, designer clothing and bush gear are sold practically everywhere. Apart from the usual kitsch there's much that's of high quality, with prices to match. Check out the huge range sold in The Rocks and Darling Harbour, then compare prices in other areas.

For Australian-made, environmentally friendly souvenirs visit the Wilderness Society Shop (☎ 9233 4674), on the 1st floor of Centrepoint, or the Australian Conservation Foundation shop (☎ 9247 4754), 33 George St, The Rocks.

The *Australian Geographic* magazine has stores full of Australiana at Harbourside (☎ 9212 6539), Darling Harbour, and in Centrepoint (☎ 9231 5055), on Pitt St.

At the Gardens Shop (☎ 9231 8125) in the Royal Botanic Gardens Visitors Centre there are souvenirs, posters and books on Australian flora.

Posters and silk-screen prints by Sydney artist Ken Done are available from the Ken Done Gallery (☎ 9247 2740), 1 Hickson Rd, The Rocks. There are also several Done & Design shops around town, including one nearby at 123 George St (☎ 9251 6099), which sell T-shirts, greeting cards etc.

The Australian Wine Centre (☎ 9247 2755), downstairs in Gold Fields House behind Circular Quay at 1 Alfred St, is open daily and has wines from every Australian wine-growing region. Tastings for the general public take place after 4 pm Friday.

Aussie Clothing

A must-buy item is an Akubra hat. These are sold everywhere tourists gather, but if you want good advice and the right size, try the Strand Hatters (☎ 9231 6884), 8 Strand Arcade on Pitt St Mall. This excellent shop sells a variety of hats, none very cheap, but the staff are friendly and knowledgeable.

RM Williams (☎ 9262 2228), 389 George St, is an established manufacturer and distributor of Aussie bush gear. Thomas Cook Boot & Clothing Company (☎ 9212 6616), 790 George St, is similar.

Opals

The opal is a popular souvenir, but buy wisely and shop around – quality and prices vary widely.

Many Sydney jewellers and duty-free shops sell opals, especially in The Rocks. These include: Opal Fields (☎ 9247 6800), 155 George St; Opal Minded (☎ 9247 9885), 36–64 George St; and Opal Beauty (☎ 9241 4050), 22 Argyle St in The Rocks Centre.

Outdoor Gear

There's a good selection of outdoor shops on Kent St near Bathurst St and the YHA Travel Centre. Among the Australian firms here are Kathmandu (☎ 9261 8901), Paddy Pallin (☎ 9264 2685) and Mountain Designs (☎ 9267 3822).

It's also worth checking out 'disposal' stores, which handle ex-army gear. They're good for rugged clothing and less hi-tech gear and can be a lot cheaper than the specialists. One of Sydney's many disposal stores is Mitchell King Camping & Disposals, which has several stores on Pitt St – the one at No 327 (☎ 9264 5440) specialises in backpacks.

Antiques

Queen St in Woollahra is the main centre for antiques in Sydney. Woollahra Antiques Centre (☎ 9327 8840), 160 Oxford St (opposite the eastern end of Centennial Park), is a conglomeration of 50 shops. Sydney Antique Centre (☎ 9361 3244), 531 South Dowling St, Surry Hills, has 60 shops.

Craft & Design

The local scene is particularly strong in ceramics, jewellery and stained glass. Call into the Arts & Crafts Society of NSW (☎ 9241 1673), in the Metcalfe Arcade, 80–84 George St, which has a gallery and sales operation. You could also try Australian Craftworks (☎ 9247 7156), 127 George St, in the old police station.

Dinosaur Designs is noted for its excellent range of inexpensive jewellery and home wares made from jewel-coloured resins, gold, silver and bone. It has two stores: Strand Arcade (☎ 9223 2953) and 339 Oxford St, Paddington (☎ 9361 3776).

The Object store (☎ 9247 7318) at Customs House sells funky creations by contemporary designers.

Duty-Free

Duty-free shops abound in the city, especially on Pitt St, and include:

Allders Duty Free (☎ 9241 5844) 22 Pitt St
Angus & Coote Duty Free (☎ 9247 7611) 19 Pitt St
City International Duty Free (☎ 9232 1555) 88 Pitt St
Downtown Duty Free (☎ 9221 4444) 105 Pitt St
Harbourside Duty Free (☎ 9283 8900) 249 Pitt St

Music

Big stores that sell recorded music include HMV Megastore (☎ 9221 2311) and Sanity (☎ 9223 8488), facing each other across Pitt St Mall. For dance and electronic music, Oxford St is the place; try Central Station Records at No 46. Brashs (☎ 9261 2555) is at 244 Pitt St. See also the *Yellow Pages* under 'Compact Discs, Records & Tapes'.

For guitars and stringed instruments, try Venue Music (☎ 9267 7288) on Druitt St, opposite the Town Hall.

Markets

Sydney has lots of weekend flea markets. The most interesting, Paddington Bazaar (☎ 9331 2646), St John's Church, 395 Oxford St, is held from 10 am to 4.30 pm on Saturday.

There are two Paddy's Markets. The one on the corner of Hay and Thomas Sts in Haymarket, in the heart of Chinatown, is a Sydney institution where you'll find the usual market fare at rock-bottom prices. It's open weekends. The other, open Friday and Sunday, is on Parramatta Rd in Flemington near Sydney Olympic Park.

In The Rocks, the top end of George St under the bridge is closed to traffic for a market (☎ 9255 1717) on weekends.

Other good markets are: Balmain Markets (☎ 0418 765 736) in Darling St, on Saturday; Glebe's weekend market (☎ 4237 7499), in Glebe Public School on Saturday; and Bondi Beach Market (☎ 9398 5486), in Bondi Beach Public School on Sunday.

GETTING THERE & AWAY
Air
Sydney's Kingsford-Smith Airport is Australia's busiest and is inadequate to handle demand, so expect delays. It's only 10km south of the city centre, which makes access easy, but this also means that flights cease between 11 pm and 5 am due to noise regulations.

You can fly into Sydney from all the usual international points and from all over Australia. Both Qantas Airways (☎ 13 1313) and Ansett Australia (☎ 13 1300) have frequent flights to other capital cities and major airports, and Impulse Airlines (☎ 13 1381) flies to Sydney from several state capitals. Regional carriers, such as Eastern Australia Airlines (a subsidiary of Qantas) and Hazelton Airlines (☎ 13 1713) fly within NSW.

Cheap international flights are advertised in the Saturday *Sydney Morning Herald.*

Bus
The private bus operators are competitive and service is usually efficient. Shop around for discounts. Compare private operator prices to the Countrylink network of trains and buses, which has discounts of up to 40% on economy fares.

Sydney Coach Terminal (☎ 9281 9366), on Eddy Ave outside Central Station, is open daily 6 am to 10.30 pm. Greyhound Pioneer (☎ 13 2030) and McCafferty's (☎ 9361 5125) have offices on Eddy Ave, while Premier (☎ 1300 368 100) and Firefly Express Coaches (☎ 9211 1644) have offices around the corner on Pitt St. Many lines stop in suburbs on the way in or out of the city, and some have feeder services from the suburbs.

See the Getting There & Away and Getting Around chapters for more information.

Train
All interstate and principal regional services operate from Central Station. Call the Central Reservation Centre (☎ 13 2232, 6.30 am to 10 pm) or contact a Countrylink Travel Centre (same central number). There are Countrylink Travel Centres on the main concourse at Central Station, at Circular Quay on Alfred St under the Cahill Expressway behind Wharf 5 (☎ 9241 3887), at Wynyard train station (☎ 9224 4744) and in the QVB arcade near Town Hall station (☎ 9267 1521). Call ☎ 13 2232 for recorded information on arrival/departure times.

See the Getting There & Away and Getting Around chapters for more information.

Car & Motorcycle
There are four main road routes out of Sydney: the Sydney-Newcastle Fwy/Pacific Hwy, which runs north to Newcastle and eventually to Brisbane (cross the Harbour Bridge and follow the Pacific Hwy to the start of the freeway in Hornsby); the Western Motorway (M4), which runs west to Penrith and the Blue Mountains and becomes the Great Western Hwy (follow Parramatta Rd west to Strathfield); the Hume Hwy, which runs south-west to Mittagong and Goulburn and on to Melbourne (follow Parramatta Rd west to Ashfield); and the Princes Hwy, running south to Wollongong and the coast (follow South Dowling St south from Surry Hills).

Rental The major car-rental companies – Avis (☎ 9353 9000), Budget (☎ 13 2727) and Hertz (☎ 13 3039) – have offices at the airport and around the city. Thrifty Car Rental is a smaller, national company that has desks at the airport (☎ 9669 6677) and an office (☎ 9380 5399) in the city at 75 William St. It offers small manual cars for $49 per day with insurance and unlimited kilometres.

The *Yellow Pages* is crammed with other outfits. Many offer deals that appear better than those offered by the major companies, but advertisements may be misleading so read the small print carefully and ring around.

Plenty of places rent older cars, which range from reasonable transport to frustrating old bombs. There are no huge bargains. Check for things like bald tyres and bad brakes *before* you sign anything – some of these outfits have all the compassion of used-car salespeople (which some of them are). Also, check the fine print regarding insurance excess – the amount you pay before the insurance takes over. It can be pretty high. One small company offering competitive rates is Bayswater Rental (☎ 9360 3622), William St, Kings Cross, which rents out small manual cars from $22 a day (for six days) with insurance and 100km/day free.

Motorcycle rentals are available from Bikescape Motorcycle Rentals and Tours (☎ 9699 4722, fax 9699 4733), on the corner of Abercrombie and Cleveland Sts, Chippendale, a five-minute walk from Central Station. Rates start from $60 per day, including gear.

GETTING AROUND

The STA controls almost all public transport in Sydney. Call ☎ 13 1500 between 6 am and 10 pm daily for information on Sydney Buses, Sydney Ferries and CityRail, or visit their separate information booths at Circular Quay. Online information is available from www.131500.com.au. Also, check the front of the A–K *Yellow Pages*. Children (under 16) pay half price on STA services.

STA Fare Deals

The composite SydneyPass offers great value if you intend to use many different forms of transport. If you just want to get to a particular place, you're better off buying a TravelPass.

SydneyPass The SydneyPass offers bus, rail and ferry transport, travel on the Sydney Explorer and Bondi & Bay Explorer buses, harbour ferry cruises and a return trip on the Airport Express. The SydneyPass costs $60/50 for adults/children (three

days), $80/70 (five days), or $90/80 (seven days). Family tickets are also available. Passes are valid for a week. The trip back to the airport is valid for two months but it must be your last trip because you have to surrender the ticket.

TravelPass This offers cheap weekly, quarterly or yearly travel on buses, trains and ferries. It's designed for commuters but is useful for visitors. There are various colour-coded tickets offering different combinations of distances and services. The Green Travel-Pass is valid for extensive bus and train travel and all ferries except the RiverCat and the Manly JetCat (before 7 pm). At $33 for a week, it's a bargain. If you buy a TravelPass after 3 pm, your week begins the next day. Travel Passes are sold at newsagents, railway stations and STA offices.

TravelTen & FerryTen The colour-coded TravelTen ticket gives a sizable discount on 10 bus trips. The blue ticket is valid for two zones and costs $9.50. The brown ticket is valid for three to five zones and costs $16. The FerryTen (from $23) also allows 10 trips.

Day Passes The BusTripper allows unlimited travel on Sydney bus routes for $8.30. The Bus/Ferry DayPass costs $12.

The CityHopper costs $6.60/5.20 peak/off peak and gives you unlimited train travel within the city centre and on all normal buses. The DayRover ($20) adds unlimited travel on ferries.

Combination Passes Several transport-plus-entry tickets are available, which are cheaper than paying separately. The ZooPass pays for your ferry to/from Taronga Zoo, the short bus ride from the wharf to the zoo entrance, zoo entry and the 'Aerial Safari' cable car ride. It costs $21/10.50 (family tickets available). There are similar passes to the National Aquarium in Darling Harbour and Oceanworld in Manly.

The Rocks and Darling Harbour also have composite tickets offering sightseeing, travel and admission to several attractions.

To/From the Airport

Sydney's Kingsford-Smith Airport is 10km south of the city centre. There are free shuttle buses between the domestic and international terminals (which are 4km apart), but only if you have a transit ticket for an onward plane journey. There is no timetable for this service – the bus picks up passengers for specific flights. For information, call ☎ 9667 9111. If you don't have a transit ticket, you can travel between terminals on the Airport Express bus for $3 (or $8 for a family).

Ansett Australia and Qantas Airways have separate domestic terminals. In the arrivals hall at the international terminal there's an airport information desk and a branch of the NSW Travel Centre. All terminals have foreign-exchange facilities.

The green-and-yellow Airport Express buses (☎ 13 1500) travel from the domestic and international terminals to Circular Quay (No 300), Kings Cross (No 350) and Darling Harbour and Glebe (No 352). One of these buses leaves the airport every 10 minutes, but to each separate destination about every 30 minutes. All drop off/pick up at Eddy Ave outside Central Station, so they're convenient for that end of town. Tickets cost $7/12 one way/return, and are valid for two months. The service runs from 5 am to 11 pm.

Kingsford-Smith Transport/Airporter (☎ 9667 0663/3800, 24 hours) runs a door-to-door service between the airport and places to stay (including hostels) in the city and Kings Cross. The fare is $6.50/10 one way/return. Heading out to the airport, you have to book at least three hours before you want to be collected.

The STA also runs buses to the airport (but they take forever), from Dee Why (No 100), Maroubra via Bondi Junction (No 353), and Railway Square (No 305). Normal STA fares for the appropriate distance/zone covered apply.

A new train service from Central Station to the airport takes 10 minutes ($9/12). These are regular commuter trains, so can get crowded and are not luggage friendly.

Depending on traffic conditions, a taxi from the airport to Circular Quay costs $20 to $25, to Central Station $15 to $20.

Bus

The bus information kiosk on the corner of Alfred and Pitt Sts (behind Circular Quay) is open daily. There are other offices on Carrington St (by Wynyard Park) and outside the QVB on York St.

Buses run almost everywhere but they're slow compared with trains. However, some places – including Bondi Beach, Coogee and the North Shore east of the Harbour Bridge – aren't serviced by trains. On the eastern-suburbs line you can get a combination bus/rail ticket from some stations, which enables you to change from a train to a bus for a destination such as Bondi Beach. This works out cheaper than buying the tickets separately.

Sydney is divided into seven zones, with the city centre as zone 1. The main bus stops in the city centre are Circular Quay, Wynyard Park on York St and Railway Square. Nightrider buses provide an hourly service after the regular buses and trains stop running.

Special Bus Services The red STA Sydney Explorer ($28/20, every 20 minutes, 8.40 am to 5.25 pm daily) operates on a two-hour circular route from Circular Quay to Kings Cross, Chinatown, Darling Harbour and The Rocks, linking many innercity attractions. There's an on-board commentary, you can get on and off as often as you like, and your ticket entitles you to discounted entry to many attractions. This is a good way to orient yourself and see a lot of sights.

The 22 Explorer stops are marked by green and red signs. You can use the Explorer ticket on ordinary buses between Central Station and Circular Quay or The Rocks until midnight and the ticket entitles you to big discounts on some tours – conditions apply. You can buy the ticket on the bus, from STA offices and elsewhere.

The Bondi & Bay Explorer (every half hour, 9.15 am to 4.15 pm daily) operates on similar lines but has a larger route, which includes Circular Quay, Kings Cross, Paddington, Double Bay, Vaucluse, Watsons Bay, The Gap, Bondi Beach and Oxford St. The circular route takes two hours, and if

SYDNEY

you want to get off at many of the 19 places of interest along the way you'll need to start early. The ticket entitles you to travel on ordinary buses south of the harbour until midnight. Ticket prices are the same as for the Sydney Explorer, or you can buy a two-day pass for $50/40 ($140 family), which gives you use of the Sydney Explorer as well. Passes valid for five or seven days area also available.

Night Buses Nightrider buses provide an hourly service after regular buses and trains stop running. They operate from Town Hall station and service suburban train stations. Return and weekly train tickets are accepted, otherwise most trips cost $3.60.

Train

CityRail (☎ 13 1500) services a substantial portion of the city. It has frequent trains and is generally much quicker than the bus. Getting around the city centre by train is feasible (if disorienting). At Circular Quay, under the Cahill Expressway behind Wharf 5, there is a CityRail booth open from 9 am to 5 pm daily.

The rail system consists of a central City Circle and a number of lines radiating out to the suburbs. The stations on the City Circle, in clockwise order, are: Central, Town Hall, Wynyard, Circular Quay, St James and Museum. A single trip anywhere on the City Circle or to a nearby suburb such as Kings Cross costs $1.60. An off-peak return trip costs $2.

Most suburban trains stop at Central Station and at least one of the other City Circle stations. If you have to change trains, buy a ticket to your ultimate destination: It's cheaper.

Trains run from around 4 am to about midnight, give or take an hour. After the trains stop, Nightrider buses provide a skeleton service.

There are automatic ticket machines at most railway stations. They accept $5 and $10 notes and all except 5c coins. You can buy an off-peak return ticket for not much more than a standard one-way fare after 9 am on weekdays and at any time weekends.

Ferry

Sydney's ferries are one of the nicest ways of getting around. The picturesque old green-and-yellow boats are supplemented by speedy JetCats to Manly and sleek River-Cats running up the Parramatta River.

All the harbour ferries (and the Cats) depart from Circular Quay. The STA, which runs most ferries, has a ferry information office (which also sells tickets) on the concourse under the Cahill Expressway opposite the entry to Wharf 4; it's open 7 am to 5.45 pm Monday to Saturday, 8 am to 5.45 pm Sunday. Many ferries have connecting bus services.

For Manly, you can choose a roomy ferry ($4/3, 30 minutes), or a JetCat ($5.20, no concessions, 15 minutes). The ferry trip is more pleasant because you can walk around and there's a snack bar. The JetCat is the only craft that runs to Manly after 7 pm, but you can take it for the normal ferry fare. If you're staying in Manly, consider buying a Manly FerryTen pass (10 trips for $34) or better still, a Green TravelPass ($33 for a week of extensive train, bus and ferry travel).

Hegarty's Ferries (☎ 9206 1167) run from Wharf 6 at Circular Quay to wharves directly across the harbour: Lavender Bay, McMahons Point and two stops in Kirribilli. These services ($2.45/1.20 one way) cater to peak-hour commuters and stop early in the evening. The Hunters Hill ferry stops at Balmain and Birchgrove.

You can catch a RiverCat upriver to the Olympic Park wharf at Homebush Bay ($3.40), and some even go as far as Parramatta ($5).

Monorail

More a tourist attraction than a kosher form of public transport, the monorail (☎ 9552 2288) circles Darling Harbour and links it to the city centre. There's a train every four minutes and the full circuit takes about 14 minutes. A single trip costs $3 (free for children who are five and under) but with the $6 day pass ($19 family day pass) you can ride as often as you like between 7 am (8 am Sunday) and 10 pm (midnight Thursday to Saturday).

Light Rail

In the 1930s Sydney had more than 250km of tramway, but by the early 1960s the last tram had lowered its pantograph and that fine metaphor for a hasty departure, 'shoot through like a Bondi tram', became meaningless. However, in 1997 the tram made a return to Sydney's streets, albeit with its name changed to Sydney light rail. It's basically another monorail operating 24 hours a day between Central Station and Pyrmont ($4 return) via Darling Harbour and Chinatown.

Car & Motorcycle

You'll need a street directory to drive around the city but with such good public transport, why bother?

The city centre has an extensive one-way-street system. Parking is hell in most of the innercity and tow-away zones lurk everywhere. Car parks in the inner area include: the Goulburn St Parking Station, corner Goulburn and Elizabeth Sts; KC Park Safe, 581 George St, near Chinatown; Grimes Parking at Gateway Plaza at Circular Quay; The Rocks Space Station, 121 Harrington St, The Rocks; and Kings Cross Car Park, corner Ward Ave and Elizabeth Bay Rd. Many maps indicate with a 'P' where you can park your car. See also the *Yellow Pages* under 'Parking Stations'.

If you have a car, make sure that your hotel has parking or you'll have to pay for commercial parking.

The new Eastern Distributor toll road should reduce travelling time between the airport and city ($3 for northbound traffic).

Taxi

Taxis can be flagged down in the city centre and the inner suburbs. You'll also often find cabs in taxi ranks at Central, Wynyard and Circular Quay train stations and at the large rank off George St in Goulburn St.

The four big taxi companies offer a reliable telephone service. They are: Taxis Combined (☎ 8332 8888); RSL Taxis (☎ 13 2211); Legion (☎ 13 1451); and Premier Cabs (☎ 13 1017).

Taxi fares are: $1 telephone booking fee, $2 flag fall and $1.17 per kilometre. The waiting fee is $0.55 a minute and there's a luggage charge (often waived) of $0.10 per kilogram for bags over 25kg. These fares apply any time of the day or night.

If you take a taxi via the Harbour Bridge or tunnel (or any other toll road), expect to pay the driver's return toll.

Water Taxi Water taxis are pricey, but a fun way of getting around the harbour. Companies include Water Taxis (☎ 9955 3222) and Harbour Taxis (☎ 9555 1155).

Bicycle

Steep hills, narrow streets and heavy traffic don't make Sydney a particularly bicycle-friendly city. Some roads have designated cycle lanes, but these often run between parked cars and moving traffic. Bicycle NSW (☎ 9283 5200), Level 2, 209 Castlereagh St, publishes a handy book called *Cycling around Sydney* ($10). It details routes and cycle paths in and around the city.

The Road Transport Authority (RTA) issues maps of metropolitan Sydney's cycle path network – call ☎ 1800 060 607 or download the maps from the Web site at www.rta.nsw.gov.au.

Bicycles can travel on suburban trains for concession rates during peak hours, and for free outside peak times. Cycling is prohibited in Darling Harbour and Martin Place.

Innes Bicycles (☎ 9264 9597), 222 Clarence St, in the city, sells bicycles and does repairs.

Bicycle Hire Check out Inner City Cycles (☎ 9660 6605), 151 Glebe Point Rd, Glebe, which rents out quality mountain bikes for $30 a day or $50 from Friday afternoon to Monday morning; rental includes helmet, lock, water bottle and pump.

Woolys Wheels (☎ 9331 2671), 82 Oxford St, Paddington, opposite Victoria Barracks, rents hybrid bikes for $30 a day (24 hours). In Manly you can hire bikes from the Manly Cycle Centre (☎ 9977 1189), 36 Pittwater Rd, for $10/25 an hour/day.

Most places require a hefty deposit but do accept credit cards.

Around Sydney

Sydney sprawls over a coastal plain, surrounded by rugged country on three sides and the South Pacific Ocean on the fourth.

The city is at the centre of the largest concentration of population in Australia. Most people live on the coast or around the lakes of the Central Coast – the slopes and forests of the Great Dividing Range have halted westwards expansion, except along a ridge-top corridor through the stunning Blue Mountains.

This might sound like a recipe for overcrowding, but the region has historic small towns, stunning waterways, uncrowded beaches, superb national parks and vast tracts of forest. The proximity of Sydney means that public transport is often good, enabling you to see a lot of the area on day trips even without your own vehicle.

Greater Sydney

Sydney's sprawling suburbs have covered much of the coastal plain, with corridor development running out along the Great Western Hwy (M4) to Penrith and south along the Hume Hwy past Liverpool. In the hilly areas to the north-west, settlement is sparser but increasing.

BOTANY BAY

It's a common misconception among first-time visitors to Sydney that the city is built on the shores of Botany Bay. Sydney is actually built around the harbour of Port Jackson, some 10km to 15km north of Botany Bay, although the city's southern suburbs now encompass the bay too.

It was at Botany Bay that Captain James Cook first stepped ashore in Australia. The bay was named by Joseph Banks, the naturalist who accompanied Cook, because of the many botanical specimens he found here. Cook's landing place is marked by monuments at Kurnell on the southern side of the bay in **Botany Bay National Park**.

HIGHLIGHTS

- Walking the coastal trail in Royal National Park
- Taking in the spectacular water views at Ku-Ring-Gai Chase National Park
- Travelling the Hawkesbury River on the *Riverboat Postman* mail boat
- Bushwalking or cycling in the scenic Blue Mountains
- Touring the limestone Jenolan Caves
- Driving along Bells Line of Road or through Kangaroo Valley
- Horse riding in the Southern Highlands
- Braving the surf at magnificent beaches along the Central Coast

The **Discovery Centre** (☎ 9668 9111) in the park has material relating to Cook's life and expeditions and information on the surrounding wetlands. It's open from 10 am to 3 pm daily (to 4 pm on weekends). There are bushland walking tracks and picnic areas in the park, which is open 7 am to 7 pm. From Cronulla train station (10km away), take bus No 987. Entry costs $5 per car.

La Perouse is on the northern side of the bay entrance, at the spot where the French explorer of that name arrived in 1788, just six days after the arrival of Cook's First Fleet. He gave the Poms a good scare because they weren't expecting the French to turn up quite so soon. La Perouse and his men camped at Botany Bay for a few weeks, then sailed off into the Pacific and were never seen again. It was not until many years later that the wrecks of their ships were discovered on a reef near Vanuatu. There's a monument at La Perouse built in 1828 by French sailors to commemorate the explorer. You can also visit **La Perouse Museum** (☎ 9311 3379), which has relics from his hapless expedition and a col-

lection of antique maps. The museum is open from 10 am to 4 pm Tuesday to Sunday ($5/3 for adults/children). Bus Nos 394 and 398 run here from Circular Quay.

WILDLIFE PARKS
In addition to the large national parks on the fringes of Sydney (see later in this chapter), there are several other places where you can see native animals, often at cuddling range.

Waratah Park
Popular Waratah Park (☎ 9450 2377), on Namba Rd, Terrey Hills, on the edge of the

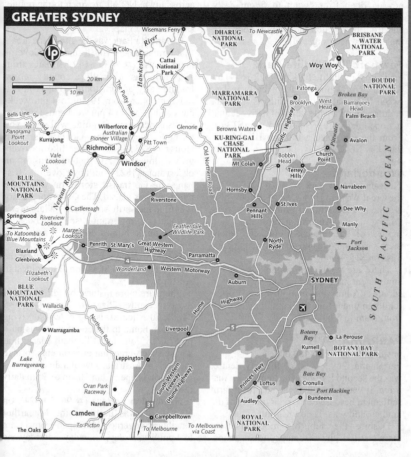

GREATER SYDNEY

Ku-Ring-Gai Chase National Park, is a good place to see native fauna. There is koala-petting hourly. It's open from 10 am to 5 pm daily ($12.90/6.50 for adults/children). You can get here on Forest Coach Lines (☎ 9450 2277) bus No 284, which meets trains at Chatswood station on the North Shore line, but there are only three buses on weekdays and fewer on weekends. A recorded message (☎ 9450 1236) gives bus times.

Koala Park

Koala Park (☎ 9484 3141), on Castle Hill Rd in West Pennant Hills in north-west Sydney, is open from 9 am to 5 pm daily ($10/5). Take a train to Pennant Hills station and from there catch the Glenorie bus (ask the driver where to get off).

Featherdale Wildlife Park

Featherdale Wildlife Park (☎ 9622 1644) on Kildare Rd, Doonside, about halfway between Parramatta and Penrith, is a 'koala cuddlery' with a wide range of native fauna. It's open daily from 9 am to 5 pm ($12/6). From the city, take a train to Blacktown, then bus No 725.

Wonderland

This amusement park (☎ 9830 9187), off the Great Western Hwy west of the city, also has the large **Australian Wildlife Park**, containing native Australian animals and a replica of an outback woolshed, where there's a 30-minute show (wildlife park admission $15/9).

There are pools and waterslides at the amusement park, so bring your swimsuit in summer. Admission to both costs $39/27 (children under four free) and they're open from 9 am to 5 pm daily.

PARRAMATTA

postcode 2124 • pop 130,000

Parramatta, 24km west of the city centre, was the second European settlement in Australia. It was selected as the site for a farm settlement because of the poor quality of the land around what is now Circular Quay.

Despite the suburb's modernisation, there's still a hint of country-town atmosphere and it retains some beautiful historic buildings.

Information

The Parramatta Visitors Information Centre (☎ 9630 3703), 353 Church St, is a couple of blocks north of the Church St pedestrian mall, just across the river. It has a walking-tour map and a good booklet, as well as other information. It's open from 10 am to 5 pm weekdays, 9 am to 1 pm weekends.

Historic Buildings

Parramatta's historic buildings are scattered across town. Not all are open to the public; the locations of those not listed here are shown on the map.

Parramatta Park was the site of the area's first farm and here you'll find **Old Government House** (☎ 9635 8149). It dates from 1799 and was originally a country retreat for the early administration, but is now a museum, open from 10 am to 4 pm weekdays and 11 am to 4 pm weekends ($6/4 for adults/concession). A guide will show you through. Nearby, the **Governor's Bath House** (1823) looks rather like an overgrown dovecote. All that remains of an observatory (1822), built by Governor Brisbane, are the **transit stones** on which the telescope was placed. The **Governor's Dairy** (1815) to the north was actually a labourer's cottage (an important discovery because early humble homes are much rarer than grand ones).

St John's Cemetery, which is south of the park on O'Connell St, is one of the oldest in Australia.

There are more historic buildings east of the city centre. **Elizabeth Farm** (☎ 9635 9488), 70 Alice St, is the oldest surviving European home in the country. It was built in 1793 by John and Elizabeth Macarthur, whose sheep-breeding experiments formed the basis of Australia's wool industry. Elizabeth Farm is open from 10 am to 5 pm daily ($6/3).

Hambledon Cottage (☎ 9635 6924), on Hassall St, was built for the Macarthur daughters' governess. It's open from 11 am to 4 pm Wednesday, Thursday, Saturday and

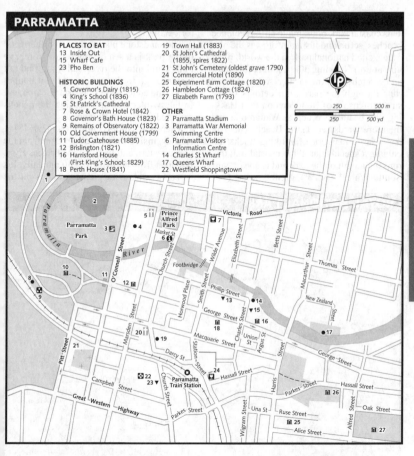

PARRAMATTA

PLACES TO EAT
13 Inside Out
15 Wharf Cafe
23 Pho Ben

HISTORIC BUILDINGS
1 Governor's Dairy (1815)
4 King's School (1836)
5 St Patrick's Cathedral
7 Rose & Crown Hotel (1842)
8 Governor's Bath House (1823)
9 Remains of Observatory (1822)
10 Old Government House (1799)
11 Tudor Gatehouse (1885)
12 Brislington (1821)
16 Harrisford House
(First King's School; 1829)
18 Perth House (1841)

19 Town Hall (1883)
20 St John's Cathedral
(1855, spires 1822)
21 St John's Cemetery (oldest grave 1790)
24 Commercial Hotel (1890)
25 Experiment Farm Cottage (1820)
26 Hambledon Cottage (1824)
27 Elizabeth Farm (1793)

OTHER
2 Parramatta Stadium
3 Parramatta War Memorial
Swimming Centre
6 Parramatta Visitors
Information Centre
14 Charles St Wharf
17 Queens Wharf
22 Westfield Shoppingtown

AROUND SYDNEY

Sunday ($3/1.50 for adults/children). **Experiment Farm Cottage** (☎ 9635 5655), 9 Ruse St, is a fine example of an early 1880s homestead, furnished in 1840s style. It's open from 10 am to 4 pm Tuesday to Thursday, 11 am to 4 pm Sunday ($5/3 for adults/concession).

Places to Eat

South of the railway line, Church St's ubiquitous fast-food joints give way to Asian restaurants and supermarkets. **Pho Ben** (☎ 9689 3310, 131 Church St) has a large, well-priced menu of Asian food.

Down on the Charles St wharf, **Wharf Cafe** does focaccia and melts for $8.50. Get a table outside. Nearby, **Inside Out** (☎ 9687 9045, 99 Phillip St) has salads for $8 to $12 and meals such as linguini with prawns and semidried tomatoes ($12).

Getting There & Away

CityRail trains run to Parramatta from Central Station or Town Hall, while regular ferries and JetCats run from Circular Quay. By car, follow Parramatta Rd west from the city centre and take either the Great Western Hwy or the quicker Western Motorway toll road.

ROYAL NATIONAL PARK

This coastal park of dramatic cliffs, secluded beaches, scrub and lush rainforest is the oldest gazetted national park in the world. It begins at Port Hacking, 30km south of Sydney, and stretches 20km farther south. A road runs through the park with detours to the small township of Bundeena on Port Hacking, the beautiful beach at Wattamolla and the more windswept Garie Beach. The park has a large network of walking tracks, including a spectacular 29km coastal trail that runs the length of the park and is one of New South Wales' (NSW) great walks. (See Lonely Planet's *Bushwalking in Australia* for details.)

The sandstone plateau at the northern end of the park is a sea of low scrub. You have to descend into the river valleys to find tall forest, or go to the park's southern boundary on the edge of the Illawarra Escarpment. In late winter and early spring the park is carpeted with wild flowers.

There's a visitors centre (☎ 9542 0648) at Audley, inside the park about 2km from the north-eastern entrance, off the Princes Hwy. It's open from 8.30 am to 4.30 pm daily. It's a scenic spot, with picnic grounds on the

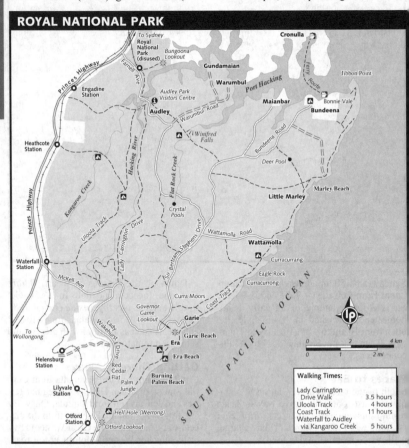

ROYAL NATIONAL PARK

Walking Times:

Lady Carrington Drive Walk	3.5 hours
Uloola Track	4 hours
Coast Track	11 hours
Waterfall to Audley via Kangaroo Creek	5 hours

Hacking River. You can hire rowboats and canoes at the Audley Boat Shed (☎ 9545 4967) for $12/24 an hour/day. Bikes cost $10 an hour, $16 for four hours.

Garie, Era, South Era and **Burning Palms** are popular surf beaches; swimming or surfing at Marley Beach is dangerous (Little Marley is safe). Garie Beach has a surf-life-saving club and **Wattamolla Beach** has a picnic area and a lagoon for gentle swimming.

A walking and cycling trail follows the Hacking River south from Audley and other walking tracks pass tranquil freshwater swimming holes. You can swim in Kangaroo Creek, but not the Hacking River.

Park entry costs $9 per car (free for pedestrians and cyclists). The road through the park and the offshoot to Bundeena are always open, but the detours to the beaches are closed at sunset.

The sizeable town of **Bundeena**, on the southern shore of Port Hacking opposite Sydney's southern suburb of Cronulla, is surrounded by the park. Bundeena has its own beaches, or you can walk 30 minutes towards the ocean to **Jibbon Head,** which has a good beach and Aboriginal rock art. Bundeena is the starting point of the 29km coastal walk.

Places to Stay

The only camp ground accessible by car is at Bonnie Vale, near Bundeena, where sites cost from $10 for two people. Free bush camping is allowed in several other areas, but you must obtain a permit from the visitors centre, where you can get information about current useable camp sites. The small, basic (no electricity or phone) and secluded *Garie Beach YHA Hostel* is near one of the best surfing beaches and has beds for Youth Hostel Association (YHA) members only ($7). You need to book; collect a key and get detailed directions from the YHA Travel Centre (☎ 9261 1111) in Sydney.

Getting There & Away

Train The Sydney-Wollongong train line forms the western boundary of the park. The closest station is Loftus, 4km from the park entrance and another 2km from the visitors centre. Bringing a bike is a good

idea because there's a 10km ride through forest on a vehicle-free track about half an hour's ride from Sutherland station. The stations of Engadine, Heathcote, Waterfall and Otford are on the park boundary and have walking trails into the park.

Train & Boat A scenic way to reach the park is to take a train from Sydney to Cronulla (changing at Sutherland on the way), then the Cronulla National Park Ferries (☎ 9523 2990) boat to Bundeena in the north-eastern corner of the park ($2.60/1.30 for adults/children). Ferries depart from the Cronulla wharf, just below the train station. Cronulla Ferries also offers Hacking River cruises on Sunday, Monday, Wednesday and Friday from March to November (daily December to February) for $12/9. The boats usually get as far as Audley (depending on the tide), but passengers cannot disembark.

Car & Motorcycle From Sydney, take the Princes Hwy and turn off south of Loftus to reach the northern end of the park. From the south, enter via Otford on the coast road north from Wollongong. It's a beautiful drive through thick bush and there are great views of the Illawarra escarpment and the coast from Bald Hill Lookout, just north of Stanwell Park, on the southern boundary of Royal National Park. There's another entrance at Waterfall, just off the Princes Hwy.

KU-RING-GAI CHASE NATIONAL PARK

This 15,000-hectare national park, 24km north of the city centre, borders the southern edge of Broken Bay and the western shore of Pittwater. It has that classic Sydney mixture of sandstone, bushland and water vistas, plus walking tracks, horse-riding trails, picnic areas, Aboriginal rock engravings and spectacular views of Broken Bay, particularly from West Head at the park's north-eastern tip. The park has over 100km of shoreline. There are several roads through the park and four entrances. Entry is $9 per car.

Kalkari Visitors Centre (☎ 9457 9853, 9457 9322) on Ku-Ring-Gai Chase Rd, about 4km into the park from the Mt Colah

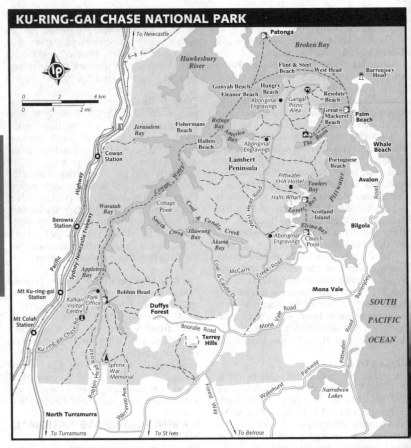

KU-RING-GAI CHASE NATIONAL PARK

entrance, is open from 9 am to 5 pm daily. From the visitors centre, the road heads to the Bobbin Head picnic area on Cowan Creek, then to the Turramurra entrance.

At Bobbin Head, Halvorsen (☎ 9457 9011) rents out rowboats for $12 for the first hour ($4 for each subsequent hour) and motorboats that seat eight for $43 ($7).

The best places to see **Aboriginal engravings** are on The Basin Track and Garigal Aboriginal Heritage Walk at West Head.

It's unwise to swim in Broken Bay because of sharks, but there are safe, netted swimming areas at Illawong Bay in the cen-

tre of the park and at The Basin, on the western side of Pittwater.

From West Head there's a fantastic **view** across Pittwater to Barrenjoey Head at the end of Palm Beach. You might see **lyrebirds** at West Head during their mating period (May to July).

Places to Stay

Camping is allowed only at The Basin. It's a 2km walk from the West Head Rd, or a ferry ride from Palm Beach. It costs $10 for two people ($15 in school holidays) and you must book and pay in advance. Cal

☎ 9974 1011 for bookings, ☎ 9451 8124 for recorded information.

The ***Pittwater YHA Hostel*** (☎ *9999 2196),* 2km south of The Basin, has arguably the best location of any youth hostel in Australia, with stunning views over Pittwater. It is isolated – the only way in is by ferry – so party animals should probably go elsewhere. The facilities are basic but comfortable. Beds cost $15, or $19 per person in a twin room; if you stay Saturday night only, rates are $20/24 respectively. Nonmembers pay $2 more. Book in advance and bring all your food. There's great bushwalking nearby (the friendly manager supplies hand-drawn maps) and you can hire canoes for $8 per person.

Getting There & Away

Bus From Wynyard Park in the city centre, take bus No 190 or L90 to Mona Vale, No 175 to Warringah Mall or L88 to Dee Why where you change to bus No 156 to Church Point. Ask for a ticket for the entire journey ($4.50). Bus No 156 runs from Manly.

Shorelink Buses (☎ 9457 8888) has a fairly frequent service from Turramurra train station to the nearby park entrance.

STA buses service the Terrey Hills and Church Point entrances, but it's quite a walk to the Pittwater YHA Hostel or the camp sites from these entrances.

Car & Motorcycle There are four road entrances to the park: Mt Colah, on the Pacific Hwy; Turramurra, in the south-west; and Terrey Hills and Church Point, in the south-east.

Boat The Palm Beach Ferry Service (☎ 9918 2747) runs to The Basin hourly from 9 am to 6 pm ($7 return). A ferry leaves Palm Beach for Bobbin Head (running on a 60km scenic route via Patonga on the northern side of Broken Bay) daily at 11 am, returning at 3.30 pm. The one-way fare is $28/14 for adults/children.

Church Point Ferries (☎ 9999 3492, 0408 296 997) departs Church Point for Halls Wharf and Scotland Island every hour (roughly on the half-hour) from 8.30 am to 6.30 pm ($6 return). Departures are timed to

The elusive lyrebird is sometimes seen at Ku-Ring-Gai Chase National Park.

coincide with buses from Wynyard and Manly.

HAWKESBURY RIVER

The Hawkesbury River enters the sea 30km north of Sydney at Broken Bay. It's dotted with coves, beaches, picnic spots and some fine riverside restaurants. The final 20km or so expands into bays and inlets like Berowra Creek, Cowan Water and Pittwater to the south, and Brisbane Water to the north before it enters the ocean. The river flows between Marramarra and Ku-Ring-Gai Chase National Parks in the south and Dharug, Brisbane Water and Bouddi National Parks to the north. Windsor and Richmond are about 120km upstream – see Macquarie Towns Area later in this chapter.

The *Riverboat Postman* (☎ 9985 7566) **mail boat** is an excellent way to get a feel for the river. It does a 40km round trip weekdays, running upstream as far as Marlow, near Spencer. It leaves Brooklyn at 9.30 am and returns at 1.15 pm. A shorter afternoon run on Wednesday leaves at 1.30 pm and returns around 4 pm. It costs $30/15 for adults/children. The 8.16 am train from Central Station gets you to Brooklyn's Hawkesbury River station in time to meet the

AROUND SYDNEY

morning boat. You may have to change at Hornsby. By car, take the Sydney-Newcastle Freeway or follow the old Pacific Hwy.

Wiseman Ferry Cruises (☎ 4575 5387) has two-hour **cruises** of the Hawkesbury, Colo and McDonald Rivers for $37.50, including a food hamper.

Houseboat Holidays

The Hawkesbury River Tourist Accommodation Centre (☎ 9985 7090) at Brooklyn can assist with finding places to stay, including houseboats. You can hire houseboats in Brooklyn, Berowra Waters, Bobbin Head and Wisemans Ferry. These aren't cheap, but renting midweek during the low season is affordable for a group. There are different types and sizes and different deals for longer rentals and weekends. As a rough guide, Holidays-A-Float (☎ 9985 7368) in Brooklyn offers four midweek days (three nights) on a six-berth boat for $850 between May and late September. Other companies include Able Houseboats (☎ 4566 4308), on River Rd, Wisemans Ferry, and Ripples Houseboats (☎ 9985 7333), 87 Brooklyn Rd, Brooklyn.

Brooklyn & Berowra Waters

The settlements along the Hawkesbury River have their own distinct character. Life in Brooklyn centres on boats and the river. The town is on the Sydney-Newcastle train line, just east of the Pacific Hwy.

The small town of Berowra Waters, farther upstream on a narrow, forested waterway, is clustered around a free, 24-hour winch ferry that crosses Berowra Creek. It's in a pretty location, and boat-hire businesses and bushwalking tracks abound.

An atmospheric place to eat is *The Restaurant on Berowra Waters (☎ 9456 1027),* open for lunch Wednesday to Saturday, dinner on Friday and Saturday and breakfast on Sunday. Bookings are essential as you must arrange a ferry pick-up. There are also several *cafes* overlooking the water.

Wisemans Ferry & Around

The tranquil settlement of Wisemans Ferry is a popular spot on the Hawkesbury River, about halfway between Windsor and the mouth of the river. A free, 24-hour winch ferry is the only means of crossing the river here.

The historic *Wisemans Ferry Inn (☎ 4566 4301)* has rooms for $55 to $65 a double. Caravan parks include *Del Rio Riverside Resort (☎ 4566 4330),* 3km south-west of the village centre (sites $19 a double).

Unsealed roads on both sides of the river run north from Wisemans Ferry to the hamlet of **St Albans**. It's a pretty drive, with bush on one side and the serene flats of the McDonald River on the other, with the occasional old sandstone house. In St Albans the friendly *Settlers Arms Inn (☎ 4568 2111)* dates from 1848 and the public bar is worth a beer. It has a few pleasant rooms from $100 to $120 a double and there's a basic *camp site* opposite the pub. There's also B&B in the old *Court House (☎ 4568 2042)* for $135 a double midweek. You can book the whole place on weekends for $900 for two nights (sleeping eight).

Note that it may be unwise to swim in the Hawkesbury River between Windsor and Wisemans Ferry during summer due to blue-green algae. Call the Environment Protection Authority (EPA) Pollution Line (☎ 9325 5555) for information.

National Parks

The **Dharug National Park** is a 14,834-hectare wilderness noted for its Aboriginal rock carvings dating back nearly 10,000 years. Forming the western boundary of the park is the dilapidated **Old Great North Road**, built by convicts in the 1820s to link Sydney and Newcastle. There's camping in the park at Mill Creek and Ten Mile Hollow.

On the south side of the Hawkesbury is **Marramarra National Park** (11,760 hectares), with vehicle access from the Old Northern Rd south of Wisemans Ferry. You can bush camp here. Contact the National Parks & Wildlife Service (NPWS; ☎ 4324 4911), 207 Albany St in Gosford, for more information.

Getting There & Away

Berowra Waters is 5km west of the Pacific Hwy; turn off the Pacific Hwy at Berowra. A scenic alternative is to take the road through the Galston Gorge north of Hornsby in Sydney's north-east. There's a train station at Berowra, but it's a 6km hike down to the ferry.

A road leads to Wisemans Ferry from Pitt Town, near Windsor. You can also get there from Sydney on the Old Northern Rd, which branches off Windsor Rd north of Parramatta.

From Wisemans Ferry you have a choice of two ferries to reach St Albans. The ferry in the west of town (at the bottom of the steep hill) takes you to St Albans Rd; the ferry on the north-east side (a short way out of town, near the park) takes you to Settlers Rd.

The Sydney-Newcastle Freeway crosses the Hawkesbury River near Brooklyn. Trains run from Central Station to Brooklyn's Hawkesbury River train station.

The Riverboat Postman runs a ferry service from Brooklyn to Patonga Beach five times a week for $15/8 return. Bookings are necessary.

There's also a daily ferry between Palm Beach, Patonga and Bobbin Head in Ku-Ring-Gai Chase National Park (see the Ku-Ring-Gai Chase National Park section earlier in this chapter). From Patonga, Busways (☎ 4368 2277) has infrequent buses to Gosford where you can catch a bus or train going north.

MACQUARIE TOWNS AREA

The river flats of the upper Hawkesbury River, under the lee of the Blue Mountains, offered the young colony fertile land for growing much-needed food. After early settlements were flooded several times, Governor Lachlan Macquarie established the five 'Macquarie Towns' on higher ground in 1810 – Windsor, Richmond, Wilberforce, Pitt Town and Castlereagh. The area is still intensively cultivated.

The upper Hawkesbury River is popular for water-skiing, but call the EPA Pollution Line (☎ 9325 5555) for information on the algae problem.

Information

The Hawkesbury Visitors Centre (☎ 4588 5895), across from the Richmond Royal Australian Air Force (RAAF) base on the Richmond-Windsor road, is the main information centre for the upper Hawkesbury River. It's open from 9 am to 5 pm weekdays, 10 am to 2 pm Saturday and 9 am to 1 pm Sunday.

Windsor has an information centre (☎ 4577 2310) in the 1843 Daniel O'Connell Inn on Thompson Square.

In Richmond, there's an NPWS office (☎ 4588 5247) at 370 Windsor St.

Windsor

Windsor, founded in 1810 on the banks of the Hawkesbury River, was the main Macquarie Town and has many fine colonial buildings. The **Hawkesbury Museum** is in the same building as the information centre. It's open daily ($5/2 for adults/children).

Other old buildings include the convict-built **St Matthew's Church** (1820), designed by convict architect Francis Greenway, as was the old **courthouse** (1822). George St has other historic buildings and the **Macquarie Arms Hotel** is reckoned to be the oldest pub in Australia, though there are a few 'oldest pubs' around. This one was built in 1815. Happily, its history hasn't gone to its head and it's still very much a small-town pub.

Windsor Cruises (☎ 9831 6630) runs tours on the Hawkesbury from Windsor.

On the edge of town is the **Tebbut Observatory** (☎ 4577 2485), featured on the $100 note. You can look through the telescopes by paying $25 for dinner at the restaurant. Bookings are essential.

Wilberforce & Around

Wilberforce, 6km north of Windsor, is a tiny town on the edge of the river-flat farmland where the **Hawkesbury Heritage Farm** (☎ 4575 1457), a collection of old buildings gathered from around the district, forms a small historic park. It includes Rose Cottage (1811), probably the oldest surviving timber building in the country (occupied by the same family until 1961). There are also native animals and regular entertainment. The farm is open from 10 am to 5 pm Thursday to Sunday ($10/6). Next to it is a **butterfly**

farm. You can get here via a CityRail train to Windsor and then by bus, but the bus isn't frequent.

The originally Presbyterian (now Uniting) **Ebenezer Church** (1809) on Coromandel Rd, 5km north of Wilberforce, is said to be the oldest church in Australia that's still used as a place of worship. The old **Tizzana Winery** (☎ 4579 1150), 518 Tizzana Rd, near Ebenezer, is open from noon to 6 pm weekends.

Pitt Town & Around

Pitt Town, a few kilometres north-east of Windsor, has the restored **Bird in Hand Hotel** (1825). North of town on the road to Wisemans Ferry is the small **Cattai National Park** (☎ 4572 3100). There are two parts: Cattai Farm, containing the remains of an old homestead (c. 1799), and, 2km east, Mitchell Park with pristine forest and walking trails. There's also canoe hire, horse riding and camping.

Richmond

Richmond is 6km west of Windsor, at the end of the CityRail line and at the start of the Bells Line of Road across the Blue Mountains. The town dates from 1810 and has some fine Georgian and Victorian buildings. These include the **courthouse** and **police station**, on Windsor St and, around the corner on Market St, **St Andrew's Church** (1845). A number of notable pioneers are buried in the cemetery at **St Peter's Church** (1841).

The Putty Road

The Putty Rd (also called the Singleton Rd) is a scenic route from Windsor to the upper Hunter Valley. The road, flanked by Wollemi and Yengo National Parks, runs through dense bush amid a sea of forest-covered ranges. On the Putty Rd, about 20km north of Windsor, there's a long descent to the lovely **Colo River**, a picturesque spot popular for swimming, canoeing and picnicking. It has a service station, shop and tourist information point and camping at the *Riverside Tourist Park (☎ 4575 5253)*, where you can hire canoes for $12 an hour.

Getting There & Away

CityRail trains run from Sydney to Windsor and Richmond, but getting to the other Macquarie Towns involves connecting with an infrequent local bus service.

From Sydney, the easiest routes to Windsor are on Windsor Rd (Route 40), the north-western continuation of Parramatta's Church St (you'll have to wind around the Church St mall), and via Penrith, heading north from either the Western Fwy or the Great Western Hwy on Route 69 (Parker St and the Northern Rd).

The Putty Rd runs from Windsor to Singleton, 160km north in the upper Hunter Valley. From Windsor, take Bridge St across the river then turn right onto the Wilberforce road (Route 69).

From Richmond, Bells Line of Road runs west to the Blue Mountains. This is a more interesting (but considerably longer) route to Katoomba than the crowded Great Western Hwy.

PENRITH & AROUND
postcode 2750

Now Sydney's westernmost suburb, Penrith is bounded on the west by the serene Nepean River (which becomes the Hawkesbury a few kilometres downstream). Across the river, the forested foothills of the Blue Mountains rise above the Nepean's river flats and the plains of western Sydney come to an abrupt end. Europeans arrived here soon after the colony was founded, in search of land to grow food. A road between Parramatta and Penrith was built in 1818.

The tourist information centre (☎ 4732 7671), open from 9 am to 4.30 pm (it closes briefly at lunchtime) daily, is in the car park of the Penrith Panthers complex.

Things to See & Do

The **Museum of Fire** (☎ 4731 3000), off Castlereagh Rd (the main road to Richmond) just east of the train line, contains displays of historic firefighting equipment and educational items about fire and its dangers. There's a graphic display on the disastrous effects of fire. The museum is open 10 am to 3 pm daily ($5/3 for adults/children).

The huge **Penrith Panthers** complex is a leagues club with glitzy surroundings, plenty of pokies, flash restaurants, a free cinema, lavish amusements such as cable water-skiing and an expensive motel (☎ 4721 7700). A visit here on the way to the Blue Mountains may give you a better appreciation of the bush.

The *Nepean Belle* (☎ 4733 1274), a paddle-wheeler, cruises the Nepean River several times a week.

Getting There & Away

Frequent CityRail trains stop at Penrith on the run between Sydney and the Blue Mountains.

The Western Motorway (M4) from Sydney runs past Penrith while the Great Western Hwy passes through. The Northern Rd (Route 69) runs south from Penrith to the towns of Camden and Picton and north to Windsor.

MACARTHUR COUNTRY

The Hume Hwy heads south-west from Sydney, with the rugged Blue Mountains National Park to the west and the coastal escarpment on the east, following a rising cor-

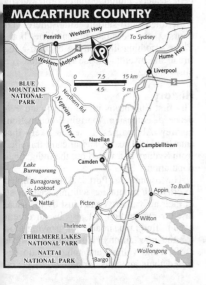

Cow Pastures & Sheep

Macarthur Country was originally called Cow Pastures because a herd of cattle that had escaped from Sydney Cove thrived here. But it was John and Elizabeth Macarthur's sheep, which arrived in 1805, that made the area famous. The couple's experiments with sheep breeding led to the development of merino sheep suited to Australian conditions, and these became the foundation of the Australian wool industry.

ridor. This cleared and rolling sheep country contains some of the state's oldest towns, although many have been swallowed by Sydney's steamrolling suburbs. If you would prefer a closer look at the countryside, take the **Northern Rd** between Penrith and Narellan (just north of Camden).

Liverpool and, 20km farther south, **Campbelltown** are unattractive outer suburbs of Sydney, though both do have some interesting old buildings.

Balloon Aloft (☎ 1800 028 568) has early morning hot-air **balloon flights** from Camden for $130. The price includes a champagne breakfast.

Camden

Camden is a large country town that's almost a dormitory suburb of Sydney. The town retains its integrity but the surrounding countryside is fast filling up with weekend attractions for Sydneysiders. **John Oxley Cottage**, on the northern outskirts, houses the Camden Information Centre (☎ 4658 1370), open from 10 am to 2.30 pm daily. The **Camden Museum** has objects and displays relating to local history. It is behind the library at 40 John St and is open from 11 am to 4 pm Thursday to Sunday ($2.50/1 for adults/children).

The Macarthurs' home, **Camden Park House** (1835), is open to the public on the last weekend in September only.

Attractions around Camden are aimed primarily at families and coach parties. **Gledswood** (☎ 9606 5111), Camden Valley Way in Catherine Field near Narellan, is an

AROUND SYDNEY

old homestead (1827) housing a winery and restaurant. There's also sheep shearing, boomerang throwing and other activities. It's open from 10 am to 5 pm daily.

Midway between Camden and Campbelltown, **Mount Annan Botanic Garden** (☎ 4648 2477) is an offshoot of Sydney's botanic gardens and displays native flora on over 400 hectares. It's open from 10 am to 6 pm daily October to March, to 4 pm April to September; admission costs $5 per car or motorcycle, $2 for pedestrians. You can get here on bus No 896, which runs more or less hourly from Campbelltown train station.

Picton & Around

South of Camden, pretty Picton is an old rural village, which was known originally as Stonequarry. Today it is coal that is mined in the area (and there are subsidence problems under those rolling hills and sheep paddocks). A number of historic buildings still stand, including the train station and the 1839 **George IV Inn** (☎ 4677 1415), which brews its own Bavarian-style beer and provides some modest accommodation ($38 a double). **Upper Menangle St** is listed by the National Trust.

Elizabeth Macarthur Agricultural Institute is a research station at 710 Morton Park Rd in Menangle, north-east of Picton. It takes in **Belgenny Farm** (☎ 4655 9651), the Macarthurs' first farm in the area and the oldest in Australia. It has open days on certain Sundays and public holidays; call for details. Most historians agree that Elizabeth Macarthur supervised most of the sheep-breeding projects while the irascible John, her husband, was embroiled in political disputes.

South of Picton in Thirlmere, the **Rail Transport Museum** (☎ 4681 8001), on Barbour Rd, has a huge collection of engines and rolling stock, with many more awaiting restoration. It's open from 10 am to 3 pm weekdays, 9 am to 5 pm weekends ($8/2). There are steam-train excursions (☎ 9744 9999) on Sunday, Monday public holidays, and Wednesday during school holidays.

Merigal Dingo Sanctuary (☎ 4684 1156), 590 Arina Rd, near Bargo, about 20km south of Picton, is run by the Australian Native Dog Conservation Society, which aims to have dingoes recognised as native fauna in need of protection. The centre is open from 10 am to 3.30 pm daily ($5/2).

Blue Mountains

The Blue Mountains, part of the Great Dividing Range, have some truly fantastic scenery, excellent bushwalks and all the gorges, gum trees and cliffs you could ask for. The foothills begin 65km inland from Sydney and rise to 1100m, but the mountains are really a sandstone plateau riddled with spectacular gorges formed over millennia by erosion. The blue haze that gives the mountains their name is a result of the fine mist of volatile oil given off by eucalyptus trees.

For more than a century, the area has been a popular getaway for people seeking to escape the summer heat of Sydney. Despite the intensive tourist development, much of the area is so precipitous that it's open only to bushwalkers.

The Blue Mountains offers two main attractions – the national parks, with their superb scenery and opportunities for walking and other activities, and the guesthouses, with their hill-station atmosphere. Of course, it's possible to combine both. There's nothing like coming back to a log fire in an Edwardian house after a hard day's bushwalking.

History

The first Europeans in the area found evidence of extensive Aboriginal occupation, but few Aborigines. It seems likely that catastrophic diseases had already travelled from Sydney and wiped out the indigenous population.

The colonists at Port Jackson attempted to cross the mountains within a year or so of their arrival, driven not just by the usual lust for exploration but also by an urgent need to find land suitable for growing food for the new colony. However, the sheer cliffs, blind valleys and tough terrain defeated their attempts for nearly 25 years.

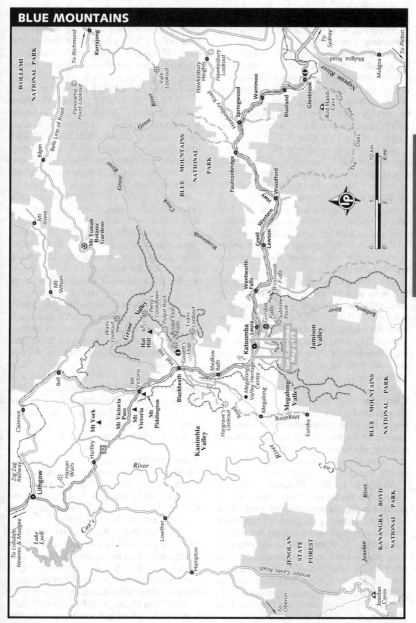

BLUE MOUNTAINS

AROUND SYDNEY

Many convicts came to believe that China, and freedom, were just the other side of the mountains.

The first crossing was made in 1813, by Blaxland, Wentworth and Lawson. They followed the ridge tops and their route is pretty much the same route of today's Great Western Hwy. The first road across the mountains was built in just six months. The great expansion into the western plains had begun.

After the railway across the mountains was completed in the 1860s, wealthy Sydney residents began to build mansions here as summer retreats from the heat and stench of Sydney town. By the turn of the 20th century, grand hotels and guesthouses had opened to cater for the increasing demand. This early tourist boom tapered off by the 1940s, but some of the old guesthouses have recently made a comeback and new resorts have been built.

One of Australia's first conservation battles was won in the Blue Mountains in 1931, when members of the Sydney Bushwalking Club came across loggers about to cut down Blue Gum Forest in the Grose Valley. They reached an agreement with the loggers to buy out their rights to the timber, and spent the next two years raising the £150 needed.

Climate

Be prepared for the climatic difference between the Blue Mountains and the coast – you can swelter in Sydney but shiver in Katoomba. However, even in winter the days are often clear and down in the valleys it can be warm.

Although the Blue Mountains are promoted as a cool-climate attraction, they're worth visiting at any time of year. With none of the summer haze, winter can be the best time for bushwalks, but beware of sudden changes in weather and come prepared for freezing conditions. Autumn's mists and drizzle can make bushwalking less attractive, but Katoomba in a thick mist is an atmospheric place.

It usually snows sometime between June and August.

Orientation

The Great Western Hwy from Sydney follows a ridge from east to west through the Blue Mountains. Along this less-than-beautiful road, the Blue Mountains towns often merge into each other – Glenbrook, Springwood, Woodford, Lawson, Wentworth Falls, Leura, Katoomba (the main accommodation centre), Medlow Bath, Blackheath, Mt Victoria and Hartley. Just west of Mt Victoria township, the road falls down Mt Victoria Pass, with sharp bends and a steep gradient. On the western fringe of the mountains is Lithgow, on a level with Penrith on the eastern side.

To the south and north of the highway's ridge the country drops away into steep valleys, including the Grose Gorge to the north and the Jamison Valley south of Katoomba. There's a succession of turn-offs to waterfalls, lookout points or scenic alternative routes along the highway.

The Bells Line of Road, much more scenic (and less congested) than the Great Western Hwy, is a more northerly approach from Sydney. From Richmond it runs north of the Grose Valley to emerge in Lithgow, although you can cut across from Bells Line of Road to join the Great Western Hwy at Mt Victoria.

Maps The NPWS Blue Mountains National Park Shop and Information Centre (see Information, following) sells maps and some books. Maps suitable for walking are also sold at information centres.

Information

There's a visitors information centre on the Great Western Hwy at Glenbrook and another at Echo Point in Katoomba. Both are open from 9 am to 5 pm daily. For phone inquiries call ☎ 1300 653 408.

The excellent NPWS centre (☎ 4787 8877) is on Govett's Leap Rd near Blackheath, about 3km north of the highway. This is the best place to ask about walks. It is open from 9 am to 4.30 pm daily. Blackheath has the closest train station to the centre.

Megalong Books (☎ 4784 1302), 82 Railway Parade in Leura, stocks books about the

Blue Mountains. It's open daily. *How to See the Blue Mountains* by Jim Smith is useful and has details of day walks, as does Neil Paton's *Walks in the Blue Mountains*. Lonely Planet's *Bushwalking in Australia* details the Blue Gum Forest walk.

You can hire camping gear from Mountain Designs (☎ 4782 5999), 190 Katoomba St, Katoomba.

National Parks

The **Blue Mountains National Park** protects large areas to the north and south of the Great Western Hwy. It's the most popular and accessible of the three national parks in the area and offers great bushwalking, scenic lookouts, breathtaking waterfalls and Aboriginal stencils.

Wollemi National Park, north of Bells Line of Road, is the state's largest forested wilderness area (nearly 500,000 hectares). It offers good rugged bushwalking and has lots of wildlife. Access is limited and the centre of the park is so isolated that a new species of tree, named the Wollemi pine, was discovered in 1994.

Kanangra Boyd National Park is southwest of the southern section of the Blue Mountains National Park. It has bushwalking, limestone caves and grand scenery including the spectacular Kanangra Walls Plateau, which is surrounded by sheer cliffs. The park can be reached by unsealed roads from Oberon or Jenolan Caves.

Entry to these national parks is free unless you enter the Blue Mountains National Park at Bruce Rd, Glenbrook, where it costs $5 per car (walkers free).

Lookouts

Blue Mountains views have been cliches for so long that it's a little surprising to find that they *are* breathtaking. Don't miss **Echo Point** at Katoomba, where you'll see the famous Three Sisters. **Cliff Drive**, running along the edge of the Jamison Valley between Leura and Katoomba, also has some great views. Make sure you get to **Govett's Leap** (near Blackheath, close to the NPWS centre) and **Evans Lookout** (north of the highway; turn off before Blackheath) for

spectacular views. Less well known but at least as spectacular are the viewpoints off Bells Line of Road, such as **Walls Lookout**. **Hawkesbury Heights**, on the road between Springwood and Bells Line of Road, has views across the Nepean River to Sydney, sometimes muddied by a cloud of tan smog.

Bushwalking

Bushwalking has been popular in the Blue Mountains for a long time. Myles Dunphy founded one of Australia's first bushwalking clubs in 1914 and the Blue Mountains was his favourite area.

There are walks lasting from a few minutes to several days. The two most popular areas, spectacular from both the cliff tops and the valleys, are the **Jamison Valley**, immediately south of Katoomba, and the **Grose Valley**, north-east of Katoomba and Blackheath. South of Glenbrook is another good area.

Visit an NPWS centre for information or, for shorter walks, ask at a tourist information centre. This is very rugged country and walkers sometimes get lost, so it's highly advisable to get reliable information, not to go alone, and to tell someone where you're going. Most Blue Mountains watercourses are polluted, so you have to sterilise water or take your own. Be prepared for rapid weather changes.

Blue Mountains Backpackers in Katoomba takes guests to trailheads. There's free parking near the trailhead for the Grand Canyon walk on Evans Lookout Rd.

There's a fairly easy three-day walk from Katoomba to Jenolan Caves along the **Six Foot Track**. The Department of Conservation & Land Management (DCLM) has a brochure detailing the walk. More challenging is the 140km **Ensign Barralier Walking Track** from Katoomba to Mittagong (see under Activities in the Southern Highlands section later in this chapter for more information).

On weekends and public holidays the NPWS runs a series of guided walks, many with an historical or ecological theme. These must be booked. Call ☎ 4787 8877 for information.

Other Activities

The cliffs, gorges and valleys of the Blue Mountains offer outstanding abseiling, rock climbing and canyoning. **Narrow Neck, Mt Victoria** and **Mt Peddington** are among the popular sites.

Cycling is permitted on most of the national park trails and, notwithstanding the hassle of carrying your bike down to the valley floor and back up, there is good riding.

Most outfits offering guided adventure activities and courses are based in Katoomba – see Activities in the Katoomba section later in this chapter. Several outfits in the Megalong Valley offer horse trail rides – see that section later in this chapter.

Organised Tours

Large tour operators running day trips to the Blue Mountains from Sydney include Australian Pacific (☎ 1300 655 965) and Gray Line (☎ 9252 4499). Both have similar day trips; a 'highlights' tour costs around $83 and a 'wilderness experience' around $123.

The Wonderbus (☎ 9555 9800), popular with backpackers, runs day tours of the Blue Mountains ($60 for students, YHA and VIP members, $65 others) and overnight trips that include the Jenolan Caves ($185/200), with dorm accommodation at the Katoomba YHA Hostel. There's an optional dawn 4WD wilderness tour. Tours depart from Sydney. Book in person at the Sydney YHA Travel Centre or the YHA hostels in Sydney. The City Host tourist information kiosk at Martin Place also takes bookings.

Oz Trek (☎ 9360 3444) does a good-value tour for $49 including some bushwalking.

Fantastic Aussie Tours (☎ 4782 1866, 1300 300 915), 283 Main St, Katoomba, runs tours departing from Katoomba including: half-day 'Blue Mountains Highlights' tours ($34/17 for adults/children), Jenolan Caves tours ($64), half-day 4WD wilderness tours ($68) and a full-day caving trips ($85).

Cox's River Escapes (☎ 4784 1621), in Leura, offers 4WD day tours of the Cox's River Valley with swimming, bushwalking and picnicking for $150.

Special Events

The region has a Yulefest in July, when many restaurants and guesthouses have good deals on 'Christmas' dinners.

Accommodation

Accommodation ranges from camp sites and hostels to expensive guesthouses and resorts. Katoomba is the main accommodation centre. Most places charge more at weekends and guesthouses tend to be booked out on long weekends. Camping is banned in some parts of the national parks and in others you need a permit, so check with the NPWS first.

Information centres (including the NSW Travel Centre in Sydney) stock copies of the free *Blue Mountains Holiday Book,* listing mid-range and top-end places. Good deals are often available. Information centres book accommodation in the Blue Mountains and will know of current specials and packages.

Getting There & Away

Katoomba, 109km from Sydney's city centre, is almost a satellite suburb. CityRail trains run more or less hourly from Central Station ($11.80 off-peak return, two hours). Countrylink buses meet trains at Mt Victoria for the run to Oberon (☎ 13 2232 for information).

By car, exit the city via Parramatta Rd and detour onto the Western Motorway toll road ($1.50) at Strathfield. The motorway becomes the Great Western Hwy west of Penrith. To reach the Bells Line of Road, exit the city on Parramatta Rd and from Parramatta head north-west on the Windsor Rd to Windsor. The Richmond Rd from Windsor becomes the Bells Line of Road west of Richmond.

Getting Around

Mountainlink (☎ 4782 3333, 1800 801 577) buses run between Leura, Katoomba, Medlow Bath, Blackheath and Mt Victoria, with some services running down Hat Hill Rd and Govett's Leap Rd, which lead respectively to Perry's Lookdown and Govett's Leap. The bus will take you to within about

1km of Govett's Leap, but for Perry's Lookdown you will have to walk about 6km from the last stop. Services are sparse, with only two buses running on Saturday on Hat Hill Rd and Govett's Leap, and none on Sunday. In Katoomba the bus leaves from the top of Katoomba St, outside the Carrington Hotel (timetables are posted there).

The Blue Mountains Bus Company (☎ 4782 4213) runs between Katoomba, Leura, Wentworth Falls and east as far as Woodford. There's roughly one service an hour from Katoomba train station.

On weekends and public holidays the Blue Mountains Explorer Bus offers all-day travel for $18/9. It departs regularly from the train station and visits the Scenic Railway, Skyway, Echo Point, Leura village and other places. It takes an hour to do the full circuit but you can get on or off and spend as much time as you like at a particular place. Contact Fantastic Aussie Tours (☎ 4782 1866), 283 Main St, Katoomba.

There are train stations in most Blue Mountains towns along the Great Western Hwy. Trains run roughly hourly between stations east of Katoomba and roughly two hourly between stations to the west.

If you're driving, parking restrictions are strictly enforced. The only car rental company is Thrifty, in Leura (☎ 4784 2888).

GLENBROOK TO KATOOMBA

From Marge's Lookout and Elizabeth's Lookout, near Glenbrook, there are good views back to Sydney. The section of the Blue Mountains National Park south of Glenbrook contains **Red Hands Cave**, an old Aboriginal shelter with hand stencils on the walls. It's an easy, 7km return walk south-west of the NPWS centre.

Springwood

The artist and author Norman Lindsay, infamous for his cheerfully erotic art, lived in Springwood from 1912 until his death in 1969. His home and studio at 14 Norman Lindsay Crescent, Faulconbridge, is now the **Norman Lindsay Gallery & Museum** (☎ 4751 1067), with exhibits of his paintings, watercolours, drawings, etchings and sculp-

tures. The beautiful grounds are great for a picnic and there's a 20-minute bushwalk trail. It's open from 10 am to 4 pm Wednesday to Monday ($7/3 for adults/children). There is a bus from Springwood train station at 10.55 am and returning at 2.43 pm weekdays.

Wentworth Falls

There are views of the Jamison Valley and of the 300m Wentworth Falls from **Falls Reserve**, the starting point for a network of walking tracks, south of the town.

In Wentworth Falls, signposted off the Great Western Hwy, **Yester Grange** (☎ 4782 2155) is the restored home of a 19th-century premier, open from 10 am to 4 pm weekdays and to 5 pm weekends ($5/2.50).

Leura

Leura is a quaint, tree-lined centre full of country stores and cafes. In Leura Strand Arcade, the Candy Store has a huge range of lollies (sweets).

Leuralla (☎ 4784 1169), at 36 Olympian Parade, is an Art Deco mansion with a fine collection of 19th-century Australian art, as well as a toy and model-railway museum. The house is a memorial to HV 'Doc' Evatt, a former Australian Labor Party leader and first president of the United Nations; it's open Wednesday to Sunday ($6/3).

Garden lovers should head to **Everglades**, a historic National Trust house with gardens designed by Paul Sorensen, a famous early 20th-century landscaper who did a lot of work in the Blue Mountains. It is open from 10 am to 5 pm daily ($5/1).

South of Leura, **Sublime Point** is a great cliff-top lookout. **Gordon Falls Reserve** is a popular picnic spot; from there you can follow the road back past Leuralla, then take Cliff Drive or the more scenic Prince Henry Cliff Walk to Katoomba's Echo Point.

Places to Stay

There are NPWS *camping areas* accessible by road at Euroka Clearing near Glenbrook, Murphys Glen near Woodford and Ingar near Wentworth Falls, but always check for updates about the accessibility of areas and tracks at the NPWS office (eg, the tracks to

Ingar and Murphys Glen may be closed after heavy rain). Get a permit to camp at Euroka Clearing from the NPWS office (☎ 4588 5247) at Richmond.

About 8km north-east of Springwood is the small, ecofriendly *Hawkesbury Heights Hostel* (☎ *4754 5621, 836 Hawkesbury Road, Hawkesbury Heights*). It sleeps 12 in twin rooms and costs $12 per person or $100 per night for the whole hostel. Booking is essential.

In Leura, *Woodford of Leura* (☎/*fax 4784 2240*, ❷ *woodford@leura.com, 48 Woodford St*) offers B&B in a stunning garden setting for $110 a double. The owners provide complimentary afternoon teas. Heading upmarket, *Leura House* (☎ *4784 2035, fax 4784 3329, 7 Britain St*) is a grand Victorian home (c. 1880) with facilities for the disabled. Weekday rates are $69 per person rising to $120 on weekends. The 210-room *Fairmont Resort* (☎ *4782 5222*, ❷ *reservations@fairmont.com.au, 1 Sublime Point Rd*) is right on the edge of the escarpment and has great views, although it is fairly impersonal. Rates are from $99 per person midweek and from $164 weekends.

KATOOMBA
postcode 2780 • pop 8300

Katoomba and the adjacent centres of Wentworth Falls and Leura form the tourist centre of the Blue Mountains. Katoomba is where the Sydney 'plains-dwellers' escape the summer heat, and has long catered to visitors. Despite the number of tourists and its closeness to Sydney, Katoomba has an uncanny atmosphere: another time, another place, accentuated by its Art Nouveau and Art Deco guesthouses and cafes, its thick mists and occasional snowfalls.

Information

The visitor information centre (☎ 1300 653 408), at the end of Echo Point Rd, about 2km from the train station down Katoomba St, is open from 9 am to 5 pm daily.

The post office is opposite the shopping centre between Katoomba and Parke Sts.

The Internet cafe, Barcode 6ix, at 6 Katoomba St, is open from 9 am to 9 pm daily.

Things to See

The major tourist attraction is **Echo Point**, near the southern end of Katoomba St about 1km from the shopping centre. Here you'll find some of the best views of the Jamison Valley and the magnificent **Three Sisters** rock formation.

The story goes that the three sisters were turned to stone by a sorcerer to protect them from the unwanted advances of three young men, but the sorcerer died before he could turn them back into humans.

Floodlit at night, the rocks are an awesome sight. A walking track follows the road and goes even closer to the edge.

West of Echo Point, at the junction of Cliff Drive and Violet St, are the **Scenic Railway** and **Scenic Skyway** (☎ 4782 2699). The railway drops 200m to the bottom of the Jamison Valley ($4/7 one way/return) where there's good bushwalking. The railway was built in the 1880s to transport coal miners and its 45° incline is one of the steepest in the world. The Scenic Skyway cable car travels some 200m above the valley floor, traversing Katoomba Falls gorge ($7 return).

The **Explorers Tree**, just west of Katoomba near the Great Western Hwy, was marked by Blaxland, Wentworth and Lawson in their crossing of the mountains in 1813.

Activities

The 12km-return **bushwalk** to the **Ruined Castle** rock formation on Narrow Neck Plateau, dividing the Jamison and Megalong Valleys, is one of the best walks - watch out for leeches after rain. The **Golden Stairs** lead down from this plateau to more bushwalking tracks.

Several companies offer **abseiling**, **rock climbing**, **canyoning** and **caving**. The competition means that the deals are usually similar – expect to pay about $89 for a day's abseiling.

High 'n' Wild Mountain Adventure (☎ 4782 6224), 3/5 Katoomba St, is run by an enthusiastic team of mountaineers and ex-travellers. It offers abseiling, climbing and various canyoning trips ($75 to $139). Half-/full-day mountain-bike tours start at

KATOOMBA

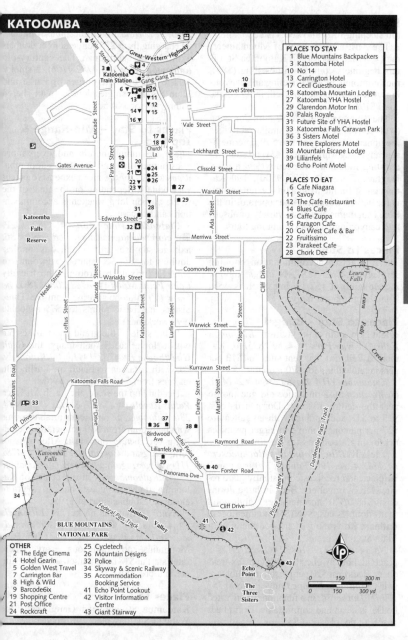

PLACES TO STAY
1 Blue Mountains Backpackers
3 Katoomba Hotel
10 No 14
13 Carrington Hotel
18 Cecil Guesthouse
18 Katoomba Mountain Lodge
27 Katoomba YHA Hostel
29 Clarendon Motor Inn
30 Palais Royale
31 Future Site of YHA Hostel
33 Katoomba Falls Caravan Park
36 3 Sisters Motel
37 Three Explorers Motel
38 Mountain Escape Lodge
39 Lilianfels
40 Echo Point Motel

PLACES TO EAT
6 Cafe Niagara
11 Savoy
12 The Cafe Restaurant
14 Blues Cafe
15 Caffe Zuppa
16 Paragon Cafe
20 Go West Cafe & Bar
22 Fruitissimo
23 Parakeet Cafe
28 Chork Dee

OTHER
2 The Edge Cinema
4 Hotel Gearin
5 Golden West Travel
7 Carrington Bar
8 High & Wild
9 Barcode6ix
19 Shopping Centre
21 Post Office
24 Rockcraft
25 Cycletech
26 Mountain Designs
32 Police
34 Skyway & Scenic Railway
35 Accommodation
   Booking Service
41 Echo Point Lookout
42 Visitor Information
   Centre
43 Giant Stairway

$55/99. Its two-day bush survival course (no sleeping bags allowed!) is $225.

The Australian School of Mountaineering (☎ 4782 2014), 166b Katoomba St, offers beginners courses on abseiling ($89), rock climbing, mountaineering and canyoning. A two-day basic rock-climbing course costs $195.

The Blue Mountains Adventure Company (☎ 4782 1271) organises similar activities (beginners abseiling course $99, intermediate canyoning trips from $145) and some interesting mountain-bike tours ($99 a day). Dogface Tours (☎ 4782 9500), 190 Katoomba St (in the Mountain Designs shop), is the newest adventure-tour operator in the Blue Mountains and has a variety of abseiling, canyoning and rock-climbing tours.

Places to Stay

There is a free accommodation booking service (☎ 4782 2857, @ info@bmbookings.com.au) at 157 Lurline St. It is open from 9 am to 5 pm daily.

Places to Stay – Budget

About 2km south of the highway, *Katoomba Falls Caravan Park* (☎ 4782 1835), on Katoomba Falls Rd, has tent sites for $12 per person and cabins for $70 a double.

Katoomba YHA Hostel (☎ 4782 1416, 66 Waratah St) is in a nice old guesthouse near the centre of town. Dorm beds cost $15 to $18 and doubles with en suites are $27 per person. A move to larger premises nearby in Katoomba St is imminent.

The VIP *Blue Mountains Backpackers* (☎ 4782 4226, 190 Bathurst Rd) is a popular place and receives consistently good reviews from travellers. Beds in large dorms cost $18 ($20 nonmembers) and good twins/doubles cost $46 ($50 nonmembers). Bathurst Rd is the western continuation of Main St.

No 14 (☎ 4782 7104, 14 Lovel St) is a peaceful, homely guesthouse run by ex-travellers. Beds cost $20 per person in doubles or twins. *Mountain Escape Lodge* (☎ 1800 357 577, 77 Darley St), in a functional, converted house, is clean and comfortable. Dorm beds cost $20; doubles cost $55.

Katoomba Mountain Lodge (☎ 4782 3933, 31 Lurline St) is a guesthouse and hostel charging from $35 per person for doubles with shared bathrooms. The century-old *Katoomba Hotel* (☎ 4782 1106), a smoky Aussie local on the corner of Parke and Main Sts, has singles/doubles with shared bathrooms for $40/60.

Places to Stay – Mid-Range & Top End

There are many motels and even more guesthouses in and around Katoomba. Rates at most of the more expensive places vary widely, depending on the time of the week, and on long weekends accommodation can be scarce.

Clarendon Motor Inn (☎ 4782 1322, @ clarendon@pnc.com.au, 68 Lurline St), half guesthouse, half motel, has singles/doubles for $58/78 (shared bathroom) or $88/118 (private bathroom). The friendly *Echo Point Motel* (☎ 4782 2088, 18 Echo Point Rd), a stone's throw from the Three Sisters, has basic rooms for $75 a double ($90 weekends).

In the style of the grand guesthouses but with a lower tariff than many, the *Cecil Guesthouse* (☎ 4782 1411, 108 Katoomba St), with a larger frontage on Lurline St, charges from $40/75 with breakfast.

Heading up the scale, the plush Art Deco *Palais Royale* (☎ 4782 7888, fax 4782 7444 230 Katoomba St) has comfortable rooms with bathroom from $89 per person, including a very hearty breakfast. After a major refit, the grand *Carrington Hotel* (☎ 4782 1111, @ carrington@thecarrington.com.au 15–47 Katoomba St), in the centre of Katoomba, transports guests back to an era of elegance. Doubles start at $195.

Even further upmarket is *Lilianfels* (☎ 4780 1200, @ reservations@lilianfel.com.au), on Lilianfels Ave, one of the Blue Mountains' most luxurious resorts, where rates start at $181 per person including dinner and breakfast.

Places to Eat

Katoomba St, between Gang Gang and Waratah Sts, has plenty of good places to eat. The bright, Art Deco *Savoy (12 Katoomba St)* has an interesting menu of focaccia, pasta and Asian-inspired food. It's pleasant and has reasonable prices. Salads cost $7.50 and pastas start at $8.50.

The eternally popular *Blues Cafe (57 Katoomba St)* has mostly vegetarian (and vegan) food – steamed vegies and brown rice with tofu and peanut sauce costs $9. It has Art Deco decor, but nearby is Katoomba's undisputed Art Deco masterpiece, the *Paragon Cafe (65 Katoomba St)*. While the menu offers only a little more than you'll find in NSW country-town cafes, the surroundings are as wonderful as the handmade chocolates. It is open during the day Tuesday to Sunday.

On the other side of the street, *The Cafe Restaurant* has sandwiches and kangaroo burgers ($8.90), and is open for breakfast. *Caffe Zuppa (36 Katoomba St)* has several choices of home-made soup daily ($7) as well as pastas (such as vegetarian ravioli with chive sauce) and a good choice of bagels and pizzette.

Farther down Katoomba St, *Fruitissimo (175 Katoomba St)* is a lively vegetarian cafe offering pasta for $7.50, focaccia for $8, juices and good-quality fresh fruit. Nearby, the sociable *Parakeet Cafe (195 Katoomba St)* has vegie burgers for $8.50, lamb cutlets for $12.50. There are tables outside. Across Waratah St, the Thai *Chork Dee (216 Katoomba St)* has *pad king* (chicken with ginger) for $10.60 and vegetarian dishes for around $8; it's open for dinner only.

Near the station, *Cafe Niagara (92 Main St)* is an Art Deco cafe with a varied menu. Try the Niagara burger, with pesto and mozzarella ($10.90); there are great desserts and cakes.

Entertainment

On Friday night *Cafe Niagara* has a cabaret and drag show. *Parakeet Cafe* has live entertainment on Friday and Saturday night. The green-tiled *Carrington Bar (15 Katoomba St)* is a lively spot in the evenings. For local bands, try the *Katoomba Hotel*, on the corner of Parke and Main Sts, on weekends, or *Hotel Gearin*, opposite the station. The *Blues Cafe* sometimes has jazz.

If you want to experience the thrills of the Blue Mountains without leaving the comfort of a cushioned seat, *The Edge Cinema (☎ 4782 8900, 225–237 Great Western Hwy)* shows a 40-minute Blue Mountains documentary, *The Edge*, as well as current releases on a giant screen ($12.50/8.50 for adults/children).

Getting Around

The Blue Mountains Bus Company (☎ 4782 4213) runs from opposite the Carrington Hotel to the Scenic Railway approximately hourly until about 4.30 pm on weekdays and a few times on Saturday ($3). Mountainlink (☎ 4782 3333) runs a service between Echo Point and Gordon Falls via Katoomba St and Leura Mall. There is roughly one service an hour midweek, fewer on weekends. See also Getting Around at the start of the Blue Mountains section for information about the Blue Mountains Explorer Bus.

Cycletech (☎ 4782 2800), 182 Katoomba St, rents rigid-fork mountain bikes for $15 a half-day, $25 a full day and $45 for two days. Suspension bikes cost a bit more.

BLACKHEATH & AROUND
postcode 2785 • pop 3800

Blackheath, 10km north-west of Katoomba on the Great Western Hwy, is a good base for visiting the Grose and Megalong Valleys.

There are superb lookouts east of town, among them **Govett's Leap** with the adjacent **Bridal Veil Falls** (the highest in the Blue Mountains) and **Evans Lookout** (turn off the highway south of Blackheath). To the north-east, via Hat Hill Rd, are **Pulpit Rock**, **Perry's Lookdown** and **Anvil Rock**.

A long cliff-edge track leads from Govett's Leap to Pulpit Rock and there are walks down into the Grose Valley. All involve at least a 300m descent and ascent. Get details on walks and trail conditions from the NPWS centre. Perry's Lookdown is at the beginning of the shortest route to the beautiful **Blue Gum Forest** at the foot of the valley – a full day's return walk or a good overnight hike if you want to camp. To the west and south-west of Blackheath

AROUND SYDNEY

lie the Kanimbla and Megalong Valleys, with yet more spectacular views from places like **Hargrave's Lookout**.

Places to Stay & Eat

The nearest NPWS camp site is *Acacia Flat* in the Grose Valley, near the Blue Gum Forest. It's a steep walk down from Govett's Leap or Perry's Lookdown. You can camp at *Perry's Lookdown*, which has a car park and is a convenient base for walks into the Grose Valley.

Blackheath Caravan Park (☎ 4787 8101), on Prince Edward St off Govett's Leap Rd about 600m from the highway, has tent sites for $7 a single and vans from $38 a double. Nearby, *Lakeview Holiday Park* (☎ 4787 8534), also on Prince Edward St, has cabins from $50 a double.

The cosy *Gardners Inn* (☎ 4787 8347), on the Great Western Hwy in Blackheath, is the oldest hotel (1831) in the Blue Mountains, and charges $35/60 for singles/doubles with shared bathrooms, including breakfast. *Jenby-Rimbah Lodge* (☎ 4787 7622, 336 Evans Lookout Rd) is an eco-tourism lodge in bushland with good self-contained cabins (sleeping four) from $98. If you're looking for luxury and tranquillity in a stunning garden setting, head for *Parklands* (☎ 4787 7771), on Govett's Leap Rd, where weekday doubles start from $205. On weekends, two nights for two people costs $530; a gourmet breakfast basket is included.

Several cafes are clustered along the highway and Govett's Leap Rd, including *Wattle Cafe*, which serves hamburgers for $2.50 and has a potbelly stove. The *Banksia* has bagels with interesting fillings for $8.90 and excellent coffee.

Two top Sydney restaurateurs run *Vulcan's* (☎ 4787 6899, 33 Govett's Leap Rd), a cosmopolitan city-style cafe in the mountains. It is open weekends only; booking is essential.

Cleopatra (☎ 4787 8456), on Cleopatra St, is one of NSW's top restaurants, winner of many awards. There's also accommodation, with midweek packages ranging from $175 to $220 per person including meals.

MEGALONG VALLEY
postcode 2785

Unless you walk or take Katoomba's Scenic Railway, about the only chance you'll get to see what the gorges of the Blue Mountains look like from below is via the Megalong Valley. It feels like rural Australia here, a big change from the quasi-suburbs strung out along the ridge tops. It is largely cleared farmland but still beautiful. The road down from Blackheath passes through pockets of **rainforest**; you can taste the Blue Mountains' beauty by following the 600m Coachwood Glen Nature Trail, 2km before the small settlement of Werribee.

Megalong Valley Heritage Centre (☎ 4787 8188) is a display farm with activities ranging from sheep herding to whip cracking, horse and harness shows, animal feeding and shearing. It's open from 10 am to 5 pm daily; day passes cost $9.95 (family $29.95), half-day passes $7. There is also accommodation in bunkhouses; dorm beds cost $15. Two-day bush trail rides cost $195.

There are several **horse riding** outfits, such as Werriberri Trail Rides (☎ 4787 9171), on Megalong Rd near the heritage centre, which offers three-hour rides for $52. Packsaddlers (☎ 4787 9150), run by one of the district's longest-established families, at the end of the valley in Green Gully, offers riding and accommodation.

MT VICTORIA
postcode 2786 • pop 880

Mt Victoria is a small village, 16km northwest of Katoomba, with some historic buildings and a semirural atmosphere. At 1043m it's also the highest point in the mountains. It has been popular as a holiday spot for a long time and author Henry Lawson worked here as a house painter, decorating the houses that his father built. Today the town is classified by the National Trust.

Everything is an easy walk from the train station, where the **Mt Victoria Museum of Australiana** is open from 2 to 5 pm weekends ($2/0.50 for adults/children). Interesting buildings include the Victoria & Albert guesthouse, the 1849 Tollkeeper's Cottage and the 1870s church.

Mt Vic Flicks (☎ 4787 1577) is a cinema of the old school, with 'usherettes', a piano player and door prizes. It shows mainstream films and the more popular arthouse releases. On Thursday it costs $5.50; on Saturday night $7.50 ($5.50 children).

Off the highway at **Mt York** there's a memorial to the European explorers who first crossed the Blue Mountains. A short stretch of the original road crosses the mountains here.

Places to Stay
The fine old *Hotel Imperial (☎ 4787 1878, 1 Station St)* has doubles from $88. Nearby, the *Victoria & Albert (☎ 4787 1588, 19 Station St)* is a guesthouse in the grand old style. B&B costs from $49.50 per person. The guesthouse also has a cafe and a good licensed restaurant.

Another old-style guesthouse is *Manor House (☎ 4787 1369),* on Montgomery St, with rooms from $79 to $90 per person, including dinner and breakfast. The Duke of York, later King George VI, had afternoon tea here in 1927.

HARTLEY HISTORIC SITE
In the 1830s, after the Victoria Pass route made it easier to travel inland from the coast, increasing numbers of travellers crossed the Blue Mountains. However, the discomforts of the old road via Mt York were soon replaced by the discomforts of being bailed up by bushrangers. The government established Hartley, 10km north-west of Mt Victoria, as a police post and the village became a popular place to break the journey, partly because it was safe and partly because of the pubs. Some fine sandstone buildings were constructed, notably the Greek Revival courthouse (1837). Many remain today, although the village is now deserted.

The NPWS information centre (☎ 6355 2117) in the Farmer's Inn is open from 10 am to 1 pm and 2 to 4.30 pm daily. You can wander around the village for free but to enter specific buildings you have to take a guided tour ($4/3 for adults/children), with a minimum group size of six. Countrylink buses stop nearby.

JENOLAN CAVES
South-west of Katoomba and on the western fringe of Kanangra Boyd National Park are the Jenolan Caves (☎ 6359 3311), the best-known limestone caves in Australia. One cave has been open to the public since 1867, although parts of the system are still unexplored. Three caves are open for independent viewing and you can visit a further nine by guided tour. There are about 10 tours from 10 am to 5 pm daily, with an evening tour at 8 pm Saturday. Tours last one to two hours and prices start from $12 and rise to $50. During holiday times it's advisable to arrive early, as the best caves can be 'sold out' by 10 am; better still, book ahead.

Walks
There's a network of walking trails through the bush surrounding the Jenolan Caves.

The 42km **Six Foot Track** from Katoomba to the Jenolan Caves is a fairly easy three-day walk (it can be done in two days if you are energetic). The NPWS has a detailed brochure, produced by DCLM. Great Australian Walks (☎ 9555 7580) has guided walks along the Six Foot Track with accommodation for $370. They carry everything for you.

Organised Tours
See Organised Tours at the start of the Blue Mountains section for information on the popular Wonderbus tour. Fantastic Aussie Tours (☎ 4782 1866) has day tours to the caves from Katoomba for $64 (one cave) or $73 (two caves). Walkers can be dropped off at and collected from the Six Foot Track at Jenolan for $36, but you have to book.

Places to Stay
On the road from Hartley about 8km north of the caves, *Jenolan Caves Cottages (☎ 6359 3311, ✉ jencaves@jenolan.org.au)* has cottages (sleeping six) for $80 per night. *Jenolan Cabins (☎ 6335 6239, 42 Edith Rd),* off the Oberon road, has cabins (sleeping six) for $89 to $95 per night.

In Oberon, about 30km north-west of the caves, there are other, cheaper options – see the Central West chapter.

BELLS LINE OF ROAD

This back road between Richmond and Lithgow is the most scenic route across the Blue Mountains. It's highly recommended if you have your own transport. There are fine views towards the coast from Kurrajong Heights, orchards around Bilpin and Shipley and sandstone cliff and bush scenery all the way to Lithgow. This road was constructed in 1841 by Archibald Bell, a local landowner, as an alternative route across the mountains.

Mt Tomah Botanic Garden

Midway between Bilpin and Bell, Mt Tomah Botanic Garden (☎ 4567 2154) is a cool-climate annexe of Sydney's Royal Botanic Gardens. As well as native plants there are exotic species including a magnificent display of rhododendrons. The gardens are open daily; admission is $5 per car or motorcycle, $2 for pedestrians and cyclists.

Mt Wilson

Mt Wilson is 8km north of Bells Line of Road; the turn-off is 7km south-east of Bell. Like Katoomba, Mt Wilson was settled by people with a penchant for things English, but unlike Katoomba, with its guesthouses and Art Deco cafes, Mt Wilson is a spacious village of hedgerows, lines of European trees and houses with big gardens. Near the Post House there's an information board with details of gardens open to the public and some short walks in the area.

About 1km from the village centre is the Cathedral of Ferns, a lovely remnant of rainforest thick with tree ferns.

The Post House (☎ 4756 2000) serves teas and can arrange B&B accommodation, or you could try Blueberry Lodge (☎ 4756 2022), on Waterfall Rd, with self-contained chalets sleeping up to six and costing $140 a double (more on weekends).

Zig Zag Railway

The Zig Zag Railway (☎ 6353 1795) is at Clarence, about 10km east of Lithgow. It was built in 1869 and was quite an engineering wonder in its day. Trains descended from the Blue Mountains by this route until 1910. A section has been restored and steam and diesel trains run daily. The fare for the 12km trip is $13/6.50 for adults/children.

LITHGOW

postcode 2790 ● pop 20,400

Nestled in the western foothills of the Blue Mountains, the Lithgow Valley was first settled by Europeans in the 1820s, but the town didn't begin to grow until the coal was mined in the 1870s to supply the trains crossing the mountains on the Zig Zag Railway. Today Lithgow is a pleasant rural town, with some nice restored buildings.

The Lithgow Visitor Information Centre (☎ 6353 18590), with super-helpful staff, is in the old train station on the Great Western Hwy just north of the turn-off into town. It's open from 9 am to 5 pm daily, and has maps plus lists of local attractions and accommodation. It also has information on sites and attractions around Lithgow.

Eskbank House

This gracious home (☎ 6351 3557) was built by the founder of Lithgow's coal industry in 1842. It now houses a museum and is open from 10 am to 4 pm Thursday to Monday ($2). Australia's first steelworks were established in Lithgow in the 19th century, but all that remain are a few crumbling buildings in Blast Furnace Park off Inch St, although there are plans to develop it.

Places to Stay

The Lithgow Caravan Park (☎ 6351 4350), on Cooerwull Rd, has tent sites for $10 for two people, on-site vans for $30 and self-contained cabins for $50.

Several pubs have accommodation, including the Grand Central (☎ 6351 3050), on the corner of Main and Eskbank Sts, with singles/doubles for $20/40. Motels include the Lithgow Valley Motel (☎ 6351 2334), off the highway on Cooerwull Drive, with rooms from $40/56. At Clarence, Zig Zag Lodge (☎ 6355 2683, 94 Donald Rd) has B&B for $80 a double.

Getting There & Away

Countrylink buses (☎ 13 2232) connect with some trains and run to Orange, Bathurst

Dubbo, Coonabarabran, Mudgee, Gulgong, Forbes and Parkes, but not daily.

Lithgow is on the main western train line to Bathurst, Orange and Dubbo. CityRail trains also run from Sydney.

Lithgow is on the Great Western Hwy, which runs between Sydney and Bathurst. You can head south on smaller roads to Oberon (where still smaller roads lead south to Goulburn) and north to Mudgee and Gulgong (turn off the highway about 7km on the Bathurst side of town).

AROUND LITHGOW

At Lidsdale, on the Mudgee road about 10km north of Lithgow, a road degenerates into the rough track running 30-odd kilometres to **Newnes**, a ghost town. Ruins of the **Newnes Oil Shale Mine**, established in 1906, are worth a visit. There's a 5km walk to a disused railway tunnel full of glow-worms and access to the wild Wollemi National Park. An 11km walking track leads north to the ghost town of **Glen Davis** where there's a museum open on weekends. There are camping areas at both Newnes and Glen Davis.

At the former **Mt Piper Power Station** there are interactive displays on the production and use of electricity and free tours of the power station.

There are fine views from **Hassan Walls Lookout**, 5km south of town. **Blackfellows Hands Reserve**, 24km north of Lithgow off the Wolgan Rd, features Aboriginal rock paintings.

Southern Highlands

The fertile Southern Highlands was one of the first inland areas to be settled by Europeans. Most of it was quickly cleared of unruly native foliage to make way for agriculture and English-style villages. This development was early enough in Australia's history for the settlers to regard themselves as English landed gentry rather than Australian farmers and their unease at being so far from home can be understood amid this landscape of bare hills, brooding pines and stone buildings.

As well as being of historical interest, the Southern Highlands gives access to the excellent Morton National Park. The country north of the Hume Hwy is more rugged and there's an interesting drive to the Wombeyan Caves and on to Bathurst.

Information

The area's main source of information is the Southern Highlands Visitors Information Centre (☎ 4871 2888) in Mittagong; it's open from 8 am to 5.30 pm daily. It also provides a free accommodation booking service (☎ 1300 657 559). Craigie's *Visitors Map of the Southern Highlands* ($5) covers the area in detail.

Activities

There is some good bushwalking in the area, especially in Morton National Park. One of the longest trails is the **Ensign Barralier Walking Track**, which begins near Mittagong at Lake Alexandra and winds 140km

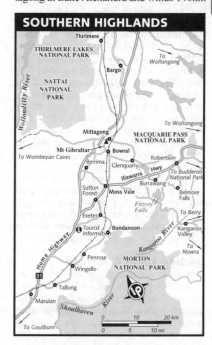

SOUTHERN HIGHLANDS

north through wild country to Katoomba. It takes seven to nine days and passes through the privately owned ghost town of **Yerranderie**. Robert Sloss has written a booklet containing detailed track notes; it's available from the Southern Highlands Visitors Information Centre for $6.90 (it can mail credit-card orders). Information centres in the Blue Mountains may also stock it.

Horse riding is offered on many properties in the highlands. Caringal Holiday Farm (☎ 4886 4234), not far from Fitzroy Falls, charges $25 an hour for riding, $30 for lessons. Other outfits include Birrabongie (☎ 4877 1114), in Berrima, which has hour-long trail rides for $25, and Maple Downs Tourist Park (☎ 4861 6075) in Bowral.

Special Events
The Mittagong Country Fair is held in late March and the Bowral Tulip Festival is held in late September. Over the Queen's Birthday long weekend in June, the village of Burrawang holds a folk-music festival.

Accommodation
In the 1920s a bout of nostalgia for 'home' afflicted the area, resulting in lavish country guesthouses catering to wealthy Sydney residents. The few guesthouses that remain are popular. The highlands can be a bleak place in winter, with grey skies and winds off the snow, so log fires and hearty meals have their attraction and certainly offer a contrast to Sydney, not far away on the Hume Hwy. As in the Blue Mountains, many guesthouses celebrate Christmas in winter.

The larger places are almost resorts and the words 'exclusive' and 'luxury' figure prominently in their advertising. Tourism NSW information centres and some travel agents in Sydney have brochures and will know about packages and special deals.

Getting There & Around
Bus Long-distance buses running on the Hume Hwy between Sydney and Melbourne call in at Mittagong, but most don't go on to Bowral or Moss Vale. The visitors information centre in Mittagong sells tickets for most buslines; you can buy Countrylink

tickets at the train station, a few blocks away. Buses don't come off the highway into Mittagong unless someone has booked a ticket. Except for Countrylink, whose buses stop at the train station, buses stop at the visitors information centre.

Berrima Coaches (☎ 4871 3211) runs fairly frequent weekday services between Mittagong, Bowral and Moss Vale, with a few continuing on to Berrima, Sutton Forest, Exeter and Bundanoon. On Saturday morning, Berrima Coaches has services between Mittagong, Bowral and Moss Vale. Kiama Coaches (☎ 4232 3466) has buses between Wollongong and Moss Vale, some running via Bundanoon.

Train CityRail trains run to Mittagong, Bowral and Moss Vale. Some Countrylink trains on the Sydney-Canberra run stop at these stations and at Bundanoon; the XPT (express train) to/from Melbourne also stops at one or more of them. Check with CityRail and Countrylink for schedules.

Car & Motorcycle The Hume Hwy runs past Mittagong, which is 1½ hours from Sydney, and Bowral. The Illawarra Hwy links the area with the coast and runs through Moss Vale.

MITTAGONG & BOWRAL
postcode 2575/2576 • pop 20,000
These two large towns, surrounded by dairy farming and stud cattle country, have almost blended into each other. **Moss Vale**, just south of Bowral, may eventually do the same.

If you're driving between Bowral and Mittagong, take the scenic route over **Mt Gibraltar**, which gives good views down the valley.

Sir Donald Bradman began his cricketing career in Bowral. The large **Bradman Museum** (☎ 4862 1247), on St Jude St a few blocks east of the main street, is in a purpose-built pavilion beside a cricket ground and contains plenty of memorabilia. You can see videos of 'The Don's' career and other pieces of cricketing history. The museum is open from 10 am to 5 pm daily ($7/3 for adults/children).

Our Don Bradman

Sir Donald Bradman is probably the greatest batsman cricket has ever seen, and is an Australian sporting legend and national treasure. Born in Cootamundra in central west New South Wales in 1908, the young Bradman practised for his illustrious cricketing career by hitting a golf ball against a corrugated metal tank using a cricket stump as a bat. In this way he developed his footwork, his quick eye and judgment of bowling. He became a brilliant outfielder and is considered by many to have been the greatest natural batsman in the history of cricket.

Bradman took the cricket world by storm, scoring 19 centuries in Test matches against England between 1928 and 1948. Known to Australians as 'The Don' or simply 'Our Don Bradman', he was instrumental in lifting the spirit of an entire nation after WWII. He captained the 1948 Test team, still regarded as Australia's best-ever side. He retired the same year with a Test batting average of 99.9! The average would have been over 100 had Sir Donald not been dismissed for a duck (0) in his last innings, and it's a mark of the man's character that he didn't play another match to boost the average.

KN

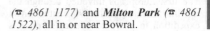

AROUND SYDNEY

Places to Stay

The *Mittagong Caravan Park* (☎ 4871 1574), on the old highway, has tent sites for about $12, on-site vans from $30 and cabins from $47. *Moss Vale Village Park* (☎ 4868 1099), off Argyle St (the Illawarra Hwy) south of the town centre, is similarly priced.

The *Mittagong Hotel* (☎ 4871 1923), on the old highway, has singles/doubles from $20/40. On the highway in Mittagong, motels include the *Melrose* (☎ 4871 1511) and the *Mittagong* (☎ 4871 1277), which charges from $50 a double. In Bowral there's a swag of more expensive places; the *Oxley View* (☎ 4861 4211), on Moss Vale Rd, has rooms with spa baths from $70/80.

Braemar Lodge (☎ 4871 2483), off the old highway just north of Mittagong, is a big old mansion in large grounds with doubles for $75 to $100, including breakfast. There's also an Indian restaurant.

In Robertson, on the Illawarra Hwy between Bowral and the coast, is *Ranelagh House* (☎ 4885 1111), built in 1924. Deer and peacocks roam the extensive grounds and apparently a friendly ghost walks the hallways. B&B rates are $55 per person on weekdays.

Top-end places to stay include *Links House* (☎ 4861 1977), *Berida Manor* (☎ 4861 1177) and *Milton Park* (☎ 4861 1522), all in or near Bowral.

WOMBEYAN CAVES

These interesting limestone caves (☎ 4843 5976), 65km north-west of Mittagong, are reached by an even more interesting mountain road. The caves are in a pretty little valley with mown lawns shaded by poplars and pines. The surrounding bushland is a nature reserve with some walking trails and plenty of wildlife. You can walk to a swimming hole at Limestone Canyon. Guided tours of the caves cost $12/6/30 for adults/children/families, and there's one cave you can inspect by yourself for $10. Wombeyan is open from 8.30 am to 5 pm daily.

Places to Stay

At the Wombeyan *camping reserve* next to the caves there are tent sites for $12, caravan sites for $15, on-site vans for $45 and cabins with en suites for $65. There's a kiosk and a well-equipped communal kitchen for campers.

On the Mittagong road, just before the steep ascent into the Wombeyan Nature Reserve, *Wollondilly Camping Ground* (☎ 4888 9239) has some lovely camping areas on the banks of a broad, shallow river. It also rents out tents. Off the road, back towards Mittagong, is *River Island Nature Retreat (☎ 4888 9236)*, with camping (powered sites $10) and vans ($59). There's a small store here.

Getting There & Away

From Canberra or Melbourne, the Goulburn/Taralga route is quickest and involves only 4km of narrow, winding road. From Sydney, take the road running west from Mittagong. This route is direct but involves about 45km of narrow, steep and winding mountain road – very scenic but slow. It's a popular drive; watch out for oncoming cars at blind corners, especially on weekends.

Fuel is available at the camping reserve.

BERRIMA
postcode 2577

The first Europeans travelled through the Berrima area early in the 19th century on an expedition to prove to Sydney's convicts that China (and thus freedom) did not lie on the other side of the Great Dividing Range.

The site for Berrima was chosen by explorer Thomas Mitchell and the town was founded in 1829. It blossomed as a stopping-place on the way to the wide lands west of the mountains. However, the road proved too steep for easy travel, bushrangers infested the route and eventually the railway bypassed the town. Berrima's population dropped to just eight people by 1900, and consequently the town suffered little from further development. Today the population is under 800 and the village is heritage classified.

The best of its old buildings is the neo-classical **Berrima Courthouse**, built in 1838. The court now houses an excellent little museum (☎ 4877 1505) and for $3/2 for adults/children you can see an audiovisual on Berrima's history and visit the court-room, set up – complete with dummies and a soundtrack – as it was during the trial of a woman who murdered her husband with an axe. The courthouse is open from 10 am to 4 pm daily and also has tourist information.

Berrima Museum (☎ 4868 2230), at the other end of the main street opposite the Al-

paca Centre, houses a local history collection. It's open from 10 am to 4 pm on weekends ($2/1). The nearby **Surveyor General Inn** claims to be Australia's oldest continuously operating hotel (ho-hum). The first owner of the pub built himself a large house on Wilkinson St, **Harper's Mansion** (☎ 4861 2402), where a maze was being built at the time of writing. It will be open daily.

Places to Stay

The *White Horse Inn (☎ 4877 1204)*, on Market Place, was built in 1832, but has newer motel rooms from $85. So too does the *Berrima Bakehouse Motel (☎ 4877 1381)*, which charges from $73 midweek to $110 for doubles. The *Surveyor General Inn (☎ 4877 1226)*, on the main street, has doubles for $50 midweek ($70 weekends), including breakfast. Ask the information centre about other places offering B&B, most of which are pricey.

BUNDANOON & AROUND
postcode 2578 • pop 1500

Bundanoon is a village off the Hume Hwy, midway between Sydney and Canberra. Tourists discovered the town early and in the 1920s it was the guesthouse capital of the Southern Highlands, with over 50 guest-houses. There are far fewer today but you can still experience some of that stuccoed charm.

Ye Olde Bicycle Shoppe (☎ 4883 6043), next to the post office and not far from the train station, has a cafe and rents out bikes from $20 per day; cycling is a popular way to get around the area's villages.

Bundanoon's main attraction is its proximity to the northern escarpments of **Morton National Park**, and there are a number of lookouts and walking trails within easy reach of the town.

Places to Stay

In a large, leafy yard, *Bundanoon YHA Hostel (☎ 4883 6010)*, on Railway Ave about 1km east of the station, is an old boarding house. Dorm beds cost $16, twins/doubles cost $20 per person.

Most other places are cheaper midweek than on weekends, when you might have to take a package, including meals. **Bundanoon Country Hotel** (☎ 4883 6005), on Erith St across the tracks from the train station, is a well-equipped place charging from $46 to $58 per person. The 1897 **Killarney at Bundanoon** (☎ 4883 6224), on Ellsmore Rd, is a retreat centre in six hectares of garden. There are no phones or TVs in the rooms and guests can partake in meditation classes. It costs $95 per person midweek (including all meals, mainly vegetarian). **Mildenhall** (☎ 4883 6643, 10 Anzac Parade) has B&B from $75 and offers weekend packages.

Getting There & Away

Countrylink runs to Wollongong daily via Moss Vale. Taking a train to Wollongong then a bus through Macquarie Pass National Park is a long but interesting way to get here from Sydney.

Bundanoon is on the Sydney-Canberra train line.

MORTON NATIONAL PARK

This wilderness area in the Budawang Range, which covers 162,386 hectares, has magnificent sandstone cliffs and waterfalls that fall to the forests deep in the valleys below. It is, however, a very rugged area and you should always seek advice and record your proposed walk with the NPWS visitors centre (☎ 4887 7270), at Fitzroy Falls near the park entrance. Pamphlets ($5) at the NPWS list shorter walks in Morton National Park (and other nearby national parks). For longer bushwalks you'll need specific topographical maps. Ask at the NPWS about camping in the valleys below the escarpments – you'll probably have to walk in, although there is a camp site with facilities at Bundanoon. The closest road access to the park is around Bundanoon and Fitzroy Falls and on the road from near Kangaroo Valley to Tallowa Dam on the Shoalhaven River. There's also the road that runs to Sassafras (surrounded by the park) from either Nowra or Braidwood.

The spectacular **Fitzroy Falls** have an 82m drop and the less well-known **Twin Falls** are about 1km from here along the eastern track. **Glow-worm Glen**, best visited at night, is a half-hour walk from the end of William St in

Bundanoon. In the south of the park is the **Pigeon House**, a curiously shaped mountain. See under Ulladulla in the South Coast chapter for information on climbing it.

Twin Falls Bush Cottages (☎ 4887 7333), on Throsby Rd at Fitzroy Falls, are self-contained and sleep six people in two bedrooms or up to four in a single-bedroom cabin. They are on their own patch of bushland. Weekend rates are $250 a double for two nights or up to $320 for four people. Weekday rates are slightly lower.

On the north-east edge of Morton National Park is the smaller **Budderoo National Park**, with more waterfalls, lookouts and walking trails. On the west side of the park is the **Minnamurra Rainforest Area** (see under Kiama & Around in the South Coast chapter for more information). Access to both is from Robertson to the north or from Jamberoo near Kiama.

KANGAROO VALLEY
postcode 2577

From Fitzroy Falls to Kangaroo Valley the road climbs down the steep escarpment. Kangaroo Valley is a lovely place, largely cleared but with steep, forested mountains and escarpments encroaching onto the valley floor.

You enter the valley through the castellated **Hamden Bridge** (1897), a few kilometres north of the township of Kangaroo Valley. Near the bridge is **Pioneer Farm Settlement** (☎ 4465 1306), an old homestead with historic displays and some native animals in a refuge. Markets are held here on the last Sunday of the month.

The Shoalhaven and Kangaroo Rivers are popular for **canoeing**, and Kangaroo Valley Safaris (☎ 4465 1502) rents out two-person canoes for $35 a day and will organise transport to/from a specified point for $10.

In Kangaroo Valley township, **Glenmack Caravan Park** (☎ 4465 1372) is a pleasant place to pitch a tent ($6 per person) and has cabins from $45. It also has limited tourist information.

The road from Kangaroo Valley to Berry is beautiful. Take the turn-off to the left just out of Kangaroo Valley township on the road to Nowra. This narrow road takes you up through thick forest to a neatly farmed plateau, then plunges down again through the forest. Take it easy – it's about 20km of narrow, winding road and there are school buses travelling along it too.

Illawarra Coast

pop 365,000

Illawarra comprises the coastal strip and the spectacular escarpment behind it, which runs from Royal National Park south past the cities of Wollongong and Port Kembla.

The region was explored by Europeans in the early 19th century, but apart from timber cutting and dairy farming there was little development until the escarpment's coalfields attracted miners. By the turn of the 20th century Wollongong was a major coal port. Steelworks were developed in the 1920s and today the region is one of the country's major industrial centres.

Despite the industry, there is spectacular natural scenery and some great beaches.

WOLLONGONG & AROUND

postcode 2500 • pop 180,000

Wollongong, 80km south of Sydney, is the state's third-largest city and sprawls south to the biggest steelworks in Australia at Port Kembla. There are some excellent surf beaches, especially north of the centre where the Illawarra Escarpment draws closer to the coast. The hills behind provide a fine backdrop, great views over the city and coast and good walks.

Wollongong is a hard-working industrial city without the edgy weirdness of inner Sydney – a day trip to Wollongong can be a good break. It's easily reached by train from Sydney, an interesting ride through tunnels and the bushland of the Illawarra Escarpment. Suburbs such as Bulli offer plenty of sand and waves and most have train stations.

Orientation & Information

Crown St is the main commercial street and between Kembla and Keira Sts is a two-block pedestrian mall. Keira St is part of the

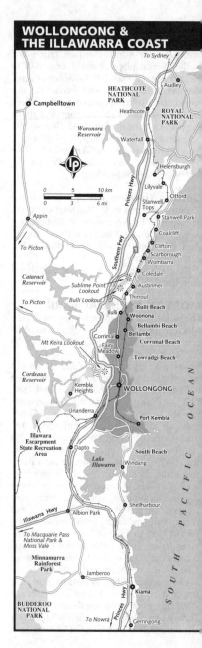

WOLLONGONG & THE ILLAWARRA COAST

Princes Hwy. Through-traffic bypasses the city on the Southern Fwy.

The tourist information centre (☎ 4228 0300), on the corner of Crown and Kembla Sts, is open from 9 am to 5 pm weekdays, 9 am to 4 pm Saturday and 10 am to 4 pm Sunday. The post office is on Crown St.

SpidrWeb Connections (☎ 4225 8677), 67 Kembla St, offers Internet/email access.

Bushcraft on Stewart St has hiking and camping gear.

Things to See & Do

The fishing fleet is based in the southern part of Wollongong's harbour, **Belmore Basin**, which was cut from solid rock in 1868. There's a fishing cooperative (with a fish market, cafe and the Harbour Seafood Restaurant) and an 1872 lighthouse on the point. Nearby, on the headland, is the newer Breakwater Lighthouse.

North Beach, north of the harbour, generally has better surf than the south Wollongong City Beach. The harbour itself has beaches that are good for children. Other beaches run north up the coast.

The interesting **City Gallery** (☎ 4228 7500), on the corner of Kembla and Burelli Sts, is the largest regional gallery in the country. Its collection focuses on 20th-century Australian painting and sculpture, and Aboriginal paintings. It's open from 10 am to 5 pm Tuesday to Friday, noon to 4 pm weekends (free).

The **Illawarra Museum** (☎ 4228 0158), 11 Market St, contains a reconstruction of the 1902 Mt Kembla village mining disaster and other exhibitions. It's open from noon to 3 pm Thursday, 1 to 4 pm weekends ($2/0.50 for adults/children).

Wollongong Botanic Gardens, on Murphy's Ave in Keiraville, north-west of the centre, have tropical and temperate plants and a lily lake; they are open daily.

The enormous **Buddhist Temple** (☎ 4272 0600), a few kilometres south of the city, is open to visitors daily except Monday.

North of the City Wollongong sprawls north, nearly to the edge of Royal National Park, but the beachside suburbs are almost in-

dividual towns. **Bulli** and **Thirroul** (where DH Lawrence lived during his time in Australia; the cottage where he wrote *Kangaroo* still stands) are both popular. In Bulli the Black Diamond District Heritage Centre (☎ 4267 4312), at the old train station, is open from 10 am to 4 pm on Sunday. At **Coalcliff** (appropriately named – coal was mined near this cliff for most of the 19th century), the road heads up the escarpment. A short way along, near **Stanwell Park**, it enters thick forest and you drive through the Royal National Park.

Up the coast there are several excellent beaches. Those with good surf include **Sandon Point**, **Austinmer**, **Headlands** (only for experienced surfers) and **Sharkies**.

On the road to the village of **Otford** and Royal National Park, the **Lawrence Hargrave Lookout** at Bald Hill above Stanwell Park is a superb cliff-top viewing-point. Hargrave, a pioneer aviator, made his first attempts at flying in the area early in the 20th century. Hang-gliders fly there today and the Sydney Hang Gliding Centre (☎ 4294 9994) offers tandem flights ($175) and courses.

Symbio Koala Gardens (☎ 4294 1244), on Lawrence Hargrave Drive in Stanwell Tops (above Stanwell Park), has koalas, kangaroos and other animals. Near Otford, Otford Valley Farm Riding School (☎ 4294 2442) is one of several outfits offering horse riding in the area.

South of the City Just south, **Lake Illawarra** is very popular for water sports including windsurfing. South of Lake Illawarra, **Shellharbour**, a popular holiday resort, is one of the oldest towns along the coast. It was a thriving port back in 1830, but it declined after the construction of the railway lines. The name Shellharbour comes from the number of shell middens (remnants of Aboriginal feasts) that the early Europeans found here. There are good beaches on the Windang Peninsula north of the town.

In **Albion Park** on the second Sunday of the month (every Sunday in January and all long weekends) you can ride an old tram or steam train at the **Illawarra Light Railway Museum** (☎ 4256 4627), Tongarra Rd. Admission is free; rides cost up to $2.50/2.

AROUND SYDNEY

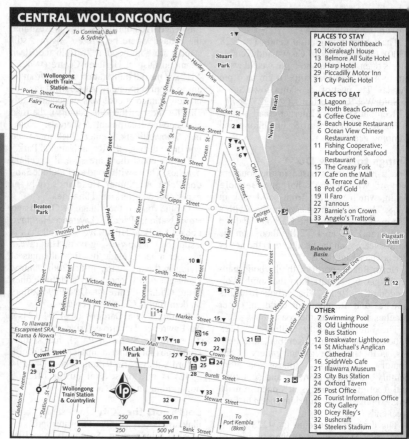

CENTRAL WOLLONGONG

PLACES TO STAY
2 Novotel Northbeach
10 Keiraleagh House
13 Belmore All Suite Hotel
20 Harp Hotel
29 Piccadilly Motor Inn
31 City Pacific Hotel

PLACES TO EAT
1 Lagoon
3 North Beach Gourmet
4 Coffee Cove
5 Beach House Restaurant
6 Ocean View Chinese Restaurant
11 Fishing Cooperative; Harbourfront Seafood Restaurant
15 The Greasy Fork
17 Cafe on the Mall & Terrace Cafe
18 Pot of Gold
19 Il Faro
22 Tannous
27 Barnie's on Crown
33 Angelo's Trattoria

OTHER
7 Swimming Pool
8 Old Lighthouse
9 Bus Station
12 Breakwater Lighthouse
14 St Michael's Anglican Cathedral
16 SpidrWeb Cafe
21 Illawarra Museum
23 City Bus Station
24 Oxford Tavern
25 Post Office
26 Tourist Information Office
28 City Gallery
30 Dicey Riley's
32 Bushcraft
34 Steelers Stadium

Illawarra Escarpment

This state recreation area (SRA), which takes in land donated by the Broken Hill Proprietary (BHP) company, is good for bushwalking. There's no vehicle access. The park is a number of separate sections from Bulli Pass to Bong Bong; it isn't very large but the country is spectacular. Contact the NPWS (☎ 4229 4756) for information on bush camping.

Views

The most popular viewpoint in the area is the spectacular **Bulli Lookout**, high on the escarpment off the Princes Hwy, with enormous views down to the coastal strip and out to sea. Nearby, **Sublime Point** and **Bald Hill Lookout** in Stanwell Tops are similarly breathtaking. **Mt Keira Summit Park**, Queen Elizabeth Drive on Mt Keira, offers an ever higher viewpoint.

Special Events

A big surf-lifesaving carnival is held on Australia Day (26 January).

Places to Stay

The tourist information centre books accommodation and will know of any specials

Places to Stay – Budget

You have to go a little way out before you can camp. The city council runs *caravan parks* on the beach at Corrimal (☎ 4285 5688), near the beach on Farrell Rd in Bulli (☎ 4285 5677) and on Fern St in Windang (☎ 4297 3166), with beach and lake frontage. From central Wollongong, Corrimal is about 6km north, Bulli 11km north and Windang 15km south, between Lake Illawarra and the sea. All charge about $17 for camp sites (two people) and from $55 for vans or cabins, with prices rising sharply during school and Christmas holidays. Buses run from the train station to within walking distance of all these.

There are quite a few privately owned caravan parks in the area – the tourist information centre has details.

Keiraleagh House (☎ 4228 6765, 60 Kembla St), north of Market St, is a large, rambling hostel catering mainly to long-term students but also to shorter-term backpackers. It has dorms for $15 or singles for $25/30 without/with bath.

Places to Stay – Mid-Range & Top End

Several pubs have fairly cheap accommodation, such as the central *Harp Hotel (☎ 4229 1333, 124 Corrimal St)* near Crown St, which charges $70/85 for newly renovated rooms with TV and bathroom.

About the only inexpensive motel in the area is the *Cabbage Tree Motel (☎ 4284 4000, 1 Anama St),* behind the Cabbage Tree Hotel in Fairy Meadow, off the Princes Hwy 3.5km north of the city centre. Rooms cost $55/65. Most buses heading north from the train station go to Fairy Meadow.

Piccadilly Motor Inn (☎ 4226 4555, 341 Crown St), near the train station, has rooms for $60/65. The *City Pacific Hotel (☎ 4229 7444, 112 Burelli St)* has good-value budget rooms for $49/60 in the old part of the hotel; in the new section standard doubles start at $115.

Belmore All Suite Hotel (☎ 4224 6500, 39–41 Smith St) has serviced apartments from $100 to $115. The top place to stay is *Novotel Northbeach (☎ 4226 3555, 2–14 Cliff Rd),* with standard rooms from $156 to $600 with ocean views, but there are often special deals.

Places to Eat

For good coffee, snacks, cakes and meals try *Tannous,* a Lebanese cafe on the corner of Crown and Corrimal Sts. Various shish kebabs, felafel and other takeaways cost $4. Eat-in meals come with large serves of hummus, tabouli and bread.

There are plenty of other places. *Cafe on the Mall,* on the corner of Church and Crown Sts, opens long hours for snacks and meals. Breakfasts are $6.50. *Barnie's on Crown,* on the mall near Kembla St, is an Italian restaurant with three-course lunch specials for $9.90; it also does good cakes.

Pot of Gold (146 Crown St) is a Mexican place with main courses for around $12.50. Across Kembla St is *Il Faro,* with pasta and pizza.

The Greasy Fork (☎ 4229 3651, 26 Market St), west of Corrimal St, is better than its name might suggest. Pasta mains cost $15 to $25, chicken schnitzel $18.50.

Popular with the Italian community, *Angelo's Trattoria (28 Stewart St)* serves moderately priced Italian food, steaks and seafood. There's no sign over the door – walk along the veranda past Portofino Lounge to the back.

At Belmore Basin, *Harbourfront Seafood Restaurant* is open daily for lunch and dinner with mains for $21 to $22. More seafood is available at the *Lagoon (☎ 4226 1677)* in Stuart Park behind North Beach. Snapper fillets cost $23.50. This licensed restaurant has a great location and opens daily for lunch and dinner.

On Bourke St at North Beach, there are several *cafes* serving breakfast and light meals. Round the corner, *Beach House,* on Cliff Rd, serves mostly seafood; king prawns cost $25. Next door, the *Ocean View* Chinese restaurant is cheaper, and offers Cantonese and Thai cuisine.

Entertainment

This is a steel town where people let their hair down on weekends. Several pubs in the centre of town usually have bands on then.

AROUND SYDNEY

Your best chance of hearing an interesting young band is at the *Harp Hotel* on Corrimal St on Friday and Saturday, or at the *Oxford Tavern (47 Crown St)* on Wednesday, Friday and Saturday. *Dicey Riley's (333 Crown St)* has Irish music on Thursday and rock/pop covers on Friday and Saturday. There are many clubs and other pubs with live entertainment.

Getting There & Away
Bus The bus station (☎ 4226 1022) is on the corner of Keira and Campbell Sts. There are three daily services to Sydney ($11 one way), and one to Canberra ($28 one way) that runs through Moss Vale and the Southern Highlands.

Greyhound Pioneer's (☎ 13 2030) Sydney-Melbourne coastal route runs through Wollongong and it also has direct buses to Brisbane. Pioneer Motor Service (☎ 13 3410) – a Nowra company, not the national giant – runs through Wollongong along the south coast as far as Eden ($47) and also connects with buses to Canberra.

Countrylink runs buses to Moss Vale from outside the train station.

Train Many trains run to/from Sydney ($6.60 one way, 1½ hours) and a fair number continue south along the coast to Kiama, Gerringong and Bomaderry (Nowra).

From Saturday to Tuesday, a tourist train known as the Cockatoo Run (☎ 1800 643 801) travels inland across the Southern Highlands from Port Kembla to Moss Vale ($11/20 one way/return) or Robertson ($10/18).

Car & Motorcycle The Princes Hwy (a freeway near Wollongong) runs north to Sydney or you can follow the coast road north through Otford and Royal National Park, rejoining the highway near Sutherland. The highway also runs south to Kiama, the south coast and eventually Melbourne.

The Illawarra Hwy runs up the escarpment to the Southern Highlands.

Getting Around
Two local bus companies service the area: Rutty's (☎ 4271 1322) and John J Hill

(☎ 4229 4911). The main stop is on Crown St, where it meets Marine Drive, next to the beach. You can reach most beaches by rail and trains are fairly frequent.

Although cycling is definitely urban in this area, bringing a bike on the train from Sydney and riding around is a good idea. A cycle path runs from the city centre north to Bulli and south to Port Kembla.

Central Coast & Lake Macquarie

pop 260,800
The Central Coast is a strange combination of the beautiful and the awful – superb surf beaches, lakes and national parks combined with huge swathes of rampant suburban housing. There are more urban areas around Lake Macquarie, immediately to the north, which blend into the sprawling city of Newcastle. While you're stuck in one of the Central Coast's suburban-style traffic jams, you might ponder the possibility of this situation spreading over the entire east coast of Australia. It's a depressingly likely scenario.

The Central Coast's symbol for tourism is the pelican and the huge birds are everywhere. They paddle around in search of a meal or glide overhead, looking about as manageable as jumbo jets.

Orientation
The Central Coast includes some lovely inland waterways as well as the long string of surf beaches. Broken Bay in the south is the beautiful mouth of the Hawkesbury River, with many wide bays and inlets, including Brisbane Water, which runs up to Gosford. Next north is Tuggerah Lake, which meets the sea at The Entrance. North of Tuggerah Lake is the smaller Lake Budgewoi near Toukley, and just north again is Lake Munmorah. These three lakes are actually contiguous. A few kilometres north of Lake Munmorah is Lake Macquarie, which runs up to outer Newcastle.

West of the lakes in the low Watagan Mountains are 13 state forests running north

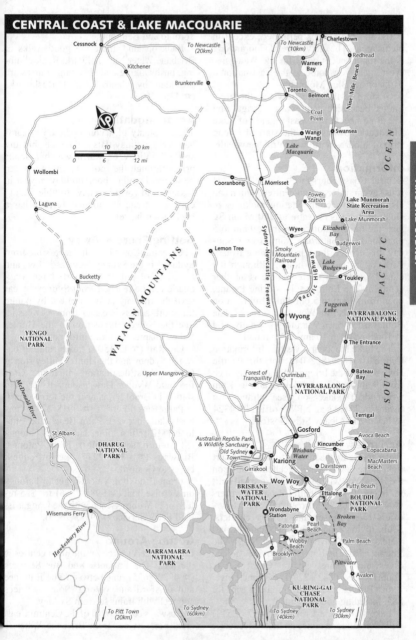

CENTRAL COAST & LAKE MACQUARIE

AROUND SYDNEY

Cessnock
Kitchener
Brunkerville
To Newcastle (20km)
To Newcastle (10km)
Charlestown
Redhead
Warners Bay
Toronto
Belmont
Coal Point
Wangi Wangi
Swansea
Lake Macquarie
Nine Mile Beach
OCEAN
Wollombi
Cooranbong
Morrisset
Power Station
Lake Munmorah State Recreation Area
Lake Munmorah
Laguna
Wyee
Elizabeth Bay
Budgewoi
PACIFIC
Lemon Tree
Smoky Mountain Railroad
Lake Budgewoi
Toukley
Bucketty
WATAGAN MOUNTAINS
Sydney-Newcastle Freeway
Pacific Highway
Tuggerah Lake
WYRRABALONG NATIONAL PARK
Wyong
YENGO NATIONAL PARK
The Entrance
Upper Mangrove
Forest of Tranquility
Ourimbah
WYRRABALONG NATIONAL PARK
Bateau Bay
SOUTH
McDonald River
Terrigal
St Albans
Gosford
Avoca Beach
DHARUG NATIONAL PARK
Australian Reptile Park & Wildlife Sanctuary
Old Sydney Town
Kariong
Kincumber
Brisbane Water
Copacabana
MacMasters Beach
Girrakool
Davistown
Woy Woy
Wisemans Ferry
BRISBANE WATER NATIONAL PARK
Umina
Ettalong
Putty Beach
BOUDDI NATIONAL PARK
Wondabyne Station
Broken Bay
Patonga
Pearl Beach
Hawkesbury River
Wobby Beach
Palm Beach
MARRAMARRA NATIONAL PARK
Brooklyn
Pittwater
KU-RING-GAI CHASE NATIONAL PARK
Avalon
To Pitt Town (20km)
To Sydney (60km)
To Sydney (40km)
To Sydney (30km)

0   10   20 km
0   6   12 mi

to the Hunter Valley. There are walking trails, and camping is permitted, except in picnic areas. The old village of Cooranbong is the main access point for the Watagans. West again you come to the vast national parks of the Blue Mountains.

Gosford is the main town in the area. Larger beachside centres are Terrigal and The Entrance. On the eastern side of Lake Macquarie, Swansea is the start of a long strip of suburbs north to central Newcastle.

Information
Central Coast Tourism (☎ 1800 806 258) runs several information centres, which can also help with accommodation bookings. In Gosford there is a centre at 200 Mann St, near the train station, open from 9 am to 5 pm Monday to Saturday, 9 am to 3 pm Sunday. In Terrigal, there is a centre at Rotary Park, open the same hours, although it's closed Sunday in winter. There is another centre at The Entrance, in Marine Parade, open from 9 am to 5 pm daily. Information booths are also at Woy Woy (18–22 The Boulevarde), open 9 am to 5 pm daily, and at Toukley, open 10 am to 3 pm daily.

The Lake Macquarie Visitors Information Centre (☎ 1800 802 044), on the Pacific Hwy north of the bridge in Swansea, is open from 9 am to 5 pm weekdays and to 4 pm weekends. The lake's only sea entrance is at Swansea. There's an NPWS office (☎ 4324 4911) at 207 Albany St in Gosford.

Activities
Water sports are the main activities, with surf right along the coast and excellent boating on the lakes. You will be able to hire small craft in many towns. Central Coast Charters (☎ 4363 1221), 38 Mirreen Ave, Davistown, offers river cruises and fishing charters. Scuba diving is popular in the Central Coast waters and Pro Dive (☎ 4334 1559), 96 The Entrance Rd, The Entrance, provides guided dives and lessons. Central Coast Kayak Tours (☎ 4381 0342), 227 The Round Drive, Avoca Beach, has sea-kayaking day trips for $85, including gourmet lunch.

Lake Macquarie Cruises (☎ 4973 2513) will take you for a cruise on Lake Macquarie

($14 for 2½ hours), with pick-up from Toronto and Belmont.

Back on land, there are good walks in Brisbane Water National Park. Rock climbing, bushwalking and abseiling courses are provided by Central Coast Bushworks (☎ 4363 2028).

Accommodation
There's plenty of accommodation in caravan parks, holiday flats and motels, but any sort of holiday or warm weather sends prices through the roof and vacancies can be scarce. Families book holidays a year in advance and you might have trouble finding even a tent site in summer. Terrigal has a backpacker hostel.

Getting There & Away
The Central Coast is easily accessible from Sydney via the Sydney-Newcastle Fwy and a variety of public transport. Lake Macquarie can be reached from Sydney by car (exit the freeway at Wyong) but by public transport, access is easier from Newcastle. See the Newcastle section in the Hunter Valley chapter for more information.

CityRail (☎ 13 1500) trains running between Sydney and the Hunter Valley stop at Central Coast destinations, including Gosford and Wyong. Hawkesbury River train station in Brooklyn is near the ferry wharf.

Palm Beach Ferries (☎ 9918 2747) runs boats daily between Palm Beach and Ettalong ($12 return, nine daily) and Patonga ($12 return, seven daily). From Patonga, Busways (☎ 4368 2277) has infrequent buses to Gosford.

From Brooklyn, you can get to Patonga on a cruise boat (☎ 9985 7566) for $15 return or to Wobby Beach with the Dangar Island Ferry Service (☎ 9985 7605).

Getting Around
Local bus services cover the main centres in the area. The Entrance Red Bus Services (☎ 4332 8655) runs between The Entrance and Gosford and Wyong. Some services connect with trains to/from Sydney.

Busways covers most of the Central Coast area. For services from Brisbane Water to

Wyong call ☎ 4368 2277. For services from Wyong to Lake Macquarie, Swansea, Belmont and Charlestown call ☎ 4392 6666.

Toronto Bus Service (☎ 4959 1233) has services from Toronto to Wangi Wangi and Coal Point on Lake Macquarie, to Charlestown and to the Newcastle suburbs of Glendale and Shortland. STA urban buses run between Newcastle and the northern end of the lake.

This isn't the easiest place to drive around, partly because many roads are too small for the amount of traffic they carry and partly because you have to negotiate suburban shopping centres every few kilometres. You'll also need a detailed map, such as the National Roads & Motorists Association's (NRMA) *Central Coast Holiday Map,* because the signposting gets you to Gosford and Wyong but not to many other places.

GOSFORD & AROUND
postcode 2250

Gosford, the largest town in the area, is 12km inland on the shores of Brisbane Water, about 85km north of Sydney. Europeans first settled this area in the 1820s, attracted by the timber, and boat building followed. After the construction of the railway from Sydney in the 1880s, tourism began and large guesthouses were built.

Gosford is easily accessible by train from Sydney or Newcastle and is a sensible base from which to explore the region.

Brisbane Water National Park

On the north side of the Hawkesbury River, across from Ku-Ring-Gai Chase National Park, Brisbane Water National Park is 9km south-west of Gosford. It extends from the Pacific Hwy in the west to Brisbane Water in the east but, despite its name, the park has only a short frontage onto that body of water.

This park, which is rugged sandstone country, is known for its wild flowers in early spring and there are many walking trails. South of the township of Kariong is the turn-off for the **Bulgandry Aboriginal Engraving Site**, where there are interesting rock carvings.

The main road access is at Girrakool; travel west from Gosford or exit the Sydney-Newcastle Fwy at the Calga interchange. Wondabyne train station, on the Sydney-Newcastle line, is inside the park near several walking trails (including part of the Great North Walk). You must tell the guard if you want to get off at Wondabyne and travel in the rear carriage. Ferries from Palm Beach run to Patonga; ferries from Brooklyn run to Wobby Beach on a peninsula south of the park near some walking trails.

For more information contact the NPWS office (☎ 4324 4911) in Gosford.

Old Sydney Town

Off the freeway 9km south-west of Gosford, Old Sydney Town (☎ 4340 1104) is a major

---

Great North Walk

There are plenty of transport options for getting from Sydney to Newcastle – planes, trains and automobiles for starters. But have you ever considered going by foot along the Great North Walk?

The 14-day walk begins from the centre of Sydney and after a short ferry ride, follows natural bushland almost the entire way to the city of Newcastle. While not strictly a wilderness walk, it has much to offer visitors and can be walked in any season. It has been sited to pass through almost every type of environment found close to Sydney.

The 250km track is the result of an ambitious undertaking by two Sydney bushwalkers. After having explored and planned a walk from Sydney to Newcastle, they then canvassed support for a walking track, obtaining grants from the Bicentennial Committee in 1988. They realised that for the track to be successful, it had to be supported by a government department, and so they had the track adopted by the Department of Conservation & Land Management (DCLM).

The best information on this track comes from the well-researched guide *The Great North Walk,* by Garry McDougall & Leigh Shearer-Heriot, the walk's originators. Maps to the entire route are produced in brochure form by DCLM.

reconstruction of early Sydney, with street theatre that depicts events from the colony's early history. It's open from 10 am to 4 pm Wednesday to Sunday, and daily during school holidays ($19/11 for adults/children). Busways buses run from Gosford station (10.15 am daily) and several tours run from Sydney.

Other Attractions

West of Gosford on the Pacific Hwy in Somersby, the **Australian Reptile Park & Wildlife Sanctuary** (☎ 4340 1146) has native animals, birds and reptiles. It's open from 9 am to 5 pm daily ($12.95/6.50 for adults/children). Another attraction is the **Forest of Tranquillity** (☎ 4362 1855), a private forest reserve and wildlife sanctuary west off the freeway at Ourimbah. It's open from 10 am to 5 pm Wednesday to Sunday, daily in school holidays ($8/4).

The historic MV *Lady Kendall* (☎ 4323 1655) has 2½-hour cruises of Brisbane Water from Gosford Wharf at 10.15 am and 1 pm Saturday to Wednesday, daily during school holidays. There's also parasailing and water-skiing on Brisbane Water.

South of the Brisbane Water National Park is **Patonga**, a small fishing village on Broken Bay, with camping at *Patonga Caravan Park* (☎ 4379 1287). Off the road to Patonga, **Warrah Lookout** has great views over Broken Bay.

Not far away, but screened from the housing estates of Umina and Woy Woy by a steep road over Mt Ettalong, is **Pearl Beach**, a lovely National Trust hamlet on the eastern edge of the national park. The only way to stay here is to rent a holiday house or apartment and there aren't many of them.

TERRIGAL & AROUND
postcode 2260

Terrigal, on the ocean about 12km east of Gosford, is probably the most upmarket of the Central Coast's beachside towns. The big *Holiday Inn Resort* (☎ 4384 9111) dominates the foreshore; double rooms start from $205. *Terrigal Beach Backpackers* (☎ 4385 3330, 10 Campbell Crescent), a YHA hostel

one block from the beach, has dorm beds for $17, doubles for $44.

North of Terrigal, **Bateau Bay** is adjacent to the southern section of the small **Wyrrabalong National Park**. It's popular for surfing and the beach is patrolled. There are several caravan parks in the area.

Bouddi National Park

Bouddi National Park, 19km south-east of Gosford, extends south from MacMasters Beach to the north head of Broken Bay. It also extends out to sea in a marine reserve; fishing is prohibited in much of the park. Vehicle access is limited but there are walking trails leading to the various beaches. The park is in two sections on either side of Putty Beach, which has vehicular access. The Maitland Bay Centre has information on the park but it is only open on weekends and holidays. There's camping in the park at Little, Putty and Tallow Beaches, but you must book through the NPWS office (☎ 4324 4911) in Gosford.

THE ENTRANCE & NORTH
postcode 2261

The Entrance, on the Tuggerah Lake sea inlet, is the only place you need to visit if you want to see the best and worst of the Central Coast. It's a large urban area of relentlessly cheerful cream brick and introduced palm trees, plastic chairs on footpaths, happy urchins and beer-bellied parents – all on a supremely beautiful lake and a superb surf beach.

At 3.30 pm daily the **pelicans** are fed on the beachfront near the visitors information centre. The **Entrance Boatshed** (☎ 4332 2652), beside the bridge, rents out bikes, canoes, rowboats and motorboats.

On the peninsula north of The Entrance is the northern section of the small **Wyrrabalong National Park**, with walking trails and diverse flora habitats. North of the park are the towns of **Toukley** and **Budgewoi**, popular bases for boating and fishing on the nearby lakes. The **Munmorah SRA** runs up the coast for 12km. There are well-equipped *camping areas* at Freemans and Frazer Beaches but they fill up at peak times; book at the office (☎ 4324 4911) off the road south of Elizabeth Bay. Day-use fees are $5 per car/motorbike; camping costs $17.50 for two people for the first night, $10 for subsequent nights plus $2 per extra person.

Places to Stay

At The Entrance on the northern side of the bridge at the end of the spit, which separates the sea from the lake, *Dunleith Caravan Park (☎ 4332 2172)*, Hutton Rd, is close to the surf and has good facilities. Powered sites cost from $20, on-site vans from $50 and self-contained cabins from $70. The place is packed at peak times. Other caravan parks include *Blue Bay (☎ 4332 1991, 14 Narrawa Ave)* and *Pinehurst (☎ 4332 2002, 11 The Entrance Rd)*.

The *Entrance Hotel (☎ 4332 2001)*, near the waterfront, has singles/doubles for $35 per person including breakfast.

LAKE MACQUARIE

Lake Macquarie, Australia's largest saltwater lake, covers four times the area of Sydney Harbour and is a popular centre for sailing, water-skiing and fishing. It lies north of Munmorah Lake, separated by a narrow strip of land, and extends up to outer Newcastle. The suburban development here is a little older than that on the Central Coast and there's a little more room to move.

The main centres on Lake Macquarie are **Charlestown** and **Belmont**, both outer suburbs of Newcastle, and **Swansea**, a longtime holiday resort for holiday-makers from Newcastle; it too is now merging into the city's sprawl. The Lake Macquarie visitors centre (☎ 1800 802 044) is on the Pacific Hwy just north of Swansea. Caravan parks here are cheaper than farther south.

Nine Mile Beach runs north from Swansea to **Redhead**, where there's a *caravan park (☎ 4944 8306)* near the beach. The western shores of Lake Macquarie are relatively undeveloped but they certainly aren't virgin bush.

On **Wangi Point**, on the west shore, opposite Swansea, there are walking trails through the bush and a *caravan park (☎ 4975 1889)*. Also on the point is **Dobell House** (☎ 4975 4115) where artist William Dobell lived and worked. It's open from 2 to 4 pm on Sunday.

Vales Point power station (☎ 4352 6111) and the adjacent colliery are at the south end of the lake. Call to arrange a visit. The area's two other power stations aren't open to visitors.

AROUND SYDNEY

Hunter Valley

The Hunter Valley is best known for its wines, with about 60 vineyards in the lower Hunter (mainly around Cessnock and Pokolbin) and half a dozen more in the upper Hunter (around Denman). Coal is another important commodity, Newcastle taking its name from the industrial city in England. The first export of coal sailed in 1814 in exchange for a cargo of rum. Electricity also flows out of the Hunter Valley – 75% of the state's power is generated here.

For a relatively small area, the Hunter Valley includes some diverse landscapes. West of Newcastle there's a large urban conglomeration (linked by poorly maintained roads clogged with irritating traffic); farther west, beyond Cessnock, you come to the lower-Hunter wineries, nestled in gentle hills and rolling farmlands. The Hunter Valley also has rugged ranges harbouring lush stands of temperate rainforest in the Barrington Tops National Park, and some of the oldest towns in the country.

On the coast there are excellent surf beaches, the tranquil waterways of Myall Lakes National Park (an estuarine lakes system) and popular Port Stephens, a large bay that is home to dolphins – see the North Coast chapter for more information on these destinations.

History

The Hunter Valley was settled early in the history of New South Wales (NSW) as it offered a large expanse of relatively flat land, with coastal access. Before the Great Dividing Range was crossed such land was at a premium, attracting a growing influx of graziers, timber cutters and coal miners.

Finding a route from the Hunter Valley to the plains beyond the mountains proved almost as difficult as crossing the Blue Mountains. For thousands of years, Aborigines had used the rocky gorges of what is now the Goulburn River National Park as a route between the interior and the Hunter Valley (and thus the sea). Europeans, however, encumbered by their wagons, flocks and herds, had to settle for the long, steep climb up the Liverpool Range near present-day Murrurundi. The New England Hwy closely follows one of the first routes out of the Hunter Valley.

Vines were first planted in the valley in the 1820s, and by the 1860s there were 2000 hectares under cultivation. A Hunter sparkling wine made its way to Paris in 1855 and was favourably compared with the French product. However, most Hunter wineries gradually declined, and it wasn't until the 1960s that wine making again became an important industry.

The Golden Grape Estate, on Oakey Creek Rd near Pokolbin, has a museum

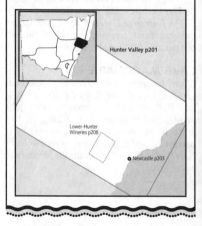

Hunter Valley p201

Lower-Hunter Wineries p208

Newcastle p203

HUNTER VALLEY

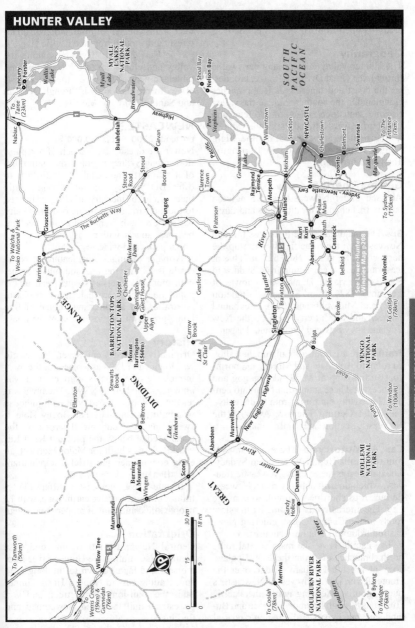

See Lower Hunter Wineries Map p208

HUNTER VALLEY

devoted to the history of wine making in the area. It's open from 10 am to 5 pm daily.

Geography

The Hunter Valley cuts a triangular swathe through the Great Dividing Range, broadest on the coast and tapering as it approaches Denman. On the southern side of the valley rise the sandstone ranges of Wollemi and Goulburn River National Parks; the valley's northern side is bordered by the high, rugged ranges leading up to Barrington Tops National Park.

Getting There & Away

Air See under Newcastle and Singleton later in this chapter for air routes and fares.

Bus The major interstate lines pass through Newcastle on their Pacific Hwy run up the north coast. Kean's (☎ 1800 625 587) has at least one bus a day running from Sydney to Scone ($37) via the Hunter Valley towns of Cessnock ($24 from Sydney), Singleton ($28) and Muswellbrook ($31). Greyhound Pioneer and McCafferty's run up the New England Hwy between Sydney and Brisbane.

Train There are trains running up the valley en route to Armidale and Moree, and north-coast trains stop at Maitland, Dungog and Gloucester. These trains don't run into central Newcastle, but trains from Sydney do – see under Getting There & Away in the Newcastle section later in this chapter.

Car & Motorcycle There are several routes into the Hunter Valley from Sydney. The quickest is the Sydney-Newcastle freeway, which doesn't actually reach Newcastle but stops short near Minmi, west of the city. The alternative is to come by the slow roads of the Central Coast, entering Newcastle through its southern suburbs.

The Pacific Hwy, the main coastal route north, branches off from the New England Hwy at the big Hexham Bridge over the Hunter River, just north-west of Newcastle's outer suburbs. Heading north, the Pacific Hwy runs through Raymond Terrace and Bulahdelah, but bypasses the region's coastal attractions. See under The Bucketts Way later in this chapter for information on an interesting diversion from the Pacific Hwy.

The New England Hwy runs along the valley and climbs up to the New England tableland near Murrurundi; the other western exit from the valley is through Denman and Sandy Hollow to Merriwa.

NEWCASTLE

postcode 2300 • pop 140,000

Newcastle doesn't have much of a reputation among Sydney people – they still think of it as a dirty industrial city with little to offer. But Sydneysiders are wrong. While there is a lot of industry, it's largely limited to the outskirts of town; the rest of the city has some superb architecture and excellent beaches, and is within easy access of national parks and wineries.

A major distinguishing feature of Newcastle is its thriving arts and music scene, with more working artists per head of the population living here than anywhere else in Australia, and an amazing choice of live home-grown music most nights of the week.

History

Originally named Coal River, Newcastle was founded in 1804 as a place for the most intractable of Sydney's convicts and was known as 'the hell of NSW'. The breakwater out to Nobbys Head with its lighthouse was built by convicts. The Bogey Hole, a swimming pool cut into the rock on the ocean's edge below the pleasant King Edward Park, was built for Major Morriset, an early commander and strict disciplinarian. It's still a great place for a dip.

In late 1989, Newcastle suffered Australia's most destructive earthquake, with 12 people killed and a lot of property damaged.

Orientation

Central Newcastle sits on the end of a peninsula separating the Hunter River from the sea, and tapers down to the long sand spit heading east to Nobbys Head. Hunter St is the 3km-long main street, and is a pedestrian mall between Newcomen and Perkins Sts.

Across the railway lines (there's a footbridge beginning in Hunter Mall) is the waterfront and the Queens Wharf complex. The swimming beaches are on the other side of the peninsula, a short walk from the city centre.

Just across the Hunter River (by now a wide estuary called Port Hunter) from Queens Wharf is Stockton, a modest town with beaches and striking views back to the city of Newcastle.

Information

The Newcastle Visitor Information Centre (☎ 4974 2999) is at 363 Hunter St. It's open from 9 am to 5 pm weekdays and from 10 am to 3.30 pm weekends. Pick up an excellent heritage walk map here (free).

Beaches

Surf beaches are a major attraction. Newcastle's favourite surfing son is former world champ Mark Richards, and many surfers come here to seek out the breaks where Richards cut his teeth. The main beach, **Newcastle Beach**, is just a couple of minutes' walk from the city centre. It has an ocean pool and good surf. Just north of here is **Nobbys Beach**, which is more sheltered. At the northern end of Nobbys Beach is a fast left-hander known as **the Wedge**. The most popular surfing break is about 2km south at **Bar Beach**, which is floodlit at night in summer. Nearby **Merewether Beach** has two huge pools. Bus No 207 runs to Merewether Beach every half-hour ($2) via Bar Beach – catch it at the railway station bus stop.

Museums & Galleries

The **Newcastle Regional Museum**, in a superbly restored former brewery at 787 Hunter St in Newcastle West, opens from 10 am to 5 pm daily except Monday. Admission is by donation. It includes the Supernova hands-on science display. The **Fort Scratchley Maritime & Military Museum** opens from 10 am to 4 pm Tuesday to Sunday. Admission to the museum is free, but it costs $1 to explore the tunnels under the fort, which are said to run all the way to King Edward Park. Fort Scratchley overlooks Nobbys Head, and was originally built to look out for invading Russians.

The excellent **Newcastle Regional Art Gallery** is on Laman St next to Civic Park. It's open from 10 am to 5 pm, Tuesday to

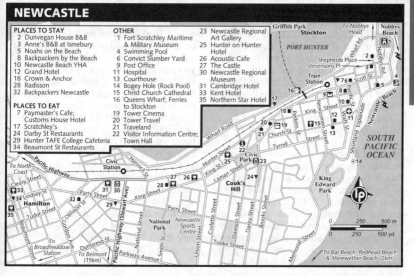

NEWCASTLE

PLACES TO STAY
2 Dunvegan House B&B
3 Anne's B&B at Ismebury
5 Noahs on the Beach
8 Backpackers by the Beach
10 Newcastle Beach YHA
12 Grand Hotel
18 Crown & Anchor
28 Radisson
32 Backpackers Newcastle

PLACES TO EAT
7 Paymaster's Cafe;
  Customs House Hotel
17 Scratchley's
24 Darby St Restaurants
29 Hunter TAFE College Cafeteria
34 Beaumont St Restaurants

OTHER
1 Fort Scratchley Maritime
  & Military Museum
4 Swimming Pool
6 Convict Slumber Yard
9 Post Office
11 Hospital
13 Courthouse
14 Bogey Hole (Rock Pool)
15 Christ Church Cathedral
16 Queens Wharf; Ferries
  to Stockton
19 Tower Cinema
20 Tower Travel
21 Traveland
22 Visitor Information Centre;
  Town Hall

23 Newcastle Regional
  Art Gallery
25 Hunter on Hunter
  Hotel
26 Acoustic Cafe
27 The Castle
30 Newcastle Regional
  Museum
31 Cambridge Hotel
33 Kent Hotel
35 Northern Star Hotel

Sunday (free). There are several private galleries on nearby Cook's Hill.

Convict Lumber Yard

This site on Scott St, filled with excellent interpretive sculptures and some historic buildings such as the paymaster's cottage (now a cafe), was once a convict lumberyard enclosed by massive log walls. It's the earliest surviving example of a convict industrial workplace and gives an interesting insight into the foundation of Newcastle as a convict settlement.

Blackbutt Reserve

The reserve (☎ 4952 1449) covers 182 hectares of bush at New Lambton Heights, approximately 10km south-west of the city centre. It has bushwalks, aviaries, wildlife, fern houses and a koala enclosure. The reserve is open from 9 am to 5 pm daily (free). Bus Nos 232 and 363 run past the upper entrance, Nos 216 and 217 past the lower ($2).

Organised Tours

Hunter Valley Day Tours (☎ 4938 5031) provides personalised tours to Barrington Tops National Park, Port Stephens and other destinations. A couple of outfits offer infrequent cruises up the Hunter River. *Lady Joy,* run by Hunter River Cruises (☎ 4982 8352), departs from Queens Wharf and provides a variety of cruises such as Newcastle to Morpeth ($40 return), and *William IV* (☎ 4926 1200), a replica of an old paddle-wheel steamship, which leaves from near Queens Wharf at 11 am and 2 pm on the third Sunday of the month.

For winery tours, see under Lower-Hunter Wineries later in this chapter.

Special Events

Newcastle certainly likes a festival and there's always something happening, so ask at the information centre for details. The Maritime Festival (☎ 4929 2588) is held at the end of January, with harbour and foreshore-focused activities, such as an across-the-harbour swim. Surfest, held at Newcastle Beach in March, is the longest-running professional surfing competition in Australia.

Call ☎ 0412 127 525 for details. Also in March is the Jazz & Arts Festival (☎ 4969 3354), held in Beaumont St, Hamilton, while the Newcastle Jazz Festival (☎ 4963 1515) is held in August at the City Hall.

Places to Stay

There's a surprising lack of accommodation for such a big city, so it's wise to book on weekends and during holiday periods.

Stockton is handy for Newcastle by ferry but it's 20km by road. *Stockton Beach Caravan Park (☎ 4928 1393)* is on the beach at Pitt St. Tent sites cost $13 and cabins start at $40, increasing to $75 with en suite. There are several caravan parks south of Newcastle, around Belmont and on the ocean at Redhead Beach.

Newcastle Beach YHA (☎ 4925 3544, 30 Pacific St) has a great position close to the city centre and beaches. It's in a beautiful heritage building with a very swish common room – timber-panelled walls, French doors, billiard table, open fireplace, the works. Dorm beds cost from $17 and doubles are $44 (plus $3 for non-YHA members).

Close by is the Nomads *Backpackers by the Beach (☎ 4926 3472, 34 Hunter St),* a relaxed place with dorm beds from $15 and doubles from $40.

Backpackers Newcastle (☎ 4969 3436, 42–44 Denison St, Hamilton) occupies a couple of fine old weatherboard houses. Dorm beds cost $17, doubles cost $40 and you can hire surfboards for $5 a day. Any bus heading along Hunter St can drop you at the nearby Regional Museum, or you can phone for a free pick-up from town.

Dunvegan House B&B (☎ 4929 4103, 4 Shepherds Place), a homely and relaxed place with a lovely, bright living area, offers rooms with double/queen-size beds for $130/145. From an earlier era, *Anne's B&B at Ismebury (☎ 4929 5376, 3 Stevenson Place)* is a pleasant Federation terrace house with doubles from $98.

Crown & Anchor (☎ 4929 1027), corner Hunter and Perkins Sts, has singles/doubles for $30/40. *Grand Hotel (☎ 4929 3489),* corner Bolton and Church Sts, has large rooms with bathroom for $50/60.

There's a string of cheapish motels along the Pacific Hwy at Belmont, about 15km south of town, such as the *Lake View Motor Inn* (☎ *1800 678 154, 749 Pacific Hwy)*, with rooms for $55/60.

Noahs on the Beach (☎ *4929 5181)* faces the ocean on Shortland Esplanade. The rooms, some with views, cost from $105 to $125. The *Radisson* (☎ *4926 3777)*, corner King and Peel Sts, charges from $105 a double ($89 weekdays) – good value if you don't mind windows that don't open.

Places to Eat
What it lacks in accommodation options, Newcastle certainly makes up for in places to eat. During term, the best deal in town is to be found at *Hunter TAFE College* on Parry St. The cafeteria operated by the college's catering and hospitality school offers main courses for $4 and desserts for $2.

Beaumont St in Hamilton has the greatest concentration of restaurants. Once known as 'Little Italy' for its profusion of Italian eateries, it's now taken on a more multicultural flavour, with restaurants like *Anatolia*, a good Turkish restaurant at No 63, where most meals are under $10, and *Gandha's* Indian restaurant, upstairs at No 54.

But if Italian is what you're after, try *Trieste* (☎ *4961 4257)*, a colourful and atmospheric place that has pasta for $10 to $15 and other mains for $16 to $19. Another good, slightly cheaper option is *Antonio's Cafe* (☎ *4969 7100, 52 Cleary St)*, just off Beaumont St.

Newcastle's other main restaurant strip is closer to the city on Darby St. The choices include *Lan's* (☎ *4929 1565)*, a Vietnamese restaurant, *Al-Oi* (☎ *4929 3610)*, for Thai food, and *Taj Takeaway* (☎ *4929 4265)*, for Indian. *Goldbergs'* (☎ *4929 3122, 137 Darby St)* is one of the more popular spots in town and is a great place to have a long brekky over morning papers. It's also open for lunch and dinner, with evening mains for $8 to $15.

The harbour foreshore offers a third area where you're spoilt for good food choices (and views). *Paymaster's Cafe* (☎ *4925 2600, 18 Bond St)* is a charming, double-storey historic building (1879) where the paymaster for the railway station employees used to live. It's open for lunch daily and dinner from Wednesday to Saturday. Evening mains on the innovative menu cost from $18 to $22, but vegetarians may go wanting.

Close by, *Customs House Hotel* (☎ *4925 2585, 1 Bond St)* is another terrific place for dinner, with mains from $10 to $20, good daily seafood specials and pub-priced drinks. Again though, vegetarians may miss out.

Just down from Queens Wharf, you can sit out over the water at *Scratchley's* (☎ *4929 1111)*, a superb, breezy place, specialising in seafood. Mains cost from $15 to $24, and there's a takeaway section.

Entertainment
Newcastle has a busy home-grown music scene, with live bands playing somewhere in town most nights. The weekly *That's Entertainment* paper gives some indication of the massive choice available. Pick up a copy from the tourist centre.

One of the best rock venues to check out is the *Cambridge Hotel*, on the corner of Hunter and Denison Sts, the pub where silverchair was launched. The *Hunter on Hunter Hotel* (417 Hunter St), is another pub that promotes local rock talent. The *Kent Hotel* and the *Northern Star Hotel*, both on Beaumont St, have jazz, while the *Acoustic Cafe* (410 King St), at the Star Hotel, covers pretty much all types of music.

The *Castle* is a popular nightclub on King St. It's open from Wednesday to Sunday, with live bands downstairs and a disco upstairs.

There are a number of cinemas in the city, such as *Tower Cinema* (☎ *4926 2233, 185–187 King St)*, close to the mall.

Getting There & Away
Air Aeropelican (☎ 13 1300) flies between Sydney and Belmont ($92), just south of Newcastle, about 12 times a day. Eastern Australia Airlines (☎ 13 1313) also has daily flights to Sydney ($114), while Impulse Airlines (☎ 13 1381) flies between Newcastle and Port Macquarie ($174), Coffs Harbour ($219), Brisbane ($267), Canberra ($240) and Melbourne ($362). Eastern and Impulse

use the airport at Williamtown, north of Newcastle.

Bus Between Sydney and Newcastle you're better off taking the train, but if you're heading up the coast, buses offer a much better service. Most long-distance buses stop at the bus terminal at the train station. Cheapish fares from Newcastle include: Sydney ($22), Port Macquarie ($31), Byron Bay ($59) and Brisbane ($60). Traveland (☎ 4926 2000), at 285 Hunter St near Darby St, handles bookings for most major bus companies.

Sid Fogg's (☎ 4928 1088) runs up the valley to Dubbo ($46) three times a week, and its buses go to Canberra ($45) during school holidays. Book at Tower Travel (☎ 4926 3199), 245 Hunter St on the corner of Crown St. Rover Motors (☎ 4990 1699) runs to Cessnock ($8.80). Port Stephens Coaches (☎ 4982 2940) has 11 weekday buses to Nelson Bay and Shoal Bay ($8.40, 1½ hours), and four on weekends and public holidays.

Train CityRail (☎ 13 1500) runs from Sydney to Newcastle about 25 times daily, taking nearly three hours. The one-way fare is $15.20; an off-peak return is $18. Other trains heading north on the lines to Armidale and Murwillumbah bypass central Newcastle, stopping at suburban Broadmeadow, just west of Hamilton. Frequent buses run from here to the city centre. An XPT (express train) from Central Station to Broadmeadow takes about 2¼ hours and costs $24.

Car As well as all the regular car-hire companies, you can hire cars from budget joints such as Cheep Heep (☎ 4961 3144) at 141 Maitland Rd, Islington.

Getting Around
To/From the Airport Port Stephens Coaches stop at Newcastle airport (Williamtown) on most runs to Nelson Bay. The trip takes 35 minutes and costs $4.60. Local bus Nos 348, 349, 350 and 358 stop outside Belmont airport ($2, one hour).

Bus STA buses cover Newcastle and the eastern side of Lake Macquarie. Fares are time based, with a minimum fare of $2. The ticket is valid for one hour, which is long enough to get anywhere you want around the city. An all-day BusTripper ticket costs $7 and is valid on STA buses and ferries. Most services operate half-hourly. Phone the Travel Information Centre (☎ 4961 8933) between 8.30 am and 4.30 pm for timetables. For sightseeing, try route No 348, 350 or 358 to Swansea, No 306, 307 or 327 to Speers Point or No 363 to Belmont.

Taxi For a cab, phone Newcastle Taxis (☎ 4979 3000) – there are depots at the railway stations.

Ferry There are ferries to Stockton from Queens Wharf approximately half-hourly from 5.15 am to midnight Monday to Saturday. They stop at 10 pm on Sunday. The ferry office on Queens Wharf has timetables.

MAITLAND
postcode 2320 • pop 50,200
Maitland has been a large town since the early days of European settlement in the Hunter Valley. It was long seen as a more desirable address than Newcastle and even had brief dreams of rivalling Sydney as the colony's most important city.

One of Maitland's most famous citizens was Les Darcy, a boxer who was a national hero before dying – perhaps under suspicious circumstances – in the USA in 1917.

Orientation & Information
Maitland's main street is High St, which follows the winding route of the original trail through the town. Part of the street is now the Heritage Mall, so driving through town is not simple. The information centre (☎ 4933 2611) is just off the highway on the corner of High St. It's open from 9 am to 5 pm daily and there's also a cafe on the premises.

Things to See & Do
The city's 19th-century wealth is reflected in the elaborate Georgian and Victorian buildings that remain. The extraordinary **Masonic Lodge** on Victoria St and the **courthouse** (1895) at the western end of High St are

some of the many interesting old buildings in Maitland.

East Maitland, which was established in 1833 after floods in the original town, has its share of old buildings, such as the **old jail** and the nearby **courthouse** on John St, and the **Lands Department offices** on Newcastle St. The nearby village of **Morpeth**, once the area's main river port, is also well endowed with architectural gems, especially along Swan St.

The **City Art Gallery**, open from 1 to 4 pm weekdays, from 1.30 to 5 pm on Saturday and from 10.30 am to 5 pm on Sunday, is in Brough House (1870) on Church St. Admission is free.

Tiger Moth Joy Flights (☎ 4932 8888), based at the Royal Newcastle Aeroclub outside Maitland, has half-hour **flights** for $95 in open-cockpit biplanes.

Special Events
The Maitland Show, held in February, is one of the biggest in the state.

Places to Stay & Eat
The Imperial Hotel (☎ 4933 6566, 458 High St) has been well renovated, with better-than-average pub rooms for $35/50 a single/double (B&B). You need to book here, though, as there aren't many rooms. Downstairs, *Shenanigans* is a good place for some tucker and a pint or two of Guinness.

There's plenty of other pub and motel accommodation, such as the *Endeavour Motel (☎ 4933 5488, 243 Newcastle St)* in East Maitland, which has rooms for $67/79 including a light breakfast.

Cintra (☎ 4932 8483) is a massive old Victorian house on Regent St, with lovely gardens and a terrific billiards room. Rooms cost $65/110 with cooked breakfast – good value for such a historic place. It opens on weekends.

Aberglasslyn House (☎ 4932 7396), a few kilometres out of town in Aberglasslyn Lane, is an incredible sandstone mansion overlooking the Hunter River. Accommodation costs from $185 a double, with weekend packages available. You have to see this place to believe it.

There are several Chinese restaurants and other eateries, but fewer interesting places to eat than you would expect in a large town near the wineries. The *Old George & Dragon Restaurant (☎ 4933 7272, 48 Melbourne St, East Maitland)* is in a restored pub dating from the 1830s and offers Anglo-French food. Allow around $55 per head.

Getting There & Away
Sid Fogg's (☎ 4928 1088) has bus services to Dubbo, while Rover Motors (☎ 4990 1699) does the run to Newcastle.

Trains to the north coast stop at Maitland and there are Newcastle-Maitland services.

LOWER-HUNTER WINERIES
With around 60 vineyards concentrated in a small, pretty area, the lower-Hunter wineries are a popular tourist destination, especially for weekenders from Sydney. If you can, visit midweek.

At most wineries you can just drop in, but some also have tours. They include McWilliams Mt Pleasant Estate (11 am daily); Tyrrell's (1.30 pm daily); and Tinkler's Vineyard (11 am weekends).

The largest concentration of wineries is around Pokolbin Village, but be sure to venture farther afield to wineries such as Audrey Wilkinson on De Beyers Rd, with its excellent 360° views of the area; Briar Ridge farther south on Mt View Rd; and wineries in the Lovedale area such as Wandin Valley Estate on Wilderness Rd and newcomer Gartelmann on Lovedale Rd.

Pick up a copy of the comprehensive *Hunter Valley Wine Country* booklet from one of the region's tourist centres for further options.

Orientation
Most lower-Hunter wineries are north-west of Cessnock (population 18,000), the closest town to the winery area. Although it's a good base for winery visiting, Cessnock isn't especially attractive. Pokolbin, among the wineries, is a purpose-built general store, restaurant, cafe, resort and conference centre.

Broke is a hamlet on the north-western edge of the vineyards. Farther south, getting

HUNTER VALLEY

LOWER-HUNTER WINERIES

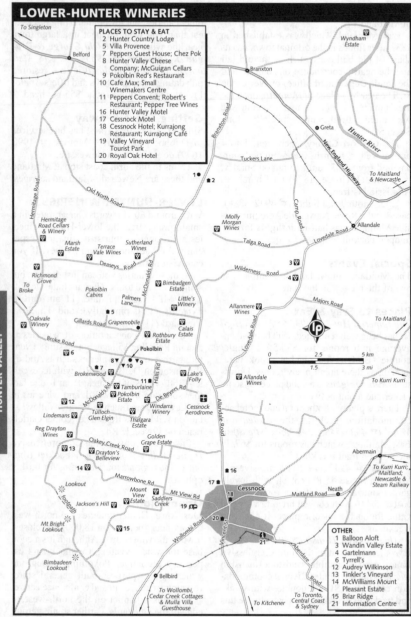

PLACES TO STAY & EAT
2 Hunter Country Lodge
5 Villa Provence
7 Peppers Guest House; Chez Pok
8 Hunter Valley Cheese
   Company; McGuigan Cellars
9 Pokolbin Red's Restaurant
10 Cafe Max; Small
   Winemakers Centre
11 Peppers Convent; Robert's
   Restaurant; Pepper Tree Wines
16 Hunter Valley Motel
17 Cessnock Motel
18 Cessnock Hotel; Kurrajong
   Restaurant; Kurrajong Café
19 Valley Vineyard
   Tourist Park
20 Royal Oak Hotel

OTHER
1 Balloon Aloft
3 Wandin Valley Estate
4 Gartelmann
6 Tyrrell's
12 Audrey Wilkinson
13 Tinkler's Vineyard
14 McWilliams Mount
   Pleasant Estate
15 Briar Ridge
21 Information Centre

HUNTER VALLEY

into the ranges, is picturesque little Wollombi. A scenic but bumpy road runs between the two, and Wollombi is also accessible from Cessnock and Sydney.

Information
The region's efficient information centre (☎ 4990 4477), on Aberdare Rd in Cessnock (the way into town from Sydney), opens from 9 am to 5 pm, Monday to Friday, from 9.30 am to 5 pm on Saturday and from 9.30 am to 3.30 pm on Sunday. Drop in for its comprehensive brochures before setting out for the wineries. Free maps are also available.

Steam Railway
The Richmond Vale Railway Museum (☎ 4937 5344), 4km south of Kurri Kurri on Mulbring Rd, operates an old steam-driven coal train on 3.5km of track between the mines at Pelaw Main and Richmond Main. It's open from 10 am to 5 pm, with departures every hour from 10.30 am, on the first three Sundays of each month ($10/5 for adults/children, which entitles you to ride the train as many times as you like).

Ballooning
Balloon Aloft (☎ 1800 028 568) has flights over the valley for $200/225 per person on weekdays/weekends. This includes an hour flight at sunrise followed by a cooked, champagne breakfast.

Organised Tours
Hunter Valley Day Tours (☎ 4938 5031) has a range of excellent tours leaving daily from Newcastle, Cessnock and other Hunter centres, including wine- and cheese-tasting tours priced from $70 per adult. A less expensive option is Hunter Vineyard Tours (☎ 4991 1659), which charges $45, or $29 without lunch.

Grapemobile (☎ 4991 2339) offers one-day bike rides around the wineries for $98 per person, including all equipment, tour guide and lunch.

Special Events
The Hunter Valley Vintage Festival in February and March attracts hordes of wine en-

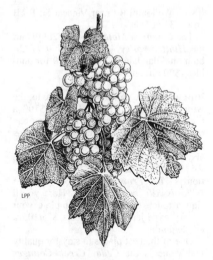

LPP

thusiasts for wine tasting, and grape-picking-and-treading contests. This is a hectic time in the valley as the harvest is in full swing. Accommodation can be scarce, but with planning you can pick up some good package deals. In September there's the Wine & Food Affair.

Places to Stay
There's an amazing array of superb accommodation options in this area – we can't list everything here, so contact the Cessnock or Maitland information centres for other options. Bear in mind that most accommodation, including pubs, is more expensive at weekends, when you might have to take a two-night package. Bookings are advised.

Cessnock The *Valley Vineyard Tourist Park* (☎ 4990 2573), Mt View Rd, has tent sites for $12, on-site vans from $35 and cabins from $55.

There's no hostel accommodation in town, but there are some reasonable deals at the pubs. The *Royal Oak Hotel* (☎ 4990 2366, 221 Vincent St)* has singles/doubles for $25/40, increasing to $30/45 on weekends. Rooms are better than average at the well-renovated *Cessnock Hotel* (☎ 4990 1002).

HUNTER VALLEY

It's on Wollombi Rd near Vincent St; B&B costs $35 per person.

The *Cessnock Motel* (☎ 4990 2699) and the *Hunter Valley Motel* (☎ 4990 1722), both on Allandale Rd, charge $59 for doubles ($90 on Saturday night).

Vineyards You can stay at, or close to, the wineries. Most go for well over $100 a night on weekends, but midweek you can often get a good deal at places such as *Hunter Country Lodge* (☎ 4938 1744), about 12km north of Cessnock on Branxton Rd ($95 a double, B&B). Another good option is *Villa Provence* (☎ 4998 7404, 15 Gillards Rd), near Pokolbin. Here you'll find a touch of France to complete your winery experience. B&B costs $75/105 a single/double.

One of the best places to stay for quality and value is the *Cedar Creek Cottages* (☎ 4998 1576) on Wollombi Rd, 18km from Cessnock. These self-contained timber slab cottages are in a delightful, peaceful setting, and have verandas overlooking the owners' vineyards. Doubles cost $90/130 on weekdays/weekends.

About another 10km on, just out of Wollombi, *Mulla Villa Guesthouse* (☎ 4998 3254) is a superb convict-built homestead, with wide verandas from which to contemplate the surrounding sounds of nature. B&B costs $95 per person midweek, while weekend packages cost $195 per person, including all delicious meals.

The indulgence market is definitely cornered by the Peppers Group, with *Peppers Guest House* (☎ 4998 7596), on Ekerts Rd, a luxurious retreat with plenty of personal touches, and the more intimate but equally divine *Peppers Convent* (☎ 4998 7764), on Halls Rd. The prices reflect the extravagance of these places, with a midweek B&B stopover costing from $257 and $296 respectively per double, and weekend packages starting at $688 (dinner included) and $632.

Places to Eat
Cessnock The *Oak Brasserie* at the Royal Oak Hotel in Cessnock has a reputation for fine food, with most mains costing from $10 to $15.

For something more upmarket, the *Kurrajong Restaurant* at the Cessnock Hotel is excellent. Two courses from the innovative menu will set you back $38 per person, and three, $45.

Next door, the *Kurrajong Cafe* is a good place for coffee, brekky and the morning newspapers.

Vineyards Many wineries have cafes or restaurants, but if you are watching your budget, a cut lunch will have to be the go. A good place to stock up on picnic supplies is at the *Hunter Valley Cheese Company* at McGuigan Cellars, on McDonalds Rd. There's also a good *bakery* here.

At Pokolbin Village, *Pokolbin Red's Restaurant* (☎ 4998 7977) has an interesting menu; mains cost $18 to $26. *Cafe Max* (☎ 4998 7899), in the Small Winemakers Centre on McDonalds Rd near Pokolbin, charges similar prices. It's an inviting place, with an eclectic menu, and you can bring your own (BYO) alcohol, but it's only open on Saturday.

Well-regarded *Chez Pok*, at Peppers Guest House, offers a menu influenced by French, Italian and Asian cuisines. Main courses cost $24 to $28.

For the ultimate dining experience try *Robert's Restaurant* (☎ 4998 7330) at Pepper Tree Wines on Halls Rd, where the atmosphere, cuisine, wine list and service are superb. Mains cost $29.

Getting There & Around
Rover Motors (☎ 4990 1699) runs between Newcastle and Cessnock frequently on weekdays, less often on Saturday and not at all on Sunday ($8.80). Sid Fogg's (☎ 4928 1088) runs up the valley on its route from Newcastle to Dubbo. See Getting There & Away at the start of this chapter for Kean's service from Sydney to various towns in the Hunter Valley.

You can hire bicycles from Grapemobile (☎ 4998 7639), on the corner of McDonalds and Gillards Rds near Pokolbin. It charges $15/25 for a half/full day.

SINGLETON
postcode 2330 • pop 12,000

Europeans first came to this area in 1820 and farms soon sprang up on Patricks Plains. By 1835 the village that was later to be called Singleton was established.

The information centre (☎ 6571 5888), at 57 George St (the New England Hwy), is open from 9 am to 5 pm daily.

In the old courthouse by beautiful Burdekin Park, a **museum** with displays on local history opens from noon to 4 pm on weekends and from 10 am to 1 pm Tuesday ($3/1 for adults/children). For other early buildings, take a stroll down George St.

The **Royal Australian Army Infantry Corps Museum** (☎ 6570 3257) is at Singleton Army Camp. As well as guns there are memorabilia from most wars that the Australian infantry has been involved in. The camp is 4km from Singleton; from Maitland take the New England Hwy. The museum opens from Wednesday to Sunday (closed November; $3/2).

Singleton also claims to have the world's largest sundial.

Places to Stay

The *Country Acres Caravan Park* (☎ 6572 2328), on Maison Dieu Rd, has powered sites for $15 for two, on-site vans from $25 and cabins for $40.

The *Caledonian Hotel* (☎ 6572 1356), on the highway near the town centre, has singles/doubles for $15/35. Things should be quieter at one of the pubs along John St, such as *The Criterion Hotel* (☎ 6571 2712), which charges $20 per person. There's also a choice of motels, both on the highway and in town, such as the *Benjamin Singleton Motel* (☎ 6572 2922, 24 George St), which charges $55/65, plus $5 on weekends.

Getting There & Away

Yanda (☎ 13 1313) flies between Sydney and Singleton weekdays for $210. The airport is at Whittingham, just east of town.

UPPER-HUNTER WINERIES

With far fewer wineries, the upper Hunter is less visited than the lower, but the country is pretty and the wineries are well worth seeing. Most upper-Hunter wineries are close to the small town of Denman, such as picturesque Rosemount Estate, but don't miss James Estate, tucked away in a beautiful valley near the hamlet of Sandy Hollow. Verona Winery is just north of Muswellbrook.

Denman
postcode 2328 • pop 1500

Denman is a sleepy little place close to the forested sandstone ranges bordering the southern side of the Hunter Valley.

The information centre (☎ 6547 2731) is on the main street at the Old Carriage Restaurant.

Places to Stay The *Denman Van Village* (☎ 6547 2590, 10 McCauley St) has sites for $13, on-site vans from $28 and cabins from $38. The *Denman Hotel* (☎ 6547 2207) has pub rooms for $15 per person, and the pleasant *Royal Hotel* (☎ 6547 2226) nearby charges $15/25 a single/double. The friendly *Denman Motor Inn* (☎ 6547 2462) charges from $48/58.

Ask the information centre about B&B accommodation in the area.

Getting There & Away Sid Fogg's (☎ 4928 1088) buses stop at Denman ($24) three times a week on the Newcastle-Dubbo run. The fare from Denman to Dubbo is $33.

MUSWELLBROOK
postcode 2333 • pop 10,700

Like other towns in the Hunter Valley, Muswellbrook has some interesting old buildings, surrounded by spreading residential areas.

Bridge St (the New England Hwy) is Muswellbrook's main shopping street. The information centre (☎ 6541 4050), along with a wine-tasting room, is at 87 Hill St, which runs off Bridge St. It's open from 9.30 am to 4.30 pm daily. There's a National Parks & Wildlife Service (NPWS) office (☎ 6543 3533) on the corner of Francis St and Maitland Rd.

The **Weidman Cottage Heritage Centre**, on Bridge St near the centre of town, has displays on the area's history. It's open Saturday morning (free). **St Alban's Church** on Brook St dates from 1867. It's quite small and dark, which makes the stained glass blaze on sunny days.

Historic *Eatons Hotel* (☎ 6543 2403), on the main street at the northern end of town, charges $20/30 a single/double.

SCONE

postcode 2337 • pop 4500

Scone (ryhmes with 'tone') is a pleasant, old, upper Hunter town known for its horse studs – there are more than 40 in the area. Like Muswellbrook, Scone is a handy jumping-off point for the upper-Hunter wineries.

About 25km north-east of Scone, just off the interesting road across to Barrington Tops and Gloucester, **Belltrees** is an old sheep station with a grand homestead. The family of Patrick White, Australia's Nobel Prize–winning author, has owned the property for 150 years, and it appears as 'Kudgeri' in White's novel *The Eye of the Storm*. Belltrees is open for inspection by arrangement, and there's a guesthouse on the property – see under Places to Stay later in this section.

Orientation & Information

Kelly St (the New England Hwy) is the main shopping street. Liverpool St runs off Kelly St and becomes the road to Merriwa.

The information centre (☎ 6545 1526) is off Kelly St on the north side of the town centre, near the *Mare & Foal* statue.

Horse Studs

The information centre can arrange visits to some of the area's horse studs outside the August/September foaling season.

Burning Mountain

Coal seams beneath this mountain were burning when the first Europeans arrived in the area (they thought it was an active volcano), and calculations based on the burning rate of a metre per year suggest that the fire started as long as 6000 years ago. The mountain is a nature reserve, and a 3km round-trip walking track leads through

---

Australian Stock Horses

Although it wasn't formally defined as a breed until 1971, the Australian stock horse participated in most of the major events of European-Australian history. Originally called Walers (from New South Wales), the breed served as cavalry horses in India, South Africa and during WWI. They carried the 4th Australian Light Horse regiment in the world's last cavalry charge at the taking of Beersheba in 1916.

The headquarters of the Australian Stock Horse Society (☎ 6545 1122) is in Scone at 48 Guernsey St.

---

some diverse terrain up to the smoking vents. The turn-off from the New England Hwy to Burning Mountain is about 20km north of Scone.

Activities

Mountain Cattle Drives (☎ 6546 5246), about 75km from Scone, has received good reports for its eight-day trips, which will cost aspiring cowboys and cowgirls $549.

Special Events

Horse Week, with equestrian competitions and displays, is held in mid-May.

Places to Stay

There are a couple of caravan parks: The *Scone* (☎ 6545 2024) has sites for $12 and cabins from $30 (BYO linen), and the smaller *Highway* (☎ 6545 1078) has sites for $12 and on-site vans from $25.

The rural *Scone YHA Hostel* (☎ 6545 2072) occupies the old schoolhouse at Segenhoe, 8km east of town. Dorm beds in this historic building cost $15 and doubles cost $16 per person (plus $3 for nonmembers). The owners will pick you up from Scone for $5 and there's free use of bikes.

The lovely *Belmore Hotel* (☎ 6545 2078), on Kelly St not far from the information centre, is a pleasant place, with a fine beer garden. It has singles/doubles for $15/30. The equally attractive *Royal Hotel* (☎ 6545 1305), on the corner of Kelly and

St Aubins Sts, has pub rooms for $20/25 and motel-style rooms for around $40/50.

Airlie House Motor Inn (☎ 6545 1488), on the highway near the town centre, charges from $67/76, and also has a restaurant in a large Victorian house on the premises.

Belltrees Country House (☎ 6545 1668), on Belltrees property 25km north-east of Scone, is a very comfortable guesthouse, charging from $185 per person including dinner, B&B.

Places to Eat

The *Station Gallery & Cafe*, at the railway station, opens for lunch and tempting Devonshire teas ($6).

Across from the interesting Art-Deco Civic Theatre on Kelly St, the *Summerhouse Cafe* is a pleasant place for coffee, cake and light meals on weekdays.

On Kelly St across from the Village shopping centre is *Asser House*, an appealing cafe in a lovely historic building. It's open for lunch Monday to Saturday; mains cost $9 to $12.

Getting There & Away

Kean's (☎ 1800 625 587) buses run from Sydney to Scone ($37). Greyhound Pioneer and McCafferty's do the Sydney-Brisbane run along the New England Hwy, which is also the route many drivers take through the valley, stopping at Scone along the way.

MERRIWA

postcode 2329 • pop 1000

Merriwa is very much a country town immune to the Hunter Valley's creeping urbanisation. You have now entered pastoral country, a feature of this area since the 1820s.

The information centre (☎ 6548 2607) is on the main street (Bettingpon St) and is theoretically open daily.

This is a sandstone region and there are several early stone buildings here and in the surrounding area. The **Colonial Cottage Museum**, on the main street, is in one such building, a quite modest structure built in 1847.

Goulburn River National Park, 35km south-west of town, protects the upper reaches of the Goulburn River (which flows into the Hunter River east of Denman). The park follows the river as it cuts its way through sandstone gorges. This was the route used by Aborigines travelling from the plains to the sea, and the area is rich in rock art. You can camp here – some sites have pit toilets and barbecues. Access is from the road running south to Wollar and Bylong; all roads in the park are dry-weather roads only. The Mudgee NPWS office (☎ 6372 7199) has more information.

Places to Stay & Eat

The *Fitzroy Hotel* (☎ 6548 2258), a fine old sandstone pub, charges $20/30 a single/double, and the *Royal Hotel* (☎ 6548 2235) charges $15/30. Both are on the main street. *El Dorando Motel* (☎ 6548 2273) is on the main street east of the shopping centre and charges $45/53. For a mock Spanish-American motel it's quite a nice place.

The *Merriwa Bakery* on the main street sells some of the best pies in the land.

Getting There & Away

Sid Fogg's (☎ 4928 1088) buses stop in Merriwa between Dubbo ($30 from Merriwa) and Newcastle ($31).

Merriwa is a modest travel crossroads, with roads leading to the upper Hunter, Gulgong, Mudgee, Dubbo, and Coonabarabran.

THE BUCKETTS WAY

This old road is an alternative to the Pacific Hwy as a route north of Newcastle, branching off the highway about 15km north of Raymond Terrace and rejoining it just south of Taree. This road is longer and narrower than the highway, but it carries much less traffic and passes through some interesting country.

Stroud

postcode 2425 • pop 600

Stroud is a small village but it's the main town in this part of the Karuah Valley. The newsagent on the main street (☎ 4994 5117) serves as the town's information centre.

Founded by the Australian Agricultural Company in 1826, Stroud has several convict-built buildings such as **Quambi**, once a company residence and now a museum (open from 10 am to 4 pm Wednesday and Sunday). Next door to Quambi is the Anglican church, and in its graveyard are some interesting old headstones, including one that pronounces, rather ominously, 'Vengeance is Mine, Saith the Lord'.

The road running past Quambi leads to **Silo Hill**, where there are some wheat silos built in the early days of the Australian Agricultural Company. These aren't your ordinary, phallic silos – they are buried in the hill and you can climb down into one of them, if you're game.

The Australian Agricultural Company

By the 1820s, the idea that New South Wales might be a good place to make money had filtered back to Britain. Floated in 1825, the Australian Agricultural Company raised £1,000,000 from British investors, a colossal sum, and was granted a huge tract of land from Port Stephens north to the Manning River. The company also took over the Hunter coalfields and renamed the port Newcastle. A manager and workers (including convicts who were essentially slave labour) were sent out to farm sheep and cattle, and they began in the Karuah Valley around the company-built village of Stroud, named for the landscape's resemblance to the English Cotswolds.

Unfortunately, while the country is lush, well watered and beautiful, the soil lacks essential trace elements and, along with the sheep, the company failed to thrive. Just about every other form of agriculture was tried, including growing silkworms, but the land refused to nurture cash crops.

Taking up more land in the Tamworth area (which didn't look like England at all) proved to be more successful, but the company's plans for a closely settled private empire with an English social structure never materialised. Today the company still owns large properties in Queensland and the Northern Territory.

Farther down the main street is the old **courthouse**, which you can inspect by arrangement with the Historical Society (☎ 4994 5400).

Special Events Stroud's annual brick-throwing contest, held in mid-July, is an international affair, linked to similar contests in the English, US and Canadian villages of the same name (female contestants throw rolling pins!).

Places to Stay There's a basic but pretty *camping area* at the showgrounds, near the river. The pleasant old *Central Hotel* (☎ 4994 5197) is the only hotel in town and has standard singles/doubles for $20/40.

In the hamlet of Booral, 7km south of Stroud, *Gundayn House* (☎ 4994 9246), Lowes Lane, is an impressive Georgian B&B charging $89 per person. It's a non-smoking, nondrinking, vegetarian establishment.

The *Girvan YHA Hostel* (☎ 4997 6639) is about 15km from Stroud on the Bulahdelah road (turn east off The Bucketts Way at Booral). For more information about Bulahdelah see the North Coast chapter.

Getting There & Away Countrylink buses stop in Stroud on the weekday run between Newcastle and Taree.

Gloucester
postcode 2422 • pop 2500

Gloucester is a busy country town on the banks of the Gloucester River. The tourist information centre (☎ 6558 1408) is in the centre of town on the corner of Church and Denison Sts.

The **museum**, at the southern end of Church St, opens on Thursday and Saturday, plus Tuesday during school holidays.

There are extensive **state forests** in the area offering good walks and drives, and good views abound from **Mograni Lookout**, 5km east on The Bucketts Way.

The Barrington River, which rises in the Barrington Tops National Park and flows down past Barrington, just north-west of Gloucester, is popular for **white-water** canoeing. There are several companies offering canoe trips, including the Barrington Outdoor Adventure Centre (☎ 6558 2093), which has one-day trips ($99), and Barrington River Lodge (☎ 6558 4316).

Places to Stay *Gloucester Holiday Park* (☎ 6558 1720), on Denison St, has sites for $12 and cabins from $30. The *Avon Valley Inn* (☎ 6558 1016), on Church St, has singles/doubles for $20/30, and there's also *Gloucester Country Lodge Motel* (☎ 6558 1812), near the golf course, charging $60/68.

Getting There & Away Northbound trains stop at Gloucester, but coming in the other direction you'll have to change to a bus at Taree. The buses run on weekdays. Countrylink buses stop in Gloucester on the weekday run between Newcastle and Taree.

The Bucketts Way runs south to Stroud and beyond, and winds east to the Pacific Hwy just south of Taree. From near Barrington, you can head north on a partly sealed road to Walcha or branch off to Terrible Billy (great name!), from where a sealed road runs to Tamworth. If you keep heading west from Barrington, you'll be on a spectacular unsealed road that winds past Barrington Tops National Park, eventually reaching the New England Hwy near Scone.

BARRINGTON TOPS NATIONAL PARK

Barrington Tops National Park is a World Heritage wilderness area centred on the rugged Barrington Plateau, which rises to almost 1600 metres around Mt Barrington and Carey's Peak. The 'tops' are a series of monolithic hills known as 'bucketts', a corruption of an Aboriginal word meaning 'big rock' (hence the road called The Bucketts Way). The park also takes in the Gloucester Tops just to the north. There are good walking trails, but be prepared for snow in winter and cold snaps at any time. Drinking water must be boiled.

Vegetation in the park ranges from subtropical rainforest in the lower reaches of the park to snow-gum country on the exposed peaks. The slopes in between are dominated

by ancient, moss-covered Antarctic beech forest. The park can be reached from the towns of Dungog, Gloucester and Scone. The NPWS office (☎ 4987 3108) in Raymond Terrace has more information.

Places to Stay

The *Gloucester River Camping Area*, 31km from the Gloucester-Stroud road, is the main camp site within the park. *Barrington Guest House* (☎ 4995 3212), 43km from Dungog on the southern edge of the park, has a spectacular setting beneath the plateau escarpment. It has lovely cottages that cost from $129 per person per night, and guesthouse rooms with/without en suite from $99/69. Packages with all meals included are available, as well as trail rides for $15 an hour.

WOKO NATIONAL PARK

Smaller than nearby Barrington Tops National Park, Woko is similarly undeveloped and rugged, and also protects rainforests as well as other vegetation types. Access is from Gloucester, about 30km to the southeast; head for Rookhurst and take the left fork shortly after. There are *camp sites* on the banks of the Manning River near the park entrance, and some good swimming holes. The NPWS office (☎ 4987 3108) in Raymond Terrace has more information.

DUNGOG
postcode 2420 • pop 2500

The quiet country town of Dungog, in the steep hills to the north of the Hunter Valley, is the closest town to the southern side of Barrington Tops National Park. There are also many state forests in the area. Established in the 1830s as a military post with the task of eradicating bushrangers (it failed), Dungog is today a service centre for the area's farms.

There are several small, pretty villages in the area, such as **Clarence Town**, **Gresford** and **Paterson**, but getting to them on the winding roads can be time-consuming.

Places to Stay

The *Tall Timbers* (☎ 4992 1547) motel, on Dungog's main street, has singles/doubles for $50/65. Along the Chichester Dam road, running north from Dungog, there are several farmstay options, such as *Ferndale Park Camping Reserve (☎ 4995 9239),* which charges $5 per adult per night to camp. Camping is also permitted in the area's state forests.

Getting There & Away

Trains on the main northern line stop at Dungog.

Dungog is about 20km west of Stroud (the turn-off from The Bucketts Way is at Stroud Road, 7km north of Stroud), or you can get here from Singleton on the Gresford road.

North Coast

The New South Wales (NSW) north coast stretches from Port Stephens to the Queensland border at Tweed Heads. Most places north of Coffs Harbour, especially Byron Bay, are travellers meccas, but it's worth taking your time on a trip north from Sydney as there are excellent beaches and rugged bushland all the way. There are also some interesting places in the ranges behind the coast.

The Central Coast, between Sydney and Newcastle, is covered in the Around Sydney chapter.

Accommodation
This area of NSW is very popular, especially the far northern regions. During peak times (Christmas, January, Easter and school holidays), it's important to book ahead and to bear in mind that prices can skyrocket. Many places also increase their prices on weekends.

Getting There & Around
Air See the Port Macquarie, Coffs Harbour, Grafton, Byron Bay and Lismore sections later in this chapter for details of flights and fares.

Bus & Train Bus companies travelling the Pacific Hwy route to Brisbane include Greyhound Pioneer (☎ 13 2030), McCafferty's (☎ 13 1499) and Premier Motor Service (☎ 13 3410). They stop at all the resort towns except Port Stephens and Forster-Tuncurry. Some typical fares from Sydney are Port Macquarie $50 (seven hours), Coffs Harbour $57 (9½ hours) and Byron Bay $69 (13 hours). The fare through to Brisbane is $71 (16 hours). Port Stephens and Forster-Tuncurry have their own bus services to Sydney, provided by local companies (see those sections later in this chapter).

The nightly XPT (express train) from Sydney to Brisbane runs up the coast. Connecting buses at Casino run to Lismore, Ballina, Byron Bay, Mullumbimby and Tweed Heads/Coolangatta. Another XPT makes a

HIGHLIGHTS
- Swimming with dolphins at Port Stephens
- Visiting the koala hospital in Port Macquarie
- Soaking up the peaceful ambience of beautiful Bellingen
- Walking in Dorrigo National Park, the most accessible of Australia's World Heritage rainforests
- Seeing Grafton's magnificent jacaranda trees in full bloom in late October
- Looking down on Cape Byron from a tandem hang-glider
- Watching the sunrise from the summit of Mt Warning
- Visiting one of the many great weekend markets at The Channon, Byron Bay, Lismore, Nimbin and Bellingen

daylight run from Sydney to Murwillumbah, from where connecting buses run to Tweed Heads/Coolangatta and Surfers Paradise.

Car & Motorcycle The Pacific Hwy runs all the way up the coast. It is steadily being upgraded to cope with the ever-increasing traffic. The long-term goal is to provide a four-lane highway all the way from Sydney to Brisbane.

Lower North Coast

The coast from Port Stephens north to Port Macquarie is easily accessible from Sydney, but doesn't attract as much attention as the resort towns farther north.

PORT STEPHENS

Port Stephens is a huge sheltered bay about an hour's drive north of Newcastle. It occupies a submerged valley that stretches more than 20km inland. It's a popular boating and fishing spot and is well known for its resident dolphins.

Port Stephens is a good weekend getaway from Sydney, about three hours away by bus, and is much less developed than the Central Coast.

History

Captain James Cook sighted the entrance to Port Stephens in 1770, but the colony of NSW was seven years old before the first survey of the area was made – the first official survey, that is. Escaped convicts had made it up here five years earlier and were living with local Aborigines in what must have seemed like heaven after their captivity in Sydney.

Orientation & Information

Port Stephens has a long way to go before it's in the same league as the crowded Central Coast, but it's headed in the same direction, with land sales and new housing estates everywhere. The largest town on Port Stephens is Nelson Bay (population 7000), near the south head. The tourist office (☎ 4981 1579) at the end of the main street, near the d'Albora Marina complex, is open from 9 am to 5 pm weekdays and to 4 pm on weekends.

Just east of Nelson Bay, and virtually merged with it, is the less-commercial Shoal Bay, with its long, sheltered beach and great views across to hilly islands. It's a short walk to the surf at Zenith Beach.

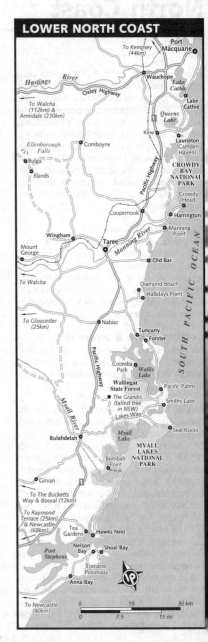

LOWER NORTH COAST

NORTH COAST

Back down the Tomaree Peninsula from Shoal Bay is Anna Bay, with access to both bay and ocean beaches. Samurai Beach, at the northern end of One Mile Beach on Anna Bay (some way east of the town of the same name), is a nudist beach. One Mile Beach is one of the area's best surf beaches. On the west side of Anna Bay township, the wide Stockton Beach runs all the way back to Newcastle. Watch out for vehicles – 4WDs are allowed on the beach here (permits are available from the tourist office). The stretch of coast between Shoal Bay and Anna Bay is occupied by tiny Tomaree National Park.

Things to See & Do

The restored 1872 **Inner Lighthouse** at Little Beach has displays on the area's history. There's also a cafe here, with good views.

There's a huge range of **cruises** on offer, so many that the cruise boats have their own wharf and booking centre, east of the d'Albora Marina. Some boats cruise around Port Stephens, with good chances of seeing dolphins (and even swimming with them if the boat has a net; *Moonshadow* is one that does), and others head across to Myall Lake.

Sail Cruise Port Stephens (☎ 4982 2399) rents out **yachts** for a minimum of two days from $360 (to sleep four). Aqua Action (☎ 4984 7433) has **paraflying** for $50, or you can learn to water-ski with Bay Barefoot & Water-ski School (☎ 4981 9409) for $100 an hour.

At Nelson Bay, Pro Dive (☎ 4981 4331), at d'Albora Marina, and Dive Nelson Bay (☎ 4981 2491), in Stockton St, run **diving** courses and rent out equipment. *Advance II* (☎ 018 494 386) is a motor/sailing yacht that has live-aboard dive courses for up to four people – pricey but fun.

Near the Salamander shopping centre, **Toboggan Hill Park** (☎ 4984 1022) is a great place for family outings. There's rock climbing, minigolf, a 1km toboggan track and numerous other attractions. Admission is $18 ($12 for children aged between four and seven), which includes use of all park facilities and three toboggan rides.

Places to Stay

During summer, Port Stephens gets very busy, especially on weekends, when it's not uncommon for people to miss out on a bed. Make sure you book ahead.

Camping The closest caravan parks to Nelson Bay are *Halifax Holiday Park* (☎ 4981 1522), at Little Beach on Nelson Head about 2km north of town, and the council-run *Shoal Bay Holiday Park* (☎ 4981 1427). Both have sites for $16 and cabins from about $40, but are expensive at peak times.

Hostels There's a YHA hostel section in the *Shoal Bay Motel* (☎ 4981 0982), on the beachfront road. Dorm beds cost $19 ($16 for YHA members) and there are family rooms for $24 ($21 for members); these rates can rise during school holidays.

Samurai Beach Bungalows (☎ 4982 1921), just east of Anna Bay on the corner of Frost Rd and Robert Connell Close, offers an opportunity for backpackers to go bush. Dorm beds cost $16 and doubles cost from $45. There's free use of surfboards and bikes can be hired for $10 a day. Buses from Newcastle run past the door.

Motels & Rental Accommodation Motel units at *Shoal Bay Motel* (☎ 4981 1744) start at $59 ($75 on weekends), increasing to $150 ($165) in peak season!

Aloha Villa Motel (☎ 4981 2523, 30–34 Shoal Bay Rd) charges $95 a double during the week and $145 on weekends, all year round. This is a tranquil, inviting place, although there is some traffic noise.

Nelson Towers Motel (☎ 4984 1000), well positioned opposite the marina, has standard rooms from $99 and rooms with water views from $170.

KD Winning Real Estate (☎ 4981 1999), at 19 Stockton St, has a huge listing of apartments. Other agents in town also have listings.

Places to Eat

Good, cheap meals are available at the large *RSL Club* between Nelson Bay and Shoal Bay and at the *Bowling Club* on Stockton St.

NORTH COAST

The *Big Fish Table Cafe*, also on Stockton St, is a gorgeous little place filled with mosaic tables and all the colours of the ocean. Drop in for a coffee, delicious gourmet salad or other yummy fare.

The d'Albora Marina complex has several excellent places, including alfresco dining at *Rob's on the Boardwalk* (☎ 4984 4444), open for breakfast on weekends, lunch Monday to Saturday and dinner Wednesday to Saturday. Evening mains on the innovative, although distinctly nonvegetarian menu, cost $18 to $23.

Fisherman's Wharf Seafoods, west of the marina, is the place for all your (raw) seafood needs, but drop into *Bub's* close by for some great fish and chips.

Upstairs in the complex across from the tourist office, *Noodle Fusion* (☎ 4981 0014) has a yummy selection of Asian dishes, many for around $10.

Getting There & Away

Port Stephens Coaches (☎ 4982 2940) has a daily service to Sydney ($26) and frequent buses to Newcastle ($8.40). If you're heading north up the coast, it's easiest to backtrack to Newcastle and catch a long-distance bus from there.

If you want to drive north up the coast from Nelson Bay, you'll have to backtrack a long way to the Pacific Hwy at Newcastle or Raymond Terrace, or join the highway north of Raymond Terrace by taking the partly unsealed road via Medowie.

Port Stephens Ferry Service (☎ 4981 3798) operates between Nelson Bay and Tea Gardens, across the bay, at 8.30 am, noon and 3.30 pm daily ($15/8 for adults/children).

Getting Around

It's worth hiring a bike, as there is a good network of bike paths in the area. Nelson Bay Sports (☎ 4981 2333), opposite the tourist office, has a good selection, plus in-line skates if that's your preferred mode of transport.

BULAHDELAH & AROUND

postcode 2423

A small town on the Myall River and the Pacific Hwy, Bulahdelah is the jumping-off point for Myall Lake and, a little way north of town, the Lakes Way route to Seal Rocks and Forster-Tuncurry. Some interesting old towns, such as Stroud, and the spectacular Barrington Tops National Park are inland from Bulahdelah, but they're more easily reached from towns in the Hunter Valley (see the Hunter Valley chapter for information).

There's a tourist office (☎ 4997 4981) on the corner of Pacific Hwy and Crawford St in Bulahdelah; it opens from 9 am to 5 pm daily.

Looming over the town is **Mt Alum**, the largest above-ground deposit of alum (a salt used in various industrial processes) in the world. The mining has ceased and the mountain is now the **Bulahdelah Mountain Park**, with some walking trails to historic sites. The entrance is a couple of blocks from the highway, on the same street as the police station.

Places to Stay

The *Alum Mountain Caravan Park* (☎ 4997 4565) and several motels are all just highway stops. Campers are better off heading to one of the nearby beaches at Seal Rocks or Myall Lakes National Park. Ask at the Forestry Commission office (☎ 4997 4206), near the

The Grandest Tree

The mists that often wreath Mt Alum occur throughout the surrounding area, and the combination of warmth and moisture is ideal for lush forests. Not far from Bulahdelah, The Grandis, the tallest tree in New South Wales, towers over dense rainforest.

This 400-year-old flooded gum (*Eucalyptus grandis*) is an awesome sight. On a humid, misty day, with the strange calls of whip birds echoing off palm trees and tall timber, the atmosphere is almost primeval. With its immensely tall, straight trunk it's amazing that The Grandis and some of its slightly shorter cousins survived the logging that continues in this area.

To get here, take the Lakes Way and then the signposted turn-off 12km from Bulahdelah. The Grandis is 6km farther on, down a bumpy all-weather road.

entrance to Bulahdelah Mountain Park, or at the Bulahdelah tourist centre for information on camping in the area's state forests.

There are two *houseboat* hire places in Bulahdelah – see the Myall Lakes National Park section for details.

The very rustic and basic *YHA Hostel* (☎ 4997 6639) near the tiny hamlet of Girvan, about 20km west of Bulahdelah on the winding back road to Booral, occupies an old school and has beds for $8 ($10 non-members). There are hot showers but pit toilets. It's a pleasant, secluded spot with good walks in the surrounding forests. Great Lakes Coaches goes past the hostel on its Newcastle-Bulahdelah run on weekdays when school's in. If you're driving, look out for the YHA sign at the highway turn-off 3km south of Bulahdelah. Ring first.

Getting There & Away
Great Lakes Coaches (☎ 4983 1560) services Bulahdelah on its daily run between Forster and Sydney ($31 from Sydney) via Newcastle ($15).

MYALL LAKES NATIONAL PARK
This park is one of the most popular recreation areas in the state. The large network of coastal lakes is ideal for water sports. Canoes, windsurfers and runabouts can be hired at **Bombah Point**, the park's main settlement. The best beaches are in the north around the hamlet of **Seal Rocks**, and there are good walks through coastal rainforest at **Mungo Brush** in the south.

Places to Stay
There are several National Parks & Wildlife Service (NPWS) *camp sites* around the park, including a good one at Mungo Brush. Camping fees are $5 for two people, plus a $7.50 once-only park-use fee. Sites can be scarce at peak times. Contact the NPWS office (☎ 4987 3108) in Raymond Terrace for more details. At Bombah Point, *Myall Shores* (☎ 4997 4495) has tent sites from $18 a double, bungalows for $50 and cabins for $77. There's also a shop and a restaurant.

There are caravan parks and motels in Tea Gardens and Hawks Nest. *Hawk's Nest*

Beach Caravan Park (☎ 4997 0239) has just a narrow band of bush separating it from a good surf beach. Tent sites cost $17 a double; cabins cost from $75/45 with/without en suite.

Several outfits rent out houseboats to cruise the lakes. In Bulahdelah, *Myall Lakes Houseboats* (☎ 4997 4221, 90 Crawford St) has an ageing fleet including two-person boats that cost from $200 to $370 for three midweek nights, depending on the season. *Luxury Houseboat Hire* (☎ 4997 4380), on Myall Marina, has a newer fleet of more up-market boats. Its two- to six-person boats cost from $490 to $1025 for three midweek nights. It's best to ring for a price list, as there's a bewildering array of rates.

Getting There & Away
There is road access to the park from Tea Gardens in the south and from Bulahdelah on the Pacific Hwy. You can drive from Tea Gardens to Bulahdelah via the Bombah Point ferry. The ferry runs half-hourly from 8 am to 6 pm, shuttling between the ocean and the western sides of the park. The fare is $3 per car. Great Lakes Coaches has a daily service from Newcastle to Tea Gardens for $14.60.

SEAL ROCKS
postcode 2423
Seal Rocks is a small hamlet on a great beach at the northern end of Myall Lakes National Park. There's a shop, a few houses and not much else. The actual rocks are some distance offshore.

Humpback **whales** swim past Seal Rocks and can sometimes be seen from the shore. There is good **surf** just south of Seal Rocks at Treachery Beach.

The simple *Seal Rocks Camping Reserve* (☎ 4997 6164) is a bit of a walk from town, but is next to an excellent beach. Sites cost $10.50 and there are on-site vans from $32. It's the sort of place you might stay at for a week in summer. There's also the privately run *Treachery Camp* (☎ 4997 6138) behind Treachery Beach.

Seal Rocks is 11km down a partly sealed road from the Lakes Way; turn off at Bungwahl, which is about 30km from Bulahdelah.

FORSTER-TUNCURRY

postcode 2428 • pop 22,815

Forster and Tuncurry are twin towns on either side of the sea entrance of Wallis Lake. The area boasts great beaches, good fishing and water sports, so it's packed with holiday-makers in summer.

Orientation & Information

Forster (pronounced fos-ter), on the southern side of the entrance, is much the larger of the two towns. It lies at the northern tip of a narrow spit of land between Wallis Lake and the ocean, and has about two-thirds of the population and most places of importance to travellers.

The Lakes Way leads into town from the south, first becoming MacIntosh St then turning sharply left into Head St, which runs east to a large roundabout that marks the city centre. The helpful information centre (☎ 6554 8799), set back from the lake on Little St, just south of the roundabout, is open from 9 am to 5 pm daily. The post office, near the roundabout, is on the corner of Little and Wallis Sts. Head St continues east from the roundabout and crosses the long Wallis Lake bridge to become Manning St, the main street through Tuncurry.

Things to See & Do

The area has many attractions, including the walking track that leads to a lookout on top of **Cape Hawke**, a few kilometres south-east of town.

There's a **museum** on Capel St in Tuncurry (off South St, which runs off Manning St), open Sunday afternoon ($2/1 for adults/children).

A **market** is held at the reserve at the bridge end of Head St in Forster on the second Sunday of the month.

The **lake** is great for paddling and there are some excellent **ocean beaches** right near the town. Nine Mile Beach at Tuncurry is consistently the best for surf, but Forster and Pebbly Beaches can also be good. There are large swimming **pools** at Forster Beach and near the harbour entrance in Tuncurry.

Amaroo II (soon to be the upgraded *Amaroo III*) is run by Amaroo Cruises (☎ 0419

333 445), which has a daily two-hour coffee **cruise** ($18/10). Dolphin Watch Cruises (☎ 6554 7478) has two-hour **dolphin-watching** cruises ($35/15). Most of the marinas along Little St hire out boats and other forms of water transport.

Action Divers (☎ 6555 4053), on the main street in Tuncurry, and the Forster Dive Centre (☎ 6554 5255), at the Aussie Boatshed on Little St, offer **diving** and dive courses. Popular dives in the area include the SS *Satara*, the largest diveable wreck on the east coast of Australia (this is a deep dive; advanced certificate required), and Seal Rocks, where there are grey nurse sharks.

Organised Tours

Boomerang 4WD Tours (☎ 6554 0757) offers half- and full-day ecotours, such as bird-watching breakfasts ($25) and rainforest-and-river tours in Wallingat State Forest ($65).

Special Events

The annual Oyster Festival is held in early October.

Places to Stay

The towns get packed out in summer, especially the two weeks following Boxing Day. Most places require a minimum one-week stay over Christmas and Easter.

Camping There are almost 20 camping and caravan parks in the area. In the middle of Forster and a short walk from the lake and ocean, the council-owned *Forster Beach Caravan Park* (☎ 6554 6269) has sites for $15.50, rising to $19.50 at Christmas and during school holidays. Cabins with en suites cost from $40. There are several places with lake frontage south of town along the Lakes Way. *Tuncurry Beach Caravan Park* (☎ 6554 6440), on Beach St, has both lake and ocean frontages.

Hostels The friendly, YHA-affiliated *Dolphin Lodge* (☎ 6555 8155, 43 Head St) is in a renovated block of flats; all rooms have their own bathroom. It's very clean and airy and has a surf beach pretty well at its back door, from where you should be able to see dolphins. Dorm beds cost $16 ($18 non-members) and doubles $20 per person. Boogie boards and surfboards are free and you can hire bikes for $12 a day.

Guesthouses The *Tudor On West* (☎ 6554 8766, 1 West St) is a lovely looking place with a good restaurant and rooms from $115 ($15 more for terrific ocean views).

Hotel & Motels The *Lakes & Ocean Hotel* (☎ 6554 6005), on Little St near the information centre, has a top position overlooking the lake. Singles/doubles cost $28/35 in the low season – not bad value for the view and your own balcony.

There are about 20 motels in town that can get very expensive at peak times, but in the low season there are some good deals, with doubles advertised for as little as $40 at motels along the main drag.

The *Great Lakes Motor Inn* (☎ 6554 6955, 24 Head St) is a good budget option close to the Forster town centre and beach. Budget doubles cost from $40; deluxe doubles cost $53.

Rental Accommodation There are a lot of holiday apartments. The cheapest go for around $100 a week in the low season and about $300 at Christmas, but you can pay an awful lot more. Agents include Ray White (☎ 6554 6611) at 27 Wharf St, Forster.

Places to Eat
There are several excellent restaurants overlooking Wallis Lake from Memorial Dr, which runs parallel to Wharf St, the main shopping street in Forster. These include the atmospheric *Divino Italian Brasserie* (☎ 6557 5033), with outdoor seating and an enticing menu including plenty of vegetarian options. Mains cost around $15 to $17.

Close by are two good seafood options: *Cid's Seafood Restaurant & Grill* (☎ 6554 8055), 1st floor, Pacific Arcade, Wharf St, a spacious place with lovely views and a good menu, including seafood paella ($19.50); and the smaller *Oyster Rack* (☎ 6557 5577), Shop 6, Pacific Arcade, Memorial Dr.

El Barracho Mexican (☎ 6554 5573, 5/12 Wharf St) is a fun place with good food. Mains cost around $12.

The *Lakes & Ocean Hotel* has pub meals, including steaks, for $7 to $10. You can eat in the beer garden overlooking the lake.

Down at Green Point, off the road to Pacific Palms about 8km south of Forster, the *Green Point Restaurant & Gallery* (☎ 6557 6222) is open for dinner Thursday to Saturday (bookings required) and for lunch and Devonshire tea Wednesday to Sunday. You can bring your own (BYO) alcohol.

Getting There & Away
Great Lakes Coaches has daily buses to Newcastle ($25) and Sydney ($40). Some services to Newcastle connect with trains to Sydney. There are also buses from Tea Gardens (on Port Stephens). Eggins Coaches (☎ 6554 8699) runs north to Taree ($9) four times on weekdays and twice on Saturday. The bus stop is outside the information centre.

Forster-Tuncurry is off the Pacific Hwy, on the scenic but winding Lakes Way, which leaves the highway at Bulahdelah and rejoins it about 20km south of Taree.

THE MANNING VALLEY
The Manning Valley extends from the Manning River delta (near Old Bar and Harrington) west through farmland to Taree and Wingham, then through forests to the Bulga and Comboyne plateaux. About 150km of the meandering Manning River is navigable.

History
Explorer John Oxley was the first European to visit the valley (1818), although Cook had sailed past in 1770 and renamed mountains in the area. In 1829 Governor Ralph Darling set the Manning River as the northernmost limit of the colony, but this was ignored by the cedar cutters. A land grant to William Wynter in 1831 saw permanent European settlement on the Manning River.

Taree
postcode 2430 • pop 18,000
It's hard to get excited about Taree, the largest town and service centre of the

NORTH COAST

Manning Valley – although the **Big Oyster**, by the highway just north of town, surely ranks among the most bizarre of Australia's many 'big' things. It's a tribute to the area's large oyster-farming industry.

Taree's long main street is Victoria St (what used to be the Pacific Hwy); the centre of town is probably the block between Pulteney and Manning Sts, although the shops continue a long way east. A block south of Victoria St is the Manning River, and the narrow **Queen Elizabeth Park** runs along the bank for the length of the city centre.

The Manning Valley Tourist Information Centre (☎ 6552 1900), on the old Pacific Hwy about 3km north of the town centre, is open from 9 am to 5 pm daily.

The **Manning Regional Art Gallery** is on Macquarie St, which runs off Victoria St near the main shopping centre. It's open from 1 to 4 pm Wednesday and Sunday and 10 am to 4 pm Thursday to Saturday.

Manning Point Marine **River Cruises** (☎ 6553 2683) offers trips on the Manning River, including three-hour Devonshire-tea cruises ($15) and four-hour 'trap-a-crab' seafood tours ($55).

Places to Stay Taree's two caravan parks, *Taree (☎ 6552 1751)* and *Twilight (☎ 6552 2857)*, on the highway north and south of town respectively, have sites for about $15 and cabins from about $28.

The *Exchange Hotel (☎ 6552 1160)*, on the corner of Victoria and Manning Sts, has rather grim singles/doubles for $14/25, although the pub itself is inviting. A block away on the corner of Pulteney and Victoria Sts, *Fotheringhams Hotel (☎ 6552 1153)*, also known as Fogg's, has slightly better rooms opening onto a balcony for $15/30.

Motel enthusiasts can take their pick of the 20-odd in town, such as the good-value *Rainbow Gardens Motel (☎ 6551 7311, 28 Crescent Ave)*, which has doubles for $45 including a continental brekky.

Manning River Holidays Afloat (☎ 6552 6271), on the Old Pacific Hwy, has houseboats for hire. Low-season prices start at $320 for a six-berth boat for the weekend.

Places to Eat A good spot for breakfast or lunch, or a coffee and yummy cake, is *Scenes Sidewalk Cafe*, near the main shopping drag on the corner of Manning and Albert Sts.

Two very good pub options include *Plates*, a cosy dining room at the Exchange Hotel, and the *Royal Brasserie (☎ 6552 1242)*, at the lovely wooden Royal Hotel on Victoria St, where mains cost $9 to $15. There's also a pleasant outdoor eating area here overlooking the river.

You'll find standard club grub at *Benny's Bistro* in the Returned & Services League (RSL) on Pulteney St. If you want to dine in a bit more style, head for *Laurent's (☎ 6552 5022)* at the Caravilla Motor Inn, just north of the town centre on the main street. Its interesting menu includes crocodile, emu and kangaroo as well as European fare (mains cost $13 to $21).

Getting There & Away Most long-distance buses stop at the Mobil service station on Victoria St. Great Lakes Coaches has a daily service to Newcastle ($27), which leaves from the train station on Olympia St.

If you're driving north to Port Macquarie, consider making an inland detour through Wingham to Wauchope, passing through some interesting villages and great scenery. It would, however, mean missing out on the drive through Crowdy Bay National Park.

Wingham
postcode 2429 • pop 4900

Wingham is a quiet town serving the upper Manning Valley. It has a long association with the timber industry. The main streets surround **Central Park**, a large grassy square that was once the town's common and still hosts cricket matches. The huge brush-box log on the common is a memorial to Cook but it could equally be a memorial to the Manning Valley's vanished forests. On Farquar St is the **museum** (☎ 6553 5823), open from 10 am to 4 pm daily.

Just east of the town centre down Farquar St is a picnic spot on a bend in the wide Manning River and **Wingham Brush**, a seven-hectare vestige of rainforest. It's a

The amazing scene from Evans Lookout, Blue Mountains National Park

RICHARD I'ANSON

ines of vines in the grape-groovy Hunter Valley

RICHARD I'ANSON

Surf-side greens at relaxed Crescent Head

Surf rafting, Diggers Beach, Coffs Harbour

The view of Mt Warning from Watego's Beach, Byron Bay

pretty place, alive with bird calls and the twitter of flying foxes.

Wingham's **market** is held on the second Saturday of the month on Wynter St, near the Wingham Hotel.

Places to Stay There are no camping areas close to town. The *Australian Hotel (☎ 6553 4511)*, facing Central Park on the corner of Farquar and Bent Sts, has singles/doubles for $20/36. Cheaper, but less inviting, is the *Wingham Hotel (☎ 6553 4007)*, across the park on the corner of Isabella and Wynter Sts – it's made of timber, unusual for a large hotel. There's also the *Wingham Motel (☎ 6553 4295)*, on Bent St near the Australian, with rooms for $45/55.

Getting There & Away Trains between Sydney and Brisbane run through Wingham. You'll find the station at the western end of Isabella St.

Mountains & Forests

Inland from Wingham there is some wild and rugged bushland, but it's less well known than the forests of Walcha in New England. Woko National Park is west of Wingham, but is more easily reached from Gloucester (see the Hunter Valley chapter for information).

There are quite a few small communities in the area with alternative-lifestyle tendencies, especially around Elands and Bulga. There are also plenty of art and craft galleries – the Taree information centre has a brochure.

The Bulga Plateau is worth a visit to check out the spectacular **Ellenborough Falls**, which plunge 160m in one dramatic drop. The falls are about 25km west of Comboyne. In the same area you can visit **Blue Knob Lookout** and the **Wautui Falls**.

Places to Stay The *Lizzard Island Lodge (☎ 6550 4188)* at Comboyne is a collection of old timber mill buildings converted into accommodation. A dormitory-style building that sleeps 14 costs $200 a night, or there's a self-contained cabin overlooking the Thone River for $80 a double.

Near Comboyne is the *Comboyne Hideaway (☎ 6550 4230)*, which has quality accommodation and excellent views through valleys to the ocean. Dinner B&B packages cost from $175 a double in the homestead or in one of three self-contained cottages.

There are various *farmstays* in the area – contact the Taree information centre for a complete list.

Beaches

On the coast south of the Manning River's southern arm and 16km from Taree is **Old Bar**, a village with a popular surf beach. Accommodation is available at the *Old Bar Beachfront Holiday Park (☎ 6553 7274)*, with sites from $15 and cabins from $39. For holiday apartments contact LJ Hooker (☎ 6553 7133). Just south of Old Bar is **Wallabi Point**, where there's a lagoon for swimming.

Near the south side of the northern arm is **Manning Point**, a hamlet serving the oyster farms along the river. Manning Point is on a large, flat, river island that supports intensive dairy farming. There are several *caravan parks* in the area. Across on the north bank is **Harrington**, a small village (turn off the highway at Coopernook). There's swimming in the lagoon and surf beaches nearby. Harrington is developing into a small resort town and there are plenty of *motels* and *caravan parks*.

Crowdy Head is a small fishing village 4km north-east of Harrington. The views from the old lighthouse on the high head are superb, out to the limitless ocean, down to the deserted beaches and back to the apparent wilderness of the coastal plain and mountains. The only place to stay is the pleasant *Crowdy Head Motel (☎ 6556 1206)*, which charges from $55/60 for singles/doubles.

North of Harrington and Crowdy Head, **Crowdy Bay National Park** backs onto a long and beautiful beach that sweeps north to **Diamond Head**. A rough road leads into the national park from just before Crowdy Head village. You can also enter from Laurieton at the north end of the park. There are basic, pretty *camp sites* at Diamond Head and Indian Head, but you need to bring water. Camping fees are $5 a double, plus a $7.50 once-only park-use fee. Contact the NPWS office (☎ 6584 2203) in Port Macquarie for more information.

North of the national park and accessible from the Pacific Hwy at Kew is **Camden Haven**. This area is composed of Laurieton, North Haven and Dunbogan, villages clustering around the wide sea entrance of Queens Lake, and there are good beaches. North Brother Mountain towers over Camden Haven. There are walking trails in the state forests behind Laurieton. *Beachfront Caravan Park (☎ 6559 9193)*, in North Haven, has sites from $12.50 and cabins from $40, and is right behind a good surf beach.

North of here the coast road runs past **Lake Cathie** (pronounced cat-eye), both a town (with accommodation) and a lake with shallow water suitable for kids. The road then enters the sprawling outer suburbs of Port Macquarie.

PORT MACQUARIE
postcode 2444 • pop 31,000
Port Macquarie, usually called just Port, is at the southern end of the state's subtropical coast. Winters are cool but short, while summers can be sticky.

Although tourist development has been gaining momentum for over 20 years, the city still has a relaxed small-town feel. With surf beaches, the winding lower reaches of the Hastings River and its tributaries, and some excellent bush in the mountains behind the coast, this is a good place to unwind.

History
Port Macquarie was the third town to be established on the Australian mainland following Oxley's visit to the area in 1818. Governor Lachlan Macquarie established a penal settlement here in 1821, designed as punishment for convicts who found life in Sydney Cove too easy.

Orientation & Information
The city centre is at the mouth of the Hastings River, on the south side. Running south from the city centre is a long string of excellent beaches.

The Port Macquarie Visitor Information & Booking Centre (☎ 6581 8000, 1800 025 935), in the town centre on Clarence St, is open from 8.30 am to 5 pm weekdays and 9 am to 4 pm on weekends. There's an NPWS office (☎ 6584 2203) at 152 Horton St.

Historic Buildings & Museums
Few buildings from the early days of the penal settlement still stand. Most survivors are near the city centre. They include: **St Thomas' Church** (1828), on William St near Hay St ($1/0.30 for adults/children); the **Garrison** (1830), on the corner of Hay and Clarence Sts, now housing some cafes; the recently restored **courthouse** (1869), across the road on Clarence St, open from 10 am to 4 pm Monday to Saturday ($2/0.50); and the nearby building at 22 Clarence St housing the **museum** (1830), open from 9.30 am to 4.30 pm Monday to Saturday, from 1 pm on Sunday ($4/1).

The old pilots cottage above Town Beach is now a **Maritime Museum**, open from 10 am to 4 pm daily ($2).

Observatory
The small observatory at the beach end of Lord St is open Wednesday and Sunday. You can look through the telescope from 7.30 to 9.30 pm in winter and from 8.15 to 10 pm in summer ($2/1).

Koalas
Koala habitats and new housing developments compete for space in this area, and guess who loses out? Koalas living near urban areas are at risk from traffic and domestic animals and many end up at the **Koala Hospital** (☎ 6584 1522) off Lord St, about 1km south of the town centre. The convalescent koalas are in outdoor enclosures and you can visit them daily; the best times to drop in are when they're being fed, at 7.30 am and 2.50 pm. Tours of the hospital are by arrangement only.

You can meet undamaged koalas and other animals at **Kingfisher Park** (☎ 6581 0783), off the Oxley Hwy, and at **Billabong Koala Park** (☎ 6585 1060), farther out of town at the Pacific Hwy interchange. Both are open daily.

PORT MACQUARIE

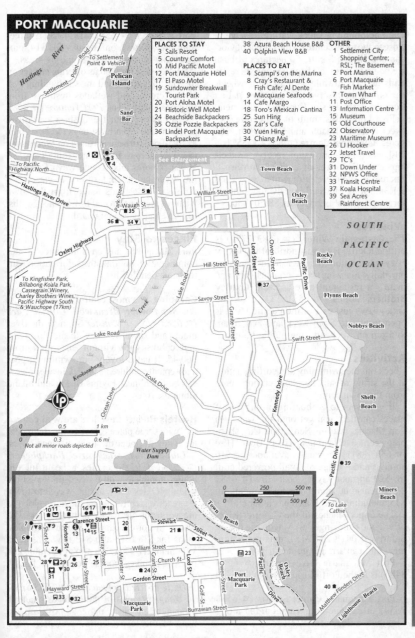

PLACES TO STAY
3 Sails Resort
5 Country Comfort
10 Mid Pacific Motel
12 Port Macquarie Hotel
17 El Paso Motel
19 Sundowner Breakwall Tourist Park
20 Port Aloha Motel
21 Historic Well Motel
24 Beachside Backpackers
35 Ozzie Pozzie Backpackers
36 Lindel Port Macquarie Backpackers

38 Azura Beach House B&B
40 Dolphin View B&B

PLACES TO EAT
4 Scampi's on the Marina
8 Cray's Restaurant & Fish Cafe; Al Dente
9 Macquarie Seafoods
14 Cafe Margo
18 Toro's Mexican Cantina
25 Sun Hing
28 Zar's Cafe
30 Yuen Hing
34 Chiang Mai

OTHER
1 Settlement City Shopping Centre; RSL; The Basement
2 Port Marina
6 Port Macquarie Fish Market
7 Town Wharf
11 Post Office
13 Information Centre
15 Museum
16 Old Courthouse
22 Observatory
23 Maritime Museum
26 LJ Hooker
27 Jetset Travel
29 TC's
31 Down Under
32 NPWS Office
33 Transit Centre
37 Koala Hospital
39 Sea Acres Rainforest Centre

NORTH COAST

Nature Reserves

The **Kooloonbung Creek Nature Reserve** is close to the town centre on the corner of Gordon and Horton Sts. Its 50 hectares of bush are home to many bird species and there are trails and boardwalks (suitable for wheelchairs). In the reserve is a cemetery dating from the early days of European settlement.

Five kilometres south of the centre, between Miners Beach and Pacific Dr, **Sea Acres Rainforest Centre** (☎ 6582 3355) is a 70-hectare flora and fauna reserve protecting a small pocket of coastal rainforest. There's an ecology centre with displays and a 1.3km-long elevated boardwalk, suitable for wheelchairs. Entry costs $8.50/4.50.

Wineries

The **Cassegrain Winery** (☎ 6583 7777) is off the Pacific Hwy just north of the Oxley Hwy intersection. It's open from 9 am to 5 pm daily for wine sales and tastings and there's a restaurant here as well. **Charley Brothers Wines** (☎ 6581 1332), on the Oxley Hwy just east of the Pacific Hwy, is open from 1 to 5 pm weekdays and 10 am to 5 pm on weekends and public holidays.

Activities

Check out the **swimming** and **surfing** action at the string of surf beaches running south from the town centre.

If you want to go **boating**, a number of places can help you get onto the water. At Port Marina, near the Settlement City shopping centre, Hastings River Boat Hire (☎ 6583 8811) has canoes available for $10 an hour and a range of small powered craft for $20 an hour. Gypsy boat Hire (☎ 6583 2353) rents out small boats for six hours for $45, including fuel. It also has other craft.

The upper reaches of the Hastings River offer good canoeing. Port Macquarie Canoe Safaris (☎ 0419 237 315) rents out equipment and can arrange guided trips.

Port Macquarie Dive Centre (☎ 6583 8483) is at the Port Marina near Settlement City.

Port Macquarie Camel Safaris (☎ 6583 7650) offers one-hour **camel rides** along Lighthouse Beach for $22/14.

Organised Tours

Port Explorer (☎ 6581 2181) has a three-hour tour of town on Tuesday for $14, plus other day tours in the surrounding areas.

There are several boats offering cruises on the Hastings River and the surrounding system of creeks and wetlands upstream from Port Macquarie. The *Port Venture* (☎ 6583 3058) has two-hour Devonshire-tea cruises at 10 am and 2 pm most days ($17), as well as five-hour barbecue cruises on Wednesday ($32). Waterbus Everglade Tours (☎ 6582 5009) explores inland waterways, known as the Everglades, and offers a variety of cruises. These boats leave from the town wharf at the western end of Clarence St. Just roll up and pay as you board.

Places to Stay

Port Macquarie has an abundance of accommodation options; the information centre has a detailed list.

Camping The most central caravan park is the *Sundowner Breakwall Tourist Park (☎ 6583 2755, 1 Munster St)*, near the river mouth and Town Beach, with sites from $15 and cabins with/without en suites from $60/45. It has a lovely big swimming pool and separate children's pool. Cheaper places can be found near Flynns Beach and inland along the river.

Hostels Budget travellers are well catered for, with three places close to the town centre. They all meet the long-distance buses.

Lindel Port Macquarie Backpackers (☎ 6583 1791) occupies a beautiful old house (complete with pressed-tin walls) beside the Oxley Hwy on the way into town. It's readily identifiable by the large globe of the world outside. It's clean, homely and well run, with dorm beds for $16 and doubles/twins for $38 ($18 and $42 if you're not a VIP member). There's a pool, pool table and free use of bikes, boogie boards and fishing gear.

Ozzie Pozzie Backpackers (☎ 6583 8133, 36 Waugh St), part of the Nomads chain, is a clean, bright place in a good position, just west of the town centre. Travellers rave about the cleanliness of the bathrooms! Dorm beds cost $16, twin beds $18 and family rooms $50.

YHA-associate *Beachside Backpackers* (☎ *6583 5512, 40 Church St*) is a clean, friendly and popular place where dorm beds cost $16 ($18 nonmembers). There's free use of bikes and boogie boards.

B&Bs About 5km south of the town centre, *Azura Beach House B&B* (☎ *6582 2700, 109 Pacific Dr*) is a lovely, ultramodern home charging between $110 and $135 a double.

Dolphin View B&B (☎ *6582 3561, 53 Matthew Flinders Dr*) has a fantastic beachfront position on Lighthouse Beach, about 7km from the centre. Make sure you go for one of the two rooms with a view. Singles/doubles cost $75/105.

Hotels The single pub in town is the *Port Macquarie Hotel* (☎ *6583 1011*), at the north end of Horton St. Rooms cost $25/40, or $30/45 with a bathroom.

The lovely old Royal Hotel, next door to the Port Macquarie Hotel, was being redeveloped into offices, restaurants, a nightclub, apartments and a luxury hotel at the time of writing.

Motels There might not be many pubs in town but there are plenty of motels – 36 at last count. The cheapest are those farthest from the beaches, especially along Hastings River Dr.

One of the best, inexpensive options is the friendly *Port Aloha Motel* (☎ *6583 1455, 3 School St*). The rooms are large and sunny and most have their own balcony, many with excellent views. Doubles cost $55 to $75. Another good, bright and breezy option is the *Historic Well Motel* (☎ *6583 1200, 1 Stewart St*), built on the site of the Port Macquarie Gaol, the original well forming part of the motel. Almost every room has great views over parkland to the ocean and Hastings River. Good-value doubles cost $65 to $85.

The *Mid Pacific Motel* (☎ *6583 2166*), on the corner of Clarence and Short Sts, is a high-rise building with great views over the river. Doubles cost $85, plus $20 in peak periods.

Farther east on Clarence St, *El Paso Motel* (☎ *6583 1944*) is an old-style motel that's been renovated. (It won't be long before motels like this get National Trust listing for their unique architecture.) The experience will set you back $87 for a standard double, increasing to $97 for the deluxe model.

The resort-like *Country Comfort* (☎ *6583 2955*), on the corner of Buller and Hollingworth Sts on the waterfront, charges $103 a double ($113 with a river view). This is much better value than the more expensive *Sails Resort* (☎ *6583 3999*), on the waterfront near Settlement City. Doubles cost from $172 without a view and from $202 with a view of the water.

Rental Accommodation There are a great many apartments and holiday flats. They are expensive at peak times, but in the low season you'll be able to find a two-bedroom apartment for between $200 and $400 a week. Letting agents include LJ Hooker (☎ 6583 3044), on the corner of William and Horton Sts. Its accommodation booklets have comprehensive listings.

Places to Eat

For breakfast, try *Zar's Cafe* on William St, which has bacon and eggs for $5. *Cafe Margo*, in the historic Garrison building on the corner of Hay and Clarence Sts, is another good option, with tables outside and brekky all-day.

Port is the perfect setting for seafood and you won't find it any fresher than at the *Port Macquarie Fish Market*, by the river on Wharf St. If you want your seafood cooked, *Macquarie Seafoods*, on the corner of Clarence and Short Sts, does excellent fish and chips. For something a bit more upmarket, try *Scampi's on the Marina* (☎ *6583 7200*), close to Settlement City on Park St. This is a relaxed, inviting BYO restaurant with an excellent choice of daily seafood specials for around $19 and a seafood platter for one ($40).

Another place to splurge is *Cray's Restaurant & Fish Cafe* (☎ 6583 7885, 74 Clarence St), overlooking the river, with mains from $16 to $24. There's a good cluster of restaurants at this end of Clarence St, including *Al Dente* (☎ 6584 1422), an atmospheric place offering a great outlook over the river and good Italian food. Pasta dishes cost $13 to $16, other mains $17 to $22.

Toro's Mexican Cantina (☎ 6583 4340, 22 Murray St) is an inviting spot with great Mexican-theme decor. Main courses cost from $11 and it's BYO.

Good-value Chinese meals can be had at *Sun Hing* (☎ 6583 5667, 112 William St), which has MSG-free lunches from $3.80, while the *Yuen Hing* (☎ 6583 2269), on Horton St, offers 10-course banquets for $11 per person (minimum three people). Now there's value. A cheap Thai option is *Chiang Mai* (☎ 6583 1766, 153 Gordon St), where most dishes are under $10.

Entertainment

The nightclub *TC's* is on William St and *Down Under* nightclub is around the corner on Short St. The *RSL Club* at Settlement City has free live bands on Friday and Saturday nights, and you'll also find *The Basement* nightclub here.

Getting There & Away

Air Eastern Australia Airlines (☎ 13 1313) flies to Sydney at least three times daily for $188. Impulse Airlines (☎ 13 1381) flies to Sydney for $180, as well as to Brisbane ($259), sometimes via Coffs Harbour and Coolangatta. The Impulse agent is Jetset Travel (☎ 6584 1411) on the corner of Horton and William Sts.

Bus Greyhound, Premier Motor Service and McCafferty's all use the bus stop at the Transit Centre in Hayward St. Sample fares include Newcastle ($31), Sydney ($40), Byron Bay ($50) and Brisbane ($50). Kean's (☎ 1800 625 587) runs to Coffs Harbour ($20), Bellingen ($25), Dorrigo ($27), Armidale ($40) and Tamworth ($57). Port Macquarie Bus Service (☎ 6583 2161) runs to Wauchope four times a day for $7.

Train The nearest station is at Wauchope, 19km inland. The fare from Sydney is $62. An extra $5 will get you into Port Macquarie on the Countrylink bus that meets the train arriving at 5.59 pm.

Car & Motorcycle The next major town on the Pacific Hwy is Kempsey, about 50km north. The Oxley Hwy runs west from Port Macquarie through Wauchope and eventually reaches the New England tableland near Walcha. It's a spectacular drive.

The Settlement Point ferry operates 24 hours, crossing to the north side of the Hastings River. It costs $2 per car. To get to the ferry, keep going past the RSL Club and follow the signs to Settlement Point, from where two interesting roads lead north. A very rough dirt road (4WD only) runs along the coast, past Limeburners Creek Nature Reserve to Point Plomer (good surf) and Crescent Head, from where you can rejoin the highway at Kempsey. The second road, Maria River Rd (unsealed but fine for a 2WD) takes a more inland route to meet the Crescent Head to Kempsey road.

Getting Around

Hertz (☎ 6583 6599) car rental is at 102 Gordon St. Hibbard Car & Bike Hire (☎ 6584 9887) offers seven-day car hire from $25 per day.

Graham Seers Cyclery (☎ 6583 2333) at Port Marina rents bikes for $20 a day.

WAUCHOPE

postcode 2446

Wauchope (pronounced war-hope) is a timber town of long standing. The town's main attraction is the big **Timbertown** historic park (☎ 6585 2322), with the emphasis on the history of the timber industry. It's one of the better theme parks and is well worth visiting. Admission is free, but there are individual attractions that you pay for.

Places to Stay

The *Rainbow Ridge Hostel* (☎ 6585 6134), 11km west of town on the Oxley Hwy, was once the only hostel between Sydney and Queensland. It's still an old-style hostel –

quiet, friendly and definitely not the place for party animals. There are bushwalks nearby, including a six-hour climb to the top of Bago Bluff. Dorm beds cost $10 or you can camp for $5 per person.

Coming from Wauchope, the hostel's driveway is on the right just before the Comboyne turn-off; keep a look-out after you cross the Mahers Creek bridge. Ask around town for information on school buses running out this way – one of them tends to connect with the afternoon train.

In Wauchope, the *Hastings Hotel (☎ 6585 2003)*, on the main street near the train line, has singles/doubles for $25/45. There are also a couple of motels on the main street, charging around $45/55: the *Wauchope (☎ 6585 1933)* and *The Broadaxe (☎ 6585 1355)*, near Timbertown. There's also a *caravan park* at The Broadaxe.

Getting There & Away

See the Port Macquarie section earlier in this chapter for information on buses.

Wauchope is on the main train line between Sydney ($58) and Murwillumbah or Brisbane.

Mid-North Coast

MACLEAY VALLEY

Rising in the New England tableland, the Macleay River flows east through the fertile Macleay Valley, entering the sea near South West Rocks (although until a flood in 1893 its entrance was farther north near Grassy Head). The main town in the valley is Kempsey, on the Pacific Hwy and about 20km inland from the nearest ocean beach at Crescent Head. There are long, uncrowded beaches north and south of Crescent Head.

Before Europeans arrived, the valley was owned by the Dainggatti people, but in 1827 the penal settlement in Port Macquarie established a camp in the valley to cut cedar and rosewood. Land grants were made in 1835 and the town of Kempsey (named after the Kempsey Valley in Worcestershire, England) was established by 1840. Beef cattle and dairying were early agricultural ventures

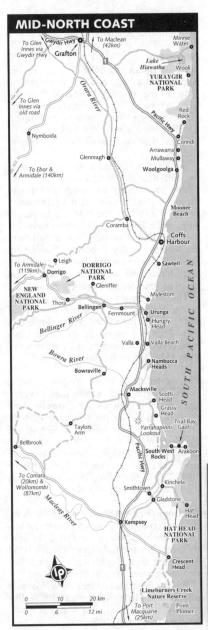

and they remain the mainstay of the area, with further contributions from tourism.

Kempsey
postcode 2440 • pop 8630
Kempsey is a large rural town serving the farms of the Macleay Valley. As the main town between Port Macquarie and Coffs Harbour, it's a handy place to stock up on supplies for a stay at the beaches east of here and the mountainous national parks to the west.

Kempsey is now the home of the Akubra hat, although this wasn't the firm's birthplace. Unfortunately, the factory isn't open to the public, but a video at the information centre shows how the hats are fashioned from rabbit-fur felt, and shops in town sell them. Another Australian icon to hail from the Macleay Valley is country singer Slim Dusty. His songs such as 'Pub with No Beer' and 'Duncan' are known even to people who claim no knowledge of country music.

The information centre (☎ 6563 1555), off the highway at the southern entrance to town, is open from 9 am to 5 pm weekdays and 10 am to 4 pm weekends. There's also a **museum** here, open from 10 am to 4 pm daily ($3/1 for adults/children).

Places to Stay There are five caravan parks, all with sites, on-site vans and cabins, including *Sundowner Caravan Park* (☎ 6562 1361), on the Pacific Hwy, with sites for $15 and cabins for $30. *Pearl Perch Hotel* (☎ 6562 4586), in the town centre near the bridge, where the Armidale road splits from the Pacific Hwy, charges $20/25 a single/double. There is other pub accommodation and 10 motels.

Getting There & Away Kempsey is on the north coast train line and the major bus companies stop here on the Sydney to Brisbane run. See the following Crescent Head and South West Rocks sections for information on local bus services.

By car, there's an interesting and largely unsealed route running west to Wollomombi (on the Dorrigo to Armidale road); head north-west to Bellbrook.

Crescent Head
postcode 2440 • pop 1100
This small village, 20km south-east of Kempsey, has both a quiet front beach and a surf-washed back beach. There's quite a lot of new holiday development, but the village is far enough off the highway to remain relaxed. South of the town is the **Limeburners Creek Nature Reserve** (☎ 6583 5866), with walking trails and camp sites. North of town is Hat Head National Park.

Places to Stay Right on the beach, *Crescent Head Holiday Park* (☎ 6566 0261) has sites from $15 and cabins from $49. It will take weekly bookings only during holiday periods.

There are plenty of holiday apartments in town that are often better value than a cabin at the caravan park if you're staying a few nights. In the low season, they're generally available by the night, but during holiday periods you have to rent by the week. The cheapest (two-bedroom) apartment costs $165 a week ($60 a night) at off-peak times. See one of the two estate agents (☎ 6566 0500, 6566 0306) on the main street for further information.

Bush & Beach Retreat (☎ 6566 0235) is about 4km north of town on Loftus Rd (turn off the main road at the Mediterranean Motel), with bushland behind and the beach not far away. It's a modern building in 'colonial' style with B&B packages starting at $75 a double. *Killuke Lodge* (☎ 6566 0077) is 3km south of Crescent Head on the Point Plomer road and has accommodation in good cottages from $275 a double per week ($595 at peak times).

Getting There & Away If you're driving, the turn-off to Crescent Head is near the information centre in Kempsey. King's (☎ 6562 1228) has three buses each weekday from Kempsey and two on Saturday ($5.70). They leave from Belgrave St.

Hat Head National Park
This coastal park of 6500 hectares runs north from near Hat Head to Smoky Cape (south of Arakoon), protecting scrubland,

swamps and some excellent beaches backed by significant dune systems. Birdlife is prolific on the wetlands. Rising up from the generally flat landscape is Hungry Hill, near Hat Head, and sloping Hat Head itself, where there's a walking track.

Surrounded by the national park, the village of **Hat Head** is much smaller and quieter than Crescent Head. *Hat Head Holiday Park (☎ 6567 7501)* is close to a beautiful sheltered bay. Sites cost from $13 a double and en suite cabins from $50.

You can *camp* at Hungry Head, 5km south of Hat Head. There are pit toilets, no showers and you'll need to take your own water.

The park is accessible from the hamlet of Kinchela, on the road between Kempsey and South West Rocks. It's possible to get a lift on a school bus from Kempsey to Hat Head. Phone Hat Head Holiday Park for details.

South West Rocks
postcode 2431 • pop 3500

This small resort town lies on the coast near the mouth of the Macleay River and is popular with fishing and water-sports enthusiasts. The information centre (☎ 6566 7099) shares the old Boatman's Cottage at Horseshoe Bay with a small **maritime museum**. Both are open from 10 am to 4 pm daily. The information centre has details of a **historic walk** around town.

There's excellent diving at **Fish Rock Cave**, south of Smoky Cape. South West Rocks Dive Centre (☎ 6566 6474) and Fish Rock Dive Centre (☎ 6566 6614) organise dives in the area. The Macleay River enters the sea a few kilometres from South West Rocks at New Entrance. The boat shed here is the departure point for **river trips** on the *Macleay Discoverer* (☎ 6566 6863).

Horseshoe Bay Beach Park (☎ 6566 6370) is a lovely little place running along the slope behind pretty Horseshoe Bay, near the town centre. Sites cost from $16 and on-site vans from $37. Prices almost double in summer and vacancies are rare at Christmas and other major holidays.

The *Bay Motel (☎ 6566 6909),* close to the beach on Prince of Wales Ave, has

doubles for $50 ($90 at peak times). Raine & Horne Real Estate (☎ 6566 6116) at 1/11 Prince of Wales Ave has a choice of rental houses and apartments.

King's runs two buses a day (weekdays only) from Kempsey ($8.10).

Trial Bay & Arakoon State Recreation Area

About 3km east of South West Rocks is Trial Bay, named after the brig *The Trial,* which was stolen from Sydney by convicts in 1816 and wrecked here. The setting is dominated by **Trial Bay Gaol**, which overlooks the bay from the headland. This imposing edifice was a prison in the late 19th century and housed German internees during WWI. The jail is now a museum, open daily ($4/2).

The beaches on the ocean side of the peninsula are unsafe, but those on the bay side are safe and good.

On the shores of the bay behind the old jail is *Arakoon State Recreation Area (SRA;* ☎ *6566 6168),* a pleasant spot with tent sites from $10. You'll pay more for waterfront sites, and double during school holidays and summer. During the peak season you can hire catamarans and other boats on the beach here. Close to the camping area is *The Kiosk (☎ 6566 7100),* a licensed (to serve alcohol) restaurant with a lovely outdoor eating area. It's open daily for breakfast and lunch, and for dinner Thursday to Saturday.

NAMBUCCA HEADS
postcode 2448 • pop 6000

This quiet resort town has a fine setting overlooking the mouth of the Nambucca (pronounced nam-buk-ka) River.

The Nambucca Valley was owned by the Gumbainggir people when the European timber cutters arrived in the 1840s – the name means 'many bends'. There are still strong Aboriginal communities in Nambucca Heads and up the valley in Bowraville.

Orientation & Information

The town is 1km or so off the Pacific Hwy, and the road in, Riverside Dr, runs alongside the wide estuary of the Nambucca River, then climbs a steep hill to Bowra St, the main shopping street. A right turn onto Ridge St at the top of the hill leads through the old part of town to the beaches.

The Nambucca Valley Information Centre (☎ 6568 6954), on the Pacific Hwy just south of the Riverside Dr turn-off, is open from 9 am to 5 pm daily.

Things to See & Do

The town's **Headland Museum** is on Liston St, opposite the turn-off to Main Beach. As well as displays on local history, the museum has 'many other interesting exhibits difficult to place into categories'! The $1 admission charge is a small price to pay.

Among the places offering **boat hire** are Nambucca Boat Shed (☎ 6568 5550), on the waterfront at Gordon Park.

Main Beach, the patrolled surf beach, is about 1.5km east of the centre. Follow Ridge St and fork left onto Liston St when it splits. To get to Nambucca River mouth (where there is good surf for experienced surfers), turn off Bowra St at the Mobil station onto Wellington Dr, which winds down past scenic Gordon Park. There's a good walk along the **Vee Wall** breakwater at the river entrance, where hundreds of concrete blocks and rocks used in the construction of the wall have been painted graffiti-style by locals and visitors – feel free to create your own masterpiece.

Back in town, the **Mosaic Wall** is another work of art. Created by a local artist using materials such as tiles and broken crockery, this 60m fantasy sculpture outside the police station on Bowra St is well worth a visit.

Places to Stay

Camping There are several caravan parks. As usual, prices rise in holiday periods and you might have to stay by the week at peak times.

The *White Albatross (☎ 6568 6468)* is near the river mouth at the end of Wellington Dr. There's a lagoon for swimming as well as

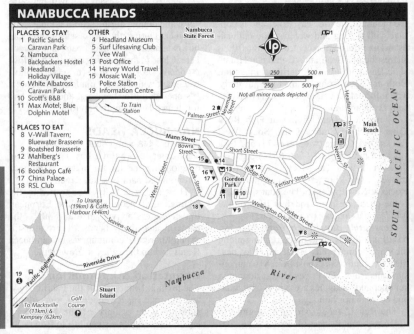

NAMBUCCA HEADS

PLACES TO STAY
1 Pacific Sands Caravan Park
2 Nambucca Backpackers Hostel
3 Headland Holiday Village
6 White Albatross Caravan Park
10 Scott's B&B
11 Max Motel; Blue Dolphin Motel

PLACES TO EAT
8 V-Wall Tavern; Bluewater Brasserie
9 Boatshed Brasserie
12 Mahlberg's Restaurant
16 Bookshop Café
17 China Palace
18 RSL Club

OTHER
4 Headland Museum
5 Surf Lifesaving Club
7 Vee Wall
13 Post Office
14 Harvey World Travel
15 Mosaic Wall; Police Station
19 Information Centre

the surf beach. Sites cost from $16 (there's a campers kitchen), on-site vans start at $25 and en suite cabins at $52. Near the main surf beach are the similarly priced *Headland Holiday Village* (☎ 6568 6547) and the lovely, leafy *Pacific Sands* (☎ 6568 6120).

There are other caravan parks farther out. Near the small town of Valla Beach, off the highway 8km north of Nambucca Heads, the *Valla Beach Resort* (☎ 6569 5106) is on a lagoon not far from the surf. It has its own bar and restaurant. Sites cost from $12, cabins from $37.

Hostels The *Nambucca Backpackers Hostel* (☎ 6568 6360) is a quiet place tucked away behind the town at Newman St. It's a 1km walk through bush to the beach. Dorm beds cost $15, doubles $34, with discounts for longer stays. The managers can meet the buses/trains and also lend snorkel gear and boogie boards.

B&Bs Formerly an old hotel, *Scott's B&B* (☎ 6568 6386, 4 Wellington Dr) has been well renovated by its lovely Irish owners into a comfortable weatherboard guesthouse. Off-peak rates are $60/70 a single/double, plus $10 for a room with a view.

Motels Sharing a good view are a couple of cheap (outside holiday times) motels: *Max Motel* (☎ 6568 6138) and *Blue Dolphin Motel* (☎ 6568 700), next door. Both places are on Fraser St, the southern continuation of Bowra St, and both charge around $45 a double.

Places to Eat
The *RSL Club* has a prime site by the river at the foot of Bowra St and turns out some of the cheapest meals in town. *China Palace* (☎ 6568 6956, 19 Bowra St) is a spacious and bright place with some interesting Singaporean and Malaysian dishes alongside Chinese standards. Mains ($8 to $12) are good value. Close by, opposite the police station, the *Bookshop Cafe* has a nice atmosphere, and yummy focaccia and coffee.

Mahlberg's Restaurant (☎ 6568 5533), a little way east along Ridge St, is a lovely

BYO restaurant open for dinner from Wednesday to Sunday. Mains on the Mediterranean-influenced menu cost around $18.

There are some other good places down by the river along Wellington Dr. The *Boatshed Brasserie* (☎ 6568 9292) turns out a three-course meal for $23.50 and has seating right by the river. It also does takeaways. Farther on, the *V-Wall Tavern* is worth a visit just for the great views of the river mouth. You can choose between pub meals at the snack bar and a multicultural menu at the *Bluewater Brasserie* (☎ 6568 6394), where mains cost from $13 to $19.

Getting There & Away
Most long-distance buses stop on the highway at the bus shelters just south of the Aukaka Caravan Park, on the Pacific Hwy north of the information centre. Harvey World Travel (☎ 6568 6455), on Bowra St opposite the police station, handles bookings. Fares to Sydney start at $45; to Byron Bay it's $40.

Newman's (☎ 6568 1296) has four buses a day to Coffs Harbour ($7). Joyce's (☎ 6655 6330) buses run from Nambucca to Bellingen ($10). These local services leave from outside the police station on Bowra St and run only on weekdays.

The train station is about 3km out of town: follow Bowra St then Mann St. The fare to Sydney is $75. The hostel picks up guests (for a fee); otherwise there's no transport between the station and town.

AROUND NAMBUCCA HEADS
The main roads running up the Nambucca Valley turn off from the old town of **Macksville**, on the highway about 12km south of Nambucca Heads. Taylors Arm, about 25km west of Macksville, is the home of the **Pub with No Beer**, immortalised in a song by Slim Dusty, one of the first Australian songs to sell well overseas – it stayed at the top of the Irish charts for more than two months! There's plenty of beer there now and often acoustic music at weekends. Near Taylors Arm, Bakers Creek Station (☎ 6564 2165) offers horse riding through the mountains for $60 per half-day, including lunch.

South of Macksville, off the road to the seaside village of **Scotts Head** (good surf), an unsealed road leads up through the Way Way State Forest to **Yarrahapinni Lookout**, which has great views down to the coast and back into the hinterland.

Bowraville
postcode 2449

This small town is very different from its booming coastal neighbours. It's a close-knit community of old families, the descendants of the cedar cutters who arrived in 1842, and the Aborigines who are somewhat longer-established residents.

Along the main street you'll find several interesting craft shops and the excellent **Bowraville Folk Museum** (☎ 6564 8200), open from 10 am to 3 pm on Tuesday, weekends and school holidays, and 10 am to 12.30 pm on Wednesday and Friday ($1/0.50 for adults/children). Even if you aren't interested in the museum, have a look at the wonderful Max Hill Memorial Gates at the entrance.

On Saturday morning the popular **Bowraville Country Market** is held in a building on the main street. The market has its own tearooms, a great place to meet locals.

The annual **Back to Bowra Festival** is held over the October long weekend. Among the many events is billy-cart racing.

Places to Stay The *Bowra Hotel* (☎ 6564 7041), on High St, is a nice old pub with accommodation for $15 per person, including breakfast. The rooms open up onto a wide veranda with views over town to the surrounding hills.

Getting There & Away Newman's has a daily bus service (school days only) leaving from Nambucca Heads at 3 pm ($3.60). By car you can get here from Macksville and interesting back roads lead north to Bellingen and Dorrigo and south to Taylors Arm.

Urunga
postcode 2455 • pop 2600

The small coastal town of Urunga, 20km north of Nambucca Heads, lies at the mouth of the Bellinger and Kalang Rivers, which meet just a few hundred metres from the sea. The estuary is a popular fishing spot and there is a surf beach close by at **Hungry Head**.

On the highway close to the town centre turn-off is the Bellingen Shire Tourist Information Centre (☎ 6655 5711), open from 9 am to 5 pm Monday to Saturday and 10 am to 2 pm on Sunday. There is a bus waiting area out the front.

There are several caravan parks in the area, including *Urunga Heads Holiday Park* (☎ 6655 6355), well situated on Morgo St next to Urunga Lagoon, with tent sites from $13 and on-site vans from $30. *Ocean View Hotel* (☎ 6655 6221) is a fine old pub overlooking the estuary with pub singles/doubles for $25/40, including breakfast.

Mylestom
postcode 2454

About 5km north of Urunga and just south of the big Raleigh Bridge over the Bellinger River is the turn-off for the **Raleigh Winery** (☎ 6655 4388), open for tastings and sales from 10 am to 5 pm daily. North of this bridge you come to the turn-off for Mylestom, which is about 5km east of the highway.

This quiet hamlet is in a great location on the north bank of the Bellinger River estuary and also has good ocean beaches.

Places to Stay & Eat Close to the beach, *North Beach Caravan Park* (☎ 6655 4250) has sites from $10 and on-site vans from $25.

Riverside Lodge (☎ 6655 4245) is a peaceful and homely backpacker hostel on the main street (River St) across from the river. Dorm beds cost $15 and there are discounts for longer stays. The owners can help organise activities such as white-water rafting and horse riding, and there are bikes to explore the area.

Also on River St, *Rivers* (☎ 6655 4416) is a BYO restaurant with a lovely outlook and plenty of seafood on the menu; mains cost $17 to $22. It's open for lunch Thursday to Sunday and for dinner Thursday to Saturday.

BELLINGEN

postcode 2454 • pop 2600

This lush small town sits on the banks of the lovely Bellinger River, inland from the Pacific Hwy just north of Urunga. It's a laid-back place with a great vibe and is a centre for the sizable artistic/alternative population living in the surrounding valleys.

The valley was part of the extensive territory of the Gumbainggir people until European timber cutters arrived in the 1840s. The first settlement here was at Fernmount, about 5km east of Bellingen, but later the administrative centre of the region was moved to Bellingen. River craft were able to come up here until the 1940s, when dredging was discontinued. Until tourism boomed at Coffs Harbour in the 1960s, Bellingen was the most important town in this area.

Orientation

The main road from the Pacific Hwy to Dorrigo and beyond becomes Hyde St through town. Next to the post office, Bridge St leads across the river to North Bellingen and Gleniffer.

Things to See

The small **museum** behind the old wooden library on Hyde St is open from 10 am to 4 pm Tuesday and Thursday, until noon on Wednesday, and from 10 am to noon and 2 to 4 pm on Friday ($2). Talking to the volunteers who staff the museum can be as informative as looking at the exhibits.

The magnificent **Hammond & Wheatley Emporium** on Hyde St is worth a look. Formerly an old department store, it's been very well restored and now houses a shop, art gallery and cafe.

There are plenty of other craft shops in town, and a short way out on the road east to the highway is the **Old Butter Factory**, which houses several craft workshops and galleries.

A huge colony of **flying foxes** lives in a small patch of remnant rainforest on Bellingen Island, near the caravan park, during the breeding season from December to March. There are also **platypus** living in the river nearby.

The community **market**, held on the third Saturday of the month, is a major event, with more than 250 stalls. People from all over the valley show up and there's live music.

Organised Tours

Gambaarri Tours (☎ 6655 4195) can explain how the Gumbainggir people lived in the valley and has tours to the Gleniffer area.

Special Events

You'll find a multicultural mix of music and performances at the annual Global Carnival in early October and a strong line-up of jazz names at the Jazz Festival in late August. Accommodation is scarce at these times, so make sure you book ahead.

Places to Stay

Right next to Bellingen Island (and the bats) on Dowle St, *Bellingen Caravan Park* (☎ 6655 1338) has tent sites for $10 and self-contained vans for $40.

Bellingen YHA Backpackers (☎ 6655 1116) is a great place to hang out. It occupies a beautifully renovated weatherboard house on Short St, behind the Federal Hotel. It has big open balconies overlooking the river. Dorm beds cost from $16, doubles $36, and you can also camp. The owners will pick you up from Urunga by arrangement.

There is good pub accommodation at the *Federal Hotel* (☎ 6655 1003) on Hyde St for $20/35 a single/double. *Bellingen Valley Motor Inn* (☎ 6655 1599) is just west of town on the road to Dorrigo and has doubles for $75.

Definitely one of the best places to stay in this region is *Koompartoo Retreat* (☎ 6655 2326), self-contained accommodation on the corner of Rawson and Dudley Sts on the southern edge of Bellingen. It has stylish, cosy timber chalets with private balconies set in two hectares of gorgeous bushland with all the sounds of nature close by. Excellent-value singles/doubles cost $80/95. Plan to stay for a while, because you won't want to leave.

Rivendell (☎ 6655 0060, 10 Hyde St) is a very pleasant B&B close to the centre of town. It charges $85/95.

NORTH COAST

For a bit of a splurge, stay at *Casabelle Country Guest House* (☎ 6655 0155, 0500 550 155), about 1km out of town on the road to Gleniffer. This splendid retreat, with Tuscan/Mediterranean influences, was built by its owners with love, and it shows. Rooms cost $110/150.

Places to Eat

Bellingen has a good choice of excellent eating places. The atmospheric *Carriageway Cafe*, in the Hammond & Wheatley Emporium, is a good place to head for coffee and cake. A personal favourite is the *Lodge 241 Gallery Cafe* in the superb old Masonic Lodge. It's a terrific light and airy place with high ceilings and great food. Try the vegetarian's breakfast ($7.50) or pop in for lunch.

The bistro at the *Federal Hotel* is open daily and has good pub meals, with nothing over $10.

There are several places on Church St including the *Good Food Shop*, which has vegetarian takeaways and organic produce, and the *Cool Creek Cafe* (☎ 6655 1886), a good-vibe BYO place where the staff really care about food.

Shanti Cafe (☎ 6655 9950), on Wheatley St in North Bellingen near the roundabout, is a great little vegetarian restaurant with most mains, such as curries and Indonesian stir-fries, costing around $10. It's open for dinner from Wednesday to Sunday. For a divine pizza experience, try *Bare Nature Cafe* (☎ 6655 1551, 111 Hyde St).

Getting There & Away

The bus stop is on the corner of Church and Hyde Sts, diagonally opposite the courthouse. Kean's stops at Bellingen on its Port Macquarie–Tamworth run, and also offers short trips, including to Coffs Harbour and Dorrigo (both $10). Jessup's (☎ 6653 4552) also operates between Coffs Harbour and Bellingen, with buses leaving Bellingen at 8 and 9.30 am and Coffs Harbour at 8.50 am, and 2 and 3.45 pm (weekdays only). Joyce's (☎ 6655 6330) has three runs each weekday between Bellingen and Nambucca Heads.

Bellingen is about 12km west of the Pacific Hwy; turn off just south of the Raleigh Bridge. From Bellingen the road climbs steeply to Dorrigo – a spectacular drive. From Dorrigo you can continue west to the Armidale to Grafton road. A network of unsealed roads leads south to Bowraville and some tiny mountain settlements.

AROUND BELLINGEN

If you have transport, there are some beautiful spots waiting to be discovered in the surrounding valleys. The most accessible is the tiny hamlet of **Gleniffer**, 10km to the north and clearly signposted from North Bellingen. There's a good swimming hole in the **Never Never River** behind the small Gleniffer School of Arts at the crossroads.

If you want to sweat, tackle the **Syndicate Walking Trail**, a strenuous 15km walk from Gleniffer to the Dorrigo Plateau, following the route of a tramline once used by timber cutters. There's a very steep 1km climb on the way up. To get to the start, take the Gordonville Rd, turning into Adams Lane soon after crossing the Never Never River. The walking track commences at the first gate.

There are a couple of good places to stay around Gleniffer. *Crystal Creek Farm Hideaway* (☎ 6655 1090), off the Promised Land road, has a self-contained cottage for $90 per day, while *Blue Gum* (☎ 6655 1592) is a stylish B&B with singles/doubles for $55/80. It's closer to town on the Bellingen road.

The **Kalang Valley**, south-west of town, and the **Thora Valley**, about 10km west of town, are also worth exploring. People who pursue alternative lifestyles represent the majority around here. Bellingen Canoe Hire (☎ 6655 8510) at Thora hires out canoes and equipment for $35 a half-day. There's a good chance of seeing platypus if you're out on any of the local rivers around dawn or dusk.

DORRIGO
postcode 2453 • pop 1192

This mountain town, close to the edge of the Great Dividing Range's eastern escarpment, was one of the last places to be settled by Europeans in the eastwards push across the New England tableland. It had the usual cedar-cutting pioneers and was on a railway line to Glenreagh to the north.

Today Dorrigo is a quiet country town with wide streets and a few architectural reminders of its history. It remains an important stop on the road between Armidale and the coast. As the largest town on the Dorrigo Plateau, it makes a good base for visiting the area's outstanding national parks.

There is an information centre (☎ 6657 2486) at 36 Hickory St, open from 10 am to 4 pm daily. The proposed **Steam Railway Museum** appears no closer to opening than it was 10 years ago. There is a long line of steam engines queued up at the old train station, just out of town on the road to North Dorrigo. A few kilometres north of town on the road to Leigh are the picturesque **Dangar's Falls**.

Places to Stay

The *Commercial Hotel/Motel (☎ 6657 2003)* is a good budget option with motel singles/doubles for $32/38. The nearby *Dorrigo Hotel/Motel (☎ 6657 2017)* charges $45 in the motel and $35 for a pub room.

Dorrigo Mountain Resort (☎ 6657 2564), just out of town on the Bellingen road, has sites from $12.50 and self-contained cabins from $46 (linen supplied). A little farther on, *Lookout Motor Inn (☎ 6657 2511)* is set in large grounds with lovely views. It charges from $60/70.

Gracemere Grange (☎ 6657 2630), signposted from the road past Dorrigo National Park, is a homely little cottage with a great front porch from which to ponder luscious pastures. Rooms cost $40/70, and there's also a backpacker B&B deal for $20. Pick-ups from Dorrigo are possible by arrangement.

Places to Eat

People come from far and wide to eat at *Misty's (☎ 6657 2855, 33 Hickory St)*. It's a charming little restaurant in a renovated weatherboard house and the food is great value. Mains, from a small but innovative blackboard menu, cost $14 to $19. It's open for dinner Thursday to Sunday and for lunch on Sunday.

The *Dorrigo Hotel/Motel* has $5 lunches every day and a good evening menu with a decent vegetarian selection such as eggplant

and risotto balls ($7). Not to be outdone, the *Commercial Hotel/Motel* offers daily lunches for $4.90!

Getting There & Away

Kean's uses Dorrigo as a meal stop on its Port Macquarie–Tamworth run. It also offers short trips such as Bellingen to Dorrigo ($10).

Coffs Harbour is about 60km away via Bellingen, or there's an interesting, partly unsealed route via Leigh and Coramba. You can continue west to Armidale via Ebor.

DORRIGO NATIONAL PARK

This is the most accessible of Australia's World Heritage rainforests and well worth a visit. The **Rainforest Centre** (☎ 6657 2309), at the park entrance, has information about the park's many walks and is open from 9 am to 5 pm daily. There's also an elevated walkway (Skywalk) over the rainforest canopy. You can see right down to the ocean on a fine day. A walking track leads to the Glade rest area, from where there's a 5.5km walk through the forest. It's well worth making the drive down to the Never Never rest area in the heart of the national park, from where you can walk to waterfalls or begin longer walks. Bush camping is permitted in some areas – call the Rainforest Centre for more details. The turn-off to the park is just south of Dorrigo.

COFFS HARBOUR

postcode 2450 • pop 60,000

Coffs Harbour is the biggest town between Newcastle and the Gold Coast, and an important regional centre. There's a string of fine beaches north of town and it's a good base for exploring the many attractions of the hinterland, but the town is poorly planned and disjointed, making it difficult to get around without a car. Still, this hasn't stopped it being a popular holiday destination.

History

Originally called Korff's Harbour, the town was settled in the 1860s. The jetty was built in 1892 to load cedar and other logs – it fell into disrepair some years ago but now is restored to its former glory. Bananas were first grown in the area in the 1880s but no-one made much money from them until the railway came to town in 1918.

Banana growing is still big business, but these days tourism is the mainstay of the local economy.

Orientation

The Pacific Hwy is called Grafton St and then Woolgoolga Rd on its run north through town. The city centre is around the junction of Grafton and High Sts. High St east of Grafton St has been transformed into a mall.

You have to take the highway to get to the beaches and resorts north of Coffs Harbour. About 5km south is Sawtell, a sprawl of housing developments that merge into Coffs Harbour, but with great surf beaches.

Information

The Visitor Information Centre (☎ 6652 1522) is north of the town centre on the corner of Rose Ave and Marcia St.

The main post office is on the ground floor of the Palms Centre shopping complex in the mall. There's another post office at the jetty, opposite the Pier Hotel.

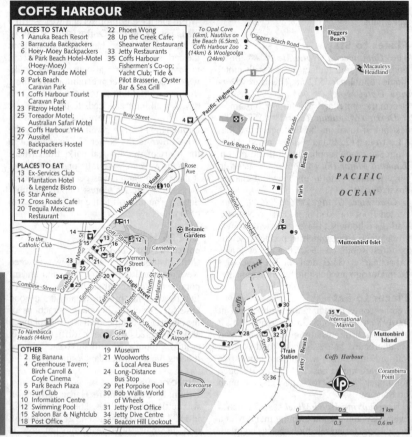

COFFS HARBOUR

PLACES TO STAY
1 Aanuka Beach Resort
3 Barracuda Backpackers
6 Hoey-Moey Backpackers & Park Beach Hotel-Motel (Hoey-Moey)
7 Ocean Parade Motel
8 Park Beach Caravan Park
11 Coffs Harbour Tourist Caravan Park
23 Fitzroy Hotel
25 Toreador Motel; Australian Safari Motel
26 Coffs Harbour YHA
27 Aussitel Backpackers Hostel
32 Pier Hotel

PLACES TO EAT
13 Ex-Services Club
14 Plantation Hotel & Legendz Bistro
16 Star Anise
17 Cross Roads Cafe
20 Tequila Mexican Restaurant

22 Phoen Wong
28 Up the Creek Cafe; Shearwater Restaurant
33 Jetty Restaurants
35 Coffs Harbour Fishermen's Co-op; Yacht Club; Tide & Pilot Brasserie, Oyster Bar & Sea Grill

OTHER
2 Big Banana
4 Greenhouse Tavern; Birch Carroll & Coyle Cinema
5 Park Beach Plaza
9 Surf Club
10 Information Centre
12 Swimming Pool
15 Saloon Bar & Nightclub
18 Post Office
19 Museum
21 Woolworths & Local Area Buses
24 Long-Distance Bus Stop
29 Pet Porpoise Pool
30 Bob Wallis World of Wheels
31 Jetty Post Office
34 Jetty Dive Centre
36 Beacon Hill Lookout

To Opal Cove (6km), Nautilus on the Beach (6.5km), Coffs Harbour Zoo (14km) & Woolgoolga (24km)

Diggers Beach Road
Diggers Beach
Macauleys Headland

Bray Street
Pacific Highway
Park Beach Road
Ocean Parade
Park Beach

Rose Ave
Marcia Street
Woolgoolga Road

SOUTH PACIFIC OCEAN

Botanic Gardens
Cemetery
Coff Street
Mooree St
Vernon Street
Grafton Street
Gordon Street
East Street
Combine Street
Curacoa Street
High Street
North St
Hardacre St
Albany Street
Hogbin Dve
Orlando Street
Park Street
Edinburgh Street

Muttonbird Islet

To the Catholic Club
To Nambucca Heads (44km)
Golf Course
To Airport

Coffs Creek
International Marina
Muttonbird Island

Train Station
Racecourse
Coffs Harbour
Corambirra Point

0   0.5   1 km
0   0.3   0.6 mi

NORTH COAST

The Harbour

The International Marina, protected by the northern breakwall, is home to a sizable commercial fishing fleet. There are good views from Beacon Hill Lookout above the harbour at the top of Edinburgh St and from Corambirra Point on the south side of the harbour.

Muttonbird Island

The harbour's northern breakwall continues out to Muttonbird Island, a nature reserve named after the 12,000-odd pairs of muttonbirds (wedge-tailed shearwaters) that call it home from late August until April. The island is dotted with their nesting burrows and the chicks emerge during December and January.

Beaches

The main town beach is Park Beach, which is patrolled from October to April and during school holidays – be careful though, as there are some rips here. Jetty Beach is not a bad spot for a dip, and it's safer than Park Beach. If you've got wheels, you'd be better off heading to beaches north of town. Diggers Beach, reached by turning off the highway near the Big Banana, has a nude section. Other good spots are Moonee Beach, about 14km north of town, and Emerald Beach, 6km farther on.

North Coast Botanic Gardens

The botanic gardens, at the end of Hardacre St, are well worth a visit. It's hard to believe that part of the site was once the town tip. The immaculately maintained gardens contain many endangered species, and areas have been planted to re-create the region's different forest types. There's also a boardwalk over the mangrove swamp bordering Coffs Creek, information on plants used by Aborigines and a 'sensory garden'. The gardens are open from 9 am to 5 pm daily. Admission is by donation.

Coffs Creek

The gardens can be visited as part of the excellent Coffs Creek Walk, an easy 3.5km stroll along the creek bank that starts opposite the council chambers on Coff St and finishes near the Pet Porpoise Pool.

Coffs Harbour Historical Museum

The museum, 191 High St, has exhibits including the old 'optic' from the South Solitary Island lighthouse and displays on the Aboriginal and European history of the area. It's open from 1.30 to 4 pm Tuesday to Thursday and Sunday ($2/0.50 for adults/children).

Big Banana

This award-winning piece of kitsch was once voted Australia's silliest attraction by a travellers' poll. It stands by the highway on the northern edge of town. Guided Plantation Tours (☎ 6652 4355) has a mini-railway that runs through the plantations and theme park. Entry to the Big Banana complex is free, but it costs $10/6 to take the tour. There's also a toboggan ride worth checking out ($4 for one ride, less for more) and an ice-skating rink.

Animal Acts

The Pet Porpoise Pool (☎ 6652 2164), next to Coffs Creek on Orlando St, has shows at 10.30 am and 2.15 pm daily for $12.50/5.50. Coffs Harbour Zoo (☎ 6656 1330) is on the highway at Moonee, 14km north of Coffs. The emphasis is on native animals and the koalas are 'presented' at 11 am and 3 pm daily ($12/6).

Activities

There's a huge range of things to do. The Marina Booking Centre (☎ 6651 4612), at the harbour, has information about what's available. You'll find the best deals at the hostels.

White-Water Rafting The Nymboida River inland from Coffs Harbour offers some of the best white-water rafting in Australia. There are a couple of long-established outfits that get consistently good feedback. WOW Rafting (☎ 6651 4066) has day trips for $139 and overnight trips for $295, fully catered. Wildwater Adventures (☎ 6653 3500) offers similar deals, plus four-day trips for $480.

NORTH COAST

Surfing The Coffs Harbour surf club is at **Park Beach**. The best surfing is around Macauley's Headland, between Park Beach and **Diggers Beach**, reached by turning off the highway opposite the Big Banana. For those who haven't ridden a board before, East Coast Surf School (☎ 6651 5515) charges $25 per lesson.

Boating There's a growing band of boats offering an assortment of trips. You can go deep-sea fishing on the *Adriatic III* (☎ 6658 4379) for $60 per person (six hours) or the *Cougar Cat 12* (☎ 6651 6715).

Whale Watching Humpback whales are often sighted off Coffs Harbour during their northbound migration in June and July and during their southern migration from September to November. When there are whales around, you'll find plenty of boats to take you out for around $35, such as the *Pacific Explorer* (☎ 0418 663 815).

Diving There's interesting diving around the Solitary Islands, a few kilometres up the coast. The Diver's Depot (☎ 6652 2033) does an introductory dive for $125, including equipment, and a four-day accreditation course for $285. Jetty Dive Centre (☎ 6651 1611) at 396 High St is a long-established business that also rents out snorkelling gear ($15 a day).

Horse Riding There are a number of places offering horse riding. Wyndyarra Estate (☎ 6653 8488) has received glowing reports from our readers. Two-hour horse rides cost $30 and leave at 8.30 am and 3.30 pm daily. Popular rides include 'Swim on the Horses' or 'Misty Rainforest Ride'.

Organised Tours

Half a dozen companies run 4WD tours around the region's forests, such as 4WD Adventure Safaris (☎ 6655 9477). The hostels normally have special deals.

Gambaarri Tours (☎ 6655 4195) has excellent, informative half-day trips to a number of Aboriginal sites on the coast between Red Rock and Valla ($50).

Special Events

The Gold Cup, Coffs Harbour's premier horse race, is run on a Thursday in early August. It's a big day out, capping off a big week of entertainment. The harbour is the finishing point of the Pittwater (Sydney) to Coffs Harbour yacht race that sets sail on 28 December.

Places to Stay

Except in the hostels and hotels, expect prices to rise by about 50% in school holidays and by as much as 100% at Christmas/New Year.

Camping The huge *Park Beach Caravan Park* (☎ 6648 4888), on Ocean Parade, is right next to the beach and has tent sites from $13 a double, on-site vans from $28 and en suite cabins from $40. *Coffs Harbour Tourist Caravan Park* (☎ 6652 1694), on the highway a couple of blocks north of the town centre, is slightly cheaper. There are plenty of other places along the highway north and south of town.

Hostels There are four good places to choose from. The *Coffs Harbour YHA* (☎ 6652 6462, 110 Albany St), not far from the city centre, is a friendly place with dorm beds for $15 and doubles for $38. Use of bikes and surfboards is free, and the hostel bus does beach runs.

Aussitel Backpackers Hostel (☎ 6651 1871, 312 High St) is close to the jetty restaurants and harbour. It's well run and has dorm beds for $15, doubles for $38 (plus $2 for nonmembers) and family rooms for $48.

Behind the dunes at Park Beach is *Hoey-Moey Backpackers* (☎ 6651 7966). It has dorm beds for $15 and doubles for $36.

Barracuda Backpackers (☎ 6651 3514, 19 Arthur St) is a long way from anywhere out near the Park Beach Plaza, but this hasn't stopped the rave reviews from our readers. It has a pool, spa and good facilities; dorm beds cost $18, doubles $40.

B&Bs About 7km south of town, *Illoura* (☎ 6653 1690 after 4 pm), on South Boambee Rd (get full directions when you book), has great views, wildlife and one guest suite for $85/110 a single/double. No children under 16 are permitted.

Hotels Many of the town's hotels have accommodation. In the low season you're better off hunting around for a motel with deals, but pub prices tend to stay the same year-round, so they can be great value in summer.

Officially on Moonee St (although it appears to be on Grafton St), *Fitzroy Hotel* (☎ 6652 3007) is an old-style neighbourhood pub with singles/doubles for $20/35. Down near the harbour on High St, the *Pier Hotel* (☎ 6652 2110) has a few large, clean rooms for $20 per person.

Motels & Resorts There's a string of motels on Grafton St, on the southern approaches to town, such as *Toreador* (☎ 6652 3887) and the quaint *Australian Safari Motel* (☎ 6652 1900). Outside school holidays, prices are around $45 a double.

There's another bunch of motels in a better area around Park Beach that have similar rates, such as *Ocean Parade Motel* (☎ 6652 6733), although expect to pay around $75 at peak times.

Most of the resorts are off the highway past Korora, about 5km north of Coffs Harbour. Novotel's *Opal Cove* (☎ 6651 0510), 6km north of town, is a huge, quite sterile development that includes a residential suburb and a par-three golf course. Rooms cost $160 to $300 per night. Just north of here is the long-running *Nautilus on the Beach* (☎ 6653 6699), with two-bedroom self-contained villas from $270 a day and motel units from $125 (up to $210).

Aanuka Beach Resort (☎ 6652 7555) is more discreet than some of the others, tucked away at Diggers Beach. It has holiday villas from $190 (two bedroom, low season) to $400 (three bedroom, high season) a day.

Rental Accommodation There is a huge range of holiday apartments and houses. The cheapest of the two-bedroom apartments goes for around $70 a night in the low season (less by the week), and $140 a night in the high season. There are many that are vastly more expensive and a lot of places are available only by the week in the high season. The visitor information centre has a free booking service (☎ 1300 369 070) and there are plenty of real estate agents, such as Park Beach Realty (☎ 6652 5374), with listings.

Places to Eat
Some of the best cheap eats can be found in the clubs, such as the giant *Ex-Services Club*, on the corner of Grafton and Vernon Sts, and the *Catholic Club*, on High St, about 1km inland from Grafton St.

City Centre The mall is full of cafes and takeaway joints that cater for the town's office population at lunchtime. Drop into the *Lucky Kids Cafe* for all your kebab, Mexican, carvery, and fish and chip needs. All the pubs in this area have counter meals. The best deals are at the Plantation Hotel on Grafton St, where *Legendz Bistro* has mains from $4.50 and an excellent cut of rump steak for $7.50.

Cross Roads Cafe, on Vernon St, is a fun place filled with '50s memorabilia. It serves American-style hot dogs and burgers. On Park Ave across from Woolworths, *Phoen Wong* (☎ 6652 3246) has Chinese smorgasbords for $13.50 on Friday and Saturday nights. Its usual menu includes quite a few vegetarian dishes for under $7. The popular and cosy *Tequila Mexican Restaurant*, just east of the mall on High St, has most mains costing from $13 to $16.

Star Anise (☎ 6651 1033, 93 Grafton St) has received excellent reviews. The small but innovative menu changes every two weeks, with mains around the $20 mark. It's open for lunch Thursday and Friday and dinner from Wednesday to Sunday.

Jetty For choice, you can't beat the cluster of restaurants at the jetty end of High St.

Foreshores Cafe (☎ 6652 3127) is the place to head for a good-value breakfast in a friendly environment. It's open from 7.30 am daily and has bacon and eggs for $5. The excellent *Tahruah Thai Kitchen* (☎ 6651 5992), near the Pier Hotel, has a selection of filling stir-fries for around $10 in a lively, friendly environment.

There are a couple of great places in the Coffs Promenade building opposite Aussitel Backpackers. *Up The Creek Cafe (☎ 6652 5517)* is a friendly, colourful place with indoor and outdoor seating overlooking Coffs Creek. Next door, the *Shearwater Restaurant (☎ 6651 6053)* opens for breakfast and lunch daily, and for dinner from Wednesday to Saturday. Dinner mains cost $16 to $18.

Harbour The harbour is the place to go for seafood. *Coffs Harbour Fishermen's Co-op* has a good takeaway section and a sushi/sashimi bar as well as uncooked seafood. The nearby *Yacht Club* has $5.50 lunches daily and *Tide & Pilot Brasserie, Oyster Bar & Sea Grill (☎ 6651 6888)* offers fantastic views up the coast; mains cost $16 to $23.

Entertainment

There's something happening every night, although the pickings are fairly slim early in the week. Thursday's edition of the *Coffs Harbour Advocate* has the week's listings.

The *Plantation Hotel (☎ 6652 3855)*, on Grafton St, is a popular venue, with live bands from Wednesday to Saturday night. Big-name touring bands play at the *Sawtell RSL Club (☎ 6653 1577)*, 5km south of town, or at the *Ex-Services Club (☎ 6652 3888)*, on Vernon St. Lesser lights play at the *Greenhouse Tavern (☎ 6651 5488)*, just off the highway at the junction with Bray St.

There used to be a few nightclubs in town, however all but one have been closed down due to rowdiness. The survivor is the *Saloon Bar & Nightclub* (although the sign out the front says Coffs Pool Bar & Nightclub), on Grafton St near the city centre. It's open Wednesday through Saturday.

There are two *Birch Carroll & Coyle cinemas (☎ 6651 6444)* in Coffs Harbour and the independent *First Avenue Cinema (☎ 6653 3119)* in Sawtell, which shows mainstream and alternative movies.

Getting There & Away

Eastern Australia Airlines (☎ 13 1313) offers five flights a day to Sydney ($199),

while Impulse Airlines (☎ 13 1381) flies to Brisbane ($218) via Coolangatta.

All long-distance bus services on the Sydney-Brisbane run stop opposite the Toreador Motel on Elizabeth St, which is a small service road running parallel to Grafton St. Fares from Coffs Harbour include: Byron Bay ($40), Brisbane ($42), Nambucca Heads ($15) and Port Macquarie ($27).

Ryan's (☎ 6652 3201) buses run several times daily (except Sunday) to Woolgoolga ($14) via beachside towns off the highway. It also has two services a day between Coffs Harbour and Grafton. These services leave from the stop at the car park next to Woolworths on Park Ave.

The train station (☎ 6652 2312) is near the harbour at the end of High St. The fare to Sydney is $75.

If you're driving north, the back road to Grafton via Coramba and Glenreagh passes through some pretty country and is a pleasant alternative to the Pacific Hwy.

Coffs Harbour is reportedly a good place to pick up a ride along the coast on a yacht or cruiser. Ask around or put a notice in the yacht club at the harbour. Sometimes the hostels know of boat owners who are looking for crew.

Getting Around

As well as the major car-rental companies there are some local outfits offering cheaper rates – just make sure you read the fine print. Coffs Harbour Rent-A-Car (☎ 6652 5022) has cars from $39 a day.

Coffs District Taxi Network (☎ 13 1008, 6658 5922) operates a 24-hour service. There's a taxi rank on the corner of High and Gordon Sts. Bob Wallis World of Wheels (☎ 6652 5102), near the harbour on the corner of Collingwood and Orlando Sts, rents out bikes.

COFFS HARBOUR TO GRAFTON
Glenreagh
postcode 2450 • pop 300
On the inland route that follows the train line between Coffs Harbour and Grafton, Glenreagh is a small village on the Orara River. Glenreagh had a gold rush in the

1880s and it was a railway junction town until the Dorrigo line closed in the 1970s.

Take the left turn from the Coffs Harbour to Glenreagh road just past Coramba, then turn right on Bushmans Range Rd and you'll come to **George's Goldmine** (☎ 6654 5355), which is actually the old Bayfield Mine. Tours of the mine ($9/4.50 for adults/children) are held through the day, starting at 10.30 am, with the last tour at 3 pm. It's open from Wednesday to Sunday.

Woolgoolga
postcode 2456 • pop 4000
The small resort town of Woolgoolga is notable for its fine surf beach. It has a sizable Sikh community whose *gurdwara* (place of worship) is the impressive **Guru Nanak Temple**, overlooking the highway on the southern side of town. The temple is not to be confused with the shabby **Raj Mahal**, another Indian-style temple farther north near the roundabout that has two elephant statues out the front.

The *Woolgoolga Beach Caravan Park* (☎ 6654 1373) is on the beach and has tent sites from $15 and small cabins from $35. There are quite a few motels along the highway, including *Woolgoolga Motor Inn* (☎ 6654 1534), many of them advertising doubles from $42.

For Indian food try the *Maharaja Tandoori Indian Restaurant* (☎ 6654 1122), across from the temple. Near the beach opposite the caravan park you'll find the popular *Bluebottles Brasserie* (☎ 6654 1962).

The long-distance buses pass through Woolgoolga. There are local services to Coffs Harbour, Grafton and nearby beaches.

Arrawarra
This quiet seaside village 1km off the highway has yet another great beach, some bushland that is noisy with birds, the inlet of a small creek and a very pleasant caravan park close to the water, *Arrawarra Beach Holiday Park* (☎ 6649 2753). Sites cost from $10, cabins from $42. A short way south is **Mullaway**, and **Corindi** is a few kilometres north; you have to return to the highway to get to either.

Red Rock
Six kilometres off the highway by the ocean, Red Rock is a sleepy village, a little larger than Arrawarra. It's both relaxed and neat, with well-mown lawns and tidy holiday houses. The small Redbank River enters the sea here and there's a beautiful inlet just across from *Red Rock Caravan Park* (☎ 6649 2730), where sites cost from $12 and cottages cost $45 to $85.

Yuraygir National Park
Yuraygir (20,000 hectares) is the southernmost of a chain of coastal national parks and nature reserves that runs almost all the way north to Ballina. The beaches are outstanding and there are some stretches of forest offering bushwalks. The park is in three sections, from Red Rock to the Wooli River (turn off the highway just north of Red Rock); from the township of Wooli to the Sandon River (turn off the highway 12km south of Grafton); and from near Brooms Head to Angourie (accessible from those towns). There is no vehicle access between the sections; on foot you'd have to cross the sizable Wooli and Sandon Rivers.

Walkers can bush camp and there are basic *camping* areas at Station Creek in the southern section, at the Boorkoom and Illaroo rest areas in the central section and on the north bank of the Sandon River, and at Red Cliff at the Brooms Head end of the northern section. These are accessible by car; there are also walk-in camp sites in the northern section: Plumbago Headland, Shelly Head and Shelly Beach.

Nearby Towns There are a number of small holiday settlements surrounded by the park. **Wooli** and **Minnie Water** are reached from a road running off the highway 12km south of Grafton or, if you're coming from the north, from Ulmarra.

Wooli is a straggling holiday hamlet, not especially attractive, but there are the usual great beaches and the very clean Wooli River, which you can apparently canoe up for 20km. Wooli's big event is the Goanna Pulling Championship, held on the Queen's Birthday long weekend in June. This is not something the Royal Society for the Prevention of Cruelty to Animals need be concerned about – it's a tug-of-war between contestants with a leather strap around their heads.

You can stay at *Wooli Caravan Park* (☎ 6649 7671), which has sites for $11 and on-site vans for $30, or *Wooli Hotel/Motel* (☎ 6649 7532), which has singles/doubles in motel units for $40/50.

Minnie Water, 12km or so north on the other side of **Lake Hiawatha**, is smaller but nicer. The *caravan park* (☎ 6649 7693) has sites from $10 and cabins from $33 a double.

Brooms Head, on the coast 25km southeast of Maclean, remains a quiet hamlet, popular with locals. It has good beaches (lagoon and ocean), a few holiday units, a *caravan park* (☎ 6646 7144) and proximity to the national park, both north and south of the town.

The Solitary Islands

This group of five islands is strung out along the coast offshore from Yuraygir National Park. It's a marine park at the meeting place of warm tropical currents and the more temperate southern currents, with some interesting varieties of fish and coral because of the unusual conditions. Cruises and dive boats from Coffs Harbour come here.

Far North Coast

As well as great beaches and a subtropical climate, rivers are a feature of this area (which is also known as the Northern Rivers district), with the mighty Clarence, Richmond and Tweed Rivers sprawling through rich deltas. They are wide, deep and blue – most un-Australian.

Winters are a bit of a nonevent in this part of the world. Even in June and July, daytime temperatures normally reach around 25°C, although nights can be cool (locals think the nights are cold and shiver in woollies). By September it's beach weather.

GRAFTON
postcode 2460 • pop 17,310

Grafton is a graceful old country town on the banks of the wide Clarence River. The

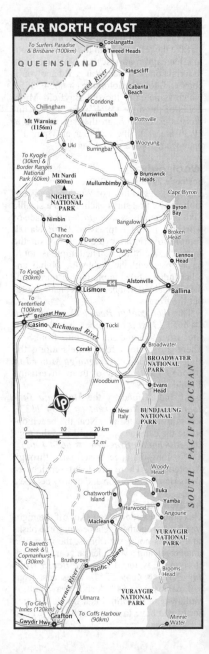

FAR NORTH COAST

town is famous for its fine trees, particularly the spectacular jacarandas, which carpet the streets with mauve flowers in late October. Although there isn't a lot to do or see here, this isn't a tourist town or a retirement ghetto and that makes a nice change from some of the sprawling coastal developments. The town lies at the centre of a rich agricultural district – beef cattle inland and sugar cane in the Clarence River delta.

Inland from Grafton are the Washpool and Gibraltar Range National Parks (see the New England chapter for information on these parks).

Orientation & Information

The Pacific Hwy bypasses Grafton and you enter the town on a double-decker (road and rail) bridge.

Clarence River Tourist Centre (☎ 6642 4677), on the highway south of the town near the turn-off to the bridge, is open from 9 am to 5 pm daily. There's an NPWS office (☎ 6642 0613) at 50 Victoria St.

Things to See & Do

Pick up a free heritage trail leaflet from the tourist centre, as it has a **walking tour** around Grafton's old buildings. Victoria St

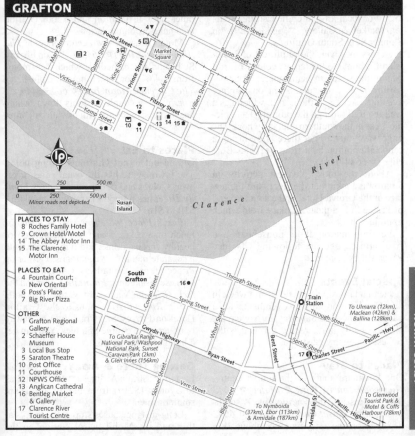

GRAFTON

PLACES TO STAY
8 Roches Family Hotel
9 Crown Hotel/Motel
14 The Abbey Motor Inn
15 The Clarence
   Motor Inn

PLACES TO EAT
4 Fountain Court;
   New Oriental
6 Poss's Place
7 Big River Pizza

OTHER
1 Grafton Regional
   Gallery
2 Schaeffer House
   Museum
3 Local Bus Stop
5 Saraton Theatre
10 Post Office
11 Courthouse
12 NPWS Office
13 Anglican Cathedral
16 Bentleg Market
   & Gallery
17 Clarence River
   Tourist Centre

Market Square

Clarence River

Susan Island

South Grafton

Train Station

To Ulmarra (12km),
Maclean (42km) &
Ballina (128km)

To Gibraltar Range
National Park, Washpool
National Park, Sunset
Caravan Park (2km)
& Glen Innes (156km)

Gwydir Highway

To Nymboida
(37km), Ebor (113km)
& Armidale (187km)

To Glenwood
Tourist Park &
Motel & Coffs
Harbour (78km)

Pacific Highway

0   250   500 m
0   250   500 yd
Minor roads not depicted

NORTH COAST

is worth a look, with the old post office, courthouse and police station, shaded by big trees. On the corner of Victoria and Duke Sts is the **Anglican Cathedral**, in spare 1930s style and with older buildings in the grounds. **Saraton Theatre**, on Prince St, is a restored movie theatre where you can still see the flicks most nights.

Fitzroy St runs off Prince St and has some interesting houses, including the one that's home to the **Grafton Regional Gallery**, at No 158, open from 10 am to 4 pm Wednesday to Sunday (admission by donation). A bit farther on, **Schaeffer House** is where you'll find the local **museum**, open from 1 to 4 pm, Sunday and Tuesday to Thursday ($2). For local art and craft, visit the **Bentleg Market & Gallery** (☎ 6643 2929), on Skinner St in South Grafton.

Across the river, the rainforest of **Susan Island** is home to the largest colony of fruit bats in the southern hemisphere. Their departure is a spectacular sight on summer evenings. Access to the island, which has a walking trail through the rainforest and picnic areas at the southern end, is by boat. The only way you can get there is by hiring a canoe/aluminium boat from Seelands Boat Hire (☎ 6644 9381).

About the most pleasant activity in Grafton is looking at the river, and the terrace at the Crown Hotel at the southern end of Prince St is a pleasant place from which to do just that.

For information about houseboats and river cruises, see the following Clarence River Valley section.

Special Events

A Jacaranda Festival is held over a week in late October and early November, with a parade on the first Saturday in November. Grafton's July horse racing carnival is the richest in country Australia.

Places to Stay

One kilometre south of the tourist centre, **Glenwood Tourist Park & Motel** (☎ 6642 3466) is just off the Pacific Hwy's southbound arm. **Sunset Caravan Park** (☎ 6642 3824) is on the Gwydir Hwy about 3km west of the tourist centre. Both have tent sites for around $11.50 and Glenwood has self-contained cabins, as well as motel units from $45.

Crown Hotel/Motel (☎ 6642 4000) is a pleasant place overlooking the river, with pub singles/doubles for $20/30 ($30/40 with private bathroom) and motel units for $45/55. See if you can get a room overlooking the river. If it's one of the small pub rooms you'll have French doors opening onto a long, wide veranda. The pub beds could be newer, but it's a clean and friendly place.

Another nice old pub in the same area is **Roches Family Hotel** (☎ 6644 2866, 85 Victoria St). It has rooms from $24/30. Most other pubs in Grafton and South Grafton also have accommodation.

Motels near the town centre include **The Abbey Motor Inn** (☎ 6642 6122), on Fitzroy St behind the cathedral, which has rooms from $54/64. For something more plush, try **The Clarence Motor Inn** (☎ 6643 3444, 51 Fitzroy St), a couple of doors down, which has impressive rooms with private balconies for $84/89.

Places to Eat

Dining out is not Grafton's strong point. The town centre has the usual cafes, takeaways, clubs and pub meals. **Roches Family Hotel** has a good bistro, with meals for $10 to $16.

Poss's Place (88 Prince St) is open for lunch on weekdays and has a selection of healthy snacks, drinks and light meals, with a separate menu for vegetarians. Farther up Prince St, past the railway viaduct, are two Chinese restaurants: **Fountain Court** and the **New Oriental**. Mains cost $9 to $13 at both.

Big River Pizza, opposite the Grafton Hotel on Fitzroy St, is mainly a takeaway but there are a couple of tables. You can get a bowl of pasta for $6.

Getting There & Away

Eastern Australia Airlines (☎ 13 1313) flies to Sydney ($219) from the airport 10km south of town.

Long-distance buses stop at the train station and the Mobil petrol station on the highway in South Grafton, not far from the tourist centre.

Countrylink buses run up the Gwydir Hwy to Glen Innes ($24) on Tuesday, Thursday and Saturday and can drop you near Washpool and Gibraltar Range National Parks.

Most local buses leave from King St, a block back from the Market Square shopping centre, not far from the corner of Pound St. Ryan's has two services a day between Grafton and Coffs Harbour, running via Red Rock and Woolgoolga.

King Brothers (☎ 6642 3111) runs to Maclean ($5.80 one way) and Yamba ($7) several times daily. Its buses leave from outside the Saraton Theatre.

The train station is just south of the bridge. The fare from Sydney is $81.

The Pacific Hwy runs north to Maclean and south to Coffs Harbour. Near Grafton there are several scenic routes that parallel the highway and involve ferry crossings, such as Grafton to Maclean via the north bank and the Lawrence ferry. There's also a ferry crossing between the highway and the north bank road at Ulmarra.

There's an interesting route from Grafton to Armidale via Nymboida and Ebor, passing turn-offs to Dorrigo and the New England and Cathedral Rock National Parks. Heading west to Glen Innes, the Gwydir Hwy passes through the superb Washpool and Gibraltar Range National Parks.

Getting Around
Grafton Radio Taxis (☎ 6642 3622) runs 24 hours.

CLARENCE RIVER VALLEY
The Clarence River rises in Queensland's McPherson Ranges and runs south through the mountains before thundering down a gorge in the Gibraltar Range west of Grafton. It then meanders serenely to the sea at Yamba, watering a beautiful and fertile valley along the way.

The delta between Grafton and the coast is a patchwork of farmland in which the now immense and branching Clarence River forms about 100 islands, some very large. If you're driving, the profusion of small bridges and waterways makes it hard to keep track of whether you're on an island or the mainland.

This is the start of sugar-cane country and also the beginning of Queensland-style domestic architecture: wooden houses with high-pitched roofs perched on stilts to allow air circulation in the hot summers. The burning of the cane fields (May to December) adds a smoky tang to the air. Reeves Cane Farm (☎ 6647 7215) has free one-hour tours on Friday at 2 pm – ring ahead.

There are several outfits that can help to get you cruising on the lower Clarence River, such as Captain-a-Cruiser (☎ 6645 8067), which rents out a six-berth cruiser from around $540 a weekend or $1080 a week plus fuel, and Clarence Riverboats (☎ 6647 6232), at Brushgrove to the north-east.

Inland from Grafton
The Clarence River is navigable as far upstream as the village of **Copmanhurst**, about 35km north-west of Grafton. The *Rest Point Hotel (☎ 6647 3125)* has singles/doubles for $20/30. Farther upstream the Clarence River descends rapidly from the Gibraltar Range through the rugged **Clarence River Gorge**, a popular but potentially dangerous site for white-water canoeing.

Private property flanks the gorge. On the south side the land is owned by the Winters family, who allow day visitors and have cabin accommodation at *Winters' Shack (☎ 6647 2173)*. Access is via Copmanhurst. It's best to ring first to get permission and to arrange for the gates to be unlocked. On the north side, *Wave Hill Station (☎ 6647 2145)* has homestead or inexpensive cottage accommodation and regular 4WD or horse-riding trips to the gorge. These trips cost $200 for the day, so a group of four would pay $50 each.

Ulmarra
postcode 2462 • pop 500
On the Pacific Hwy about 15km north of Grafton, Ulmarra is a National Trust-classified village founded in the 1850s by early cane planters. Today the town has an abundance of craft and antiques shops. The

Commercial Hotel (☎ 6644 5305) has limited accommodation for $25/40, including brekky. A vehicle ferry (not suitable for caravans) crosses the Clarence here.

Maclean
postcode 2463 • pop 3000
This pretty old town has strong Scottish roots and at Easter it holds a Highland Gathering. Maclean is at the junction of the Clarence River's main and south arms, where the river begins its lazy sprawl over the delta, and is home to a prawn-fishing fleet. It's a quiet place with excellent river views and great sunsets.

The **Maclean Historical Society**, in the Stone Cottage Museum on Wharf St, tells the story of the Northern Rivers district and is open from 1 to 4 pm Wednesday and Saturday, and from 10 am Friday ($2). **Maclean Lookout**, about 2km from the town centre on Wharf St, has views over the Clarence River and the cane fields. There's a Cane Harvest Festival in September.

Historic Gables B&B (☎ 6645 2452, *2b Howard St*) is a lovely heritage-listed place, with huge open living areas and bedrooms. Good-value rooms cost $65/88.

Yamba
postcode 2464 • pop 4000
Yamba is a thriving little resort town on the south head of the Clarence River's wide estuary, with beaches on three sides. There are lots of motels, holiday apartments and housing developments for retirees. Indeed, it would be a pleasant place to retire to, with reputedly the warmest winters in the state.

Fishing is the favourite pastime – you can choose between beach, rock and estuary fishing. Oyster Channel Boat Hire (☎ 6646 0263) hires out tackle as well as boats. The Yamba-Iluka ferry runs cruises up the river on Wednesday, Friday and Sunday, departing at 11 am and returning at 3 pm ($15/7.50 for adults/children).

Places to Stay There are a few caravan parks, including *East's Calypso Holiday Park* (☎ 6646 2468), right in town and overlooking the small harbour. Tent sites cost from $13 ($22 at peak times) and cabins from $36 ($50). The *Pacific Hotel* (☎ 6646 2466, *1 Pilot St*), superbly located high above Yamba Beach, has backpacker accommodation in twin rooms for $17.50 per person.

Yamba's six or so motels have relatively low rates outside peak times. The inviting *Aston Villa* (☎ 6646 2785), on Mulgi St (the inland continuation of Coldstream St, which crosses Yamba St), charges from $49 a double.

About 10km out of Yamba, set deep in the cane fields and on the banks of the Clarence River, is the lovely, rambling *Wynyabbie House B&B* (☎ 6646 0168). You can fish from the jetty or hang out on the wide verandas overlooking the river and lush gardens. Singles cost $60 and doubles start at $90 – the only downside is that the bedrooms are quite dark.

Places to Eat There are two great restaurants on Clarence St opposite the Pacific Hotel. The bright and breezy *Beachwood Cafe/Restaurant* (☎ 6646 9258) has mains for around $19. Next door is the similarly priced *Restaurant Castalia* (☎ 6646 1155). For something less upmarket, grab a good burger at *Two Fat Men* on Yamba St.

Getting There & Away Yamba is 15km east of the Pacific Hwy; turn off at the Harbord Island bridge intersection north of Maclean. King Brothers runs to Maclean and Grafton several times daily.

A ferry runs to Iluka, on the north bank of the Clarence River, four times a day for $3.50 one way (children $1.75).

Angourie
Five kilometres south of Yamba, Angourie is one of the far north coast's top spots for experienced surfers, but beware of rips. Also here is the Blue Pool, a quarry next to the beach filled with fresh water from a spring.

Iluka
postcode 2466 • pop 1800
North across the river from Yamba, Iluka remains something of a backwater. It's home to

a small commercial fishing fleet and recreational fishing is the main activity. The town adjoins the southern end of Bundjalung National Park and a section known as the **Iluka Rainforest** has World Heritage listing. A short walking trail from the town centre to Iluka Bluff takes you through the rainforest.

To get here from Yamba it's either a short ferry ride or, if you have a car, a long drive back to the highway, a total trip of about 40km.

BUNDJALUNG NATIONAL PARK

Stretching from Iluka north to Evans Head and covering 17,700 hectares, Bundjalung has long beaches, a river and a patch of rainforest at Woody Head, at the southern end of the park near Iluka.

Nearby is the large Woody Head *camping* area, leased from the NPWS and run privately. It has a few more facilities than most NPWS camping areas – including a kiosk and cabins – but there's no electricity, so you're spared the worst of the holiday hordes. Still, at peak times you'll need to book (☎ 6646 6134). Sites cost $10 a double and cabins start at $50. There are also simple camp sites at Black Rocks, Boorooa, Jerusalem Creek and Yabbra, with pit toilets but no water.

There are three access points for the park: from near Iluka, near Evans Head and, for the middle of the park, Gap Rd, which runs off the Pacific Hwy about 5km south of Woodburn.

NEW ITALY MUSEUM

This bizarre exhibition is on the highway about 10km south of Woodburn. The small museum traces the exciting events of the Marquis de Ray's plan to colonise the New Guinea island of New Ireland and how the tattered survivors of that fiasco ended up here. There's also an Italian Pavilion with a lot of information on the various provinces of Italy. Admission is free.

The museum has a coffee shop and there's a licensed Italian restaurant nearby. Behind all this is the **Gurrigai Aboriginal Arts & Crafts** shop, selling some local work along with pieces from the outback.

EVANS HEAD

postcode 2473 • pop 2500

A fishing town at the mouth of the Evans River, Evans Head has a pretty location and accommodation at *Hotel Illawong* (☎ 6682 4222), on the main shopping street, for $20/40 a single/double. The *Silver Sands Caravan Park & Camping Reserve* (☎ 6682 4212), just down the street, is lovely and green. Tent sites cost $9 and units with en suites start at $35.

Evans Head is 10km east of the highway; turn off at Woodburn.

BROADWATER NATIONAL PARK

Extending from north of Evans Head to Broadwater, this small coastal park (3750 hectares) protects a 7km stretch of beach backed by coastal heath. You can drive through the park on the roads between Evans Head and Broadwater. Camping is not allowed in the park.

BALLINA

postcode 2478 • pop 16,500

Ballina is a busy resort town at the mouth of the Richmond River, 30km south of Byron Bay. The emphasis around here is on family holidays and the main attractions include water sports and fishing. It's also (in)famous for its Big Prawn, which would have to be one of the most amusing of Australia's 'big' things.

Orientation & Information

The Pacific Hwy runs into town from the south (passing the Big Prawn) and becomes River St, the long main street.

The information centre (☎ 6686 3484), just past the old post office (now the courthouse) at the eastern end of River St, opens from 9 am to 5 pm weekdays and until 4 pm on weekends.

Museum

The interesting **Naval & Maritime Museum**, behind the information centre, houses one of the three balsawood rafts that drifted across the Pacific from Ecuador to Australia on the Las Balsas expedition in 1973, coming ashore at Ballina after 177 days. It's open from 9 am to 4 pm daily and admission is by donation.

Beaches

The popular **Shelly Beach**, east of the town centre, is the closest patrolled beach to town. To get there, take the first turn right (coming from Ballina) after the Shaws Hotel turn-off. This road also passes **Lighthouse Beach**. The small beach curving around **Shaws Bay Lagoon** is a safe spot for kids to swim.

Cruises

The MV *Richmond Princess* (☎ 6687 1216, or book at the information centre) has two-hour cruises at 10 am on Wednesday and 2 pm on Thursday ($9.50).

The MV *Bennelong* (☎ 0414 664 552, or book at the information centre) also has a variety of cruises, including a day cruise up the river to Lismore ($55/20 for adults/children). These cruises leave from near the RSL Club.

You'll find all sorts of small boats for hire at Ballina Quays Marina (☎ 6686 4289), off the highway south of the Big Prawn.

Activities

Ocean River Riding (☎ 017 108 468) is popular for its two-hour horse rides on the beach ($50/30). Ballina & Evans Head Surf School (☎ 6682 4393) has group lessons for $20 (1½ hours), or for $35 you can get one-on-one tuition.

Places to Stay

Nearly half of all visitors to Ballina stay with friends or relatives. It's that sort of town. Prices at most places rise sharply at peak times.

Camping There are 10 camp sites to choose from. The closest to the town centre is *Ballina Central Caravan Park* (☎ 6686 2220), on River St, a block east of the information centre. It has tent sites from $13 and cabins

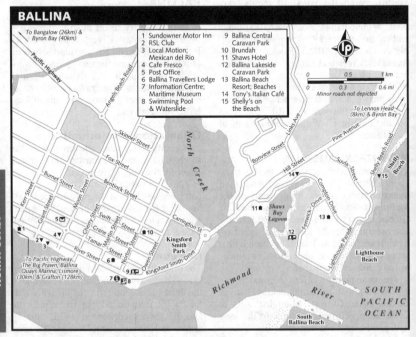

BALLINA

1 Sundowner Motor Inn	9 Ballina Central
2 RSL Club	Caravan Park
3 Local Motion;	10 Brundah
Mexican del Rio	11 Shaws Hotel
4 Cafe Fresco	12 Ballina Lakeside
5 Post Office	Caravan Park
6 Ballina Travellers Lodge	13 Ballina Beach
7 Information Centre;	Resort; Beaches
Maritime Museum	14 Tony's Italian Café
8 Swimming Pool	15 Shelly's on
& Waterslide	the Beach

To Bangalow (26km) &
Byron Bay (40km)

Pacific Highway

Angels Beach Road

0   0.5   1 km
0   0.3   0.6 mi
Minor roads not depicted

To Lennox Head
(8km) & Byron Bay

Skinner Street

North Creek

Fox Street

Bonview Street

Links Ave

Pine Avenue

Suvla Street

Shelly Beach Road

Shelly Beach

Burnet Street

Bentinck Street

Hill Street

Compton Drive

14

Kerr Street
Grant Street
Moon Street
Cherry Street
Crane Street
Swift Street
Tamar Street
Martin Street
Norton Street

11 Shaws Bay Lagoon

Fenwick Drive

13

Carrington St

Kingsford Smith Park

12

River Street

Owen Street

Lighthouse Parade

Lighthouse Beach

To Pacific Highway,
The Big Prawn, Ballina
Quays Marina, Lismore
(30km) & Grafton (128km)

Kingsford Smith Drive

7 9 8

Richmond

River

SOUTH
PACIFIC
OCEAN

South
Ballina Beach

NORTH COAST

with/without en suites from $55/30. The best location is to be found at ***Ballina Lakeside Caravan Park*** (☎ *6686 3953)*, which borders Shaws Bay Lagoon off Fenwicke Dr. It has sites from $11 and en suite cabins from $50.

Flat Rock Camping Park (☎ *6686 4848)*, about 5km north of town on the road to Lennox Head, is a terrific little camping area (tents only) just 100m from good surf. Sites cost from $12 to $14. There are hot showers, toilets, laundry and barbecues.

Hostels The YHA-associated ***Ballina Travellers Lodge*** (☎ *6686 6737, 36–38 Tamar St)* is a good, modern hostel. Dorm beds start at $15. Bikes and boogie boards can be hired ($1 an hour) and there's also a pool. This place also has motel-style doubles for $49 (around $62 at peak times).

B&Bs It's wise to make reservations at ***Brundah*** (☎ *6686 8166, 37 Norton St)*, a magnificently restored Federation home with large verandas overlooking lovely gardens. Singles/doubles cost $90/120. There are only two rooms.

Motels There are plenty of motels along the Pacific Hwy and River St, such as the good-value ***Sundowner Motor Inn*** (☎ *6686 2388)*, on the corner of River and Kerr Sts, which charges $40/49.

Near both Shaws Bay Lagoon and Lighthouse Beach, ***Ballina Beach Resort*** (☎ *6686 8888)* is free of traffic noise and has good facilities. Accommodation includes doubles from $99 and family units from $149.

Houseboats Off the highway south of the Big Prawn, ***Ballina Quays Marina*** (☎ *6686 4289)* rents out houseboats. Prices start at $235 weekdays in the low season ($390 in the high season) for up to four people. The longer you hire, the cheaper it gets, and with over 100km of navigable river, there's plenty of space to explore.

Places to Eat

For breakfast (from 7.30 am), lunch and snacks, ***Shelly's on the Beach*** (☎ *6686 9844)* is *the* place to go. It's a lovely kiosk-style cafe overlooking Shelly Beach with superb views of the sea and, sometimes, dolphins. It also opens for dinner on Friday and Saturday during the warmer months, with mains costing $10 to $16.

Another inviting spot is ***Beaches*** at Ballina Beach Resort, with pleasant undercover outdoor areas. The menu incorporates local ingredients such as Davidson plums and macadamia nuts and there's also a good selection of seafood. Mains cost around $20.

The stark and modern ***RSL Club***, somewhat reminiscent of a giant luxury yacht, has a prime position on the river bank on the corner of Grant and River Sts. The downstairs bistro is good value and has seating on a deck over the water.

Tony's Italian Cafe (☎ *6686 6602, 3 Compton Dr)* is very popular with locals. It's BYO and has a great open-deck dining area overlooking Shaws Bay. Mains cost $16 to $19.

Cafe Fresco (☎ *6686 2411, 177 River St)* is a licensed place with a Modern Australian menu and mains costing $10 to $19. There's a string of small restaurants on the other side of River St, including ***Local Motion*** (pasta) and ***Mexican del Rio***.

Getting There & Away

Most long-distance buses stop at the Big Prawn Tourist Complex, on the highway just west of town. Blanch's (☎ 6686 2144) has six buses a day to Lennox Head ($4.20) and Byron Bay ($6.60), leaving from the bus stop on Tamar St. Kirklands (☎ 6622 1499) also uses this stop for its regular buses to Lismore ($9.10).

If you're heading to Byron Bay, take the coast road through Lennox Head. It's much prettier than the highway and much shorter as well. Macadamia-nut fans might want to stick to the highway though, as there's the Macadamia Castle north of Ballina.

AROUND BALLINA

Inland from Ballina, the closely settled country of the north-coast hinterland begins, with winding, hilly roads running past tropical fruit farms, tiny villages and the occasional towering rainforest tree that somehow escaped the wholesale clearing of forest, which once covered the area.

Lennox Head
postcode 2478
Lennox Head, 11km north of Ballina and 18km south of Byron Bay, is the name of both the small, pleasant town with a fine beach and the dramatic headland (a prime hang-gliding site) that overlooks it. It has some of the best surf on the coast, particularly in winter. **Lake Ainsworth**, just back from the beach, is a freshwater lake, good for swimming and windsurfing. Its dark colour is due to tea-tree oil, supposedly good for the skin and hair, seeping in from the surrounding vegetation.

Places to Stay The basic *Lake Ainsworth Caravan Park* (☎ 6687 7249) has tent sites for $13 and cabins with/without en suite from $45/30.

Across the road is the YHA-affiliated, purpose-built *Lennox Head Beach House* (☎ 6687 7636). It's very clean and very friendly. Both Lake Ainsworth and the beach are seconds away and you can use all of its sporting equipment, such as a catamaran, windsurfer, boards and bikes ($5 for as long as you stay). Dorm beds cost $17 and there's a double for $40 ($19/44 for nonmembers). It also offers a free neck/back massage on Thursday – now that's service!

There are a couple of motels such as the *Lennox Head Motel* (☎ 6687 7257, 49 Ballina St), well situated near the beach, with singles/doubles from $50/60.

Places to Eat The *7 Mile Cafe* (☎ 6687 6210, 41 Pacific Parade) is a delightful place just across the road from the beach. It has airy eating areas and great food, and is open for lunch Friday to Sunday, and dinner Wednesday to Saturday; evening mains cost $17 to $26.

Mi-Thai in the main shopping area serves up great Thai food, with mains for $11 to $16. Just down the street, *Lennox Health Foods* makes delicious smoothies and other healthy tucker.

Getting There & Away Premier Motor Service buses go through Lennox Head about three times a day – the bus will stop by request – and Blanch's stops here on Ballina–Byron Bay run.

BYRON BAY
postcode 2481 • pop 5200
Byron Bay, one of the most popular stops on the whole east coast, is a relaxed seaside town with superb beaches and a great climate – warm in winter, hot in summer. Despite the moans of longtime locals that tourism is over the top, the atmosphere remains fairly laid-back.

Byron Bay is a meeting place of alternative cultures. It's almost a place of pilgrimage for surfers thanks to the superb surf below Cape Byron and is also close to the 'back-to-the-land' lifestyles pursued in the beautiful far north coast hinterland. There are good music venues, wholefood and vegetarian eateries, off-beat people, distinctive craft and clothes shops, a thriving fashion and surf industry and activities ranging from didgeridoo making to trapeze lessons

The Byron Bay market, held in Butler St on the first Sunday of each month, is one of a series around the area at which the counterculture (almost establishment up here!) gets a chance to meet and sell its wares.

Orientation
Byron Bay is 9km north-east of the Pacific Hwy turn-off at Bangalow, or 6km east of the turn-off farther north. Jonson St, which becomes Bangalow Rd, is the main shopping street. The corner of Jonson and Lawson Sts is pretty well the town centre. South of the centre, along Tallow Beach, is the satellite development of Suffolk Park.

Information
The helpful staff at the Byron Bay Visitor Centre (☎ 6685 8050), on Jonson St in the old cottage outside the train station, are kept busy answering questions from 9 am to 5 pm daily At the bus stop outside you'll find a listing of bus times, fares and other information.

You can store bags at the Byron Bus & Backpacker Centre (☎ 6685 5517), close by

BYRON BAY

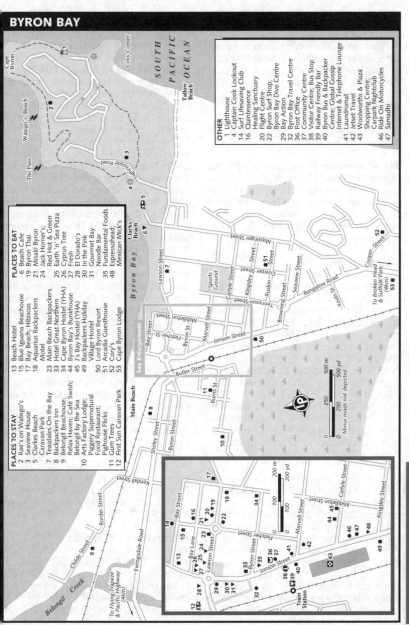

PLACES TO STAY
2 Rae's on Watego's
3 Seaview House
5 Clarkes Beach Caravan Park
7 Teasdales On the Bay
8 Backpackers Inn
9 Belongil Beachouse;
   Relax Haven; Café Swish;
   Belongil by the Sea
10 Arts Factory Lodge;
   Piggery Supernatural
   Food Restaurant;
   Pighouse Flicks
11 Gin Trees
12 First Sun Caravan Park

13 Beach Hotel
15 Blue Iguana Beachhouse
17 Bay Beach; Hibiscus
18 Aquarius Backpackers
   Motel
23 Main Beach Backpackers
33 Hotel Great Northern
34 Cape Byron Hostel (YHA)
44 Byron Bay's Bunkhouse
   J's Bay Hostel (YHA)
49 Backpackers Holiday
   Village Hostel
50 Lord Byron Resort
51 Arcadia Guesthouse
52 Cory's
53 Cape Byron Lodge

PLACES TO EAT
6 Beach Café
19 Byron Thai
21 Misaki Byron
24 Jack Horner's;
   Red Hot & Green
25 Earth 'n' Sea Pizza
26 Cyprus Tree
27 Fresh
28 El Dorado's
30 In the Pink
31 Gourmet Bay
   Noodle Bar
35 Fundamental Foods
48 Espressohead;
   Mexican Mick's

OTHER
1 Lighthouse
4 Captain Cook Lookout
14 Surf Lifesaving Club
16 Quintessence
   Healing Sanctuary
20 Flight Centre
22 Byron Surf Shop;
   Byron Bay Dive Centre
29 Bay Action
32 Byron Bay Travel Centre
36 Post Office
37 Community Centre
38 Visitor Centre; Bus Stop
39 Railway Friendly Bar
40 Byron Bus & Backpacker
   Centre; Global Gossip
   Internet & Telephone Lounge
41 Laundromat
42 Jetset Travel
43 Woolworths & Plaza
   Shopping Centre;
   Carpak Nightclub
46 Ride On Motorcycles
47 Samadhi

on Jonson St, for $2 a day, as well as buy tickets and book tours.

Read the quirky weekly *Echo* to get an idea of the way of life around here; the *Byron Shire News* mostly presents the view from the other side of the fence.

Internet Resources Global Gossip Internet & Telephone Lounge (☎ 6680 9140), close to the bus stop, is one of several Internet places in town.

Travel Agencies Travel agents include the Byron Bay Travel Centre (☎ 6685 6733) in Palm Court, opposite the Hotel Great Northern on Jonson St, Jetset Travel (☎ 6685 6554), on Marvell St near the corner of Jonson St, and the Flight Centre (☎ 6685 5440), on Lawson St.

Cape Byron

Cape Byron was named by Cook after the poet Byron's grandfather, who had sailed around the world in the 1760s. One spur of the cape is the most easterly point of the Australian mainland. You can drive right up to the picturesque 1901 **lighthouse**, one of the most powerful in the southern hemisphere. There's a 3.5km walking track around the cape from the **Captain Cook Lookout** on Lighthouse Rd. It's circular, so you can leave bikes at the start (but it'd be a good idea to use bike locks). There's a good chance of seeing wallabies and bush turkeys in the final rainforest stretch. There is also a herd of feral goats, descendants of an early lighthouse-keeper's flock, which have lived here for about 80 years.

From above you can often see schools of dolphins surfing through the waves. During the season (best in June and July) whales swim past, sometimes quite close to shore. The area around the lighthouse (where the best lookouts are) closes at 5.30 pm.

If you were to sail due north from Cape Byron, the next landmass you'd meet would probably be eastern Siberia; heading south, the ocean rolls all the way down to Antarctica. Chile is the next stop east, but heading west you'd probably end up on the beach in front of the Belongil Beachouse!

Beaches

The Byron area has a glorious collection of beaches, ranging from 10km stretches of empty sand to secluded little coves. **Main Beach**, immediately in front of the town, is a good swimming beach and sometimes has decent surf. The sand stretches 50km or more, all the way up to the Gold Coast, interrupted only by river or creek entrances and a few small headlands.

The eastern end of Main Beach, curving away towards Cape Byron, is known as **Clarks Beach** and can be good for surfing. The headland at the end of Clarks Beach is called The Pass and the best surf is off here and at **Watego's Beach**, next door. Farther around is **Little Watego's Beach**, almost at the tip of the cape. Dolphins are common, particularly in the surf off Watego's and Little Watego's Beaches.

South of Cape Byron, **Tallow Beach** stretches 7km down to a rockier stretch of shore around Broken Head, where a succession of small beaches dot the coast before opening on to **Seven Mile Beach**, which goes all the way to Lennox Head, another 10km south.

The Suffolk Park area, behind Tallow Beach, is about 5km south of central Byron Bay. Another kilometre down the Byron to Lennox Head road is the turn-off to Broken Head Caravan Park. About 200m before the caravan park, the unsealed Seven Mile Beach Rd turns off south and runs behind the rainforest of the Broken Head Nature Reserve. This road ends after 5km, but several tracks lead from it through the forest to the Broken Head beaches: **Kings** and **Whites Beaches** are just two good ones. Both are nude beaches (but be discreet).

A bike path runs all the way from Byron Bay to Suffolk Park.

Alternative Therapies

There are at least two places with relaxing flotation tanks: Samadhi (☎ 6685 6905), on Jonson St opposite Woolworths, and Relax Haven (☎ 6685 8304), at the Belongil Beachouse. At Relax, you get an hour in the tank and a one-hour massage for $40 – excellent value.

The wierd and wonderful Nimbin Museum

LEANNE LOGAN

ape Byron's 1901 lighthouse

JOHN HAY

Clarks Beach from The Pass, Byron Bay

Sawn Rocks, at the northern end of Mt Kaputar National Park

Several other places offer massage, acupuncture and alternative therapies; other outfits drift into the fuzzier edges of alternative thought. If you need your chakra realigned, contact Quintessence Healing Sanctuary (☎ 6685 5533), at 8/11 Fletcher St.

Activities

There's plenty to do in and around Byron; check with the visitor centre for further options, such as white-water rafting, parasailing, horse riding and Tiger Moth joy flights.

Surfing Most hostels have free boards for guests. Otherwise it's around $20 a day to hire a board from places like the Byron Surf Shop (☎ 6685 7536), on Lawson St near Fletcher St, or Bay Action (☎ 6685 7819), at 14 Jonson St. Many places require a $400 deposit (cash or credit card).

Several places offer lessons, such as the Byron Bay Surf School (☎ 1800 707 274), which has three-hour group lessons ($30 per person) daily. Private lessons are also available. Another good option is Black Dog Surfing (☎ 6685 8858).

North Coast Surfaris (☎ 1800 634 951) offers five-day surfing trips up the coast from Sydney to Byron Bay, stopping at out-of-the-way surf spots. Its bus leaves Sydney every Monday from Central Station. The price of $385 includes camping and surfing gear and all meals. You just need to bring a sleeping bag and pillow.

Diving Divers come to Byron Bay to visit the **Julian Rocks Marine Reserve**, 3km north of Cape Byron. Cold southerly currents and warm northerly ones meet here, attracting a profusion of marine species from both. The most popular of the dives is the **Cod Hole**, known for its huge moray eels and blue groper. There's keen competition between the growing number of dive operators wanting to take you out there, so ask around to see who has the best deals. Two operators worth checking out are Byron Bay Dive Centre (☎ 6685 7149), on the corner of Fletcher and Lawson Sts, and Sundive (☎ 6685 7755), in the Cape Byron Hostel complex on Middleton St.

Whale & Dolphin Watching Humpback whales can often be seen off Cape Byron during their northerly migration in June/July and again on their return journey between September and November. Marine Charter Service (☎ 6685 6858) has whale-watching trips from charter fishing boats.

Dolphins are much easier to find. The highly recommended Byron Bay Sea Kayaks (☎ 6685 5830) gets lots of takers for its breakfast with the dolphins off Main Beach ($35). Dolphin Kayaking (☎ 6685 8044) offers great value at $25 for three hours.

Flying This area is great for hang-gliding. Flight Zone (☎ 6685 8768) and Byron Bay Hang-Gliding School (☎ 015 257 699) do half-hour tandem flights for $85 and $95 respectively. Both also offer tuition. They operate either from Cape Byron or from Lennox Head – ring early to find out when and where the action is.

Skylimit (☎ 6684 3711) has a trike (ultra-light aircraft) flights starting at $105 for half an hour. Byron Bay Skydiving Centre (☎ 6684 1323) has tandem skydiving; prices start at $230 for a 25-second free fall.

Byron Air Charter (☎ 6684 2753) has joy flights as well as charters. A 20-minute flight works out at $25 per person if there are three of you ($75 for the plane). It operates from Tyagarah airport, midway between Byron Bay and Brunswick Heads.

Trapeze Potential circus stars can head out to the Flying Trapeze (☎ 6685 8000), west of town at the Byron Bay Beach Club, Bayshore Drive. The operators offer the opportunity to make your first catch on a flying trapeze at the end of a two-hour lesson ($25). It gets rave reports.

Didgeridoo Playing Gondwana Gifts (☎ 6685 8866), 2/7 Byron St, has free didgeridoo lessons from 3.45 pm Monday to Friday. They're popular, so make sure you book.

Organised Tours

Byron Bay Bush Tours (☎ 6685 6889) and Jim's Alternative Tours (☎ 6685 7720) both run day tours of the spectacular north coast hinterland for $25, including pick-up. Jim's also has trips to The Channon markets on the second Sunday of each month and to Bangalow on the fourth Sunday.

Forgotten Country Ecotours (☎ 6687 7845), which offers one- to three-day nature-based tours to places like Bald Rock National Park (see the New England chapter for more information on this park), comes highly recommended by our readers.

Special Events

There's a massive Blues Festival held over the Easter long weekend in April – more than 10,000 people attend, so it's a good idea to book accommodation. Other happenings include the Byron Food & Wine Festival in June and the Writers Festival in August. Contact the visitor centre for more details.

Places to Stay

There's an astonishing array of excellent accommodation, so check with the visitor centre for other options not listed here. It's a good idea to book, especially at peak times. Prices often increase dramatically during Christmas, January, Easter and school holidays.

Camping During holidays the best sites will probably be taken and around Christmas/January and Easter you'll be lucky to find *any* kind of site. If you need camping equipment, try Byron Bay Disposals in the Plaza shopping centre on Jonson St.

The council has four caravan parks, all next to beaches. *First Sun Caravan Park* (☎ 6685 6544) is well located on Main Beach and is very close to the town centre, but it's badly in need of some trees. Powered sites start at $15.50 for two, rising to $26 at peak times. The cheapest cabins cost from $50 in the low season to $60 at peak times. *Clarkes Beach Caravan Park* (☎ 6685 6496) is off Lighthouse Rd about 1km east of the town centre – it has plenty of trees and similar prices.

Other options include *Suffolk Park Caravan Park* (☎ 6685 3353) and, farther south again, the small *Broken Head Caravan Park* (☎ 6685 3245), which is behind a pop-

ular surf beach and close to Broken Head Nature Reserve.

Hostels The moment travellers step off the bus they will be aware of fierce competition between the town's numerous hostels: Awaiting them will be a line-up of touts. Most hostels offer fairly similar packages, with free use of bikes and surfboards, and all are of a very high standard.

There are two YHA-affiliated hostels. *J's Bay Hostel* (☎ 6685 8853, 1800 678 195), on the corner of Carlyle and Middleton Sts, is spotless and well equipped, with rooms laid out around a couple of central courtyards – one contains a heated swimming pool. Dorm beds cost from $18 (plus $2 for nonmembers) and there are doubles for $48 ($53 with en suite). The setup and costs are similar at *Cape Byron Hostel* (☎ 6685 8788, 1800 652 627), 200m closer to the beach on Middleton St.

Aquarius Backpackers Motel (☎ 6685 7663, 1800 028 909, 16 Lawson St) is a very well appointed hostel with small dorms, each with its own en suite bathroom, TV and fridge. Dorm beds cost $20.

If you're looking for the spirit of Aquarius, the place to head is the amazing *Arts Factory Lodge* (☎ 6685 7709), on Skinners Shoot Rd, with its permaculture gardens, clever recycled furnishings and creative energy. There's always something going on: didgeridoo making, music, yoga etc. Accommodation choices range from tent sites ($13) to tepees and converted double-decker buses ($24). Dorm beds cost $22 and doubles start at $60. Philosophically sound food is available at the adjoining Piggery Supernatural Food Restaurant (see Places to Eat).

It's a toss up as to which of the beach hostels is actually the closest to the sea. The modern *Backpackers Inn* (☎ 6685 8231, 29 Shirley St), about 500m from the town centre, is one of the contenders. Dorm beds cost $17 to $20; doubles cost from $42.

Lovely *Belongil Beachouse* (☎ 6685 7868), on Childe St, is definitely the pick of the bunch if you don't mind being away from the town centre. It has stylish accommodation, is well run, relaxed and friendly, and the excellent Cafe Swish is on the premises (see Places to Eat). Beds in small dorms cost $17 and basic doubles are $45. There are also large doubles with en suite and spa for $90.

Backpackers Holiday Village Hostel (☎ 6685 8888, 1800 350 388), just past Woolworths on Jonson St, is a clean, friendly, well-equipped place with a small pool and spa. Dorm beds cost $19, doubles $47 ($65 with en suite). *Byron Bay's Bunkhouse* (☎ 6685 8311, 1 Carlyle St) has a very pleasant common area and dorm beds for $12 to $20.

Other good places include *Main Beach Backpackers* (☎ 6685 8695, 1800 150 233), in the old council chambers on Lawson St; the homely *Blue Iguana Beachouse* (☎ 6685 5298), opposite the surf club on Bay St; and *Cape Byron Lodge* (☎ 6685 6445, 78 Bangalow Rd), 2km south of the town centre.

B&Bs For those watching their budget, *Gum Trees* (☎ 6685 7842, 5 Burns St) is a good option. It offers basic but homely accommodation from $35/50 for singles/doubles.

Arcadia Guesthouse (☎ 6680 8699, 48 Cowper St) is a lovely home with wide hallways and inviting living areas. Prices range from $60 to $170 (plus $10 for breakfast), depending on the season and the room.

If you'd like a room with a view, head to *Seaview House* (☎ 6685 6468, 146 Lighthouse Rd), which has its access on Lee Lane. Comfortable rooms with decks cost $100 a double (ask for one with a view).

For those with deeper pockets, *Cory's* (☎ 6685 7834, 21 Cooper St) is a beautifully restored early-20th-century home with original features such as pressed-tin walls. Rooms cost from $185 to $250 a night.

Hotels & Motels The *Hotel Great Northern* (☎ 6685 6454), on Jonson St, has doubles for $50.

Motels such as *Bay Beach* (☎ 6685 6090, 32 Lawson St) and *Hibiscus* (☎ 6685 6195, 33 Lawson St), both close to the beach, have doubles from around $89.

Lord Byron Resort (☎ 6685 7444, 120 Jonson St) is good value – doubles with private balconies start at $94.

At the luxury end of the market, there's the accommodation wing at *Beach Hotel* (☎ 6685 64020), on Bay St. Downstairs rooms open onto lush gardens with a heated pool, while the 1st-floor rooms have ocean views. Standard rooms start at $165 and luxury rooms with spa at $210. For something more intimate but equally luxurious, *Teasdales On the Bay* (☎ 6685 5125, 44 Lawson St) is a peaceful place with hints of the Orient. Standard rooms cost $220 to $300 ($260 to $350 for the penthouse suite).

At the absolute top end is *Rae's on Watego's* (☎ 6685 5366), a gleaming-white fantasy palace overlooking Watego's Beach. The rooms here are incredible, with rates starting at a mere $300 (increasing to $850 – yes, that's per night).

Rental Accommodation The least-expensive holiday houses cost from around $300 a week in the low season, increasing to $1000 at peak times. Letting agents include Elders (☎ 6685 6222), on Jonson St near the train station.

Belongil by the Sea (☎ 6685 8111), next to the Belongil Beachouse hostel, has self-contained cabins (including cooking facilities) from $90 a double (rising to $140 at peak times).

Byron Bay Rainforest Resort (☎ 6685 6139), south of town on Broken Head Rd, is designed and run by wheelchair users for travellers with disabilities. Rates start at $90 for a self-contained, three-person cabin.

Places to Eat

People don't come to Byron Bay to spend time slaving over a hot stove. Places to eat are everywhere in the town centre and the choice is overwhelming. Vegetarians are well catered for.

Fast Food The local council continues its resolve to keep the major junk-food dealers out of town, encouraging interesting, small takeaway places. The northern end of Jonson St is the place to look, where options include a couple of *kebab joints*, Mexican food at *El Dorado's* and Thai noodle dishes and stir-fries at *Gourmet Bay Noodle Bar*.

Cyprus Tree on Bay Lane does souvlakis and home-made Greek dips, while *Earth 'n' Sea Pizza* on Lawson St is more imaginative than most pizza parlours, with creations like 'Mullumbimby Madness' (vegetarian) and the 'Krakatoa' (enough chilli to spark an eruption). One reader swore this place served up the best pizza they'd ever eaten. Try *In the Pink* on Jonson St for the best ice cream in town.

Cafes The *Beach Cafe*, overlooking Clarks Beach, is *the* place to go for breakfast. It opens at 7.30 am and stays open for lunch. It's set up like a kiosk, with a good outdoor seating area, and set breakfasts for around $12. As cute as its name, *Jack Horner's*, in Lawson Arcade off Lawson St, is another good place for brekky.

Cafe Swish, at the Belongil Beachouse, is an inviting spot, serving up delicious, healthy food between 8 am and 9 pm. In spring and summer, an added bonus is its 'Jazz @ Sunset'. At the southern end of Jonson St, *Espressohead* is a terrific little spot for a coffee.

Fundamental Foods, next to the post office on Jonson St, has a good range of yummy tucker as well as organically grown fruit and vegetables.

Restaurants On the corner of Bay Lane and Jonson St, *Fresh* (☎ 6685 7810) is a popular, chic place, open all day, with excellent evening meals such as Thai green curry ($13) and nasi goreng ($18). *Red Hot & Green* (☎ 6685 5363), an inviting Thai restaurant tucked away just off Bay Lane, is highly recommended. Mains cost $10 to $16.

The *Beach Hotel* on Bay St has a wide range of snacks, such as nachos, for $9.50 and more substantial meals like char-grilled cuttlefish ($12.50) and steaks (from $14.50). An old favourite in town is *Mexican Mick's* (☎ 6680 9050, 109 Jonson St), a licensed place open for dinner.

For some good Japanese, head to *Misaki Byron* (☎ 6685 7966), on Fletcher St. Mains cost $10 (home-smoked salmon roll) to $30 (mixed fish, sushi and sashimi platter). Regular sushi and sashimi dishes cost $19.

Out at Watego's Beach, the gorgeous restaurant at *Rae's on Watego's* is a good place for a splurge, with its great views and luxurious atmosphere. Mains on the predominantly seafood menu cost $30 to $35. It's open for dinner nightly and for lunch on weekends.

Foremost among the good vegetarian options is the *Piggery Supernatural Food Restaurant* (☎ 6685 5833), out at the Arts Factory Lodge – it's every bit as cosmic as the name suggests. It's open from 6 pm daily; delicious fare costs $7 to $13. *Byron Thai* (☎ 6685 8453, 31 Lawson St) is an inviting place with an unusually large vegetarian selection. Mains cost around $10.

Entertainment

The busy nightlife is another of Byron Bay's major drawcards. You'll find a gig guide in the *Byron Shire News*, published on Wednesday.

The *Railway Friendly Bar* (☎ 6685 7662) has live music most nights, while *Beach Hotel* and *Hotel Great Northern* have live bands from Thursday to Saturday nights and sometimes on Sunday afternoon.

Next to the Arts Factory in the old piggery is the *Pighouse Flicks cinema*. Call the movie hotline (☎ 6685 5828) to find out what's on.

For some techno trance into the wee hours, head to the *Carpark Nightclub* at the Woolworths complex.

Getting There & Away

The closest airport is at Ballina, but most people use the much larger airport at Coolangatta on the Gold Coast in Queensland. There are frequent direct flights from both Sydney and Melbourne.

All the major bus companies come through Byron Bay, stopping at the main bus stop on Jonson St. Typical fares are Brisbane ($20), Sydney ($69), Coffs Harbour ($40) and Surfers Paradise ($20). You can travel all the way up to Cairns for $170 passing Airlie Beach ($127) on the way.

Blanch's serves the local area with destinations such as Mullumbimby ($4.20) and Ballina ($6.60).

Byron Bay is on the Sydney to Murwillumbah train line, with a daily train in each direction plus several rail/bus services. From Sydney ($92) the quickest service is the 7.05 am XPT (express train), which reaches Byron Bay at 7.30 pm. This train continues to Murwillumbah and connects with a bus to Brisbane. The southbound train stops in town at 10 pm.

Getting Around
Earth Car Rentals (☎ 6685 7472) has older cars from $35 a day (including 100km free), more recent vehicles from $45 and new cars from $60. Jetset Travel (☎ 6685 6554) rents out small current-model cars for $37 a day plus 12c per kilometre after the first 100km free. Add about $10 to these prices if you want to reduce the insurance excess to below $3000.

Ride on Motorcyles (☎ 6685 6304), on Jonson St opposite Woolworths, hires out motorbikes from $100 a day. You need a motorbike licence (Australian or foreign).

The hostels lend bikes of varying quality to guests. Byron Bay Bicycles (☎ 6685 6067), in the Plaza shopping centre on Jonson St, has good single-speed bikes for $16 a day, including helmet, and geared bikes for $20 a day.

If you need a cab, call Byron Bay Taxis (☎ 6685 5008).

BRUNSWICK HEADS
postcode 2483 • pop 1700
Brunswick Heads is a small fishing town that's popular for family holidays. It's quite a pleasant place, with the Brunswick River, famous for its mud crabs and fresh oysters, and a good beach, but nearby Byron Bay overshadows its modest attractions.

Places to Stay & Eat
On Fingal St, *The Terrace Reserve Caravan Park* (☎ 6685 1233), is close to the beach (via a footbridge) and the town centre. Sites cost $13 for two people, rising to $18 at peak times, and cabins with en suites cost $42 ($83).

The pick of the four motels in town is the *Heidelberg Holiday Inn* (☎ 6685 1808, 2 The Terrace), close to both the beach and river. Singles/doubles start at $47/50, twice that at peak times.

The *Hotel Brunswick* (☎ 6685 1236), Mullumbimby St, is a superb pub overlooking the Brunswick River. As well as being a fine place for an ale or two, it houses the *Blue Water Grill* bistro, which serves delicious, generous meals such as pastas, seafood and steak for around $15. The indoor dining room has a lovely ambience, or you can dine alfresco under the poinciana trees.

Getting There & Away
Long-distance buses on the Sydney-Brisbane runs can drop you here. The fare from Byron Bay is $7 with Kirklands.

THE TWEED COAST
The Pacific Hwy north of Brunswick Heads curves inland to Murwillumbah then back to the coast at Tweed Heads. There's also a route along the Tweed Coast, which is a little shorter but probably slower.

It won't be many years before the stretch of coast between Brunswick Heads and Tweed Heads is overrun by housing estates, in the all-too-familiar process whereby a superb area is ruined by tasteless developers and short-sighted local governments. Meanwhile, there are still large gaps between the cream-brick ghettos, and a series of fine beaches.

The coastal road is sealed north of **Wooyung**, where there's a basic *camping* area; the Wooyung turn-off from the highway is about 7km north of Brunswick Heads. Next stop north is **Pottsville**, a residential development. After Pottsville you come to **Cabarita Beach** (also known as Bogangar), which has good surf, usually even when other areas are quiet.

At Cabarita Beach there's a good purpose-built hostel, the *Emu Park Backpackers Resort* (☎ 6676 1190). It's one of the cleanest hostels around and the rooms are large. Dorm beds cost $15 and there's a 'stay two nights, get the third night free' deal outside peak periods. Bikes and boards are free and the beach is a minute away. The staff will drop you off at Mt Warning and pick you up

NORTH COAST

after your climb for about $60 – not bad among several people. They will also pick you up free from Coolangatta, Murwillumbah or Kingscliff if you stay for more than one night.

Close to Cabarita Beach is **Cudgen Lake**, where you can hire catamarans and windsurfers ($15 an hour) and canoes (from $6 an hour). The hire shop is part of *Cabarita Gardens Lake Resort (☎ 6676 2000)*, a motel and apartment complex on Tamarind Ave, with doubles for $75 to $95. **Kingscliff** is next north and is almost an outer suburb of Tweed Heads. It's a little older than the beachside developments farther south.

TWEED HEADS
☎ 07 • postcode 2485 • pop 10,300
Sharing a street with the more developed Queensland resort of Coolangatta, Tweed Heads marks the southern end of the Gold Coast strip. The north side of Boundary St, which runs along a short peninsula to Point Danger above the mouth of the Tweed River, is in Queensland. This end of the Gold Coast is much quieter than the resorts closer to Surfers Paradise.

Orientation
Tweed Heads' older town centre is quite a compact area north of the river. Coming from the south, after the new bypass road branches off, the Pacific Hwy crosses the river on narrow Boyds Bay Bridge and becomes Wharf St, the long main street.

Information
The Tweed & Coolangatta Traveller Information Centre (☎ 5536 4244), at the northern end of Wharf St, is open from 9 am to 5 pm daily. There's also an information centre (☎ 5536 7765), on Warner St in Coolangatta, open from 8 am to 4 pm weekdays and 10 am to 4 pm on Saturday.

Things to See & Do
The towering **Captain Cook Memorial** straddles the state border at Point Danger, named by Cook after he nearly ran aground there. The 18m-high monument was completed in 1970 (the bicentenary of Cook's

visit) and is topped by a laser-beam lighthouse visible 35km out to sea. There are views over the Tweed Valley and the Gold Coast from the **Razorback Lookout**, 3km from Tweed Heads.

There are several good **beaches**, most in Queensland. Coolangatta's Kirra Point is famous for its surf, and Rainbow Bay, on the northern side of Point Danger, is another patrolled beach.

On Kirkwood Rd in South Tweed Heads, the **Minjungbal Aboriginal Cultural Centre** (☎ 5524 2109) has exhibits on the Minjungbal people, who once owned this area. You can buy authentic souvenirs. The nearby *bora* ground is a traditional ceremonial site. The centre is open 10 am to 4 pm daily ($6). A boardwalk runs through the adjacent Ukerebagh Island Nature Reserve.

The **Tweed Maritime Museum**, on Kennedy Dr in Tweed Heads West, has old photos and other bits and pieces and is open on Tuesday and Friday afternoon ($1/0.50 for adults/children).

Tweed Endeavour Cruises (☎ 5536 8800) has a 1½-hour **cruise** ($22/11) and a four-hour river-and-rainforest cruise with a seafood buffet lunch ($48/24).

Places to Stay
Accommodation in Tweed Heads spills over into Coolangatta and up the Gold Coast, where the choice is more varied.

There are many caravan parks in the area. One of the most pleasant is *Tweed Billabong Holiday Park (☎ 5524 2444)*, on Holden St, which has sites from $17 and basic cabins with en suite from $45. Much posher (and more expensive) cabins are also available. *Boyds Bay Holiday Park (☎ 5524 3306)*, on Dry Dock Rd, is another good option, with tent sites from $11 and cabins from $38.

A good hotel option just over the border is the *Coolangatta Sands Hotel (☎ 5536 3066)*, on the corner of Griffith and McLean Sts, which has rooms for $20 per person.

Tweed Coast Backpackers Motel (☎ 5524 2111), on the corner of Pacific Hwy and Soorley St, is a good budget choice. Dorm beds cost $15, doubles from $35. The owners can pick you up from the Transit Centre.

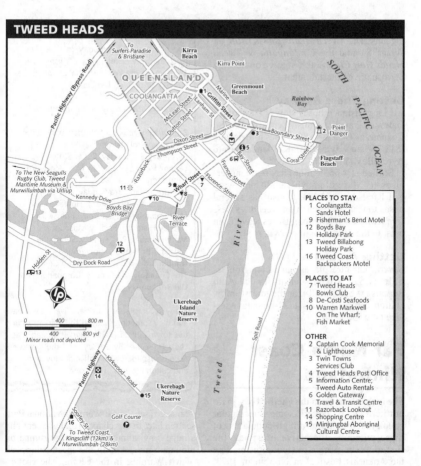

TWEED HEADS

PLACES TO STAY
1 Coolangatta
  Sands Hotel
9 Fisherman's Bend Motel
12 Boyds Bay
  Holiday Park
13 Tweed Billabong
  Holiday Park
16 Tweed Coast
  Backpackers Motel

PLACES TO EAT
7 Tweed Heads
  Bowls Club
8 De-Costi Seafoods
10 Warren Markwell
  On The Wharf;
  Fish Market

OTHER
2 Captain Cook Memorial
  & Lighthouse
3 Twin Towns
  Services Club
4 Tweed Heads Post Office
5 Information Centre;
  Tweed Auto Rentals
6 Golden Gateway
  Travel & Transit Centre
11 Razorback Lookout
14 Shopping Centre
15 Minjungbal Aboriginal
  Cultural Centre

The motels along Wharf St have been feeling the pinch since the completion of the bypass road and you'll find doubles advertised for as little as $35. Try the basic but clean *Fishermen's Bend Motel* (☎ 5536 1842, 163–165 Wharf St). For another $5 you'll get a hearty cooked breakfast as well.

Places to Eat

For inexpensive fare, try *Tweed Heads Bowls Club* (☎ 5536 3800), on Wharf St, which has specials, such as weekday roast lunches, for under $5; other clubs in town are also sources of cheap eats. For something more upmarket, try *Warren Markwell On The Wharf* (☎ 5536 1160, 118 Pacific Hwy), which has a good selection of dishes for $15 to $30 and a great outlook over the river. Directly opposite, the same owner runs a fish market where you can buy fresh seafood or have it cooked to take away. There's a similar setup at *De-Costi Seafoods* (☎ 5599 2343, 2 River Terrace).

Entertainment

The large *Twin Towns Services Club*, on the corner of Wharf and Boundary Sts, and *The New Seagulls Rugby Club*, on Gollan

NORTH COAST

Dr in West Tweed Heads, have regular touring acts. The **Tweed Heads Bowls Club**, on Wharf St, and the **Coolangatta & Tweed Heads Golf Club**, south of town on Soorley St, also have entertainment.

Getting There & Away
All long-distance buses stop at the Golden Gateway Travel & Transit Centre on Bay St. Coachtrans (☎ 5588 8700) goes to Brisbane ($13/26 one way/return). Kirklands goes to Byron Bay ($15.10).

Surfside (☎ 5536 7666) has frequent services to Murwillumbah ($3.80 one way) and Kingscliff ($3.10). It also has several buses to Cabarita Beach on weekdays (less frequently on weekends). Buses leave from outside the Tweed Mall on Wharf St.

Getting Around
Several car-hire places have cars from as little as $20 a day, such as Tweed Auto Rentals (☎ 5536 8000), at the tourist information centre. There's a 24-hour taxi service (☎ 5536 1144).

Far North Coast Hinterland

The area inland from the Pacific Hwy in far northern NSW covers some spectacular country. It's home to a high population of those pursuing alternative lifestyles, the first of whom were attracted to the area by the Aquarius Festival at Nimbin in 1973. They have become a prominent and colourful part of the community.

The country between Lismore and the coast was once known as the Big Scrub, an inadequate description given that it must have been close to paradise at the time of European incursion. Much of the 'scrub' was cleared for farming after the loggers had removed the prized red cedar. These days the region is marketed as Rainbow Country.

Geography
The northern part of the hinterland was formed by volcanic activity some 20 million

Markets & Music

The alternative community can be seen in force at the weekend markets listed below. The biggest market is at The Channon, between Lismore and Nimbin.

Bangalow 4th Sunday of the month, sports oval
Brunswick Heads 1st Saturday, behind the Ampol petrol station
Byron Bay 1st Sunday, Butler St Reserve
Lennox Head 5th Sunday, Lake Ainsworth foreshore
Lismore 1st and 3rd Sunday, Lismore shopping square; 5th Sunday, Heritage Park
Mullumbimby 3rd Saturday, Brunswick Valley Historical Society Museum
Murwillumbah 2nd Sunday, Sunnyside Plaza; 4th Sunday, showgrounds
Nimbin 3rd Sunday, Community Centre
The Channon 2nd Sunday, Coronation Park
Uki 3rd Sunday, old buttery

Many accomplished musicians live in the area and they sometimes play at the markets or in the town pub after the market (notably at Uki). The *Echo* (Byron Bay) and the *Lismore Echo* newspapers give notice of most musical and cultural events in the area.

years ago (see the Mt Warning National Park section later in this chapter) and is essentially a huge bowl almost completely rimmed by mountain ranges, with the spectacular peak of Mt Warning in the centre. The escarpments of the McPherson and Tweed Ranges form the north-western rim, with the Razorback Range to the west and the Nightcap Range to the south-west. The area's three national parks – Border Ranges, Mt Warning and Nightcap – are all World Heritage areas, as are some smaller nature reserves.

The country south of here is a maze of steep hills and beautiful valleys, some still harbouring magnificent stands of rainforest, others cleared for cattle grazing and plantations, especially macadamia nuts and avocados. Coffee is a new crop that is showing a lot of promise.

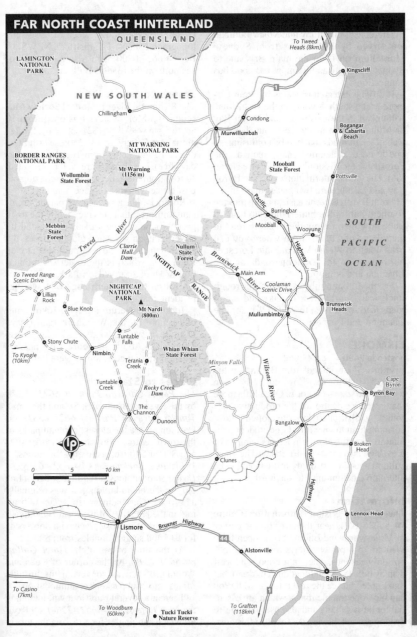

FAR NORTH COAST HINTERLAND

QUEENSLAND

To Tweed Heads (8km)

LAMINGTON NATIONAL PARK

Kingscliff

NEW SOUTH WALES

Chillingham

Condong

Murwillumbah

Bogangar & Cabarita Beach

MT WARNING NATIONAL PARK

Mooball State Forest

BORDER RANGES NATIONAL PARK

Mt Warning (1156 m)

Wollumbin State Forest

Pottsville

Uki

Pacific

Burringbar

Mooball

Wooyung

SOUTH

Mebbin State Forest

Tweed

River

Clarrie Hall Dam

Nullum State Forest

Brunswick

Main Arm

PACIFIC

NIGHTCAP

River

Coolaman Scenic Drive

OCEAN

To Tweed Range Scenic Drive

RANGE

Highway

NIGHTCAP NATIONAL PARK

Mt Nardi (800m)

Mullumbimby

Brunswick Heads

Lillian Rock

Blue Knob

Wilsons

To Kyogle (10km)

Tuntable Falls

Whian Whian State Forest

Minyon Falls

Cape Byron

Stony Chute

Nimbin

Terania Creek

River

Byron Bay

Tuntable Creek

Rocky Creek Dam

The Channon

Dunoon

Bangalow

Broken Head

0   5   10 km
0   3   6 mi

Clunes

Pacific

Lennox Head

Lismore

Bruxner   Highway

Highway

44

Alstonville

Ballina

To Casino (7km)

1

To Woodburn (60km)

To Grafton (118km)

Tucki Tucki Nature Reserve

NORTH COAST

Getting There & Around

Lismore, Mullumbimby and Murwillumbah are served by XPT trains from Sydney; Murwillumbah is on the main Brisbane to Sydney bus route and Lismore has good bus connections.

If driving, the area is accessible from Lismore in the south, Kyogle in the west, Murwillumbah in the north-east and Byron Bay or Mullumbimby in the east, but there's a web of small roads that can be confusing, so you'll need a detailed map, such as the Forestry Commission's Casino Area map ($6). The tourist information centres in Byron Bay and Lismore are two places that sell it.

From Byron Bay the easiest route into the southern half of the hinterland is to head to Bangalow then follow the Lismore road to the village of Clunes, from where you can head north to Whian Whian State Forest or north-west on the Dunoon road for The Channon and Nimbin.

From Mullumbimby, a scenic but rough track leads north-west to Uki and small roads lead south-west to Whian Whian, The Channon and Lismore.

LISMORE

postcode 2480 • pop 43,000

Lismore, 35km inland from Ballina on the Bruxner Hwy to New England, is the main town of the state's far north. Once little more than a service centre for the productive surrounding district, it has developed into a cosmopolitan town with a large student population from the Northern Rivers campus of the University of New England. The local cultural agenda is strongly influenced by the alternative community to the north.

Information

The Lismore Visitor Information Centre (☎ 6622 0122), near the river on the corner of Molesworth and Ballina Sts, is open from 9.30 am to 4 pm weekdays and 10 am to 3 pm on weekends. There's a good rainforest display here ($1/0.50 for adults/children), but make sure you see the real thing as well. You can buy topographic maps, which are essential for bushwalking and also useful if you're driving around the narrow roads in this area.

The Big Scrub Environment Centre (☎ 6621 3278), at 123 Keen St, also sells topographic maps. The district's NPWS office (☎ 6627 0200) is in Alstonville, east of Lismore on the road to Ballina.

Things to See & Do

The **Richmond River Historical Society Museum**, 165 Molesworth St, is open from 10 am to 4 pm weekdays ($2). Close by, the **Regional Art Gallery**, at 131 Molesworth St, is open the same hours from Tuesday to Saturday (free). Local artists are well represented. Across from the gallery is the interesting old post office with its iron-lace dome.

Rotary Park is a six-hectare patch of remnant rainforest that survived while the town grew around it. The park is dominated by towering hoop pines and giant fig trees. It's about 3km east of the information centre on Rotary Dr, which is the easterly continuation of Uralba St. **Wilson Park**, off Wyrallah Rd on the southern edge of town, has resident koalas.

Tucki Tucki Nature Reserve, 16km south of Lismore on the Woodburn road (leave Lismore on Wyrallah Rd), is a koala reserve. There's an Aboriginal **bora ring** nearby, where initiation ceremonies were held.

Places to Stay

The *Palms Caravan Park* (☎ 6621 7067), by the river on Brunswick St, and the small *Tourist Caravan Park* (☎ 6621 6581), on Dawson St, are the closest caravan parks to the town centre. They charge $15 for sites and $36 or $40 (respectively) for cabins.

Lismore Backpackers (☎ 6621 6118, 14 Ewing St) occupies Currendina Lodge, a fine old weatherboard building. It was originally a hospital – Currendina means 'place of healing' in the language of the local Bundjalung Aborigines. It's a cosy place with dorm beds for $15 and singles/doubles from $20/32.

At the time of research, *Hotel Gollan* (☎ 6621 2295), on the corner of Keen and Woodlark Sts, was converting its upstairs rooms into backpacker accommodation.

There are several pubs in town, including the *New Tattersalls* (☎ 6621 2284), on Keen St, which has singles for $15, and the lovely

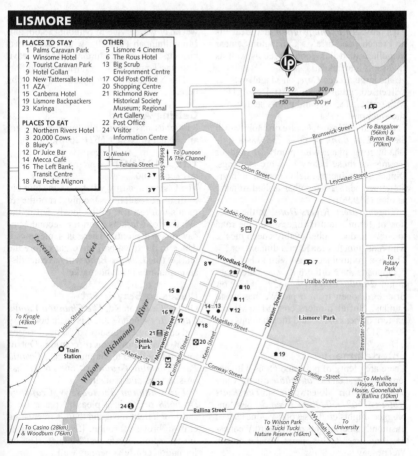

LISMORE

PLACES TO STAY
1 Palms Caravan Park
4 Winsome Hotel
7 Tourist Caravan Park
9 Hotel Gollan
10 New Tattersalls Hotel
11 AZA
15 Canberra Hotel
19 Lismore Backpackers
23 Karinga

PLACES TO EAT
2 Northern Rivers Hotel
3 20,000 Cows
8 Bluey's
12 Dr Juice Bar
14 Mecca Café
16 The Left Bank;
  Transit Centre
18 Au Peche Mignon

OTHER
5 Lismore 4 Cinema
6 The Rous Hotel
13 Big Scrub
  Environment Centre
17 Old Post Office
20 Shopping Centre
21 Richmond River
  Historical Society
  Museum; Regional
  Art Gallery
22 Post Office
24 Visitor
  Information Centre

Winsome Hotel (☎ 6621 2283, 75 Bridge St), which charges $20/25 for singles/doubles.

The rooms at the *Canberra Hotel (☎ 6622 4736, 77 Molesworth St)* have been very well renovated, each having its own theme, such as the 'Picasso Room'. Guests have private access and the rooms are quiet. Prices are $59/69.

The more central of the 10 motels include *Karinga (☎ 6621 2787, 258 Molesworth St)* and *AZA (☎ 6621 9499, 114 Keen St),* which both charge $50/60.

Melville House (☎ 6621 5778, 267 Ballina St), a B&B, charges from $40/55 for singles/doubles with shared bathroom, up to $90/110 with en suite. Farther east in the suburb of Goonellabah, *Tulloona House (☎ 6624 2897, 106 Ballina Rd)* is a National Trust-classified Victorian mansion with a massive garden. The rooms are huge and furnished with antiques. B&B doubles cost $95.

Places to Eat

The place for the cheapest brekky in town is *Bluey's,* on Woodlark St, where bacon and eggs costs just $2.95. *Dr Juice Bar (142 Keen St)* is a deservedly popular spot that serves up excellent vegetarian and vegan

NORTH COAST

food, smoothies and juices. It's open weekdays only. *Au Peche Mignon* is a great little French patisserie on Carrington St near Magellan St. It has good coffee as well as croissants and cakes.

The large *Mecca Cafe*, on Magellan St, is a licensed, great-looking Art Deco place, with burgers ($5.50) and mains such as nachos and pasta ($8).

Close to the Transit Centre on Molesworth St, *The Left Bank (☎ 6622 2338)* is a stylish, inviting place with plenty of outdoor seating for those balmy Lismore evenings. Dinner mains include delicious lemon myrtle fettuccine ($15) and char-grilled Atlantic salmon ($19.90).

The *Northern Rivers Hotel*, at the junction of Terania and Bridge Sts on the road to Nimbin, does unbelievably cheap meals, with roast lunches for $2 and dinners for $3. This is a good place to go with kids.

Opposite the Northern Rivers is the vegetarian *20,000 Cows (☎ 6622 2517)*, on Bridge St, open from 6 pm Wednesday to Sunday. Buffet dinners cost $18, Middle Eastern dishes cost $6 and Indian mains cost $9 to $12.

Entertainment

There are plenty of pubs and clubs with entertainment, such as *Powerhouse* at the Canberra Hotel on Molesworth St. *The Rous Hotel (☎ 6621 5044, 44 Keen St)* has 'unplugged' nights on the second Wednesday of the month, poets nights on the third Wednesday and Irish/Celtic jams on the fourth Wednesday.

The *Lismore 4 cinema (☎ 6621 2361)* is diagonally opposite The Rous on the corner of Keen and Zadoc Sts.

Getting There & Away

There are daily flights to Brisbane (Ansett Australia) and Sydney (Ansett and Hazelton Airlines).

Kirklands is based here and runs buses around the immediate area as well as farther afield. Destinations include Byron Bay ($10.90), Mullumbimby ($11.70) and Brisbane ($29.70). There's a handy service to Tenterfield in New England on weekdays.

Marsh's Bus Service (☎ 6689 1220) has a weekday bus service to Nimbin ($8.60) and Murwillumbah ($14.20), with another two buses to Nimbin on Saturday. All buses leave from the Transit Centre on Molesworth St.

The XPT train from Sydney ($92) stops here.

Getting Around

Kirklands has urban-area buses, and there are 24-hour taxis (☎ 6621 2618).

THE CHANNON
postcode 2480

The Channon, a tiny village off the Nimbin to Lismore road, hosts the biggest of the region's markets (or, as the locals call it, the 'Mother of Markets'), on the second Sunday of each month. There is sometimes a dance in the town hall the night before the market (the *Lismore Echo* will have details) and often music at the market.

Places to Stay & Eat

On The Channon Rd, *The Channon Village Campsite (☎ 6688 6321)*, is basic but pretty and costs $5 per person. You'll need to ring to let them know you're coming. Out of town on the road to Terania Creek, *Terania Park Camping Ground (☎ 6688 6121)* has on-site vans and tent sites.

The Channon Teahouse & Craftshop (☎ 6688 6276) is a pleasant place for a snack or a light meal and there's interesting craft to browse through. It's open from 10 am to 5 pm daily except Monday. The information centre is here as well.

For top bush tucker, head to the *Channon Tavern (☎ 6688 6165)*, a great pub in the old butter factory.

NIGHTCAP NATIONAL PARK

This park of nearly 5000 hectares is a World Heritage area of outstanding beauty. There are three main sections.

The **Terania Creek** area, accessible from The Channon, protects a stunningly beautiful rainforest valley (some of the brush-box trees are estimated to be more than 1500 years old) and very diverse bird and animal species. From the picnic area, a 700m walk leads to **Protesters' Falls**, named after the environmentalists whose 1979 campaign to stop logging was a major factor in the creation of the national park.

Mt Nardi (800m), a steep rise 12km from Nimbin, has thick forest and good views. There are several walking trails that lead from the summit, including a 1km walk to Mt Matheson and the beautiful **Pholis Walk**, off the track to Mt Matheson. The views from **Pholis Gap** are particularly spectacular. From Mt Matheson, an 8km track connects with the **Nightcap Track**, a packhorse trail that was once the main route between Lismore and Murwillumbah.

The western end of the park around **Mt Burrel** (933m) is accessible only to experienced walkers.

NIMBIN
postcode 2480 • pop 1300

The Aquarius Festival of 1973 transformed the declining dairy town of Nimbin, 30km north of Lismore, into a name almost synonymous with Australia's 'back-to-the-land' counter-culture movement. It's still a very active alternative centre and there are many communes in the area. You're still likely to be asked if you want to buy some green (marijuana) as you walk along the street.

Orientation & Information
Despite the size of its reputation, Nimbin is a tiny village – admittedly somewhat larger than life. Cullen St is the main street.

The Nimbin Tourist Connexion (☎ 6689 1764), at the northern end of Cullen St, has tourist information. The staff are helpful and friendly and can also sell Willing Workers On Organic Farms (WWOOF) memberships – there are over 90 participating farms in the Nimbin region.

Look out for a copy of the booklet *Nimbin & Environs* for $3. It has guides to local sights and services and gives the local history. *Nimbin News,* the community newspaper, is also essential reading.

Things to See & Do
The weird and wonderful **Nimbin Museum** is on Cullen St – just look for the building

with the painted combi van crashing through it. It's worth a visit for the conversations you'll have before you get through the door. Admission is by donation.

Many people come to the area to visit **Djanbung Gardens** (☎ 6689 1755), a permaculture education centre established by Robyn Francis, a disciple of permaculture guru Bill Mollison. The gardens are a five-minute walk from the town centre on Cecil St; there are guided tours at 10.30 am on Tuesday and Thursday ($10).

The town's biggest employer is the **Rainbow Power Company** (☎ 6689 1430). The address (No 1 Alternative Way) says a fair bit about the organisation. It designs and produces what it calls 'appropriate home-energy systems' that use sun, wind and water to generate electricity. These systems are sold all over the world. You can visit the complex, which is behind the caravan park – it's open from 9 am to 5 pm weekdays and until noon on Saturday.

Visitors are welcome to attend a **drumming session** in the town hall on Thursday morning; pay $5 and you can join in the dancing. There's also a monthly party happening somewhere in town to celebrate the relevant month's star sign – contact the Tourist Connexion for further details.

Nimbin holds a **market** on the third Sunday of the month at the Community Centre. You may catch a band playing afterwards.

Organised Tours
Nimbin Explorer Tours (☎ 6689 1557) has two-hour culture and history tours of the Nimbin area for $18.

Special Events
There's an annual Mardi Grass Festival at the end of April, which culminates in the famous Marijuana Harvest Ball.

Places to Stay
The basic *Nimbin Holiday Caravan Park* (☎ 6689 1402) is right next to the local swimming pool and close to the bowling club – head north down Cullen St, curving right past the Nimbin (Freemasons) Hotel. Sites cost $14, on-site vans $32.

NORTH COAST

Granny's Farm (☎ *6689 1333)* is a relaxed hostel surrounded by farmland, with platypus in the nearby creek. It also has a saltwater swimming pool. Dorm beds cost $15, doubles $35. You can also camp by the creek for $8 per person. To get there, go north along Cullen St and turn left just before the bridge over the creek.

The Rectory (☎ *6689 0303, 23a Cullen St),* next to the Anglican church, has budget guesthouse accommodation in an old Queenslander-style house for $35 a double ($120 per week).

On the road into town from Lismore, *Grey Gum Lodge* (☎ *6689 1713)* is a pleasant old weatherboard house with a great veranda out the front where meals are served. Singles/doubles cost $25/45 (plus $5 for breakfast). Other meals are also available, and it's licensed.

Places to Eat

The inviting *Rainbow Cafe,* in the centre of town on Cullen St, has no doubt had some serious assaults on its range of delicious cakes. It also has various vegetarian snacks and meals for around $6. *The Cage,* at the Community Centre, also on Cullen St, is another good option for vegetarians; it's generally open only on weekdays. The food is a treat, especially the lovely laksa.

Close by, *Nimbin Pizza & Trattoria* has pasta starting at $8.50.

Oasis Cafe, next to the Tourist Connexion, serves up good coffee, cake and savoury pastries. Also good for a coffee is the *Nimbin Espresso Bar,* at the other end of Cullen St.

Entertainment

If there's a *dance* at the town hall, don't miss the opportunity to meet up with the friendly people from the country around Nimbin.

The *Nimbin (Freemasons) Hotel* often has music and the *Bush Theatre & Cafe,* at the old butter factory near the bridge at the northern end of town, has films at 7.30 pm on Friday and Saturday and at 6.30 pm Sunday.

Getting There & Away

The Nimbin Shuttle (☎ 6680 9189) operates between Byron Bay and Nimbin ($12),

leaving from the main bus stop on Jonson St in Byron Bay at 10 am daily (except Sunday). Marsh's Bus Service calls at Nimbin on its Murwillumbah to Lismore route.

The main routes to Nimbin are from Lismore to the south and off the Murwillumbah to Kyogle road, 23km west of Uki.

AROUND NIMBIN

The country around Nimbin is superb. **Nimbin Rocks,** an Aboriginal sacred site, lies about 6km south of town, well signposted off Stony Chute (Kyogle) Rd. **Hanging Rock Creek** has falls and a good swimming hole; take the road through Stony Chute for 14km, turn right at the Barker's Vale sign, then left onto Williams Rd; the falls are nearby on the right.

See the Nightcap National Park section earlier in this chapter for information on Mt Nardi.

BANGALOW

postcode 2479

This lovely little town in the hills, about 14km inland from Byron Bay, has a good choice of eateries for a town of its size, as well as antique and craft shops. On the fourth Sunday of the month, there's an excellent **market** at the sports oval.

Places to Stay

Nestled on Byron Creek's banks, *Riverview* (☎ *6687 1317, 99 Byron St)* is a delightful, well-restored house with polished floorboards, wide verandas and lovely gardens. B&B costs from $80/120 a single/double.

Two kilometres out of Bangalow, just off Possum Creek Rd, *Possum Creek Lodge* (☎ *6687 1188)* is a lovely old homestead perched high on a ridge with terrific 360° views. Rates for a double start at $145 midweek, including a delicious breakfast served on the veranda.

Places to Eat

There's a good cluster of cafes and restaurants on the main street (Byron St), such as the *Urban Cafe* (☎ *6687 2678),* a nice bright spot for lunch, with burgers for around $8 and other dishes such as Thai chicken salad for $10. It's also open daily except Monday for breakfast, and for dinner from Thursday to Saturday.

Ruby's Restaurant (☎ 6687 2180) is at the lovely Bangalow Hotel, which still retains much of its 1940s charm. Mains cost $13 to $16. Its open-air deck is perfect for dining on balmy evenings.

A terrific restaurant for dinner is *Wild About Food (☎ 6687 2555)*, an inviting BYO place with changing art exhibitions. It specialises in seafood; mains on the innovative menu cost $13 to $18.

A few doors up is *The Get Stuffed Gourmet* and *I Scream For Sweets*. They really love their food in this town.

MULLUMBIMBY
postcode 2482 • pop 2700

This pleasant little town, known simply as Mullum, is in subtropical countryside 4km off the Pacific Hwy between Bangalow and Brunswick Heads. The distinctive cone of Mt Chincogan is just outside the town. Perhaps best known for its marijuana ('Mullumbimby Madness'), it's a centre for a long-established farming community as well as for the alternative folk from nearby areas.

Burringbar St is the main shopping street, which runs off Dalley St, the main road through town.

Things to See & Do

There's a short **walk** through rainforest by the Brunswick River.

The **Brunswick Valley Historical Society Museum** (☎ 6684 1149), open from 11 am to 3 pm on Friday and from 9 am to noon on market days, is off the southern end of Stuart St in the old post office.

Although none are very grand, Mullumbimby has some nice old buildings and their setting in this quiet town makes them seem even finer. **Cedar House**, at 140 Dalley St, has been recommended for National Trust listing. It houses an antique shop.

Places to Stay

North of Mullumbimby, 12km out on Main Arm Rd, *Maca's Camping Ground (☎ 6684 5211)* is an idyllic place. On a macadamia-nut plantation, under the lee of hills lush with rainforest, it's a relaxed spot with a lot of room to move. While it's nothing like a commercial caravan park, the facilities are quite good, with a communal kitchen, hot showers and a laundry. It costs $6/2 for adults/children and you'll need to bring your food. To get here, take Main Arm Rd out of Mullumbimby, go through Main Arm, then Upper Main Arm, and Maca's is on the right just past the school. There are blue 'Camping' signs at the intersections pointing the way.

Back in town, accommodation is available at the inviting *Commercial Hotel (☎ 6684 3229)*, on the corner of Burringbar and Stuart Sts, where singles/doubles cost $25/40 (shared bathroom). The *Mullumbimby Motel (☎ 6684 2387, 121 Dalley St)* has rooms starting at $40/45 (about $75 at peak times).

Places to Eat

The appropriately named *Popular Cafe*, on Burringbar St, charges just $2 for great burgers, with a choice of beef, chicken, bacon, fish, tofu, steak, soy or egg. *Buon Appetito*, on Stuart St, serves up kebabs (including a vegetarian option) during the day for around $4.50, and pizzas to eat there or take away. Also on Stuart St, *Cafe Al Dente (☎ 6684 3676)* is a bustling, cosmopolitan place with an inviting Mediterranean menu. Mains cost $9 to $15.

There's a good Thai menu at *Cafe Tee Pee (☎ 6684 2618, 72a Burringbar St)*, where mains cost $10 to $13. The *Commercial Hotel* and the *Chincogan Tavern*, on the corner of Dalley and Burringbar Sts, have inexpensive counter meals and live music a couple of nights a week.

Getting There & Away

No buses go through town – you have to travel to Brunswick Heads ($4) with Brunswick Valley Coaches (BVC; ☎ 6685 1385) to connect to any other town, including Byron Bay. Kirklands picks up from Brunswick Heads to go to Lismore ($11.70) and Brisbane ($23.60). Mullumbimby Travel (☎ 6684 1089), on Stuart St, is the Kirklands agent. There are approximately four Kirklands buses a day, but only some of the BVC buses connect to them, so be sure to call and check the times.

Mullumbimby is on the Sydney ($92) to Murwillumbah railway.

The most direct road route to Mullumbimby from the Pacific Hwy turns off just south of Brunswick Heads, but it's worth taking the longer but prettier Tunnel Rd route, which leaves the highway north of Brunswick Heads, near the Ocean Shores turn-off. There's also the Coolaman Scenic Drive, which leaves the highway between Bangalow and the Byron Bay turn-off. For a superbly scenic drive to Uki and Mt Warning, head out to Upper Main Arm, pass Maca's Camping Ground (see Places to Stay earlier in this section for directions) and follow the unsealed road through the Nullum State Forest. Keep to the main road and watch for signposts at the few ambiguous intersections. It's a narrow road and steep where it crosses the range, but in dry weather it's OK if you take it easy and watch out for logging trucks. Don't try it after rain or you stand a good chance of sliding off the mountain.

WHIAN WHIAN STATE FOREST

Whian Whian State Forest is west of Mullumbimby and adjoins the south-eastern side of Nightcap National Park. On the south-eastern side of the state forest, **Minyon Falls** plunges 100m into a rainforest gorge and the surrounding area is a flora reserve with several walking tracks.

Access to the reserve is from Minyon Dr, which cuts across the south-eastern corner of the state forest. Peates Mountain Rd runs off Minyon Dr and heads north to **Peates Mountain Lookout**, with views to the coast and on to *Rummery Park*, a Forestry Commission camp site with pit toilets and cold showers. Koalas live in the nearby forest. The eastern end of the Nightcap Track walking trail emerges on the road beyond Rummery Park.

The south-western corner of Whian Whian is the **Big Scrub Flora Reserve**, the largest surviving chunk of the vegetation that once covered the Richmond Valley.

UKI
postcode 2482 • pop 200

Uki (pronounced uke-eye) is a pretty village dominated by the peak of Mt Warning. It's most famous for its big market, held at the old buttery on the third Sunday of the month. The Trading Post (☎ 6679 5351) restaurant is a helpful information centre.

At *Uki Village Guesthouse (☎ 6679 5777)*, next to the Trading Post in an old weatherboard home, B&B costs from $45 a double.

The licensed *Trading Post* serves light meals and Devonshire teas daily except Monday and is open for dinner on Saturday.

There are a number of other places to stay in the area, including the *Midginbil Hill Farm Resort (☎ 6679 7158)*, with B&B for $100 a double ($160 including dinner). Activities include horse riding ($20) and canoeing on the Clarrie Hall dam.

Marsh's Bus Service stops at Uki on the run between Murwillumbah and Lismore, weekdays only.

Uki is on the main road between Murwillumbah and Kyogle. The turn-off to Mt Warning is 4km north of Uki; the turn-off to Blue Knob and Nimbin is 23km south-west of Uki.

MT WARNING NATIONAL PARK

The dramatic peak of Mt Warning (1156m) dominates the whole district. It was named by Cook as a landmark for avoiding Point Danger off Tweed Heads. The mountain is the former central magma chamber of an immense volcano formed more than 20 million years ago. It once covered an area of more than 4000 sq km, stretching from Coraki in the south to Beenleigh in the north and from Kyogle in the west to an eastern rim now covered by the ocean. Erosion has since carved out the deep Tweed and Oxley Valleys around Mt Warning, but sections of the flanks survive as the Nightcap Range in the south and parts of the Border Ranges to the north.

The road into the national park runs off the road between Murwillumbah and Uki. It's about a 4.5km walk from the car park to the summit, much of it through rainforest.

The final section is steep (to put it mildly), so allow five hours for the return trip and take water. If you're on the summit at dawn you'll be the first person on the Australian mainland to see the sun's rays that day! The trail is well marked, but you'll need a torch if you're climbing at night (to reach the summit at dawn).

Even if you don't want to climb Mt Warning it's worth visiting for the superb rainforest in this World Heritage area. There's a short walking track near the car park.

Places to Stay

You can't camp at Mt Warning but the *Mt Warning Caravan Park & Tourist Retreat (☎ 6679 5120)*, on the Mt Warning approach road, has tent sites ($12), on-site vans (from $30) and cabins ($40 to $60). There are kitchen facilities and a well-stocked kiosk.

Getting There & Away

Marsh's Bus Service can drop you at the turn-off to Mt Warning. From there it's about a 5km walk to the base of the mountain. The bus leaves Murwillumbah at around 7 am and can pick you up from the turn-off at about 4 pm. Call to confirm these times as they can change.

MURWILLUMBAH

postcode 2482 • pop 9000

Murwillumbah is in an area of banana and sugar-cane plantations in the broad Tweed Valley, and is the main town in this part of the north coast hinterland. It's also within reach of Mt Warning and the spectacular NSW-Queensland Border Ranges. You can cross into Queensland by the Numinbah Rd through the ranges between the Springbrook and Lamington areas.

Information

The tourist information centre (☎ 6672 1340), on the Pacific Hwy near the train station, incorporates the NPWS office, so there's plenty of information on the national parks in the area as well as a great rainforest display. It's open from 9 am to 4.30 pm daily.

Things to see & Do

The excellent **Tweed River Regional Art Gallery** is just up Tumbulgum Rd from the hostel. As well as a portrait collection and works relating to the Tweed area, there are often interesting temporary exhibitions. It's open from 10 am to 5 pm Wednesday to Sunday (free). The gallery administers Australia's richest prize for traditional portraiture: the $100,000 Doug Moran Prize. The works of past winners are on display.

The **Tweed Historical Museum** is on Queensland Rd and is open from 11 am to 4 pm on Wednesday and Friday ($2). The century-old **Condong Sugar Mill** (☎ 6672 2244), 5km north of Murwillumbah, has guided tours ($4/2.50 for adults/children) daily during the crushing season, from approximately July to November.

Tropical Fruit World, well signposted off the highway about 15 minutes north of Murwillumbah, is a good place to take the kids, with some rides and native animals as well as many varieties of tropical fruit (and ice cream to die for). It's open from 10 am to 5 pm daily ($20/12, or $50 for families).

Places to Stay

The *Mt Warning/Murwillumbah YHA Backpackers (☎ 6672 3763, 1 Tumbulgum Rd)* has a great location beside the Tweed River, with views over to Mt Warning from the veranda. Owner Tassie runs a friendly house with lots of activities, including free canoes and a rowing boat plus bike hire for $5 a day. Dorm beds cost $18, singles/twins $21/36. If you stay two nights, they'll throw in free transport to and from Mt Warning, which is a good deal as it's not easy to get there without your own transport.

Several pubs have accommodation, including the solid, recently renovated *Imperial Hotel (☎ 6672 1036)*, on Murwillumbah St across from the post office. Singles/doubles cost $20/34.

Motels include the *Murwillumbah Motor Inn (☎ 6672 2022)*, on the corner of Wollumbin and Byangum Sts, which has doubles for $62 to $77, or the more basic *Town Motel (☎ 6672 1633)*, on Wharf St, where you can score a double for $50.

NORTH COAST

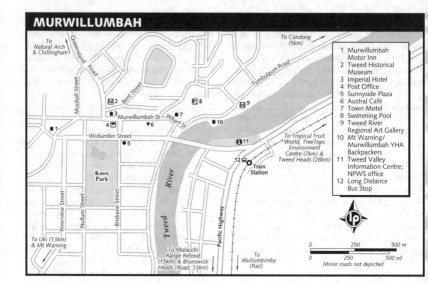

MURWILLUMBAH

1	Murwillumbah Motor Inn
2	Tweed Historical Museum
3	Imperial Hotel
4	Post Office
5	Sunnyside Plaza
6	Austral Café
7	Town Motel
8	Swimming Pool
9	Tweed River Regional Art Gallery
10	Mt Warning/ Murwillumbah YHA Backpackers
11	Tweed Valley Information Centre; NPWS office
12	Long Distance Bus Stop

Seven kilometres north of town near Condong, *TreeTops Environment Centre* (☎ 6672 3068), on Clothiers Creek Rd, has a gallery, an excellent restaurant (dine alfresco or fireside, depending on the weather) and five delightful timber lodges in a lovely setting. B&B doubles cost $150 to $220.

Malacchi Range Retreat (☎ 6677 1031) has a magnificent two-bedroom house with superb views over lush rainforest. There's a minimum two-night stay and it costs $200 per night between four people midweek ($150 for two adults), which is great value. The property is 15km south of Murwillumbah on Dixons Rd.

Places to Eat

The *Eatery*, at the Town Motel, is open for lunch every day and dinner on Friday and Saturday. It has a good Aussie menu and is BYO; evening mains cost $12 to $16.

For some great old-fashioned baked goods in a 1950s setting, try the *Austral Cafe* on Murwillumbah St.

Getting There & Away

This is the end of the northern rail line from Sydney ($98). There's a daily train that connects with a bus to the Gold Coast and Brisbane.

Murwillumbah is served by nearly all the buses on the Sydney ($69) to Brisbane ($19) coastal run. Marsh's Bus Service operates a weekday bus to Uki ($4.80), Nimbin ($10.30) and Lismore ($14.20). It leaves from opposite the Sunnyside Plaza at 7 am.

BORDER RANGES NATIONAL PARK

The Border Ranges National Park, a World Heritage Area of 31,500 hectares, covers the NSW side of the McPherson Range, which runs along the NSW-Queensland border, and some of its outlying spurs. The park's wetter areas protect large tracts of superb rainforest and it has been estimated that a quarter of all bird species in Australia can be found in the park.

There are three main sections. The eastern section, which includes the escarpments of the massive Mt Warning caldera, is the most easily accessible, via the Tweed Range Scenic Drive. The smaller central section is accessible from the Lions Rd, which turns off the Kyogle-Woodenbong road 22km north of Kyogle. The large and rugged western section is almost inaccessible except to well-equipped bushwalkers, but there are good views of its peaks from the Kyogle to Woodenbong road.

The **Tweed Range Scenic Drive** – gravel but useable in all weather – loops through the park from Lillian Rock (midway between Uki and Kyogle) to Wiangaree (north of Kyogle on the Woodenbong road). The signposting on access roads isn't good (when in doubt take roads signposted to the national park), but it's well worth the effort of finding it. The road is unsuitable for caravans and large vehicles.

The road runs through mountain forest most of the way, with steep hills and breathtaking lookouts over the Tweed Valley to Mt Warning and the coast. The adrenaline-charging walk out to the crag called **The Pinnacle** – about half an hour's walk from the road and back – is not for vertigo sufferers! At **Antarctic Beech** there is, not surprisingly, a forest of Antarctic beeches. Some of these trees are more than 2000 years old. From here, a walking track (about 5km) leads down to **Brindle Creek**, where there is stunningly beautiful rainforest and a picnic area. The road also runs down to Brindle Creek.

From the **Sheepstation Creek** camp site a walking track connects with the Caldera Rim Walk (three or four days) in Lamington National Park, over the border in Queensland.

Mebbin State Forest is by the eastern section of the Border Ranges National Park – this is the bush you will see if you dare to look down when you're on The Pinnacle.

Places to Stay

There are a couple of NPWS *camp sites* on the Tweed Range Scenic Drive. *Sheepstation Creek* is about 15km north of the turnoff at Wiangaree, and *Forest Tops* is 6km farther on, high on the range. There are toilets but no showers and a camping fee of $3 per person is required. Tank water might be available but it's best to BYO. There's free camping at *Byrill Creek*, on the eastern side of Mebbin State Forest.

New England

New England is the area on top of the Great Dividing Range, stretching north from around Newcastle to the Queensland border. It's a vast tableland of sheep and cattle country with many good bushwalking areas, photogenic scenery and, unlike much of Australia, four distinct seasons. If you're travelling along the eastern seaboard, it's worth taking a longer route through an inland area like New England now and then to get a glimpse of noncoastal Australia – which has a different way of life, is at least as scenic as the coast and suffers from a great deal less tourist hype.

History

Graziers first came to New England in the 1830s in search of new land. At the time it was illegal for colonists to venture beyond the Hunter Valley and these graziers became known as squatters because they 'squatted' on land that didn't belong to them. Although they were technically outlaws, many were eventually granted long leases on huge tracts of land and became influential citizens of the colony.

New England was once called New Caledonia and that name should have stuck because of the large numbers of Scottish people involved in the area's settlement. Place names reflect this association – Armidale, Inverell and Glen Innes, which even has its own ring of Celtic-style 'standing stones'.

Geography

North of Armidale the plateau rises steeply and snowfalls are common in winter. The eastern edge of the tableland ends at a steep and often densely forested escarpment, dropping down to the coastal plains below. Along this edge is a string of fine national parks, some of them World Heritage areas. Gorges and waterfalls are common features and most parks offer at least basic camping. The western side of the tableland drops down to the plains.

HIGHLIGHTS

- People watching at the Tamworth Country Music Festival
- Appreciating autumn colours in Armidale
- White-water rafting on the Nymboida River
- Gazing on the impressive Wollomombi Falls, especially after rain
- Visiting the spectacular World Heritage-listed national parks, such as Gibraltar Range and Washpool

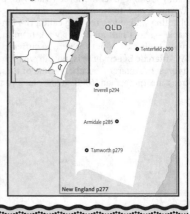

Activities

Bushwalking Most of New England's national parks offer walking.

White-Water Canoeing & Rafting The Nymboida River is popular for both canoeing and white-water rafting. Every summer, water is released from Copeton Dam (near Inverell), turning part of the Gwydir River into a challenging white-water course.

Two companies that offer rafting in New England are WOW Rafting (☎ 6651 4066) and Wildwater Adventures (☎ 6653 3500), both based in Coffs Harbour (see the North Coast chapter).

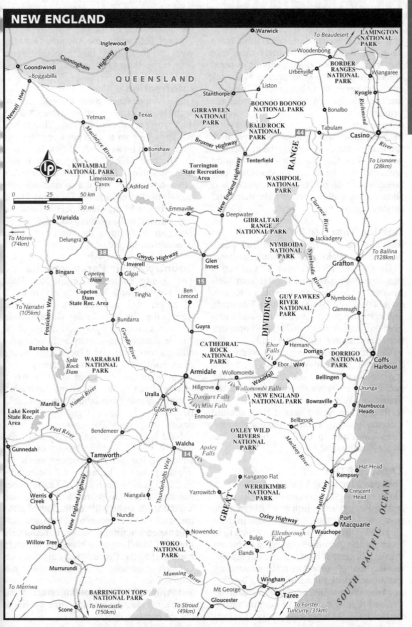

Horse Riding Steve Langley (☎ 6732 1599), based near Glen Innes, arranges 'pub crawls on horseback', lasting from three days to a week. These leisurely rides take you from village to village, staying at pubs, and cost around $1000 per person for a week (including everything but booze). The rides are suitable for any standard of rider (or drinker).

Fishing Trout fishing is popular and there are many stocked streams – the closed season is from the Queen's Birthday long weekend in June to the Labour Day long weekend in October. Other species are also fished. Information centres have maps and further details.

Getting There & Away

The airports at Armidale and Tamworth provide daily links to Sydney and Brisbane.

Greyhound Pioneer and McCafferty's buses run through New England from Melbourne or Sydney to Brisbane. Kean's (☎ 1800 625 587) runs between Tamworth and Port Macquarie via Armidale and Coffs Harbour. Kirklands (☎ 6622 1499) operates between Lismore and Tenterfield.

Countrylink trains run from Sydney to Tamworth ($67) and Armidale ($75). Countrylink buses connect with the trains for the run from Tamworth to Inverell along the Fossickers Way and from Armidale to Tenterfield up the New England Hwy. A third Countrylink bus service passes through Glen Innes and Inverell on the route between Grafton and Moree.

TAMWORTH

postcode 2340 • pop 35,000

On the dry western slopes of the Great Dividing Range, Tamworth has little in common with the other major towns in New England. This is cattle country, which ticks over to the plaintive twang of country music. The area's 'heritage' doesn't revolve around Scottish ancestors and misty moors, but around steel guitars and riding boots.

In the 1960s a Tamworth radio station organised regular concerts of country music, and in 1973 the first Australasian Country Music Awards were held. These are now the centrepiece of the big Country Music Festival, held around the Australia Day long weekend in January (see Special Events later in the Tamworth section).

Information

Guitar-shaped things are all the rage, starting with the tourist information centre (☎ 6755 4300), on the corner of Peel and Murray Sts. It's open 8.30 am to 4.35 pm weekdays and 9 am to 5 pm on weekends. Pick up a map of the Heritage Walk (1½ hours), which begins at the junction of Brisbane St and Kable Ave in the city centre. You'll also find information on the longer Kamilaroi Walking Track, which begins at the Oxley Scenic Lookout, high on a hill at the northern end of White St. There are also maps of day tours that can be done around the area.

Country Music Paraphernalia

The Country Collection, on the New England Hwy in South Tamworth, 4.5km south of the centre, is not hard to spot – out the front is the 12m-high **Golden Guitar**. Inside is a wax museum displaying effigies of 20 Aussie country-music stars and, incongruously, a rock, gem and mineral display. It's open daily ($4/2 for adults/children).

For some more serious country-music history, head to the excellent **Australian Country Music Foundation Museum** at 93 Brisbane St. It's open 10 am to 2 pm Monday to Saturday ($5/3).

Near the corner of Kable Ave and Brisbane St you'll find the **Hands of Fame**, which are handprints of country music luminaries. Not to be outdone, Tattersall's Hotel on Peel St has **Noses of Fame**! Other country music memorabilia you'll see around town include the **collection of photos** at the Good Companions Hotel, the **guitar-shaped swimming pool** at the Alandale Flag Inn Motel, and the **Hawking Brothers memorial** at the Country Capital Motel on Goonoo Goonoo (pronounced gun-na-g'noo) Rd.

Tamworth's four **recording studios** are open for inspection by appointment – ask at the information centre.

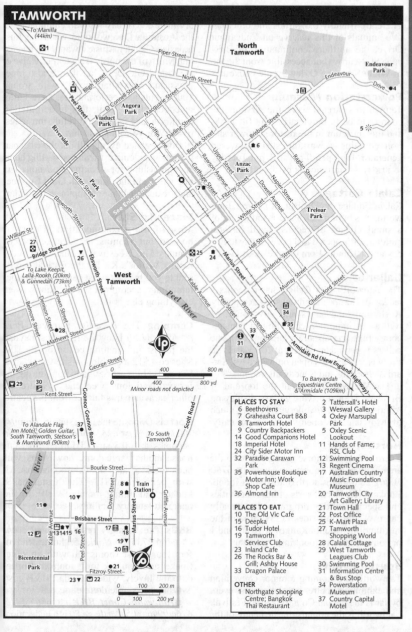

TAMWORTH

To Manilla
(44km)

North
Tamworth

Piper Street

Bligh Street

North Street

Peel Street

Connell Street

Endeavour

Endeavour
Park

Drive

Angora
Park

Macquarie Street

Viaduct
Park

Griffin Lane

Darling Street

Brisbane Street

Riverside

Carter Street

Park

Bourke Street

Upper Street

Rawson Avenue

Anzac
Park

Napier Street

Raglan Street

Ebsworth Street

Carthage Street

Fitzroy Street

White Street

Dowell Avenue

Treloar
Park

William St

Bridge Street

Ebsworth Street

Marius Street

Hill Street

Roderick Street

To Lake Keepit,
Lalla Rookh (20km)
& Gunnedah (73km)

West
Tamworth

Kable Avenue

Peel Street

Byrnes Avenue

Murray Street

Chelmsford Street

Gipps Street

Crown Street

Denison Street

Belmore Street

Mathews Street

Peel River

East Street

Armidale Rd (New England Highway)

Park Street

George Street

Kent Street

Goonoo Goonoo Road

0   400   800 m
0   400   800 yd
Minor roads not depicted

To Banyandah
Equestrian Centre
& Armidale (109km)

To Alandale Flag
Inn Motel, Golden Guitar,
South Tamworth, Stetson's
& Murrurundi (90km)

Scott Road

To South
Tamworth

Peel River

Bourke Street

Dowe Street

Train
Station

Griffin Avenue

Marius Street

Brisbane Street

Kable Avenue

Peel Street

Bicentennial
Park

Fitzroy Street

0   100   200 m
0   100   200 yd

PLACES TO STAY
6 Beethovens
7 Graheasha Court B&B
8 Tamworth Hotel
9 Country Backpackers
14 Good Companions Hotel
18 Imperial Hotel
24 City Sider Motor Inn
32 Paradise Caravan
    Park
35 Powerhouse Boutique
    Motor Inn; Work
    Shop Cafe
36 Almond Inn

PLACES TO EAT
10 The Old Vic Cafe
15 Deepka
16 Tudor Hotel
19 Tamworth
    Services Club
23 Inland Cafe
26 The Rocks Bar &
    Grill; Ashby House
33 Dragon Palace

OTHER
1 Northgate Shopping
   Centre; Bangkok
   Thai Restaurant
2 Tattersall's Hotel
3 Weswal Gallery
4 Oxley Marsupial
   Park
5 Oxley Scenic
   Lookout
11 Hands of Fame;
    RSL Club
12 Swimming Pool
13 Regent Cinema
17 Australian Country
    Music Foundation
    Museum
20 Tamworth City
    Art Gallery; Library
21 Town Hall
22 Post Office
25 K-Mart Plaza
27 Tamworth
    Shopping World
28 Calala Cottage
29 West Tamworth
    Leagues Club
30 Swimming Pool
31 Information Centre
    & Bus Stop
34 Powerstation
    Museum
37 Country Capital
    Motel

Oxley Marsupial Park

There are friendly kangaroos and other native animals at this reserve on Endeavour Drive, the northern continuation of Brisbane St. Nearby (but accessible from the top of White St) is the **Oxley Scenic Lookout**.

Powerstation Museum

Tamworth's streets were the first in the country to be lit by electric light (in 1888) and this museum in the restored power station contains a working steam-powered generator. It's open 9 am to 1 pm Tuesday to Friday – admission is by donation.

Calala Cottage

Calala Cottage, on Denison St in West Tamworth, was built in 1875 and is today part of a small cluster of reconstructed historic buildings. It's open 2 to 4 pm Tuesday to Friday and 10 am to 4 pm on weekends ($4/1).

Galleries

The **Tamworth City Gallery** has a good selection of European paintings, contemporary Australian landscapes and silverware, as well as an important collection of contemporary fibre art (tapestries, applique etc). The gallery is behind the library at 203 Marius St. Entry is free and it's open on weekdays, Saturday morning and Sunday afternoon.

The **Weswal Gallery**, at the top end of Brisbane St, is a private gallery displaying painting, pottery, jewellery and crafts, much of it for sale. It's open 9 am to 5 pm daily.

Horse Riding

There are several horse riding outfits in the area. Banyandah Equestrian Centre (☎ 6760 3006), 20 minutes north of town on Moonbi Lookout Rd, has all sorts of horse activities and special holiday programs. It normally has two-hour trail rides ($25) through the surrounding Moonbi Ranges at 10 am and 1 pm on weekends – bookings necessary.

Special Events

Tamworth is becoming a major convention and exhibition centre, but the biggest event by far is the annual Country Music Festival. Tamworth is the country-music centre of the nation, an antipodean Nashville. Each January there's a 10-day festival, culminating in the Australia Day weekend when the Australasian Country Music Awards are handed out. Much of the music is pretty derivative of the Grand Ole Opry, but there's also bluegrass and Australian styles. With around 1000 events and performances, there's a lot to choose from. Still, this is definitely a country-music festival, not a folk-music festival. Wear your fanciest shirt.

Horse-related events fill out the calendar, including a racing carnival and cutting horse championships for working stockhorses in February, and the Tamworth Gold Cup race and the quarter-horse championships in May.

Places to Stay

Most of the accommodation in town is booked out months in advance for the Country Music Festival in January. If out of luck, a Visitor's Kit for the festival can be sent to you by the tourist centre – it outlines temporary accommodation options when everything else is full.

Camping The *Paradise Caravan Park* (☎ 6766 3120) is by the river, just beyond the tourist information centre on Peel St. Sites cost $12 a double, on-site vans start at $31 and cabins are $50 (add 25% during the festival and long weekends). There are other caravan parks farther from the centre.

Hostels Opposite the train station, *Country Backpackers* (☎ 6761 2600, 169 Marius St) occupies a 100-year-old former boarding house and has large dorms downstairs, with beds for $15, and smaller rooms upstairs, with beds from $18. The hostel has a kitchen and dining room as well as coin-operated laundry facilities.

B&Bs The lovingly restored *Beethovens* (☎ 6766 2735, 66 Napier St) homestead offers four guest rooms, all with en suites (make sure you ask for a room that opens onto the lovely, wide veranda). B&B costs $90/110 per single/double.

Graheasha Court B&B (☎ 6766 5115, 6766 9996, 105 Carthage St) is a Federation-era home with (very feminine) bedrooms for $80 a double. Better value is the separate studio loft with en suite for $100.

Lalla Rookh (☎ 6768 0216), on Werris Creek Rd in Duri, 20km south of Tamworth, is a modern home chock full of antiques and old books. B&B costs $86 a double.

Farmstays About 50km from town near Dungowan, *Leconfield (☎ 6769 4230)* is a jackaroo and jillaroo school. The owners offer an excellent-value 11-day program for $550, which includes all food, accommodation, horse riding and activities such as milking cows and mustering. Call for directions, or they'll pick you up from Tamworth for free.

Hotels The *Tamworth (☎ 6766 2923)*, on Marius St opposite the train station, is the pick of the pubs in town. It's been well renovated with plenty of inviting eating areas. Singles/doubles go for $28/36. Other city-centre pubs include the *Good Companions (☎ 6766 2850)* on Brisbane St ($20/40) and the *Imperial (☎ 6766 2613)*, on the corner of Brisbane and Marius Sts ($25/40).

Motels Tamworth's dozens of motels are concentrated along the New England Hwy in South Tamworth and on the way out to Armidale. At off-peak times, doubles can be found for $45 at motels such as the *Almond Inn (☎ 6766 1088, 389 Armidale Rd)*. If you can afford a bit more, the *City Sider Motor Inn (☎ 6766 4777, 237 Marius St)* is much better value, with spacious, light rooms for $62/72. Tamworth's, top-of-the-range, almost five-star hotel is the *Powerhouse Boutique Motor Inn (☎ 6766 7000)*, Marius St, where rooms cost $105 to $180.

Places to Eat
Like most country towns, the clubs are the place to go for the best meal deals. These include the *Tamworth Services Club* on Marius St and the *RSL Club* (which excels in fish dishes), near the Hands of Fame on Kable Ave. Pubs, such as the *Tudor* on Peel St, which has $5 lunch specials, are also good value.

If the clatter of poker machines is not your scene, there are plenty of cafes and small restaurants. One of the most popular is the slick *Inland Cafe (☎ 6761 2882, 407 Peel St)*, a stylish place perfect for breakfast (from 7 am) or some delicious cake ($6) and coffee. It's also open for lunch daily and dinner from Thursday to Saturday.

Another good downtown spot with similar opening hours is *The Old Vic Cafe (☎ 6766 3435, 261 Peel St)*, where dark-wood furniture contributes to the cosy atmosphere. Lunch mains cost $7 to $15.

There's good Indian food at *Deepka (☎ 6766 1771, 23 Brisbane St)*, where most mains cost around $11. *Dragon Palace (☎ 6766 6999, 528 Peel St)* is one of the best regarded Chinese restaurants in town. Mains cost $9 to $19. If Thai's more your thing, try the excellent *Bangkok Thai Restaurant (☎ 6761 3098)* at Northgate Shopping Centre. There are plenty of mains for around $10 and it's also a good option for vegetarians.

Those with a cowboy/cowgirl fantasy can head out to *Stetson's (☎ 6762 2238)*, behind the McDonald's on Goonoo Goonoo Rd, which offers a 'Wild West dining adventure' to go with your $20 (massive) steak.

Definitely one of the best places to dine is the *Work Shop Cafe (☎ 6766 7000)* at the Powerhouse Motel. There's an excellent outdoor eating area, the service is first rate and the food's not bad either (although vegos may be left wanting). Mains cost $14 to $21.

Another good upmarket option is *The Rocks Bar & Grill (☎ 6762 0033, 83–85 Ebsworth St)* at Ashby House. Barramundi's a speciality ($20) and other mains cost $15 to $20.

Entertainment
There's usually some live music happening somewhere in town just about every night. The *Imperial* and the *Good Companions* ('the Goodies') often have bands. Backpackers are drawn to the attractive *Tamworth Hotel*, and the *West Tamworth Leagues Club* on Phillip St is also popular. The *RSL Club* is a happening venue for country and western music, especially during the festival.

The *Regent Cinema* (☎ 6766 3707), on the corner of Kable Ave and Brisbane St, has daily screenings and $6 sessions before 6 pm, Monday to Wednesday.

Getting There & Away
Impulse Airlines (☎ 13 1381) has six services a day between Tamworth and Sydney ($179), as well as flights to Brisbane ($240). Eastern Australia Airlines also operates on the Tamworth to Sydney route.

Kean's (☎ 1800 625 587) operates a bus service from Tamworth to Scone ($15), and other services from Scone to Sydney ($37). Other lines also come through on the run from Brisbane to Sydney. Buses stop at the information centre.

Tamworth is a stop on the Sydney-Armidale train line. The train station on Marius St has a Countrylink Travel Centre (☎ 6766 2357).

Getting Around
Tamworth Bus Service buses run from Kable Ave in the city centre down Goonoo Goonoo Rd to the Golden Guitar and beyond (weekdays and Saturday morning only). The information centre has timetables.

The major car-rental companies have agencies: Avis (☎ 6760 7404), Budget (☎ 6766 7255), Hertz (☎ 6761 5545) and Thrifty (☎ 6765 3699).

You can often find a taxi on Fitzroy St near the corner of Peel St. If not, phone Tamworth Radio Cabs (☎ 6766 1111).

WALCHA
postcode 2354 • pop 1800
Walcha is a small town set in pretty, rolling country on the edge of the Great Dividing Range. It lies on the Oxley Hwy about 50km east of the New England Hwy (turn off at Bendemeer). The information centre (☎ 6777 1075) is in the old primary school on the highway, called Fitzroy St as it runs through town. It's open 9 am to 4.30 pm weekdays only.

Explorer John Oxley passed through the area in 1818 and in the 1830s. It was the first part of the tablelands to be invaded by graziers bringing their herds and flocks up from the Hunter Valley. The town dates from 1845 and the 1854 **Catholic church** on South St is one of the oldest remaining buildings. **Langford**, on the southern side of the town, is a very impressive old homestead.

Walcha is the nearest town of any size to Oxley Wild Rivers and Werrikimbe National Parks. Streams in the area are well stocked with trout and the season opens in October.

Places to Stay & Eat
The *Walcha Caravan Park* (☎ 6777 2501) has tent sites for $8 and cabins from $30. The *New England Hotel/ Motel* (☎ 6777 2532) on Fitzroy St has good-value motel rooms for $38/48 a single/double, while the *Walcha Motel* (☎ 6777 2599), also on the main street, charges $50/60. *Fenwicke House* (☎ 6777 2713) is a gallery and tea-room in an old house at 23E Fitzroy St, with accommodation for $35 per person, including cooked breakfast.

The old, atmospheric *Royal Walcha Road Hotel* (☎ 6777 5829) is about 20km west on the road to Tamworth and has rooms for $60 per person, including breakfast.

The *Figtree Coffee Shoppe*, on Fitzroy St, is the place to go for good country tucker or delicious banana & mango smoothies ($4).

Getting There & Away
It seems a long way out of their way, but Kean's (☎ 1800 625 587) buses will come here on request on the run from Tamworth to Port Macquarie (via Armidale and Coffs Harbour).

If you're heading to Armidale, there's a pretty back road from Walcha to Uralla.

OXLEY WILD RIVERS NATIONAL PARK
This park of scattered sections (90,270 hectares in total) east of Armidale and Walcha contains some dramatic waterfalls and gorges. **Wollomombi Falls**, 40km east of Armidale, are among the highest in Australia, with a drop of 220m; the spectacular **Apsley Falls** are 18km east of Walcha at the southern end of the park. Down at the bottom of the gorges is a wilderness area accessible

from Raspberry Rd, which runs off the Wollomombi to Kempsey road. The Armidale National Parks & Wildlife Service (NPWS) office (☎ 6773 7211) has information.

Bloomfield's Crossing (☎ 6777 9189) is 35km north-east of Walcha and close to the park. It's a five-bedroom, self-contained house that sleeps up to 12. Rates are $80/130 a single/double. B&B is also available for $90/150 and extra meals are available (lunch $15 and dinner from $35).

WERRIKIMBE NATIONAL PARK

This rugged and spectacular park (35,180 hectares) has remote gorge walking as well as more gentle walks around the visitor areas. Access is via the Kangaroo Flat road, about 50km east of Walcha off the road to Wauchope. The Armidale NPWS office has information.

URALLA

postcode 2358 • pop 2500

A small town on the New England Hwy, Uralla is a good place to break the journey. The information centre (☎ 6778 4496) is on the highway and opens 10 am to 5 pm daily. A **market** is held on Salisbury St, across the road from the centre, on the second Saturday of each month.

Captain Thunderbolt (the dashing name taken by young Fred Ward when he turned bushranger) roamed through much of New England in the 1860s, and you'll see many sites, such as caves, rocks and lookouts, with a claimed association to the rebel.

Thunderbolt was a popular hero and seems to have performed many acts of kindness as well as robbery. He was killed by police near Uralla in 1870, and there's a **statue** of him on the highway in the town centre. The bushranger's simple **grave**, still sometimes honoured with flowers, is in the cemetery. Whether or not Thunderbolt's body lies in the grave is another matter: There's a persistent rumour that he was seen in Canada many years after the funeral.

The impressive, three-storey **McCrossin's Mill Museum**, on Salisbury St, has some Captain Thunderbolt artefacts. It's open from noon to 5 pm daily ($3.50/1 for adults/children). There's also a **Brass & Iron Lace Foundry** and museum at 6 East St, which has been operating since 1872 ($3/1), and **Hassett's Military Museum** on the highway, both open daily. Burnet's Bookshop is a large antiquarian and second-hand bookshop on the main street.

There's a **fossicking area** with a picnic spot about 5km north-west of Uralla on the Kingstown road. Also in the area is Mt Yarrowyck, with some Aboriginal **cave paintings** that can be visited. The information centre has detailed directions.

Places to Stay & Eat

In a quiet spot near a creek, *Uralla Caravan Park* (☎ 6778 4763, 17 Queen St) has tent sites for $9.50, on-site vans for $22 and en suite cabins for $35.

Thunderbolt Inn (☎ 6778 4048), on the New England Hwy (called Bridge St through town), is a good pub with singles/doubles for $20/30.

Probably the best motel value in all of New England can be found at *The Bushranger Motor Inn* (☎ 6778 3777, 37–41 Bridge St). The well-appointed rooms are huge and all have baths (or spas for slightly more); singles/doubles cost from $58/64. You needn't go far for dinner – the excellent *Stoker's on Bridge* is in an historic building on the premises, open nightly except Sunday. Mains cost $13 to $15.

Espresso Caffe, at the information centre, opens daily and has good coffee and light meals.

GOSTWYCK

If you're beginning to wonder how New England came by its name, visit Gostwyck, a little piece of England 11km east of Uralla. This hamlet is comprised of the buildings and cottages of the Gostwyck sheep station. It's unusual for an Australian village to conform to the English pattern of the squire's house surrounded by the cottages of the labourers. There are long avenues of tall trees and a gorgeous vine-covered chapel.

If you're heading to Armidale, you don't have to return to the highway. There's a more interesting back road (partly unsealed), which passes turn-offs for the **Mihi Falls**, near Enmore, and **Dangar Falls**, south of Dangarsleigh.

At the Dangars Falls turn-off you'll see a refreshingly eccentric **war memorial**, which was erected by a local landowner in honour of the people of the British Empire who 'went west' during WWI. You enter through a gate labelled Nirvana. A corporal with the same surname as the landowner is listed first on the honour roll, out of alphabetical order.

ARMIDALE
postcode 2350 • pop 22,270

The regional centre of Armidale is a popular place to stop. The altitude (1000m) means it's pleasantly cool in summer and frosty (but often sunny) in winter. The town is famous for its gorgeous autumn colours, which are at their best in late March and early April.

The town centre is attractive, with the Beardy St pedestrian mall and some well-kept old buildings. It's also a lively place, thanks to the large student population at the University of New England (UNE). Education is big business in Armidale, and there are large private boarding schools. They include The Armidale School (TAS), the imposing buildings and grounds of which can be seen along the road to Dorrigo.

Information
The information centre (☎ 6772 4655) is just north of the city centre near the corner of Marsh and Dumaresq Sts (pronounced duma-reck) Sts. It's open 9 am to 5 pm weekdays, until 4 pm on Saturday and 10 am to 4 pm on Sunday.

The NPWS office (☎ 6773 7211) is in the State Government building at 87 Faulkner St. Harvey World Travel (☎ 6774 8888) is at 109 Dangar St.

Historic Buildings
Pick up some brochures detailing the Heritage Walking Tour and the Heritage Drive from the enthusiastic staff at the information centre; just strolling down the mall is enough to whet your appetite for historic buildings. Another great way to see the

town is on the (free) Armidale Heritage Trolley Tour (☎ 1800 627 736, or book at the information centre).

Folk Museum
This well-presented museum is on the corner of Faulkner and Rusden Sts and opens from 1 to 4 pm daily. Admission is free, but donations are appreciated. The museum has an annexe in the village of Hillgrove, 30km east of Armidale, with exhibitions relating to rural industries and mining. It's open 10 am to 5 pm Friday to Monday.

Aboriginal Cultural Centre & Keeping Place
Although there are changing exhibitions, the main purpose of the cultural centre is to preserve traditions and provide facilities for study. The centre is on Kentucky St and you can visit from 9 am to 5 pm on weekdays and from 2 to 5 pm on weekends.

New England Regional Art Museum
This excellent gallery on Kentucky St houses the large Howard Hinton collection as well as more recent acquisitions. Only a small proportion of the collection can be displayed at any one time, so there are frequent changes. The museum opens from 10 am to 5 pm daily and admission is free.

University of New England
This university's administration building is **Booloominbah**, an enormous house built by a land baron in 1888; it once housed the entire university. A large stained-glass window depicts events in the life (and death, in 1885) of General Charles Gordon, one-time British governor-general of Khartoum, in the Sudan, Africa. There is a guided tour (☎ 6773 3909) of the building every Monday at 12.30 pm ($3.50). Behind Booloominbah is a **deer park**, where you'll also meet wallabies.

There are several **museums** at UNE. The Zoology Museum in the Department of Zoology opens on weekday afternoons. Admission is free, as it is at the Museum of Antiquities in the arts building, also open on weekdays.

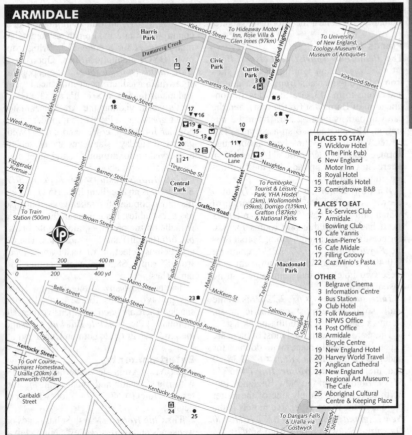

ARMIDALE

PLACES TO STAY
5 Wicklow Hotel
   (The Pink Pub)
6 New England
   Motor Inn
8 Royal Hotel
15 Tattersalls Hotel
23 Comeytrowe B&B

PLACES TO EAT
2 Ex-Services Club
7 Armidale
   Bowling Club
10 Cafe Yannis
11 Jean-Pierre's
16 Cafe Midale
17 Filling Groovy
22 Caz Minio's Pasta

OTHER
1 Belgrave Cinema
3 Information Centre
4 Bus Station
9 Club Hotel
12 Folk Museum
13 NPWS Office
14 Post Office
18 Armidale
   Bicycle Centre
19 New England Hotel
20 Harvey World Travel
21 Anglican Cathedral
24 New England
   Regional Art Museum;
   The Cafe
25 Aboriginal Cultural
   Centre & Keeping Place

Market

A market is held in the mall in Beardy St on the last Sunday of the month.

Activities

Pick up a free copy of *Fishing in the New England Region* from the information centre, a great guide to angling in the area. The Armidale Golf Course (☎ 6772 5837) charges $16 for 18 holes and hires out clubs.

The Armidale Walking Track takes you through parks to the Armidale State Forest. The information centre sells a good range of maps covering the region's national parks.

Organised Tours

Highly recommended, Wilderness Rides (☎ 6778 2172) offers two-, three- and five-day horse rides through the Blue Mountain Gorge, near Enmore. It charges $85 per person per day, which includes all horse riding, food and tent accommodation.

Waterfall Way Tours (☎ 6772 2018) provides personalised natural history tours of three World Heritage National Parks.

Special Events

Armidale's spectacular Autumn Festival is a one-day event in March, with a street parade, live music and various stalls set up along Dumaresq Creek near the information centre.

Places to Stay

The *Pembroke Tourist & Leisure Park* (☎ 6772 6470), on Grafton Rd, has sites from $13, on-site vans from $30 a double and cabins from $43. Grafton Rd is the continuation of Barney St (to the east), and the caravan park is about 2.5km from the bus station. The park is also an associate YHA hostel, with a lot of bunk beds in one huge dorm, costing $16 ($14 for YHA members). There isn't a lot of privacy, but the facilities are quite good.

Wicklow Hotel (☎ 6772 2421), also known as the Pink Pub, is on the corner of Marsh and Dumaresq Sts (you can't miss it). It has comfortable pub rooms for $20 per person. Farther south along Marsh St is the *Royal Hotel* (☎ 6772 2259), charging $30/40 a single/double. The problem with these two hotels is that semitrailers grind past all night.

Tattersalls Hotel (☎ 6772 2247) is on the mall, so it has almost no traffic noise. Rooms cost $25/40, including breakfast.

There are 22 motels, and most of them are expensive. The only places with doubles for under $50 are the *Rose Villa* (☎ 6772 3872) and the *Hideaway Motor Inn* (☎ 6772 5177). Both are on the New England Hwy north of town. Definitely one of the better options of the more expensive motels is the *New England Motor Inn* (☎ 6771 1011, 100 Dumaresq St), with rooms from $60/70.

Comeytrowe B&B (☎ 6772 5869, 184 Marsh St) is a lovely heritage-listed house with elegant bedrooms and a wide veranda, from which you can enjoy the pretty cottage garden. Rates are $65/95.

Places to Eat

The central streets have a wide variety of good eating places. The best place to start is the East Mall. *Cafe Midale*, an inviting place with stylish decor on Beardy St, is a good place for breakfast and light meals (around $7). Two doors up, *Filling Groovy* is a hip little joint – a great place for smoothies, good coffee and gourmet rolls.

At the other end of the mall, *Jean-Pierre's* (☎ 6772 2201), an odd combination of a country-town cafe and French restaurant, has main courses for around $15. Bring your own (BYO) alcoholic drinks. Opposite is *Cafe Yannis* (☎ 6771 5801), a large, popular spot with a Mediterranean-influenced menu and mains for $11 to $18. It's also BYO.

It's worth visiting the Art Museum for *The Cafe* alone, a light-filled, modern spot, popular for lunch, coffee and cakes (Wednesday to Sunday). Baguettes and bruschetta are served up for around $6, and other delicious mains cost about $9.

Caz Minio's Pasta (☎ 6771 4555, 201A Brown St) is an excellent little BYO place – it's most popular for takeaways, but also has a few tables. It's unique in that all pasta is made on the premises, along with bread, *biscotti* (biscuit) and other goodies. There's a delicious selection of pasta and sauces from $5 (up to $8.50) as well as other Italian dishes.

The popular *bistro* at the Wicklow Hotel has pub-type mains for $14 to $16, and snacks. There are good, inexpensive meals to be found at the *Armidale Bowling Club* and the *Ex-Services Club*, both on Dumaresq St.

Entertainment

The *UNE* is Armidale's entertainment hub, with films, theatre and music. Call the Tattersalls Hotel (☎ 6772 2247) for 'what's on' details.

The *Club Hotel* on Marsh St has bands on weekends and there's Harley's Nightclub at the *New England Hotel* ('the Newie') on the corner of Dangar and Beardy Sts. Check the *Armidale Express* newspaper for other venues.

The *Belgrave Cinema* (☎ 6772 2856, 6773 3833 for program information, 137 Dumaresq St) shows mainstream and art-house films.

Getting There & Away

Eastern Australia Airlines (☎ 13 1313) flies to Sydney ($197) and Impulse Airlines (☎ 13 1381) services Brisbane ($240).

Countrylink, McCafferty's and Greyhound Pioneer buses service Armidale, and

Kean's runs down to Coffs Harbour and Port Macquarie via Dorrigo. Examples of fares with Greyhound are Sydney $53, Brisbane $48, Tamworth $20, Glen Innes $25 and Port Macquarie $40. All buses stop at the information centre.

The train fare from Sydney is $75.

Getting Around
For a taxi, phone Armidale Radio Taxis (☎ 6771 1455).

Armidale Bicycle Centre (☎ 6772 3718), 248 Beardy St (near Allingham St), hires out bikes for $5 an hour, $20 a day or $50 a week. Failes Cycleway runs past the information centre out to UNE, a ride of 5km, mainly through parkland.

AROUND ARMIDALE
Saumarez Homestead
On the New England Hwy between Armidale and Uralla, Saumarez (☎ 6772 3616) is a beautiful house that contains the effects of the rich pastoralists who built it. Tours ($7) take place at 10.30 am and 2 pm weekdays, more often on weekends. One day in May a fair is held at the homestead, with hay rides and other entertainment. Saumarez is closed from June to September.

Views & Waterfalls
The Armidale area is noted for its magnificent gorges and impressive waterfalls. These include the **Wollomombi Falls** (see the Oxley Wild Rivers National Park section earlier in this chapter), and the **Ebor Falls**, near the hamlet of Ebor. Closer to Armidale, off the road heading south to Gostwyck, are **Dangars Falls**.

NEW ENGLAND NATIONAL PARK
Right on the escarpment, New England National Park is a spectacular park of 30,000 hectares with a wide range of ecosystems. It's good for bushwalking, with 20km of walking tracks. Access is from near Ebor, and there are *camp sites* with cabins near the entrance; book through the Dorrigo NPWS office (☎ 6657 2309).

Close by, an excellent new place is *Yaraandoo (☎ 6775 9219)*, an environmen-

tal interpretive centre on Point Lookout Rd, which caters to large groups as well as individual travellers. Dormitory-style accommodation costs $65 per person per day, including all meals.

Another accommodation option is the *Little Styx River Cabins*, dating from the 1930s, when they housed workers at a timber mill. Cabins sleep up to 10 people and are comfortable, but very basic, and have no electricity. The cabins are close to the start of some walking trails in the national park and cost $40 a double and $5 for each additional person. Book through the Armidale tourist information centre on ☎ 6772 4655.

CATHEDRAL ROCK NATIONAL PARK
Cathedral Rock National park is also near Ebor, off the Ebor to Guyra road. It's a small park (6500 hectares) with photogenic granite formations.

GUY FAWKES RIVER NATIONAL PARK
Protecting the rugged gorges of the Guy Fawkes River, this park of 35,630 hectares offers canoeing as well as walking, with camping on the pleasant river flats. Access (not always easy) is from Hernani, 15km north-east of Ebor, and it's 30km to the Chaelundi Rest Area, with *camp sites* and water. The Dorrigo NPWS office (☎ 6657 2309) has information.

GUYRA
postcode 2365 • pop 2000
This small town (altitude 1320m) is at the top of Devil's Pinch Pass, about 25km north of Armidale. It gets pretty cold in winter. Guyra sits at the beginning of the highlands of the New England tablelands, and nearby is Chandlers Peak (1564m). The country and western tear-jerker 'Little Boy Lost' tells of the desperate search for a child who went missing 'in the wild New England ranges' near Guyra in 1960. The town was deserted during the four days it took to find him.

The **Guyra & District Historical Society Museum** has filled the old council chambers with pioneering memorabilia. It's open by appointment (☎ 6779 1420). **Mother of Ducks** is a waterbird sanctuary on the western edge of town. A path through the golf course leads to a viewing platform.

The strange **balancing rock** can be seen by the highway 12km before Glen Innes.

Places to Stay

The *Crystal Trout (☎ 6779 1241)* caravan park is on the highway south of town, and there's pub accommodation at the *Royal Hotel (☎ 6779 1005)* for $15/25 a single/ double and *Hotel Guyra (☎ 6779 1018)* for $15/30. There are also a couple of motels.

The Quarters (☎/fax 6779 4243) is a farmstay, originally shearers accommodation, on a property called Cabar Feidh 20km north of Guyra. Self-contained accommodation costs $16 per person per night in a dinky house that sleeps up to 15 ($5 extra for linen). A kitchen and living room occupy a second house, and a laundry and two bathrooms, a third.

GLEN INNES

postcode 2370 • pop 6250

This highland town regards itself as the Celtic capital of New England. It does have strong Scottish roots – but having bilingual (English and Gaelic) street signs is stretching things a bit far.

Orientation & Information

The New England Hwy becomes Church St as it goes north through town and the Gwydir Hwy winds east-west from Meade St, turning right into Church St at the roundabout, then left into Ferguson St. Grey St, which runs parallel to Church St, is the main shopping precinct.

The information centre (☎ 6732 2397), on Church St near the town centre, is open 9 am to 5 pm on weekdays and 9 am to 3 pm weekends. There's an NPWS office (☎ 6732 5133) on the New England Hwy at the junction with Oliver St.

Things to See & Do

This area was once known as the Land of the Beardies because of two hirsute stock-men who lived on an early station and augmented their wages by selling advice to new settlers. The **Land of the Beardies History House** (☎ 6732 1035), in the old hospital (1875) on the corner of Ferguson St and West Ave, is a big folk museum open from 10 am to noon and 2 to 5 pm weekdays, and 2 to 5 pm weekends ($4).

Grey St is well worth strolling down for its almost complete Victorian and Edwardian streetscape – above shop-front level, anyway. The Club Hotel (1906), the National Bank (1890), the town hall (1888; see the proscenium arch in the ballroom), the courthouse (1874) and the post office (1896) stand out. The information centre has a good Heritage Walk brochure for $0.50.

The excellent **Aboriginal Cultural Centre** (☎ 6732 5960), south of the town centre on the New England Hwy, houses an art and craft gallery where local indigenous artworks are on display. There are also 'bush tucker' gardens surrounding the centre – if these arouse your curiosity, you can try some bush food at the Koori Cuisine Cafe, also on the property.

Overlooking the town from the Centennial Parklands off the eastern end of the Gwydir Hwy, the **Glen Innes Standing Stones**, erected in 1990, are based on the Ring of Brodgar in Scotland's Orkney islands. The 33 huge 'stones' (they weigh up to 30 tonnes) were erected in recognition of the town's Celtic roots. The traditional plan, with its astronomical/mystical significance, is overlaid with other stones representing the Southern Cross.

The information centre has a map and brochure of fossicking areas in the district, including **Dwyers Fossicking Reserve**, where you can fossick and camp for a small fee ($5 per person, payable in an honesty box).

Special Events

Glen Innes is big on festivals. A Celtic Festival is held on the first weekend in May and Minerama, a gem and mineral festival, is held on the second weekend in March. On the second weekend in October the town celebrates the Land of the Beardies Festival.

Places to Stay

The town's five caravan parks are dotted along the New England Hwy. You'll find tent sites at the *Poplar Caravan Park* (☎ 6732 1514) for $8, on-site vans for $28 and cabins with en suites for $38.

The best deals are at the pubs on Grey St. The impressive *Club Hotel* (☎ 6732 3043), on the corner of Wentworth St, has singles/doubles for $25/38, or $30/48 with cooked breakfast. The *Imperial* (☎ 6732 3103) and the *Royal* (☎ 6732 3179) both charge $20/35.

The *Amber Motel* (☎ 6732 2300, 135 Meade St) is a good, inexpensive motel without the highway noise, with rooms from $45/48 (just beware the gas heaters). Most other motels are on Church St.

Diarmid's B&B (☎ 6732 5701, 15 Torrington St), off Church St, was once the parsonage and is now the delightful home of Lynn Talbott, Ian MacDiarmid and Micky (the dog). It's worth staying here for Lynn's cooking alone, especially the Celtic afternoon tea (included in price). Rooms cost $65/90 and come with a guarantee that you'll be spoilt.

The *Red Lion Tavern* (☎ 6733 3271), in the village of Glencoe, 22km south of Glen Innes, is a fine old pub with loads of atmosphere. En suite accommodation costs $35/55, including a continental breakfast.

Places to Eat

The *Popular Cafe*, an old-style country cafe on Grey St, is good for brekky and burgers. Cosy *Cafe Heritage* (215 Grey St) has a varied lunch menu. Mains cost $7 to $9; good burgers and focaccia cost around $6.

The *Dragon Court*, a good Chinese restaurant on Grey St near Wentworth St, is licensed to serve alcohol. There's a cheaper Chinese place farther up Grey St.

The *Hereford Steakhouse* (☎ 6732 2255), at the Rest Point Motel on Church St, is popular with locals for its steaks. It offers a two-course special (entree and main) for $20.

Getting There & Away

Impulse Airlines (☎ 13 1381) flies to Sydney at least twice daily for $199.

Greyhound buses stop near the information centre on the run between Sydney ($53) and Brisbane ($48). McCafferty's buses stop at the Ampol petrol station on Church St. Countrylink (☎ 13 2232) buses come through on the runs from Armidale to Tenterfield and from Grafton to Inverell and Moree. Black & White (☎ 6732 3687) has a bus to Inverell ($16) from Sunday to Friday.

If you're driving or riding east on the Gwydir Hwy to Grafton, note that Glen Innes has the last fuel for 130km. The Gwydir Hwy to Grafton is a scenic road, but to get off the beaten track take the Old Grafton Rd: it turns off the Gwydir Hwy about 40km east of Glen Innes. The road, mostly unsealed but in fair condition, passes through a convict-built tunnel, and there are good camping and fishing spots along the river.

GIBRALTAR RANGE & WASHPOOL NATIONAL PARKS

These two national parks – dramatic, forested and wild – lie between Glen Innes and Grafton off the Gwydir Hwy. Together they form a World Heritage area, although it's only a decade or so since Washpool was saved from logging by a protest campaign. Except for the rest areas near the entrance, most of Washpool is a wilderness of lush rainforest and river gorges offering challenging bushwalking (there's no vehicle access); Gibraltar Range is drier country and features granite outcrops.

Countrylink buses running along the Gwydir Hwy between Glen Innes and Grafton stop at the Gibraltar Range visitors centre, the start of a 10km track to the Mulligans Hut rest area, and at the entrance to Washpool. It's about 3km farther to the Bellbird and Coombadjha rest areas, where you can camp and take a 10km walking trail. NPWS offices in Grafton (☎ 6640 3910) and Glen Innes (☎ 6732 5133) have more information.

NYMBOIDA NATIONAL PARK

The Nymboida River and its tributary, the Mann River, flow through this wilderness and offer excellent canoeing and white-water rafting (best organised in Coffs Harbour).

NEW ENGLAND

Although much of the park is rugged wilderness, the river banks are good places to camp but there are no facilities. To get there, head east from Glen Innes on the Gwydir Hwy for 45km, turn off onto the Narlala road and travel for another 35km. You can reach the eastern end of the park from Jackadgery, farther east on the highway. The NPWS offices in Glen Innes and Grafton have more information.

TENTERFIELD
postcode 2372 • pop 3300
If you're heading north, Tenterfield is the last sizable town before the Queensland border. Sitting at the junction of the New England and Bruxner Hwys, it is also something of a travel crossroads. It's easily accessible from Lismore, so if you're staying on the far north coast it's worth a visit to see something of what the locals call the 'real' Australia.

Tenterfield touts itself as the town where Australia's path to Federation began because of a speech made here by former NSW premier Sir Henry Parkes in 1889.

Information
The information centre (☎ 6736 1082) is on the New England Hwy (Rouse St) to the south of the town centre.

Things to See
The School of Arts, on the corner of Rouse and Manners Sts, is where Parkes made his famous speech. It's now a library, housing a small **museum** with exhibits relating to the politician's career. It's open from 9 am to 5 pm weekdays.

Centenary Cottage, on the corner of High and Logan Sts, houses local history exhibits, and **Petrie Cottage**, next door, is an early worker's cottage that has been restored. Both are open from 10 am to 4 pm Wednesday to Sunday. Nearby, on High St, the old, stone **Saddler's Shop** is worth visiting for a yarn with the saddler. The shop once belonged to the grandfather of Australian entertainer Peter Allen, who sang about it in the song 'Tenterfield Saddler'.

The disused **train station**, near the western end of Manners St, is a fine building dating

from 1886 and houses a collection of railway memorabilia. The courthouse (1885) and post office (1881) are also worth a look.

Thunderbolt's Hideout, where bushranger Captain Thunderbolt supposedly did just that, is 11km out of town.

The New England Hwy runs north from Tenterfield to the Queensland towns of Stanthorpe and Warwick. Between the state border and Stanthorpe are **Girraween National Park** and the **wineries** of the granite belt.

Organised Tours
Woolool Woolool Aboriginal Culture Tours runs tours to nearby Bald Rock and Boonoo Boonoo National Parks. The information centre handles bookings.

Special Events
The Autumn Colours Festival is held in the second half of April. Events at the festival include a big bush dance at the showgrounds.

Places to Stay

Near the old train station at the western end of Manners St is *Tenterfield YHA Lodge* (☎ 6736 1477). Most rooms have a couple of single beds and a double bed. Shared rooms go for $16 per person, doubles cost $36 and there's also a family room for $45. This place is also a small caravan park, with sites for $12, on-site vans from $24 and more expensive cabins. The managers can arrange work on fruit and vegetable farms in the area.

Several pubs have accommodation. On Manners St, the *Exchange Hotel* (☎ 6736 1054) has singles/doubles for $20/40 and the *Telegraph Hotel* (☎ 6736 1015) charges $18/28. The Telegraph Hotel also has motel units for $33/41. There's a string of motels on Rouse St, south of Manners St.

Mirrambeena Cabins (☎ 6736 2063), 13km from Tenterfield on Black Swamp Rd, offers excellent bushwalking and self-contained accommodation for $75 a double.

Getting There & Away

As well as the buses running along the New England Hwy between Sydney and Brisbane, Kirklands (☎ 6622 1499) runs to Lismore ($22.30) and from there to the coast (weekdays only).

If you've driven or ridden across from the coast or up the relatively busy New England Hwy, a journey west from Tenterfield is a delight – the Bruxner Hwy is a wide, almost deserted road. It runs west to Boggabilla, on the Newell Hwy, and heading east it twists and turns over the ranges to Casino, then on to Lismore.

BALD ROCK NATIONAL PARK

Bald Rock National Park (5450 hectares) is about 30km north of Tenterfield on an unsealed road that continues into Queensland. Lying not on the escarpment but in granite country, Bald Rock is a huge monolith that has been compared to Uluru. There are several walks to the summit: an easy two-hour walk, a long seven-hour walk and a steep straight-up climb. From the top, you're rewarded with great views. There's a basic *camping area* near the base with pit toilets and gas barbecues.

Access is from Tenterfield, off the unsealed route to Warwick. This is a pretty drive, but be careful: Although the road is wide and smooth, it has a thick coating of fine dust that gives no traction if you have to brake or swerve.

BOONOO BOONOO NATIONAL PARK

Near Bald Rock, Boonoo Boonoo (pronounced bun-na-b'**noo**) is an area of pretty forest with a 210m waterfall. There are facilities at the rest area near the falls and *camp sites* along the Boonoo Boonoo River.

CASINO

postcode 2470 • pop 10,350

Casino is more renowned for its title of Australia's Beef Capital than its tourist attractions. However, if you're after an insight into a great agricultural tradition, Casino Beef Week runs between late May and early June. The information centre (☎ 6662 1572) is on the highway just after the bridge crossing the Richmond River.

The Fossickers Way

This interesting (and almost traffic-free) road begins high in the hills at Nundle, passes through Tamworth and then skirts the western edges of the ranges, passing through rolling cattle country that's lower and drier than the tablelands. Between Manilla and Warialda the road runs between the foothills of the Great Dividing Range to the east and the rugged Nandewar Range to the west.

The Fossickers Way is named because of the many sites where you might discover anything from fossilised wood to diamonds. You'll need a licence to fossick, available from courthouses and many tourist offices for about $4.

NUNDLE

postcode 2340 • pop 350

The lovely little township of Nundle lies in the valley of the Peel River, 63km southeast of Tamworth. There was a major gold rush in the surrounding hills in the 1850s, and you can still fossick for gold, sapphires and other semiprecious stones.

The town's information centre is at the Nundle Country Cafe (☎ 6769 3158) on Jenkins St (the main street) – you can also hire fossicking gear here. It's open 7 am to 7 pm daily. The **Court House Museum**, also on the main street, opens on Sunday afternoon ($1/0.50 for adults/children).

The hamlet of **Hanging Rock** overlooks Nundle from the hills about 10km to the east. You can camp here by the Sheba Dams, which were built during the gold rushes.

Places to Stay & Eat

There's a *caravan park* (☎ 6769 3355) in town by the Peel River and good accommodation at the *Peel Inn Hotel* (☎ 6769 3377), Jenkins St, for $30/40 a single/double.

An out-of-town alternative is the *Dag Sheep Station* (☎ 6769 3234), 12km southeast of town on the Crawney road. It's run by a former Oz Experience driver who figured he could have more fun showing backpackers the ropes in the bush. The Dag is a 16,000 hectare sheep-and-cattle-grazing property, and accommodation is in the old shearers quarters. A bed costs $15, dinner is available for $7 and breakfast (including yummy pancakes) costs $4.

To indulge, stay at the *Jenkins Street Guest House* (☎ 6769 3239), which offers luxury accommodation in a superbly renovated historic bank. En suite rooms cost $100/140, including a continental breakfast. Just be warned – you may never want to leave this place. There's also an excellent *restaurant* downstairs, open daily for morning and afternoon tea (scrumptious cakes for $6), lunch on weekends, and dinner Friday and Saturday (every night for house guests).

Getting There & Away

There's a sealed road from Nundle to Tamworth. A largely unsealed and hilly road runs to Walcha, passing through some lovely forest. Other minor roads head south-east to Nowendoc, then on to Taree and Gloucester, offering spectacular drives that skirt the Barrington Tops National Park. You can also head south to Scone from Nundle.

MANILLA
postcode 2346 • pop 2300

Manilla lies 45km north-west of Tamworth at the junction of the Namoi and Manilla Rivers. The name is a corruption of the name of the local Aborigines, the Manellae people.

Manilla developed as a place to stop on the main route to the grazing lands of the Namoi Valley and the north-west in the early days of European expansion.

The information centre (☎ 6785 1113) is at the Big Fish Centre at 79 Arthur St (the road into town from Tamworth). It's open 9 am to 8 pm daily. The **Royce Cottage Museum**, on Manilla St (the main street), comprises several old buildings and opens from 2 to 4 pm on Monday, Wednesday and Friday ($2).

Dutton's Meadery (☎ 6785 1148), on Barraba St on the northern side of town, is well worth a visit. It has a quirky shop/museum/pub where you can sample meads and melomels (meads fermented with fruit juices) and perhaps buy a bottle. The meadery opens daily and you're sure of a good chat with Mr Dutton.

If you're into paragliding or hanggliding, this is one of the best areas in Australia to do it. The national **paragliding championships** are held here every year in February/March.

Warrabah National Park, 35km northeast of Manilla, is centred on a gorge in the Namoi River and has bushwalking, climbing, canoeing and basic camp sites. There's a challenging three-day canoe trip from the village of Retreat, east of the park, to Lowry Creek within the park – a 250m drop over 15km, with plenty of rapids. It's for experienced canoeists only.

Places to Stay

A few kilometres before Manilla on the road from Tamworth, you'll see a sign with the youth hostel symbol directing you to a rest area. There's no youth hostel.

Manilla St's four pubs all have accommodation and there's the *Manilla Motel* (☎ 6785 1306) on the corner of Namoi and Court Sts, which has singles/doubles for $40/50.

The Myall Creek Massacre

In 1838, not far from present-day Bingara, stockmen from the Myall Creek station rounded up 28 men, women and children, hacked them to death with knives and swords, then made a half-hearted attempt at burning the bodies.

What is unusual about the Myall Creek massacre is not that it happened but that we know about it – the stockmen were whites, their victims Aborigines. By a series of accidents, a report of the massacre reached Governor Gipps and he ordered that the stockmen be prosecuted. Amidst shocked protests from across the colony, seven of the murderers were hung. It was the first and one of the last times that whites were hung for the murder of Aborigines.

Historians assume that such massacres were routine in the 'clearing' of new grazing lands (the Myall Creek stockmen had apparently been involved in at least one other massacre), but because the new frontiers kept pushing way past the reach of the law – and because the new settlers saw Aborigines as vermin to be casually eradicated – little concrete evidence is available.

Massacres such as Myall Creek weren't just the work of semibarbaric station workers, who were in any case usually following at least implicit orders. Myall Creek was owned by Henry Dangar, an educated Englishman who had helped set up the huge Australian Agricultural Company holdings in the Hunter Valley, New England and the north-west. His voice was amongst the loudest protesting against the trial, and he raised money to pay for his stockmen's defence.

BARRABA

postcode 2347 • pop 2370

Barraba lies amid prime sheep country on the upper reaches of the Manilla River. There's an information centre (☎ 6782 1255) in a shop near the war memorial on Queen St, the main street. Ask here about having the **museum** opened for you.

Andy's Backpackers Lodge (☎ 6782 1916, 98 Queen St) is a good place to kick back for a few days and experience life in a country town. There's a permaculture garden, an inviting common room with a piano and a host of creative activities going on. Beds cost $15, which also allows you to help yourself to breakfast, and there's normally somebody putting a meal together in the evening – contributions welcome.

Blue Gum (☎ 6782 1067), on Fitzroy St, is one of two caravan parks in town. There are also several pubs with accommodation and the *Barraba Motel* (☎ 6782 1555), on Edward St, which has singles/doubles for $47/55.

Oz Experience comes through town four times a week or you can catch the Countrylink bus from Tamworth.

BINGARA

postcode 2404

Bingara, on the Gwydir River, is even smaller than Barraba. Finch St, the main street, is planted with orange trees as a war memorial. The oranges are left untouched until a special ceremony in July when they are picked by school children.

The council-run tourist information centre (☎ 6724 0066) is at 64 Maitland St, next to the newsagent. Pick up a brochure about the fossicking sites in this geologically diverse area. There's a **museum** in the old Satter's Hotel on Maitland St, open 2 to 4 pm Wednesday to Saturday ($2). The Imperial Hotel has information on **canoeing** on the Gwydir River (peaceful most of the year, highly exciting in late spring) and can help with canoe hire. **Copeton Dam State Recreation Area**, a large dam popular for boating, is about 45km east of town.

Places to Stay

The pleasant *Riverside Caravan Park* (☎ 6724 1209) has a good position on Keera Rd near the bridge. It has tent sites for $9 and on-site vans from $25. The 1879 *Imperial Hotel* (☎ 6724 1629) has good backpacker accommodation. It charges $10 for a dorm bed and $15/25 for singles/doubles, all including light breakfast. The managers can help you organise outings and activities in the district.

The *Fossickers Way Motel* (☎ 6724 1373) is on Finch St and has rooms from $48/54.

There's a *caravan park* (☎ 6723 6269) at the Copeton Dam.

INVERELL
postcode 2360 • pop 10,000

A large, pleasant country town with some impressive public buildings, Inverell is at the centre of a sapphire-mining area. Other stones, such as diamonds, are also found.

Until they are cut, sapphires aren't especially impressive. There's a story, probably questionable, that a few years ago the council was resurfacing a stretch of road and one truckload of gravel had a bluish look to it. 'Couldn't be, there's too many of the bastards,' was the road crew's verdict, but who knows?

Information

The information centre (☎ 6728 8161), in a converted water tower on Campbell St, is open 9 am to 5 pm weekdays and until noon on weekends. Pick up a map of the area's fossicking sites and if you think you've found a sapphire, any of the town's jewellers will help you evaluate it.

Things to See & Do

The **Inverell Pioneer Village**, opposite the racecourse on the Tingha road, is a pleasant place to stroll around. It's open 2 to 4 pm on Sunday and Monday and 10 am to 5 pm the rest of the week. You can fossick here and damper (bush bread) is served for afternoon tea on Sundays. Admission costs $5/2 for adults/children.

There are some interesting old buildings in town as well, such as the superb **courthouse** (1886) on Otho St and the nearby **town hall**. Around the corner in Evans St, Butler Hall now houses the impressive **Inverell Art Centre**, open 10 am to 5 pm weekdays and until 2 pm on Saturday (admission by gold coin donation). Special exhibitions fostering local art are a regular feature.

The **Draught Horse Centre & Museum** (☎ 6722 1461), 4km east of town off Glen Innes Rd, is open 10 am to 4 pm Thursday

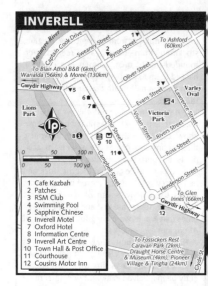

INVERELL

To Ashford (60km)

To Blair Athol B&B (6km), Warialda (56km) & Moree (130km)

Gwydir Highway

Varley Oval

Lions Park

Victoria Park

To Glen Innes (66km)
Gwydir Highway

To Fossickers Rest
Caravan Park (2km),
Draught Horse Centre
& Museum (4km), Pioneer
Village & Tingha (24km)

1 Cafe Kazbah
2 Patches
3 RSM Club
4 Swimming Pool
5 Sapphire Chinese
6 Inverell Motel
7 Oxford Hotel
8 Information Centre
9 Inverell Art Centre
10 Town Hall & Post Office
11 Courthouse
12 Cousins Motor Inn

to Monday. Five different breeds of these gentle animals live here. Admission is $5/2.

About 5km south of Inverell off the Tingha road, the **Goonoowigall Bushland Reserve** surrounds the site of Ferndale, which is a small settlement that became derelict early this century. There are several short walking tracks and quite a lot of wildlife in the bush.

Special Events

Inverell's Sapphire City Floral Festival is held over 10 days in October. There's a wide range of events and a parade.

Places to Stay

The best and friendliest of the town's five caravan parks is *Fossickers Rest Caravan Park* (☎ 6722 2261), 2km east of town on the road to Lake Inverell. It has shady sites for $10 and en suite cabins from $35.

In the centre of town on Otho St, the *Oxford Hotel* (☎ 6722 1101) has B&B from $26/42 for singles/doubles. Next door, the *Inverell Motel* (☎ 6722 2077) charges from $48/58. For something a bit more upmarket, try *Cousins Motor Inn* (☎ 6722 3566) on Glen Innes Rd, with rooms for $69/79.

Six kilometres west of town on Warialda Rd, *Blair Athol B&B* (☎ *6722 4912)* is a lovely, turn-of-the-century manor set in two hectares of botanical gardens. It's worth staying here for the gardens alone and the accommodation is quite nice. Doubles start at $95.

Places to Eat
For brekky, *Patches*, on the corner of Byron and Vivian Sts, is good. *Cafe Kazbah* *(☎ 6721 1199),* corner Byron and Lawrence Sts, is an inviting spot for lunch (or dinner, Wednesday to Saturday); mains cost $7 to $11.

The *RSM Club* on Evans St has very cheap tucker in the family restaurant and more expensive meals in the Anzac Restaurant. *Sapphire Chinese (☎ 6722 2266, 23 Byron St)* has mains for $8 to $14 and pretty good options for vegetarians.

Getting There & Away
Harvey World Travel (☎ 6722 3011), at 17 Byron St (opposite the Coles supermarket), sells tickets for Impulse Airlines flights to Sydney (from $219).

Buses stop at the information centre on Campbell St. Countrylink has services along the Fossickers Way to Tamworth and to Grafton via Glen Innes. Harvey World Travel can organise bus bookings. Black & White (☎ 6732 3687) runs to Armidale ($30) via Glen Innes ($16) when school's in.

AROUND INVERELL
The **Dejon Sapphire Centre** (☎ 6723 2222), on the Gwydir Hwy 19km east of Inverell, is a working sapphire mine that offers tours at 10.30 am and 3 pm daily ($5).

The **Gilgai winery** (☎ 6723 1204), about 10km south of Inverell on the Bundarra road, is open for tastings and sales from 10 am to 6 pm Monday to Saturday and from noon on Sunday.

Green Valley Farm (☎ 6723 3370) is 10km south-east of Tingha. It has children's rides, a museum (featuring grotesqueries such as an eight-legged kitten and 'Siamese' pigs) and a small zoo. Basic cabin accommodation is available.

North towards the Queensland border, approximately 25km from Ashford, **Kwiambal** (pronounced Ki-am-bal) **National Park** covers 2626 hectares of woodland and features impressive waterfalls and waterholes. In the park are the **Limestone Caves** – Main Cave is over half a kilometre long and leads on to Great Cave, which is almost as large. Close by on the Macintyre River are the **Macintyre Falls**, with some rugged gorges, swimming holes and *camp sites*.

Central West

The central west takes in some of the richest farmland in Australia. Although the area has an aura of being utterly typical, it is unique in New South Wales (NSW), and perhaps Australia, for its relatively close settlement and liberal sprinkling of fair-sized towns. The central west is solid, respectable and, above all, rural. With some notable exceptions, such as the Western Plains Zoo in Dubbo, there isn't a lot in the way of tourist-oriented attractions – but this in itself is an attraction.

History
Much of the central west was owned by the Wiradjuri people before Europeans arrived.

Soon after explorers Gregory Blaxland, William Wentworth and William Lawson found a path through the Blue Mountains in 1813, the young colony began to expand onto the inland plains. A road across the mountains was built in just two years and Governor Lachlan Macquarie ordered the founding of Bathurst – Australia's first inland town (if you don't count Sydney's satellite villages) and the first to be built on a river that flowed towards the inland.

Settlement was at first restricted because the government was concerned about convicts escaping into the vast inland, and because the size and purpose of the colony was still a matter of debate – did Britain really *want* a huge colony on this continent? The government would have to administer and police new settlements, and this could be an expensive business if they spread too far. Anyway, the new road over the Blue Mountains was too rough to provide ready access to the Sydney markets. Sections were so steep that wagons had to be hauled up and down, and it wasn't until the Victoria Pass route was built in the 1830s that coaches were able to cross the mountains.

Despite these obstacles, cattle and sheep were moved into the new country, and before long Europeans were widely but thinly spread. Little is known of their adventures,

HIGHLIGHTS

• Travelling through time at the Gulgong Pioneer Museum

• Coming face to face with the big cats at Western Plains Zoo

• Visiting the many wineries in the region

• Downing a beer in a country pub

• Exploring the Abercrombie Caves

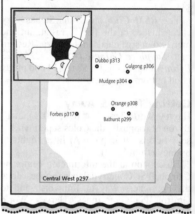

as they were mainly illiterate shepherds and drovers, but there must have been some interesting stories told in the pubs of Bathurst town.

Although most land had been taken up by squatters, the white population remained small until a string of gold rushes began at Ophir in 1851. For the next 50 years the hint of gold sent diggers pouring from one hastily built town to another, with the lucky and the disillusioned staying behind to farm or develop the township.

Geography
The area is bounded on the east by the Great Dividing Range and to the west by the vast outback plains. North of Dubbo, the Liverpool Range separates the central west from

the more sparsely populated north-west of the state, and in the south the Murrumbidgee River marks the beginning of the Riverina. Geographically, the central west is a diverse area, including some of the Great Divide's high tablelands (around Bathurst and Orange), the western slopes (all the way from Mudgee, south to Cootamundra) and the flatter land farther west, tailing off into the dry western plains.

The Lachlan River, rising in the Great Dividing Range near Crookwell and flowing west through Cowra, Forbes and Condobolin, runs through the heart of the area

and passes through varied but always beautiful country. Like most of the state's inland rivers, it eventually enters the Murray River (via the Murrumbidgee) and reaches the sea in South Australia (SA).

Getting There & Around

The central west region is well served by air. From Dubbo ($184 from Sydney) there are flights to several places in the central west and the far west of the state.

The major bus companies have services through the central west region on routes between Sydney and Broken Hill or Adelaide,

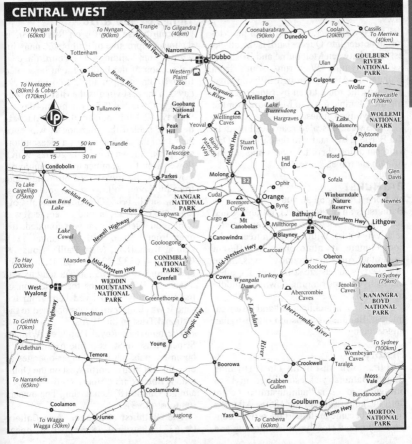

CENTRAL WEST

and from Brisbane to Melbourne or Adelaide. Local companies include Rendell's Coaches (☎ 1800 023 328). Sid Fogg's (☎ 1800 045 952) runs from Newcastle as far as Dubbo.

Trains run from Sydney to Lithgow ($24), Bathurst ($35), Orange ($42) and Dubbo ($62). From those centres, connecting buses run to most other towns, including Cowra ($49 from Sydney), Forbes ($59), Grenfell ($56) and Mudgee ($42).

From Sydney the main route into the central west is the one used by the first Europeans to enter the area. Follow the Great Western Hwy to Bathurst, at the junction of the Mid-Western Hwy and the Mitchell Hwy.

The Newell Hwy, running from the Victorian border into Queensland, is the quickest route between Melbourne and Brisbane.

The Olympic Way runs south from Bathurst to Albury, through hilly country. This was the route taken by runners carrying the Olympic torch to Melbourne for the 1956 Olympic Games.

In the west, unsealed roads lead north to the Barrier Hwy and into the far west. Driving conditions here take on some aspects of outback travel.

BATHURST
postcode 2795 • pop 30,100

Bathurst is an old town laid out on a grand scale, and its Victorian streetscape is still relatively intact. With European trees and a cool climate, its atmosphere is different from other Australian country towns. Some of the city's streets are still lit by old, often ineffective lamps running down the middle of the road.

As well as its architectural and historical interest, Bathurst is a bastion of Australian motor racing.

History

The first town west of the Great Dividing Range, Bathurst was established in 1815 but remained a small administrative centre until the gold rushes of the 1850s. After the rushes it became an important service centre for the now closely settled farming and grazing lands. Cobb & Co moved the headquarters of its coach company here in 1861.

Orientation & Information

The city is laid out on a large grid of wide streets. William St between Durham and Keppel Sts is the main shopping area.

The friendly Bathurst Visitor Information Centre (☎ 6332 1444), 28 William St, opens from 9 am to 5 pm daily. The Land Information Centre (☎ 6332 8200), on Panorama Ave, produces many of Australia's maps and opens for map sales on weekdays. Camping supplies are available from Camping World on William St.

Things to See & Do

The **courthouse** (1880), on Russell St, is the most impressive of Bathurst's many interesting old buildings. The court, the central section of the building, can be visited from 10 am to 1 pm and 2 to 4 pm weekdays. In the east wing is the **Historical Museum** (☎ 6332 4755), open Tuesday to Sunday ($2/1 for adults/children). **Machattie Park**, behind the courthouse, was once the site of the jail and is now a pleasant formal park, known for its begonias which flower from late summer to early autumn.

Most of the town's old buildings date from the boom following the gold rushes, but the small, brick **Old Government Cottage** (☎ 6332 4755) behind 1 George St was built soon after Bathurst was founded. It's open from 1.30 to 3.30 pm Sunday ($1). Dating from 1845, **Miss Traill's House & Garden** (☎ 6332 4232), 321 Russell St, opens from 10 am to 3 pm Tuesday to Saturday ($5/3). It contains the collection of the Lee family, who lived here from the time it was built until it was donated to the National Trust in the 1970s.

The renovated **Royal Hotel**, on William St near Russell St, is a fine example of a boom-era pub, but it no longer operates as one. Six kilometres north-west on the Ophir road is **Abercrombie House** (☎ 6331 4929), a huge, Gothic 1870s mansion. The owners run tours ($5/3).

The **Bathurst Regional Art Gallery** (☎ 6331 6066), 70–78 Keppel St, opens from 10 am to 5 pm Tuesday to Saturday and from 2 to 5 pm Sunday. Grace Cossington Smith, whose paintings of the Sydney Harbour Bridge under construction defined the event for many Australians, is well represented.

Ben Chifley, prime minister from 1945 to 1949, lived in Bathurst and **Ben Chifley's Home** (☎ 6332 1444), 10 Busby St, opens from 2 to 4 pm Monday to Saturday and 10 am to noon Sunday ($2.50/1.25). The Chifley government's initiatives in welcoming European refugees as immigrants were important to Australia's cultural and economic development. Before entering politics Chifley had been a train driver and he maintained a simple lifestyle even when in office.

Near the city centre is the 6.2km **Mount Panorama Motor Racing Circuit**, the venue for several of Australia's most popular motor races: the Bathurst Motorsport Spectacular in October; the FAI 1000 for 5L production cars, held in November; and motorcycle racing over Easter. You can drive around the tight, steep circuit, which is a two-way public road. The **National Motor Racing Museum** (☎ 6332 1872), on Pit Straight, opens from 9 am to 4.30 pm daily ($5/1.50).

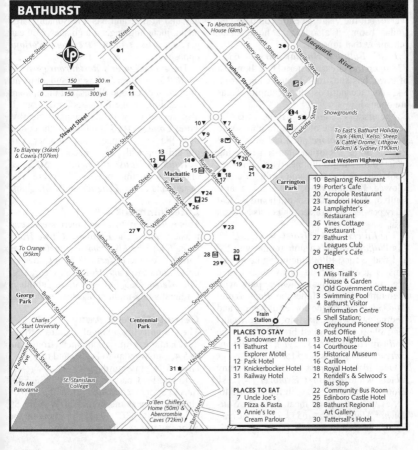

BATHURST

PLACES TO STAY
5 Sundowner Motor Inn
11 Bathurst Explorer Motel
12 Park Hotel
17 Knickerbocker Hotel
31 Railway Hotel

PLACES TO EAT
7 Uncle Joe's Pizza & Pasta
9 Annie's Ice Cream Parlour
10 Benjarong Restaurant
19 Porter's Cafe
20 Acropole Restaurant
23 Tandoori House
24 Lamplighter's Restaurant
26 Vines Cottage Restaurant
27 Bathurst Leagues Club
29 Ziegler's Cafe

OTHER
1 Miss Traill's House & Garden
2 Old Government Cottage
3 Swimming Pool
4 Bathurst Visitor Information Centre
6 Shell Station; Greyhound Pioneer Stop
8 Post Office
13 Metro Nightclub
14 Courthouse
15 Historical Museum
16 Carillon
18 Royal Hotel
21 Rendell's & Selwood's Bus Stop
22 Community Bus Room
25 Edinboro Castle Hotel
28 Bathurst Regional Art Gallery
30 Tattersall's Hotel

Also on Mt Panorama, the 52-hectare **Sir Joseph Banks Nature Park** (☎ 6333 6286) has native animals and walking trails (open from 9 am to 3.30 pm daily). **Bathurst Goldfields** (☎ 6332 2022), a reconstruction of an early gold-mining town, is open weekdays for guided tours – call to find out times, as they vary.

The **Sheep & Cattle Drome** (☎ 6337 3634), 6km from Bathurst on the Limekilns road, is an indoor display of various facets of agriculture, including shearing and sheepdog working. Call for show times ($10/5).

Places to Stay

During the motor racing, accommodation is scarce, but the visitors centre can help you find a room; it also runs a home-share scheme at that time.

East's Bathurst Holiday Park (☎ 6331 8286), on the Great Western Hwy 4km east of town, has sites for $13 and cabins from $42. At race periods other camping areas are opened.

The visitors centre has listings of B&Bs and farmstays. One of the more impressive B&Bs is *Strathmore* (☎ 6332 3252, 202 Russell St), a Victorian mansion charging $85/100 for singles/doubles with bathroom. Bookings are essential and children aren't allowed. *Yarrabin* (☎ 6337 5712) is a farm south of Bathurst offering full board for $90 a day per person. Horse riding costs an extra $15.

The *Knickerbocker Hotel* (☎ 6332 4500, 134 William St) has en suite rooms with TV and fridge for $40/60, including breakfast. This is good value, as many rooms have been recently renovated. Other pubs with accommodation include the *Park Hotel* (☎ 6331 3399), on the corner of Keppel and George Sts, which has motel-style rooms for $39/60 with cooked breakfast, and the *Railway Hotel* (☎ 6331 2964, 157 Havannah St), with rooms for $15/30.

One of the cheapest of Bathurst's many motels is the *Bathurst Explorer* (☎ 6331 2966, 357 Stewart St), with rooms for $40/50, as well as a good meal deal. The *Sundowner Motor Inn* (☎ 6331 2211, 19 Charlotte St) is well located. Rooms start at $72.

Places to Eat

On the corner of William and Howick Sts, the *Acropole* is a large cafe-cum-restaurant with some Greek dishes on the menu, including a decent moussaka. Close by at No 76, *Porter's Cafe* is a good place for breakfast.

For wood-fired pizza or large servings of inexpensive pasta, try *Uncle Joe's Pizza & Pasta*, opposite the post office on Howick St.

The small *Ziegler's Cafe* on Keppel St has a shaded garden and an interesting, contemporary menu of not-too-expensive dishes. On George St near the corner of Russell St there's a group of eating places, including the Thai *Benjarong* restaurant. It's open for dinner Tuesday to Sunday and for lunch Tuesday and Friday, and has a reasonably large menu, including vegetarian dishes. You can get a sugar fix at *Annie's Ice Cream Parlour* opposite.

The *Lamplighter's Restaurant* (☎ 6331 1448, 128 William St) has a standard menu of meat and seafood dishes, but the opulent surroundings make for a good night out. It also serves tasty lunch specials. Nearby, *Vines Cottage* (☎ 6331 6470), on the corner of William and Keppel Sts, is another in an old building with period decor.

Tandoori House (94 Bentinck St) has a cheap lunch-time buffet. There are also restaurants at the *Leagues* and *RSL* clubs.

Entertainment

This is a student town and there are several music venues. The *Edinboro Castle Hotel* ('The Eddy'; 134 William St) sometimes has bands, as do the *Tattersall's Hotel*, on Keppel St, and the *Park Hotel*, on George St. The *Metro* (183 George St) nightclub is Bathurst's late-night spot, closing at 5 am.

Getting There & Away

The Countrylink Travel Centre (☎ 13 2232), at the train station, opens from 8 am to 5.45 pm Monday to Friday and from 9.45 am to 5.15 pm Saturday.

Rendell's Coaches (☎ 1800 023 328) runs to Sydney and Dubbo from the stop on Howick St near the corner of William St. Selwood's (☎ 6362 7963) stops here on the Sydney-Orange run. Greyhound Pioneer stops at the Shell petrol station, which is on Durham St.

Countrylink buses run from the train station west to Orange and east to Lithgow and Sydney.

Small towns in the area have community buses into Bathurst, most only once a week or so. The Community Bus Room, where you can wait for buses, is in the car park under the shopping centre on Howick St. Call ☎ 6331 3322 for more information.

Bathurst is on the main western train line, with daily trains to Sydney and Dubbo, and connections to Broken Hill and beyond. Countrylink buses connect with some suburban services from Sydney.

The Great Western Hwy from Sydney enters Bathurst from the east. The Mitchell Hwy heads north-west to Orange, then north to Dubbo and Bourke. The Olympic Way runs south-west from Bathurst to Cowra, eventually reaching Albury. The Mid-Western Hwy (the same road as the Olympic Way until Cowra) runs south-west to West Wyalong and on to Hay.

Getting Around
Taxis (☎ 6331 1511) run 24 hours a day. Bathurst Coaches runs a local bus service, which stops outside East's Bathurst Holiday Park every day except Sunday. Grab a timetable from the tourist office.

AROUND BATHURST
The high, cold tablelands around Bathurst were some of the first inland areas of Australia to be settled by Europeans, and there are some interesting old villages. The Around Orange section later in this chapter covers some villages to the north-west of Bathurst.

Carcoar
Sitting on the Belubula River, 52km southwest of Bathurst, this pretty village was established in 1839. It has many wonderful old buildings and has been classified by the National Trust. Enterprise Stores (☎ 6367 3085), on Belubula St, has tourist information, and **Stoke Stable Museum** is in the stables of the old Stoke Hotel. *Olde Fossickers Inne Caravan Park* (☎ 6367 3081)

has sites for $10. There are singles/doubles for $20/38 at the *Royal Hotel* (☎ 6367 3009), and B&B at the *Dalebrook Guesthouse* (☎ 6367 3149) from $80 a double.

Rockley
Rockley is a little old village about 40km south of Bathurst, with some nice stone buildings and several craft and antique shops. There's a **museum** in the old mill.

Oberon
Thriving Oberon, 43km south-east of Bathurst, is an elevated (1113m) rural town surrounded by farmland and extensive pine plantations. Oberon and Katoomba are the only towns in NSW other than the ski resorts to regularly receive heavy snowfalls. Oberon makes a reasonable base for visiting the Jenolan Caves and the Kanangra Boyd and Blue Mountains National Parks.

Cobweb Craft Shop (☎ 6336 1895), on Oberon St (the main street), provides tourist information. The *Jenolan Caravan Park* (☎ 6336 0344) has tent sites for $10 for two people, on-site vans for $30 and cabins for $55. The *Royal* (☎ 6336 1011) and *Tourist* (☎ 6336 1378) hotels have rooms for $20 a person, and there are several motels.

On Tuesday, Friday and Sunday, Countrylink buses run from opposite the hardware store on Fleming St to Mt Victoria in the Blue Mountains, where they connect with trains to Sydney.

Abercrombie Caves
This group of about 50 caves is less well known than the Jenolan Caves but is worth visiting. The Grand Arch is one of the world's largest natural tunnels and even the side tunnels are huge – in the Hall of Terpsichore you can still see the dance floor installed by miners last century. The Archway cave is open from 10 am to 5 pm daily ($10/5 for adults/ children). To visit Bushranger's Cave you must take a guided tour. It leaves at 2 pm daily ($12/6). There's swimming near the caves and fossicking at Grove Creek.

There are *camp sites* for $10 and *cabins* from $40. For tour and accommodation information and bookings, call ☎ 6368 8603.

Abercrombie Caves are 15km south of Trunkey (another of the area's old villages) and 70km south-west of Bathurst.

Crookwell & Around

Crookwell is the largest town on the high, cold plateau extending south to Goulburn. It's a pleasant place, 45km north of Goulburn and nestled in a highland valley. Crookwell Promotion Centre (☎ 4832 1988), 44 Goulburn St, has tourist information and maps. **Stephenson's Mill Museum**, in a restored flour mill (1871) on Roberts St, has exhibits on local history. Popular activities in the area include trout fishing and fossicking. Crookwell's agricultural show is held in February, and over the Anzac Day long weekend in April, during the Autumn Festival, several of the town's gardens are open to the public.

Small villages dot the area around Crookwell, most founded in the early 19th century. Sheep in the surrounding paddocks produce small quantities of very fine wool.

A network of small roads offers interesting drives. From Goulburn you can cut through this area to Bathurst or Lithgow – not a bad 'back-door' route to the Jenolan Caves and the Blue Mountains, although some causeways flood after heavy rain. The route via **Taralga** involves a steep ascent from the valley where the Bummaroo Bridge crosses the Abercrombie River. The valley is a beautiful place but the road isn't suitable for caravans. You also meet semitrailers pounding along these unsealed roads, so take care.

Places to Stay The small, basic *Crookwell Caravan Park* (☎ 4832 1230), near the town centre on the Laggan-Taralga road, has sites for $8.50. There's accommodation at several pubs in town, including the *Criterion Hotel* (☎ 4832 1031) on Goulburn St and the *Crookwell Hotel Motel* (☎ 4832 1016), which also has motel units for $30/35 a single/double. The *Uplands Pastures Motel* (☎ 4832 1999), a few hundred metres off the main street on the Taralga road, is good value, with units for $58/68.

In Taralga the *Argyle Inn* (☎ 4840 2004), on Orchard St, has rooms for $25 per person including a light breakfast.

If you're interested in staying on a farm, contact the Crookwell Promotion Centre for details.

BATHURST TO MUDGEE

The road running to Mudgee curves east to run past towns on the western edge of the huge Wollemi National Park, one of the parks that protect the Blue Mountains. The Mudgee National Parks & Wildlife Service (NPWS; ☎ 6372 3122), 72 Church St, has information on this section of Wollemi.

Sofala

The picturesque village of Sofala, on the fast-flowing Turon River, is an old gold town, unusual for its large number of preserved timber buildings. It was the location for Peter Weir's 1974 film *The Cars that Ate Paris*. The general store (☎ 6337 7025) has information, including the useful booklet *A Pleasant Walk Around Sofala* ($1). The store is an amazing place, thoroughly cluttered with new and ancient stock. The Sofala Souvenir Shop houses the post office.

Places to Stay & Eat Contact June at the general store for information on accommodation. Camping is free down by the river – cross over the bridge from town and go left down the dirt road about 50m up from the bridge. The *Old Miner's Cottage* has simple rooms for $20 a night and the *Old Parsonage* has rooms for $25/50, including a light breakfast. Rooms are also available at the *Old Schoolhouse* for $20 per person and the *Royal Hotel*. The *Sofala Souvenir Shop* has 'Evanshire teas' and a variety of meals. There's also the licensed *Cafe Sofala*, open Friday to Sunday.

Getting There & Away Sofala is on the road between Mudgee and Bathurst. School buses and a weekly community bus offer the only public transport to Bathurst.

Hill End

In 1871 Hill End was one of the state's largest inland towns, with thousands of miners working a rich reef of gold. Deep mining required money, so, unlike other gold rushes, the Hill End rush attracted investors and speculators as well as diggers. Just two years later the gold ran out and the town declined rapidly.

Today, Hill End is almost a ghost town and most of its buildings are gone. Luckily, the town was visited by the photographer Beaufroy Merlin (see the boxed text 'The Holterman Collection' in this chapter), and in many empty spaces along the streets there are photos showing the vanished buildings. Hill End isn't quite deserted and the small community lives in an enviably pretty setting.

On the hill at the edge of town is the old hospital, now a museum and information centre (☎ 6337 8206), open from 9.30 am to 12.30 pm and 1.30 to 4.30 pm daily. Ask here about tours of the Bald Hill mine. In the hospital's old morgue, *Jill's Bazaar* offers light meals and second-hand goods.

Places to Stay There are two *camping* areas close to the town centre; book at the information centre. The *Royal Hotel* (☎ 6337 8261), the only surviving pub of the 28 that were once here, has singles/doubles for $30/45. There's also the *Holiday Ranch* (☎ 6337 8224), which costs from $15 per person.

Getting There & Away Hill End is accessible by unsealed roads from Mudgee (72km) and Bathurst (77km). The Bathurst road is a 'bridle track' and a popular 4WD route. The 2WD route from Bathurst is via Sofala. The road is narrow and winding and carries some speedy local traffic, so take care. Also watch out for horses and wandering cattle.

A weekly community bus runs to Bathurst, usually on Friday morning, returning to Hill End in the afternoon.

Lake Windamere

This water-storage dam on the Cudgegong River, about 25km south-east of Mudgee, is accessible from the Ilford-Mudgee road (not to be confused with the Ilford-Kandos-Mudgee road). Boating and fishing are popular and *Tabrabucca Lodge* (☎ 6358 8414),

south of the lake, has basic accommodation for $25 per person. There's also a *camping* area. BYO food.

Rylstone & Kandos

Rylstone is a pretty village, with some fine sandstone buildings, including the police station and St Malachi's Church. Kandos is a larger town; it has a cement industry. Access to Wollemi National Park from these towns is on rough roads – seek local knowledge before using them. The small *Apex Caravan Park* is in Rylstone. There's also a basic *camping* area at Dunns Swamp (Kendells Weir), which is accessible from Rylstone, but you might have to walk in.

MUDGEE
postcode 2850 • pop 9000

The Mudgee area was explored by Europeans in the 1820s and a small town grew up in the 1840s, expanding rapidly with the gold rushes of the 1850s. Today Mudgee is an interesting old town and a thriving centre for the nearby wineries. It's a popular weekend getaway for well-heeled visitors who come to taste the wine and honey. It's a pleasant and interesting place to explore.

Orientation & Information

Mudgee is about 120km north of Bathurst and Lithgow, on the banks of the Cudgegong River. Most wineries are north of the river. The main shopping street is Church St.

The information centre (☎ 1800 816 304), on Market St near the old police station, is open daily.

Work Despite the number of wineries in the area there isn't much casual grape-picking work available, as most is done by locals and is 'pre-booked'. The four-week picking season is around February and March.

Wineries

Most of the area's wineries are small and locally owned. The harvest season is later than in the Hunter Valley because of Mudgee's higher altitude.

Craigmoor (☎ 6372 4320), 4km north of Mudgee, has produced a vintage every year

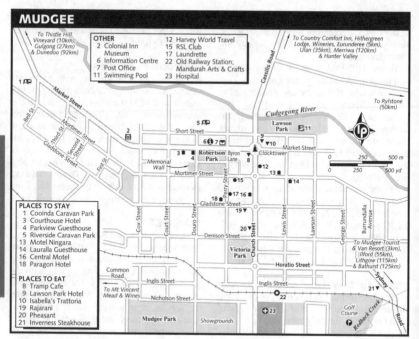

MUDGEE

OTHER
2 Colonial Inn Museum
6 Information Centre
7 Post Office
11 Swimming Pool
12 Harvey World Travel
15 RSL Club
17 Laundrette
22 Old Railway Station; Mandurah Arts & Crafts
23 Hospital

PLACES TO STAY
1 Cooinda Caravan Park
3 Courthouse Hotel
4 Parkview Guesthouse
5 Riverside Caravan Park
13 Motel Ningara
14 Lauralla Guesthouse
16 Central Motel
18 Paragon Hotel

PLACES TO EAT
8 Tramp Cafe
9 Lawson Park Hotel
10 Isabella's Trattoria
19 Rajarani
20 Pheasant
21 Inverness Steakhouse

since 1858, making it the second-oldest continuously operating winery in Australia. It now incorporates the well-known **Montrose** and **Poet's Corner** labels. You can see the original cellar and some antique wine-making equipment. The restaurant here is one of the area's best.

Botobolar and **Thistle Hall** both specialise in organically produced wine.

The tourist office provides a full list of the area's wineries and their opening times.

Other Attractions
It doesn't take long to realise that this is Henry Lawson country. The celebrated bush poet and short-story writer spent most of his childhood in and around Mudgee.

The information centre has details of a drive that takes in locations featured in Lawson's work. They include the **Old Bark School** at Eurunderee, where he began his schooling in 1876. Eurunderee is just north of Mudgee, off Henry Lawson Drive.

The **Colonial Inn Museum**, on Market St west of the information centre, re-creates several rooms of a 19th-century pub and has a large collection of early photos. Many fittings came from the old Budgee Budgee Inn, popularly believed to be the wine shanty involved in Henry Lawson's story 'The Loaded Dog'.

Lawson Park is a pleasant spot for a family picnic by the river at the top of Church St. **Mandurah** is an interesting arts and crafts co-op at the impressive old train station; it's open daily.

Special Events
The Mudgee Wine Festival, which continues through most of September, is the area's major event. Unfortunately, it occurs at the same time as another wine festival in the Hunter Valley. If you have to choose between the two events, the quality of the wine is perhaps better at the longer-established Hunter Valley festival but the Mudgee area

is more pleasant. This is a real rural festival and it coincides with the advent of spring.

Places to Stay

If you come to Mudgee on a weekend or during the wine festival you should book. Most prices stay the same all year.

The *Mudgee Cooinda* (☎ 6372 1236), Bell St, and *Riverside* (☎ 6372 2531, 22 Short St) caravan parks both have sites and cabins, and Cooinda has on-site vans as well. Riverside also has mountain-bike rental. *Mudgee Tourist & Van Resort* (☎ 6372 1090) is a few kilometres south-east of the centre of Mudgee on Lions Drive.

There are some above-average pubs. The *Paragon Hotel* (☎ 6372 1313), on the corner of Gladstone and Perry Sts, has clean, comfortable rooms for $28 per person including a big breakfast.

The *Courthouse* (☎ 6372 2068), on Market St, has double rooms for $40.

The cheapest motel in town is the *Central Motel* (☎ 6372 2268, 120 Church St), with singles/doubles for $35/45 and a family room for $55. *Motel Ningara* (☎ 6372 1133), on the corner of Mortimer and Lewis Sts, charges from $58/64. Top of the range is the big *Country Comfort Inn* (☎ 6372 4500), on Cassilis Rd north of the river, charging from $95 a room.

On the corner of Market and Douro Sts, across from Robertson Park, *Parkview Guesthouse* (☎ 6372 4477) has good doubles from $120, including a three-course breakfast. All the bedrooms have attached bathrooms and there is a guest kitchen.

Lauralla (☎ 6372 4480), on the corner of Lewis and Mortimer Sts, is an impressive Victorian home offering B&B for $100 a double during the week.

Thistle Hill Vineyard (☎ 6373 3546), on McDonald's Rd about 10km west of Mudgee, has a cottage for rent, which sleeps six.

There are many other guesthouses, most charging around $120 a double. Contact the information centre for a complete listing.

Places to Eat

Mudgee has a huge range of eating options. As well as the usual takeaways, cafes, Chinese restaurants and pubs, there are some places to eat that are a cut above the usual country-town standard.

The Tramp Cafe, through the archway at 61 Market St, is a pleasant spot for breakfast and light snacks. *Isabella's Trattoria*, on Market St, is a fairly smart, new Italian place with a large range of focaccia and good coffee.

For dinner, the *Rajarani* Indian restaurant, on Gladstone St, is open from Tuesday to Sunday. The *Red Heifer* restaurant at the Lawson Park Hotel, on the corner of Church and Short Sts, is a popular steakhouse, with good lunch specials. The licensed *Inverness Steakhouse* (☎ 6372 1701, 18 Sydney Rd) occupies a fine old coaching inn on the edge of town. It's open for dinner Wednesday to Saturday and for lunches on weekends.

Lauralla guesthouse's *Grapevine Restaurant* (☎ 6372 4480) has a good reputation for its $25 set meals; booking is essential. The *Pheasant* on Church St is a coffee shop by day, with lunch specials, and a licensed restaurant at night.

Out of town, the *Craigmoor Restaurant* (☎ 6372 4320), at the historic Craigmoor Winery, is one of the best places to eat in the area. The restaurant is on a mezzanine floor of the old cellars and has a varied menu, with cheaper lunch specials. It's open for lunch on weekends and for dinner on Friday and Saturday. *Augustine Winery* (☎ 6372 6816), George Campbell Dr, also has a good restaurant open for lunch daily and dinner on Friday and Saturday. Bookings are essential for both places.

Getting There & Away

Hazelton Airlines flies to Sydney most days ($160).

Countrylink has two buses daily to Lithgow, linking with the Sydney trains. The combined train/bus fare from Sydney to Mudgee is $42. The bus continues to Gulgong and beyond.

Harvey World Travel (☎ 6372 6077), near the gigantic clock on Church St, is the Countrylink agent. Buses depart from near the post office and from the old train station.

CENTRAL WEST

Getting Around

Harvey World Travel rents out a Falcon or Commodore for $94 a day, including 200km free, and other deals are possible. It's advisable to book in advance, especially on weekends.

Mudgee Radio Taxis (☎ 13 1008) can usually be found on Mortimer St near Church St.

GULGONG

postcode 2852 • pop 2000

Gulgong was known as 'the Hub of the World' during the roaring days of gold fever. It later called itself 'the town on the $10 note', but since the introduction of the plastic $10 note, it isn't.

History

Gulgong was created almost overnight in the rush that began in 1870. After 1880 the rush tapered off, but it left behind a well-established town that is today classified by the National Trust.

Author Henry Lawson spent part of his early childhood in the area after his parents followed the rush to the goldfields. Not that Lawson's memories of Gulgong were rosy; it was here that he learned to dislike the squalor, meanness and brutalising hard work and poverty of the goldfields. A bitterness that never quite faded, and a belief in the essential worth of everyday life, were instilled in Lawson here.

Gulgong's history is unusually well documented for a gold town. As well as Henry Lawson's writings, the novel *Robbery Under Arms* by Rolfe Boldrewood is partly set here. British novelist Anthony Trollope dropped in and wrote about what he saw, several journalists reported the rush and there are the wonderful photos of the Holterman Collection.

Orientation & Information

The main street of modern Gulgong is Herbert St, which leads south to Mudgee. The original main street was Mayne St, a delightful, narrow, old street that winds across town from the Wellington road. Near the junction with Herbert St is the old Opera House, built during the gold rush. The information centre (☎ 6374 1202), 109 Herbert St, opens daily.

Things to See

The **Gulgong Pioneer Museum** on Herbert St is one of the best country-town museums in the state. The huge collection of the important and the trivial borders on chaos, but it's all fascinating. Photographs of early Gulgong from the Holterman Collection are displayed, and there are also pin-up photos of the stars who drove the diggers wild at the local opera. The museum opens from 9

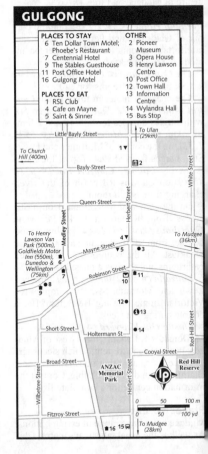

GULGONG

PLACES TO STAY	OTHER
6 Ten Dollar Town Motel;	2 Pioneer
Phoebe's Restaurant	Museum
7 Centennial Hotel	3 Opera House
9 The Stables Guesthouse	8 Henry Lawson
11 Post Office Hotel	Centre
16 Gulgong Motel	10 Post Office
	12 Town Hall
PLACES TO EAT	13 Information
1 RSL Club	Centre
4 Cafe on Mayne	14 Wylandra Hall
5 Saint & Sinner	15 Bus Stop

am to 5 pm daily ($4/2 for adults/children – a bargain).

The **Henry Lawson Centre**, 147 Mayne St, houses part of the collection of the Henry Lawson Society. It also has a good selection of Lawson's works for sale. The centre opens from 10 am to 1 pm Sunday to Tuesday and from 10 am to 3.30 pm Wednesday to Saturday ($3).

Special Events

The second weekend in June is the time for the big Henry Lawson Festival, which celebrates the author's birthday. There is music, dramatisations of Lawson stories at the Opera House, and literary awards, some sponsored by Norwegian organisations – Lawson's father was a Norwegian immigrant. Sheepdog trials, parades and many other events make this a hectic weekend for the many people who attend.

Gulgong also hosts a popular folk-music festival over the New Year period.

Places to Stay

The *Henry Lawson Van Park* (☎ 6374 1294), on Mayne St, is a little way out of town on the road to Wellington. Tent sites cost $5 per person and it also has overnight vans and family cabins.

The better hotels are the *Post Office Hotel* (☎ 6374 1031, 97 Herbert St), with basic pub accommodation, and the *Centennial* (☎ 6374 1241, 141 Mayne St), with en suite rooms from $40 a double. Across the road from the Centennial, the *Ten Dollar Town Motel* (☎ 6374 1204) has units from $69. The *Gulgong Motel* (☎ 6374 1122, 71 Medley St) does doubles with breakfast from $53, and the *Goldfields Motor Inn* (☎ 6374 1111), on the road to Wellington, has doubles from $57.

The *Stables Guesthouse* (☎ 6374 1668, 149 Mayne St) is a pleasant B&B. On weekdays, singles/doubles cost $75/105.

Places to Eat

Cafe on Mayne has good snacks and a fine balcony view. *Saint & Sinner*, on Mayne St, is a country cafe with interesting paintings. *Phoebe's Restaurant*, at the Ten Dol-

The Holterman Collection

Rediscovered in 1951, the Holterman Collection is an extremely important record of early settlement and goldfields life captured on thousands of photographic plates taken by Beaufroy Merlin and Charles Bayliss.

Merlin had been working as a travelling photographer for many years when he met Bernard Holterman in 1871. Holterman was a digger who had just struck it extremely rich and was interested in photography. He commissioned Merlin to produce an extensive series of photographs of New South Wales and Victoria, which he later used as a touring exhibition in Europe. Merlin died two years into the project, but the work was continued by Bayliss. It culminated in the building of a 25m-high tower to take panoramic shots of Sydney, using huge plates – one measured 1.5m across! The bulk of the collection is now housed in Sydney's Mitchell Library.

lar Town Motel on Medley St, is a good dinner option, or try the *RSL Club*, Herbert St.

Getting There & Away

The Countrylink service to Mudgee continues to Gulgong ($45 from Sydney). The post office takes bookings.

ORANGE

postcode 2800 • pop 35,000

The city of Orange is in a fertile agricultural area, but the crops grown do not include oranges – the city was named after Prince William of Orange. Cool-climate fruit and vegetables are the area's main produce.

Although it's now larger than Bathurst, Orange didn't have the administrative importance of its neighbour and it lacks the grand buildings, but it is a pleasant city of wide streets and parks. The altitude (950m) means that there are four distinct seasons, including cold winters, which bring occasional snowfalls.

History

Land grants were made in the area in the early 1830s, but Orange didn't appear until the 1840s, and it remained a small village until the 1851 gold rush at nearby Ophir. By the 1880s Orange was a large and prosperous town, shipping fruit to the Sydney markets on the new railway line. Orange was briefly considered as the site for the national capital, but Victoria didn't want the capital to be so close to Sydney and so far from Melbourne.

Orientation & Information

Suburban Orange sprawls over quite a large area, but the city centre, with its grid-pattern streets, is fairly compact and easy to get around. Summer St is the main street and the town centre begins just west of the train line.

The big Orange Visitors Centre (☎ 6361 5226), on Byng St near the railway line, opens from 9 am to 5 pm daily. It has a range of handy brochures, including a walking tour of the city and winery tours around the district. It also rents gold pans.

OCTEC, 247 Anson St, provides Internet access for $6 an hour. It opens from 9 am to 5 pm weekdays.

Work The autumn apple-picking season lasts for about six weeks. The harvest officer at the Employment National office (☎ 1300 720 126), on Anson St, can help you find work. Some orchards have accommodation.

Things to See

The excellent **Orange Regional Gallery** (☎ 6361 5136) in Civic Square (behind the visitors centre) has an ambitious, varied program of exhibitions. It's open from 11 am to 5 pm Tuesday to Saturday and 2 to 5 pm on Sunday and holidays (free).

The **Botanic Gardens** are on Clover Hill (with good views of the city), a couple of kilometres north of the city on Kearneys Drive. The gardens were established in 1981 to preserve the native woodlands of the area and to grow other plants suited to this cool climate. This is an interesting project, as most botanic gardens in the state were established long ago and are rigidly formal, echoing the gardens back 'home' in Britain (**Cook Park** in central Orange is a good example).

Many craftspeople live in the area and there are several outlets in town. The **Guildry** arts and crafts shop in Cook Park on Summer St opens daily.

Orange has some interesting old buildings, including the old **Town Hall** (1887) and the former **Union Bank**, both on Byng St.

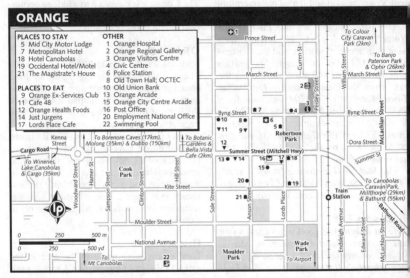

ORANGE

PLACES TO STAY	OTHER
5 Mid City Motor Lodge	1 Orange Hospital
7 Metropolitan Hotel	2 Orange Regional Gallery
18 Hotel Canobolas	3 Orange Visitors Centre
19 Occidental Hotel/Motel	4 Civic Centre
21 The Magistrate's House	6 Police Station
	8 Old Town Hall; OCTEC
PLACES TO EAT	10 Old Union Bank
9 Orange Ex-Services Club	13 Orange Arcade
11 Cafe 48	15 Orange City Centre Arcade
12 Orange Health Foods	16 Post Office
14 Just Jurgens	20 Employment National Office
17 Lords Place Cafe	22 Swimming Pool

Banjo Paterson

Andrew Barton ('Banjo') Paterson remains the bestselling poet in Australia 60 years after his death. If you know *Waltzing Matilda* you know a poem by 'the Banjo'. His popular ballads include *The Man from Snowy River* and *Clancy of the Overflow*.

Paterson was born near Orange in 1864 and grew up there and on stations around Yass, but was sent to an exclusive Sydney boarding school at an early age. He worked as a solicitor but became bored and spent the rest of his life in adventurous activities such as reporting on the Boer War, breaking horses in Egypt during WWI, pearl diving at Broome and shooting crocodiles in the Northern Territory.

Paterson's cheerful doggerel is in stark contrast to the more sombre work of Henry Lawson, although they shared an obsession with bush themes. The poets were not friends and at one time engaged in a rhyming debate. Paterson has a point when, in 'An Answer to Various Bards', he complains about Lawson and his ilk:

KN

> With their dreadful, dismal stories of the overlander's camp
> How his fire is always smoky and his boots are always damp;
> And they paint it so terrific it would fill one's soul with gloom,
> But you know they're fond of writing about 'corpses' and 'the tomb'.
> So, before they curse the bushland they should let their fancy range,
> And take something for their livers, and be cheerful for a change.

Paterson's range of experience was much wider than Lawson's, but his poetry is one-dimensional and often verges on the jingoistic. It's Paterson who is quoted when advertisers want to add a tinge of 'the real Australia'.

> And of course there's no denying that a bushman's life is tough
> But a man can easy stand it if he's built of sterling stuff.

Poet Banjo Paterson was born on Narrambla Station near Orange in 1864. The site of the station is now **Banjo Paterson Park**, about 3km north-east of Orange on the Ophir road, with picnic facilities.

Special Events

The Orange National Field Days, held during the third week in October, are the largest in the state. It's your chance to catch up on the world of tractors and chemical sprays, and to see events such as sheepdog trials.

Places to Stay

About 2km north-east of the city centre, *Colour City Caravan Park* (☎ 6362 7254), on Margaret St, has tent sites for $7.50, on-site vans for $25 a double and self-contained units for $40 a double, plus $6 for each extra person. There's also the *Canobolas Caravan Park* (☎ 6362 7279, 166 Bathurst Rd), south-east of the city centre, with sites for $8.

Hotel Canobolas (☎ 6362 2444, 248 Summer St) is a rarity in rural Australia: a hotel built specifically to provide accommodation. There is a ballroom and several other grand public rooms. Time has taken its toll, but the clean rooms are better than average pub rooms. With singles/doubles for $30/50, and $50/70 with bathroom, it's worth a try.

The *Metropolitan Hotel* (☎ 6362 1353), on the corner of Byng and Anson Sts, has rooms for $32/50 with breakfast. The *Occidental Hotel/Motel* (☎ 6362 4833), on the corner of Kite St and Lords Place, has good-value motel units for $45.

Most of the other motels are quite expensive. The central *Mid City Motor Lodge* (☎ 008 047 906, 245 Lords Place) is run by the Orange Ex-Services Club and charges $65/75.

Duntryleague Country Club (☎ 6362 3602), at the golf club on Woodward St, has rooms from $60/75. Duntryleague is an old mansion built in 1876, with the golf course constructed in its grounds in 1920.

The visitor centre has a list of B&Bs and farmstays in the district. Pick of the B&Bs are *The Magistrate's House* (☎ 6361 2510, 177 Anson St), with large suites with spas for $95/125, and *Strathroy Guesthouse B&B* (☎ 6361 4493, 24–26 Spring St), in an 1875 mansion with a beautiful, big garden. Rooms here cost from $75/85.

Places to Eat

For a good, cheap breakfast *Lords Place Cafe (211 Lords Place)* is the choice; it has an interesting collection of magazines to read.

Cafe 48 (48 Sale St) is a colourful BYO restaurant with a varied menu including curries and pasta.

There are many places along Summer St. *Just Jurgens* (☎ 6361 4999) Thai restaurant, next to the Orange Arcade, is a small but busy place with an excellent green curry in coconut sauce. For a smoothie or lentil burger, try *Orange Health Foods (143 Summer St)*. For Japanese takeaway, head for *Shinsu Mura* in the Orange City Centre arcade. The *Orange Ex-Services Club*, on Anson St, has a bistro and a restaurant.

Next to the Botanical Gardens, the friendly *Bella Vista* (☎ 6361 2858), a cafe overlooking Mount Canobolas, is an excellent spot to enjoy some good food and sample the local wines.

Highly recommended is the *Pippin Cafe* (☎ 6365 6190) at the Cargo Road Winery, 12km west of Orange on the Cargo Rd. Displaying interesting regional artwork, this place combines a great view with fine food and wine for a reasonable price. It's open from 11 am to 5 pm on the weekend.

Getting There & Away

You can buy bus and train tickets from the Countrylink Travel Centre (☎ 6361 9500) at the train station near the town centre.

Hazelton Airlines (☎ 6361 5888) flies to Sydney ($151) daily. The airport is 13km south-east of Orange. Shuttle buses leave from Harvey World Travel on Summer St.

Rendell's Coaches (☎ 1800 023 328) runs to Dubbo ($30) and Sydney ($30) daily. There's also a service to Canberra ($35) on Monday and Friday. Rendell's stops at the train station. Selwood's Coaches (☎ 6362 7963) also runs to Sydney daily from the station. Countrylink buses run to Parkes, Forbes, Dubbo, Bathurst and Lithgow.

XPTs (express trains) between Sydney and Dubbo stop here, as does the *Indian Pacific*, which runs west to Perth.

The Mitchell Hwy runs south to Bathurst and north to Wellington and Dubbo. Smaller roads run west to meet the Newell Hwy near Parkes and Forbes.

AROUND ORANGE
Mt Canobolas

Mt Canobolas (1395m) is a steep, extinct volcano 20km south-west of Orange. The views stretch a long way across the western plains, and in winter there's often snow on the peak. It's now a State Recreation Area (SRA) – you can drive to the top and there are a couple of walking tracks.

At the bottom of the mountain is **Lake Canobolas**, where you can see deer and lots of birds. Cabins are available at the *Mountain Tea House* (☎ 6365 3227) for $120 for four people. It's next to the main access road to the SRA. You can camp near the teahouse or in the SRA at Federal Falls.

Borenore Caves

About 17km north-west of Orange, these caves can be explored without a guide, but you'll need a torch (flashlight). You can camp nearby. From Orange, take the Mitchell Hwy (Woodward St) and turn off onto Forbes Rd.

Millthorpe & Around

Millthorpe is a neat village 29km south-east of Orange. On a winter's day it's somewhat reminiscent of a northern English village. The *Old Mill Cafe* (☎ 6366 3188) has tourist information and is open for lunch daily. There are several craft and antique shops, and there's B&B accommodation in the impressive old Bank of NSW building *Rosebank* (☎ 6366 3191, 40 Victoria St). Singles/doubles cost $95/140 (more on the weekend). Children aren't allowed here but they're allowed in the adjoining cottage, though it's more expensive. There's also pub accommodation at the *Railway Hotel* (☎ 6366 3157) and the *Commercial Hotel* (☎ 6366 3014). Each charges $20 per person.

Closer to Orange, **Byng** was settled by Cornish miners and retains some old buildings, notably the church (1872). The village is only accessible by dirt roads from Ophir or the Mitchell Hwy near **Shadforth**, another early village.

Molong is a larger town 35km north-west of Orange on the Mitchell Hwy. Molong boasts more early buildings and craft shops. The **Molong Historical Museum** (1856), on the corner of Gidley and Riddell Sts, opens on Sunday afternoon. East of Molong, off the Orange road, is the grave of Yuranigh, an Aboriginal guide on several of Major Mitchell's explorations. You can still see carvings on several nearby trees.

Ophir

The Ophir goldfield was the scene of Australia's first gold rush, and was quickly followed by other rushes in NSW and Victoria.

The Ophir field yielded nuggets rather than gold dust, so luck played as large a part as hard work. However, the easy pickings at Ophir were soon worked out, and most diggers had moved to other fields a year after the rush began. After the diggers left, deep mining was begun at Ophir, and continues today at Doctors Hill. A few fossickers still come here, and small finds by visitors aren't uncommon. You can buy a licence and a pan at the Gallery of Minerals in Orange (on the Mitchell Hwy on the eastern side of town); the gallery will help you identify your finds.

Ophir's diggings didn't develop into a permanent town. The rugged, bush-covered area is now a recreation reserve, with walk-

---

Gold!

Australia's first gold rush began at Ophir in 1851. There had been regular finds of alluvial fields before the Ophir rush, but the government had not broadcast the information, fearing the wholesale movement of population and the influx of foreigners that a gold rush would produce. Labour was needed to work the sheep stations, not to hunt for gold. Also, it wouldn't do for working people to get rich quickly!

However, in 1851 the government needed help with a stagnant economy and offered a reward to the discoverer of payable gold. Edward Hargraves, who had been on the Californian goldfields, found gold in Lewis Ponds Creek, and his associate William Tom found more nearby. Tom's father suggested the name Ophir (the biblical name for King Solomon's mines) for the field.

The government had been right to fear the consequences of a rush, as the fiercely independent 'diggers' (a word used for the first time on Ophir) from all over the world brought fresh political ideas into Australia. These democratic stirrings were to culminate in Australia's first and only popular revolt, the 1854 Eureka Rebellion on the Ballarat goldfields in Victoria.

The Ophir rush lasted only a year, but gold fever had hit New South Wales. Tens of thousands of diggers moved constantly from field to field for the rest of the century.

CENTRAL WEST

---

ing and fossicking the main activities. Signs of the diggers' activities remain, with mine shafts dotted all around the area (be careful – they're unmarked).

There are several walking trails and the Orange Visitors Centre has a map. Noel Rawlinson runs tours of Gunnadoo gold mine ($8/4 for adults/children); call ☎ 6366 0445 for information.

Places to Stay You can *camp* at Fitzroy Bar at the junction of Lewis Ponds and Summer Hill Creeks, the site of the diggers' tent-town. There are toilets and drinking water.

Getting There & Away From Orange, head east on March St. Be careful on the access roads – they're unsealed but carry speedy local traffic. Some sections of road within the Ophir area are steep, and unsuitable for caravans. Several creek crossings are impassable after heavy rain.

Wineries

Many wineries around Orange are open for sales and tastings, including **Cargo Road Winery** (☎ 6365 6100) and **Canobolas-Smith** (☎ 6365 6113), both open weekends and holidays and both on the road running south-west from Orange to Cargo. **Highland Heritage Estate** (☎ 6361 3612), 3km east of Orange on the Mitchell Hwy, is open daily.

The Orange Visitors Centre has a map with detailed directions to the wineries.

WELLINGTON

postcode 2820 • pop 5600

Wellington was the first settlement to be established west of Bathurst and was an important stopping place for settlers heading into the interior.

Orientation & Information

The town meanders along the east bank of the Bell River, which joins the Macquarie River just north of the town centre. Nanima Crescent curves past Bell River; Cameron Park runs down to the river from Nanima Crescent, and across the river is the pleasant Pioneer Park.

Next to the library in Cameron Park, Wellington Travel (☎ 1800 621 614) is also a helpful information centre. It's open from 9 am to 5 pm daily.

Things to See

The **Oxley Museum**, in an impressive old bank on the corner of Warne and Percy Sts, opens from 1.30 to 4.30 pm Sunday to Friday. There's a **lookout** on Mt Arthur in the forested Catombal Range, about 1km west of town along Maughan St.

Special Events

The horse-racing carnival in March culminates in the running of the town's answer to the Golden Slipper (Australia's premier event for two-year-olds), the Wellington Boot.

Places to Stay

There are several caravan parks. In town a good one is the **Riverside** (☎ 6845 1370), by the highway on the north bank of the Macquarie River. The best one is **Caves Caravan Park** (☎ 6845 2970) at nearby Wellington Caves. Both have tent sites for $10.

The heritage-style **Wellington Hotel** (☎ 6845 2083), on Swift St near the train station, is probably the nicest of the pubs and charges $25/35 for singles/doubles with breakfast.

Motels in Wellington include the **Garden Court** (☎ 1800 677 426, 7–9 Lee St), with rooms from $45/55, and the **Bridge** (☎ 6842 2555, 1–5 Lee St), by the river (from $49/59).

The information centre has details of the many farmstays and B&Bs in the area.

Getting There & Away

All long-distance buses leave from the post office. Greyhound Pioneer runs between Sydney ($48) and Wellington daily, arriving and departing early in the morning. Rendell's has a cheaper and more convenient daily service to Sydney ($45) and a service to Canberra on Monday, Wednesday and Friday ($45).

The Mitchell Hwy runs north to Dubbo and south to Orange. There is a sealed road east to Gulgong via Lincoln and Goolma. To Parkes, you can take the Mitchell south to Molong and head west from there, or there's a shorter, prettier drive through the hills via the village of Yeoval.

AROUND WELLINGTON

The **Wellington Caves**, off the highway 8km south of Wellington, are the region's main attraction. Cathedral Cave contains the largest stalagmite in the southern hemisphere. Caves can be visited on guided tours at 9, 10 and 11 am and 2, 3 and 4 pm. They cost $9.50/6 for adults/children. Across the road are the recently opened Japanese Gardens.

About 25km south-east of Wellington **Lake Burrendong** is a large water-storage dam, which is popular for water sports. I you want to stay, **Burrendong Park** (☎ 6846 7435) has camping sites ($9 for two), on-site vans ($30) and cabins ($45).

DUBBO

postcode 2830 • pop 38,000

One of the larger towns in the state, Dubbo is a rural centre and a transport crossroads on the farthest fringes of the central west region. Go north or west from Dubbo and you'll find that the population density drops dramatically and the outback begins.

John Oxley passed through in 1817 and graziers took up land in the area only a few

years later. The village of Dubbo appeared by 1850 and first took on its role as a highway stop in the 1860s, catering to the people rushing to the Victorian goldfields.

Orientation & Information

Dubbo's grid-pattern city centre lies just east of the Macquarie River, with parkland bordering both banks of the river.

The Mitchell and Newell Hwys cross at a roundabout just west of the river. The Newell Hwy becomes Whylandra St, then Erskine St as it bends east around the top end of the city centre; the Mitchell Hwy becomes Cobra St

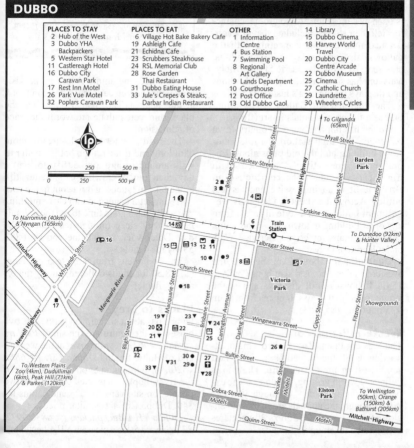

DUBBO

PLACES TO STAY	PLACES TO EAT	OTHER
2 Hub of the West	6 Village Hot Bake Bakery Cafe	1 Information
3 Dubbo YHA	19 Ashleigh Cafe	Centre
Backpackers	21 Echidna Cafe	4 Bus Station
5 Western Star Hotel	23 Scrubbers Steakhouse	7 Swimming Pool
11 Castlereagh Hotel	24 RSL Memorial Club	8 Regional
16 Dubbo City	28 Rose Garden	Art Gallery
Caravan Park	Thai Restaurant	9 Lands Department
17 Rest Inn Motel	31 Dubbo Eating House	10 Courthouse
26 Park Vue Motel	33 Jule's Crepes & Steaks;	12 Post Office
32 Poplars Caravan Park	Darbar Indian Restaurant	13 Old Dubbo Gaol

14 Library
15 Dubbo Cinema
18 Harvey World Travel
20 Dubbo City Centre Arcade
22 Dubbo Museum
25 Cinema
27 Catholic Church
29 Laundrette
30 Wheelers Cycles

and skirts the city centre to the south. The main shopping street is Macquarie St, which runs between the two.

The main information centre (☎ 6884 1422), at the top end of town on the corner of Macquarie and Erskine Sts, opens from 9 am to 5 pm daily.

The library on Talbragar St provides Internet access ($5 for 30 minutes). There is a laundrette on Brisbane St near the corner of Bultje St. Travel agents in town include Harvey World Travel (☎ 6881 8144) on Macquarie St.

Things to See & Do

The large **Old Dubbo Gaol** on Macquarie St is open as a museum. 'Animatronic' characters tell their stories, including that of a condemned man due for a meeting with the gallows, also on display ($6/3 for adults/children). Also on Macquarie St, the **Dubbo Museum** has some re-creations of old shops and displays on the area's history ($5/1).

The **Regional Art Gallery**, 165 Darling St, has a theme of animals in art (free).

Dubbo has impressive, old country-town buildings. The **train station** is a fine sandstone building and the old **pubs** along Talbragar St are suitably adorned with iron-laced verandas. The **courthouse** on Brisbane St is an impressive neoclassical edifice. Across the street is the **Lands Department** building, in a style different from any other building in town. The information centre has maps for both a Heritage Walk and a Heritage Drive.

Dundullimal, about 2km beyond the Western Plains Zoo, is a slab house built in 1840. It houses craft displays and is the venue for animal shows. It opens from 9 am to 5 pm daily ($5.50/3).

Western Plains Zoo

The Western Plains Zoo, Dubbo's major attraction, is off the Newell Hwy about 4km south-west of the town centre. The zoo is definitely worth visiting, but don't come expecting a safari park – although you can drive through, the animals are in moated enclosures and much of the zoo's 300 hectares seems to be taken up with roads.

Slab Houses

Slab houses – the Australian equivalent of US log cabins – were the earliest form of permanent European housing in the newly settled areas of New South Wales. The slabs were rough-cut tree trunks laid vertically around the frame, sometimes with mud packed into the inevitable gaps.

A slab house offered more protection than a tent but didn't require the time, tools or skills necessary for a more refined finish. Brick houses had to wait until the district was sufficiently populated to support a kiln, and stone buildings were almost exclusively the preserve of the gentry and the government.

Slab houses such as Dundullimal rarely survive, but you occasionally see more recent barns or shepherds huts made from slabs.

Of course, the animals' loss is the visitors' gain and you certainly get a good look at the inmates. The Bengal tigers and the black rhinoceros alone are worth the price of admission.

The road around the enclosures is about 6km long and if it isn't too hot it's better to walk around or hire a bike ($10 for half a day) than join the crawling cars. Better still, hire a bike in Dubbo and ride out to the zoo.

If you get a chance, do an early morning zoo walk. It's a good time to see the animals before they sleep through the heat of the day. Dates vary, so call the zoo (☎ 6882 5888) for details.

The zoo opens from 9 am to 5 pm daily ($16/8.50 for adults/children; family tickets are available).

Places to Stay

Dubbo has about six caravan parks. The two closest to the centre are the small *Poplars* (☎ 6882 4067), near the river at the western end of Bultje St, and *Dubbo City* (☎ 6882 4820), on Whylandra St on the west bank of the river. Poplars has sites for $11 for two people, on-site vans for $23 and cabins for $40. Dubbo City has similar prices.

Dubbo YHA Backpackers (☎ 6882 0922, 87 Brisbane St) is a pleasant YHA hostel just north of the railway line. From the bus station, head west on Erskine St. Dorm beds cost $15 and there are a few twin rooms ($30) and a family room ($40). The managers can advise on travel in the area and farther west, and they do free trips to the sheep and cattle markets on Monday, Thursday and Friday. Guests get a 10% discount on zoo tickets and bikes can be hired for $6 a day, which is much better value than the zoo's bikes.

Nearby is the *Hub of the West* (☎ *6882 5004, 79 Brisbane St)*. The accommodation resembles spartan student lodgings, but it's clean and perfectly adequate, though hardly inspiring, especially when school groups or shearers stay. Singles/doubles with shared bathrooms cost $25/45 and dorm bunks are $10 a head.

The *Castlereagh Hotel* (☎ *6882 4877),* on the corner of Talbragar and Brisbane Sts, is good. You don't want a room directly above the bar and you shouldn't expect everything to work perfectly, but it's clean and friendly, and many rooms have attached bathrooms. Rooms cost from $30/60, including a large cooked breakfast.

The *Western Star* (☎ *6882 4644, 62 Erskine St)* has good rooms for $30/50. Its meals are also recommended.

There are nearly 40 motels, mostly along Cobra St and the Newell Hwy. On long weekends and at other peak times they fill up quickly. The new *Rest Inn* (☎ *6882 9211),* on Whylandra St west of the centre just over the bridge, is a good deal, with rooms from $39 and family rooms for $55. In town, the *Park Vue* (☎ *6882 4253, 131 Bourke St)* is another decent cheapie, with rooms for $40/48.

Places to Eat
The 24-hour *Bus Stop Cafe*, at the bus station on Erskine St, is good value, with an all-you-can-eat salad bar for $6 and hot meals for $8.

The *Ashleigh Cafe* on Macquarie St is a good spot for breakfast, as is the *Village Hot Bake Bakery Cafe* *(113 Darling St),* near the bus station.

The *Dubbo Eating House* *(270 Macquarie St)* is recommended for big eaters. It does a cheap smorgasbord lunch and dinner. Most dishes are Asian but there is a bit of Anglo tucker as well. The bistro at the opulent *RSL Memorial Club* on Brisbane St is very popular; mains cost under $10.

Most hotels do meals. The *Castlereagh* is the pick, with cheap weekday counter lunches. *Scrubber's Steakhouse* (☎ *6882 9776, 69 Wingewarra St)* serves light meals during the day and $16 steaks at night.

To escape the mixed-grill menus, head for the southern end of Macquarie St. You'll find good coffee and tasty meals at the *Echidna Cafe* (☎ *6884 9393, 35/177 Macquarie St),* trendy pancakes at *Jule's Crepes & Steaks* (☎ *6882 9330, 213 Macquarie St)* and curries at the *Darbar Indian Restaurant* (☎ *6884 4338, 215 Macquarie St).* There's Thai food at the *Rose Garden* (☎ *6882 8322, 208 Brisbane St),* next to the Catholic church with the ski-jump spire.

Vegetarians will find a good range of snacks at *Pure and Natural* in the Dubbo City Centre Arcade.

Getting There & Away
Eastern Australia Airlines and Hazelton Airlines fly to Dubbo. The standard fare to Sydney is $184. Hazelton also flies to Broken Hill ($263).

The bus station (☎ 6884 4199) is on Erskine St and is open from 9 am to 5.30 pm and 11 am to 3 am weekdays, and 9 am to noon Saturday. It's easiest to make bus bookings there.

Most major bus companies pass through along the Newell Hwy, but the local company, Rendell's (1800 023 328), often has the cheapest fares to Sydney ($45). Sid Fogg's runs to Newcastle ($48) three times a week.

XPTs run to Sydney four times daily ($62).

Dubbo is at the junction of the Newell and Mitchell Hwys, so travellers who are heading for Sydney, Adelaide, Melbourne and Brisbane pass through.

Getting Around
Wheelers Cycles (☎ 6882 9899), on the corner of Bultje and Brisbane Sts, rents out mountain bikes for $15 a day.

PARKES
postcode 2870 • pop 10,500

Like many towns in the central west, Parkes began as a gold-rush settlement. A visit to the diggings by NSW premier Sir Henry Parkes in 1871 prompted the locals to change the name of their village from Currajong and name the main street after Parkes' wife, Clarinda. It's said that Parkes influenced the decision to route the railway through the town, so this sycophancy paid off.

Today, Parkes is at the junction of the railway line between Sydney and Perth and the line between Melbourne and Brisbane, and is a major freight terminal. The town is also an important rural centre.

Orientation & Information

From the south, the Newell Hwy takes a twisting route through the centre of Parkes, becoming Grenfell St, Welcome St and finally joining Clarinda St, the main shopping street, to begin its run north to Dubbo. This is a three-way intersection, with Dalton St, the road running west to Condobolin, also joining Clarinda St here. South of this intersection, Clarinda St curves eastwards and becomes the main route to Orange.

The Parkes information centre (☎ 6861 2365), in Kelly Reserve by the highway on the Dubbo side of the town centre, opens from 9 am to 5 pm Monday to Friday and from 10 am to 4 pm on the weekend.

Museums

On the Dubbo side of town, **Pioneer Park** (☎ 6862 3732) contains farm relics from around the area. It's open from 2 to 4 pm Tuesday, Thursday and Saturday ($1.50/0.60 for adults/children).

Vintage cars are on show from 10 am to 4 pm Monday to Saturday at **Parkes Motor Museum** (☎ 6862 1975), on the corner of Bogan and Dalton Sts ($2/1).

Parkes Radio Telescope

The Parkes Radio Telescope, built by the Commonwealth Scientific and Industrial Research Organization (CSIRO) in 1961, is 6km east of the Newell Hwy, about 20km north of Parkes. It has helped Australian radio-astronomers become world leaders in their science, and brought pictures of the Apollo 11 moon landing. Over half the known pulsars (incredibly dense neutron stars) have been discovered at Parkes.

Although the telescope is off-limits, you can get close enough for a good look. There's an interesting visitors centre (☎ 6861 1777), with hands-on displays and screens that show you what the astronomers see; it's open from 8.30 am to 4.30 pm daily (free).

Special Events

There's a Country Music Jamboree on the Labour Day long weekend in early October, when there's also an antique motorcycle rally. A large agricultural show takes place in late August.

Places to Stay

On the corner of Victoria and Albert Sts, **Spicer Park Caravan Park** (☎ 6862 1654) has sites for $14. **Currajong Caravan Park** (☎ 6862 3400) is by the Newell Hwy, 300m north of Kelly Park and the information centre; powered sites cost $15 and there is a pool. **Parkes Overnighter Caravans** (☎ 6862 1707, 48 Bushman St), west of the centre, has sites for $12, and **Parkes Highway Caravan Park** (☎ 6862 1108), on the Newell Hwy near the train station, has sites for $11.

All except Spicer Park have on-site vans ($28 to $32) and all have cabins for around $40 a double. The Spicer Park cabins are the best equipped.

Most pubs have accommodation. The rooms at the **Parkes Hotel** (☎ 6862 2498, 1 Welcome St) are a bit better equipped than most and cost $28/35 a single/double. Others are the **Royal** (☎ 6862 2039), the **Cambridge** (☎ 6862 2098) and the **Commercial** (☎ 6862 1526), all on Clarinda St and charging around $20/30.

Parkes is well supplied with motels. The good value **Clarinda Motel** (☎ 6862 1655, 72 Clarinda St), south of the centre, has small but reasonable rooms for $48/53. There are several other places charging about the same, including the **Coachman** (☎ 6862 2622, Welcome St). Of the more upmarket places, the **All Settlers Motor Inn** (☎ 6862

2022, 20 Welcome St), across from Cooke Park, is a fair example and costs $68/78.

Getting There & Away
Hazelton Airlines flies to Sydney three times a day.

Countrylink buses run to Cootamundra and Dubbo (both $16 one way). It runs daily to Sydney and twice a week to Canberra.

The *Indian Pacific* train stops here on the run between Sydney and Perth. The Sydney-Broken Hill Western Explorer also stops en route.

As well as the Newell Hwy, smaller roads run east to Orange and west to Condobolin and into the far west.

FORBES
postcode 2871 • pop 8500
Smaller than nearby Parkes, Forbes has retained much of its 19th-century flavour and is worth exploring.

John Oxley was the first European through the area, on his 1817 expedition. During the gold rush of 1861 the town boomed, shrinking rapidly a few years later when the gold ran out.

Orientation & Information
Forbes has two main roads: Dowling St (the Newell Hwy) and, parallel, Rankin St.

The cheerful information centre (☎ 6852 4155), in the old train station just off the highway at the northern end of town, opens from 9 am to 5 pm daily.

Things to See & Do
The **Town Hall** faces Victoria Park, forming a nice town square. The park is also flanked by the **courthouse** (1880) and the **Vandenberg Hotel**, less grandiose but better proportioned than other hotels in town. At the tower atop the **Albion Hotel** on Lachlan St a watch was kept for Cobb & Co coaches. The Albion also contains the interesting **Bushrangers Hall of Fame** in the old tunnels beneath the pub. The **Lands Office** (now the state government offices) on Camp St is a fine wooden building, designed for the climate.

Osborne Hall on Cross St was the dance-hall of the Osborne Hotel and now houses the **Forbes Museum** (☎ 6852 1694) of local history, with Ben Hall relics. It's open from 3 to 5 pm daily October to May, and from 2 to 4 pm June to September ($2/1 for adults/children).

The **Lachlan Vintage Village**, 1km south beside the Newell Hwy, has some original and some re-created buildings. The village (☎ 6852 2655) is on the site of the old goldfields; you can pan for gold. It's open from 9.30 am to 5.30 pm daily ($8/4).

Just off the Newell Hwy about 4km south of Forbes, **Gum Swamp** is a wetland area that is home to many species of birds.

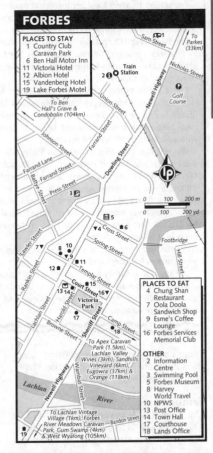

FORBES

PLACES TO STAY
1 Country Club Caravan Park
6 Ben Hall Motor Inn
11 Victoria Hotel
12 Albion Hotel
15 Vandenberg Hotel
19 Lake Forbes Motel

PLACES TO EAT
4 Chung Shan Restaurant
7 Oola Doola Sandwich Shop
9 Esme's Coffee Lounge
16 Forbes Services Memorial Club

OTHER
2 Information Centre
3 Swimming Pool
5 Forbes Museum
8 Harvey World Travel
10 NPWS
13 Post Office
14 Town Hall
17 Courthouse
18 Lands Office

Ben Hall, Jesse James & Elvis

Ben Hall (1838–65) lived and died at a time when the ordinary people of Australia were beginning to see themselves as a people; a time when the concepts of social and political democracy and suspicion of authority were becoming ingrained in the national character.

However, political and economic power was still wielded by a British-oriented elite. Land and power were apportioned to people of 'quality' (or at least wealth), and it was still expected that the British class system would take root in Australia. If ordinary colonials were not sufficiently servile it was because they were crude and uneducated. The legal system was well equipped to deal with such upstarts.

Ben Hall's parents had been convicts and he grew up with a hatred of the prevailing system and of police in particular. He lived a reasonably respectable life, working as a stockman and leasing a cattle-run, until his wife left him – for a policeman! Enraged, he joined Frank Gardiner and John Gilbert and turned to bushranging.

From 1861 to 1865 they terrorised and mocked the gentry of a large area in the central west. During this period, Hall is credited with 613 armed robberies. Compare this with US outlaw Jesse James: Over 16½ years he is credited with only 27 armed robberies!

The band's exploits smacked of larrikinism – capturing and ridiculing police (led by English noble Sir Frederick Pottinger), forcing respectable folk to get drunk and sing songs, stealing racehorses, giving alcohol and cigars to the poor – and above all demonstrating that it was possible to flout the conventions of society.

This band of bushrangers saw themselves as latter-day Robin Hoods, and to the local people they were heroes. The police were unable to capture them because no-one would inform on them, until 1865 when the government began to punish people who associated with Hall and his cronies.

Ben Hall was shot dead by police on 5 May 1865, but just how he was killed is uncertain. The official story is that he died while resisting arrest, but popular legend has it that he was shot while sleeping. His bullet-riddled body was displayed in Forbes as a warning to would-be renegades, but people openly mourned his death at his funeral and his status as a folk hero grew. Flowers are still sometimes placed on his grave in the Forbes cemetery.

A bitter folk song, *The Streets of Forbes*, gives the popular version of his career and death.

In Farnell St in Forbes there's a replica of a house associated with another apparent rebel beloved of the common folk and still loudly mourned – Elvis Presley's Graceland, built, somewhat appropriately, by the local undertaker.

TC

There's a hide to watch them from; sunset and sunrise are the best times. Bring plenty of insect repellent.

Wineries

The **Sandhills Vineyard** (☎ 6852 1437), which is about 6km north-east of town off Orange Rd (the continuation of Camp and Bridge Sts), opens for tastings from 9 am to 5 pm Monday to Saturday and from noon to 5 pm Sunday. You might want to take a look at the wine museum here.

Lachlan Valley Wines (☎ 6852 3983), on Wandary Lane, which splits from the Cowra road just after the Apex Caravan Park, opens from 9 am to 5.30 pm daily.

Places to Stay

The *Country Club Caravan Park* (☎ 6852 1957), on Sam St north of town, has sites for $12. *Forbes River Meadows Caravan Park* (☎ 6852 2694), by the Lachlan River on the Newell Hwy south-west of town, has sites for $9 and on-site vans for $25 and cabins from $35. *Apex Caravan Park* (☎ 6852 1929), also by the Lachlan River but south-east of town near the Cowra road, has sites for $11 and cabins for $28/35.

The impressive *Albion Hotel* (☎ 6852 1881, 135 Lachlan St) has better-than-average rooms for $15/30 a single/double, plus $5 for breakfast. Also on Lachlan St, the *Victoria Hotel* (☎ 6852 1269) has rooms with bath for $40. Most motels are pricey. A couple of cheaper ones are the *Ben Hall Motor Inn* (☎ 6851 2345, 5–7 Cross St), with units for $45/52 and *Lake Forbes Motel* (☎ 6852 2922, 8 Junction St), with units for $47/54.

Places to Eat

For cheap, quick meals try *Esme's Coffee Lounge* on Templar St or the *Oola Doola Sandwich Shop*, close by on Rankin St. The *Balcony Restaurant* at the Albion Hotel serves good food and has a nice balcony outlook onto Lachlan St.

There are several Chinese places, including the *Chung Shan*, which has lunch specials. The *Services Memorial Club*, on the corner of Sheriff and Templar Sts, has a large restaurant.

Getting There & Away

Harvey World Travel (☎ 6852 2344), 6 Templar St, handles bus bookings.

Greyhound Pioneer and McCafferty's buses pass through Forbes. Countrylink buses stop at the train station and run to Orange, Parkes and Condobolin.

Forbes is on the Newell Hwy. Smaller roads head east to Canowindra and Cowra, south to Grenfell and west to Condobolin and into the far west.

Getting Around

Forbes Bus Lines (☎ 6852 1663) runs local buses. Car-rental companies Budget (☎ 6852

2245) and Hertz (☎ 6852 1755) have agents in town. Phone (☎ 6852 2222) for a taxi.

CONDOBOLIN & AROUND
postcode 2877 • pop 3500

Condobolin is a medium-sized town on the Lachlan River. It's the service centre for farms in the Lachlan Valley.

There were once many Chinese living in the area and there's a restored section of Chinese graves in the town's cemetery.

The 40-hectare **Gum Bend Lake**, 3km west, is a venue for water sports. In town, Taylor's Marine, on Lachlan St, hires watersports equipment. About 8km north of Condo is **Mt Tilga**, officially the geographical centre of NSW. There's a road to the bottom and you can climb to the top of the mountain.

Places to Stay

The shaded *Riverview Caravan Park* (☎ 6895 2611), on the banks of the Lachlan River south of the bridge, has sites for $10.

The pubs have accommodation and the *Condobolin Hotel* (☎ 6895 2040) has motel-style single/double units for $40/45. Two motels – *Condobolin Motor Inn* (☎ 6895 2233), which charges $55/62, and the *Allambie* (☎ 6895 2722), charging $54/60 – are on William St.

Getting There & Away

Condobolin Travel (☎ 6895 2988), on Bathurst St, handles train and bus bookings.

Countrylink buses run to Cootamundra ($50) via Lake Cargelligo, West Wyalong and Temora, and to Parkes, Forbes and Orange.

The *Indian Pacific* train stops every Sunday and Wednesday on its way to Sydney. The *Outback Explorer* runs to Sydney every Friday.

Roads run east to the Newell Hwy at Parkes or Forbes, and south to the Newell Hwy at West Wyalong. You can drive west to Lake Cargelligo and on to the Riverina and the far west. There are also some interesting routes north.

NORTH OF CONDOBOLIN

North of Condobolin, the farmland begins to blur into the outback. If you're heading

CENTRAL WEST

north to the Barrier Hwy there are several routes from Condobolin that don't involve backtracking to the Newell Hwy. These are all at least partly unsealed, so check conditions before setting out, drive carefully and take a good map.

To Cobar, the road runs through **Bobadah** (no fuel or accommodation) and **Nymagee**, a hamlet with basic services including the *Nymagee Hotel* (☎ 6837 3854). You can also get to Cobar on the Kidman Way. **Mt Hope** consists of the *Royal Hotel* (☎ 6897 7984), a petrol station and a shop. It's a friendly hamlet (population 12) on the Kidman Way and used to be a large copper-mining town.

To get to Nyngan head directly north from Condobolin (if you have a good map) or, for a better road, drive east towards Parkes and turn off to **Tullamore**, a fair-sized village about 80km north-east of Condobolin, with a pub, fuel and shops. Farther on is **Tottenham**, a smaller but nicer place. There's a pub here as well.

COWRA

postcode 2794 • pop 9100

Cowra developed because it was on the only easy crossing of the Lachlan River for some way. The town straggles up the side of a steep hill above the river. The main landmark is a set of traffic lights, on the corner of Kendal (the Mid-Western Hwy) and Brisbane Sts.

The information centre (☎ 6342 4333), on the highway west of the shopping centre across the bridge, opens from 9 am to 5 pm daily.

During WWII, the prisoner-of-war (POW) camp at Cowra was the scene of the Cowra break-out. The **Japanese War Cemetery** is a few kilometres north of town on Binni Creek Rd (Brisbane St).

Japanese Garden

Built as a token of Cowra's connection with Japanese POWs (but with no overt mention of the war or the break-out), the garden and the attached cultural centre are worth visiting. The large garden, serene and beautifully maintained, was a gift from the Japanese government. The cultural centre is a peaceful

The Cowra Break-Out

During WWII the large prisoner-of-war (POW) camp at Cowra held mainly Italian and Japanese prisoners. In the early hours of 5 August 1944 the Japanese prisoners overran their section of the camp and nearly 400 went over the wire in an escape attempt that never had a chance of succeeding. Of the 230 Japanese who died, many had committed suicide.

The official report of the Cowra break-out (available at the information centre for $2.50) makes interesting reading. It's strange that amid the racist propaganda of WWII, the inquiry into the break-out was concerned about how much force was used on the escapees and whether the Japanese dead were treated with respect. Soldiers hunting the escapees were armed only with bayonets until a soldier was killed.

The book *Die Like the Carp* (also available at the information centre) tells the story of the break-out.

place, with displays of modern Japanese art, some modern Japanese kitsch and some antiques. There's a collection of *ukiyo-e* paintings, depicting everyday events in the lives of ordinary people in pre-industrial Japan.

The garden opens from 8.30 am to 5 pm daily ($7/4 for adults/children).

The garden is at the top of Bellevue Hill, a steep kilometre or so north up Brisbane St. Nearby is the **Bellevue Hill Flora & Fauna Reserve**, a complete contrast to the formality of its neighbour.

Steam Museum

Cowra Steam Museum (☎ 6341 1052), on Campbell St, opens from 9.30 am to 4.30 pm on weekends and holidays ($5). From here, the Lachlan Valley Railway Society runs steam trains two or three days a month to Blayney and Canowindra.

War, Rail & Rural Museum

This interesting museum includes a large POW display as well as lots of railway and farming memorabilia. It's good fun and there's lots of 'hands-on' stuff for kids. The museum is 3km from town on the Mid-Western Hwy and is open from 9 am to 5 pm daily ($7.50/5).

Special Events
The agricultural show and Sakura Matsuri, the Cherry Blossom Festival, are held in October.

Places to Stay
The riverside *Cowravan Park* (☎ *6342 1058)*, on Lachlan St south of Kendal St, has sites for $11 and cabins for $45.

Most hotels have accommodation, including the big *Imperial Hotel* (☎ *6342 1588, 14 Kendal St)* with basic singles/doubles for $25/40.

Motels include the *Cowra Motor Inn* (☎ *6342 2799, 3 Macquarie St)*, with rooms for $38/48, and the *Aalana* (☎ *6341 1177, 161 Kendal St)*, with units for $68/78. The *Vineyard* (☎ *6342 3641)* is a small place about 4km south-west of town on Chardonnay Rd, away from highway noise. It has rooms for $75/85.

Places to Eat
Most eateries are on Kendal St. The pies at *Royce's Bakery* score well in the Great Aussie Meat Pie competition. The *Garden of Roses* cafe has sandwiches, burgers and pizza. Nearby, the *Hoong Hing* Chinese restaurant opens for lunch and dinner daily.

Ilfracombe (☎ *6341 1511, 127 Kendal St)*, east of the traffic lights, is a historic cottage housing an excellent upmarket restaurant, with a cosy cafe in its next-door extension. The restaurant, open for dinner Wednesday to Saturday, has a French-based menu using local produce and serves local wines. The cafe opens for lunch and dinner Tuesday to Saturday. For Japanese food, try *Chabana* (☎ *6341 2233)* at the Japanese Garden. It also has a standard cafe menu.

Getting There & Away
Rendell's Coaches runs Monday and Friday to Orange ($25) and Canberra ($30), from the information centre. Greyhound Pioneer stops at the Mobil petrol station, near the information centre, on its Melbourne-Brisbane run. Countrylink runs between Bathurst and Cootamundra, and stops on Macquarie St near the corner of Kendal St.

Lachlan Travel (☎ 6342 4000), 61 Kendal St, sells tickets and is the Countrylink agent.

Cowra is on the Mid-Western Hwy, which runs west through Grenfell. The Olympic Way runs south-west to Young and Wagga Wagga. Smaller roads run south to the Hume Hwy at Yass, south-east to Crookwell and Goulburn, north to Canowindra and north-west to Forbes.

AROUND COWRA
To the west of Cowra the Lachlan River flows through picturesque, fertile farmland. The road to Forbes (turn off the Mid-Western Hwy about 5km south of Cowra) runs along the Lachlan River and is a nice drive. At Paynters Bridge, about 45km on from the turn-off, cross the Lachlan to visit **Eugowra**, a rambling village in the shadow of bush-clad hills. Eugowra was held up by Ben Hall in 1863, and there is a re-enactment every October. Granite quarried here was used to build the new Parliament House in Canberra. You can also get here from Canowindra, via a road along the Lachlan River's north side.

Canowindra
The sprawling town of Canowindra, about 30km north of Cowra, is a service centre for the surrounding rich farmlands. Curving Gaskill St, the main street, follows the route of a bullock-cart track. In 1863 bushranger Ben Hall held up the town for three days.

Schneider's Bakery, on Gaskill St, has limited tourist information and good pies; it's open daily. Fossil finds from a rich, 360-million-year-old fossil bed discovered in the area are in the new **Age of Fishes Museum** (☎ 6344 1008) on Gaskill St. It's open from 10 am to 4 pm on the weekend, but there's often someone there during the week ($5/3 for adults/children; includes a tour and talk). It also arranges visits to the fossil sites.

Canowindra's main attraction is **ballooning**. In April, it holds a popular balloon festival. Several outfits offer flights; Balloon Aloft (☎ 1800 028 568) charges $175 for a flight and champagne breakfast.

Places to Stay By the river near the top of Gaskill St, *Canowindra Caravan Park* (☎ 6344 1272) has sites for $5. *Canowindra Hotel (☎ 6344 1407)*, on Gaskill St near the park, has singles/doubles for $20/35. *Blue Jacket Motel (☎ 6344 1002)*, on the Cowra road a couple of kilometres from the village centre, charges $50/58.

Getting There & Away Countrylink buses stop on the corner of Gaskill and Blatchford Sts at the northern end of town.

Wyangala Waters State Recreation Area

Taking in Wyangala Dam south-east of Cowra, this SRA (☎ 6345 0877) is popular for windsurfing, swimming, canoeing and sailing. Accommodation includes tent sites, a caravan park, cottages and cabins.

Conimbla National Park

This small park (7590 hectares) is in two sections, only one of which has ready access. There's some pleasant forest and, in the spring, wildflowers.

There's camping within the park along Barryrennie Rd, the main access road. *Barryrennie Camping Ground (☎ 6342 9239)*, at the south-eastern end of the park, is a simple place geared to bushwalkers and has basic facilities. The owners are friendly and can help with information about the park. Sites cost $5 per person.

The park can be reached from Gooloogong to the north (on the Cowra-Forbes road) or from Cowra – head west towards Grenfell for 9km and turn right at the signposted turn-off.

Nangar National Park

Even smaller than Conimbla, this park (4000 hectares) is 15km east of Eugowra on the road to Cudal and Orange. Despite its size there is diverse vegetation and it offers some tough bushwalking. There are no facilities and only foot access.

Grenfell

Grenfell is a quiet country town today, but in 1867 there were 10,000 diggers here searching for gold. Main St curves through the town centre and has some beautiful old buildings, notably the banks. Running parallel is tiny George St, the original (and even more curved) main street where a couple of the original buildings still stand.

Tourist information is available from the Wool & Craft Centre on Main St; it's open from 10 am to 4 pm daily.

The town's main claim to fame is that Henry Lawson was born here in 1867, although he and his family left for the goldfields near Gulgong when he was an infant. A memorial marking Lawson's birthplace is off the highway at the eastern edge of town; turn off just before the railway crossing. The annual **Henry Lawson Arts Festival** is held around the writer's birthday on 17 June.

For something completely different, Grenfell hosts the **National Guinea Pig Races** during Easter and in June.

Places to Stay The *Exchange Hotel* (☎ 6343 1034) has rooms for $20 per person, including breakfast, while the recently renovated *Royal Hotel (☎ 6343 1412)* charges $15/25 for singles/doubles, including breakfast. The *Grenfell Motel (☎ 6343 1333)* charges $45/55. All are on Main St.

An interesting B&B is *Grenfell House (☎ 6343 2235, 7 Weddin St)*, in a meticulously restored Victorian convent. Rooms cost from $50 per person.

Weddin Mountains National Park

Nineteen kilometres south-west of Grenfell, Weddin isn't large (8361 hectares), but it's a rugged place with lots of wildlife, Aboriginal sites and some good walking trails. *Holy Camp* in the north-west and *Seatons Camp* in the north-east are camping areas; both have road access and you can walk between them. The NPWS office (☎ 6851 4429) in Forbes has more information.

WEST WYALONG & AROUND
postcode 2671 • pop 3800

West Wyalong, a middling-size town on the Newell and Mid-Western Hwys, is a rare example of stubbornness winning out over bureaucracy. A settlement grew here during a gold rush late last century, but the government decided that Wyalong, a few kilometres east, was to be the town. A grid of streets was laid out, official buildings were erected and the government waited for the population of West Wyalong to get the message and move. It didn't. West Wyalong is still the larger town and its Main St follows the same curving path it did when it was a bullock track.

The 'sometimes-open' information centre (☎ 6972 3645) is in an old railway carriage in McCann Park, on the Mid-Western Hwy.

Things to See & Do

The Bland District (West Wyalong is part of this unfortunately named shire) **museum**, at the eastern end of Main St, has a collection of photos of the goldfields and the town's development. It's open from 2.30 to 5 pm Monday to Saturday and 10 am to 12.30 pm Sunday ($3/0.50 for adults/children).

The local Aboriginal Land Council has a **craft and artefact shop** at 76 Main St, towards the eastern end.

When it's full, **Lake Cowal** is the largest freshwater lake in the state. The area is an animal sanctuary and the lake supports plenty of birdlife, but getting to see it isn't simple. The lake is surrounded by farmland and even the usually accurate National Roads & Motorists Association (NRMA) map has problems with the tangle of backroads and farm tracks around the lake; don't travel on them after heavy rain. A road leading in the general direction of the lake leaves the Newell Hwy about 15km north of Marsden. Good luck.

Places to Stay

There are two caravan parks: the *Ace* (☎ 6972 3061), on the corner of the Newell and Mid-Western Hwys, and the *West Wyalong* (☎ 6972 3133), Neeld St. Both have sites for $11, cabins and on-site vans.

Tattersalls Hotel (☎ 6972 2030), on the corner of Main and Monash Sts, has OK pub rooms for $25. Also on Main St, the 'dry' (no alcohol is served) *Metropolitan Hotel* (☎ 6972 0400, 156 Main St) has been renovated recently. Singles/doubles cost $25/35 and family rooms $65.

The *Charles Sturt Motor Inn* (☎ 6972 2422), on Main St, is good value at $45/55.

Places to Eat

The *New Paragon Cafe* is West Wyalong's typical main-street, greasy-spoon cafe. A bit more upmarket is *Tamara's Metropolitan Cafe & Restaurant*, in the Metropolitan Hotel. It's open for three meals a day.

The pubs on Main St have cheap counter meals. Tattersalls Hotel has specials for $5. There's also the *Jan Wah* Chinese restaurant on Main St, and the *Services & Citizens Club* on Monash St.

In Wyalong you can buy meals at a 24-hour petrol station.

Getting There & Away

Countrylink buses run to Cootamundra and Condobolin. The stop is on Church St off Main St, around the corner from the post office. Harvey World Travel (☎ 6972 2744), next to the post office, takes bookings.

YOUNG

postcode 2594 • pop 12,000

Young, Australia's 'cherry capital', is on the edge of the western slopes of the Great Dividing Range. East of here is rolling country; to the west the plains of the Riverina begin.

Cherries were first planted here in around 1860 by Nicole Jasprizza, who arrived during one of the central west's many gold rushes. His orchard was an immediate success and expanded rapidly.

Today there are about 130 orchards producing a large proportion of Australia's crop and earning Young its 'cherry capital' tag. Prunes are also an important local industry, but 'prune capital' doesn't have quite the same ring.

The notorious 'White Australia policy' of Australia's early years had its origins near Young – goldfield riots at Lambing Flat in 1861 led to the government restriction on Chinese immigration, a classic example of blaming the victim.

Information

The tourist information centre (☎ 6382 5433), near the creek on Short St (the

CENTRAL WEST

Olympic Way as it enters town from the south), opens from 9 am to 5 pm Monday to Friday and 9.30 am to 4 pm on the weekend.

Work The cherry harvest is in November and December. In January other stone fruits are harvested and in February the prune harvest begins. The Employment National office (☎ 13 3400), 187 Boorowa St, can help you find fruit-picking work.

Wineries
This area produced wine grapes from the 1880s until the 1930s, when the more profitable cherry orchards took over. In the 1970s the Barwang vineyard was established, and there are now about 15 small vineyards in the area, with a couple you can visit for tastings and sales. **Woodonga Hill** (☎ 6389 2972), north-east of Young on the Cowra road, opens daily; **Demondrille Vineyards** (☎ 6384 4272), south on the Prunevale road near Kingsvale, opens Friday to Sunday.

Other Attractions
The **Lambing Flat Folk Museum** (☎ 6382 2248), on Campbell St, displays artefacts from the goldfields. It's open from 10 am to 4 pm daily ($2/0.50 for adults/children).

The information centre can tell you about **orchards** open for inspection and where you can pick your own fruit. **JD's Jam Factory**, just out of town on the Grenfell road, is worth a stop to have a look at a small jam factory in operation (free). You can also sample or buy some of the produce.

The **Millard's Building** is on Boorowa St opposite the town hall. It was once a huge department store, built by Edward Millard who started out as a 'carpenter, joiner and undertaker'.

Special Events
The Cherry Festival is held on the last weekend in November and the first weekend in December – but if you want to see the trees in blossom, come in early October.

The Young Show is held in late September. The Young-Burragong Picnic Races are held in October, and this is one of the largest picnic race meetings in the state.

Places to Stay & Eat
North of the town centre, *Young Caravan Park* (☎ 6382 2190), on Zouch St, has tent sites for $10, on-site vans from $33 and self-contained units from $42.

The *Australian Hotel* (☎ 6382 5544) on Boorowa St, has singles/doubles for $25/35, including breakfast. The *Commercial Hotel* (☎ 6382 5899), on the corner of Boorowa and Main Sts, has rooms for $20 per head. Motels include the *Cherry Blossom* (☎ 6382 1699), the *Colonial* (☎ 6382 2822) and the *Goldrush* (☎ 6382 3444). None stands out and all are in the $55/70 bracket.

The information centre has details of B&Bs and farmstays in the area.

Eating options in Boorowa Street include *The Cherrywood Gourmet Kitchen*. For dinner, head for the *Mandarin Court Chinese Restaurant* or *Matilda's Restaurant* in the Commercial Hotel.

Getting There & Away
Buses stop at the old train station on Lovell St. Countrylink buses run to Cootamundra and Bathurst; Greyhound Pioneer runs to Melbourne and Brisbane. Lachlan Travel (☎ 6382 4340), 12 Boorowa St, sells tickets.

The Olympic Way runs north-east from Young to Cowra and south to Cootamundra. Smaller roads run north to Grenfell, west to Temora and south-east to Yass.

COOTAMUNDRA
postcode 2590 • pop 8240
Cootamundra, by the Cootamundry Creek and with the smaller Muttama Creek flowing through town, is a service centre for surrounding farmland and an important railway junction. The town, founded around 1860, was known as Cootamundry until the 1950s, when the current name was introduced.

The town's neat grid of streets contains many fine examples of Federation-style houses and a few earlier Victorian gems. Cootamundra is in the foothills of the Great Dividing Range. In winter it sometimes snows.

Orientation & Information
Parker St is the main shopping street, and its intersection with Wallendoon St, where

you'll find the impressive post office, town hall and several banks, is the centre of town. At the train station on Hovell St there's a tourist office (☎ 6942 4212), open from 10 am to 4 pm daily.

Things to See & Do

Donald Bradman, Australia's greatest cricketer, was born here in 1908. His birthplace, the old weatherboard hospital at 89 Adams St, is now a **museum** (☎ 6942 2744). It's open from 8.30 am to 4.30 pm daily ($2/free for adults/children). The Bradmans moved to Bowral when The Don was still very young, and it's there that he learned his craft.

The climate means that European trees flourish (the elms along Cooper St are over 100 years old) and there are several quite formal parks. **Albert Park** is on Hovell St near the train station and **Jubilee Park**, on the other side of the city centre, has an Olympic-size swimming pool dating from 1935. It also features the **Captains' Walk**, a series of busts of Australia's cricket captains. Just south of town, across the Cootamundry Creek, **Pioneer Park** is a nature reserve taking in some hilly bushland with picnic places, good views and a short walking trail.

Cootamundra is best known for the **Cootamundra wattle** *(Acacia baileyana);* its profuse yellow flowers are a sign that winter is nearly over. Although native to this area, Cootamundra wattle has been planted throughout the cooler areas of southern Australia. The Wattle Time Festival is held in August.

Places to Stay & Eat

In pretty Jubilee Park, beside the Muttama Creek, *Cootamundra Caravan Park (☎ 6942 1080)* has sites for $10, on-site caravans for $26 and cabins for $42.

The *Globe (☎ 6942 1446)* and *Albion (☎ 6942 1177)* hotels are both on the corner of Parker and Wallendoon Sts. The Globe has rooms for $25 to $45 per person. The Albion has singles/doubles with bathrooms for $25/35. There are several motels, including the *Wattle Tree (☎ 6942 2688)* on Wallendoon St, not far from the train station, which charges from $43/53.

There aren't many places to eat in Cootamundra. *Country Cuisine* on Parker St has coffee and light meals. Also on Parker St, *Mo's Restaurant* has a pleasant courtyard and good food. *Cootamundra Country Club*, on Hurley St, and the town's pubs also have meals.

Getting There & Away

There's a Countrylink Travel Centre (☎ 6940 1246) at the train station.

Countrylink buses meet the train and run to Bathurst ($35 one way) via Cowra, Dubbo via Forbes and Parkes, Condobolin via West Wyalong and Lake Cargelligo, and Balranald via Griffith.

XPTs running between Sydney and Melbourne stop here twice daily.

The Olympic Way runs north-east to Young and south-west to Junee and Wagga Wagga. Smaller roads run north-west to Temora and south to the Hume Hwy.

North-West

This wedge of New South Wales (NSW), between New England and the Mitchell Hwy, is flat and dry, but largely fertile country, especially in the broad valley of the Namoi River. Cattle and cotton are the main industries.

Many of the towns in the area are small, relaxed places, still conscious of the hard work that went into their establishment, and aware that their status as outposts of settlement gives them an importance greater than their size. It's only since WWII that good roads have linked many towns, and even today they can be isolated by floods.

Except for visitors to the Warrumbungle National Park and the steady stream of traffic on the Newell Hwy, the north-west doesn't see many tourists.

Geography

Unlike other regions west of the Great Dividing Range, there are few significant foothills in the north-west. The Warrumbungle and Nandewar Ranges straddle the fertile Namoi Valley, whose river meanders west onto the plains to join the Barwon River, which becomes the Darling River – which eventually joins the Murray River and flows to South Australia (SA).

Much of the area is a vast artesian basin, and there are hot artesian baths in Moree and Lightning Ridge. Bore water is often too salty for human consumption, and even potable water can taste strongly of sulphur – if you let it stand for a while, the gases dissipate and the taste fades.

Getting There & Away

Yanda and Eastern Australia airlines (book through Qantas – ☎ 13 1313), and Hazelton Airlines (book through Ansett – ☎ 13 1300) are among the airlines serving the north-west.

Towns on the Newell Hwy are served by Brisbane to Melbourne or Adelaide buses. Countrylink connects most other towns in the area with Sydney, usually with a train/bus combination via Dubbo, Tamworth or Moree.

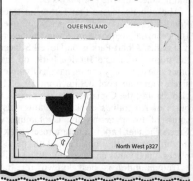

North West p327

Explorer trains from Sydney run north as far as Moree ($81).

The Newell Hwy, running through the north-west, is a good road that provides the quickest route between Melbourne and Brisbane. The Castlereagh Hwy, forking off the Newell Hwy at Gilgandra, runs north into opal country towards the Queensland border. The Mitchell Hwy heads through Nyngan, and the Gwydir Hwy runs from Collarenebri through to New England.

GUNNEDAH
postcode 2380 • pop 10,000

Gunnedah is a large country town on the Oxley Hwy at the edge of the Namoi Valley's plains. Back in the hills to the north-east is Lake Keepit, a big dam on the Namoi River, which provides water for irrigating the region's cotton crops.

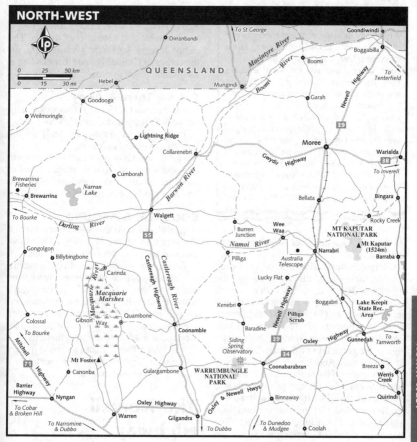

NORTH-WEST

0 25 50 km
0 15 30 mi

QUEENSLAND

To St George

Dirranbandi

Goondiwindi

Boggabilla

Macintyre River

Boomi

Boomi River

Hebel

Mungindi

To Tenterfield

Newell Highway

Goodooga

Garah

Weilmoringle

Lightning Ridge

Moree

Gwydir Highway

Warialda

To Inverell

Collarenebri

Barwon River

Cumborah

Bellata

Bingara

Brewarrina Fisheries

Narran Lake

Rocky Creek

Brewarrina

Walgett

To Bourke

Darling River

Wee Waa

MT KAPUTAR NATIONAL PARK

Burren Junction

Namoi River

Mt Kaputar (1524m)

Gongolgon

Billybingbone

Pilliga

Narrabri

Barraba

Australia Telescope

Macquarie River

Carinda

Castlereagh Highway

Castlereagh River

Lucky Flat

Boggabri

Lake Keepit State Rec. Area

Macquarie Marshes

Kenebri

Pilliga Scrub

Newell Highway

Colossal

Gibson Way

Quambone

To Bourke

Coonamble

Baradine

Oxley Highway

Gunnedah

To Tamworth

Siding Spring Observatory

Oxley

Highway

39

34

Mt Foster

WARRUMBUNGLE NATIONAL PARK

Coonabarabran

Breeza

Werris Creek

Mitchell Highway

Canonba

Gulargambone

71

Barrier Highway

Nyngan

Oxley & Newell Hwys

Quirindi

To Cobar & Broken Hill

Oxley Highway

Binnaway

Warren

Gilgandra

To Dubbo

To Dunedoo & Mudgee

Coolah

To Narromine & Dubbo

NORTH-WEST

Information
The Gunnedah Visitors Centre (☎ 6740 2230) is in Anzac Park, just south of the railway lines from the town centre. It's open from 9 am to 5 pm weekdays and 10 am to 3 pm weekends.

Things to See & Do
Just uphill from the visitors centre is the **Water Tower Museum**, open from 2 to 5 pm on Saturday, while opposite is the **Dorothea Mackellar memorial**. The poet's work *My Country* contains arguably the most famous stanza in Australian poetry:

I love a sunburnt country,
A land of sweeping plains,
Of ragged mountain ranges,
Of droughts and flooding rains.

You can listen to a recording of Mackellar reading her poem on local radio 88FM. It's a very short-range transmitter – you have to be within 100m of the statue. The information centre has free copies of the poem.

At the visitors centre, pick up a copy of the **town tour** map. There are also brochures detailing the Lands Department's **Bindeah Walking Track**, which leads from the visitors centre to Porcupine Lookout.

Ode to a New Country

While many Australians know the second verse of *My Country*, the one that begins 'I love a sunburnt country', not many know the whole poem, which is a declaration of independence from 'The love of field and coppice/Of green and shaded lanes'. These sentiments weren't very remarkable in Australia in the early 1900s, when writers and painters had already staked Australia's claim to an individual identity. However, Dorothea Mackellar came from a wealthy, landed family, the sort of people who looked to England as 'home'. That she wrote poetry not just extolling the Australian landscape but comparing it more than favourably to England was a sign that the new nation had found its feet.

On the way you might see some kangaroos and koalas.

Gunnedah Rural Museum, on the Oxley Hwy to the west of the town, boasts 'the largest gun display in northern NSW' as well as antique farm equipment. It's open from 9 am to 3 pm daily ($4/2 for adults/children).

On the corner of Abbott and Little Conadilly Sts, across from the police station, is the **grave site of Cumbo Gunnerah**, an 18th-century Aboriginal leader known as Red Kangaroo. His burial place is marked by a bronze cast of the carved tree that once stood over the site. It's rare to have any physical reminder of individual Aborigines who lived before European contact. The events of Cumbo Gunnerah's life are related in *The Red Chief* by Ion Idriess, available at the information centre.

Lake Keepit, 35km north-east of Gunnedah, is a popular holiday centre, with boating and other activities.

The village of **Breeza**, 42km south-east of Gunnedah, is the disputed birthplace of bushranger Ben Hall, and a mural here shows the events of Hall's last years.

Places to Stay & Eat

The large *Lake Keepit State Recreation Area* (☎ 6769 7605) has sites from $11.50 and en suite cabins for $68. There's also camping at the *Tourist Caravan Park*

(☎ 6742 1372), pub accommodation at the *Regal Hotel* (☎ 6742 2355) for $25/45 a single/double and a number of motels. The richly decorated *Classic Visions Cafe*, on the corner of Conadilly and Chandos Sts, is an inviting place to drop in for lunch.

Getting There & Away

Yanda Airlines (☎ 13 1313) flies twice daily between Sydney and Gunnedah for $252.

Trains stop in Gunnedah ($67) on the way from Sydney to Moree.

The Oxley Hwy runs east to Tamworth and south-west to Coonabarabran. Smaller roads run north to Boggabri and Narrabri, and south to Coolah and the Hunter Valley.

BOGGABRI & AROUND

Boggabri, 40km north-west of Gunnedah on the road to Narrabri, is a sleepy little town that manages to support three old pubs.

Gin's Leap, about 6km north of Boggabri, is a sheer rockface with great views from the top. (There are probably as many gin's leaps in Australia as there are bushrangers' caves – many cliffs seem to have presented themselves as suicide places for Aboriginal women, at least in white imaginations.)

The **Wean Picnic Races** are held in July and attract large crowds. The racetrack is about 22km east of Boggabri.

The Newell Highway

GILGANDRA

postcode 2827 • pop 2700

Gilgandra is a sizeable town on the Castlereagh River, at the junction of the Newell, Castlereagh and Oxley Hwys. During WWI, Gilgandra was the starting point for the Cooee March, when 26 volunteers set off for Sydney to enlist. Along the way they attracted 237 others, and all of them were duly shipped to the trenches.

The visitors centre (☎ 6847 2045) and a small **museum** ($2) are in Coo-ee March Memorial Park on the Newell Hwy south of the town centre.

The privately run **Gilgandra Observatory** (☎ 6847 2646), on Willie St, has a 31cm telescope. It's open from 7 to 10 pm (from 8.30 pm during daylight saving) every evening except Sunday. It also has an audio-visual display of the moon landings and other space flights ($8/5 for adults/children).

Places to Stay
There are three caravan parks, including the *Rotary Caravan Park (☎ 6847 2423)* by the river across the bridge from town. Tent sites cost $10 a double and cabins start at $35.

On the main street, the *Golden West Hotel (☎ 6847 2109)* has singles/doubles for $15/30. Nearby, and marginally better, the *Royal Hotel (☎ 6847 2004)* charges $15/25, which includes a help-yourself continental breakfast.

As Gilgandra is a junction town, there are plenty of motels, most charging around $50 for doubles.

Getting There & Away
The major buslines stop here on their Newell Hwy services. Countrylink buses run to Lightning Ridge ($42) and Dubbo ($9).

The Newell Hwy runs north-east to Coonabarabran (this section of it doubles as the Oxley Hwy) and south to Dubbo; the Castlereagh Hwy runs north to Coonamble; and the Oxley Hwy runs west to Warren and Nyngan. A smaller road runs south-east to Dunedoo and Mudgee.

COONABARABRAN
postcode 2357 • pop 3000
Coonabarabran (pronounced **coo-na-bar-ra-brn**) is a country town that has retained its shady main street (John St), despite the street being both the Newell and Oxley Hwys.

As well as serving as a base for visits to the Warrumbungle National Park, Coonabarabran is a handy stop roughly halfway between Brisbane and Melbourne (although motels tend to be cheaper farther south in Gilgandra). It's about 450km from Sydney, a fairly easy day's drive.

The town's name comes from Cooleburbarun, a squatting lease that was taken up in 1839, 20 years after John Oxley's party made the first European foray into the homelands of the Kamilario people.

Information
The information centre (☎ 6842 1441), on John St a few blocks south of the clocktower, opens from 9 am to 5 pm daily. There's also a National Parks & Wildlife Service (NPWS) office (☎ 6842 1311) on Cassilis St.

The Ryder Brothers sports store on John St sells everything you've forgotten to bring for your camping trip to the Warrumbungles. It's a pleasantly chaotic old shop.

Things to See & Do
The area's main attraction is the nearby national park. Mike Caruana (☎ 6842 3560) offers **scenic flights** over the Warrumbungle Range for $55 per person (minimum two people).

Places to Stay
Just north of the town centre, *John Oxley Caravan Park (☎ 6842 1635)* has sites from $13.50 and cabins from $39 a double. There's another caravan park, the *Wayfarer (☎ 6842 1773)*, a few kilometres south of town, charging similar prices.

The *Imperial Hotel (☎ 6842 1023)*, across from the clocktower, is a well-maintained, family run pub with singles/doubles for $26/40 (including breakfast), as well as backpacker accommodation for $20 per person. Other pubs in town also have accommodation. The *Country Gardens Motel (☎ 6842 1711)*, on the corner of John and Edward Sts, has good rooms from $52/55. It occasionally indulges in price wars with the town's 11 other motels.

Places to Eat
There are the usual country-town cafes, pub meals ($4 lunch specials at the *Imperial Hotel*) and motel dining rooms, such as the *Gunyah Restaurant* at the Country Gardens Motel, where main courses cost $14 to $17. The big *Golden Sea Dragon (☎ 6842 2388)* Chinese restaurant, on John St near the information centre, offers a $10.50 two-course meal deal. *Jolly Cauli* is a cosy cafe on John St with a pleasant outdoor eating

area and a good lunch menu. The smoothies ($3.20) are large and refreshing. It also offers Internet surfing for $5 an hour.

Getting There & Away
Yanda Airlines (☎ 13 1313) flies between Sydney and Coonabarabran ($312).

The major buslines stop here on their Newell Hwy services. Countrylink buses meet some trains at Lithgow and run to Coonabarabran via Mudgee from Sunday to Friday.

The Newell Hwy runs north to Narrabri and south to Gilgandra, and the Oxley Hwy runs north-east to Gunnedah. Smaller roads run west to Warrumbungle National Park and on to the Castlereagh Hwy at Gulargambone, and north to Baradine and Pilliga.

WARRUMBUNGLE NATIONAL PARK
The Warrumbungle Range makes an abrupt appearance in the midst of the region's gentle slopes. It was formed by volcanic activity an estimated 13 million years ago, and has been eroded into a strikingly rugged mountain range. In 1818 explorer John Oxley described the Warrumbungle Range as:

...lofty hills arising from the midst of lesser elevations, their summits crowned with perpendicular rocks, in every variety of shape and form that the wildest imagination could paint...

The national park (20,900 hectares) is popular with sightseers, bushwalkers and rock climbers. There are many walking trails, both short and long. You need to see the rangers at the informative visitors centre (☎ 6825 4364), open daily, before undertaking the longer walks or rock climbing. Park entry fees are $5 per vehicle.

There's a great range of flora and fauna, with spectacular displays of wildflowers in the spring. (Wildflowers aren't the only plants to thrive in the area – the national park grew by 620 hectares in 1993, when land confiscated from a marijuana-grower was added to it.)

Summers can be hot but it usually cools down at night, and while winter days are often sunny, there can be heavy night frosts. The best time to visit is spring or autumn.

For more information on the park, *Warrumbungle National Park* by Peter Fox is an excellent guide put out by the NPWS. It's available at the tourist information centre for $11.95. Lonely Planet's *Bushwalking in Australia* details the Grand High Tops walk.

Observatories
The elevation, remoteness and clear skies of the Warrumbungles make them a perfect place for stargazing, which is why the Australian and British governments chose to locate one of the world's most precise large telescopes here. The Anglo-Australian Telescope, with its 3.9m mirror, is at **Siding Spring Observatory**, 23km west of Coonabarabran on the road to the national park. The visitors centre, open from 9.30 am to 4 pm daily, hosts the 'Exploring the Universe' exhibition of hands-on displays and videos ($5/3/12 for adults/children/families). You can ride the lift to a viewing gallery inside the telescope building (free), but there are no public viewing facilities.

If you want to view the stars, call in at the **Skywatch Observatory**, 2km from Coonabarabran on the Warrumbungles road. It has a planetarium and astronomy exhibition for day visitors, open from 2 to 5 pm daily, and astronomy sessions after dark. Day admission is $6, or $10 including an astronomy session.

Places to Stay
The national park has powered *camp sites* for $15 a double, plus $3 for each extra person, and unpowered sites for $10, plus $2 for each extra person. Most of the park's camping areas are accessible by car. Hikers are charged $2 per night for bush camping. The *Woolshed* is a bunkhouse designed for groups (minimum 20 people), costing $4.50 per person.

The *Warrumbungles Mountain Motel* (☎ 6842 1832), 9km west of Coonabarabran on the road to the national park, has singles/doubles for $49/55.

Tibuc (☎ 6842 1740, best to call after hours) is an organic farm on the boundary of the park, with accommodation in mud-brick buildings. The facilities range from no electricity to solar system or mains power. Each building costs $72 per night (less for longer stays) and sleeps up to six people. Catering facilities are provided, but you need to bring your own linen and bedding. The turn-off to the farm is 17km from Coonabarabran on the road to the park. Tibuc is popular and books out during school holidays.

On the western side of the park, *Gumin-Gumin* (☎ 6825 4368) is a beautiful old 1870s homestead with self-contained accommodation for $65 a double.

Getting There & Away

The park entrance is 33km west of Coonabarabran, and most people come via that town, but you can also get here on smaller roads from Gulargambone or Coonamble, both on the Castlereagh Hwy to the west of the park.

THE PILLIGA SCRUB

This 400,000-hectare forest and its large koala population is between Coonabarabran and Narrabri – it has an interesting history that you can read about in Eric Rolls' outstanding book *A Million Wild Acres*. Rolls says that the early settlers cleared the land and wiped out the small marsupials that would have eaten many of the tree seedlings. After the farms failed because of unsuitable soils, the new forest exploded into life.

Baradine, north-west of Coonabarabran, is the main town in this part of the world, and roads running into the Pilliga Scrub run east from here and from Kenebri, 20km farther north. The Forestry Office in Baradine (☎ 6843 1607), open from 9 am to 4 pm weekdays, has maps of drives through the Scrub. The hamlet of **Pilliga**, 50km north of Kenebri, remains much as it ever was.

NARRABRI

postcode 2390 • pop 7300

As in so many other areas of the north-west, Major Thomas Mitchell made the first European foray and was quickly followed by others who took up land as squatters. Mitchell's visit was perhaps inevitable, but it was sparked by the capture of George Clark, a runaway convict who had lived with Aborigines for six years. The unfortunate Clark was sent to Norfolk Island, but before leaving he told of rich lands and a big river flowing to an inland sea.

Split by the Namoi River and the Narrabri Creek, this old town is today in danger of becoming just another stop on the busy Newell Hwy. There are good places for picnics in the riverside parks.

The visitors centre (☎ 6799 6760), on the Newell Hwy near the town centre, has maps of drives and walks around town. It's open from 9 am to 5 pm weekdays and 9 am to 1 pm weekends. There's an NPWS office (☎ 6799 1740) in Maitland St (the main street).

There's good fossicking, especially for agates and petrified wood, near the township of **Bellata**, 40km north of Narrabri on the Newell Hwy.

Places to Stay & Eat

There are several caravan parks in town. The *Council Caravan Park* (☎ 6792 1294), a block back from the highway, has a camping area by the river; sites cost $14.50, cabins $30. The *Narrabri Motel & Caravan Park* (☎ 6792 2593), on the highway south of the town centre, has the cheapest motel rooms in town; singles/doubles cost $39/45. *Como* (☎ 6792 3193), Fraser St, offers B&B for $75 a double in the homestead, or $80 in the separate cottage.

Watson's Kitchen is a lovely double-storey bakery/cafe in Maitland St. The upstairs balcony is great for lunch or a snack.

Getting There & Away

Eastern Australia (☎ 13 1313) flies between Sydney and Narrabri ($218) at least once a day.

The major buslines stop here on their Newell Hwy services. Countrylink buses run to Wee Waa and other small towns.

The train running between Sydney and Moree stops here.

The Newell Hwy runs north to Moree and south to Coonabarabran. Smaller roads run south-east to Gunnedah, west to Wee

NORTH-WEST

Waa and on to Walgett, and north-east to Mt Kaputar National Park.

AUSTRALIA TELESCOPE

The Australia Telescope, 25km west of Narrabri, comprises eight radio telescopes that form the Paul Wild Observatory. Six of them are here: five are on a 3km stretch of 'railway' track (which they can be moved along) and the sixth is a few kilometres away. There's another receiver near Siding Spring in the Warrumbungle National Park and the last is a long way south, near Parkes. When all the receivers operate together, the effective diameter of the telescope is 320km!

It began operating in 1990 and helps keep Australia at the forefront of radio astronomy. One of the many wonderful facts about radio astronomy: all the radio telescopes in the world have collected less energy than is released by a raindrop falling to earth.

The visitors centre (☎ 6790 4070), with hands-on displays and videos, is near the railway track. The centre is open from 8 am to 4 pm daily but is staffed only on weekdays and school-holiday weekends.

MT KAPUTAR NATIONAL PARK

A rugged park on the westernmost spur of the Nandewar Range, Mt Kaputar National Park (36,800 hectares) is popular for bushwalking, rock climbing and, between August and October, wildflowers. Mt Kaputar rises to 1524m and snow has been known to fall on its peak. A road (unsuitable for caravans) runs close to the summit. From the Doug-Sky Lookout near the summit you can see 10% of NSW.

There are two established camp sites with good facilities: **Dawsons Springs** and **Bark Hut**, both accessible from the road up the mountain. A tent site for two costs $15, payable at the self-registration box near the entrance. There are also cabins at Dawsons Springs – you have to book through the NPWS office (☎ 6799 1740) in Narrabri and there's a minimum stay of two nights ($50 a double per night). The road to Mt Kaputar runs north-east from Narrabri.

Sawn Rocks, at the northern end of the park, is a spectacular 40m cliff formed of octagonal columns of basalt. The site is signposted off the Bingara road about 40km north-east of Narrabri. There's a 900m walking trail that starts at the car park (suitable for wheelchairs).

WEE WAA

postcode 2388 • pop 2000

Wee Waa (pronounced wee-wor) is a quiet little town. It was the first settlement to be established in the Namoi Valley and the grand Imperial Hotel was the first three-storey building erected in the north-west.

Cotton was planted near Wee Waa in the 1960s and its success sparked widespread planting throughout the area. Cotton is planted from late September to the end of October, the bolls begin to open in late February and the picking season is April and May. Guided tours of farms and gins (processing plants) can be organised (☎ 6795 4292) – there are two tours a day during the picking season, at 10 am and 2 pm.

Cubbaroo (☎ 6796 1741), 45km west of Wee Waa, is the area's only winery; it's open from 11 am to 11 pm Wednesday to Sunday.

MOREE

postcode 2400 • pop 10,000

Moree was first settled in the 1840s and is the largest town on the north-west plains. It is the centre of a cotton and grain-growing district. The lush gardens of Moree's residential districts are in striking contrast to the bare surrounding plains.

The information centre (☎ 6752 7479), on the corner of the Newell and Gwydir Hwys, is open from 9 am to 5.30 pm weekdays, and to 1 pm weekends.

Things to See & Do

Moree's **Spa Baths** (☎ 6752 7480), on Anne St, claim some fairly unlikely miracle cures, but they certainly are a good way to get the cricks out of your back after a long day in a bus or car. The baths are filled with hot (41°C) artesian water, which pours out of a bore at the rate of 13 million litres a day. The spa is open from 6 am to 8.30 pm weekdays and 7 am to 7 pm weekends ($3.50/1.70 for adults/children).

The new **Moree Plains Gallery**, in an impressive old building on the corner of Frome and Heber Sts, specialises in Aboriginal art. The gallery is open from 10 am to 4 pm daily.

There are several other interesting buildings near the art gallery. These include the **Lands Department Office** on Frome St and the nearby **courthouse**.

Places to Stay

Caravan parks include the *Mehi River Van Park* (☎ 6752 7188), on the river at the eastern end of Alice St. Sites cost $17, on-site vans $30 and cabins $48.

The *Victoria Hotel* (☎ 6752 5177), on Gosport St, and the *Moree* (☎ 6752 1644), on Alice St, certainly aren't the cheapest in the country – the Victoria charges $25/50 a single/double, and the Moree $30/45. There are no fewer than 19 motels to choose from, mostly on the Newell Hwy (Frome St) and Warialda St, on the southern side of town.

Welcannah (☎ 6754 6533) is a traditional Australian homestead 24km south of Moree on Halls Creek Rd, which runs off the Newell Hwy. Its facilities include a swimming pool and tennis court. B&B costs $55/90.

Getting There & Away

The major buslines stop here on their Newell Hwy services. Most buses leave from Wadwell's Coach Terminal (☎ 6752 4677) on Heber St, across from the art gallery, and you can buy most tickets here.

Moree is the terminus of the passenger rail line from Sydney ($81).

The Newell Hwy runs north to the Queensland border at Boggabilla and south to Narrabri. The Gwydir Hwy runs east to Warialda and Inverell. Heading west on the Gwydir Hwy to Collarenebri you pass through about 140km of flat scrubland, beautiful in the spring with lush growth and wildflowers. There's no petrol available between Moree and Collarenebri, and there are several unsealed sections. Heading north, small roads run to Boomi near the state border or, branching off at Garah, to Mungindi.

BOGGABILLA & GOONDIWINDI

Boggabilla is overshadowed by the more substantial town of Goondiwindi, 10km across the Queensland border. Goondiwindi is a pleasant town and has quite a few accommodation options – ask for details at the information centre (☎ 4671 2653) in McLean St, open from 9 am to 5 pm daily. As a starting point, the impressive wooden *Victoria Hotel* (☎ 07-4671 1007, 81 Marshall St)* has singles/doubles for $25/45. The giant *New Bridge Garage*, on the Goondiwindi bypass, is reputed to be the busiest truck stop in the southern hemisphere and offers fuel, meals and showers.

The Castlereagh Highway & Westwards

The large slice of country between the Castlereagh and Mitchell Hwys is a flat artesian basin. In spring this is a beautiful area, with the vast, steamy plains bursting into life. Much of the area is black-soil country, with the dry outback beginning as you approach the Mitchell Hwy.

WARREN
postcode 2824 • pop 2200

This small town on the Macquarie River takes its name from an old meaning of the word: a park noted for wildlife. It must have been an attractive town once, but unfortunately the old buildings along the main streets have been stripped of their verandas and balconies. The visitor information centre (☎ 6847 3181), on the main road next to the old post office, is open from 10 am to 5 pm weekdays and 9 am until noon Saturday.

The Macquarie Marshes once extended south to near Warren, but dams and irrigation projects are shrinking these huge wetlands. **Tiger Bay Wildlife Park**, off the Oxley Hwy 1km north-east of Warren, has been created to provide birds and other wildlife with a refuge. There's a hide from which many species can be seen.

NORTH-WEST

In town, pleasant **Macquarie Park** runs along the river and there's a good walk, starting near the bridge. **Warren Weir**, 5km to the south, is a good spot for a picnic, and you can also camp here, although there are no facilities.

Places to Stay

There are two motels: the *Macquarie Motor Lodge* (☎ 6847 4396) has singles/doubles for $58/68 and the *Warren Motor Inn* (☎ 6847 4404) has rooms for $50/60. Pub accommodation at the *Club House Hotel* (☎ 6847 4923) costs $25 per person. There are also a couple of caravan parks. Ask at the information centre about camping on the district's many stock routes.

THE MACQUARIE MARSHES

This huge wetlands area was thought by Captain Oxley to be the beginning of the inland sea that he had been sent down the Macquarie River to find in 1818. Captain Charles Sturt came the same way in 1828, but it was a drought year and the dry marshes clearly were not part of a sea. To avoid the marshes Sturt headed north and came upon the Darling River, which he realised joined the Murray River (and thus flowed into the ocean), and so ended the whitefellas' inland-sea dreaming.

Birdlife on the marshes is varied and prolific, with native and migratory species breeding here. In the 1930s one casual observer reckoned that 3000 birds flew overhead in an hour. The wetlands have suffered from the damming of rivers and are receding, but while the skies are no longer dark with birds there are still plenty to be seen. The best time to visit is during the breeding season, generally in spring but varying according to the water level. Phone the NPWS (☎ 6842 1311) in Coonabarabran for details.

The main nature reserve on the marshes is on the west side, about 100km north of Warren and off the sealed road from Warren to Carinda. From here the unsealed Gibson Way runs east to Quambone and it's along here that you're most likely to see birds. A sealed road runs from Quambone back to Warren, so you can make a round trip. The Gibson Way floods in a good season, but usually doesn't just close because of rain. Other unsealed roads in this area should be treated with caution as this is black-soil country and you can easily get bogged.

Places to Stay

On the Gibson Way 110km north of Warren, *Willie Retreat* (☎ 6824 4361) has self-contained accommodation in the former shearers quarters at 'Willie' Station. It can accommodate up to 20 people in bunk beds for $25 per person per night.

COONAMBLE

postcode 2829 • pop 3058

The first Europeans into this area arrived in 1817, just three years after the Blue Mountains were crossed, but the town wasn't established until 1855. You're well into the north-west when you get to Coonamble, and there's a relaxed feel to things. There isn't much to see but it's a pleasant place to wander around.

The Castlereagh Hwy runs through town and the town centre is between the Castlereagh River and the Warrena Creek. The local roadhouse sells all the necessities of life: 'Fuel, Food, Ammo'.

The **museum** on Aberford St is in the old police station and is open from 10 am to 4 pm weekdays. **St Barnabas** is a big, wooden Anglican church on the corner of Aberford and Namoi Sts. The **Ellimatta Centre** is run by the Aboriginal community and sells arts and crafts. It's on the main street (Castlereagh St), opposite the medical centre.

Places to Stay

The *Riverside Caravan Park* (☎ 6822 1926), on the highway south of the centre, has sites only for $10 a double.

The impressive *Sons of the Soil Hotel* (☎ 6822 1009), on Castlereagh St, has singles/doubles for $20/25, including breakfast. A block back from Castlereagh St on the corner of Taloon and Namoi Sts, the quieter *Club House Hotel* (☎ 6822 1663) charges $20/35 (the doubles have en suites). The *Coonamble Motel* (☎ 6822 1400) is on the highway just south of the town centre and charges $38/48. There are a couple of other motels a little farther out.

Getting There & Away

Countrylink buses stop here on the run between Dubbo and Lightning Ridge.

The Castlereagh Hwy runs north to Lightning Ridge and south to Gilgandra. Smaller roads run south-east to the Warrumbungle National Park and Coonabarabran.

WALGETT

postcode 2832 • pop 2094

The small town of Walgett is near the junction of the Namoi and Barwon (a tributary of the Darling) Rivers. Walgett and the Barwon River feature in Banjo Paterson's poem *Been There Before*. Other than this, there isn't a lot of interest in this run-down little town. Steel shutters on shop windows (but, surprisingly, not on the bank windows) indicate that break-ins are a problem. Despite this, it's a friendly place and locals are happy to tell you about the sights. There's an information centre (☎ 6828 1399) in the council chambers on Fox St (the Castlereagh Hwy).

History

Charles Sturt's 1829 expedition up the Castlereagh River brought the first Europeans to this area. Squatters followed quickly and Walgett takes its name from Walchate, a cattle station established here in the 1830s. Covering 13,000 hectares, it could support only 300 head of cattle! At this time the area was a centre for Aboriginal corroborees, but the coming of the squatters soon put an end to that. Even running 0.02 of a cow per hectare was a good enough excuse to drive the Aborigines from their lands.

By the 1880s, paddle-steamers were travelling up the Darling River to Walgett, bringing in supplies and taking wool downstream.

Mechanical shears were invented on Euroka Station near Walgett in the 1870s, and Australia's first artesian bore was sunk in the area at around the same time.

Places to Stay & Eat

On the Castlereagh Hwy north of the town centre, *Roontheben Caravan Park* (☎ 6828 1771) has sites for $12 and cabins for $25. The *Oasis Hotel* (☎ 6828 1394), on Fox St, has singles/doubles for $30/40. Motel options include the *Walgett Motel* (☎ 6828 1355) with rooms from $44/53.

The *RSL Club* on Fox St has a dining room, various pubs and motels have meals, and there's a Chinese restaurant and the odd cafe and takeaway.

Getting There & Away

Hazelton Airlines (☎ 13 1300) flies to Sydney most days ($374). The Coolabah Motel (☎ 6828 1366) on Fox St is the local agent.

Countrylink buses stop here on the run between Dubbo and Lightning Ridge. Book at the Duncan & Duncan garage (☎ 6828 1781) on Fox St.

The Castlereagh Hwy runs north to Lightning Ridge and Queensland, while the Gwydir Hwy goes north-east to Collarenebri and Moree. No petrol is available along the 143km of scrub country between Collarenebri and Moree.

Sections of the road west to Brewarrina are unsealed and impassable in wet weather.

AROUND WALGETT

If you think Walgett is a small place, check out some of the other towns nearby.

As well as the opal fields around Lightning Ridge, there are the smaller **Grawin**, **Glengarry** and **Sheepyard** opal fields, west of Cumborah, a hamlet 47km north-west of Walgett on the secondary Walgett-Goodooga road. You can have a drink with the opal miners at the Glengarry Hilton, or at the Club in the Scrub at Grawin.

West of these fields is **Narran Lake**, virtually inaccessible but home to a rich variety of birdlife in good seasons. If you want to visit, phone the landowner (☎ 6874 4957) for permission and directions. The best route is off the Brewarrina to Goodooga road.

Collarenebri is 75km north-east of Walgett on the Moree road. Its name is an Aboriginal word meaning 'place of many flowers', and in spring that is very appropriate. The weir near town is supposed to be one of the best fishing holes in the state. There are gravel pits suitable for fossicking 10km out of town on the Lightning Ridge road. The Great Raft Race is held on the river in March. **Tattersalls Hotel-Motel** (☎ 6756 2205) has pub singles/doubles for $20/30 and motel rooms for $50/59. **Camping** is permitted at several sites along the river.

BREWARRINA
postcode 2839 • pop 1500

Brewarrina (known locally as Bree) is a pleasant little town with some pride in its history, both Aboriginal and European. The town is bright with coral-tree blossom from July to September.

The shire council offices (☎ 6839 2106) on Bathurst St (the main street) can help with local information.

One of the most important Aboriginal sites in the country is the **Brewarrina Fisheries** (Ngunnhu), a series of rock traps on the Darling River where, perhaps for thousands of years, the Ngemba people caught fish to feed the huge intertribal gatherings that they hosted. Adjacent to the fisheries is the excellent **Aboriginal Cultural Museum** (☎ 6839 2421), open from 8.30 am to 5 pm weekdays ($6).

The **Settlers Museum**, behind the well-maintained courthouse on Bathurst St, is also worth a visit. It's open from 2 to 3 pm Friday ($3).

Places to Stay & Eat

The council **caravan park** (☎ 6839 2883) has sites for $15; it's by the swimming pool on Church St. There's another **camping** place on the river 6.5km upstream from Brewarrina. The **Hotel Brewarrina** (☎ 6839 2019) has accommodation and pub meals. The **Swan Crest Motel** (☎ 6839 2397), opposite the fish traps on the corner of Sandon and Doyle Sts, has rooms for $45/50.

The **De-Luxe Cafe**, on Bathurst St, is a great old country-town cafe, with lots of the original shop fittings, including a sign boasting 'Iced Fountain Drinks. We Excel in Sundaes, Cleanliness & Civility'.

Getting There & Away

Hazelton Airlines (☎ 13 1300) connects Brewarrina with Sydney ($374).

Countrylink buses run between Dubbo and Brewarrina.

You can reach Brewarrina by road from Bourke, Coolabah or Byrock (both via Gongolgon), and from Walgett. The Walgett road includes some long unsealed sections of black soil – great when it's dry, impassable in the wet. The track north to Goodooga also has a long unsealed section. Tracks through the Macquarie Marshes area also lead here, but you'll need a good map and local advice.

LIGHTNING RIDGE
postcode 2834 • pop 3100

Like Coober Pedy in SA, Lightning Ridge is a scruffy little town, entirely dependent on opal mining and the tourism that has followed. It doesn't have the sense of otherworldly desolation that marks Coober Pedy, but it's a hot, unwelcoming stretch of landscape nevertheless. Although the entire town is geared towards relieving you of some cash, Lightning Ridge is no slick tourist trap. It has a decidedly eccentric feel to it and there are some interesting characters to meet. In busy times its population almost triples.

Opal mining is still the domain of the 'battler', the little bloke or 'sheila' whose hard work and tenacity pays off – sometimes. For those who don't make it, scraping a living among rusting car bodies and extremely basic huts is not considered socially demeaning. Towns like Lightning Ridge (and there aren't many) are the last refuge of 'the bushie', usually down on their luck but infinitely resourceful and wary of authority. These 'true-blue' types sell their finds to visiting opal buyers who set up shop in motel rooms, and the meeting of these two very different worlds is an odd contrast. Some buyers come all the way from Hong Kong to buy black opals, the speciality of the area.

Most claims are 50 sq metres and no-one can hold more than two claims.

Orientation & Information

Bill O'Brien's Way, the road in from the highway, becomes Morilla St, which is the main street. The corner of Morilla and Opal Sts is pretty much the centre of town. The official tourist information centre (☎ 6829 1462) is in the Lightning Ridge Mining Centre, on the left on the way into town from the highway, but you can get tourist information from practically anyone in town.

Things to See & Do

On the north and west sides, the town is surrounded by intensively mined opal fields. Be careful walking around the diggings, as they're riddled with deep, unmarked holes; young children are especially at risk. Dropping anything down a hole won't make you popular if someone is working at the bottom.

The **Walk-In Mine**, north of town off Gem St, is open daily ($6) and you can see a video on opal mining. Nearby **Spectrum Mine** also has a video (hourly from 10 am to 4 pm; free). Off the track that goes to the Walk-In Mine is **Bevan's Black Opal & Cactus Nursery**. It has many species of cactus including some very old plants. **The Big Opal**, off Bill O'Brien's Way, has a mine tour at 10 am (and another at 2 pm, subject to sufficient numbers) daily. The **Bottle House** on Opal St is built from bottles and contains mining memorabilia as well as souvenirs and opals.

If you need to relax, the 42°C **hot artesian baths** at the northern edge of town on Pandora St are free and open 24 hours. As well as miners and jewellers, Lightning Ridge is home to many artists and craftspeople. John Murray's engaging paintings and limited-edition prints of outback life, along with some B&W photos, are displayed at his **gallery** on Opal St near the corner of Morilla St.

Opals

The main business in town is selling opals and there are outlets everywhere. In some showrooms you can see $5000 opals on display. If you want to buy something, take your time and look at as many places as possible.

Organised Tours

Black Opal Tours (☎ 6829 0368) runs two-hour tours of the town and surrounding opal fields and mines ($20) at 10 am and 2 pm daily (best to take the morning one, before the heat kicks in).

Buying Opals

There are various grades and types of opals. Top of the heap are black opals, which are solid opals (called stones) consisting of a black 'potch' overlaid by 'colour'. (The best quality are more expensive than diamonds.) Grey and white opals are the same, but the potch is grey or white. Solid crystals are clear or opaque opals without any potch.

Prices can be astronomical – up to $3000 a carat for a black opal – but you can pay as little as $50 for a stone of lower quality. The price depends on flaws and the brilliance of the colour. The variation in shades of colour is enormous, and if you're lucky, the one you like won't be one of the most expensive.

Much less expensive are nonsolid opals. Doublets are precious opals stuck (by a jeweller, not by nature) to a potch of nonprecious opal. Domed doublets are worth more than flat doublets because the section of precious opal is thicker. Triplets are flat doublets with a dome of glass or quartz crystal stuck on top, protecting and magnifying the opal.

Special Events

The Great Goat Race is held at Easter along with horse races, and the Opal & Gem Festival is held at the end of July.

Places to Stay

The big *Motor Village* (☎ 6829 0304), on Morilla St, has tent sites for $9 and cabins from $45 ($51 with en suite). The *Tram-o-Tel* (☎ 6829 0448), on Morilla St, has self-contained accommodation in old trams for $20/30 a single/twin. One is a St Kilda Beach (Melbourne) tram!

There are two motels, the *Black Opal* (☎ 6829 0518), on the corner of Morilla and Opal Sts, and the *Wallangulla* (☎ 6829 0542), on the corner of Morilla and Agate Sts. Both charge around $50/60 for singles/doubles and neither is very luxurious.

Places to Eat

The best deals in town are to be found at the huge *Bowling Club* on Morilla St, where the bistro has a selection of meals starting at

$6.50. *Wong's Chinese* on Opal St is your standard country town Chinese restaurant. If you strike it rich, the smartest restaurant in town is *Nobby's* in the Motor Village complex, where mains cost $18 to $23.

Getting There & Away

Hazelton Airlines (☎ 13 1300) flies to Sydney ($374). Buy tickets at the Lightning Ridge Newsagency (☎ 6829 1182), on Morilla St next to the post office.

Buses run north and south along the Castlereagh Hwy, including the Countrylink service to Dubbo ($53). Book at the Opal Cave (☎ 6829 0333) at 51 Morilla St, opposite the post office. Grahams Coaches (☎ 07-4630 4188) have a service from Lightning Ridge to Toowoomba ($75 one way) in Queensland on Monday, Wednesday and Friday. Buses leave from Pip's Place, in the industrial estate opposite the tourist office.

The Castlereagh Hwy runs south to Walgett and on to Dubbo. North of Lightning Ridge the road leads eventually to the Queensland town of St George.

NORTH-WEST

Far West

The far west of New South Wales (NSW) is the state's 'empty quarter', but this vast expanse of dry country is one of the most interesting areas in the state and is much more diverse than it first appears.

South of the Darling River, much of the land is taken up by cattle and sheep stations and saltbush scrub, and the horizons are vast. Elsewhere there's a surprising amount of bush, with low, tenacious trees surviving in the harsh climate. Towards the north-western corner, the long ridges of sand dunes that make up so much of central Australia begin. The bushes and wild flowers supporting the dunes can be quite beautiful.

The outback is sparsely populated but the people you meet are often much larger than life – they have room to grow, sometimes in pretty quirky ways.

Geography & Climate

Nearly all of the far west comprises the Murray-Darling Basin: red- and black-soil plains riddled with usually dry waterways and claypans. In the north-west corner the sandy plains of outback Australia begin.

From November to February this area, especially the north, is almost impossibly hot. By 9 am the thermometer is nudging 100°F in the shade and by 10 am the Celsius landmark, 40°C, is passed. That leaves another 10 hours of daylight for the current record, 51.7°C, to be broken. Air-con helps to make this season more tolerable. In winter nights can be chilly, with frosts, but the days are usually warm and sunny.

Getting There & Away

Broken Hill is the main centre for air traffic in the region, but small charter planes serve much of the area.

Major bus lines operate along the Barrier Hwy and Kidman Way, while Countrylink buses run up the Mitchell Hwy.

The *Indian Pacific* train stops at Broken Hill en route from Sydney to Adelaide and Perth.

HIGHLIGHTS

- Taking in outback landscapes, especially at sunset
- Camping under the stars on the banks of the Darling River in Kinchega National Park
- Bushwalking in Mootwingee National Park
- Staying underground at White Cliffs
- Uncovering the extraordinary archaeological record at Mungo National Park

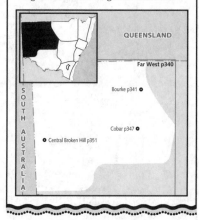

QUEENSLAND

Far West p340

Bourke p341 ●

Cobar p347 ●

● Central Broken Hill p351

SOUTH AUSTRALIA

If you're driving, two long, sealed roads cut through the far west: the Barrier Hwy, running from Cobar west to Broken Hill and on to South Australia (SA); and the Mitchell Hwy, beginning in Dubbo and running through Nyngan to Bourke, then straight up into Queensland. The sealed Kidman Way runs from near Jerilderie in the south, up through Cobar and Bourke, to the Queensland border and beyond.

You'll see a lot more of the outback if you venture off the sealed roads. As long as conditions are dry (which is the usual state of affairs out here) you won't get into too much trouble on the main roads if you have good maps, drive carefully and are prepared for

FAR WEST

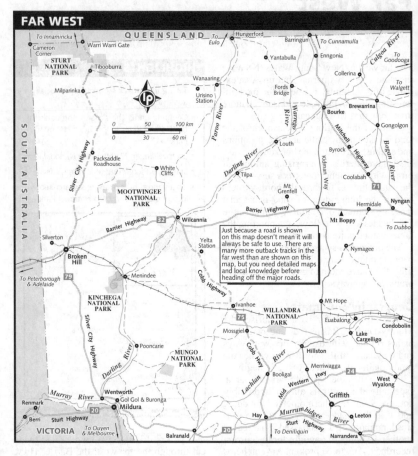

FAR WEST

Just because a road is shown on this map doesn't mean it will always be safe to use. There are many more outback tracks in the far west than are shown on this map, but you need detailed maps and local knowledge before heading off the major roads.

minor breakdowns. See the boxed text 'The Road to Ruin' in the Getting Around chapter for more information on outback driving.

BOURKE
postcode 2840 • pop 3500

Nearly 800km north-west of Sydney, Bourke is on the edge of the outback; 'back of Bourke' is synonymous with The outback, the back of beyond. A glance at the map will show just how outback the area beyond Bourke is – settlements of any sort are few and far between and the country is flat and featureless as far as the eye can see.

Its very remoteness attracts a steady stream of visitors. Bourke is a surprisingly pretty town and the surrounding country can be beautiful – the sheer space is exhilarating.

History

The Ngemba people lived in a large area centred on the Brewarrina Fisheries, a series of rock traps on the Darling River, and including Bourke and Louth. Other peoples in the area were the Barranbinja, Kula, Valaria, Kamilaroi and Wiradjuri. Early European explorers observed that local Aborigines lived in permanent structures.

The first Europeans to see this area were the members of explorer Captain Charles Sturt's party of 1828. Sturt didn't think much of the country and Major Thomas Mitchell's party of 1835 didn't manage to explore much of the area. Still, by 1860 there were enough graziers in the area for a paddle-wheeler to risk the difficult journey up to Bourke. By the 1880s, many of the Darling River's 200 paddle-steamers were calling at Bourke to take wool down to the river ports at Echuca (for Melbourne) and Morgan (for Adelaide). It was possible for wool to be in London just six weeks after leaving Bourke – somewhat quicker than a sea-mail parcel today!

Bourke is still a major wool-producing area, but droughts and low prices have forced farmers to look to other products, such as cotton and rockmelons. There's even a vineyard.

Quite a few famous Australians have passed through Bourke at one time or another. Author Henry Lawson lived at the Carriers Arms Hotel in 1892 while painting the Great Western Hotel. Fred Hollows, the ophthalmic surgeon whose philanthropic work in Third-World countries made him a national hero, chose to be buried here in the 'land without fences'.

Orientation & Information

The Mitchell Hwy winds through town then heads out across the old bridge to North Bourke (just a pub) 6km away. The shopping centre is on Oxley St between Sturt St and Richard St (the highway); the courthouse is on the corner of Richard and Oxley Sts.

Stuart Johnson's helpful Tourist Information Centre (☎ 6872 1222) is at the bus depot (the old train station) on Anson St. It's open from 9 am to 5 pm Monday to Saturday and 12.30 to 5 pm Sunday (closed on Sunday from November to March). Pick up a leaflet called *Bourke Mud Map Tours*, detailing a town walk and drives to places in the district.

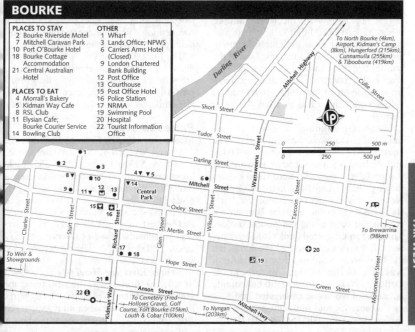

BOURKE

PLACES TO STAY
2 Bourke Riverside Motel
7 Mitchell Caravan Park
10 Port O'Bourke Hotel
18 Bourke Cottage Accommodation
21 Central Australian Hotel

PLACES TO EAT
4 Morrall's Bakery
5 Kidman Way Cafe
8 RSL Club
11 Elysian Cafe; Bourke Courier Service
14 Bowling Club

OTHER
1 Wharf
3 Lands Office; NPWS
6 Carriers Arms Hotel (Closed)
9 London Chartered Bank Building
12 Post Office
13 Courthouse
15 Post Office Hotel
16 Police Station
17 NRMA
19 Swimming Pool
20 Hospital
22 Tourist Information Office

To North Bourke (4km), Airport, Kidman's Camp (8km), Hungerford (215km), Cunnamulla (255km) & Tibooburra (419km)

Darling River

Mitchell Highway

Cullie Street

Short Street

Tudor Street

Darling Street

Mitchell Street

Warraweena Street

Oxley Street

Wilson Street

Tarcoon Street

Sturt Street

Charles Street

Richard Street

Glen Street

Mertin Street

Hope Street

Anson Street

Kidman Way

Central Park

0   250   500 m
0   250   500 yd

To Brewarrina (98km)

To Weir & Showgrounds

To Cemetery (Fred Hollows Grave), Golf Course, Fort Bourke (15km), Louth & Cobar (100km)

To Nyngan (203km)

Mitchell Hwy

Green Street

Moncomeeth Street

FAR WEST

Bourke Courier Service (☎ 6872 2092), near the Elysian Cafe on Oxley St, is the agent for Countrylink and Hazelton Airlines.

Work Limited seasonal work is available in the Bourke area: picking grapes (December to January), picking rockmelons (November or December), picking citrus fruits (May to October) and cotton chipping (weeding; November or December). You'll notice that nearly all these activities take place in summer and it can be *hot*! For fruit-picking work contact Back o' Bourke Fruits (☎ 6872 1888) or for cotton chipping work contact Darling Farms (☎ 6872 2833) or Clyde Agriculture (☎ 6872 2258).

Things to See & Do
There are plenty of reminders of the time when the big paddle-wheelers were the town's lifeline. The impressive three-tiered **wharf** at the northern end of Sturt St is a faithful reconstruction of the original, which was built in 1897, and, on the river, the *Jandra* is a replica of an 1895 paddle-wheeler.

Just north of town, the **North Bourke Bridge** (1883) once lifted to let the steamboats through. It also obligingly bends to avoid the pub on the north bank. One of the reasons that boats can no longer navigate the river is the concrete weir built downstream from the town in the 1940s. It replaced a wooden weir that tilted to allow the boats through.

Many old buildings in town are reminders of Bourke's important past. The **courthouse** (1900) on the corner of Oxley and Richard Sts has a shady courtyard and is topped by a spire with a crown on it – signifying that it can hear maritime cases! Next door is an older courthouse, very similar in design to the court at Brewarrina. Across the road is the **old police station**. The **London Chartered Bank** (1888), farther west, is a very impressive old building, but the bank went bust just a few years after it was built. The State Offices, once the **Lands Office** (1900), is an elegant but simple structure of wood and corrugated iron.

The only big old **pubs** left are the Post Office Hotel, on Oxley St, and the Central Australian Hotel, on the corner of Richard and Anson Sts. A small old pub, the Carriers Arms on the corner of Mitchell and Wilson Sts, was a watering hole of the writer Henry Lawson, but it's now closed. The North Bourke Hotel is a good place to go to meet the locals. The Port O'Bourke Hotel on Mitchell St is comparatively sedate.

Cotton is picked in March and April. From about May to August you can see the cotton gin in action by phoning Clyde Agriculture (☎ 6872 2528), or ask at the tourist office about tours of the plantations and gins.

Organised Tours
Back O'Bourke Mini Bus Tours offers excellent town and surrounding area tours from 2 to 5 pm Monday to Saturday, April to October ($15/7 for adults/children). Longer tours can also be arranged. Contact the information office for more details.

Special Events
The Agricultural Show is held in April, with important ram and bull sales as well as a sideshow alley. At Easter there's a fishing competition with other events such as woolbale rolling and egg-and-spoon races.

The Mateship Festival, held in late June, derives its name from Henry Lawson's literary theme of male bonding in the bush, a powerful strain in Aussie culture. Events are similar to those at the Easter festivities.

Places to Stay
In town, the *Mitchell Caravan Park* (☎ 6872 2791), on Mitchell St, has tent sites for $8, vans from $25 and cabins from $35. Eight kilometres north of Bourke on the Cunnamulla Rd, *Kidman's Camp* (☎ 6872 1612) is much larger and on the river. Tent sites cost $8 and on-site vans $25/35 a single/double.

The best of Bourke's hotels is the recently renovated *Port O'Bourke* (☎ 6872 2544, 32 Mitchell St). The rooms are good value at $31/46.

Bourke Riverside Motel (☎ 6872 2539, 3 Mitchell St) occupies the historic Telegraph Hotel. It's a friendly place and the dynamic owners have created a beautiful garden setting and some unique accommodation.

Budget doubles cost $55 while superb heritage suites cost $80.

Another good option is **Bourke Cottage Accommodation** (☎ *6872 2837, 51 Hope St*). There is a choice of two renovated cottages in the middle of town, both equipped with everything you could need. Rates are $50 for one person, plus $10 for each additional person.

Places to Eat

Bourke has several cafes, such as the pleasant **Kidman Way Cafe**, on Mitchell St next to the Towers Drug Co building (1890), and the **Elysian Cafe**, Bourke's country-town cafe on Oxley St.

Morrall's Bakery on Mitchell St has great pies and a good choice of breads.

The best place for dinner is the **Port O'Bourke Hotel**. It has a much better restaurant than you would expect to find in such a small and remote town. Main courses cost around $15.

There's typical club grub at the nearby **RSL Club** and the **Bowling Club** on Richard St has a Chinese restaurant.

Getting There & Away

Hazelton Airlines flies several times a week to Dubbo, where it connects with another service to Sydney ($295 one way).

The only bus is the Countrylink service to Dubbo ($53), which connects with a train to Sydney. It *might* be possible to go along on the twice-weekly mail runs to Wanaaring and Brewarrina. These tend to head out to the town in the afternoon, then make deliveries to stations the next day. The post office (☎ 6872 2017) can put you in touch with the contractors.

The Mitchell Hwy, which runs south to Nyngan and north to Cunnamulla in Queensland, the Kidman Way, which runs south to Cobar, and the road east to Brewarrina are the only sealed roads in the area.

AROUND BOURKE

Somewhere that is 'around Bourke' can be as far away as the old Urisino post office, more than 200km west on a dirt road. The Mud Map Tours brochure details some trips.

If you don't already have a map, pick one up from the National Roads & Motorists Association (NRMA) office on Richard St.

If the roads are dry, all the places mentioned in the following sections can be visited in a normal car. *Wherever* you're going, however, check current conditions with the locals, preferably the police, and carry plenty of water. If you're heading off a main route, let someone know what you're doing and take spare parts.

The climb up **Mt Oxley**, 30km south-east of Bourke off the Brewarrina road, is worth the effort for the views, especially at sunset. There are more good views and abundant flora at **Mt Gundabooka**, about 70km to the south-west off the Kidman Way. The rock pools here almost always have water in them and the mountain is thought to have been of religious significance to Aborigines, whose cave paintings can still be seen. Watch carefully for the turn-offs from the Kidman Way, as they're poorly signposted. Before you go, visit the tourist office in Bourke to pick up a key for Mt Oxley or the NPWS office at 21 Mitchell St for the Mt Gundabooka key (needed to open gates).

Fords Bridge, about 60km north-west on the road to Hungerford, is apparently a top spot for yabbying.

On the Mitchell Hwy 78km south of Bourke, the interesting hamlet of **Byrock** is worth a stop. The friendly **Mulga Creek Hotel-Motel** (☎ *6874 7311*) has singles/doubles for $38/50 and camp sites for $10. The manager is a good source of information. Check out the Mulga Walk and the 'rock-hole' – a natural gilgai (water hole) formed in a table of granite. It's a short walk from the hotel and you can have a swim.

The **Cornerstone Community**, between Bourke and Wanaaring, is a sort of Christian kibbutz on a cotton farm. This is the site of the Pera Bore, the first artesian water supply in the area. Visitors are welcome; the tourist office has more details.

The hamlet of **Enngonia** is 95km north of Bourke on the Mitchell Hwy and has accommodation at the **Oasis Hotel/Motel** (☎ *6874 7577*). Singles/doubles cost $15/30. The sand hills around here are covered with flowers in

Shinglebacks

Shingleback lizards are slow-moving, stumpy critters that love to lie on the road, and are so ugly that they're cute. Locals call them bog-eyes or stumpies, depending on where you are. When approached, a shingleback will open that big mouth wide and show its blue tongue and crimson gullet.

If you poke a finger too close to one, it might just chomp onto it. They aren't poisonous, but they have a very strong grip. Locals kill them to get them off, but the National Parks & Wildlife Service advises resting your hand on the ground and hoping that the lizard will eventually get bored and let go. It can take a while.

spring, and you'll see lots of birdlife if there's any water in the surrounding swamps. On the first weekend in September, up to 2000 people arrive for the annual races.

Farther north, almost on the Queensland border, **Barringun** is a hamlet with a pub (once frequented by Boer War soldier and poet Harry 'The Breaker' Morant), a roadhouse and not much else.

Writer Henry Lawson walked from Bourke to **Hungerford** in 1892 and he wasn't all that impressed with what he saw there. Read about it in his story *Hungerford*. The population today is about 10, but the beautiful old *Royal Mail Hotel* (☎ 07-4655 4093) is still going strong. It has rooms that sleep four for $10 per person, tent sites for $2 and overnight vans for $5. The Hungerford Field Day in July attracts thousands of visitors and the Sports Day in October is also popular. Hungerford straddles the Queensland border, and just over the border is the small **Currawinya National Park**, where large lakes provide a habitat for many birds.

DARLING RIVER

The Darling River first takes its name just north-east of Bourke, after the Barwon is joined by the Culgoa and Bogan Rivers. It flows south-west across NSW and meets the Murray River at Wentworth. Although it passes through some of the driest country in the state, the Darling River usually has at least some water in it and its banks are lined with massive river red gums. With the Murray, the Darling forms one of the world's longest exotic rivers – that is, one that for much of its length flows through country from which it receives no water.

The road that runs along the south bank of the Darling River is the main route downstream from Bourke. It's possible to drive all the way along it to Wentworth, although the road is unsealed and impassable after rain. Apart from kangaroos and emus, you won't encounter much along the way.

Fort Bourke, signposted off the Louth road about 15km south-west of Bourke, is a replica of the crude stockade built by Major Mitchell in 1835 to guard his stores while he took a boat down the Darling River. The area is a wildlife refuge with lots of water birds.

The tiny town of **Louth**, about 100km from Bourke, hosts up to 4000 people during the annual race meeting on the second Saturday in August. The town's landing strip is crowded with planes, racehorses outnumber the usual population and a score of bookmakers turn over hundreds of thousands of dollars.

Louth Cabin Park (☎ 6874 7416) has a choice of cabins (singles only) for $30 or a cottage for $40.

About 90km downstream is **Tilpa**, where the classic bush *Tilpa Hotel* (☎ 6837 3928) has meals, fuel, accommodation and, of course, beer.

From Tilpa, the Darling River flows down to **Wilcannia**, then through a system of lakes at **Menindee**, surrounded by **Kinchega National Park**. These places are accessible by sealed roads from Broken Hill.

Beyond Menindee, another 125km of dirt road brings you to **Pooncarie**, a pretty hamlet and a jumping-off point for Mungo National Park. From Pooncarie, a sealed road runs to **Wentworth**, not far from the city of Mildura in Victoria. See the Riverina chapter for information on Wentworth.

BOURKE TO TIBOOBURRA

The lonely road running west from Bourke to Tibooburra is an adventurous drive.

Wanaaring, about 190km west of Bourke, may well be tiny but it's the largest settlement for a long way. There's accommodation at the *Outback Inn* (☎ 6874 7758), where singles/doubles cost $25/50, and you can buy fuel and provisions at Cooper's Corner. Paroo Sports Day is held during the September-October school holidays.

To the west, the scrub thins and there are some large claypans that fill with birds after rain. Between Wanaaring and Tibooburra, **The Big Shed** (☎ 08-8091 6826) at Reola Station is a popular attraction. This huge shearing shed features a 16-stand circular shearing board and holds 4,000 sheep. Sheep are mustered by gyrocopter. Visitors are welcome; admission is $10.

After you pass the turn-off to Milparinka the country changes and you drive past the small mesas of the eastern half of **Sturt National Park**.

CORNER COUNTRY

The far western corner of the state is a semi-desert of red plains, heat, dust and flies. To quote Henry Lawson (1893), 'There are no 'mountains' out west, only ridges on the floor of hell'. But it's worth seeing for its interesting physical features and prolific wildlife. As well as kangaroos and emus, watch out for goannas and other lizards on the road and even big wedge-tailed eagles, which take a long time to get airborne. Running along the Queensland border is the dingo-proof fence, patrolled every day by boundary riders who each look after a 40km section.

Tibooburra
☎ 08 • postcode 2880

Tiny Tibooburra, 335km north of Broken Hill and the hottest town in the state, boasts two fine sandstone pubs, a couple of petrol stations, a small shop or two, a police station, a bush hospital and even a tiny outdoor cinema. Tibooburra is the closest town to Sturt National Park and there's a large and helpful NPWS office (☎ 8091 3308) in town, open from 8.30 am to 5 pm daily.

Tibooburra used to be called The Granites after the granite outcrops nearby, which are good to visit on a sunset walk.

Places to Stay & Eat There's camping in the national park just north of town at *Dead Horse Gully*; fees are $5 for two people. In town, *The Granites Caravan Park* (☎ 8091 3305) has sites for $10, an on-site van for $26, cabins for $36 and motel units from $46.

Both the pubs, the *Family Hotel* (☎ 8091 3314) and the *Tibooburra Hotel* (☎ 8091 3310) have accommodation. The Family Hotel has singles/doubles for $20/35 and motel units for $55/60, while the Tibooburra rooms cost $30/40. Both bars have character and are worth a beer; the Tibooburra has more than 60 well-worn hats on its wall. They also have good counter meals and outside tables.

Milparinka

Milparinka is very nearly a ghost town. Not much remains of the gold town, which once had a population of 3000, except the pub, the courthouse, and a few occupied houses. The courthouse is a fine sandstone building with a very solid sandstone dunny out the back.

Members of Charles Sturt's expedition team from Adelaide, searching for an inland sea, were forced to camp near here for six months in 1845. The temperatures were extreme, the conditions terrible and their supplies inadequate. Ask at the pub for directions to the grave of James Poole, Sturt's second-in-command, who is buried about 14km north-west of the settlement. Poole died of scurvy.

The only fuel between Milparinka and Broken Hill is at the Packsaddle roadhouse, about halfway along the partially sealed Silver City Hwy.

Sturt National Park

Taking in both gibber plains and the edge of the great Strzelecki Desert, this huge park (over 340,000 hectares) was once a pastoral lease.

The park has 300km of driveable tracks, camping areas and walks. It's recommended that you inform the ranger at Tibooburra before venturing into the park.

At **Cameron Corner** there's a post to mark the place where Queensland, SA and NSW meet. It's a favourite goal for visitors

FAR WEST

and a 4WD is not always necessary to get there. In the Queensland corner, the *Corner Store* (!) does fresh sandwiches, homemade pies and even ice cream. Everybody coming by the Corner stops here and they have good advice on road conditions. You can also buy fuel here.

THE BARRIER HIGHWAY

The Barrier Hwy, running from Nyngan west through Cobar, Wilcannia and Broken Hill, is the far west's main road and is the main route to Adelaide.

Nyngan

postcode 2825 • pop 2700

Nyngan is at the junction of the Barrier and Mitchell Hwys and is also close to the centre of NSW; a cairn marks the exact spot 72km south of the town. Tourist information is available from Nyngan Video Parlour (☎ 6832 1155), on the main street.

Major Mitchell's party passed through in 1835, but the town didn't begin to grow until the 1880s. The great flood of 1990, when the Bogan River overwhelmed the town and the entire population was evacuated by helicopter, still looms large in local memory. You can see photos of the flood at the **Railway Station Museum**. It's open from 10 am to 4 pm daily ($2/0.50 for adults/children).

Places to Stay & Eat There are a couple of caravan parks; the nicest is the *Riverside* (☎ 6832 1729) west of town and, as its name suggests, next to the river. Unpowered sites cost $10 for two people, on-site vans $30 and cabins from $35.

Barrett's Hotel (☎ 6832 1028, 64 Nymagee St), a big old place across the railway line from the main street, has pub accommodation, as does the friendly *Australian Hotel* (☎ 6832 1108, 42 Nymagee St). Both charge $20 per person, with breakfast. On the main street, the *Overlander Hotel* (☎ 6832 1535, 89 Pangee St) has singles/doubles for $25/35. For the cheapest motel, remember the *Alamo Motor Inn* (☎ 6832 1660, 14 Pangee St). Rooms cost $41/51.

Elle's Restaurant in the Overlander Hotel is open daily for lunch and dinner and there's a *Chinese restaurant* at the Nyngan Bowling Club.

Getting There & Away Countrylink buses run to Dubbo, Broken Hill, Brewarrina and Bourke.

As well as the highways, a fairly well-travelled and almost fully sealed road runs south through Tottenham to Bogan Gate, on the road between Parkes and Condobolin. See North of Condobolin in the Central West chapter for more information on routes in this area.

Cobar

postcode 2835 • pop 5500

Right on the edge of the outback, beyond the fences but before the low bush tails off into saltbush, the town of Cobar is at the beginning of the Barrier Hwy, which runs west to Broken Hill, some 455km away. Semi-arid woodland is the main vegetation in the area and there's a quiet beauty to the rolling sea of tough little trees. Sheep manage to eke out an existence on the clearer sections, in competition with destructive feral goats and pigs. After rain, the flood plains of the usually dry creeks come alive with flowers.

History Like Broken Hill, Cobar is a mining town, but here copper is the mainstay. Rich copper ore was discovered in 1871 and for the next 40 years the town grew steadily.

In the 1920s, the two biggest mines, Great Cobar and the Cornish, Scottish & Australian (CSA), closed down and Cobar began to decline. The CSA was reopened in the 1960s and is now 1km deep. The new Elura mine, 47km west of Cobar, is currently exploiting a rich plug of zinc, lead and silver. Gold is also mined in the area. Cobar has alluvial gold but there was no gold rush here because of the lack of water, which is essential for gold panning!

Information The helpful information centre (☎ 6836 2448) is at the eastern end of town in the same building as the Cobar Regional Museum. There's a NPWS office (☎ 6836 2692) at 19 Barton St.

Things to See & Do The excellent **Cobar Regional Museum**, open daily, is well worth seeing. It's housed in the former head office of the Great Cobar Copper Mining Company and many of the displays reflect this association. The hospital train carriage is interesting and there are also good displays on the environment, local Aboriginal life and the early Europeans. Don't miss it ($5/3 for adults/children).

Next to the museum is the **Stele monument**, dedicated to the town and its mining past. Pick up a walking-tour map of the town from the information centre. There are a surprising number of interesting buildings, most fairly modest. An exception is the enormous **Great Western Hotel** (1898), which has perhaps the longest pub veranda in the state.

Weather balloons are released at 9 am and 3 pm from the meteorological station on the edge of town, off the Louth road.

There are no tours of the mines, but ask at the information centre as this might change. Mining skills are displayed at the national rock-drilling championships in September.

Staff from the information centre lead **walking tours** ($5/3) at 7 am daily and you'll see lots of birdlife; bookings are essential.

Places to Stay The *Cobar Caravan Park* (☎ *6836 2425*) has sites for $10.50, on-site vans from $25 and cabins from $35. Several pubs have accommodation, including the *New Occidental* (☎ *6836 2111*), which has singles/doubles for $10/28.

The *Great Western* (☎ *6836 2053*) has motel-style units for $35, including cooked breakfast.

The *Cross Roads* (☎ *6836 2711*), on the Louth road, is a quiet motel with a pool. Units go for $50/58.

Places to Eat The 24-hour Bogas and Caltex *petrol stations* have grills and snacks. Truckies seem to prefer the Caltex.

Under the Great Western Hotel, *The Hi Way Takeaway* has pizzas and some pretty greasy takeaways. Better is *Ingrid's Country Kitchen (32 Linsley St),* which serves coffee and meals such as quiche and lasagne. It is also a craft and souvenir shop. The *Golf Club* and the *Ex-Services Club* also have meals.

The best place to eat is *Longworth (55 Linsley St)*, a licensed restaurant in a beautiful old house. It's open for dinner Tuesday to Saturday.

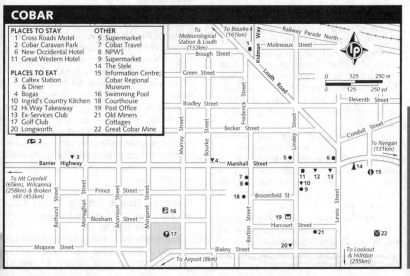

COBAR

PLACES TO STAY	OTHER
1 Cross Roads Motel	5 Supermarket
2 Cobar Caravan Park	7 Cobar Travel
6 New Occidental Hotel	8 NPWS
11 Great Western Hotel	9 Supermarket
	14 The Stele
PLACES TO EAT	15 Information Centre;
3 Caltex Station	Cobar Regional
& Diner	Museum
4 Bogas	16 Swimming Pool
10 Ingrid's Country Kitchen	18 Courthouse
12 Hi Way Takeaway	19 Post Office
13 Ex-Services Club	21 Old Miners
17 Golf Club	Cottages
20 Longworth	22 Great Cobar Mine

Getting There & Away The Barrier Hwy runs east to Nyngan and west to Wilcannia, while the Kidman Way runs north to Bourke and south through Mt Hope to Hillston.

Buses stop at the Mobil petrol station, from where there's a daily service to Dubbo. Pioneer buses run to Sydney and Adelaide daily.

Kidman Country

The fully sealed Kidman Way stretches from Jerilderie in the south to Queensland in the north. Its name pays tribute to Sir Sidney Kidman who, at the time of his death in 1935, was the greatest pastoral landowner in Australia, with an interest in over 90 stations covering 337,000 sq km – equal to almost half of New South Wales.

Sid Kidman's rags-to-riches story began in 1870, when he ran away from home at age 13 with a one-eyed horse and 10 shillings in his pocket. Heading north from Adelaide to join his brothers on the Barrier Range, young Sid made mental notes of the country and the information passing stockmen gave him about the country he hadn't yet seen. He never forgot any of it and was later able to manage the movement of stock over large areas because he knew where there would be feed and water.

Kidman proved to be a natural stock trader. By 1895 he had bought his first cattle station. He eventually established two strings of stations. The north-south chain was from Queensland to Adelaide, and the central chain from the Northern Territory to Adelaide. By moving stock from one station to another in times of drought, he was able to avoid severe losses.

Kidman kept to the straight and narrow – he didn't drink or swear and inspired tremendous loyalty in those who worked for him. He was a generous man who gave to many causes and at the time of his death was the best known Australian in the British Empire and the USA.

Did he have any bad habits? Well, it depends how you classify 'late-rising' and the ability to fall asleep at any time.

Around Cobar

East of Cobar, the Barrier Hwy passes the curiously named **Mt Boppy**, site of a huge gold mine. **Hermidale**, about 100km east of Cobar, is a railway-side hamlet consisting of a few houses and a shop.

Mt Grenfell Historic Site Taking in part of the Mt Grenfell station, this site protects Aboriginal rock art in several caves along a well-watered gully, an important place for the local Wongaibon people. Apart from the art, the site is worth visiting for the chance to walk through some pretty country on the 5km walking track.

You'll probably see feral goats and perhaps pigs in the area and there are also plenty of kangaroos and emus. From about July onwards you'll see father emus herding their broods of chicks. If a couple of males are travelling together, they can have quite a kindergarten to look after.

To get here, travel west from Cobar on the Barrier Hwy and turn off after 40km. The site is another 32km away on a good dirt road. There's water at the site but camping is not allowed.

Wilcannia
postcode 2836 • pop 900

Today, the small town of Wilcannia on the banks of the Darling River 195km east of Broken Hill, is little more than a refuelling stop. It's hard to imagine that back in the 1880s, the boom years on the Darling River, Wilcannia was the third-busiest port in Australia – dubbed the 'Queen City of the West'.

Some of the old buildings remain, such as part of the old wharf, the impressive sandstone police station and courthouse on Reid St, and the Athenaeum Chambers, also on Reid St and housing the local **museum**.

Limited visitor information is available at the golf club.

Places to Stay & Eat The *Victory Caravan Park*, across the bridge and down by the river, has tent sites for $8.

There are only two motels, *Grahams* (☎ 8091 5040) and the *Wilcannia* (☎ 8091 5802), both charging around $50/60 for singles/doubles. For fast food, try the basic cafe at the petrol station. The *Golf Club* is the only place to eat out.

Getting There & Away From Wilcannia you can take the Barrier Hwy east to Cobar or west to Broken Hill. There's a good road (mostly sealed) north to White Cliffs, and the Cobb Hwy leads south.

THE COBB HIGHWAY

The Cobb Hwy runs south from Wilcannia through Ivanhoe, Hay and Deniliquin to Moama (and Echuca) on the Victorian border. It's a handy route.

The 190km of road between Wilcannia and Ivanhoe is mostly unsealed and passes through some of the emptiest country in the state, although there are a few stations off the road.

Tiny **Ivanhoe** is the largest town for a very long way. It's built on the railway line (there's even a 'suburb' called Railtown) rather than on a river, and it isn't especially interesting – but, with a pub (accommodation), a friendly club (meals), a petrol station (NRMA affiliate), a caravan park ($5 for a tent site), a bush hospital and a few shops, it can be very useful.

South of Ivanhoe, the Cobb Hwy is sealed for the 50km run to **Mossgiel**, just a pub on the corner of the road running east to Willandra National Park and Hillston – this road closes at a hint of rain. The Cobb Hwy is again unsealed from Mossgiel to **Booligal**, a tiny town on the Lachlan River with a pub and some basic services. The historic **One Tree Hotel**, on the highway 38km north of Hay, is now a private home.

WHITE CLIFFS

☎ 08 • postcode 2836 • pop 150

There are few stranger places in Australia than the tiny opal-mining town of White Cliffs, 97km north-west of Wilcannia. The town is surrounded by some of the harshest country the outback has to offer and many residents have gone underground to escape the heat. Although the town is still a major opal producer, it's a fair bet that tourism brings in almost as much money these days.

The town centre, such as it is, is on flat land south of the main digging area. There's a pub, a post office and a corner store selling fuel and provisions. At the digging area, there are thousands of holes in the ground and miners' camps surrounded by car graveyards (which seem to be a necessary part of opal mining). The two bare hills, Turley's Hill (with the radio-telephone mast on top) and Smith's Hill (south of the centre), are relatively densely populated and command the plains like diminutive city-states.

You can fossick for opals around the old diggings, but keep a close eye on kids around those deep, unfenced holes. There are a number of opal showrooms and underground homes open for inspection. **Jock's Place** on Turley's Hill is worth seeing. Jock has a jumble of relics from the area and what he doesn't know about opal mining isn't worth knowing.

In the centre of town is the **solar power-station** (it drives a steam-turbine) where emus often graze out the front. The station is open for inspection at 2 pm daily and is worth a visit if only to see the guide in action. Bill Finney goes through a lot of shirts!

Places to Stay & Eat

White Cliffs gets busy during holiday periods, so it's advisable to book ahead if you'll be visiting then.

There's a very uninspiring little *camping area* (☎ 8091 6688) next to the swimming pool on the road to Mootwingee. Sites cost $4 per person and showers are $1.

The *White Cliffs Hotel* (☎ 8091 6606) has basic singles/doubles with air-con that are reasonable value at $20/30. A cooked breakfast costs $8. The management is friendly and other meals are available (although pricey).

The most interesting place to stay is *PJ's Underground* (☎ 8091 6626) on Turley's Hill. Energetic owners Peter and Joanne Pedler have performed miracles in converting their old mine workings into a cool sanctuary with whitewashed walls, beautiful stone floors and elegant furnishings. Rates are $65/90, including breakfast. Self-caterers can pay $2 to use the barbecue in

FAR WEST

the evening; others can pay $27 for a two-course or $33 for a three-course meal.

The other underground option is the *White Cliffs Underground Motel* (☎ 1800 021 154), which is popular with tour groups. Custom-built with a tunnelling machine, the place is quite a maze (you get a map when you check in) but it's surprisingly bright, comfortable and not at all claustrophobia-inducing. The rooms are simple and very quiet, with several metres of rock separating rooms. Rooms with bathroom cost $52/79. Meals cost $8 for a continental breakfast, $14 for a cooked breakfast and $25 for a three-course, set-menu dinner.

Getting There & Away
The emergence of White Cliffs as a tourist destination has led to an upgrading of the road south to Wilcannia. Most of the 97km was sealed at the time of research. All other roads out of White Cliffs are unsealed. Information on road conditions is posted outside the general store.

MOOTWINGEE NATIONAL PARK
Mootwingee National Park lies in the rugged Bynguano Ranges, 131km north-east of Broken Hill. The area teems with wildlife and is a place of exceptional rough beauty. In spring the roads can be like country lanes, flanked by 'hedges' of blue and white flowers.

The reliable water supply in the range was vital to Aborigines in the area and there are important **rock carvings** and **cave paintings**. Some cave paintings have been badly damaged by vandals and the major site is now controlled by the Aboriginal community and is off-limits to visitors except on escorted tours on Wednesday and Saturday morning ($15/5 adults/children) between April and November. The NPWS office (☎ 8088 5933) in Broken Hill has details.

There are walks through the crumbling sandstone hills to rock pools, which often have enough water for swimming, and rock paintings can be seen in the areas that are not off-limits.

There's a *camping area* ($10 for two people) at Homestead Creek, with toilets, showers and gas barbecues. Water for drinking may not always be available; fuel and food are not available in the park. You should collect firewood from the signposted areas near the park entrance.

Getting There & Away
There are no sealed roads to Mootwingee, which means the park is inaccessible in wet weather. Most people head out to Mootwingee from Broken Hill. The turn-off is 56km north of town along the Silver City Hwy and then it's a farther 68km to the park entrance along a good unsealed road. The back road to White Cliffs is also good but tends to stay muddy longer after rain and has a number of creek crossings – these are usually dry but fill quickly after rain, and, even when the water has gone, deep drifts of mud remain.

BROKEN HILL
☎ 08 • postcode 2880 • pop 23,000
Broken Hill is an oasis in the wilderness. It's a fascinating town, not only for its comfortable existence in an extremely unwelcoming environment, but also for the fact that it was once a one-company town that spawned one equally strong union. Some of the state's best national parks are in the area, plus some interesting near-ghost towns.

Elements of 'traditional' Australian culture that are disappearing in other cities can still be found in Broken Hill: hard physical work, hard drinking and the sensibilities that come with easy access to a huge, unpopulated landscape. The less-attractive aspects of this culture have been considerably mellowed by the city becoming a major centre for naive arts, most of it local. This is a surprising but delightful development.

History
The Broken Hill Proprietary Company (BHP), after which the town was named, was formed in 1885 after a boundary rider, Charles Rasp, discovered a silver lode. Other mining claims were staked, but BHP was always the 'big mine' and dominated the town. Charles Rasp went on to amass a personal fortune and BHP, which later di-

versified into steel production, became Australia's largest company.

Early conditions in the mine were appalling. Hundreds of miners died and many more suffered from lead poisoning and lung disease. This gave rise to the other great force in Broken Hill, the unions. Many miners were immigrants – from Ireland, Germany, Italy and Malta – but all were united in their efforts to improve mining conditions.

The first 35 years of Broken Hill saw a militancy rarely matched in Australian industrial relations. Many campaigns were fought, police were called in to break strikes and though there was a gradual improvement in conditions, the miners lost many confrontations. The turning point was the Big Strike of 1919–20, which lasted for over 18 months. The miners won a great victory, achieving a 35-hour week and the end of dry drilling, which was responsible for the dust that afflicted so many miners.

The concept of 'one big union', which had helped to win the strike, was formalised in 1923 with the formation of the Barrier Industrial Council. It still largely runs the town.

Today the richest silver, lead and zinc deposit in the world is still being worked, but lead and zinc have assumed a greater importance in the Silver City, as Broken Hill is known. There's enough ore left to ensure approximately five years of mining, but new technology has greatly reduced the number of jobs in the mines.

Orientation

The city is laid out in a straightforward grid pattern and the central area is easy to walk around. Argent St is the main shopping street and the blocks between Bromide and Iodide Sts make up downtown Broken Hill.

Information

The big Visitor Information Centre (☎ 8087 6077), on the corner of Blende and Bromide Sts, opens from 8.30 am to 5 pm daily. This is where the buses arrive and there's a bus booking agency, a cafeteria and Hertz car rental on the premises. Also here is the Broken Hill Interpretive Centre, with displays on all aspects of Broken Hill and the area, and information on walks around the city. The Heritage Trails Map is a good buy ($2).

Bizbyte, 435 Argent St, provides Internet access for $7 an hour. It's open from 9 am to 5.30 pm weekdays.

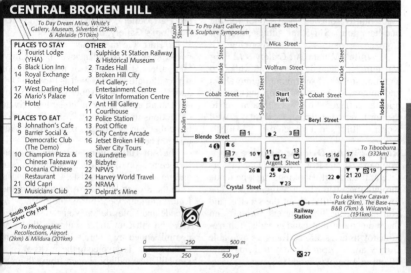

CENTRAL BROKEN HILL

PLACES TO STAY
5 Tourist Lodge (YHA)
6 Black Lion Inn
14 Royal Exchange Hotel
17 West Darling Hotel
26 Mario's Palace Hotel

PLACES TO EAT
8 Johnathon's Cafe
9 Barrier Social & Democratic Club (The Demo)
10 Champion Pizza & Chinese Takeaway
20 Oceania Chinese Restaurant
21 Old Capri
23 Musicians Club

OTHER
1 Sulphide St Station Railway & Historical Museum
2 Trades Hall
3 Broken Hill City Art Gallery; Entertainment Centre
4 Visitor Information Centre
7 Ant Hill Gallery
11 Courthouse
12 Police Station
13 Post Office
15 City Centre Arcade
16 Jetset Broken Hill; Silver City Tours
18 Laundrette
19 Bizbyte
22 NPWS
24 Harvey World Travel
25 NRMA
27 Delprat's Mine

To Day Dream Mine, White's Gallery, Museum, Silverton (25km) & Adelaide (510km)
To Pro Hart Gallery & Sculpture Symposium
Kaolin Street
Lane Street
Mica Street
Bromide Street
Wolfram Street
Oxide Street
Sulphide Street
Chloride Street
Cobalt Street
Sturt Park
Cobalt Street
Iodide Street
Kaolin Street
Beryl Street
Blende Street
To Tibooburra (332km)
Argent Street
Crystal Street
To Lake View Caravan Park (2km), The Base B&B (7km) & Wilcannia (191km)
South Road / Silver City Hwy
To Photographic Recollections, Airport (2km) & Mildura (201km)
Railway Station
0 250 500 m
0 250 500 yd

The Royal Automobile Association of South Australia (☎ 8088 4999), 261 Argent St, provides reciprocal service to members of other auto clubs. If you're venturing into the outback areas of SA you'll need a Desert Parks Pass, which is sold here.

There's a laundrette on Argent St just east of the West Darling Hotel.

If you find injured wildlife, contact Rescue & Rehabilitation of Australian Native Animals (RRANA; ☎ 8087 7753) at the veterinary clinic in South Rd.

Time Broken Hill operates on SA time (Central Standard), which is half an hour behind the time in the rest of the state. Towns near Broken Hill *don't* follow the Silver City's lead, keeping NSW time instead.

Mines

There's an excellent underground tour at **Delprat's Mine** (☎ 8088 1604) Monday to Saturday, where you don miners' gear and descend 130m for a tour lasting nearly two hours ($23/18 for adults/students). Children under six are prohibited. To get there, go up Iodide St, cross the railway tracks and follow the signs – it's about a five-minute drive.

Day Dream Mine, established in 1881, is 33km from Broken Hill, off the Silverton road. Sturdy footwear is essential for the one-hour tour ($11/5 for adults/children). Contact the visitors centre for bookings.

At **White's Mineral Art Gallery & Mining Museum**, 1 Allendale St, you can walk into a mining stope and see mining memorabilia and minerals. It has a craft shop and crushed mineral collages. Follow Galena St out to the north-west for 2km or so. Whites is well worth visiting and it's open daily ($4).

Royal Flying Doctor Service

You can visit the Royal Flying Doctor Service at the airport. Bookings must be made through the Visitor Information centre. The tour includes a film about the service, and you inspect the headquarters, aircraft and the radio room that handles calls from remote towns and stations. Tours are available from 9 am to 5 pm Monday to Friday and 10 am to 4 pm weekends ($3).

The Flying Doctor

The Royal Flying Doctor Service (RFDS) was founded by John Flynn 'of the Inland' in 1927. He envisioned a 'mantle of safety' for isolated properties in outback Australia, and with the development of simple, inexpensive short-wave radios (at first pedal-powered), much of the country suddenly had access to emergency health care in hours instead of after days of hard travelling.

Today the service responds to emergencies and holds regular clinics in even the tiniest and remotest towns – and it's all free. That's why you should drop a few coins into a RFDS donation box.

School of the Air

You can sit in on School of the Air, which broadcasts to kids in isolated homesteads at 8.30 am sharp on weekdays. The one-hour session costs $3; book through the visitors centre. You can visit even when school is out, as a tape-recording is played for visitors during vacations.

Galleries

Broken Hill seems to inspire artists and there's a plethora of galleries, including the **Pro Hart Gallery**, 108 Wyman St, and **Jack Absalom's Gallery**, 638 Chapple St.

Pro Hart, a former miner, is Broken Hill's best-known artist and a local personality. His gallery displays his own work, minor works of major artists (such as Picasso, Dali and Rouault) and a superb collection of Australian art. It's one of the largest private collections in the country. You can also see his collection of antique baby rattles. Admission costs $2.

The **Ant Hill Gallery**, opposite the visitors centre on Bromide St, features local and major Australian artists.

In the **Broken Hill City Art Gallery**, in the Entertainment Centre on the corner of Blende and Chloride Sts, you can see *Silver Tree*, an intricate silver sculpture that was commissioned by Charles Rasp. One room of the gallery is devoted to the artists of Broken Hill. The gallery is open from 10 am to

ollowing the form, White Cliffs

esert sculpture, Broken Hill

Mootwingee National Park

The Bread Knife, Warrumbungle National Park

The still quiet of a Murray River dawn

5 pm weekdays and 1 pm to 5 pm weekends ($3). There are more galleries at Silverton.

Make sure you have a look inside the residential entrance of Mario's Palace Hotel on the corner of Argent and Sulphide Sts.

Sculpture Symposium

In 1993 12 international sculptors were invited to record their impressions of Broken Hill at a hill-top site 8km north-west of town. After seeing paintings by local 'brushmen of the bush', it's interesting to see how foreign artists responded to this limitless landscape. They certainly don't see it full of cuddly marsupials and laconic stockmen! To get here, follow Kaolin St out of town on to Nine Mile Rd and the sculptures are signposted to the right. From the lower car park it's a 20-minute climb to the sculpture site. Bring water in summer. There's wheelchair access to the sculptures from the upper car park, but you need to get the keys for the gate from the visitors centre.

Apart from the sculptures, there are excellent views over the plains and this is a good place to watch one of Broken Hill's famous sunsets.

Historic Buildings

The **Afghan Mosque** is a simple old corrugated-iron building dating from 1891. Afghani cameleers helped to open up the outback and the mosque was built on the site of a camel camp. It's on the corner of William and Buck Sts in North Broken Hill and opens from 2.30 to 4.30 pm Sunday. It no longer functions as a mosque.

The **Trades Hall**, on the corner of Sulphide and Blende Sts, is a wedding-cake building, totally incongruous both in its setting and in relation to its function.

Other Attractions

The excellent **Photographic Recollections** exhibition is a fascinating pictorial history of Broken Hill. It's at the old Central Power Station on Eyre St in Broken Hill South and opens from 10 am to 4.30 pm weekdays; 1 pm to 4.30 pm weekends ($4).

The **Sulphide St Station Railway & Historical Museum** is in the Silverton Tramway

Company's old station on Sulphide St. The tramway was a private railway running between Cockburn (SA) and Broken Hill via Silverton until 1970. Also in the complex is a mineral display and a hospital museum. It's open from 10 am to 3 pm daily ($2).

The **Silver City Mint & Art Centre**, 66 Chloride St, opens from 10 am to 4 pm daily (free).

Organised Tours

There are two-hour guided walks of Broken Hill from the tourist centre at 10 am on Monday, Wednesday, Friday and Saturday. Plenty of companies offer tours of the town and nearby attractions, some going farther out to White Cliffs, Mootwingee National Park and other outback destinations. You'll pay about $25 for a tour of Broken Hill or Silverton and $85 for a trip to Mootwingee or Kinchega National Parks. The visitors centre has information and takes bookings.

Several outfits have longer 4WD tours of the area. Goanna Safaris (☎ 8087 6057) has 4WD outback tours that get good reports from travellers. Corner Country Adventure Tours (☎ 8087 5142) specialises in trips to Tibooburra and Sturt National Park.

Special Events

There's a country music festival, camel races and rodeo in early October.

Places to Stay

On Adelaide Rd north-west of town, *Broken Hill City Caravan Park* (☎ 8087 3841) has sites for $12, on-site vans from $29 and cabins from $34. *Lake View Caravan Park* (☎ 8088 2250, 1 Mann St) has slightly cheaper prices.

The YHA-affiliated *Tourist Lodge* (☎ 8088 2086, 100 Argent St) has a small pool. Dorm beds cost $15, singles/doubles $18/30 or $22/36 with air-con. Bike rental costs $15 a day.

The *Black Lion Inn* (☎ 8087 4801), across from the visitors centre, has reasonable rooms for $18/28 (no air-con in the single rooms).

The elegant *Royal Exchange Hotel* (☎ 8087 2308), on the corner of Argent and

Chloride Sts, has rooms for $24/40 or $34/50 with attached bathroom, fridge and TV. All rooms have tea- and coffee-making facilities and you help yourself to breakfast downstairs.

Farther west on Argent St, *Mario's Palace Hotel* (☎ *8088 1699*) is an impressive old pub (1888) in its own right, but its coating of murals makes it extraordinary. All rooms have ceiling fan (as well as air-con), fridge, TV and tea- and coffee-making facilities; some have a phone. Rooms cost $30/40 or $40/50 with attached bathroom. There are also some family rooms. You might want to check out your room before taking it as some have very thin walls.

Offering more-standard pub accommodation is the *West Darling Hotel* (☎ *8087 269*) on the corner of Argent and Oxide Sts. This is yet another fine old pub (1883), but the rooms are nearer their original condition (perfectly reasonable, but you might want to check the bed). There's a variety of rooms, including some interconnecting family ones. A few have attached bathrooms and go for $45 a single or double. Rooms with shared bathroom (some have a shower attached but no toilet) cost $23/36.

It's hard to understand why anyone would opt for a motel in a town with so many interesting places to stay. Still, there are 14 to choose from and the visitors centre has a list of places and prices.

There are some beautiful cottages for rent around town. *Broken Hill Historic Cottages* (☎ *1800 639 696*) and *Broken Hill Miners Cottages* (☎ *8087 8488*) provide cottage-accommodation booking services. The cottages have just about everything you could need and sleep up to six people. Rates start at around $65 per night, or $350 per week.

A good-value B&B is *The Base* (☎ *8087 7770*), located in the old Royal Flying Doctor base just over 7km from town. It's in a bush setting with lots of space, making it ideal for families. Doubles cost $52 plus $8 for each child.

Places to Eat

Broken Hill is a club town if ever there was one. They welcome visitors – you just sign the book at the front door and walk in. The *Barrier Social & Democratic Club* ('The Demo'; *218 Argent St*) starts early with breakfast from 6 am (7 am at weekends). The *Musicians Club* (*267 Crystal St*) is slightly cheaper.

There are lots of pubs too – this is a mining town. Many pubs have cheap counter meals. The locals' choice is the *West Darling Hotel*. Main courses cost $10 to $13 and the serves are huge.

The *Champion Pizza & Chinese Takeaway*, behind Pizza Hut on Sulphide St, does an all-you-can-eat Chinese buffet for $7.50 after 6 pm. There's a cluster of places at the eastern end of Argent St. The *Oceania Chinese Restaurant* is popular, with cheap lunch specials and main courses from around $8, and the *Al Dente* is a small Italian place offering home-made pasta and pizza.

Vegetarians need not despair. *Johnathons Cafe* (*198 Argent St*) has a tasty daily vegetarian special, as well as good sandwiches and smoothies.

Entertainment

Maybe it's because this is a mining town that plays hard or maybe it's because there are so many nights here when it's too hot to sleep, but Broken Hill stays up late. There isn't a great deal of formal entertainment, but you can find pubs doing a roaring trade almost until dawn on Thursday, Friday and Saturday.

The Demo often has music and sometimes good bands. The *Rising Sun Hotel* (*2 Beryl St*) gets very lively; bands play on weekends.

Two-up (gambling on the fall of two coins) is played at the Musicians Club on Friday and Saturday nights. Broken Hill claims to have retained all the atmosphere of a real two-up 'school', unlike the sanitised versions played in casinos.

Getting There & Away

Standard one-way air fares from Broken Hill include $180 to Adelaide, $592 to Melbourne via Sydney and $363 to Sydney, via Dubbo.

Greyhound Pioneer buses run daily to Adelaide ($60), Mildura ($42) and Sydney

($96). Buses depart from the visitors centre, where you can book seats.

A Victorian government V/Line bus runs to Mildura ($42) on Wednesday and Friday. Book at the train station.

The *Indian Pacific* passes through Broken Hill on its way between Sydney and Perth. It leaves Broken Hill at 5 pm on Sunday and Wednesday and arrives in Sydney at 9.15 am the next day ($108 economy). It leaves for Adelaide ($54) and Perth (from $262) at 10 am on Tuesday and Friday.

There's a slightly faster and marginally cheaper daily service to Sydney. This is a Countrylink bus departing Broken Hill daily at 4 am (groan) and connecting with a train at Dubbo, arriving in Sydney at 8.45 pm.

The Countrylink booking office at the train station (☎ 13 2232) opens weekdays. Travel agents, such as Jetset Broken Hill and Silver City Tours (☎ 8087 3310), on Argent St near the corner of Oxide St, make Countrylink bookings.

For drivers, the Barrier Hwy runs east to Wilcannia and Cobar and west into SA. The Silver City Hwy runs south to Wentworth and, mostly unsealed, north to Tibooburra.

Getting Around

The Legion, Sturt, and Musicians clubs have a free bus to drive you home after a night's drinking. It leaves hourly between 6 pm and midnight. Phone ☎ 8088 1777 to arrange a pick-up.

Murton's Citybus (☎ 8087 3311) operates four routes around Broken Hill. Pick up a timetable at the visitors centre.

Hertz (☎ 8087 2719) has an office at the visitors centre, which is open daily. Other car-rental companies include Avis (☎ 8087 7532), 121 Rakow St; Budget (☎ 13 2727), 338 Crystal St; and Thrifty (☎ 8088 1928), 190 Argent St.

Call ☎ 8088 1144 or ☎ 8087 2222 for a taxi. There's also a taxi office on Argent Lane.

SILVERTON

☎ 08 • postcode 2880 • pop 50

Silverton, 25km north-west of Broken Hill, is an old silver-mining town. Its fortunes peaked in 1885, when it had a population of 3000 and public buildings designed to last for centuries, but in 1889 the mines closed and the population (and many of the houses) moved to the new boom-town at Broken Hill.

Today it's an interesting little ghost town, used as a setting in films such as *Mad Max II* and *A Town Like Alice*. A number of buildings still stand, including the old jail (now the museum) and the Silverton Hotel. The hotel is operating and displays photographs taken on the film sets. There are also a couple of art galleries. The pub and galleries have a walking-tour map. Several artists, including Peter Browne and John Dynon, have studios here.

Bill Canard (☎ 8088 5316) runs a variety of **camel tours** from Silverton. The camels are often hitched up near the hotel or the visitors centre. You can take a 15-minute tour of the town for $5, a one-hour ride for $20 or a two-hour sunset ride for $40/$20 adults/children. There are also overnight treks ($150/75).

There's accommodation at *Penrose Park* (☎ *8088 5307*), signposted to the right as you approach town from Broken Hill. Camp sites cost $3 per person or you can bed down in a choice of 'bunkhouses' – $20 with kitchen, $15 without. There are coin-operated showers and there is water for washing, but bring or boil your drinking water.

The road beyond Silverton becomes bleak and lonely almost immediately, but the **Umberumberka Reservoir**, 13km from Silverton, is a popular picnic spot.

MENINDEE

☎ 08 • postcode 2879 • pop 500

This small town on the Darling River is 112km south-east of Broken Hill on a good sealed road. It's right by the big Menindee Lakes and Kinchega National Park.

Explorers Burke and Wills stayed at Maidens Hotel on their ill-fated trip north in 1860. The hotel was built in 1854 and has been with the same family for about 100 years; it has a courtyard, which is a nice spot for a drink on a hot day.

The town has a small but reasonably well-stocked supermarket, so you don't need to bring too many supplies. The Tourist Information Centre on Yartla St is open from 9 am to 5 pm weekdays and 10 am to 1 pm weekends.

The **Menindee Lakes** are natural lakes on the meandering Darling River, but they have been dammed to ensure year-round water. They offer the parched folk of Broken Hill a chance for watersports and this area can be crowded on summer weekends. The Broken Hill Yacht Club is not far out of Menindee.

Places to Stay

Menindee has pub accommodation at the historic *Maidens Hotel* (☎ 8091 4208), which has singles/doubles for $17/38, and at the *Albermarle Hotel* (☎ 8091 4212), which has rooms for $25/30, including breakfast. Just across from the Maidens is the *Burke & Wills Motel* (☎ 8091 4313), charging $45/55 for singles/doubles.

There are caravan parks and cabins out of town by the lakes. There's also camping in Kinchega National Park with some excellent sites among the red gums along the banks of the Darling River. Just be careful not to set up under any branches; they can break away unexpectedly.

Getting There & Away

Menindee is on the main railway line between Sydney and Adelaide, so you can catch the *Indian Pacific* here.

A good road runs to Broken Hill, and unsealed roads on both sides of the river run south to Pooncarie and Wentworth. The road on the east bank is usually better but if there has been rain ask for advice on the best route. Another unsealed road follows the river upstream to Wilcannia.

KINCHEGA NATIONAL PARK

Kinchega National Park is close to Menindee and includes the Darling River and several of the lakes in the Menindee system. These are a haven for birdlife. The visitors centre is at the site of the old Kinchega homestead, about 16km from the park entrance, and the shearing shed has been preserved. There's bunk accommodation at the shearers' quarters (book at the Broken Hill NPWS office)

for $15 and plenty of camp sites ($5) along the river.

MUNGO NATIONAL PARK

Mungo National Park (27,850 hectares), part of the Willandra Lakes World Heritage area, is remote, beautiful and a most important place, full of great significance for the human species. The echoes of over 400 centuries of continuous human habitation are almost tangible.

The story of both Australia and its oldest inhabitants is told in the dunes of Mungo. At least 60,000 years ago, Aborigines settled on the banks of the fertile lakes, living on the plentiful fish, mussels, birds and animals. Some of the animals were much larger than their modern relatives. After 45,000 years the climate changed, the lakes dried up and the Aborigines adapted to life in a harsh semidesert, with only periodic floods filling the lakes. The constant westerly wind drifted sand from the lake bed up onto the dunes, gradually burying old camp sites.

The people maintained their culture for another 15,000 years, but it was destroyed when Europeans arrived with their sheep in the early 19th century. Along with the remains of incredibly ancient animals and people, the dunes hold tracks of the Cobb & Co coaches, which cut across the lake last century.

The park includes the dry lake bed (it sometimes fills after heavy rain) and the spectacular 'lunette', a semicircular range of sand dunes, which line the eastern side. Some of the compressed sand has weathered into shimmering white cliffs known as the **Walls of China**. This weathering process began last century after sheep destabilised the dunes, which are now moving slowly eastwards under the constant west wind, leaving exposed immensely important archaeological evidence.

There's a visitors centre (not always staffed) where you can see some of the archaeological finds. Near the visitors centre is the old woolshed from the sheep station that was established here last century. During school holidays there are organised activities, such as walks and even bush dances.

The NPWS office (☎ 03-5023 1278) at Buronga near Mildura has information.

A 60km drive circles the lunette and there are various stopping places with informative noticeboards. There are a couple of short walks, the **Grassland Nature Trail** (1km), beginning near Main Camp, and the **Mallee Walk** (500m), off the road on the east side of the lunette. You can get onto the lunette from the Walls of China and there are good dune walks from Vigars Wells on the north-east side of the lunette.

In summer, be sure to carry water with you when you go walking on the dunes.

Organised Tours
Mallee Outback Experiences (☎ 03-5021 1621); Junction Tours (☎ 03-5027 4309); and Ponde Tours Aboriginal Interpretation (☎ 03-5023 2488) are three Mildura-based companies offering tours. Harry Nanya Tours (☎ 03-5027 2076) operates from Wentworth, but if you meet him at the park (around 10 am) you can get on the tour for $20.

Places to Stay
Accommodation fills up during school holidays. There are two *camp sites* in the park: Main Camp is 2km from the visitors centre and Belah Camp is in bushland on the eastern side of the lunette, a few kilometres away. On this side of the lunette you're sheltered from the west wind, but you can hear it singing eerily along the dunes.

Camping costs $5 a night. There's also shared accommodation in the old shearers' quarters, costing $15 per person or $25 for a room to yourself. There are cooking facilities. Accommodation in the *shearers' quarters* must be booked through the NPWS office (☎ 03-5023 1278) in Buronga near Mildura.

On the Mildura road about 4km from the visitor centre is *Mungo Lodge* (☎ 03-5029 7297). Singles/doubles go for $68/78 and there's a self-contained cottage that can sleep up to six ($88 for two people and $10 for each extra person). There's also a restaurant.

Getting There & Away
Mungo Lodge has an airstrip where charter flights can land.

No fuel is available in the park or along the roads leading to it. The unsealed roads into Mungo are well maintained, but they can be closed by rain. Even after a light shower, sections are treacherous. Watch out for deep drifts of sand or soft dirt. These appear without warning and if you hit one at speed, you'll lose control over the steering. Kangaroos and emus are another hazard – or rather, you are a hazard for these locals.

Mungo is 110km from Mildura and 150km from Balranald. When calculating fuel needs don't forget the 60km or so you'll probably drive within the park.

Coming from Balranald, you can take the signposted turn-off about 15km north of town. This is Burke & Wills Rd; it's an interesting drive, but a little rough. If you want to travel on tar as far as possible, keep heading north to another signposted turn-off, 53km from Balranald.

Mungo Man

Lake Mungo is one of the country's richest archaeological sites and was added to the World Heritage List in 1981 because of its significance to Aboriginal people. In 1974 the shifting sands of Mungo revealed the remains of a male who had been covered in red ochre during a burial ritual.

This is the earliest known use of pigment for artistic, philosophical or religious purposes. Recent analysis indicates the Mungo man may be up to 68,000 years old, so his presence in Australia's south-east indicates, it is argued, that humans arrived in the north-east from Asia much earlier.

Of course, all this scientific analysis does not accord with the Aboriginal view of the Dreamtime and their creation from the land. Aborigines maintain that they have always occupied the Australian continent.

The Riverina

The Riverina takes in much of southern New South Wales (NSW), specifically the mighty Murray and Murrumbidgee Rivers and the plains created by these waterways as they changed course over the millennia. The rivers are the lifeblood of this region, comprising rich grazing and farming country. Irrigation schemes have allowed crops such as rice, lettuce and grapes to flourish in several centres here, while the small towns of the Riverina region are usually pleasant oases.

The rivers are vital too to the area's ecology, as river red gums need regular inundation to survive, though the big dams built for the irrigation schemes have limited the extent of the floods and the trees are suffering.

Away from the rivers, which are popular for fishing holidays, much of this region sees few visitors. This is part of the Riverina's attraction – you can meet locals whose daily life isn't geared to extracting dollars from your wallet.

History

The rivers of the Riverina provided an idyllic home for the Aborigines, and before Europeans arrived the area around Deniliquin was probably the most densely populated part of the continent. John Oxley, the first European to visit the area (in the early 19th century), wasn't impressed:

There's a uniformity in the barren desolation of this country which wearies one more than I am able to express...I am the first white man to see it and I think I will undoubtedly be the last.

A century later, after graziers had established sheep stations on the plains, Europeans were coming to terms with the environment:

The monotonous variety of this interminable scrub...so grave, subdued, self-centred...bespeaks an ungauged, unconfined potentiality...

Joseph Furphy, *Such is Life*, 1903

Not long after, the great irrigation schemes of the Murrumbidgee Irrigation Area (MIA)

HIGHLIGHTS

- Strolling through the Botanic Gardens in Wagga Wagga
- Sinking beers at Junee's grand pubs
- Visiting the region's wineries, especially around Griffith
- Wildlife watching at Willandra National Park
- Hot-air ballooning along the Murray River near Corowa

The Riverina p359

Griffith p372

Narrandera p368

Wagga Wagga p361

Deniliquin p382

VICTORIA

were begun and parts of the plains bloomed into fertile farmland.

To get an idea of the terrain and conditions of the Riverina, drive along the Cobb Hwy between Wilcannia and Hay. This isn't a trip to take lightly, as much of the 400km is unsealed and there are few services along the way. Imagine how the trip would have been in a bullock wagon hauling eight tonnes of wool at a rate of less than 20km a day!

Geography & Climate

To the east, the landscape is broken up by the last hills of the western slopes of the Great Dividing Range. Much of the region, however, is a huge, flat space, usually with

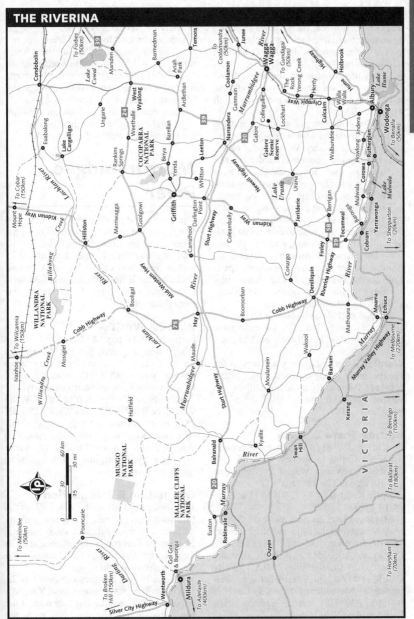

THE RIVERINA

a line of river red gums straggling along a creek on the horizon, native pines clustered on a sandy ridge overlooking grazing country or, in the west and north, expanses of saltbush or mulga.

Nor is the country far above sea level. The Murray River descends only 100m or so between Corowa and its mouth in South Australia (SA).

In the west the fences disappear and cattle grids on the road are the only sign that you are in working country. Wedge-tailed eagles waft overhead or perch awkwardly on telegraph poles – there are no peaks or tall trees for their eyries. The western grey kangaroos are dwarfed by their brothers, the big reds.

The landscape can be monotonous, but if you're after a sense of distance and space, the Riverina is the place to come. Flat horizons of 360° are common, under a hot, blue sky – some Riverina towns have more hours of sunshine per year than you might experience on the Gold Coast. The shimmering horizon blurs into mirages, and even in winter the light is blindingly strong.

Autumn nights can be cold in this region, with heavy frosts, but after the mists have burnt off, the days usually turn out beautiful.

Warning River red gums are notorious for unexpectedly dropping their huge, heavy branches. Apparently those hot, still days in summer are the most likely times for branches to fall.

Getting There & Away
Griffith and Wagga Wagga have regular passenger flights to Sydney; there are also flights from Wagga Wagga to Melbourne and Brisbane. The two main regional airlines are Kendell (☎ 13 1300) and Hazelton (☎ 13 1713).

Major bus lines running along the Newell Hwy between Melbourne and Brisbane service the Riverina, and some buses between Sydney and Adelaide pass through. There are some useful smaller lines. MIA Intercity Coaches (☎ 6962 3419) runs between Griffith and Melbourne. Fearnes Coaches (☎ 1800 029 918) services various Hume Hwy towns to Wagga Wagga.

Countrylink buses link most Riverina towns with the railway at Wagga Wagga, Cootamundra or Albury. V/Line buses run between Melbourne and the southern Riverina. Call (☎ 13 2232) for information.

The XPT (express) Sydney to Melbourne train runs through Junee, Wagga Wagga and Morgan Country. On Saturdays only there's a direct train between Sydney and Griffith.

Several highways cross the Riverina, and the Hume Hwy skirts the eastern side.

Murrumbidgee River

The Murrumbidgee River rises in the Snowy Mountains and by the time it reaches Wagga Wagga, not far from the foothills, it's already a broad river. Farther downstream its waters form part of the big MIA around Griffith, then it flows though harsher country and meets the Murray River downstream from Balranald.

WAGGA WAGGA
postcode 2650 • pop 58,000
Wagga Wagga, usually just called Wagga, is the state's largest inland city. It's a relaxed country town, with a little diversity added by the nearby Charles Sturt University.

The largest Aboriginal tribe in NSW, the Wiradjuri, lived in this area. Charles Sturt's 1829 expedition saw the beginning of European encroachment and by 1849 the town of Wagga Wagga was established. The name derives from Aboriginal words meaning 'place of many crows'.

Orientation & Information
The town centre sits on the west bank of the Murrumbidgee River. Baylis St and its northern extension Fitzmaurice St form the 2km spine of central Wagga Wagga and run from the train station to the Hampden and New Bridges over the river.

Wagga Wagga Visitors Centre (☎ 6923 5402), on Tarcutta St, opens from 9 am to 5 pm daily. Pick up a driving-tour map of the town from here. The post office, in the

Marketplace mall on Baylis St, is open from 8.30 am to 5 pm weekdays.

Civic Video, 21 Forsyth St, is open from 10 am to 10 pm daily and provides Internet access for $5 per hour.

Two camping supplies shops, Camping World and Tilly's Camping & Outdoor, are near the corner of Baylis and Tompson Sts.

Things to See & Do

The excellent **Botanic Gardens**, open daily, are south of the centre; turn south off Edward St onto Edmondson St (which be-

comes Mitchelmore St), then follow the signs. The entrance is on the right just before the archway telling you that you're entering Lord Baden Powell Drive, which leads up to a good lookout and the scenic **Captain Cook Drive**. In the gardens is a small **zoo**. Geese and peacocks roam free and there's a free-flight aviary containing some colourful native birds, although others are crowded into small cages. You can ride a model train on the first and third Sundays of the month.

The **Wiradjuri Walking Track** begins at the Wagga Wagga Visitors Centre and eventually

WAGGA WAGGA

PLACES TO STAY
1 Palm & Pawn Motor Inn
5 Romano's Hotel
6 Wagga Wagga Beach Caravan Park; Swimming Pool
10 Lagoonside B&B
13 The Manor Guesthouse
24 Charles Sturt Motor Inn
25 Country Comfort Motel
31 Victoria Hotel; Tira Thai

PLACES TO EAT
3 No 96
4 Bernie's & Tourist Hotel
8 Cafe Europa
9 Firenze
12 Locksley the Restaurant
18 Emma Chissett's
19 Indian Tavern
20 Elle's
21 Union Club Hotel
26 Nabiha's Kitchen
29 Montezuma's Mexican Restaurant

OTHER
2 Duke of Kent Hotel
7 Courthouse
11 Memorial Gardens
14 Civic Centre Theatre, Art Gallery, Library & Museum
15 Wagga Wagga Visitors Centre
16 Tilly's Camping & Outdoor
17 Camping World
22 Post Office; Marketplace Mall
23 Civic Video
27 Palladium Nightclub
28 NRMA
30 Swimming Pool
32 Red Lion Hotel

To Aurora Clydesdale Stud & Pioneer Farm (33km), Narrandera (99km) & Albury (129km)

To Charles Sturt University & Junee (41km)

Wiradjuri Reserve

North Wagga

Nurrung Street

Wilks Park

Pregan Island

Travers Street

Racecourse

Cabarita Park

The Esplanade

Tompson Street

Forsyth Street

Wagga Wagga

Spring Street

North Street

South Street

Edward Street (Sturt Highway)

Gormly Avenue

Hardy Street

Chaston Street

Train Station

Railway Street

Bolton Park

To Airport, Hume Highway & Gundagai (84km)

To Botanic Gardens & Captain Cook Drive

returns there after a 30km tour of the area, including some good lookouts. There's a shorter 10km loop past the Wollundry Lagoon. The walks can be done in stages and the visitors centre has maps. From the **beach** near Cabarita Park you can swim and fish.

The new Wagga Wagga Civic Centre houses the **Regional Art Gallery**, home to the National Art Glass collection, and the **Museum of The Riverina**. The main gallery opens from 10 am to 5 pm Monday to Saturday and from noon to 4 pm Sunday. The art glass gallery is closed on Monday and Tuesday. The museum is open from 10 am to 5 pm Tuesday to Saturday and from noon to 4 pm Sunday. Entry is free.

Wagga Wagga is a major centre for **livestock sales**, but the computerised bidding and indoor ring at the Livestock Marketing Centre in Bomen don't have quite the same atmosphere as a small town's outdoor saleyards. The sales happen a few times a month; contact the visitors centre for details.

Well worth a visit is **Wagga Wagga Winery** (☎ 6922 1221), midway between Wagga Wagga and Oura on the Gundagai road. It opens from 11 am daily for tastings and sales; meals are available for $12. Charles Sturt University is north of town, off the Olympic Way. It has a **winery** (☎ 6933 2435), open from 10 am to 4 pm weekdays and from 11 am weekends. The winery is reached through the Agriculture Research Unit, off the Olympic Way about 3km north of Wagga Wagga.

Aurora Clydesdale Stud & Pioneer Farm (☎ 6928 2215) is a working farm where you can see magnificent Clydesdales. The farm is south of the Sturt Hwy west of Wagga Wagga, about 9km west of Collingullie. The stud opens from 9 am to 4 pm daily except Thursday ($2/1 for adults/children).

Special Events

The Wagga Wagga Show, held in late September or early October, is rural NSW's largest agricultural show.

Places to Stay

Of the several caravan parks in the area, the **Wagga Wagga Beach Caravan Park**

(☎ 6931 0603, 2 Johnston St) has the best location. It's on the river next to a swimming beach and is only a couple of blocks from the town centre. You could walk here from the train and bus stations. Tent sites cost $8 and cabins start at $45 for two. There is also dorm accommodation for $10 per person.

Several pubs have accommodation, including **Romano's Hotel** (☎ 6921 2013), on the corner of Fitzmaurice and Sturt St. Good singles/doubles, some with attached bathrooms, cost $30/38. On Baylis St, the **Victoria Hotel** (☎ 6921 5233) has modest rooms from $20/30.

There are many motels to choose from. The **Palm & Pawn Motor Inn** (☎ 6921 6688), on the Olympic Way 2km north of town, is among the least expensive with rooms for $45/55. More expensive (and better) places include the **Charles Sturt Motor Inn** (☎ 6921 8088, 82 Tarcutta St), with rooms for $73/83, and the huge **Country Comfort** (☎ 6921 6444), on the corner of Morgan and Tarcutta Sts, at $84/94.

The Manor (☎ 6921 5962, 38 Morrow St) is a small, well-restored guesthouse (furnished with antiques) opposite the Memorial Gardens. B&B costs $35/80. Another B&B in a restored house is the interesting **Lagoonside B&B** (☎ 6921 1308, 1 Beckwith St), where rooms cost $73/93.

Places to Eat

Along Fitzmaurice and Baylis Sts there's a diverse range of good places to eat.

On Fitzmaurice St is **No 96**, a trendy bar where you can eat and drink if you aren't wearing runners (sneakers). It's open from 6 pm to 3 am Monday to Saturday and for lunch on Friday; pasta costs around $9.

Cafe Europa, on Johnston St just west of Fitzmaurice St, has pasta and pizza. Farther west on the corner of Johnston and Trail Sts is the upmarket **Firenze**. Wagga Wagga Writers Writers, a local literary group, sometimes holds readings here.

Scribbles (22 Fitzmaurice St) is a cheerful cafe open Thursday to Saturday. **Indian Tavern** (☎ 6921 3121, 176 Baylis St), in D'Hudson arcade, has a tandoor oven. Mains cost $7.50 to $16. It also does takeaways.

Across the street, *Emma Chissett's* (Strine for 'how much is it') serves coffee, snacks and light meals during the day.

In Neslo Arcade is *Nabiha's Kitchen*, a small Lebanese takeaway (with tables) where everything is cooked in front of you. The mostly vegetarian menu of simple, inexpensive dishes includes some Indian items, home-grown vegetables and free-range eggs. It's well worth checking out.

Meat lovers should try the *Stockyard Chargrill* in the Union Club Hotel, with steaks from $12.

For Tex/Mex, try *Montezuma's Mexican Restaurant*, where *comidas* (meals) cost $12 to $14.

The *Baylis St Bistro* at the Victoria Hotel has a good reputation, a large menu (steak costs $12.50) and dress regulations – no thongs (flip-flops), singlets or work clothes. In the Baylis Centre next door is the *Tira Thai Restaurant*, a large, plush place with main courses in the $9 to $12 range.

Bernie's at the Tourist Hotel is a vegetarian restaurant with a frequently changing menu. It's open Wednesday to Saturday.

The two finest restaurants in town are *Locksley the Restaurant (☎ 6921 4886, 137 Peter St)* and the BYO *Elles's (☎ 6925 9925)*, on the corner of Forsyth and Peter Sts. Bookings are advised as both are popular with the locals.

Entertainment
This is a student town of sorts, and a few of the pubs have bands, including the *Duke of Kent* and the *Tourist* hotels on Fitzmaurice St. The *Red Lion Hotel*, on Edward St near the train station, has live music Friday nights. On Baylis St, *The Palladium* sometimes has big-name bands and stays open until late most days of the week.

Other popular watering-holes are the *Union Club Hotel*, on Baylis St, and *Romano's Hotel* on Fitzmaurice St.

Getting There & Away
Kendell (☎ 13 1300) and Hazelton (☎ 13 1713) Airlines have air services connecting Wagga Wagga with Sydney, Melbourne, Brisbane and regional centres in NSW. The standard economy one-way/return fare to Sydney is $183/366.

Countrylink buses meet some trains and run daily to Griffith ($21) via Narrandera and Leeton, and to Echuca (Victoria) via Jerilderie, Finley, Deniliquin and Moama. They leave from the train station. Other long-distance services also leave from the station. You can book here or at a travel agent along Baylis St. Fearnes Coaches (☎ 1800 029 918) runs a service to Sydney ($40) via the Hume Hwy, stopping at most major towns, such as Gundagai, Goulburn and Mittagong.

Glass Buslines (☎ 6924 1633) runs a local service to Junee ($7) on weekdays and picks up along Baylis St.

Wagga Wagga is on the main train line between Sydney and Melbourne. The one-way economy fare to both is $72. The Countrylink Travel Centre (☎ 6939 5488), at the train station, opens from 9 am to 5 pm Monday to Friday.

Wagga Wagga is at the junction of the Sturt Hwy, which runs east to the Hume Hwy and west to Narrandera; and the Olympic Way, which runs north-east to Cootamundra and south to Albury. Smaller roads, often interesting drives, link Wagga Wagga with the small towns of this area.

Avis (☎ 6921 9977) car-rentals is near the train station at the corner of Edward and Fitzharding Sts.

AROUND WAGGA WAGGA
The Rock & Around
On the Olympic Way about 25km south-west of Wagga Wagga, The Rock is a small village near a large, craggy hill rising out of the flat plain. The town was called Hanging Rock until the boulder balanced on top of the hill fell off late in the 19th century.

Heckenberg's (☎ 6920 2218) is an interesting antique room that also provides tourist information.

The hill is in **The Rock Nature Reserve**; there's a walking trail to the summit and the return journey takes about three hours. Near the top, the going is steep and you have to be careful of falling rocks.

Three kilometres north of **Yerong Creek**, 15km south of The Rock off the Olympic

Way, *Hanericka Farmstay* (☎ 6920 3709) is a 1600-hectare complex geared mostly to overseas visitors. Singles/doubles cost $55/90, including meals and farm activities. For something simpler you could try the impressive *Yerong Creek Hotel* (☎ 6920 3515).

Galore Scenic Reserve

Henry Osborne walked from Wollongong to Adelaide in 1840 and on the way he climbed this sudden hill, exclaiming at the top, 'There's land and galore'. Now a scenic reserve, Galore Hill is worth a visit for its bush (and the plantings near the base of the hill) and for the 360° views from the platform at the top. There are toilets and fireplaces near the platform but you can't camp here. This reserve is refreshingly free of the ravages of beer parties and trail-bike vandals.

Galore Hill is 14km south of the Sturt Hwy – turn off about 60km west of Wagga Wagga; it's also accessible from Lockhart.

Lockhart

This little town is known for its beautiful, late 19th-century verandas – both sides of Green St, the main street, are lined with them. The gates to the showground, where there's an old pavilion, are concrete wool bales. The small Greens Gunyah Museum & Craft Shop opens on Wednesday and Friday to Sunday and has tourist information. Entry to the museum is $2/50c for adults/children.

Accommodation is available in the small *Lockhart Caravan Park* (☎ 6920 5119), with sites for $10.50 for two people and on-site vans for $20. Pubs such as the *Commercial Hotel* (☎ 6920 5109) have singles/doubles for $25/40 and the *Lockhart Motel* (☎ 6920 5357) has rooms for $52/58.

Ganmain

Ganmain is a sleepy village on the interesting road between Junee and Narrandera, and is accessible from Wagga Wagga via Junee or more directly via **Coolamon**, a larger, prettier place. North of Coolamon, 4km out on the Temora road, you can stay in an old railway carriage or in a self-contained cottage at *Avondale Farm* (☎ 6927 3055) for $50/80 a single/double, including breakfast.

Apart from its somnolent charm, Ganmain is notable for its hay industry. The farms have been producing high-quality wheaten hay and chaff (about 20,000 tonnes a year) since the late 19th century. The area is special because the hay is still often bound into sheaves that are stooked by hand and carted in horse-drawn wagons to be stacked into 'real' haystacks, which you can see sitting in the stubbled paddocks. There's a roadside display centre in Ganmain where you can see a video on hay production and even activate one of the old binders. The hay-cutting season is October and November.

Ganmain's other claim to fame is its meat pies, which are highly regarded in the district.

MORGAN COUNTRY

The area known as Morgan Country is a rough circle of pretty country south of Wagga Wagga, west of Holbrook and north of Albury, containing some interesting little towns, including Henty, Culcairn and Jindera.

This was once the stamping-ground of bushranger Mad Dog Morgan. Unlike Ned Kelly, Morgan was a bushranger no one respected. He began his career in Victoria in the 1850s but was captured and spent six years on a prison hulk in Port Phillip Bay (probably enough to turn anyone into a mad dog). On receiving parole he escaped and moved into NSW, where for two years he killed and looted in this small area. Declared an outlaw, he fled to Victoria (where he was still wanted) in 1865, resolving to 'take the flashness out of the Victorian people and police'. He didn't get very far. At Peechelba station, just south of the Murray River near Corowa, he was shot dead. His head was cut off and it's said that his scrotum became a tobacco pouch.

Information

For tourist information on the area, see the post office on Balfour St in Culcairn; it's open from 8 am to 5.30 pm weekdays, 9 am to 5 pm Saturday and 10 am to 1pm Sunday.

Culcairn

Culcairn was once a major overnight stop for people travelling by train between Sydney and Melbourne, and the town's main feature, the **Culcairn Hotel** (1891), reflects this status. It's a grand old hotel, the largest between the two cities until the 1930s, with a beer garden that deserves a more lavish name – there's even a fountain! Next to the pub is Scholz's Building, a long terrace of shops, and these two structures form the bulk of the town.

Across the tracks from the pub, the old stationmaster's residence has been lovingly restored as a **museum**, open from 10 am to 4 pm Saturday. There are several other historic buildings, with half the main street classified by the National Trust. On Gordon St is the artesian pumping station, first used to supply Culcairn's water in 1926.

Three kilometres east of Culcairn on the Holbrook road is **Round Hill Station** (☎ 6029 6136), featuring an enormous, old woolshed. The functions held here are sometimes open to the public (bush dances, for example).

At **Premier Yabbies** (☎ 6029 8351), about 6km south-west of Culcairn off the Walla Walla road, you can see an interesting display on yabbies ($5/2.50 for adults/children) and refreshments, including yabby sandwiches, are available. You can also catch your own yabbies. The farm opens from 10 am to 5 pm Monday and Wednesday to Saturday, and noon to 5 pm Sunday; it's closed Tuesday and throughout August. You need about an hour to do everything.

Places to Stay & Eat The small *Culcairn Caravan Park* (☎ 6029 8248), by the creek, has sites for $10 and on-site vans for $24.

The *Morgan Country Motel* (☎ 6029 8233) is good and has singles/doubles for $45/55, but it's hard to resist a night at the *Culcairn Hotel* (☎ 6029 8501); rooms cost $28/38 including a serve-yourself breakfast. The rooms are standard pub accommodation with shared bathrooms, and the decor steers an uneasy course between genuine antiques and gaudy kitsch, but the pub is big enough to take it. Tour groups stay here, so it's advisable to book.

As well as a couple of simple cafes, there's a *bistro* at the hotel and Devonshire teas and Chinese meals at the *Collector's Haven* antiques store.

Morgan's Lookout

A low hill with a cluster of huge boulders on top, this would have made a superb lookout for any bushranger. You can climb up for great views and there are gas barbecues. The lookout is about 18km south-west of Culcairn on the sealed road to Walla Walla, just past the Walbundrie turn-off. The pub in **Walbundrie** makes the modest claim of having 'the best and only beer in town'.

Henty

The Taylor Header, which revolutionised grain harvesting around the world, was invented in Henty in 1913 by Headlie Taylor. There's a display commemorating this claim to fame in Henty Memorial Park.

Each year the **Henty Machinery Field Days** are held on Tuesday, Wednesday and Thursday of the third week in September. If you're interested in farm equipment (or are interested in the people who are) this is the place to come. About 50,000 people turn up for this event, perhaps the best of its type in Australia.

Doodle Cooma Swamp is a wetlands area 2km west of town on the Pleasant Hills road.

The *Doodle Cooma Arms* (☎ 6929 3013), beside the railway line, has pub accommodation for $20 per person and the more conservatively named *Central Hotel* (☎ 6929 3149), on the main street, has singles/doubles for $25/40. Both also have meals.

Jindera

Jindera was settled by German immigrants, and the early days are remembered in the outstanding **Jindera Pioneer Museum** (☎ 6026 3622). The museum's chief exhibit is Wagners store, a country store that was left as it was when it closed in 1958 – although it must have been an old-fashioned store even then. Other displays include some buggies and wagons, including one that carried the area's first German settlers across from Adelaide. Check out the enormous builder's wagon, too. Interior scenes from the film *Mad Dan Morgan* were shot here. The museum opens from 10 am to 4.30 pm Tuesday to Sunday ($5/0.50 for adults/children).

Getting There & Away

Greyhound Pioneer buses stop in Culcairn, Henty and The Rock on their Melbourne-Brisbane run, as do Sydney to Melbourne XTP trains.

The Olympic Way runs through this area, which is also accessible from the Hume Hwy at Holbrook.

JUNEE

postcode 2663 • pop 5000

Junee, once known as the 'Rail Centre of the South', is now a small friendly country town with a disproportionate number of impressive buildings. It's well worth a stop. Tourist information is available from the Junee Tourist Information Centre (☎ 6924 4200) in the Railway Refreshment Room at the station.

Monte Cristo

The mansion of Monte Cristo (1884) was the home of Christopher Crawley, a shrewd landowner who predicted the railway's arrival in Junee and the subsequent boom in land prices. Actually, it's suspected that he was a little more than shrewd, as the railway was supposed to go through Old Junee, some way distant, but somehow ended up running through Crawley's land.

Monte Cristo isn't especially large but it's full of superb antiques collected by the owners during their 30-year restoration of the property. It had nearly been destroyed by weather and vandals, who weren't deterred by the house's reputation for supernatural goings-on.

The mansion (☎ 6924 1637) opens from 10 am to 4 pm daily; admission ($7.50/3.80 for adults/children) includes an informative guided tour. You can also wander through the outbuildings, which contain other exhibits, including a large display of old carriages and buggies.

Monte Cristo, on a hill in the town's west, is near the impressive St Joseph's Catholic Church; access is from John Potts Drive.

Railway Roundhouse

The Junee Roundhouse is the only surviving, working roundhouse in Australia. When built in 1947, its 30m turntable was the largest in the southern hemisphere. Railway enthusiasts should visit the Roundhouse Museum. As well as the large display about the history of rail in Australia, and an impressively large model-train set, there's also an interesting general transport display, including farm machinery, cars and trucks. The museum (☎ 6924 2909) is open for guided tours at 2.30 pm on Tuesday and Thursday and at 10.30 am and 2.30 pm weekends ($5/2.50).

Old Buildings

If you like pubs, lament the closing of many of Junee's watering holes. Some magnificent old pubs with massive verandas dripping with iron lace now stand empty.

The **Commercial Hotel** still has a busy bar crowded with after-work drinkers. The **Loftus** was the town's grandest hotel, with a frontage running for an entire block. It was sold in late 1999 for only $32,000!

Across the tracks, the **Junee** was built by Christopher Crawley, owner of the Monte Cristo mansion on the hill behind. The pub hasn't had a lot done to it over the years, but that just means that the original fittings are still intact. The **Locomotive** on Hill St is just a country pub, a little out of its league in this company, but it's popular. The single-storey **Red Cow** hides away on Junction St.

A number of other old buildings are worth a look, including the **railway buildings** on the small square in the centre of town. In complete contrast, next to Memorial Park is the humble building containing the **Junee Historical Museum**, open from 2.30 to 5 pm Wednesday and weekends.

Places to Stay & Eat

The small but pleasant *Willow Caravan Park* (☎ 6924 1316), at the northern end of Broadway St on the outskirts of town, charges $8 for a tent site.

There are motels, but this is a town where you should try a pub. The *Commercial* (☎ 6924 1023) is a friendly, popular place with good singles/doubles for $15/30. There's a large guests' lounge and kitchen facilities. In the bistro, standard counter-meals cost $6 to $10.

Across the railway lines, the *Junee* (☎ 6924 1124) has clean but more original rooms (complete with old iron bedsteads) for $20/30.

The *Junee Motor Inn* (☎ 6924 1266, 61 Broadway St) has rooms for $58/62.

Getting There & Away

Greyhound Pioneer buses go through Junee on the run between Melbourne and Brisbane. Junee Travel (☎ 6924 2399) on Railway Square sells tickets. Junee Buses (☎ 6924 2244), on Main St near the railway level crossing, runs weekday services to Wagga Wagga ($7 one way).

Junee is on the main Sydney to Melbourne rail line. You can get tickets at Junee Travel.

The Olympic Way runs north to Young and south to Wagga Wagga. The road from Junee west to Narrandera is interesting and there's a good drive south-east to the Hume Hwy at Gundagai, some of it alongside the Murrumbidgee River.

TEMORA
postcode 2666 • pop 4700

On the edge of the Riverina, Temora is a pleasant place, with a classic country-town main street and an air of solidity. Late in the 19th century there were over 20,000 diggers here searching for gold, but today sheep and wheat keep the town going.

The tourist office (☎ 6978 0500), in the Temora Community Centre at 182 Hoskins St (the main street), opens from 9 am to 4 pm Monday to Friday.

Things to See & Do

A number of **old buildings** reflect the prosperity of the area and its social distinctions. On one corner in the town centre is the Anglican church, backed by banks and the post office and next to the courthouse and police residence. Diagonally opposite this display of the established powers of church and state is the large Catholic church, with a school behind it, a gorgeous presbytery beside it and a pretty little park next door to that.

Taking the most prominent corner in town is a life-size statue of **Paleface Adios**,

a local horse that won 108 harness races. Temora is in harness-racing territory and there are several studs in the area.

The interesting **Temora Rural Museum**, on the Junee–Wagga Wagga road across the train line and south of the town centre, displays implements and historical items relating to the district. It's open from 2 to 5 pm daily ($3/1 for adults/children).

Temora's airport is one of the most reliably fog-free in the state and there's quite a lot of activity there, including **skydiving**. Instruction and tandem dives are available from Skydive Temora (☎ 6978 0137).

Three kilometres out north of Temora toward West Wyalong, **Lake Centenary** has swimming, fishing and water skiing. In **Barmedman**, 30km north on the West Wyalong road, there's a huge mineral-water swimming pool. Whether it has therapeutic properties is debatable, but it's a good place for a swim.

If you haven't had your fill of small Riverina villages, drop into sleepy **Ariah Park**, 35km west of Temora on the road to Griffith. It's just a hamlet in flat, red-soil country, but it has an atmosphere of times fast vanishing. Yarning on the bench outside the post office, beating the heat with a cold beer at the pub and smelling the peppercorn trees in the main street – these are activities that the theme parks and tourist towns can't quite match.

Special Events

The Trotting Club holds harness races at the showgrounds track from October to April, with the prestigious Temora Pacers' Cup run at the first meeting in February.

If you are here in late September you can attend the Temora Show.

Places to Stay & Eat

The *Temora Caravan Park* (☎ 6977 1712), near the rural museum on the Junee–Wagga Wagga road, has tent sites from $8. There's also a basic but free *camping area* (☎ 6977 1099) at the recreation ground.

Patches of Heaven (☎ 6978 1133, Hoskins St) is a good-value B&B in the defunct Federal Hotel. Nicely refurbished rooms cost $25 per person.

The *Shamrock Hotel (☎ 6977 2016, Hoskins St)*, has pub rooms and motel units, the latter for $40/50 for singles/doubles, including breakfast. The good *Goldtera Motel (☎ 6977 2433, 80 Loftus St)* charges $58/68. The other motels, the *Temora (☎ 6977 1866)*, next to the rural museum, and the *Aromet (☎ 6977 1877, Victoria St)*, are cheaper.

There are several cafes on Hoskins St. Opposite Fossey's store, the *Waratah Cafe* serves hamburgers and other snacks. The pubs have cheap counter meals, as does the *Ex-Services Memorial Club* on Baker St.

The decent *Hong Kong (133 Hoskins St)* Chinese restaurant has a karaoke unit.

Getting There & Away

Countrylink buses stop at Temora on the run between Balranald and Cootamundra via Griffith and Hay. Lynch's travel agency (☎ 6977 1296), 194 Hoskins St, sells tickets.

NARRANDERA
postcode 2700 • pop 5000

Explorer Charles Sturt passed through here on his 1829 journey down the Murrumbidgee River and many others have done so since, as Narrandera straddles the Sturt and Newell Hwys, with good connections to Sydney, Melbourne, Adelaide and Brisbane. Despite the amount of through traffic, Narrandera remains a friendly country town with good services and accommodation. It's a pleasant place to stop over for a day or two.

Orientation & Information

The Newell Hwy runs through town as Cadell St; the Sturt Hwy passes just south of it. East St is the commercial centre. The helpful Tourist Information Centre (☎ 1800 672 392), in Narrandera Park on Cadell St, opens from 9 am to 5 pm weekdays and 10 am to 4 pm weekends. Here you'll find 'the world's largest playable guitar', although you wouldn't get much of a tune out of it. The centre has a walking-tour map of the town, which takes you past many old buildings.

Things to See & Do

Behind the information centre there's a lovely **cricket ground**, complete with a small wooden grandstand. In another corner of the park is the **Mini Zoo**, consisting mainly of birds and some bored animals. There's also a **ceramic fountain**, Royal Doulton no less, perhaps one of only two in the world.

Parkside Cottage Museum is across from the park on the corner of Twynam St. The extremely diverse collection, from '1000 years of monarchy' to skis from Scott's Antarctic expedition, is in the best tradition of small-town museums. It's open from 2 to 5 pm Monday and Tuesday; from 11 am the rest of the week ($2/0.50 for adults/children).

Lake Talbot is a beautiful water spouts reserve, partly a long artificial lake and partly a swimming pool complex with some good waterslides. For $0.30 you can ride 'Rampage' – a toboggan slide where you shoot out across the pool like a skipped stone. A great way to relieve highway tensions!

Bush (including a koala regeneration area) surrounds the lake and a number of trails make up the **Bundidgerry Walking**

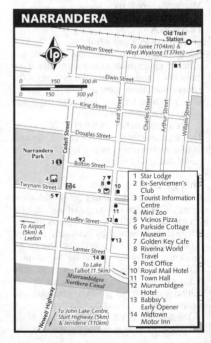

NARRANDERA

Old Train Station

To Junee (104km) & West Wyalong (137km)

Whitton Street

Elwin Street

King Street

Douglas Street

Narrandera Park

Bolton Street

Twynam Street

Audley Street

To Airport (5km) & Leeton

Larmer Street

To Lake Talbot (1.5km)

Murrumbidgee Northern Canal

To John Lake Centre, Sturt Highway (5km) & Jerilderie (110km)

1 Star Lodge
2 Ex-Servicemen's Club
3 Tourist Information Centre
4 Mini Zoo
5 Vicinos Pizza
6 Parkside Cottage Museum
7 Golden Key Cafe
8 Riverina World Travel
9 Post Office
10 Royal Mail Hotel
11 Town Hall
12 Murrumbidgee Hotel
13 Babbsy's Early Opener
14 Midtown Motor Inn

Track. The information centre has a map and brochure. The complex can be reached from the top of Larmer St, where there's a good view down the Murrumbidgee River before you take the steep road down to the lake. This is also the trackhead for the trails.

The **John Lake Centre** at the Inland Fisheries Research Station (☎ 6959 9021) opens from 9 am to 4 pm weekdays and has guided tours (on which you can see a huge Murray cod) at 10.30 am and 2 pm ($5/2.50). The turn-off to the centre is on the Sturt Hwy 4km south-east of Narrandera.

Near Painters Siding, 9km north of Narrandera, **Craigtop Deer Farm** (☎ 6959 1915) has pet deer 'available for public interaction'. It's open from 9 am to 5 pm weekdays ($3).

Special Events

In early January water-skiing championships take place on Lake Talbot. In mid-January there's a rodeo. March sees the Bush Music Festival, which explains that guitar at the information centre. In August there's the National Guinea Pig Show. In early September the town has its agricultural show. In October there's the Murrumbidgee Sheepdog Trials and the Tree-mendous Celebration (centred on Narrandera's trees but including a home-brewing competition).

Places to Stay

The information centre takes bookings for the various *farmstays* in the area.

Lake Talbot Caravan Park (☎ 6959 1302) is in a picturesque setting on a hill overlooking Lake Talbot, with dense red-gum forest stretching to the horizon. It has a good tent area ($13.50 for a site), on-site vans ($32) and self-contained brick units (from $38). It's some way from the town centre at the eastern end of Larmer St. *Narrandera Caravan Park* (☎ 6959 2955) is slightly cheaper, but it's across the river south of town.

Most of the pubs along East St have accommodation. The cheapest ($10/20 for singles/doubles) is the *Royal Mail* (☎ 6959 2007), on the corner of East St and Victoria Square; the most expensive ($20/30) is the

Murrumbidgee (☎ 6959 2011), on the corner of East and Audley Sts.

Narrandera's impressive *Star Lodge* (☎ 6959 1768, 64 Whitton St), in a fine old hotel complete with verandas and iron lace, is a beautiful B&B. Prices start at $38/58.

Narrandera has many motels. The *Midtown Motor Inn* (☎ 6959 2122), on the corner of East and Larmer Sts, is in a quiet but central location. Rooms cost from $45/55.

Places to Eat

Claiming to have the lowest prices in town, *Babbsy's Early Opener*, on East St, serves takeaway snacks from 5 am to 2.30 pm. The *Golden Key Cafe*, also on East St, is a classic small-town place with some interesting paintings. It's a good place for breakfast.

Vicinos Pizza, south of the information centre, has a wide variety of dishes, including Sunday roast lunches. The best pub meals in town are at the *Murrumbidgee Hotel* and the best Chinese is a toss-up between *Treasure Court* in the Royal Mail Hotel and the *Ex-Servicemen's Club* on Bolton St.

The beautiful restaurant at the *Star Lodge* is open from Tuesday to Sunday.

Getting There & Away

McCafferty's buses stop daily on the Melbourne to Brisbane and Sydney to Adelaide runs. Greyhound Pioneer buses stop here between Sydney and Adelaide. Countrylink buses run to Wagga Wagga (where there are trains to Sydney and Melbourne) and Griffith. Riverina World Travel (☎ 6959 1188), on East St, is a booking agent for all buslines.

As well as the highways linking Narrandera with four capital cities, smaller roads run north-west to Leeton and Griffith and east to the Olympic Way at Junee.

LEETON

postcode 2705 • pop 7000

Leeton is the MIA's oldest town and its headquarters. Although it doesn't have the range of services of Griffith, it makes a pleasant base for exploring the area. Seeds from the agricultural college were used to plant the numerous palm trees that line the roads.

Leeton was founded as an MIA town in 1913; there was no settlement here before the water came. It was the first of the Walter Burley Griffin-designed MIA towns, and it works better than nearby Griffith, partly because until relatively recently limits were placed on development. Now that restrictions have been lifted, a highway sprawl is developing.

Rice-growing began near Leeton in 1924, and today the Riverina's Ricegrowers' Co-operative exports 85% of its 1.2 million tonne crop each year.

Orientation & Information

Most streets are named after trees or local products; the main street is Pine Ave, named after the Murray pine, a native species.

The helpful Leeton Visitors Centre (☎ 6953 6481), 8–10 Yanco Ave, is in the former manager's residence of the MIA. It opens from 9 am to 5 pm weekdays, 9.30 am to 12.30 pm weekends. It has several walking-tour maps.

Things to See & Do

A number of food-processing plants have guided tours or presentations. The **SunRice Centre** (☎ 6953 0596), Calrose St, opens from 9 am to 5 pm, with presentations at 9.30 am and 2.45 pm, weekdays. The **Berri Juice Factory** (☎ 6953 3144), 37 Brady Way, has guided tours at 10.45 am weekdays. You must wear shoes on this tour.

Lillypilly Estate (☎ 6953 4069) and Toorak Wines (☎ 6953 2333) are two **wineries** near Leeton, open Monday to Saturday for tastings and on weekdays for tours – 11.30 am at Toorak Wines, 4 pm at Lillypilly Estate.

There are daily tours of the restored **Historic Hydro Motor Inn** on request; there's also a historical display and local gallery.

In **Yanco**, a village that's virtually a suburb of Leeton, is the Powerhouse Museum and mini-railway. It's open on the last Sunday of each month. Yanco was the original railhead for the MIA and the powerhouse once supplied all the area's electricity.

A few kilometres west of Yanco (the signposted turn-off is south of the town) is

Lawson in Leeton

One early resident of Leeton was Henry Lawson, who came here in 1916 in an attempt to break the cycle of poverty and drunkenness that dogged his later years. Things seemed promising: Lawson had a grant from the New South Wales government, he was 'dry', and he ran into an old mate he'd known in Bourke, when his star was on the rise. Lawson began a new series of works (the Previous Convictions stories), but he returned to Sydney after a year and died a few years later.

Yanco Agricultural High School. Visitors can drive through or, during school hours, wander around the buildings.

Whitton, 25km west of Leeton, was here before the MIA started, and there's a museum in the old courthouse and jail. It's open from 10 am to 1 pm Tuesday and from 1 to 4 pm weekends.

The north bank of the Murrumbidgee River near Leeton has several beaches and picnic areas. Ask the visitors centre for a map.

Special Events

The SunRice Leeton Festival is held over Easter in even-numbered years; the Murrumbidgee Farm Fair is held at Yanco's Agricultural College in May; and the Leeton Agricultural Show is held on the second Friday and Saturday in October. The Leeton Eisteddfod is held over three weeks in August, culminating in a big concert.

Places to Stay

Several properties in the Leeton area offer *farmstays*. The Leeton Visitors Centre has details.

Leeton Caravan Park (☎ 6953 3323), 2km south of town on Yanco Ave, has sites for $10, on-site vans for $28 and cabins for $40. The smaller *Oasis Holiday Park* (☎ 6953 3882), east on Corbie Hill Rd (off Yanco Ave), has similar rates.

The *Leeton Hotel* (☎ 6953 2027, 71 Pine Ave) charges $20/30 for singles/doubles plus $5 for breakfast. The nearby *Wade Hotel*

(☎ 6953 3266, 42 Pine Ave) also has air-con rooms for $20/25 including breakfast.

The well-positioned **Historic Hydro Motor Inn** (☎ 6953 2355) is a huge old guesthouse with a National Trust listing. Motel-style units cost $50/60 plus $10 with a cooked breakfast. Despite its restoration, the Hydro is somewhat faded. If it doesn't appeal try the **Bygalorie Motor Inn** (☎ 6953 4100, 439 Yanco Ave), with rooms for $68/75, or **Riverina Motel** (☎ 6953 2955, 1 Yanco Ave) with rooms for $63/70.

Places to Eat

Leeton doesn't have the range of eateries that nearby Griffith has. On Pine Ave there are a few cafes and coffee shops: **Cafe 119** is a gourmet deli with snacks; **Mick's Bakehouse**, at No 56, has excellent pies and varied lunch specials. **Chung Hing** and **Chan's Hong Kong** serve Chinese food. Other than that, there are counter meals and bistros in the hotels, in the motel dining rooms and in the **Leeton Soldier's Club** and the **Yanco All-Servicemen's Club**.

Getting There & Away

Countrylink buses stop daily at the visitors centre on the runs between Griffith and Cootamundra or Wagga Wagga and connect with the trains in those towns.

On Saturday there's a Sydney to Griffith train that stops in Leeton.

GRIFFITH

postcode 2680 • pop 23,000

Griffith is a small but relatively sophisticated city and the main centre of the MIA, although it is some way north of the Murrumbidgee River. The city styles itself as the wine and food capital of the Riverina, and it certainly has reason. There are vineyards, which you can visit, and Griffith's cafes and restaurants offer a variety and quality unmatched in the region. West of here you're definitely into 'steak-and-lots-of-it' country.

Griffith lies on the edge of the Great Dividing Range's western slopes. To the west the country becomes very flat and the outback begins; to the south-west is the Riverina heartland.

Like nearby Leeton, Griffith was designed by Walter Burley Griffin, the US architect who designed Canberra. Griffith does have something of Canberra's openness about it, and Griffin had similar climate and country to work with. Leafy suburbs rise up the steep hills behind the flat town centre, and Banna Ave, beginning at the circular roads of the administrative centre, is a wide boulevard. It's also a very long boulevard – too long to conveniently walk. As the railway line and canal interrupt the flow of cross-traffic, Banna Ave can be slow driving.

Information

The Griffith Visitors Centre (☎ 1800 681 141), on the corner of Banna and Jondaryan Aves, opens from 9 am to 5 pm weekdays, until 3 pm Saturday and 10 am to 2 pm Sunday; beside it is a Fairey Firefly plane perched on a pole. The district office of the National Parks & Wildlife Service (NPWS; ☎ 6962 7755) is at 200 Yambil St. The library offers Internet access ($3 per half-hour).

Work Many people come to Griffith to work on the grape harvest, which usually begins around mid-February and lasts about six to eight weeks. The citrus harvest begins in November and runs through to about March, and other crops are harvested during the year. The Griffith Employment National Office (☎ 13 3444), 108b Yambil St, will help you find harvest work.

Fewer than half the vineyards and almost none of the other properties have accommodation or even space to camp, so you'll probably have to stay in Griffith, which means that you'll need your own transport.

Things to See & Do

High on a hill north of the town centre, **Pioneer Park Museum** (☎ 6962 4196) is a re-creation of an early Riverina village that is worth seeing. There are about 40 displays, and many of the old buildings are original. The park opens from 9 am to 4.30 pm daily ($6/2.50 for adults/children). To get there from Banna Ave take Crossing St or Ulong St, then Beale Ave.

THE RIVERINA

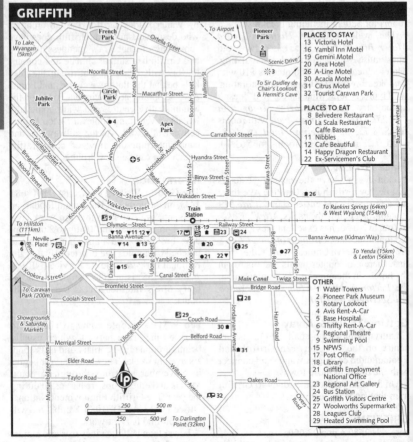

GRIFFITH

PLACES TO STAY
13 Victoria Hotel
16 Yambil Inn Motel
19 Gemini Motel
20 Area Hotel
26 A-Line Motel
30 Acacia Motel
31 Citrus Motel
32 Tourist Caravan Park

PLACES TO EAT
8 Belvedere Restaurant
10 La Scala Restaurant;
Caffe Bassano
11 Nibbles
12 Cafe Beautiful
14 Happy Dragon Restaurant
22 Ex-Servicemen's Club

OTHER
1 Water Towers
2 Pioneer Park Museum
3 Rotary Lookout
4 Avis Rent-A-Car
5 Base Hospital
6 Thrifty Rent-A-Car
7 Regional Theatre
9 Swimming Pool
15 NPWS
17 Post Office
18 Library
21 Griffith Employment
National Office
23 Regional Art Gallery
24 Bus Station
25 Griffith Visitors Centre
27 Woolworths Supermarket
28 Leagues Club
29 Heated Swimming Pool

Not far from Pioneer Park is the **Rotary Lookout**, with great views of the town and the surrounding farmland. Also up here on Scenic Hill are three **walking tracks**, Trates Loop (2km), Barinji Loop (5km) and Narinari Loop (6.5km). About 1.5km east of Pioneer Park is **Sir Dudley de Chair's Lookout**. Just below is the **hermit's cave**, home of an Italian recluse for many years – until he was interned during WWII on suspicion of being a spy.

The Art Deco **Griffith Regional Art Gallery** (☎ 6962 5991), on Banna Ave, opens from 10.30 am to 4.30 pm Tuesday to Saturday. Exhibitions change monthly and there's also a permanent collection of Australian jewellery.

The **Griffith Regional Theatre** (☎ 6962 7466), in Neville Place, has a massive, community-produced soft-sculpture curtain depicting the region and its activities. You can see it at 11 am and 2.30 and 5 pm weekdays and at 10.30 am Saturday, provided there are no productions under way. The theatre is also home to the interesting Griffith Photographic Collection. It's open from 10 am to 5 pm weekdays and 9 am to noon Saturdays.

Lake Wyangan, north of the city, is home to a lot of noisy water transport – there's a jet sprint-boat course.

On Sunday mornings, a **market** is held in Verona Place on Banna Ave; another is held in Woodside Hall at the showgrounds on the second and fourth Saturday of each month.

Wineries Although the Hunter Valley is the best-known wine-producing area in NSW, the Griffith area produces 70% of the state's wine and some of it's very good. The first winery was McWilliams (1913), with others following soon after. Many are open to visitors, although most don't open on Sunday and some don't open on Saturday. The visitors centre has information.

Special Events
The four-day Festival of Griffith is held over Easter. It's a major occasion, with events ranging from grape-treading competitions to chariot races and a Mardi Gras.

Griffith's big Festival of Gardens is held in early October and features large sculptures made from oranges and lemons.

Places to Stay
There are several caravan parks. The two most convenient for the town centre are the small *Tourist Caravan Park (☎ 6962 4537)* on Willandra Ave and the more basic camping area at the *showgrounds*, off Murrumbidgee Ave. The Tourist Caravan Park has good facilities, but we've received several complaints about the owners being rude. Powered tent sites cost $16, on-site vans cost $40 and units cost $48. At the showgrounds you'll pay $8 per person ($45 per week) for an unpowered site. Before setting up your tent check in at the office (☎ 6962 3148) in Woodside Hall, fronting the main arena.

Overlooking the town, *Pioneer Park (☎ 6962 4196)* has shared accommodation in former shearers' quarters. It costs $12 per person ($70 a week). The rooms are small and basic – this is a historic building – but there's a good communal kitchen and lounge. During the grape and fruit harvest it fills up. Unfortunately it's a steep walk from town and there's no public transport.

The *Area Hotel (☎ 6962 1322)*, on Banna Ave near Kooyoo St, is a popular pub with singles/doubles for $35/50, including breakfast. The *Victoria Hotel (☎ 6962 1299)*, a couple of blocks west, also has rooms, but the pub music is loud.

Cheaper motels include the friendly *A-Line (☎ 6962 1922)* on Wakaden St ($50/60) and the *Citrus (☎ 6962 6233)* on Jondaryan Ave (from $52/62). Other motels include the *Acacia (☎ 6962 4422)* on Jondaryan Ave (from $62/68) and *Yambil Inn (☎ 6964 1233)* on Yambil St (from $65/70). The central *Gemini Motel (☎ 6962 3833, 201–227 Banna Ave)*, has a popular bar and rooms from $60/70, but often offers a stand-by rate of $50 during the week.

Places to Eat
The district's pioneers included Italians, and Griffith still has a large Italian community. As a result, several places serve Italian food.

For breakfast, good coffee and cake or some delicious pasta, try *Caffe Bassano (453 Banna Ave)*. Nearby, down some sloping steps, the Vico family's *La Scala (☎ 6962 4322)* is perhaps the best of the Italian restaurants. The menu includes a good range of classic dishes and there's an extensive wine list. Minestrone costs $6.50, pasta costs $9 to $12, and main courses cost $16.50 to $25. It opens from 6 pm daily.

Nearby, on the corner of Banna Ave and Kookora St, is the *Belvedere Restaurant*. This has more of a cafe atmosphere and it's also a busy takeaway pizzeria, but the food is good. The prices are a little lower than La Scala's and there's a delivery service (☎ 6962 1488).

There are a few Chinese places in the same area. *Cafe Beautiful*, on the corner of Banna Ave and Ulong St, is a large, pleasant place with an extensive menu (including non-Asian dishes) and a bar. There's a buffet lunch special for $10 and dinner mains cost around $10. Across the street, the *Happy Dragon* is cheaper and has some good specials.

The *Ex-Servicemen's Club* on Jondaryan Ave has a restaurant and a bistro, and meals

THE RIVERINA

are also available at many of Griffith's other clubs, but often only on weekends.

Nibbles, on Banna Ave, has good old-fashioned hamburgers ($4 with the lot).

Entertainment

Most of the entertainment is in clubs such as the *Ex-Servicemen's* on Jondaryan Ave, the *Leagues Club* on the corner of Jondaryan Ave and Bridge Rd and, probably the most lively, the Elbow Room at the *Yoogali Club* on Leeton Rd. The *Area Hotel* and the *Gemini Motel* are popular watering holes.

Getting There & Away

Hazelton Airlines (☎ 13 1713) flies daily to Sydney; the standard one-way economy fare is $222.

The long-distance bus stop is at the Griffith Travel & Transit Centre (☎ 6962 7199), in the Mobil petrol station at 121 Banna Ave.

Greyhound Pioneer buses run to Sydney ($47), Adelaide ($91) and Canberra ($35). McCafferty's also has a daily service to those cities and is a little cheaper.

Countrylink runs to Balranald via Hay, Wagga Wagga ($45) via Leeton and Narrandera, and Cootamundra ($21) via Temora.

On Saturday there's a direct Countrylink train from Sydney to Griffith ($81, 8¼ hours).

Getting Around

Griffith has a taxi service (☎ 6964 1444). Avis (☎ 6962 6266) is at 7 Wyangan Ave; Thrifty (☎ 6962 9122) is at the airport and 2 Griffin Ave; and Hertz (☎ 6964 1233) is at the Yambil Inn Motel on Yambil St.

AROUND GRIFFITH
Cocoparra National Park

Cocoparra (8350 hectares) takes in one of the fingers of low ranges that make up the westernmost edge of hills in the state.

The park isn't large but its hills and gullies contain a fair amount of wildlife and birds. At Spring Hill picnic area in the south there's a walking trail to Falcon Falls (dry unless there has been rain). From the Binya State Forest, adjoining the south-western end of the park, there's a walking track that leads you to the top of Mt Brogden.

The camping area is on Woolshed Flat in the north of the park, not far from Woolshed Falls. Bush camping is permitted away from the roads. Bring your own water.

Access is from the unsealed (and sometimes impassable) Whitton Stock Route, which runs along the park's western edge. The stock route meets the Yenda-Ardlethan road just east of Yenda. You can also get here from the Mid-Western Hwy via a turn-off to Griffith about 15km west of Rankins Springs, a tiny town with a pub and a motel set in a beautiful horseshoe valley. See the Central West chapter for more information on towns north and east of Cocoparra National Park.

Darlington Point

Due south of Griffith and on the Murrumbidgee River, Darlington Point was an important port in the 19th century. It has dwindled to a quiet, picturesque town with good swimming beaches and red-gum forest. *Darlington Caravan Park* (☎ 6968 4237) has sites for $11 and vans for $26.

West of here, either via the Sturt Hwy or a dirt road that follows the north bank of the Murrumbidgee River, Carrathool is another pretty old port that's quietly dying. Each February a picnic race-meeting brings in a lot of visitors.

LAKE CARGELLIGO
postcode 2672 • pop 1300

Midway between Condobolin and Hillston, Lake Cargelligo (the first 'g' is soft, the second hard; the town is known locally as 'the Lake') refers to the town and the adjacent lake. The town was founded in 1879 when gold was found in the region.

Some tourist information is available from the craft shop (☎ 6898 1501) at the lake end of Foster St, the main street.

The lake is home to numerous species of birds, including swans and black cockatoos, and is popular for water sports. Next to the caravan park is a large collection of rusty old farm machinery, part of the museum.

Places to Stay

The council-run *Lake Cargelligo Caravan Park* (☎ 6898 1077) is near the sportsground, which is by the lake. From Foster St turn right at the lake. Tent sites cost $8, cabins $33.

The **Royal Mail Hotel** (☎ 6898 1006) is a solid pub with a big veranda on the main street near the lake. Singles/doubles cost $15/30, including breakfast. There are a couple of motels: the **Lake Cargelligo** (☎ 6898 1303) on Canada St charges $38/48, and the **Lachlan Way** (☎ 6898 1201), on Foster St, has rooms for $50/60.

Getting There & Away

Countrylink buses stop here daily on the run between Condobolin and Cootamundra via West Wyalong.

There are some interesting routes to and from the lake, but as far as major roads go it's quite isolated. A sealed road runs southeast to West Wyalong and partly sealed roads run east to Condobolin and west to Hillston.

HILLSTON
postcode 2675 • pop 1100

This pretty little town on the Lachlan River is known for its very long, straight main street. The local **museum**, open on Sunday, is a few blocks from the town centre on the Lake Cargelligo road. No longer in use, the Real Cafe on the main street is long past its glory days but it still has its high, pressed tin ceilings and leadlight windows. The Golden Gate milk bar opposite the Club House Hotel isn't as grand but is in better nick.

Places to Stay & Eat

At the northern end of the main street, **Hillston Caravan Park** (☎ 6967 2575) charges $9 per tent and $50 for cabins. Nearby is the **Kidman Way Motor Inn** (☎ 6967 2151), with singles/doubles for $50/60. The **Motel Hillston** (☎ 6967 2573), at the southern entrance to town, also charges $50/60. The **Ex-Servicemen's & Citizens Club** and the **pubs** have meals. At **Bill Morgan's Corner** store, lollies are still chosen from a jar, weighed out and sold in a paper bag.

Getting There & Away

Hillston is on the Kidman Way. An unsealed road heads west for about 40km to the Wil-

landra National Park turn-off, and continues on, narrower and rougher, for another 55km to Mossgiel on the Cobb Hwy. A largely unsealed road runs east to Lake Cargelligo, a nice drive through well-treed country.

Except for Kidman Way, all the roads out of Hillston can be cut off by rain.

WILLANDRA NATIONAL PARK

Like Mungo National Park, Willandra is part of a huge sheep station on a system of dry lakes. The lakes here tend to become temporary wetlands more often than Mungo's ancient basins, especially Hall's Lake, and birdlife is abundant. The plains in this area are home to many emus and kangaroos. You'll see both western greys and big reds; the latter can grow taller than 2m.

The historical interest of Willandra centres on the wool industry, although there were certainly Aboriginal civilisations in the area, probably of the same antiquity as those at Lake Mungo. The Willandra area was first grazed in the 1840s, then in 1868 some enterprising Melbourne grocers acquired several runs and formed the sheep station **Big Willandra** – the national park (about 19,400 hectares) is less than 10% of Big Willandra.

The old shearing shed, with its latitude and longitude painted on the roof to assist pilots in this featureless landscape, is still occasionally used and you can watch the shearing if you're here at the right time. The park manager has details. The nearby old shearers' quarters are not used, partly because they don't meet current union standards (which must be higher than the standards in some hostels).

A discreet distance away from the shearers' quarters is the restored homestead (1918), the third to be built on the increasingly busy station. It's a large building, with rooms for visiting wool-buyers as well as the manager's family and staff, but it's by no means palatial.

The thatched ram shed, where the kings of the station lived, is near the homestead.

There are several walking tracks in the park, none of them very long, and the Merton Motor Trail, which takes you on a loop around the eastern half of the park. The western half, beyond the stock route, has no vehicular access but you can walk here – if you're *very* sure of what you're doing.

Places to Stay

You can *camp* at the site near the homestead ($5) or, with permission, anywhere else in the park. Accommodation is available in the *old station's men's quarters* for $25 per room or there's a self-contained cottage for $40 a night. During school holidays all accommodation, including camp sites, can be booked out.

Getting There & Away

The turn-off to Willandra is on the Hillston to Mossgiel road, about 40km west of Hillston. If you're coming from Mossgiel you can take the Trida turn-off, about 10km west of the main turn-off. The unsealed Hillston to Mossgiel road is quite good between Hillston and the park turn-off, but deteriorates between the turn-off and Mossgiel. Slow down to cross cattle-grids on this section. The roads into Willandra are definitely dry-weather only; it takes less than 10mm of rain to close them. You should phone the park manager (☎ 6967 8159) to check on conditions before you arrive, and bring in enough supplies to tide you over if you are stuck – there's no shop here. The NPWS office (☎ 6962 7755) in Griffith also has information on Willandra.

HAY

postcode 2711 • pop 3800

Hay is a substantial town for this part of the world, and its position at the junction of the Sturt and Cobb Hwys makes it an important transit point.

It's very much a rural service centre and on Saturday morning the main street is full of utes (utility vans). Station hands from the big merino properties in the area make good use of the half-dozen pubs on weekends.

The Tourist & Amenities Centre (☎ 6993 4045), 407 Moppett St, just off Lachlan St (the main street), opens from 9 am to 5 pm weekdays and 9 am to noon weekends. You can pick up a drive-tour map of the town

here, although if you have time it's nicer to walk around. The centre also has clean showers and a screened picnic area; both are free and open 24 hours.

Things to See & Do

There are several impressive old buildings in town, including the **Department of Lands & Water Conservation** on Lachlan St and, around the corner in Moppett St, the **courthouse**.

Bishop's Lodge, off the highway east of the roundabout at the entrance to Hay, is a mansion built entirely of corrugated iron as a residence for the Anglican bishop. From the highway it doesn't look especially inviting, but the building faces the other way, towards the river, and there's an acclaimed heritage-rose garden at the front. Bishop's Lodge opens from 2 to 4 pm Saturday ($2). The tourist office can arrange to open it at other times. The old, renovated **train station** on Murray St is home to Hay's community radio station and a youth employment project. In a railway carriage at the station is the **Hay Internment & POW Camps Interpretive Centre**, commemorating the contribution made to the development of the area by the detainees.

The **Old Hay Gaol**, on Church St east of Lachlan St, is well worth the $1 entry fee. The gaol is small and surrounded by a wall with almost toy-like guard towers. The mu-

Dunera Boys & Hay Camp

During WWII, Hay was the site of three prisoner-of-war (POW) and internment camps. Hay's isolation and its distance from the sea and all major cities were the major factors in the decision to situate them here. The first wave of internees were the 'Dunera Boys', mainly German and Austrian Jewish intellectuals, sent out from England on board the vessel *Dunera*. Imagine their shock as they were confronted by the stark reality of the Australian bush. Later, Italian POWs replaced them and Japanese POWs were also sent here after the Cowra breakout (see the boxed text 'The Cowra Break-Out' in the Central West chapter).

seum, in the old cells, consists of a fairly random collection of the district's memorabilia and detritus. It's like a good junk shop. One cell is set up as it was when the gaol was a detention centre for wayward girls, its last incarnation before it closed in 1973. Perhaps more appalling than the dim, spartan cubicle is the fact that the cells were called cabins! Still, the place was run by the Child *Welfare* Department, perhaps another inappropriate euphemism...

Ruberto's Winery, on the highway near Bishop's Lodge, opens daily for tastings of the local product.

The **sunset viewing area**, 16km north of Hay on the Cobb Hwy, is a good place to watch the sun go down and, later, stargaze.

Special Events
On Australia Day (26 January), Hay holds a fun 'Surf Carnival' at Sandy Point beach on the Murrumbidgee River (a good place for a swim at any time). Also in January is the National Hang-gliding Championship, which includes lots of international teams.

Places to Stay & Eat
There are several caravan parks, with *Hay Plains Holiday Park (☎ 6993 1875)* on Nailor St being the closest to the town centre. The more spacious *Hay Caravan Park (☎ 6993 1415)* is on the highway (and close to the river), a little to the east.

Off the Sturt Hwy 11km east of Hay, *Bidgee Beach Camping Ground (☎ 6993 4808)* is a simple camp site on the banks of the Murrumbidgee. There are toilets and showers; tent sites cost $10, van sites $12.

Most of the pubs advertise accommodation. The big *Commercial Hotel (☎ 6993 1504)*, on the corner of Lachlan and Leonard Sts, has singles/doubles for $15/25. The *Riverina Hotel (☎ 6993 1137)*, on Lachlan St, has rooms for $20/30 including breakfast. *Hay Motel (☎ 6993 1804)*, by the roundabout, and the *New Crown Hotel/Motel (☎ 6993 1600)*, on Lachlan St, are the least expensive motels, with rooms for $45. *Sundowner Motor Inn (☎ 6993 3003)*, on the Sturt Hwy, is similar in design to the original Bishop's Lodge nearby and costs $78/85.

On Lachlan St, *Robertsons Hot Bread Kitchen* is good for sandwiches and pies, and there's also *Our Coffee Shop*, opposite the post office and open on weekdays. *Paragon Cafe* serves good, fresh Chinese food. The *Riverina Hotel* has the best pub meals in town.

Getting There & Away
Long-distance buses stop at the Caltex petrol station on the Sturt Hwy. Greyhound Pioneer and McCafferty's buses come through on the run between Adelaide and Brisbane or Sydney. Countrylink's Balranald to Cootamundra buses also stop here. There are no direct services to Melbourne. The nearest town on the Melbourne run is Deniliquin.

Traveland (☎ 6993 1974), 181 Lachlan St, handles bookings.

The Sturt Hwy runs west to Balranald and east to Narrandera; the Mid-Western Hwy runs north-east to West Wyalong; and the Cobb Hwy runs south to Deniliquin. See the Cobb Hwy section in the Far West chapter for information on the route to Wilcannia.

BALRANALD
☎ 03 • postcode 2715 • pop 1400
On the Sturt Hwy west of Hay, sleepy Balranald was once a bustling river port. Most of the town is new and not especially inspiring but there's a definite sense that you're on the brink of a vast emptiness. North of here the water dries up and the farms are enormous. Balranald is a good jumping-off point for Mungo National Park.

The information centre (☎ 5020 1599) on the main street, opens from 9 am to 4 pm weekdays and 9 am to 2 pm Saturday. Check here for road conditions before venturing into Mungo National Park.

There's a swimming and picnic area on the banks of the Murrumbidgee River at the end of We St (turn off the highway at the fire station). There are other picnic sites at Yanga Lake, 8km east along the Sturt Hwy, and the Low Level Weir, 6km west of town.

Places to Stay & Eat
The *Balranald Caravan Park (☎ 5020 1321)*, on a sharp bend in the Murrumbidgee

River close to the bridge, has tent sites for $11 and on-site vans from $28.

There are a few motels in town. *Sturt Motel* (☎ 5020 1309), on River St, and the *Shamrock Hotel/Motel* (☎ 5020 1107), on Mayall St, are far enough off the Sturt Hwy (Market St) to avoid the rumble of passing trucks.

The Shamrock has meals. *Rafferty's Coffee House*, nearby on Market St, opens during the day for snacks and light meals. The *Ex-Servicemen's Memorial Club*, on Market St, is the local favourite for reasonably priced meals.

Getting There & Away

V/Line buses stop twice weekly on the run between Melbourne and Mildura. Countrylink has daily runs, and McCafferty's and Greyhound Pioneer buses also stop here.

The Southern Riverina

Albury, the largest town on the Murray River, is covered in the South-East chapter.

COROWA

postcode 2646 • pop 5200

This sizeable river town overshadows its Victorian twin Wahgunyah, across the river. Rutherglen, the main town in Victoria's best-known wine region, is only 10km farther away.

History

The Bangerang people were living in this area when the first Europeans arrived in the 1830s. The first town to be established was Wahgunyah, then a private town on John Foord's Wahgunyah station. North Wahgunyah, today's Corowa, was also founded by Foord, but the influx of people on their way to the Beechworth goldfields, and the trade and river traffic that followed, saw Corowa become an official town.

As in many towns, the proclamation of the Colony of Victoria in 1850 and the ensuing customs hassles across the Murray River caused many people in the area to push for federation of the colonies. In 1893 a conference was held in Corowa that began the process of Federation, achieved in 1901. There had been previous conferences, but Corowa's was the first to capture the public's attention.

Another lasting product from Corowa is the famous Tom Roberts painting *Shearing the Rams*, which was researched in the woolshed of Brocklesby station.

Orientation & Information

The main street, where you'll find most of the pubs and shops, is Sanger St. It leads down to the Foord Bridge across the Murray River to Wahgunyah. Federation Ave is a leafy street cutting through town to the Mulwala road. The helpful information centre (☎ 6033 3221), in the old Memorial Hall at 88 Sanger St, opens from 10 am to 5 pm daily.

Things to See & Do

The Federation Museum (☎ 6033 1568), in an old music hall on Queen St, opposite the neat Ellerslie Gardens, opens from 10 am to noon Tuesday, and 2 to 5 pm weekends ($2). It's worth a look for the display on the history of Federation and to see some of Tommy McCrae's sketches. McCrae was a member of the Bangerang people at the time of first contact with Europeans. The sketches are among the few concrete records of an indigenous people's reaction to the European arrival.

Murray Bank Yabby Farm (☎ 6033 2922), next to the Corowa Caravan Park on the road to Mulwala, charges $10 per family for a visit. You can catch your own yabbies and cook them there. The farm opens from 11 am to 4 pm daily.

There are about a dozen wineries in Victoria's Rutherglen area that are open for tastings.

Corowa is a centre for gliding and parachuting. The National Parachute School (☎ 6033 2435) offers gliding as well as parachute jumps. Zauril Aviation (☎ 6040 4950), based in Albury, has balloon flights along the Riverina here; ask at the information centre for details.

Special Events
In January, Corowa holds the week-long Federation Festival, with parades, marching bands and general merriment.

The Rutherglen Winery Walkabout in June is the premier event on the Victorian wine-buff's calendar, and Corowa is a good place to base yourself.

Places to Stay
There are several caravan parks in the area, including *Rivergum Caravan Park (☎ 6033 1990)* on the road in from Albury, *Corowa Caravan Park (☎ 6033 1944)* on the road out to Mulwala, and *Ball Park Caravan Park (☎ 6033 1426)* on Bridge Rd. They're by the river and all have sites ($10 to $16), on-site vans ($24 to $28) and cabins ($30 to $55 a double).

Most of the pubs have accommodation, costing from $15 per person with light breakfast, including the *Star Hotel (☎ 6033 1145)* on Sanger St.

There are lots of motels and their prices rise in summer and around holidays. The cluster on the Mulwala road (Federation Ave) are in hot competition and most singles/doubles cost about $45/55.

Places to Eat
The pubs along Sanger St compete for your meal-time dollars and there are some counter-meal bargains, including $5 lunch specials at the *Star Hotel*. Check the blackboards.

The *Sanger St Deli* has light meals during the day and the various clubs have *restaurants*. *Tempura*, on Sanger St, is a more upmarket place with good food and a decent selection of local wines.

Getting There & Around
Countrylink buses stop here daily on the run between Albury and Echuca (Victoria), via Cobram (Victoria), Tocumwal, Finley and Deniliquin.

The Riverina Hwy runs east to Albury and north-west to Deniliquin. A smaller road runs west along the river to Mulwala and Tocumwal.

Phone ☎ 6033 1634 for taxis (24 hours).

MULWALA
☎ 03 • postcode 2647 • pop 1500
This small town on Lake Mulwala was the base for several big rock concerts in the 1970s, Australia's answer to Woodstock. Today it's a quiet place, somewhat overshadowed by Yarrawonga, a resort and retirement centre across the river in Victoria. Lake Mulwala, an irrigation dam on the Murray River, is a popular spot for fishing and power-boating.

There are several lakeside caravan parks, many motels and the old *Royal Mail Hotel (☎ 5744 3121)* which charges $25/30 a single/double, including breakfast.

TOCUMWAL
☎ 03 • postcode 2714 • pop 1750
Tocumwal is a small, pleasant town along the Newell Hwy and on a big bend in the Murray River. The nearest Victorian town is Cobram, but the two don't have the usual twin relationship of river towns because they're separated by a wide red-gum forest.

The Tocumwal Visitor Information Centre (☎ 1800 677 271), in the middle of town, opens from 9 am to 5 pm daily. It can book accommodation for you.

Things to See & Do
A huge statue of a **Murray cod** stands next to the information centre; in the bar of Tattersalls Hotel across the road you'll see some stuffed Murray cod almost as big. There are **riverboat cruises** on the *Matilda* ($14/8 for adults/children); book at the tourist office.

Across the river at the Time Out resort (☎ 5874 2031) there's **horse riding** for about $14 an hour for guided rides.

Tocumwal is a centre for **gliding** and you can also get your ultralight pilot's licence here. The Sportavia Soaring Centre (☎ 5874 2063) at the aerodrome (a very large airbase during WWII) has package deals including flights, tuition and accommodation. For $65 you can try a glider flight.

Just out of **Barooga**, a small town 20km east of Tocumwal, are Seppelts vineyards and the Kranmer Cellars, open all day on weekdays and afternoons on weekends.

Places to Stay

There are several basic *camp sites* by the river, such as Mulberry and Pebbly beaches, but most are across the river from town and quite a distance away on winding tracks.

There are a couple of OK caravan parks in town, but a better spot is *Bushlands on the Murray (☎ 5874 2752)*, not far east of town as the cod swims but about 3km by road. Tent sites cost $6, units $40 for two.

Farther out, in the red-gum forest by the river, is *Time Out (☎ 5874 2031)*, a large holiday resort. Take the signposted turn-off just after the first bridge on the road to Victoria and it's about 3km along a dirt road. Watch out for stray cattle. Tent sites cost $5 per person ($1 children) all year and on-site vans are $40 a double, rising to $50 from November to Easter. There's a fairly well-stocked shop out here. Free camping is allowed in the regional park, but you can't use Time Out's facilities unless you stay there.

The *Tocumwal Hotel (☎ 5874 2025)*, a nice place but with an air of importance out of proportion to the modest town, has motel-style single/double units for $40/50 with breakfast. There are several other motels, all more expensive.

Places to Eat

The interesting *Central Store Antiques*, near the information centre, has tearooms. The *Lime Tree Coffee Lounge*, nearby on the main street, serves Devonshire tea. The *River Garden* Chinese restaurant does cheap lunch specials. *Tocumwal Cafe*, on the Melbourne side of the town centre, opens for breakfast. The pubs have counter meals and the *Bowling Club* and the *Golf Club* have restaurants.

The nice old *Terminus Hotel*, near the roundabout on the Mathoura road, has a shaded beer garden.

Getting There & Away

Countrylink buses pass through Tocumwal three times weekly on the Echuca-Albury service. Victoria's V/Line buses run daily to Tocumwal from Melbourne via Seymour and Barooga. McCafferty's and Greyhound Pioneer buses stop here on their Brisbane-Melbourne run.

The bus stop is near the tourist office and you can book buses at Tezza's Gear (☎ 5874 2604), 30 Deniliquin St.

The Newell Hwy runs north to Finley and Jerilderie, and south to Melbourne. A smaller road runs east along the river to Corowa and Albury. Heading west, minor roads run to the Cobb Hwy at Mathoura, passing through a state forest full of river red gums, and indirectly to Deniliquin.

JERILDERIE

☎ 03 • postcode 2716 • pop 900

Jerilderie is a highway town on the Newell, a welcome oasis in this baking landscape.

The Kelly Gang held up Jerilderie for three days in 1879, earning themselves an Australia-wide reputation for brazenness. The speech Ned Kelly made to his captives in the Royal Mail Hotel (still operating as a pub) and the letter he wrote complaining of his treatment at the hands of the authorities aroused the suspicion that young Ned might be a latent political activist. Holding up the town sealed Kelly's fate, for the NSW government declared him an outlaw (anyone could kill him without penalty) and the colony was no longer a safe haven – he was already outlawed in Victoria.

The Willows (☎ 5886 1666), an old house (1878) by the Billabong Creek, is part museum, part souvenir shop and part tourist information centre; it serves drinks and snacks from 9.30 am to 4.30 pm daily. On the lawns of the house is a unique Jerilderie red tree, a cross between a kurrajong and an Illawarra flame tree. Nearby in Luke Park beside Jerilderie Lake is Steel Wings, a massive windmill dating from 1910.

Places to Stay & Eat

On the highway beside the pretty Billabong Creek, *Jerilderie Caravan Lodge (☎ 5886 1366)* has sites for $12, on-site vans for $27, cabins for $36 and motel units for $42 a double. The pubs have accommodation and meals and there are three or four motels, including the *Jerilderie Budget (☎ 5886 1301)*, a couple of kilometres south of the town centre, with singles/doubles for $38/45.

Old Farts in Caravan Parks

Old Farts in Caravan Parks is the name of a song by popular Australian singer John Williamson. It refers to the 'grey nomads' – retired Australians who have sold their houses, bought caravans and hit the long and dusty trail around Australia. Others migrate north to escape the harsh Victorian winter and like to take some time on the road as they head to Queensland. You will meet many in caravan parks, chatting away happily as they do their laundry and have cups of tea with perhaps something a little stronger.

These elderly nomads have all the time in the world to explore, so you'll find them all over the place. Get to know a few – you'll meet some pretty interesting folks.

The *Olive Tree Coffee & Craft Shop*, in the old post office on Jerilderie St (Newell Hwy) has good coffee and snacks. The Aboriginal art available is reasonably priced and displays the talents of local artists.

Getting There & Away

MIA Intercity Coaches stop here on the run between Griffith and Melbourne. Countrylink buses stop here on the Wagga Wagga–Echuca run. McCafferty's and Greyhound Pioneer buses stop on the Brisbane-Melbourne run.

The Newell Hwy runs north to Narrandera and south to Finley and Tocumwal. A smaller road runs west along the Billabong Creek to Conargo then south to Deniliquin, and a network of minor roads run to small villages. The Kidman Way begins 16km north-east of town off the Newell Hwy.

DENILIQUIN

☎ 03 • postcode 2710 • pop 8200

Deniliquin is a pretty, bustling town on the Edward River. It's big enough to offer most services but small enough to retain an easy-going rural feel.

History

Before whites arrived, the Deniliquin area was the most densely populated part of Australia. The flood plains and their networks of creeks and billabongs provided plenty of food, although stone for tools was hard to come by in this vast expanse of rich soil.

The Edward River was missed by Hamilton Hume's 1838 expedition; a party sent by the enterprising Ben Boyd found the river in 1842 and established a station called Deniliquin (sand hills), along with a pub. Boyd's shaky empire fell apart soon after, but a town was growing and by 1849 it was officially recognised. It initially prospered because it was at the end of major droving routes leading down from Queensland, but later wool growing and sheep breeding became important.

Orientation & Information

Deniliquin is on a bend in the Edward River. Although the town covers quite a wide area, its centre, the blocks around Napier and Cressy Sts, is compact.

The Visitors Information Centre (☎ 1800 650 712), which is part of the Peppin Heritage Centre on George St, opens from 9 am to 4 pm daily.

Things to See & Do

Deniliquin is an interesting old town and details of an **historical town walk** are available from the information centre.

The pleasant **Waring Gardens** run beside Cressy St, and an old church and hall have been converted into an arts centre here. An example of riverine wetlands is the **Island Sanctuary**, on an island in the river. There's a pleasant walking track through the sanctuary and along the river.

The **Peppin Heritage Centre** on George St is an interesting museum largely devoted to the wool industry. It's in an old school, with a classroom set up as it was in the late 19th century. It's frighteningly realistic!

Medium wools are the backbone of the Australian wool industry and the Peppin merinos that grow them were developed in the district by the Peppin family from 1862. The photos of 'Riverina Ram of the Year' winners and their owners are as interesting as the historical displays. Sheepdog displays and other events are sometimes held

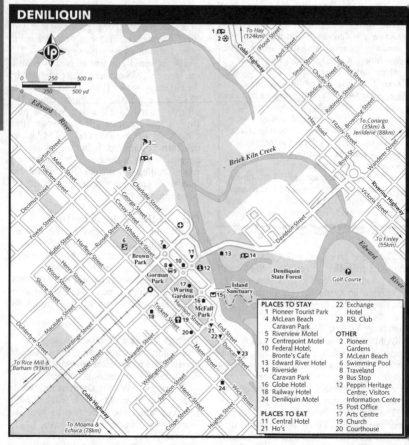

DENILIQUIN

0   250   500 m
0   250   500 yd

PLACES TO STAY
1 Pioneer Tourist Park
4 McLean Beach Caravan Park
5 Riverview Motel
7 Centrepoint Motel
10 Federal Hotel; Bronte's Cafe
13 Edward River Hotel
14 Riverside Caravan Park
16 Globe Hotel
18 Railway Hotel
24 Deniliquin Motel

PLACES TO EAT
11 Central Hotel
21 Ho's

22 Exchange Hotel
23 RSL Club

OTHER
2 Pioneer Gardens
3 McLean Beach
6 Swimming Pool
8 Traveland
9 Bus Stop
12 Peppin Heritage Centre; Visitors Information Centre
15 Post Office
17 Arts Centre
19 Church
20 Courthouse

in the old schoolyard, where there's also an old ram shed, still smelling strongly of its pampered inhabitants. The centre opens from 9 am to 4 pm daily (free).

The **SunRice Mill** is the largest rice mill in the southern hemisphere. Its visitors centre, on Saleyards Rd, has presentations at 9.30 am and 2.45 pm weekdays.

The Graeco-Roman style **courthouse** (1883) on Poictiers St is an extremely imposing building. Cases resulting from pioneering drinking habits probably formed the bulk of its work in early years. Near the courthouse is **Deniliquin Parish Church**.

Pioneer Gardens (☎ 5881 5066), on Hay Rd (Cobb Hwy), is an odd collection: a nursery, a motel and caravan park with offices in an old pub, a display of old petrol pumps and steam engines, a gallery and a craft shop.

For river swimming, try **McLean Beach**, said to be the finest riverside beach in Australia. There are picnic facilities and a walking track.

Special Events

Deniliquin now styles itself as the 'Ute Capital of the World' after its first annual 'ute muster' in 1999 attracted a world-record 2839 utes. The event is part of the Play on the Plains Festival, held on the Labour Day long-weekend in October, and also features country music.

If you want to see some champion sheep and the squatters' descendants who own them, try the Deniliquin Show (first weekend in March) or attend one of the Riverina Merino Field Days, held in various centres in mid-March.

Places to Stay

Close to the town centre and by the swimming beach, *McLean Beach Caravan Park* (☎ 5881 2448) is shady and pleasant, with sites for $12, on-site vans from $25 and cabins for $45 a double. There's also the *Riverside Caravan Park* (☎ 5881 1284, 20 Davidson St). Tent sites cost $10, single/double cabins $35/45.

About 4km north of town on Hay Rd is *Pioneer Tourist Park* (☎ 5881 0566), with tent sites for $10, caravan sites for $17 and motel-style cabins from $42.

Most hotels have accommodation. The recently renovated *Globe Hotel* (☎ 5881 2030) on Cressy St is good value, with rooms for $25 per person including a cooked breakfast. At the other pubs you're left to make your own. The *Federal Hotel* (☎ 5881 1260), on the corner of Cressy and Napier Sts, has clean rooms for $25 a head. The *Railway Hotel* (☎ 5881 1498), on Napier St a few blocks south-west of the centre, has rooms with attached bathroom for $15 per person.

The *Edward River Hotel* (☎ 5881 2065), on Davidson St, has five singles and one double room for $15 per person, including breakfast.

Among Deniliquin's many motels, the *Riverview Motel* (☎ 5881 2311) at the top end of Charlotte St probably has the best position, overlooking the river. Rooms cost $50/60. At the *Deniliquin* (☎ 5881 1820), on the corner of Crispe and Wick Sts, the rates are $52/60.

Centrepoint Motel (☎ 1800 677 490, 399 Cressy St) has a saltwater pool, free laundry and rooms for $52/62.

Places to Eat

Next to the Federal Hotel on Napier St, *Bronte's Cafe* is cosy and bright, with light meals and coffees during the day. At the Peppin Heritage Centre, *The Crossing Cafe* (☎ 5881 7827) is open daily for gourmet meals and fine local wines. The coffee's good too.

The *Exchange Hotel (116 End St)* has the most popular counter meals. The *Central Hotel*, on Napier St, has a comfortable bistro and counter lunches from $5.

The large Chinese restaurant *Ho's* is on the corner of Wellington and End Sts.

The RSL Club has the *Club Grill*, as well as the more upmarket *Ambassador Chinese Restaurant*.

Getting There & Around

Long-distance buses stop outside the defunct Bus Stop Cafe, on Whitelock St near the corner of Napier St. If you walk through the arcade near here you'll emerge on Cressy St near the Traveland (☎ 5881 7744) booking office.

Countrylink buses stop here four times weekly on the Wagga Wagga–Echuca run. McCafferty's buses stop daily on the Melbourne-Brisbane run. V/Line service runs daily to Melbourne via several other Riverina towns.

The Cobb Hwy runs south to Echuca and north to Hay. The Riverina Hwy runs southeast to Albury. Smaller roads run south-west to Barham and north-west to Balranald.

There are two taxi companies, Black & White Bonds (☎ 5881 2129) and Taits (☎ 5881 1373).

AROUND DENILIQUIN

On the Cobb Hwy 40km north of Deniliquin, **Wanganella station** is a memorial to the Peppin family's merino breeding.

Finley

Finley is a quiet rural town on the Riverina Hwy 50km east of Deniliquin. The Mary Lawson Rest Centre is a roadside stop at the southern end of the main street with a small log-cabin museum and craft shop, where you can buy tea and coffee. The *Lakeside*

Caravan Park (☎ 5883 1170) is at the other end of town. A Japanese company has established the world's first commercial liquorice farm 14km north of Finley (liquorice is usually harvested from wild plants, but the supply is dwindling).

Mathoura

On the road south of Deniliquin to Moama and Echuca is Mathoura, a tidy hamlet with a couple of small *caravan parks*. The nearby **Moira State Forest** is the largest remaining stand of river red gum anywhere, even if it is mostly regrowth. You can drive through it all the way to Tocumwal (partly on dirt roads) or take one of the scenic drives.

At **Picnic Point**, in the forest about 11km east of Mathoura, there's a swimming beach on the banks of the Murray River and several accommodation options, including the *Picnic Point Caravan Park (☎ 5884 3375)* where a tent site is $10 and cabins are from $32 a double. It hires out canoes for $5 an hour and fairly ordinary bikes for $3 an hour. Nearby, *Tarragon Lodge (☎ 5884 3387)* has accommodation for $18 per person and offers canoe trips, cycling and horse riding. It caters to groups as well as individuals, so phone first to see if there's a free place.

Picnic Point is a popular holiday spot and the sound of power boats could make it less than idyllic at peak times. On weekends and holidays a courtesy bus (☎ 5884 3290) takes people between Picnic Point and Mathoura Bowling Club daily, so you might be able to get a lift.

Moama & Echuca

Moama, the poor relation of the big Victorian town of Echuca, still lures gamblers across the bridge into NSW despite Victoria's legalisation of poker machines. Over the river in Echuca there's a lot to do and see, including the restored Port of Echuca, and plenty of accommodation, including the *Echuca YHA Hostel (☎ 5480 6522, 103 Mitchell St)*.

Countrylink buses head to Albury and Wagga Wagga four times weekly, and V/Line daily to Adelaide, Albury and Melbourne (☎ 03-5482 2576).

BARHAM & AROUND

☎ 03 • postcode 2732 • pop 1200

Barham is a small town without many attractions, but it's on the river and is popular for fishing holidays. Tourist information is available from the community centre. The Barham & District Memorial Services Club has regular entertainment, including movies; there are dress restrictions. There's plenty of accommodation in and near the town, most of it fairly expensive at weekends.

Barham is the last sizeable settlement on the NSW side of the Murray River until Wentworth. The skeins of creeks and rivers downstream from here also mean that the roads are indirect, so if you want to keep following the Murray River you'll be better off crossing over to Victoria and taking the Murray Valley Hwy to Euston/Robinvale, where you meet the Sturt Hwy.

Wakool is just a hamlet; **Moulamein** feels much larger than Wakool, although its population is only 500. Moulamein is on the Edward River and has a couple of pubs. There's accommodation at *Tattersalls Hotel (☎ 5887 5017)* for $17/33 or $20/35 in motel-style single/double cabins. The *Moulamein Caravan Park (☎ 5887 5206)* is on the edge of town by the lake; it's an inviting place but home to power boats.

Getting There & Away

The road from Barham east to Moama runs parallel to the Murray River, with several access points to the state forests along the river. It's a reasonable road, although narrow, but there's a 25km unsealed section, which is slippery after rain and also has some sand patches. The other roads through this river-riddled part of the world are similar. The unsealed section between Moulamein and Balranald is a little rocky but should be OK in the wet. If you go via Kyalite, it's all sealed and only an extra 7km.

WENTWORTH

☎ 03 • postcode 2648 • pop 1300

This old river port is overshadowed by nearby Mildura in Victoria, but it's a quiet, pleasant place to contemplate the impressive merging of the Murray and Darling

PAUL SINCLAIR

Spectacular natural sculptures known as Walls of China, Mungo National Park

PATRICK HORTON

Cruising the dusty roads in the remote far west

ROSS BARNETT

Harsh conditions take their toll, Silverton

Sunrise on the rocky coastline and stunning beach at Quondolo Point, Ben Boyd National Park

Rivers. Wentworth was originally known as The Junction because of its location and the town was shortlisted to become the new nation's capital.

The tourist information centre (☎ 5027 3624), 28 Darling St, opens from 9.30 am to 4 pm on weekdays and from 10 am to 3 pm on weekends.

You can see some local history in the **Old Wentworth Gaol** (open from 10 am to 5 pm daily; $4.50/1.50 for adults/children) and across the road in the interesting **Pioneer World Folk Museum** (open from 9 am to 5.30 pm daily; $3.50/1), which has a large collection of photos of the paddle-steamers that once made this a major port. The old paddle-steamer *Ruby* is being restored near the Darling River bridge in **Fotherby Park**, where there's a statue of Possum, one of the river's last swaggies.

The MV *Loyalty* (☎ 5027 3224), built in 1914, has two-hour **cruises** to the confluence of the Murray and Darling Rivers and Lock 10, leaving the Wentworth & District Services Memorial Club at 1.45 pm from Sunday to Friday ($14/5). There's no need to book.

Six kilometres out of town, off the road to Broken Hill, the big, startlingly orange **Perry Dunes** present the drier side of the outback.

Places to Stay
On Darling St, *Willow Bend Caravan Park* (☎ 5027 3213) has river-side sites ($10), on-site vans ($25) and cabins ($38).

Urumba Backpacker (☎ 5027 2499, 81 Darling St) is a small, relaxed backpackers in an old rectory. Beds cost $15 per person ($90 weekly); it has a work registry.

There are motels in town and on the road to Broken Hill. The best located is the *Two Rivers Motel* (☎ 1800 034 272), on the Silver City Hwy, with singles/doubles for $48/55. The *Royal Hotel/Motel* (☎ 5027 3005, 41 Darling St) is cheaper at $36/40.

Staying on a houseboat is popular. The boats accommodate from six to eight people and rates vary depending on the time of year. You usually have to stay a minimum number of nights. Expect to pay around $450 for three nights on a six-berth boat. The tourist information centre has a complete listing of boat operators.

Avoca Station (☎ 03-5027 3020), a grand homestead on the Darling River dating from 1868, has accommodation in self-contained cabins from $250 a week for two people. It also does B&B for $60/80 a night. It's about 26km north-east of Wentworth – get detailed directions when you book (essential).

Getting There & Away
Many more long-distance buses run through Mildura than through Wentworth. McCafferty's has a run between Mildura and Broken Hill that stops in Wentworth, and the Victorian V/Line bus running between Melbourne and Broken Hill also stops here.

Tom Evans runs the bus service between Wentworth and Broken Hill every Monday, Wednesday and Friday.

Coomealla Bus Lines (☎ 03-5027 4704) has a service that runs three times daily to Mildura ($3.50) from the stop opposite the Crown Hotel.

The Aboriginal owned and operated Harry Nanya Tours (☎ 5027 2076) offers day trips to Mungo National Park for $43, including lunch and morning tea.

South-East

The rugged south-eastern corner of New South Wales (NSW) is one of the state's most captivating areas. It includes the superb hiking, fishing and winter skiing regions of the Kosciuszko National Park and the Snowy Mountains (Snowies), the agricultural area west of the Snowies (but east of the Hume Hwy), the elevated but flat Monaro Tableland abutting the Snowy Mountains to the east, and towns along the Hume Hwy, from Goulburn to Albury.

Monaro Tableland

The tableland is just that – undulating, but largely flat (cyclists might not agree) and, in places, devoid of trees. Monaro is pronounced 'mon-**air**-ro'.

History

The Ngarigo people lived on the high plains at the time of the first white encroachment. Other tribal groups came up here during the annual Bogong moth harvest – a big event for many people.

Explorer John Ovens passed through in 1823 and graziers soon followed. In the 1860s there was a shortlived goldrush at Kiandra and, despite the inhospitable climate, some 20,000 diggers flocked to the area. Bushrangers, who had earlier preyed on the graziers and their herds, now became endemic. After the gold fizzled out, the area settled back into its pastoral activities. It was again disturbed when the Australian Capital Territory (ACT) was carved from the Monaro Tableland in 1908 and when the huge Snowy Mountains Hydro-electric Scheme was constructed in the 1950s and '60s.

Although the Monaro is rich in history, little of it is obvious. The goldminers established no large towns, the graziers were too few to leave much of a mark (although their cattle certainly left their mark on the

HIGHLIGHTS

- Skiing in the Snowy Mountains
- Bushwalking and mountain-biking in Kosciuszko National Park
- Attending a race day or rodeo at Gundagai, Tumbarumba or Braidwood
- White-water rafting and canoeing on the upper Murray River
- Driving the Alpine Way
- Buying fresh fruit around Batlow at harvest time
- Hooking a trout on the lakes or rivers of the Monaro Tableland

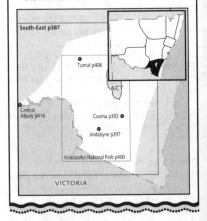

South-East p387

Tumut p406

ACT

Central Albury p416

Cooma p392

Jindabyne p397

Kosciuszko National Park p400

VICTORIA

ecology) and the towns that grew around their industry mainly did so on the lower slopes of the winter pastures.

Activities

Snow sports in the mountains to the west dominate during winter (see the Kosciuszko National Park section later in this chapter), but in the warmer months this area is perfect for bushwalking, horse riding, fishing and other water sports.

Paddy Pallin (☎ 6456 2922), in Jindabyne, hires out equipment and organises

386

activities, and there are plenty of other specialist operators.

Bushwalking The best area for summer bushwalking is the Kosciuszko National Park, but the South-East Forests National Park also provides opportunities. Remember that in the high country conditions can change rapidly and snow can fall at any time. Be prepared and don't walk alone. See if you can find a copy of *Snowy Mountains Walks*, published by the Geehi Bushwalking Club ($18.95) – National Parks & Wildlife Service (NPWS) offices should have it.

Horse Riding The Monaro is a popular place for horse riding and there are many outfits offering day rides and longer treks into the high country. Good bases for joining treks include Cooma and Jindabyne.

Water Sports Because of the huge artificial lakes – Jindabyne and Eucumbene – water sports are popular in the warmer months. You can hire boats, canoes and sailboards from caravan parks close to the water at both lakes.

Fishing is also a big attraction here. The lakes are well-stocked with trout and other

SOUTH-EAST

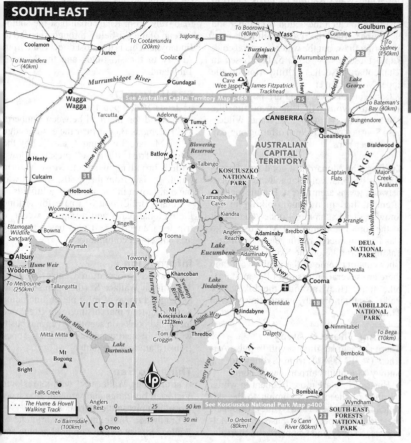

SOUTH-EAST

species (the World Fly-fishing Championship was held here in 1999), and some of the state's best fishing rivers run through the Monaro, including the Murrumbidgee, and the MacLaughlin Rivers. The rivers and creeks around Bombala are particularly prized. High Country Fly Fishing (☎ 6456 2989) in Jindabyne is one of a number of operators offering guided tours, instruction and equipment.

The Murray River rises in the Kosciuszko National Park and the 'Murray Gates', near Tom Groggin camping area, offer a great whitewater rafting experience. Upper Murray White-Water Rafting (☎ 6076 9566) in Jindabyne has one- and two-day trips. The best time to catch the action is October and November, when the river is still high from the spring thaw, but the water is not *too* cold. Rapid Descents (☎ 6072 5212), based in Khancoban, also has rafting trips on the upper Murray River.

Canoeing and kayaking are popular and in summer you'll find many outfits like Paddy Pallin (☎ 6456 2922) and Wilderness Sports (☎ 6456 2966) offering one-day and longer trips.

Cycling The Monaro is a good area for cycling as it's relatively flat and the distances between towns aren't great. But the real excitement lies in mountain-biking in the Snowies during summer – once you make it to the top. The summit of Mt Kosciuszko was first conquered by bicycle last century! Taking your bike on the Skitube up to Perisher cuts out some of the uphill work, and there are several outfits that offer mountain bike tours (they provide the bike). Try Paddy Pallin in Jindabyne and Raw NRG in Thredbo.

Getting There & Away
There are regular flights with Impulse Airlines (☎ 13 1381) from Sydney to the Snowy Mountains airport near Cooma.

Bus services are more frequent in winter because of the crowds coming to the ski-fields from Canberra and Sydney. Cooma is the main transport hub; buses from Melbourne, Sydney and Canberra run there.

If driving from Canberra, the Monaro Hwy runs down to Cooma (1½ hours). The quickest route from Sydney is to take the Hume Hwy to Goulburn, then the Federal Hwy to Canberra. A longer alternative is to take the Princes Hwy then head to Cooma from the coast at Batemans Bay or Bega. From Cooma, the Monaro Hwy heads south to Bombala and the Victorian border.

The Barry Way is a largely unsealed, narrow and winding mountain road running from near Jindabyne to Buchan in Victoria. It's a spectacular route through national parks, but it can be difficult when wet. Fuel isn't available anywhere along this road.

The Alpine Way, a spectacular mountain road, runs from Khancoban past the southern end of the ski-fields, through Thredbo to Jindabyne. This is the most direct route from Albury to the ski-fields and the Monaro Tableland.

BRAIDWOOD
postcode 2622 ● pop 1100
Braidwood, on the road between Canberra and Batemans Bay, is near the eastern edge of the Monaro Tableland. Classified by the National Trust, it's a well-preserved town with a broad main street. Most historic buildings date from the 1850s, when it was the main town in the southern goldfields.

Today, Braidwood is a base for visiting the national parks and a popular weekend trip for Canberrans. It also has a thriving arts and crafts community.

Information
Braidwood Information Centre (☎ 4842 1144) is on Wallace St (the main street). It has a good range of information, including a walking-tour map of the town (free) and maps and books on scenic drives and bushwalks in the nearby national parks. It's open from 10 am to 4 pm daily.

Things to See
A stroll along Wallace St, with its restored Victorian buildings and wrought-iron lacework, is a pleasant experience.

Braidwood Museum, at the north end of Wallace St, has displays on gold mining and local history, and the suit of armour worn by an oddly cast Mick Jagger in the 1969 film *Ned Kelly,* which was shot in Braidwood; it's open from 10 am to 4 pm daily, with a break from 12 to 1 pm on weekdays ($3/0.50 for adults/children).

There are quite a few galleries and studios. Don't miss the Italianate **Studio Altenburg** (☎ 4842 2384), in the impressive old bank (1888) on Wallace St. The gallery displays the work of local artists and craftspeople. It's open from 10 am to 5 pm daily (free).

St Andrews Church, on Elrington St, has a restored pipe organ inside and a fine collection of gargoyles leering from the tower, while **St Bede's Church**, on Wallace St, has a massive bell in the churchyard that was originally intended for St Mary's in Sydney.

Bedervale (☎ 4842 2421), an impressive homestead reached from Monkittee St, was built in 1836 to the design of John Verge, architect of Elizabeth Bay House in Sydney. It's still a working farm but opens to the public on the first Sunday of the month ($8 or $4 for the gardens).

Special Events
The Braidwood Cup, on the first Saturday in February, is one of those great country race meetings. The Braidwood Heritage Festival, a week-long event of arts and music, takes place in early April.

Places to Stay
The *Royal Mail Hotel* (☎ 4842 2488, 147 Wallace St) is an impressive old pub. Rooms with shared facilities cost $20 per person or $30 with breakfast.

Torpy's (☎ 4842 2551, 18 McKellar St) has charming colonial-style guesthouse rooms with four-poster beds for $110 a double (with full breakfast). There are also comfortable single/double motel units for $50/65 ($10 more on Saturday nights), including a light breakfast. It's just off the north end of Wallace St. *Braidwood Cedar Lodge* (☎ 4842 2244, 64 Duncan St) is a motel charging $55 a double.

There are some nice B&Bs in Braidwood, but nothing particularly cheap. The *Doncaster Inn* (☎ 4842 2356, 1 Wilson St) has

an impressive garden and restored rooms. It's a large building (once a pub and a convent) across the park from the courthouse. Costs are $55 per person ($65 on weekends). *Braidwood Country Style* (☎ 4842 2577, 91 Wallace St) is in the centre of town opposite the information centre and is the cheapest around at $65 a double (continental breakfast).

Places to Eat
The pleasant and relaxing *Cafe Altenburg*, in the courtyard of Studio Altenburg, has snacks, cakes and healthy meals at reasonable prices.

Cafe Albion, on the other side of Wallace St, has an accommodating veranda and the usual fare, while the *Boiled Lolly*, opposite, has Devonshire teas ($3) and huge jars of home-made sweets.

Torpy's Restaurant (☎ 4842 2551, 201 Wallace St), in an old house attached to the guesthouse and motel of the same name, is a nice place to dine out (Thursday to Monday). Mains range from $14 to $25 and include kangaroo and local trout, and the decor nicely captures the Braidwood experience.

Getting There & Away
Murrays bus stops daily in each direction on its run between Canberra and Batemans Bay. The bus stop is outside the post office on Wallace St.

Braidwood is on the Kings Hwy between Canberra (89km) and Batemans Bay (59km). Care should be taken on the steep, winding road to the coast.

An alternative route to the south coast at Moruya runs through Araluen and some beautiful country on the northern edge of Deua National Park. The road is sealed as far as Araluen, but after that it's not suitable for caravans. Another unsealed route heads north-east to the coast near Nowra, via Nerriga; only 4WDs should use this road when it's wet.

If you're heading to Cooma, consider taking the scenic, partly-sealed road via Numeralla. It follows the Shoalhaven River to its source, Big Badja Hill. Several sections of this road can be cut by floods, so if it has been raining be prepared to change your plans.

Goulburn and the Hume Hwy are about 86km north on a good road.

AROUND BRAIDWOOD

The superb bushwalking country of **Budawang National Park** and the southern end of **Morton National Park** is accessible from Braidwood. At 23,731 hectares, Budawang is much smaller than Morton but it offers rugged scenery and wilderness walking. There are no roads through the park, nor are there any facilities in it. The easiest access is from tiny Mongarlowe, 14km east of Braidwood.

The **Corn Trail**, in the Buckenbowra State Forest, is a 13km walking trail down the Buckenbowra River from Clyde Mountain (774m). It starts about 25km out of Braidwood, just off the Kings Hwy as it begins its steep descent to Batemans Bay. You need a shuttle (ie drop-off and pick-up) to complete this walk. The tourist offices in Braidwood and Batemans Bay have information.

The small gold rush town of **Araluen**, 27km south of Braidwood, is a centre for stone-fruit growing, particularly cherries, peaches and nectarines. **Major's Creek**, another old gold mining town 16km south of Braidwood, has a number of historic buildings and a good country pub, the *Elrington Hotel* (☎ 4846 1145), where singles/doubles cost $25/35.

LAKE EUCUMBENE

Lake Eucumbene is a massive dam, built as part of the Snowy Mountains Hydro-electric Scheme, and is adjacent to the central section of Kosciuszko National Park. Some of the lake's forested arms and inlets are scenic, although much of the area has been cleared of trees. The lake is popular for trout fishing and boating in summer and there are several small communities on the shores with camping and other accommodation.

Adaminaby
postcode 2630 • pop 230

Adaminaby (1017m) is a tiny town on the Snowy Mountains Hwy, built to replace the old town now lying beneath Lake Eucumbene 10km away. In fact, 101 buildings were moved here in 1956, when the lake flooded the original town. It's shrunk a bit since then but is still the biggest place between Cooma and Tumut and there's a good range of services. Fishing in Lake Eucumbene is a big attraction, hence the giant rainbow trout greeting visitors in the town park.

Adaminaby is the closest town to the **Mt Selwyn ski-fields** (a day-use resort; see the Kosciuszko National Park section later in this chapter for more information) and the Adaminaby Bus Service (☎ 6454 2318) runs there ($18 return) and to Cooma ($15). It also offers a charter transport service for bushwalkers in summer. You can hire ski gear at Adaminaby Ski Hire (☎ 6454 2455) on Denison St.

Places to Stay & Eat The *Alpine Tourist Park* (☎ 6454 2438), Lett St, has sites for $7 per person, on-site vans from $34 for two and a range of cabins from $34 to $75. *Tanderra Lodge* (☎ 6454 2470, 21 Denison St) charges from $40/60 for singles/doubles, including breakfast. In winter, rates are $30 per person in bunk rooms and $55/75 for singles/doubles.

The *Snow Goose Hotel/Motel* (☎ 6454 2202), Baker St, has spotless pub rooms for $20/30 and motel rooms for $30/45, both including a cooked breakfast. Winter rates are $35/55 and $45/85 respectively.

During winter these places might be booked out by groups on ski packages.

There are several cafes on Denison St, all serving smoked trout pate in various snack and sandwich forms. The Snow Goose has bistro and counter meals and is one of the few places open in the evening (till 9 pm) year-round.

Old Adaminaby & Around

Confusingly, **Old Adaminaby**, a resort town, is probably newer than Adaminaby.

Anglers Reach is a modern development on a pretty, forested arm of Lake Eucumbene, about 18km from Adaminaby. The Anglers Reach Caravan Park and Lakeside Village (see Places to Stay following) rent out boats for around $50 a day, plus fuel. They also have ski hire.

South of the lake, the Eucumbene Trout Farm (☎ 6456 8866) is a sure way to hook a trout and has horse riding suitable for beginners for $20 an hour.

Places to Stay At Old Adaminaby, the pleasant *Rainbow Pines Tourist Caravan Park* (☎ 6454 2317) has sites from $14 for two, basic on-site vans for $35 a double and a range of cabins from $50. There's also a lodge and four-bed self-contained bungalows (no en suite) for $50 a double.

The *Anglers Reach Caravan Park* (☎ 6454 2223) has tent sites for $12 and four-berth cabins for $55. The nearby *Lakeside Village* (☎ 6454 2276) has cabins for $54 a double, rising to $68 in winter.

Farmstays

A working sheep and cattle property, *Reynella* (☎ 6454 2386, ☎ 1800 029 909) offers accommodation and specialises in horse riding. You can stay in two- to six-person cabins for $120 for adults, $75 for those aged 15 to 18 and $60 for children under 15; this includes all meals and horse riding. In the ski season there are cheaper rates ($86 for adults) that don't include riding, and they also have skiing and fishing packages. Day rides are available, as well as treks of up to five days through the north of Kosciuszko National Park. A three-day ride costs $510 per person. The Reynella turn-off from the Snowy Mountains Hwy is about 8km south of Adaminaby. You can look it up on the Web at www.snowy.net.au/~reynella.

Another good place is *San Michele* (☎ 6454 2229), off the highway between Adaminaby and Cooma. It has package rates including meals and horse riding from $85 per person (minimum two-day stay). Room only is available from $35/55 a single/double. The Cooma Visitors Centre can point you towards other farmstays in the region.

COOMA

postcode 2630 • pop 8000

Cooma is the largest town on the Monaro Tableland, but it retains a small country-town feel. In the 1950s and '60s, during the construction of the Snowy Mountains Hydro-electric Scheme (for which it was the headquarters), 16,000 people crowded into the town. The streetscape has changed significantly since then; when a TV mini-series about the Snowy Mountains scheme

---

The Snowy Mountains Hydro-electric Scheme

More than 50 years after it began, the extraordinary Snowy Mountains Hydro-electric Scheme is still hailed as one of Australia's greatest engineering feats. In 1947 work began in untamed, mountainous country. Workers from around the world were recruited to the project – many from post-war eastern and southern Europe. Seventeen large dams were built (Lake Eucumbene alone could hold the water of eight Sydney Harbours), rivers were diverted and all sorts of tunnelling and building records were smashed.

The project was completed in 1974 and today provides electricity to Canberra, New South Wales and Victoria. Water from the diverted rivers irrigates the Murray, Murrumbidgee and Riverina areas inland. It's estimated that if the electricity produced by the scheme were produced by coal-fired turbines, five million tonnes of carbon dioxide would be released into the atmosphere each year.

Although little account was taken of the environmental impact of diverting the waters of the Eucumbene, Murrumbidgee, Murray, Snowy, Tooma and Tumut Rivers, the project did have an unexpected social benefit. Australia in the '50s was a parochial island and the post-war turmoil in Europe and Asia didn't do much to change that. With workers from 30 countries vital to a project that was a source of immense national pride, attitudes to new immigrants changed and Australia's multiculturalism began.

Today you can visit three power stations, as well as the information centre in Cooma. Murray 1, near Khancoban, has a good interactive visitors centre; Tumut 2, near Cabramurra, has underground tours; and Tumut 3, near Talbingo, has daily tours.

SOUTH-EAST

was being filmed in 1993, the producers chose the central Victorian town of Castlemaine to recreate Cooma's street scenes because Cooma had grown too modern.

Today, Cooma is a base for many winter skiers who, despite the town's distance from the ski-fields, stay here because of the cheaper accommodation.

Orientation & Information

The main shopping street is Sharp St, which becomes the Snowy Mountains Hwy to the west of town and the Monaro Hwy to the east.

The Cooma Visitors Centre (☎ 1800 636 525), at 119 Sharp St next to Centennial Park, is open from 9 am to 5 pm daily and has a lot of information on the area. It also makes accommodation bookings and may know of special deals being offered. The post office is at 25 Vale St. You can access the Internet at Smart Radio Systems, 26b Bombala St, for $5 an hour, or at the library on Vale St.

Snowstop Village, on Sharp St a few blocks north-east of the main shopping centre, is a handy place to hire ski gear. Most long-distance buses stop here.

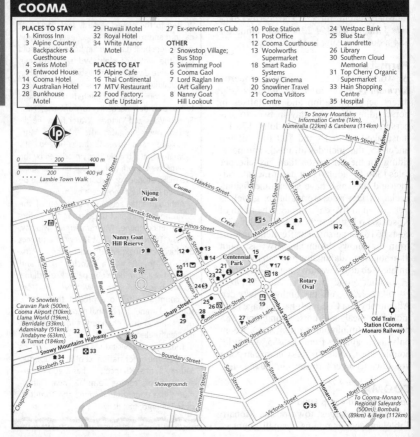

COOMA

PLACES TO STAY
1 Kinross Inn
3 Alpine Country Backpackers & Guesthouse
4 Swiss Motel
9 Entwood House
14 Cooma Hotel
23 Australian Hotel
28 Bunkhouse Motel
29 Hawaii Motel
32 Royal Hotel
34 White Manor Motel

PLACES TO EAT
15 Alpine Cafe
16 Thai Continental
17 MTV Restaurant
22 Food Factory; Cafe Upstairs
27 Ex-servicemen's Club

OTHER
2 Snowstop Village; Bus Stop
5 Swimming Pool
6 Cooma Gaol
7 Lord Raglan Inn (Art Gallery)
8 Nanny Goat Hill Lookout
10 Police Station
11 Post Office
12 Cooma Courthouse
13 Woolworths Supermarket
18 Smart Radio Systems
19 Savoy Cinema
20 Snowliner Travel
21 Cooma Visitors Centre
24 Westpac Bank
25 Blue Star Laundrette
26 Library
30 Southern Cloud Memorial
31 Top Cherry Organic Supermarket
33 Hain Shopping Centre
35 Hospital

Things to See & Do
Next to the visitors centre, in **Centennial Park**, is a series of mosaic scenes from the history of the Monaro. The park is also home to the flags of the 28 nations represented in the Snowy Mountains Hydro-electric Scheme workforce. There's also a relief map of the mountains cast in metal.

The visitors centre has a map of the **Lambie Town Walk** (4km), which takes you around the main points of interest. Interpretive boards are scattered around town to explain the local history.

The **Snowy Mountains Information Centre** (☎ 1800 623 776) is off the Monaro Hwy a couple of kilometres north of the town centre. It has models of the tunnels and power stations, a large 3-D map and a video about the project. The centre is open from 8 am to 5 pm weekdays and 8 am to 1 pm weekends (free).

The **Southern Cloud Memorial**, by the Cooma Back Creek bridge, incorporates some of the wreckage of the *Southern Cloud* – an aircraft that crashed in the Snowies in 1931, but wasn't discovered until 1958.

The old **Cooma Gaol**, on Vale St, was built in 1872 and finally closed as a correctional facility in 1998. There are guided tours of the building at 11 am and 1 pm weekdays ($6). For tickets and information, contact the visitors centre. The imposing granite **Cooma Courthouse** is set back from the road near the jail on Vale St.

On **Lambie St**, Cooma's oldest street, are several historic buildings classified by the National Trust. Lord Raglan Inn was built in 1854 and is now a gallery and cultural centre (☎ 6452 3377) for Monaro Tableland artists. It's open from 10 am to 4 pm Wednesday to Sunday (entry by donation).

The **Cooma Monaro Railway** (☎ 6452 7791) runs 45-minute train rides ($8) aboard restored 1923 CPH rail motors. The line, which closed in 1989, originally ran from Bombala to Queanbeyan. The train departs on the hour between 11 am and 3 pm weekends from October to May. In winter it runs on Sunday only.

Llama World (☎ 6452 4593), off the Snowy Mountains Hwy 19km west of Cooma, has farm tours ($10/5 for adults/children), or you can go on a walk with a llama carrying your lunch. Llama wool and wool products – even llamas – are sold. The farm opens daily during school holidays or by appointment.

Cooma is a major centre for **cattle sales** and a big sale is worth seeing. The Cooma-Monaro Regional Saleyards are just southeast of town on the Monaro Hwy.

There are several **horse riding** outfits in the area. Yarramba Trail Riding (☎ 6453 7204), on Dry Plains Rd just east of the Snowy Mountains Hwy midway between Adaminaby and Cooma, has rides along the upper Murrumbidgee River for $20 an hour or $75 for a full day including lunch. It offers tuition for novices.

Special Events
Coomafest, held over 10 days in mid-October, is a big event with street parades, bands and performing arts. The Cooma Show is held in early March and the local race day is on the first Saturday in December. Numeralla, a tiny hamlet 22km east of Cooma, hosts a popular folk festival on the Australia Day weekend in January.

Places to Stay – Budget
On the highway 1.5km west of town, *Snowtels Caravan Park* (☎ 6452 1828, 286 Sharp St) is a big, well-equipped place. It has tent/powered sites for $14/18, on-site vans from $30, cabins from $35 and self-contained flats sleeping six from $65 a double. All rates go up in winter.

Two guesthouses provide accommodation for backpackers. The *Bunkhouse Motel* (☎/fax 6452 2983), Soho St, has dorm beds for $15 in self-contained timber cabins. It's a neat, friendly place with a slightly cramped but rustic feel. You can also get singles/doubles for $25/40. The *Alpine Country Backpackers & Guesthouse* (☎ 6452 1414, 32 Massie St) has shared rooms for $15 per person ($90 weekly), and twin/doubles for $20 per person ($30 on winter weekends). There's a kitchen and dining room.

Cooma's six pubs charge from $20/30 a single/double. They include the *Australian*

Hotel (☎ 6452 1844, 137 Sharp St), which is likely to be noisy on weekends. The **Cooma Hotel** (☎ 6452 2003), on the corner of Massie and Vale Sts, is usually quieter ($25/40). The **Royal Hotel** (☎ 6452 2132, 59 Sharp St) is a beautiful old sandstone place – the oldest licensed hotel in Cooma – where you might get a room leading onto the wonderful veranda; rates are $25/35.

The **Swiss Motel** (☎ 6452 1950, 34 Massie St) has budget rooms for $30/40 including a light breakfast.

Places to Stay – Mid-Range

There are plenty of mid-range motels, charging from $40/50; the visitors centre has a full listing. Prices rise in winter.

The **Hawaii Motel** (☎ 6452 1211, 192 Sharp St) is the cheapest of the bunch ($30/45). The **White Manor Motel** (☎ 6452 1152, 252 Sharp St) is a notch higher up the scale, with rooms for $50/60.

Kinross Inn (☎ 6452 4133, 15 Sharp St), with a heated pool and neatly manicured lawn, is another highly-rated place ($55).

Entwood House (☎ 6452 3278, 25 Soho St), in a large old house near Nanny Goat Hill, has B&B for $50/90.

Places to Eat

If you're self-catering, there's a **Woolworths** supermarket on Vale St, behind the Cooma Hotel. **Top Cherry**, on Sharp St about 1km south-west of the visitors centre, sells organic fruit and vegies.

Sharp St has plenty of places to eat, mostly cafes and takeaways. The **Alpine Cafe**, on the corner of Bombala St, has breakfasts for $8. The **Food Factory**, next to the visitors centre, is a great place for filling fast food; it does huge hamburgers for as little as $2.50, pizzas and sandwiches. **Cafe Upstairs**, directly above the Food Factory, is licensed and opens from noon to around 2 am. You can get cocktails and there's a big menu, with hamburgers, pancakes and many other dishes.

MTV Restaurant (☎ 6452 2554, 86 Sharp St) serves Malaysian, Thai and Vietnamese food (hence the name), with mains for around $10 and lunch specials for $5.

Thai Continental (☎ 6452 5782, 76 Sharp St) gets good reports.

Most pubs offer counter meals. The **Royal Hotel**, on the corner of Sharp and Lambie Sts, is the pick of the bunch for a satisfying evening meal, while the **Australian Hotel**, on Sharp St, has a bistro with good-value lunchtime roasts for $5.

The big **Ex-Servicemen's Club** (☎ 6452 1144, 106 Vale St) has both a bistro (open for lunch and dinner daily) and a restaurant (Friday to Sunday) and claims to have the cheapest beer in the Monaro Tableland.

Entertainment

The pubs provide most of the evening entertainment. The **Australian Hotel** is the liveliest and has a disco on Friday nights. The **Savoy Cinema** on Commissioner St shows new-release films nightly ($8).

Getting There & Away

Impulse Airlines (☎ 13 1381) flies daily from Sydney for $195. The airport is about 10km south-west of Cooma on the Snowy Mountains Hwy.

Snowliner Travel (☎ 6452 1422), on Sharp St opposite the visitors centre, handles bus bookings. All buses except V/Line (which stops near the visitors centre) stop at the Snowstop Village.

Greyhound Pioneer runs buses to Cooma from Canberra ($25, two hours) and Sydney ($47, six hours). The Canberra to Cooma service, which continues on to Jindabyne and Thredbo, runs daily in winter and six times a week in summer.

Countrylink buses run three times a week between Canberra and Eden on the far south coast, via Cooma, Bombala, Bega and Merimbula. Victoria's V/Line has an interesting twice-weekly run between Melbourne and Canberra via Cooma. The nine-hour trip from Melbourne takes you by train to Sale, then by bus.

Adaminaby Bus Service (☎ 6454 2318) has a run between Cooma and Mt Selwyn daily during winter.

The Snowy Mountains Hwy runs northwest to Tumut (184km). The Monaro Hwy runs north to Canberra (114km) and south to

Bombala (89km); turn off 9km after Nimmitabel for Bega (112km). Other roads run west to Jindabyne (63km) and the Snowy Mountains.

If you're heading to Batemans Bay, you can travel via Numeralla to Braidwood on a partly sealed road skirting Deua National Park.

NIMMITABEL
postcode 2631 • pop 250

Pretty Nimmitabel, on the Monaro Hwy 35km south of Cooma, is a good place for a break, although its only real 'attraction' is the impressive old **windmill**. A German immigrant spent seven years building the mill in the 19th century, but when it was finished he was told he couldn't use it because the spinning sails would frighten horses!

Another thing that might frighten the horses is the more recent addition of a lifesize eight-tonne elephant on the roadside. The owner of the bakery next door took a shine to the statue and had it shipped over from Bali. There are several antique shops along the main street and a junk shop, Anything Goes (closed Tuesday and Wednesday), where you could find just about anything.

The Countrylink bus service between Canberra and Eden passes through three times a week. It stops outside the elephant.

Places to Stay & Eat
The *Royal Arms* (☎ 6454 6422), on the main road through town, is a handsome restored hotel, which is now a guesthouse and cafe. Lovely period singles/doubles upstairs cost $48/85, or $120 for the en suite double, including a cooked breakfast.

The *Tudor Inn* (☎ 6454 6204) is a cosy pub with rooms for $18/30, including continental breakfast.

The *Baker's Shop*, in the sandstone building opposite the Royal Arms, does breakfast and other meals and has a good range of breads and cakes.

BOMBALA
postcode 2632 • pop 1500

The sign at the outskirts announces that Bombala is a timber town, but it's also the centre

of a prime cattle district. It's a good base from which to explore the South-East Forests National Park, and the place to spot that elusive monotreme, the platypus. Stretches of the Bombala River in and around the town are a haven for the shy platypus – the NPWS office (☎ 6458 4080) on Maybe St (the tentatively named main street) has more information. Tourist information is available from the Mobil petrol station on Maybe St.

You can drive (or if you're feeling particularly energetic walk) the 4km up to the lookout in the bushland **Endeavour Reserve**. There are good views over the town and several short walks through the reserve.

The Bombala Agricultural Show, an annual event since 1878, is held in late March.

Places to Stay & Eat
The small *Bombala Caravan Park* (☎ 6458 3270) is pleasantly situated by the river on the northern edge of town. Unpowered/powered sites cost $12/15 for two; on-site vans cost from $30. The park allows pets; call to make arrangements.

The *Globe Hotel* (☎ 6458 3077, 101 Maybe St) has pub rooms for $20 per person.

The *Mail Coach Guesthouse* (☎ 6458 3721, 160 Maybe St) is a lovely guesthouse and restaurant in the renovated old post office. Bed and breakfast costs $55 a double; two rooms have shared facilities and two have en suite.

Maneroo Motel (☎/fax 6458 3500, 129 Maybe St) has standard single/double units for $45/50 and some slightly cheaper rooms.

Kangaroo Camp Retreat (☎/fax 6458 4444), Richardson's Rd, is about 20 minutes north-west of Bombala, just off the back road to Dalgety. There's a winery and farm here and some great high-country accommodation. B&B in the homestead is $45 per person, or $30 in the farm cottage.

There are several cafes and takeaways along Maybe St; *Lingalonga Cafe* has a deli. The *Mail Coach Inn* is a good place for dinner.

Getting There & Away
Countrylink buses run north to Cooma and Canberra, and east to Eden (via Bega).

V/Line stops here on the run between Canberra and Melbourne via Cooma. The bus stop is opposite the Bombala Hotel.

A partly sealed road runs east from Bombala to the Princes Hwy near Merimbula, and a good road off the Monaro Hwy south of Bombala runs east through the national park to the Princes Hwy near Eden. The road running south-west from Bombala through the hamlet of Delegate crosses the border and becomes the Bonang Hwy.

SOUTH-EAST FORESTS NATIONAL PARK

This amalgam of a national park (90,000 hectares) combines state forests and former smaller national parks, extending south from Nimmitabel to the Victorian border and east towards the coast near Eden. The creation of the park came in 1997 after a protracted battle between loggers and environmentalists.

There are many **picnic areas** within the park. Six Mile Creek, between Cathcart and Candelo on the Tantawangalo Mountain Rd, has camping facilities and access to walking tracks. Contact the NPWS office (☎ 6458 4080) in Bombala for more information.

JINDABYNE

postcode 2627 • pop 1670

Jindabyne is the closest town to the major ski resorts in Kosciuszko National Park. It's a sizeable place, with two modern shopping centres and a lot of new development happening. It's still relatively peaceful in summer, but in winter, when the scores of apartments and lodges fill up, the town sleeps more than 20,000 visitors!

Orientation & Information

As with so many other towns on the Monaro Tableland, today's Jindabyne is a modern incarnation of an original settlement that is now below the surface of a hydroelectric dam – in this case Lake Jindabyne.

The impressive Snowy Region Visitor Centre (☎ 6450 5600, fax 6456 1249) is on Kosciuszko Rd – the main road in from Cooma or Thredbo. It's operated by the NPWS and has information on the whole re-

gion. There are display areas, a cinema and a good cafe. It's open from 8 am to 6 pm (to 5 pm in summer) daily.

Nugget's Crossing is a well-equipped shopping centre with a supermarket, banks, the post office and numerous places to eat. It's named after a local pioneer and horseman. There's an Internet cafe (☎ 6457 1722) in the Town Centre Plaza on Kosciuszko Rd where you can get online for $12 an hour.

Ski 'n' Save Snow Centre (☎ 6456 2633), also in the Town Centre Plaza, is an excellent source of information and can organise equipment hire, accommodation, activities and transport for the region.

Summer Activities

Outside the ski season, many people come here to sail on Lake Jindabyne. Snowline Caravan Park (☎ 1800 248 148) rents out fishing boats and canoes, and you can have a crack at waterskiing for $90 per hour. Alpine Sailing (☎ 6456 1195), next door, rents out Hobie-cats and sailboards. You can take a 1½ hour cruise over the sunken Old Jindabyne on MV *Kalinga* ($20/10 for adults/children); book at the visitor centre. Fishing is popular as the lake is full of trout.

This is a prime area for horse riding. Jindabyne Trail Riding (☎ 6456 2421) has 90-minute rides for $20 including instruction for beginners. Snowy River Horseback Adventure (☎ 6453 7260), on the Barry Way about 30km south-west of Jindabyne, suits more experienced riders and has half-day rides for $60 and longer ones with overnight stops.

Upper Murray Rafting (☎ 1800 677 179) operates white-water rafting trips out of Jindabyne and Khancoban, starting near Tom Groggin. Day trips cost $120, while the two-day camping trip is $260. It's also possible to get on a half-day trip ($65) at short notice.

Several places rent out bikes including Snowy Mountain Sports (☎ 6456 2530) in the Town Centre Plaza, with mountain bikes for $30 a day, and Paddy Pallin (☎ 6456 2922).

Paddy Pallin, next to the Snowline Caravan Park, also rents out tents and other walking equipment, and offers an impressive

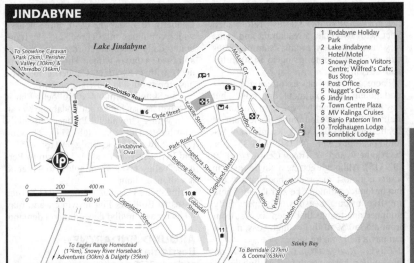

JINDABYNE

Lake Jindabyne

To Snowline Caravan Park (2km), Perisher Valley (30km) & Thredbo (36km)

Kosciuszko Road

Barry Way

Clyde Street

Jindabyne Oval

Park Road

Bogong Street

Ingebyra Street

Gippsland Street

Kalkite Street

Thredbo Tce

McLure Ct

Banjo

Paterson Cres

Cobbon Cres

Townsend St

Cobbadah Street

Gippsland Street

To Eagles Range Homestead (17km), Snowy River Horseback Adventures (30km) & Dalgety (35km)

To Berridale (27km) & Cooma (63km)

Stinky Bay

1 Jindabyne Holiday Park
2 Lake Jindabyne Hotel/Motel
3 Snowy Region Visitors Centre; Wilfred's Cafe; Bus Stop
4 Post Office
5 Nugget's Crossing
6 Jindy Inn
7 Town Centre Plaza
8 MV Kalinga Cruises
9 Banjo Paterson Inn
10 Troldhaugen Lodge
11 Sonnblick Lodge

0   200   400 m
0   200   400 yd

SOUTH-EAST

range of summer activities, including mountain-biking, white-water canoeing, abseiling, horse riding and guided alpine hikes, from leisurely day walks ($19) to seven-day walks in Kosciuszko National Park ($749). Wilderness Sports (☎ 6456 2966) in Nugget's Crossing also has organised walks and mountain-biking.

Places to Stay
The influx of snow bunnies in winter sends prices through the roof, but it's still generally cheaper in Jindabyne than at the resorts and you'll at least have a chance of finding overnight accommodation. Still, many places book out months in advance, so if you're coming to ski, plan well ahead and check out the various packages offered by the resorts and lodges.

There are two caravan parks on Kosciuszko Rd. *Jindabyne Holiday Park* (☎ 6456 2249), in town by the lake, has tent/powered sites from $13/17 for two in summer and on-site vans from $35 for two ($55 in winter). Units sleeping up to five people cost $60/100 in summer/winter.

Snowline Caravan Park (☎ 6452 2099), west of town opposite the Thredbo turn-off,

is better equipped, with a restaurant, heated amenities block, bar and backpackers accommodation. Tent/powered sites cost $15/18 for two ($27/34 in winter); a bed in a four-bed backpackers cabin costs $10 ($22 in winter; linen hire costs $4). Cabins with TV and cooking facilities cost from $36 for two in the low season.

A few guesthouses have moderate summer prices. *Jindy Inn* (☎ 6456 1957, 18 Clyde St) is the pick of the bunch with well-equipped en suite rooms for $45 a double ($40 if staying more than one night) or share rooms for only $25 per person. *Sonnblick Lodge* (☎ 6456 2472, 49 Gippsland St) and *Troldhaugen Lodge* (☎/fax 6456 2718, 13 Cobbodah St) both have B&B for $60 a double.

There's a fair range of motel-style places, some converting to long-term accommodation in winter and most offering bed and breakfast. *Lake Jindabyne Hotel/Motel* (☎ 1800 646 818), Kosciuszko Rd, a big place by the lake in the centre of town, has a heated pool, spa and sauna. Comfortable singles/doubles cost as little as $55/65 in summer, but rocket up to $150/200 in winter. Rates include a hot buffet breakfast.

The **Banjo Paterson Inn** (☎ *1800 046 275, 1 Kosciuszko Rd)* is a flash, refurbished place with two bars, a restaurant and some very nice lakeview rooms. Summer rates start at $85 a double, rising to $150 in the peak season.

There are many places offering accommodation in flats, apartments and lodges, but they can fill up quickly. Agents in Jindabyne include Snowy Mountains Reservations Centre (☎ 1800 020 622), Kosciuszko Accommodation Centre (☎ 1800 026 354), or the Alpine Resorts & Travel Centre (☎ 1800 802 315). Although getting a single night in winter is almost impossible, booking a weekend or longer shouldn't be a problem. There are five pricing seasons. Cheaper, fully equipped apartments that sleep six cost from around $350/$950 in low/high season. You can pay a hell of a lot more.

Eagles Range (☎/fax 6456 2728), on Dalgety Rd 12km south-east of Jindabyne, has purpose-built accommodation in a pleasant rural setting and activities such as horse riding. B&B in the homestead costs $37 per person in the low season and $110 for the weekend in winter. There's also self-contained chalet accommodation from $70 for a double in the low season.

Places to Eat

You'll find a variety of cafes, restaurants and takeaway places in Jindabyne, although many of the restaurants are closed outside the ski season. **Wilfred's Cafe**, in the visitor centre complex, has a great patio, good food and a broad menu. It's open from 7.30 am for breakfast. **Sundance Bakery & Cafe**, in Nugget's Crossing, is another good place for coffee, cakes, sandwiches and snacks.

Il Lago (☎ *6456 1171)*, also in Nugget's Crossing, is a good Italian restaurant. Pasta dishes cost around $13 and it also does takeaway pizzas. **Lake Jindabyne Hotel** has an excellent bistro open all year.

Getting There & Away

For transport bookings contact Ski 'n' Save (☎ 6456 2633) in the Town Centre Plaza, or Snowy River Travel (☎ 6456 2184) behind Nugget's Crossing.

Greyhound Pioneer has a direct bus from Canberra to Jindabyne ($40, three hours), which continues on to Thredbo ($44). It operates daily (except Saturday) in summer and twice a day in winter. This service connects with the Sydney-Canberra bus. The bus stop is outside the visitor centre.

The Skitube terminal at Bullocks Flat is less than half an hour from Jindabyne by car.

In winter Greyhound Pioneer runs daily shuttles to Bullocks Flat ($11), Thredbo ($17), Sawpit Creek, Smiggin Holes ($17) and Perisher Valley ($15). The trip to Perisher Valley takes 45 minutes; to Thredbo it's about an hour.

Jindabyne Coaches (☎ 6457 2117) runs buses to Bullocks Flat in winter, and may go as far as Thredbo depending on demand.

AROUND JINDABYNE
Berridale
postcode 2628 • pop 800

Berridale is a small place with a lot of accommodation and ski-hire places. In the off-season the accommodation can be great value, but book ahead in winter as it gets a lot of tour groups. Greyhound Pioneer buses between Sydney/Canberra and Thredbo stop here, so it's a feasible base for skiing if you don't have transport. Jindabyne is only half an hour away.

The **Bush Village**, just outside Berridale on the road to Jindabyne, is a re-creation of an early settlers hamlet and is open daily except Monday ($2/1 for adults/children). The **Snowy River Winery** (☎ 6456 5041), south of Berridale off the road to Dalgety, is open from 10 am to 5 pm daily. It's Australia's coolest climate winery and has a restaurant open for lunch.

Places to Stay The **Berridale Inn** (☎ *6456 3209)* is a large hotel on the main road. Motel-style rooms at the back are good value at $20 per person ($25 in winter). Tasty counter meals are available here.

Snowy Mountains Coach & Motor Inn (☎ *1800 643 753)*, on the Cooma side of town, is a quiet place charging $35/55 for singles/doubles from October to May. It becomes lively in winter but prices triple.

Ballantrae House (☎ *6456 3388, 16 Myack St)* is a pleasant B&B charging $50/90 outside winter.

Dalgety

Dalgety is only 35km from Jindabyne, but it's a sleepy rural centre rather than a resort town. There's a pub and a caravan park (☎ 6456 5000). A few kilometres west is the **Ag Barn** (☎ 6456 5102), which is basically a craft shop and cafe.

Kosciuszko National Park

NSW's largest (690,000 hectares) and most spectacular national park includes caves, glacial lakes, forest and all of the state's ski resorts, as well as Australia's highest mountain (2228m). Mt Kosciuszko (pronounced koz-zy-**os**-ko) was named by the Polish explorer Paul Edmund Strzelecki after a Polish hero of the American War of Independence.

Most famous for its snow, the national park is becoming increasingly popular in summer when there are excellent bushwalks and marvellous alpine wildflowers. Outside the snow season you can drive to within 8km of the top of Mt Kosciuszko from Jindabyne to Charlotte Pass. Thredbo is the best summer base, but if you have your own transport there are many free camping areas scattered around the park.

Orientation & Information

Mt Kosciuszko and the main ski resorts are in the south-central area of the park. From Jindabyne, Kosciuszko Rd leads to the resorts of Smiggin Holes, Perisher Valley (33km) and Charlotte Pass, with a turn-off before Perisher Valley to Guthega and Mt Blue Cow.

The Mt Selwyn resort is in the north of the park, off the Snowy Mountains Hwy west of Kiandra near Cabramurra, Australia's highest town.

The main NPWS visitors centre for the park is at Jindabyne. There's an education centre (☎ 6450 5666) at Sawpit Creek, which runs programs during school holidays (but is otherwise closed to the public), and another visitor centre at Yarrangobilly Caves (☎ 6454 9597) in the north of the park. There are park-ranger stations at Perisher Valley (☎ 6457 5214) and Thredbo (☎ 6457 6255).

Entry to the national park costs $14 per car, per day. Motorbikes pay $6 and bus passengers $6 ($2 children; this is usually included in the bus fare). There are toll booths on the Alpine Way and the road up to Charlotte Pass and you can also buy permits at Jindabyne and Thredbo. If you intend to spend a few days here, consider buying the $60 annual parks permit, which gives you unlimited access to every national park in NSW, although no other park costs as much to enter as Kosciuszko.

The Central Mapping Authority's (CMA) useful *Snowy Kosciuszko* map ($6.90) includes maps of the resorts, as does the *Snowy Mountains Tourist Atlas* ($9.95).

Flora & Fauna

There's a surprising amount of birdlife in the park, with stately eagles sweeping the sky, bright parrots, noisy kookaburras and magpies. Marsupials abound and they can be pretty tame. If you come across a native animal in need of help, contact either the NPWS or Looking After Kosciuszko's Orphans (LAKO; ☎ 6456 1313).

The rare mountain pygmy possum and yellow-and-black corroboree frog can be found in the park, though you'd be lucky to see them. In spring and mid-summer a variety of colourful alpine wildflowers carpet the mountains.

Bushwalking

Contact the NPWS visitors centres in Jindabyne or Khancoban for information on the many walks in the park.

From Charlotte Pass you can walk to the summit of Mt Kosciuszko (16km return), or take the easier walk to the summit from Thredbo (12km return). Other walking trails from Charlotte Pass include the 20km glacial lakes walk.

There are longer walks through the vast Jagungal Wilderness Area, with several

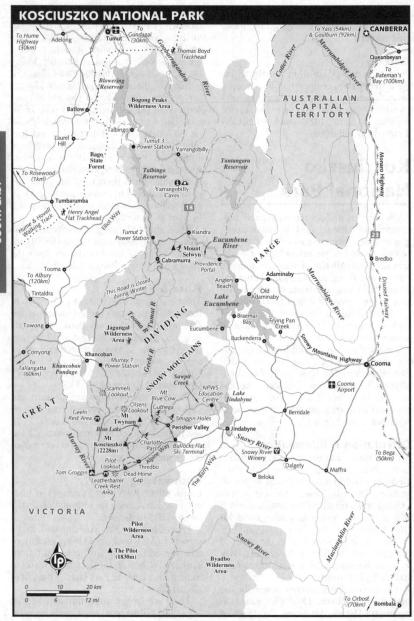

KOSCIUSZKO NATIONAL PARK

To Hume Highway (30km)

Adelong
To Gundagai (30km)
Tumut
To Yass (54km) & Goulburn (92km)
CANBERRA
Queanbeyan
To Bateman's Bay (100km)
Thomas Boyd Trackhead
Goobarragandra River
Cotter River
Murrumbidgee River

Batlow
Blowering Reservoir
Bogong Peaks Wilderness Area

AUSTRALIAN CAPITAL TERRITORY

Laurel Hill
Talbingo
Tumut 3 Power Station
Yarrangobilly
Bago State Forest

To Rosewood (1km)

Talbingo Reservoir
Yarrangobilly Caves
Tantangara Reservoir

Tumbarumba
Henry Angel Flat Trackhead
Hume & Hovell Walking Track

18

Eliot Way
Tumut 2 Power Station
Kiandra
Eucumbene River
RANGE

Mount Selwyn
Cabramurra
Providence Portal

To Albury (120km)
Tooma
This Road is closed during Winter
Anglers Beach
Adaminaby
Old Adaminaby
Murrumbidgee River

Tintaldra

Lake Eucumbene
Braemar Bay
Frying Pan Creek

Towong
Tooma R
Tumut R
Geehi R
DIVIDING

Jagungal Wilderness Area
Eucumbene
Buckenderra

Corryong
To Tallangatta (60km)
Khancoban
Murray 1 Power Station
Khancoban Pondage
SNOWY MOUNTAINS
Snowy Mountains Highway
Cooma

Scammels Lookout
Sawpit Creek
NPWS Education Centre
Lake Jindabyne
Cooma Airport

GREAT
Geehi Rest Area
Olsens Lookout
Mt Blue Cow
Guthega
Smiggin Holes
Perisher Valley
Berridale

Murray River
Blue Lake
Mt Twynam
Charlotte Pass
Bullocks Flat Ski Terminal
Jindabyne
Snowy River

Mt Kosciuszko (2228m)
Pilot Lookout
Alpine Way
Thredbo
Dead Horse Gap
Snowy River Winery
Dalgety
To Bega (50km)

Tom Groggin
Leatherbarrel Creek Rest Area
The Barry Way
Beloka
Maffra

VICTORIA
Pilot Wilderness Area
The Pilot (1830m)
Snowy River
Byadbo Wilderness Area
Maclaughlin River

Bredbo
Monaro Highway
Disused Railway
23

0   10   20 km
0   6   12 mi

To Orbost (70km)
Bombala

alpine huts available for camping, but these treks require planning (including good maps and a compass), experience and knowledge of the conditions, which can change dramatically at any time of year.

Places to Stay

Bush camping is permitted in most of the national park, but not in ecologically fragile areas (such as near the glacial lakes or other water catchment areas). Some riverside picnic areas, where you can camp, have fireplaces and pit toilets. There's a string of such camping areas along the Barry Way at the southern end of the park, and five along the Alpine Way between Bullocks Flat and Geehi. The only formal camping area is *Kosciuszko Mountain Retreat* (☎ 6456 2224), a tranquil place in bushland at Sawpit Creek along the road to Perisher Valley. It has tent/powered sites for $13/18 for two in summer and $19/30 in winter. Cabins cost from $55 a double in summer to $340 for a weekend in the winter peak.

In summer most of the resort lodges close, but good deals can be found at Thredbo and guesthouses and retreats elsewhere in the park.

In winter, the cheapest (and most fun) way to take to the slopes is to gather a bunch of friends and rent an apartment.

For the ski season, begin making inquiries as early as possible. Costs vary enormously and new rates are set before the start of each season. As rough examples, a two-bedroom apartment in Thredbo costs from about $2800 for a week during the peak ski season (roughly mid-July to early September) and a double room in a lodge costs around $1000, including some meals. It's unlikely that you'll find overnight accommodation on the mountain in peak season.

There's a good chance that you'll pay considerably less than this if you shop around. Many agents book accommodation and packages on the ski-fields. Specialists include the Snowy Mountains Reservation Centre (☎ 1800 020 622); Perisher Blue Snow Holidays (☎ 1300 655 811); and the Thredbo Resort Centre (☎ 1800 020 589). Travel agents around the country also make bookings.

SKIING & SKI RESORTS

Skiing or snowboarding in Australia can be a marginal activity. The season is short (July, August and early September) and good snow isn't always guaranteed, although the increased use of snow-making machines is making it more so. Nor are the mountains ideal for downhill skiing – their gently rounded shapes mean that most long runs are relatively easy and the harder runs short and sharp. Worse, the short seasons mean operators have to get their returns quickly, so costs are high.

The good news is that when the snow is there and the sun is shining, the skiing can be superb and the resorts are great fun. You'll find lively nightlife, decent restaurants, fine scenery and enough frightening slopes to keep you interested. The resorts tend to be particularly crowded on weekends because they're so convenient to reach, particularly from Canberra.

The open slopes are a ski-tourer's paradise – Nordic (cross-country or langlauf) skiing is popular and most resorts offer lessons and hire out equipment. The national park includes some of the country's best trails, and often old cattle-herders' huts are the only form of accommodation apart from your tent.

Group lessons, including a lift ticket, cost about $85/60 a day for an adult/child. Boots, skis and stocks can be hired for around $35 a day. It will cost less for longer periods; less, too, if you hire them away from the mountain, but if you have a problem with the fitting you may be stuck. There are hire places in towns close to the resorts and many garages hire out ski equipment and chains. Snow chains must be carried during winter even if there's no snow – heavy penalties apply if you don't.

For snow and road reports ring the various visitors centres. Thredbo (☎ 1900 934 320) and Perisher Blue (☎ 1900 926 664) have their own numbers. On the Internet try www.ski.com.au for information on all resorts.

Thredbo

Thredbo (1370m) has the longest runs (the longest is more than 3km through 670m of

SOUTH-EAST

vertical drop) and some of the best skiing in Australia. A lift day ticket costs $64, a five-day pass $275 and a five-day lift and lesson package costs $350.

Unlike the other resorts, Thredbo is also a great place to visit in summer. It's a popular bushwalking centre with excellent, scenic tracks, a good starting point for mountain-biking tours and there's even a bobsled ride. Just about everything you need to know about Thredbo is on the Internet at www.thredbo.com.au.

Although Thredbo Village covers only a small area, streets wind around the steep valley side and it's tightly packed with lodges. Pick up a map of the village in Jindabyne or Khancoban before you arrive. There's an information centre in the Valley Terminal at Thredbo Village – walk there on the wooden footbridge from the shopping centre.

The chairlift to the top of Mt Crackenback runs right through the summer ($18/9 for adults/children return). It's a very steep walk if you don't take the lift. From the top it's an easy 2km walk or cross-country ski to a good lookout to Mt Kosciuszko (which, from here, looks more like a small hill), or 6km to the top of the mountain itself. Other walks leave from the top of the lift; maps are available at the information centre. Remember to carry adequate clothing and be prepared for all conditions, even in summer.

The Thredbo Centre (☎ 6459 4100/4151) organises all sorts of activities including hiking, mountain-biking, canoeing, whitewater rafting, abseiling and horse riding. Raw NRG (☎ 6457 6282) in the Valley Terminal specialises in mountain-bike rides. A half-day ride from Dead Horse Gap down to Tom Groggin (a drop of over 1000m) costs $65 including lunch and equipment.

Special Events The hills come alive in summer: The Thredbo World Music Festival is held in mid-March; there's the Blues Festival in mid-January; and the Jazz Festival in late April/early May.

Places to Stay Accommodation at Thredbo is mostly in commercial lodges or privately owned apartments.

The Thredbo Tragedy

On the night of 30 July 1997, as hundreds of skiers slept, a tragedy engulfed the resort village of Thredbo. A hillside above the village gave way, smashing two ski lodges and cutting a trail of destruction 30m wide and 60m long.

Twenty people were buried in the wreckage. Against the odds rescue workers searched for survivors in often freezing conditions, as world attention focused on the tragedy. Then on the Saturday, 65 hours after being buried, a lone survivor was lifted free. Despite his ordeal, ski instructor Stuart Diver made a full physical recovery.

Thredbo has returned to normal, but the tragedy has prompted authorities to ensure that hillside lodges are safe and potential risk areas are shored up.

Thredbo YHA Lodge (☎ 6457 6376, 🖂 thredbo@yhansw.org.au, 8 Jack Adams Path) costs just $16 a night ($19 for non-members) or $38 a double outside the ski season, and $38 a night per person ($55 Saturday night) or $225 a week in the ski season. Not surprisingly there's stiff competition for beds in winter. A ballot is held for winter places and you have to enter by April but it's always worth checking to see if there are cancellations. There's plenty of room in the off-season. Contact the YHA Travel Centre (☎ 9261 1111) in Sydney for ballot forms.

Several Thredbo lodges have reasonable deals outside the ski season. *Bursills* (☎ 6457 6222) has singles/doubles from $59/79 with breakfast, and *Candlelight Lodge* (☎ 6457 6318) charges $60/90 for B&B.

Perisher Blue

In 1995 the resorts of Perisher Valley, Smiggin Holes, Mt Blue Cow and Guthega combined to become Perisher Blue (☎ 6459 4495, 1300 655 822), providing skiing on seven peaks across 1250 hectares, with 50 lifts and one ticketing system. Check out the comprehensive Web site at www.perisher blue.com.au.

Perisher Valley (1750m) has a good selection of intermediate runs. Smiggin Holes

(1680m) is just down the road. Guthega (1640m) is mainly a day resort best suited to intermediate and beginner skiers. It's smaller and less crowded than other places; from here, cross-country skiers head to the Main Range or Rolling Ground. Mt Blue Cow (1640m), between Perisher Valley and Guthega in the Perisher Range, has beginner to intermediate skiing. Mt Blue Cow is a day resort (no accommodation) accessible via the Skitube.

Lift day tickets cost $64/35 for adults/children); a one-day combined lesson and lift ticket costs $86/57. Add $11/7 for use of the Skitube.

Places to Stay Most accommodation is in Perisher Valley and Smiggin Holes.

In Perisher Valley, the **Sundeck Hotel** (*☎ 6457 5222, ☎ 1800 816 713*) has two-night peak-season packages for $365 including breakfast and dinner ($220 low-winter season). **Chalet Sonnenhof** (*☎ 6457 5096*) has nightly rates of $185, including breakfast and dinner in peak season, and it's one of the few Perisher lodges open in summer ($65/99 for singles/doubles with breakfast).

The Lodge (*☎ 6457 5012*) at Smiggin Holes has three-night packages including ski hire, dinner and light breakfast for $645 (peak season).

Charlotte Pass

At the base of Mt Kosciuszko, this is one of the highest (1780m), oldest and most isolated resorts in Australia. In winter you have to snowcat the last 8km from Perisher Valley. Five lifts service rather short, but uncrowded, runs and this is good ski-touring country. In summer, this is the start for a number of walks including Kosciuszko summit (18km return), the Main Range (25km) and the Blue Lake Lookout (10km).

Kosciuszko Chalet (*☎ 1800 026 369*) is a grand old place dating from the 1930s. A weekend package, including dinner, breakfast, all transport and lift passes, costs $551 in the peak season. **Southern Alps Ski Club** (*☎ 6457 5223*) has a lodge open in summer for only $24/30 a single/double with en suite. **Stillwell Lodge** (*☎ 6457 5073*) also

opens year-round. A double with dinner, bed and breakfast is $85 per person in summer.

Bullocks Flat

Bullocks Flat, on the Alpine Way between Jindabyne and Thredbo, is the site of the Skitube terminal. The Skitube train (*☎ 6456 2010*) runs from here mostly underground to Perisher Valley and Mt Blue Cow. The return fare is $22/12 for adults/children). In summer the Skitube runs to a reduced timetable but it still operates daily during school holidays.

Thredbo Diggings is a pretty but basic free camp site near the Skitube. Nearby, the **Novotel Lake Crackenback Resort** (*☎ 1800 020 524*) is an excellent complex within walking distance of the Skitube terminal. Doubles cost from $188 to $285, with lower rates for longer stays or for up to four people sharing a room. There are also winter packages, which include accommodation, some meals and lift tickets. The complex has everything you can shake a ski-pole at, and summer activities include canoeing and horse riding.

Crackenback Cottage (*☎ 6456 2198*), on the road towards Jindabyne, has B&B ($95 per person including dinner) and a cosy little restaurant.

Mt Selwyn

Mt Selwyn (1550m) is the only ski resort (*☎ 1800 641 064*) in the north of the park, halfway between Tumut and Cooma. It has 12 lifts and is ideal for beginners. Lift day tickets cost $38/19 for adults/children, and

---

Skiing's Early Days

The first people to ski in Australia were the fur hunters of Tasmania in the 1830s, who used 1m boards. Norwegians at the Kiandra gold-fields introduced skiing in New South Wales in the 1860s and the world's first ski races were held there. The skis were home-made, crude objects; the method of braking was a pole held between the two skis. Early in the 20th century the sport began to develop: lodges were built and European skis were imported.

five-day packages with lessons are $280/187. Look it up on the Web at www.selwynsnow .com.au. It's a day resort – most accommodation is in the Adaminaby area (see the Lake Eucumbene section earlier in this chapter).

To commemorate the early skiers on the Kiandra goldfields, Mt Selwyn hosts the Kiandra Goldrush in July, a race in period costume and equipment.

Cabramurra

Australia's highest town (1488m), Cabramurra has some nice views (when not enveloped in cloud) and a photo gallery in the general store, but the main reason to come up here is to visit Mt Selwyn or the nearby **Tumut 2 Power Station**. There are guided underground tours of the station on the hour between 11 am and 2 pm daily, with extra tours at 10 am and 3 pm during school holidays ($8/5 for adults/children).

Kiandra

Kiandra was a goldrush town in the 1860s, but little remains today. In winter you can pay the national park entry fee here. The **Gold Seekers Walking Track**, a two-hour return walk, leaves Elliott Way east of the Mt Selwyn turn-off.

Yarrangobilly Caves

Although not as well known as some other caves in NSW, the Yarrangobilly Caves (☎ 6454 9597) are among the most interesting. You can visit the Glory Hole by yourself between 10 am and 4 pm daily ($8/4 for adults/children), and there are guided tours of other caves at 1 pm weekdays and at 11 am, 1 and 3 pm weekends ($10/7).

There's a good NPWS visitors centre (☎ 6454 9597), some short walks and a thermal pool where you can swim in 27°C water.

You don't have to pay the park fee if you're only visiting the caves – provided you pay the caves entry fee.

Getting There & Around

Greyhound Pioneer (☎ 13 2030) is the main carrier in this area. There are services from Sydney and Canberra to Cooma and Jindabyne, from where shuttles run to the resorts in winter. In summer, buses run to Thredbo from Canberra ($44) six times a week.

In winter you can normally drive as far as Perisher Valley, but snow chains must be carried and fitted where directed. The simplest, safest way to get to Perisher Valley and Smiggin Holes in winter is to take the Skitube, a tunnel railway up to Perisher Valley and Mt Blue Cow from below the snowline at Bullocks Flat. Luggage lockers and overnight parking are available.

See the West of the Snowies section later in this chapter for western routes into the national park.

THE ALPINE WAY

From Khancoban, this spectacular route runs through dense forest, around the southern end of Kosciuszko National Park to Thredbo and on to Jindabyne. The road has been upgraded in recent years and the final sections of gravel were due to be sealed by mid-2000. Caravans and trailers can be towed on the Alpine Way but there are some very steep sections, particularly between Thredbo and Tom Groggin. Check conditions at Khancoban or Jindabyne in winter. There's no fuel available between Khancoban and Thredbo (71km). If you're driving between Khancoban and Jindabyne, you can get a free transit pass, but if you stop en route you must have a day pass ($14 for 24 hours).

Murray 1 Power Station (☎ 6076 5115), off the Alpine Way south of Khancoban, has a hi-tech, interactive visitor centre explaining the construction and role of the Snowy Mountains Hydro-electric Scheme. It's open from 9 am to 4 pm daily ($6/4 for adults/children). During summer school holidays there are guided tours on the hour from 10 am to 2 pm ($8/5).

Farther south is **Scammels Lookout**, offering superb views. There are toilets and picnic tables here. Farther on you can camp at **Geehi**, a grassy picnic area with good facilities on the Swampy Plains River.

At **Tom Groggin**, home of the original Man From Snowy River, the road skirts the upper Murray River, a clear, cool stretch that's good for a swim on a hot day. There's a good camping and picnic site here and a smaller site at Leatherbarrel Creek, about 7km farther on. After Tom Groggin the road climbs 800m to the **Pilot Lookout** (1300m), with views across a wilderness area to The Pilot (1830m), the source of the Murray River. There's another climb to **Dead Horse Gap** (1580m), named after some brumbies that froze here, then a descent to Thredbo Village (1400m), the Skitube terminal at Bullocks Flat, and Jindabyne. **Thredbo Diggings** and **Ngarigo** are two more picnic and camping areas on the banks of the Thredbo River near Bullock's Flat.

West of the Snowies

The western slopes of the Snowy Mountains are steeper than on the east, and the area is more intensively farmed, although there's still plenty of bush. The farms and small towns in the area blaze with colour in the autumn when poplars and fruit trees prepare to shed their leaves. This is a rural area with a thriving fruit-growing industry.

Getting There & Around
A Countrylink bus runs from Cootamundra to Gundagai, Tumut, Adelong, Batlow and Tumbarumba daily except Saturday. At Cootamundra it connects with the Sydney to Melbourne XPT (express) train.

If driving or motorcycling, there are several approaches to the Snowies from the west, all accessible from the Hume Hwy. The main route, the Snowy Mountains Hwy, leaves the Hume about 30km south of Gundagai and takes you to Tumut, Kiandra, Adaminaby and Cooma.

From Albury you can travel on Victoria's Murray Valley Hwy to Corryong, then head across the river to Khancoban for the Alpine Way. Another road in Victoria parallels the Murray Valley Hwy, but follows closely the south bank of the Murray. This route is longer, but perhaps more interesting, than the Murray Valley Hwy.

From Holbrook on the Hume Hwy, a sealed road runs through to Jingellic, while another sealed road runs from the Hume to Tumbarumba. From Tumbarumba you can cross the mountains on the winding Elliott Way to get to Mt Selwyn and the Snowy Mountains Hwy at Kiandra.

There's another crossing to Mt Selwyn and Kiandra just north of Khancoban, but it's usually closed in winter. Caravans can't use this road.

TUMUT
postcode 2720 • pop 6300
A mountain town in the pretty Tumut Valley, Tumut is the closest centre to the northern end of Kosciuszko National Park. In the area there are many pine plantations (timber is Tumut's biggest industry) and orchards.

Tumut was once a meeting place for three Aboriginal tribes, the Ngunawal, Walgalu and Wiradjuri. The explorers Hume and Hovell were the first Europeans to see the Tumut Valley in 1824 before farmers and graziers settled, but development of the town was slow. One of the area's most famous early residents was author Miles Franklin (her best known book is *My Brilliant Career*), who was born at Talbingo.

Information
The friendly Tumut Visitors Centre (☎ 6947 1849) is in the refurbished Old Butter Factory on Adelong Rd north of the town centre. This is also the NPWS office for the region and it has lots of information and an interesting historical display. It's open from 8 am to 5 pm (6 pm in summer) daily.

The library (☎ 6947 1969), 169 Wynyard St, has Internet access for $5 an hour.

Things to See & Do
There's a paved **river walk** along the shady west bank of the Tumut River, which is probably better than swimming in it as the water is freezing.

Opposite the visitors centre is the **Tumut Broom Factory** (☎ 6947 2804) where brooms are still made from millet; it's open from 9 am to 12.30 pm and 1.30 to 4 pm weekdays (free). The small **Tumut & District Historical Museum**, on the corner of Capper and Merivale Sts, has a room devoted to

SOUTH-EAST

Miles Franklin. The museum is open from 2 to 4 pm Wednesday, Saturday and school holidays (admission by donation).

Tumut-U-Fish (☎ 6947 4042) is a couple of dismal-looking ponds at the end of Merivale St where you can apparently catch your own trout. Entry, including rod hire, bait and cleaning is $3.50 plus $4 per fish.

Tumut is a popular spot for powered **hang-gliding**. You can take a half-hour microlight 'trike' flight out over the Tumut Valley towards Blowering Dam (part of Blowering Reservoir) for $60. Contact Air Escape (☎ 6947 1159). The airport is 3km north of town on Brungle Rd.

Selwyn Snow & Water (☎ 6947 6225), near the swimming pool on Fitzroy St, hires bikes as well as ski and water sports gear.

Special Events
The Festival of the Falling Leaf is held in late April, and there are race days in October and December.

Places to Stay
The immaculate *Riverglade Caravan Park* (☎ 6947 2528) is on the Snowy Mountains Hwy a few blocks from the town centre on the Tumut River. Tent/powered sites cost $12/16 and cabins cost from $33 a double. *Blowering Holiday Park* (☎ 6947 1383), on the Snowy Mountains Hwy 5km south of town, is well equipped and popular with backpackers working in the area. It has sites for $10, cabins from $34 ($55 in peak season) and a backpackers bunkhouse from $56 a week.

The *Oriental Hotel* (☎ 6947 1174), on the corner of Fitzroy and Wynyard Sts, has rooms for $20 per person. It's a nice old pub and the rooms lead onto the big balcony. The large *Royal Hotel* (☎ 6947 1129, 88 Wynyard St) has motel-style single/double units for $39/50 and hotel rooms for $27.50.

There are plenty of motels in town. The *Amaroo* (☎ 6947 1588, 55 Capper St) is about the cheapest, with bland rooms for

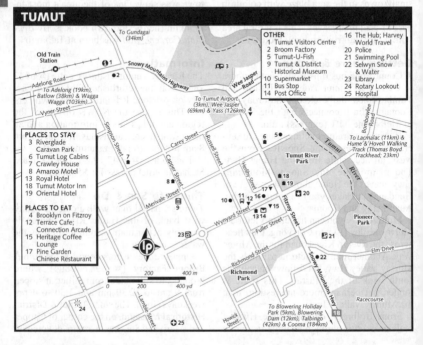

TUMUT

To Gundagai (34km)

Old Train Station

Snowy Mountains Highway

Adelong Road

To Adelong (19km), Batlow (38km) & Wagga Wagga (103km)

Vyner Street

Wee Jasper Road

To Tumut Airport (3km), Wee Jasper (69km) & Yass (126km)

Simpson Street

Carey Street

Russell Street

Bombowlee Road

To Lacmalac (11km) & Hume & Hovell Walking Track (Thomas Boyd Trackhead; 23km)

Tumut River Park

Healey Street

Capper Street

Merivale Street

Wynyard Street

Fuller Street

Fitzroy Street

Tumut River

Pioneer Park

Richmond Street

Elm Drive

Snowy Mountains Hwy

Richmond Park

Lambie Street

Howick Street

To Blowering Holiday Park (5km), Blowering Dam (12km), Talbingo (42km) & Cooma (184km)

Racecourse

OTHER
1 Tumut Visitors Centre
2 Broom Factory
5 Tumut-U-Fish
9 Tumut & District Historical Museum
10 Supermarket
11 Bus Stop
14 Post Office
16 The Hub; Harvey World Travel
20 Police
21 Swimming Pool
22 Selwyn Snow & Water
23 Library
24 Rotary Lookout
25 Hospital

PLACES TO STAY
3 Riverglade Caravan Park
6 Tumut Log Cabins
7 Crawley House
8 Amaroo Motel
13 Royal Hotel
18 Tumut Motor Inn
19 Oriental Hotel

PLACES TO EAT
4 Brooklyn on Fitzroy
12 Terrace Cafe; Connection Arcade
15 Heritage Coffee Lounge
17 Pine Garden Chinese Restaurant

0   200   400 m
0   200   400 yd

$45/50. *Tumut Motor Inn (☎ 6947 4523)*, Fitzroy St, has better rooms for $57/60.

Tumut Log Cabins (☎ 1800 625 592, 30 Fitzroy St) has comfortable self-contained cedar units by the river – good value at $55 a double. *Crawley House (☎ 6947 1246, 55 Carey St)* is a centrally located Victorian home with rooms for $30/55 including breakfast. The visitors centre can give you details on more B&Bs in the region.

Places to Eat

There are several bakeries and cake shops on or near Wynyard St. *Terrace Cafe*, in the Connection Arcade (opposite the Royal Hotel), is a great place for a coffee and light lunch. Open sandwiches cost $7. The *Heritage Coffee Lounge* opens early (7 am) for breakfast.

The pubs – no less than six of them within a block of each other – all have counter meals. The *Oriental* has $4 lunch specials and the *Royal Hotel* has meals from $6.

There are several Chinese places, including the BYO *Pine Garden (☎ 6947 1508, 47 Fitzroy St)*.

Brooklyn on Fitzroy (☎ 6947 4022, 10 Fitzroy St) is Tumut's best restaurant. Laksa costs $14 and fillet steak $20. It's open Tuesday to Saturday for dinner only.

Getting There & Away

Countrylink buses, which run to Cootamundra, Adelong, Gundagai, Batlow and Tumbarumba, stop daily (except Saturday) outside the National Bank on the corner of Russell and Wynyard Sts. Harvey World Travel (☎ 6947 3055), in The Hub centre on Wynyard St, sells tickets.

There's an interesting road from Tumut north to Wee Jasper (69km), from where you can get to Yass, and another running east through the Brindabella Range to Canberra (125km). These roads are mostly unsealed but are in reasonable condition – the visitors centre has information and maps.

AROUND TUMUT

The Thomas Boyd Trackhead of the **Hume & Hovell Walking Track** is 23km south-east of Tumut and it has camping facilities.

Blowering Reservoir, nearly 20km long, is part of the Snowy Mountains Hydroelectric Scheme. There are walks along the forested shores and numerous picnic and camping areas, and the lake is popular for water sports. You can drive or walk up to the top of the 112m-high Blowering Dam for a good view; the gates close at 4 pm. At the southern end of the reservoir is the small town of **Talbingo**, and 2km farther south is the **Tumut 3 Power Station** on Murray Jackson Drive. It's the largest of the Snowy power stations and has tours between 10 am and 2.30 pm daily ($8/5 for adults/children).

Adelong
postcode 2729 • pop 900

This neat village, 22km west of Tumut, was the centre of a goldrush after reef gold was discovered in 1857, and several buildings in the main street reflect this status. The Old Bank (1882) has tourist information, as well as an antique shop and tearooms.

Adelong Falls, 1.5km from the town centre, are more of a horizontal cascade but are worth seeing mainly for the extensive remains of the ingenious **Reefer Battery**. This set of stamping batteries, used to crush gold-bearing ore, was entirely powered by waterwheels. There are walking trails and explanatory signs among the ruins. To get there, take the right turn off the main street towards Gundagai; the turn-off to the falls is on the right.

The small, friendly *Golden Gully Caravan Park (☎ 6946 2282)*, on Victoria Hill Rd near the swimming pool, has tent/powered sites for $10/12. *Hotel Adelong (☎ 6946 2009)*, on the main street, has singles/doubles for $20/35. There are several heritage-style B&Bs in town with prices that reflect Adelong's historic quaintness. The *Old Bank (☎ 6946 2408, 47 Tumut St)* charges $65/95 on weekdays/weekends and *Beaufort House (☎ 6946 2273, 77 Tumut St)* has singles/doubles for $55/75.

There are a couple of good cafes and restaurants on the main street, including the *Old Pharmacy*. The *Miner's Plate* at the Adelong Services & Citizens' Club *(☎ 6946 2163)* serves Chinese and Australian food.

Batlow

postcode 2730 • pop 1500

Batlow, on one side of a (fruit!) bowl-shaped valley, is an apple-orchard town. Tourist information for the area (and fresh fruit) can be found at Springfield Orchard (☎ 6949 1021), just north of town.

The trees blossom in October and the apple harvest starts around mid-March (when there's a local festival), but there are also stone fruits and cherries, so picking work is usually available from December to May. The best way to find work is to approach the orchards directly – the Tumut Visitors Centre has a list.

Apple-picking aside, Batlow is a sleepy little place. If you've never seen the inside of an apple-packing factory, **Fruits of Batlow** (☎ 6949 1835), 6km south of town, is the place for a short guided tour (weekdays only).

Batlow Caravan Park (☎ *6949 1444*), by the shady creek off Kurrajong Ave, has tent/powered sites for $9/11. *Batlow Hotel* (☎ *6949 1001, 12 Pioneer St*) has singles/doubles for $20/30 ($60/80 weekly) with a cooked breakfast.

BAGO STATE FOREST

The Adelong road from Batlow to Tumbarumba slices down the western edge of the Bago State Forest, a large area of pine plantations and native hardwood stretching across to the Blowering and Talbingo Reservoirs. You can enter the forest from Laurel Hill, about 15km south of Batlow, and explore a number of walks and drives. The short stroll through a stand of **Sugar Pines** on Kopsens Rd is worthwhile, and farther in is the **Pilot Hill Forest Park** with a tidy little picnic and camping area. Heading up towards Blowering Reservoir is the **Hume & Hovell Lookout**. These roads are unsealed but in good condition.

TUMBARUMBA

postcode 2653 • pop 2000

Tumbarumba (usually called just Tumba) is a small town, though it may seem large for this part of the world. The area was first settled by graziers, who wintered their cattle here when the snows came to the high plains, and a small goldrush in the 1860s boosted the population. Today, forestry is the major industry, along with orchards growing cool-climate fruits.

Orientation & Information

The main street through town is Tumbarumba Parade, known simply as The Parade.

The best place for tourist information is the Wool & Craft Centre (☎ 6948 2805), on Bridge St at the southern end of the Parade. The Forestry Commission office (☎ 6948 2400) on Winton St has details of the area's state forests, including camp sites and walking tracks. There's free Internet access at the library (☎ 6948 2725) in the Bicentennial Gardens on Prince St.

Things to See & Do

There's a small **museum** in the Wool & Craft Centre with displays on the town's pioneer history and a nifty model of a working sawmill complete with waterwheel. It's open from 10 am to 4 pm daily except Monday (free).

Some of the district's many **orchards**, growing nuts, cherries, blueberries and apples, welcome visitors. Ask at the Wool & Craft Centre for opening times and directions. Viticulture is also taking off in the region and there are several nearby **wineries**. The closest is the Tumbarumba Wine Cellars (☎ 6948 3055) on Albury Close next to the Tumbarumba Motel. It's open for sales and tastings from noon to 4.30 pm on weekends.

Special Events

Tumbafest is a weekend of food, wine and entertainment in early February, while the Tumbarumba Rodeo is held on New Year's Day.

Places to Stay & Eat

The *Tumbarumba Creek Caravan Park* (☎ *6948 3330*), on Lauder St just off The Parade near the showground, is small but tidy and has sites for $8 and cabins from $30.

Tumbarumba Hotel (☎ *6948 2562, 20 The Parade*) has pretty basic singles/ doubles for $20/35, including a light self-serve

SOUTH-EAST

breakfast. *Cayirylys Motel* (☎ *6948 3228)*, on The Parade in the centre of town, belies the motel tag. Its cosy timber rooms are great value at $45/68, including cooked breakfast.

The *Tumbarumba Motel* (☎ 6948 2494), Albury Close, has modern rooms from $45/55.

The *Old Times Coffee Shop* and *Cayirylys Coffee Shop*, on The Parade, are good places for coffee (naturally) and light lunches. The *bowling club* (☎ *6948 2016)*, on Winton St, has Chinese meals.

Getting There & Away

Countrylink buses stop in town. From Tumbarumba, roads run west to the Hume Hwy, north to Tumut, east to the Snowy Mountains Hwy, and south to Khancoban, the Alpine Way and Corryong (in Victoria).

The ski slopes at Mt Selwyn are about an hour away on the Elliott Way. You'll need chains in winter.

AROUND TUMBARUMBA

The **Pioneer Women's Hut** (☎ 6948 2635) is in the Glenroy Heritage Reserve, 8km west of Tumbarumba on the Wagga Wagga road. The hut has historical displays on rural women's lives, crafts and a tearoom. The reserve opens from 11 am to 4 pm Wednesday and 10 am to 4.30 pm weekends.

Rosewood is a tiny place but it's big on eucalyptus oil production, thanks to a particular type of eucalypt that grows in the area. You can see the oil being distilled from leaves at a farm about 5km out of Rosewood. Call ahead for times (☎ 6948 8290) – they have to fire up the still.

There's camping at the **Henry Angel Flat Trackhead**, 7km south-east of Tumbarumba on the Khancoban road, and access to a 6km trail along Burra Creek to the **Hume & Hovell Walking Track**. Another 5km farther on there's a turn-off for **Paddy's River Falls**, 2km down a steep but sealed road. **Jingellic** is a pretty hamlet with a store, a petrol station and a pub. You can camp for no charge at Horse Creek on the eastern edge of town. The road from Jingellic to Tumbarumba is partly gravel. Watch out for logging trucks.

KHANCOBAN

postcode 2642 • pop 400

Khancoban is a small town built by the Snowy Mountains Authority to house construction workers. Towns built by public authorities are often bureaucratic monstrosities, but Khancoban is a beautiful exception. With the southern entrance to Kosciuszko National Park 5km away, it's an ideal base for exploring the Snowies and the upper Murray River.

If you're heading along the Alpine Way, there's a NPWS office (☎ 6076 9393) where you must buy your park visitor's permit. It has a good range of information, publications and a free film, and is open from 8.30 am to noon and 1 to 4 pm daily. Khancoban Roadhouse (☎ 6076 9400) has some tourist information and sells permits when the NPWS office is closed.

Activities

There's good fishing in the Khancoban Pondage and the Swampy Plains River that runs off it. Boats can be hired from the Lakeside Caravan Resort for $50/75 a half/full day.

Rapid Descents (☎ 1800 637 486) has white-water rafting trips on the upper Murray River. The one-day trip costs $120 and the two-day camping trip, covering 24km of rapids, is $280.

Khancoban Trail Rides (☎ 6076 9455), based at the Lyrebird Lodge (see Places to Stay, following), offers two-hour rides (from $40) to challenging safaris (September to April): the two-day ride costs $350; the bum-wearying 10-day ride into remote parts of the Snowies costs $1100.

Upper Murray Adventures (☎ 6076 9066), at the Lakeside Caravan Resort, can book and organise a wide range of activities including rafting, mountain-biking, skiing and hang-gliding.

Places to Stay & Eat

By the Khancoban Dam, *Lakeside Caravan Resort* (☎ *6076 9488)* is a well-equipped place with tent sites for $13, on-site vans from $25, shared loft accommodation for $15 and good cabins from $40.

Khancoban Backpackers & Fisherman's Lodge (☎ 6076 9471), Scott St, has reasonable share accommodation for $12 and singles/doubles for $17/25. You need to supply your own bedding. Book and check in at the nearby Khancoban Alpine Inn.

Khancoban Alpine Inn (☎ 6076 9471) has pleasant rooms from $49/59.

Alpine Hideaway Village (☎ 6076 9498), across the valley from the town – the road crosses the dam's spillway – has great views of the Snowies. It's a nice place, offering good accommodation in fully equipped, self-catering lodges. There's a variety of packages with overnight rates from $50/55.

Lyrebird Lodge (☎/fax 6076 9455), up the hill from Hideaway, is a smaller place offering B&B for $50/70, again with great views.

The *Alpine Inn Hotel*, Scott St, has counter meals and a daily $5 special for lunch and dinner. The *Pickled Parrot Restaurant*, in the motel section, is open for breakfast, lunch and dinner daily and is good for a more upmarket meal.

Getting There & Away
There's no regular public transport to Khancoban, but the Wayward bus stops here on its Sydney to Melbourne route.

The Hume Highway

The Hume Hwy is the busiest road in Australia, running nearly 900km from Sydney to Melbourne. It is named after Hamilton Hume, who followed roughly this route when he walked from Parramatta to Port Phillip, later the site of Melbourne, with William Hovell in 1824. Hume was a native-born Australian, while Hovell was an upper-crust Englishman, and their association was not entirely happy. Their return journey became a race to be the first in Sydney with news of new lands. Despite chicanery on Hovell's part, they both arrived at the same time.

GOULBURN & AROUND
postcode 2580 • pop 21,000
Amid sheep country, Goulburn is a big town boasting fine 19th-century buildings.

John Oxley was the first European to visit the site of Goulburn, in 1820. The town developed to serve the grazing communities on the region's high pastures and was proclaimed in 1863.

Orientation & Information
The Hume Hwy bypassed Goulburn in 1992 so the old town centre is now relatively peaceful and worth a stroll. The main shopping street is Auburn St.

The new Goulburn Visitor Centre (☎ 4823 4492), at 221 Sloane St opposite Belmore Park, has an interpretive display and plenty of regional information. It's open from 9 am to 5 pm daily. The post office is at 165 Auburn St.

Things to See & Do
Of all the impressive country courthouses in NSW, Goulburn's **courthouse** (1887) on Montague St must be the most imposing. The **old courthouse**, which did a lot of business in sentencing the bushrangers who plagued the highlands, is around the corner on Sloane St. The visitor centre has a good heritage walking-tour map of town (free).

The three-storey-high **Big Merino**, on Cowper St (the old highway) south of the centre, is claimed to be the world's biggest. It looks truly diabolical with its eyes glowing at night. By day (8 am to 8 pm) you can climb up inside and check out the view from those eyes, passing through a display on the Australian wool industry on the way (free). There's local arts and crafts on sale at the Agrodome next door.

The **Old Goulburn Brewery** (☎ 4821 6071), a large complex off Bungonia Rd, dates from 1836. As well as the brewery and museum, you can see the cooperage, the maltings, a tobacco-curing kiln and a steam-powered flour mill. Try the traditional ale in the rustic bar. It's open from 11 am daily and there are tours by appointment.

Riversdale (☎ 4821 9591), on Maude St at the north end of town by the Wollondilly River, began its career in 1840 as a coaching inn. It's now a National Trust property with fine gardens and a collection of colonial furniture, arts and crafts. It's open from

10.30 am to 4 pm weekends. **Garroorigang Historic Home** (☎ 4822 1912), about 2km from the town centre on Braidwood Rd, has had a varied history as a bullockies inn and a private boys' school. Much of the furnishings and outbuildings date back to the 1860s. The owners do an interesting one-hour guided tour for a steep $8.

About 40km south-east of Goulburn and abutting Morton National Park, **Bungonia State Recreation Area** (SRA; ☎ 4848 4277) has a dramatic forested gorge and some deep caves. Bushwalking and canoeing are popular. There's a camping ground near the main entrance with showers, but no powered sites.

Just off the highway between Goulburn and Yass, **Gunning** is a small town with restored buildings, a number of antique and craft shops and several B&Bs.

Special Events
The Australian Blues Music Festival comes to town in mid-February and the Lilac City Festival is held over the Labour Day long weekend in early October.

Places to Stay
On the old highway north of town, *Governor's Hill Carapark* (☎ 4821 7373, 77–83 Sydney Rd) has tent/powered sites for $12/16 and on-site vans/cabins for $30/37.

A number of pubs on Sloane St have accommodation and are convenient to the train station. The *Carlton Hotel* (☎ 4821 3820) has singles/doubles with en suite for $30/35 and the *Coolavin* (☎ 4821 2498, 188 Sloane St) has singles for $20.

There are plenty of motels. The *Alpine Lodge* (☎ 4821 2930, 248 Sloane St) has good value rooms for $30/40. *Country Home Motel* (☎/fax 4821 4877, 1 Cowper St), just south of town, is small and friendly with rooms for $40/50.

The rustic *Old Goulburn Brewery* (☎ 4821 6071), Bungonia Rd, has good accommodation in the renovated mews cottages for $35 per person, including breakfast.

Garroorigang (☎ 4822 1912), Braidwood Rd, has historic B&B accommodation (sleep in original 19th-century beds) for $50 per person.

The environmentally friendly *Yurt Farm* (☎ 4829 2114), on Grabben Gullen Rd 20km north of Goulburn (follow Clinton St), includes an activities camp for students, with the emphasis on learning to live simply. Travellers are welcome to stay in the yurt village (a group of basic huts around a small lake) for $11 a night if there's room; if not, you can stay in the farmhouse for $10 and do a few hours' work in exchange for meals. The farm is involved in the Willing Workers on Organic Farms (WWOOF) program, so quite a few backpackers come out here. It's a good idea to phone first to see if there's room.

Ask at the visitors centre about *farmstays* in the area.

Places to Eat
The *Paragon Cafe*, opposite the post office, is the most impressive of several cafes along Auburn St. It's licensed and has a large menu, including seafood from $14 and huge pasta dishes for $7.50.

The *Parkside Bistro* in the Goulburn Soldiers Club (☎ 4821 3300), opposite Belmore Park, has a range of meal deals and is generally excellent value. *Kinaree* (☎ 4821 2289), on Auburn St, is a good Thai restaurant. Most mains are under $10 and it's bring your own (BYO) alcohol.

The *Old Goulburn Brewery* does a three-course dinner in ambient surroundings for around $35.

Getting There & Away
Greyhound Pioneer buses between Sydney and Adelaide (via Canberra) stop outside the Goulburn train station. Murrays also run buses three times a week to Canberra and Wollongong, and Fearnes has daily services to Wagga Wagga and Sydney (stopping outside the courthouse). The visitors centre makes bookings.

Trains between Sydney and Melbourne stop here daily. The Countrylink Travel Centre (☎ 4827 1485) at the train station is open from 7.15 am to 5 pm weekdays and 6.15 to 11 am and 12.10 to 3.15 pm weekends. The one-way fare to Canberra is $12 and to Sydney $31.

SOUTH-EAST

YASS
postcode 2582 • pop 4800

The Ngunawal people occupied this area when Europeans arrived in the 1820s. Among the first to pass through were the explorers Hume and Hovell. Graziers soon followed and, by the time Hume returned to settle in the area in 1830, a town was growing on the banks of the Yass River. Yass was considered as a site for the national capital but was passed over and remains a busy rural centre.

Orientation & Information

The Yass Valley Way (the old highway) becomes Comur St, then Laidlaw St as it passes through town. Yass Visitors Centre (☎ 6226 2557), in Coronation Park on Comur St on the Sydney side of town, is open from 9 am to 5 pm weekdays and 9.30 am to 4.30 pm weekends.

The post office is in the middle of town on Comur St and the library is opposite.

Things to See

The **Yass Railway Museum** (☎ 6226 2169), on Lead St off Comur St, tells the story of Yass' trains and trams. It's open from noon to 4 pm Sunday ($3/1.50 for adults/children).

Next to the visitor centre, the **Hamilton Hume Museum** (☎ 6226 2557) has a model reconstruction of the town in the 1890s. It's open from 10 am to 4 pm weekends ($2/0.50). Hume's house, **Cooma Cottage** (☎ 6226 1470), is on the Yass Valley Way on the Sydney side of town. The original timber cottage was built in 1835. The National Trust has restored the buildings and you can visit from 10 am to 4 pm daily, except Tuesday ($4/2).

There are several **antique shops** on the main street, and at the south end of town is the **Didgeridoo Man** (☎ 6226 3011), where you can see these instruments being made.

Places to Stay

Taking up one corner of pretty Victoria Park on the Gundagai side of town, *Yass Caravan Park* (☎ 6226 1173) has tent/powered sites for $10/12 and cabins for $32 or $40 with en suite.

Several hotels on Comur St have cheap accommodation. The *Royal Hotel* (☎ 6226 1005) has rooms for only $15 per person. The *Australian Hotel* (☎ 6226 1744) has motel-style singles/doubles with en suite for $35/45.

There are quite a few mid-range motels strung out along Yass Valley Way. The *Hamilton Hume* (☎ 1800 020 559, 9 Laidlaw St), south of the centre, has rooms for $44/58 and a licensed restaurant. The *Thunderbird* (☎ 6226 1158, 264 Comur St) is central and has a pool. Rooms cost from $60/67.

The *Globe B&B* (☎ 6226 3680, 70 Rossi St) is a lovely old National Trust-classified guesthouse in a restored Victorian hotel in the middle of town; rooms cost $70/100.

Places to Eat

The *Australian Hotel* has $5 counter lunches. *Maggies*, on Comur St, serves light meals in its pleasant garden bistro. The *Yass Soldiers Club* (☎ 6226 1911), Meehan St, has a licensed bistro.

Getting There & Away

Greyhound Pioneer and V-line buses heading to Melbourne stop at the visitors centre; heading to Sydney they stop at the NRMA garage across the road. McCafferty's and Firefly services to Sydney and Melbourne stop at the Ampol petrol station. Transborder Buses (☎ 6226 1378) has daily services between Yass and Canberra ($10). They leave from Rossi St.

Trains between Sydney and Melbourne stop at Yass Junction, 2km north of town.

AROUND YASS

Burrinjuck Dam, about 57km south-west of Yass, supplies water to the Murrumbidgee Irrigation Area and its long arms wind among steep valleys. It's popular for water sports, including water-skiing and fishing, and there's wildlife in the surrounding bush. **Burrinjuck Waters SRA** (☎ 6227 8114) is about 30km from the highway and costs $5 per car to enter (for day use). There are cruises from here on the *Lady BJ* (☎ 6227 7270). There's camping ($12) and cabins, as well as boat hire.

Hume & Hovell Walking Track

This 370km walking track between Yass and Albury closely follows the historic route taken by explorers Hamilton Hume and William Hovell in their successful expedition to Port Phillip Bay (the site of present-day Melbourne) in 1824.

The party, which included another six men, took only four months to complete the return journey to Port Phillip, passing to the west of the Snowy Mountains before dropping down to the relatively flat plains through Victoria.

The walk, if you're dedicated enough to complete the entire route, takes about 21 days and winds its way through numerous state forests, along the shores of Lake Burrinjuck and Blowering Reservoir, and close to Wee Jasper, Tumut, Tumbarumba, Lankeys Creek and Woomargama. It's divided into 12 stages with six major trackheads, and there are various side trips and day walks off the main track.

The route is well-signposted and there are at least 16 camp sites along the way. You can get the kit of 10 brochures with reasonably detailed maps, track notes and historical information from the Department of Land & Water Conservation (DLWC; ☎ 9228 6111). It costs $10 to have the full kit mailed to you, or you can pick up individual stage brochures free from local tourist offices. A comprehensive guidebook is also available ($19.95).

Lake Burrinjuck Leisure Resort (☎ 6227 7271) is closer to the highway and has tent/powered sites for $12/15 and cabins with en suites for $60; you can also hire boats.

Wee Jasper

About 55km south-west of Yass, Wee Jasper is a small village in a beautiful valley near the southern end of Burrinjuck Dam. You can join the **Hume & Hovell Walking Track** here and visit the limestone **Careys Cave** on weekend afternoons. There's a store and a pub and fuel is available.

There's *camping (☎ 6227 9626)* at five bush reserves in the area, at the Fitzpatrick Trackhead of the Hume & Hovell Walking Track and at Carey's Reserve on the shores

of Burrinjuck Dam. *Wee Jasper Station (☎ 6227 9641)* has cheap shared accommodation in old shearers' quarters, and *Cooradigbee (☎ 6227 9633)* has homestead and cottage accommodation. These places cater mainly to groups, but may have something for individuals.

The road from Yass has an 8km unsealed section but it's usually pretty good. Continuing south-west to Tumut the road deteriorates for the climb out of the valley. Another unsealed road cuts across to Canberra. Both these roads are OK when dry, but check conditions after rain.

Wineries

Around **Murrumbateman**, on the Barton Hwy south-east toward Canberra, are a number of cool-climate wineries. Most are open for sales and tastings on weekends and some during the week. The Yass and Canberra visitor centres have information.

GUNDAGAI

postcode 2722 • pop 2060

Gundagai, on the Murrumbidgee River 398km from Sydney, is one of the more interesting small towns along (or bypassed by) the Hume Hwy.

The tourist office (☎ 6944 1341), on the grand main street (Sheridan St), is open from 8 am to 5 pm Monday to Friday, and 9 am to noon and 1 to 5 pm weekends.

Things to See

The long, wooden **Prince Alfred Bridge** (closed to traffic, but you can walk it) crosses the flood plain of the Murrumbidgee River. It's a reminder that in 1852 Gundagai suffered Australia's worst flood disaster; 78 deaths were recorded, but probably over 100 people drowned. There's a disused railway bridge (built 1901) here too.

Goldrushes and bushrangers were part of Gundagai's colourful early history and the notorious Captain Moonlight was tried in Gundagai's 1860 **courthouse**.

Gundagai Historical Museum (☎ 6944 1995), on Homer St, is in a modern building with an impressive old sandstone portico. It's cluttered with old photographs, household

SOUTH-EAST

The Dog on the Tuckerbox

Gundagai features in a number of famous songs, including *Along the Road to Gundagai, My Mabel Waits for Me* and *When a Boy from Alabama Meets a Girl from Gundagai*. Its most famous monument is 8km east of town just off the Hume Hwy: the Dog on the Tuckerbox memorial (made by Frank Rusconi). It's a sculpture of the dog who, in a 19th-century bush ballad (and a more recent, perhaps even better known, poem by Jack Moses), sat by and watched as its master tried to get his bullock team out of a bog. A popular tale claims that the dog was even less helpful because in the original version it apparently shat, rather than sat, on the tuckerbox!

items and farm machinery from the town's past, and is open from 9 am to 2 pm Monday to Saturday ($3/1 for adults/children). At the tourist office, **Rusconi's Marble Masterpiece** is a 21,000-piece cathedral model that took 28 years to build. Is it art? Is it lunacy? Is it worth the $1 entry fee? Probably. You even get to hear a snatch of *Along the Road to Gundagai*. It was Frank Rusconi who made the Dog on the Tuckerbox memorial.

The **Gabriel Gallery** (☎ 6944 1722), above the Mitre 10 store on Sheridan St, has a free display of historic photos. The **Mt Parnassus lookout** has good views over the town and picnic facilities. It's reached by a steep walk (or drive) up Hanley St.

Special Events

The Snake Gully Cup, in mid-November, is Gundagai's annual race day and it coincides with the Dog on the Tuckerbox festival featuring a street parade and music. It's a great country event worth catching.

Places to Stay

On Middleton Drive by the river near the south end of the Prince Alfred Bridge, **Gundagai River Caravan Park** (☎ 6944 1702) has sites for $10 and vans for $20 a double. **Gundagai Caravan Village** (☎ 6944 1057), on Junee Rd near the swimming pool, has sites for $12 and cabins from $36.

Blue Heeler Guesthouse (☎ 6944 2286, ✉ blueheel@dragnet.com.au, 145 Sheridan St) is an excellent new backpackers lodge in the refurbished Hotel Gresham. It has good kitchen and lounge areas, a balcony overlooking the street, Internet access and free bikes. Dorm beds cost $15 and doubles are $20 per person, both including a light breakfast. The owners can help find seasonal work in the surrounding orchards and farms.

The **Criterion Hotel** (☎ 6944 1048, 172 Sheridan St) has pub rooms for $20 per person. Central motels include the **Sheridan** (☎ 6944 1311), corner of Sheridan and Otway Sts, with singles/doubles for $40/55, and the **Gundagai** (☎ 6944 1066), corner of Sheridan and West Sts, with rooms for $42/50.

Places to Eat

The 1902 **Niagara Cafe** has an illustrious history (former prime minister John Curtin once visited) and is something of a gem among country town cafes, although the menu doesn't differ much from standard snacks and grills. Steak meals cost $11.50 and it's licensed.

Lacey's on the Main (128 Sheridan St), is another interesting cafe in a former laundry. As well as pizza and pasta, you can get crocodile and emu burgers. There's a **bakery** on Sheridan St (supposedly the oldest still operating in Australia) and the **Chan Kong** Chinese restaurant.

Getting There & Away

The tourist office sells bus tickets for the services that stop outside. Greyhound Pioneer buses go to Melbourne and Sydney via Canberra, and V/Line buses also stop here between Melbourne and Canberra. Countrylink runs buses north to Cootamundra and south to Tumut and Tumbarumba.

HOLBROOK & AROUND
postcode 2644 • pop 1330

The Hume runs right through this small town and it's worth a look around – it's unlikely that you'll fail to see the submarine as you pass through! This is also the best place to turn off the highway for a drive through Morgan Country to the west (see

Holbrook & Submarines

Holbrook, founded in 1858, was called Germanton until WWI, when it was thought justified to display some patriotism and opt for a name change in honour of British naval commander, Douglas Holbrook. He and his crew earned the first Victoria Crosses (VCs) of the war when their submarine sank a Turkish ship near the Dardanelles. Germanton decided to adopt Holbrook's name.

Today, a 9m model of the vessel is on display and the town has enduring links with the Australian navy's submarine corps, which donated to the town a decommissioned submarine (the top part of which is on display in a town park near the model). Holbrook's wife has been over from Britain a number of times, maintaining another link. Occasional visits by official parties of sailors have seen some riotous times in the pubs.

All this in a town more than 250km from the sea!

The Riverina chapter for information on Morgan Country). A road runs east through pretty Wontagong Valley and past the **Hume & Hovell Walking Track** at Lankeys Creek (a nice picnic spot) to Jingellic and then on to Tumbarumba or Khancoban.

Holbrook's good **Woolpack Inn Museum** (☎ 6036 2131), at 83 Albury St (the name of the highway in town), is open daily from 9.30 am to 4.30 pm ($3/1). The museum also has tourist information.

Near the museum is a short walking track, the **Ian Geddes Bushwalk**, along the banks of Ten Mile Creek.

Places to Stay & Eat

The **Riverina Hotel** (☎ 6036 2523, 131 Albury St) has singles/doubles for $20/26. **Glendale Park** (☎ 6036 2599, 61 Albury St) is one of the cheaper motels with rooms for $43/50. The **Jolly Swagman Leisure Inn** (☎ 6036 3131), on the corner of Bardwell and Albury Sts, has rooms from $55/65 and its own squash court.

Several coffee shops line Albury St, including the **Holbrook Bakery**, open daily.

The pubs have cheap counter meals and there are meals at the **Returned Servicemen's Club** in Bowler St.

Several farms in the area offer accommodation. **Glenfalloch** (☎ 6036 7203), about 9km east of the Hume Hwy down a signposted turn-off 19km north of Holbrook, is a long-established sheep station. It's a beautiful place with big elms and 200 hectares of bush. The accommodation is in bunkrooms ($17 per person) and there's a good kitchen and common room. Camp sites are also available.

Getting There & Away

V/Line coaches between Canberra and Wodonga stop outside the Westpac Bank on Albury St, as do Greyhound Pioneer buses on the Sydney-Canberra-Melbourne run.

ALBURY

postcode 2640 • pop 42,500

Albury is a major regional centre on the Murray River, just below the big Hume Weir. The city makes a convenient stopover between Melbourne and Sydney and is a good base for trips to the Riverina, the Victorian wineries around Rutherglen, the Snowy Mountains and the Victorian high country.

History

Aboriginal tribes once gathered near Albury to plan their annual expeditions into the mountains to gather Bogong moths. Europeans were attracted to the area because the Murray River was fordable here. The explorers Hume and Hovell were the first Europeans to cross the river, which they named the Hume. Well, *Hume* named it the Hume – Hovell probably disagreed with such presumption. He contented himself with carving his name into a tree on the riverbank and a plaque marks his tree, which still stands in Noreuil Park. The river was renamed by Charles Sturt when he explored the area farther downstream.

A town grew up and became an important stop-over on the route between Sydney and Melbourne. In the 1850s paddle-steamers began carrying the area's wool clip down to South Australia (SA).

Orientation & Information

The long Lincoln Causeway over the Murray River's flood plain links Albury with Wodonga, on the Victorian side of the river. Central Albury is a reasonably compact grid, but the city sprawls northwards into the residential suburb of Laverton. Dean St, where you'll find the post office, is in the main shopping strip.

The Gateway Information Centre (☎ 1800 800 743, fax 6201 0322) is part of a large 'island' complex, which includes cafes, craft shops and a brewery/restaurant. It's on the Lincoln Causeway on the Victorian side of the river and stocks loads of information on NSW and Victoria, and books accommodation. It's open from 9 am to 5 pm daily.

Cyber Heaven (☎ 6023 4320), in Kiewa St, has Internet access for $3 for 15 minutes.

Things to See & Do

The **Albury Regional Museum** (☎ 6021 4550), on Wodonga Place in Noreuil Park, is open from 10.30 am to 4.30 pm daily (free). As well as material on Aboriginal culture and early European settlement, it features the Bonegilla collection covering post-war migration.

Albury Regional Art Centre (☎ 6023 8187), 546 Dean St, has a good collection of Australian paintings, including works by Russell Drysdale and Fred Williams, and contemporary photography. The centre is open from 10.30 am to 5 pm Monday to Friday and until 4 pm weekends (free).

The paddle-steamer *Cumberoona* (☎ 1800 800 743, 6041 5558), moored on the river behind Noreuil Park, isn't the original boat (which lies at the bottom of the Darling River). It's a replica built as a community project to celebrate Australia's Bicentenary of European settlement. One-hour trips run from Thursday to Sunday, September to March ($8/4.50 for adults/children).

The **Botanic Gardens**, beside the north end of Wodonga Place, are old, formal and

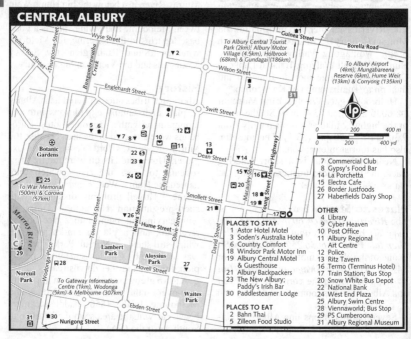

CENTRAL ALBURY

PLACES TO STAY
1 Astor Hotel Motel
3 Soden's Australia Hotel
6 Country Comfort
18 Windsor Park Motor Inn
   & Guesthouse
19 Albury Central Motel
   & Guesthouse
21 Albury Backpackers
23 The New Albury;
   Paddy's Irish Bar
30 Paddlesteamer Lodge

PLACES TO EAT
2 Bahn Thai
5 Zilleon Food Studio
7 Commercial Club
8 Gypsy's Food Bar
14 La Porchetta
15 Electra Cafe
26 Border Justfoods
27 Haberfields Dairy Shop

OTHER
4 Library
9 Cyber Heaven
10 Post Office
11 Albury Regional
   Art Centre
12 Police
13 Ritz Tavern
16 Termo (Terminus Hotel)
17 Train Station; Bus Stop
20 Snow White Bus Depot
22 National Bank
24 West End Plaza
25 Albury Swim Centre
28 Viennaworld; Bus Stop
29 PS Cumberoona
31 Albury Regional Museum

beautiful. The **Nail Can Hill Walking Track** rambles over the steep, bush-covered ridges on the western side of town. You can start from Noreuil Park or head up Dean St to the war memorial and pick up the trail there. The information centre has a map. The **Wiradjuri Walkabout** is an easy interpretive trail around Gateway Island starting from the information centre.

Zauril Aviation (☎ 6040 4950), at the airport, has sunrise **balloon flights** along the Riverina for $195.

Organised Tours

Mylon Motorways (☎ 6056 3100), 153 High St, Wodonga, runs trips including a half-day tour to Ettamogah ($28.50) and a full day in the Victorian Alps ($41). Grapevine Getaways (☎ 6023 2599) has tours to the Rutherglen wineries on weekends ($40, or $55 with lunch).

Albury Backpackers (☎ 6041 1822) has popular two-day canoe trips on the Murray River for $40. The less adventurous can take a half-day trip for $17.

Special Events

The Ngan Girra Festival is held at the Mungabareena Reserve in late November and celebrates the traditional Aboriginal gathering to feast on the Bogong moths. There's traditional music and dancing, workshops and a bushcraft display. The Albury-Wodonga Food & Wine Festival is a two-day gastronomic affair in early October.

Places to Stay

The closest caravan park to town, *Albury Central Tourist Park (☎ 6021 8420, 286 North St)* is nevertheless a couple of kilometres north of the centre. Tent sites cost $7 per person, cabins cost $38 and backpacker beds $14. *Albury Motor Village (☎ 6040 2999, 372 Wagga Rd)*, about 4.5km north of the centre, is a tidy park with pricey powered sites for $18 and cabins from $50 for two. This is also the YHA hostel, which has beds in clean dorms for $15. Local buses run past.

Albury Backpackers (☎ 6041 1822, 459 David St) is a well-run, central hostel with

dorm beds for $14 ($13 with VIP) and doubles for $32. It's just opened a newly renovated house across the road, so there are plenty of beds. As well as Internet access and free bikes, the management organises adventure activities and can help you find farm work in the area.

Soden's Australia Hotel (☎ 6021 2400), corner of Wilson and David Sts, has interesting leadlighting on its veranda. There's a warren of singles/doubles for $20/30 and equally basic rooms with bathroom for $30/40, both including continental breakfast. Rates are slightly higher on weekends.

The New Albury (☎ 6021 3599, 491 Kiewa St) has small but bright en suite rooms upstairs for $43/50. Some rooms have a balcony.

With 40 motels, Albury isn't short of rooms. Most are quite upmarket and cost upwards of $70/80, though when things are quiet many offer special rates.

Some cheaper, central motels include the *Windsor Park Motor Inn (☎ 6021 8800, 471 Young St)*, near the train station, with modern rooms for $60, and the nearby *Albury Central Motel & Guest House (☎ 6021 3127, 473 Young St)*, with more basic units from $49 a double with a light breakfast. The *Astor Hotel Motel (☎ 6021 1922)*, just north of the centre on the corner of the Hume Hwy and Guinea St, is good value at $39/49. It's part of a 24-hour pokie venue so it could be noisy.

Top places to stay include the *Country Comfort (☎ 6021 5366, fax 6041 2848)*, the tall semicircular landmark on the corner of Dean and Elizabeth Sts. Standard doubles cost $110, but there are weekend specials. *Paddlesteamer Lodge (☎ 1800 630 742, fax 6041 2161, 324 Wodonga Place)* has a pool and pleasant rooms for $87 a double.

Places to Eat

Dean St is a long strip of takeaways, cafes and restaurants. *Electra Cafe*, on the corner of Macauley St, is a trendy arthouse place with the odd household appliance stuck on the wall and a varied menu; sandwiches cost $4 and dinner mains around $15. *Gypsy's Food Bar* is a good spot for breakfast.

The *Commercial Club (618 Dean St)*, has a reputation for good food and the daily $8 self-serve buffet in the bistro is unbeatable.

La Porchetta, on the corner of Dean and David Sts, is an inexpensive pizza place with snappy service. Pasta dishes start at $6. *Paddy's Irish Bar*, at The New Albury, has a rather pricey menu of pub food (such as Guinness pie for $8), but the servings are generous.

The modern *Zilleon Food Studio (☎ 6021 8667)*, next to the Country Comfort, is an upmarket restaurant and bar with an innovative menu (mains from $22). *Bahn Thai (592 Kiewa St)*, in a beautiful Victorian house, is a good Thai restaurant open nightly. It's BYO and licensed.

Haberfields is a large dairy manufacturing a range of cheeses. You can buy them at *Haberfields Dairy Shop* on Hovell St, between David and Olive Sts. Most of the soft cheeses on sale come from elsewhere as Haberfields mainly produces cheddars and Swiss styles. You can go up to the viewing gallery in the factory and hear a commentary on the production of cheese and fruit juices while looking down on the machinery (thrilling stuff). *Border Justfoods* on Hume St sells a range of organic produce.

Entertainment

Albury's nightlife is mainly in pubs and clubs. *Paddy's Irish Bar*, in The New Albury on Kiewa St, is the latest hot spot and has your typical Irish theme bar ambience. The *Termo*, on the corner of Young and Dean Sts, has bands on weekends. The *Ritz Tavern (480 Dean St)*, has a nightclub (with tough dress regulations) on weekends. The *Commercial Club*, on Dean St, has a bar and a large area blinking and buzzing with poker machines.

Getting There & Away

Ansett Australia (☎ 13 1300), Kendell (☎ 6922 0100) and Hazelton (☎ 13 1713) airlines fly to Sydney ($235), Melbourne ($147) and Wagga Wagga ($98). Air Facilities (☎ 6041 1210) flies to Canberra ($159).

Long-distance buses running on the Hume Hwy between Sydney and Melbourne stop at the train station. Most also stop at Viennaworld (a petrol station/diner) across from Noreuil Park. Greyhound Pioneer stops only at Viennaworld and north of town at Laverton. You can book buses at the Countrylink Travel Centre (☎ 6041 9555) at the train station; it's open from 8.30 am to 5 pm weekdays and 9.30 am to 4.30 pm weekends.

Fearnes has coaches to Melbourne ($30, 4½ hours) and Wagga Wagga ($15, two hours); Greyhound has a run to Sydney ($47, 10 hours) via Canberra, and to Melbourne ($33, four hours). Countrylink runs to Echuca in Victoria via several towns in the southern Riverina three times a week. V/Line runs to Mildura ($55) and to Canberra ($25).

XPTs running between Sydney and Melbourne stop here. If you're travelling between the two capital cities, it's much cheaper to stop over in Albury on a through ticket than to buy two separate tickets. From Albury the one-way fare to Melbourne is $38.90 and to Sydney it's $81.

Getting Around

Mylon Motorways (☎ 6056 3100) has a city explorer bus that runs on a circuit through Albury and Wodonga. An unlimited day ticket costs $9.50 and you can pick up a route map from the information centre.

If you need a lift to some of the outlying areas, Snow White Bus Depot (☎ 6021 4368), 474 David St, is the pick-up point for mail, freight and passenger buses that run just about everywhere (eventually).

AROUND ALBURY

The **Ettamogah Wildlife Sanctuary**, 11km north on the Hume Hwy, is open from 9 am to 5 pm daily ($6/4 for adults/children) and has a collection of Aussie fauna including plenty of inquisitive grey kangaroos that you can feed. Most animals arrive sick or injured, so this is a genuine sanctuary. About 4km north, the lopsided **Ettamogah Pub** looms up near the highway. It's a real-life recreation of a famous Aussie cartoon pub that featured in the *Australasian Post* comic strip by Albury-born Ken Maynard. Some find it tacky and overrated, others stop and take a photo before vanishing up the highway, but it's worth popping in for a beer and a look around. There's a restaurant at the nearby **Ettamogah Winery**, which is over 100 years old – it was formerly Cooper's Winery.

About 15km farther north is **Bowna**, a town that has shrunk to a couple of buildings, including Jeff Leury's boomerang factory (☎ 6002 3240). At Bowna there's a turn-off to the *Great Aussie Camping Re-sort (☎ 6020 3236)* on the banks of the Hume Weir. This is a well-equipped but pricey place with powered sites ($15), on-site tents ($40), park units ($44) and rather elaborate self-contained 'squatter's huts' ($81). You can hire boats and there's horse riding and other activities. This road leads to **Wymah** (22km on), where you can cross by vehicle ferry to the Murray Valley Hwy on the other side of the river.

South Coast

Although it doesn't attract anywhere near as many visitors as the north coast, the south coast is well worth visiting.

As with the north coast, school-holiday periods (Christmas and Easter in particular) are the worst times to visit – accommodation gets tight and prices rise, and the beaches fill up with sun-loving families – but you can still find pockets of peaceful coastline and deserted forest at any time.

Geography & Climate
This area is a coastal strip of good beaches and bays backed by the mountains of the Great Dividing Range. South of Nowra the sandstone of the Sydney area gives way to granite and good soils, and the forests soar.

The south coast's climate is pretty good for most of the year – Batemans Bay is on an equivalent latitude to the French Riviera. You're unlikely to want to swim in winter, but summers are as hot as on the north coast and winter has its share of mild and sunny days.

Getting There & Around
Bus Nowra-based Premier Motor Service (☎ 13 3410) offers the most comprehensive services from Sydney to Eden (and on to Melbourne) and the cheapest sector fares. From Sydney fares include Batemans Bay ($30), Narooma ($40), Bega ($44) and Eden ($49). Two buses a day go as far as Eden.

Greyhound Pioneer also travels along the Princes Hwy daily between Sydney and Melbourne. Sapphire Coast Express (☎ 1800 812 135) runs from Batemans Bay through to Melbourne on Monday and Thursday only and Murrays (☎ 13 2251) has daily services between Nowra and Narooma and inland to Canberra.

Car & Motorcycle The Princes Hwy starts at Sydney's George St and continues all the way to Adelaide via Melbourne. It's known as the coastal route, but don't expect too many ocean views (although there are some

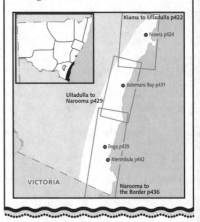

beauties): Most of the way the highway runs a little way inland. All along this route there are turn-offs to interesting places, both on the coast and up in the Great Dividing Range, where there's an almost unbroken chain of superb national parks and state forests. It's a longer, slower route between Sydney and Melbourne than the Hume Hwy, but it's infinitely more interesting.

Kiama to Ulladulla

Shoalhaven is a large municipality stretching from north of Nowra almost as far south as Batemans Bay. It takes in some great beaches, state forests and, in the ranges to the west, the big Morton National Park (see the Around Sydney chapter for more information).

This area is a popular family holiday destination, but it isn't yet as crowded as parts of the north coast and much of the tourism is confined to weekenders from Sydney.

There are regional tourist information centres in Nowra and Ulladulla, and you'll also find information on the Internet at www.shoalhaven.nsw.gov.au.

KIAMA & AROUND

postcode 2533 • pop 11,120

Kiama is a pretty town with some fine old buildings, good beaches and a sense of community. The Kiama Area Visitors Centre (☎ 4232 3322), on Blowhole Point, is open 9 am to 5 pm daily. It's near the town's major attraction, the **Blowhole**, which has drawn visitors for a century and is now floodlit at night. Beside the visitors centre is the **Pilot's Cottage Museum**, open 11 am to 3 pm Friday to Monday ($2/1 for adults/children).

The **Terrace** on Collins St is a neat strip of restored houses that date back to 1886 and are now mostly occupied by craft shops.

There's a good **lookout** from the top of Saddleback Mountain, just behind the town. From Manning St, turn right onto Saddleback Mountain Rd. There's a small enclosed **surf beach** right in town and the broad **Werri Beach**, 10km south in Gerringong.

Minnamurra Rainforest Park

This park is on the eastern edge of **Budderoo National Park** (☎ 4423 9800), about 14km inland from Kiama. There's a National Parks & Wildlife Service (NPWS) visitor centre (☎ 4236 0469) from where you can take a 1.6km loop walk on a boardwalk through the rainforest. There's a secondary 2.6km walk to the Minnamurra Falls. Admission is $9/3 per car/motorcycle, and the visitors centre sells NPWS national park passes.

On the way to Minnamurra you'll pass through the old village of **Jamberoo**, which has a nice pub.

Places to Stay

Next to the visitors centre, **Blowhole Point Caravan Park** (☎ 4232 2707) is in a terrific location if it's not too windy. It has pricey sites from $16 and on-site vans from $40.

Kiama Backpackers (☎/fax 4233 1881, 31 Bong Bong St), in the nondescript brown-brick building next to the Grand Hotel, has the usual facilities, including Internet access ($5 an hour) and free use of bikes. Dorm beds cost $15, singles are good value at $20 and doubles are $35 ($40 on weekends).

Several pubs have accommodation, including the **Grand Hotel** (☎ 4232 1037, 49 Manning St), on the corner of Bong Bong St, with small but clean singles/doubles for $25/35.

Kiama Beachfront (☎ 4232 1533, 87 Manning St), opposite the surf beach, is one of the less expensive motels in town with rooms for $45/55 ($55/65 on weekends).

Places to Eat

There are plenty of restaurants and cafes along Terralong St (the main street). The **Leagues Club** has good-value bistro meals from $7. **Cafe J**, around the corner on Collins St, is a popular place with meals for around $10.

Getting There & Away

Long-distance buses stop in Kiama (but only if there's a booking) outside the Leagues Club on Terralong St. Kiama Coachlines (☎ 4232 3455) runs out to Gerringong and Minnamurra (via Jamberoo).

Frequent CityRail trains run north to Wollongong and Sydney ($11.40) and south to Gerringong and Bomaderry/Nowra ($2).

BERRY

postcode 2535 • pop 1100

Inland and about 20km north of Nowra is the surprisingly pretty little town of Berry. Founded in the 1820s, it remained a private town on the Coolangatta Estate (see Around Nowra later in this chapter for more

KIAMA TO ULLADULLA

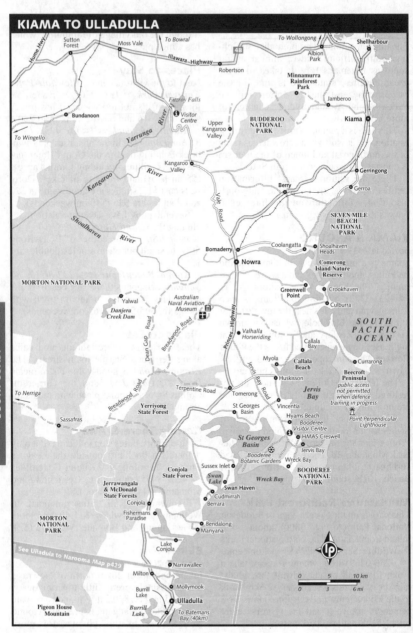

SOUTH COAST

information) until 1912. Berry's short main street (Queen St) is worth a stroll for its National-Trust-classified buildings and interesting shops and cafes.

Pottering Around (☎ 4464 2177), in the Berry Stores complex on Queen St, has some tourist information.

The **museum**, near the post office on Queen St, is in an interesting old building but it's only open 11 am to 2 pm Saturday and to 3 pm Sunday and holidays. Among the several **antique shops**, Berry Antiques stands out.

The popular **Berry Country Fair** is held on the first Sunday of the month at the showgrounds. There are several **wineries** in the area and the Berry Hotel runs a short but exceptionally good-value wine tour on Saturday at 11 am for $12.

Jasper Valley Winery (☎ 4464 1596) is only 5km south of Berry, and is open for tastings and lunches.

Places to Stay

For a small town Berry has some wonderful accommodation options, and the wandering weekenders take full advantage. Prices are between 10% and 50% higher on weekends and you'll almost certainly have to book ahead.

The *Hotel Berry* (☎ 4464 1011, 120 Queen St) is a rarity – a country pub that caters to weekending city slickers without totally losing its status as a local watering hole. Singles/doubles cost $35/50 ($45/60 on weekends). The rooms are standard pub bedrooms, but large and well presented. Why can't more pubs be like this?

The *Great Southern Hotel* (☎ 4464 1009), a newer place built in an old style, is something different again with some eccentric embellishments such as the hub-cap collection. It has motel singles/doubles at the back for $30/60.

The excellent *Bunyip Inn Guesthouse* (☎ 4464 2064, 122 Queen St), next to the Berry Hotel, is in one of the town's more impressive buildings: an old bank. There's a variety of rooms from $85/110 weekdays/weekends, including breakfast. En suite rooms start at $140/170 a double.

Nightwinds (☎ 4464 1845, 44 Clarence St) is a comfortable self-contained apartment in a friendly home with B&B for $95 a double (cheaper on weekdays).

Places to Eat

There are several cafes, including the *Postman's Ghost Coffee Lounge*, next to the museum, which has an outdoor seating area. *Berry Jetz*, opposite Berry Shops, is a health-oriented vegetarian cafe open Thursday to Monday. *Hotel Berry* has a nice courtyard dining area and meals above the usual pub standard for $10 to $18.

Salmon & Co (☎ 4464 3037), on Albert St, is one of a number of very good a la carte restaurants in town with mains for under $20.

Getting There & Away

Premier buses between Kiama and Nowra stop here on request. The main road to Kangaroo Valley and Mittagong leaves the Princes Hwy south of Berry, but there's also a scenic route to Kangaroo Valley from Berry via Woodhill and Wattamolla.

NOWRA

postcode 2541 • pop 25,000
The largest town in the Shoalhaven area, Nowra is a centre for the area's dairy farms and its increasing tourism and retirement development. It's a fairly dull town and is not, as many people expect, on the coast – the nearest beach is at Shoalhaven Heads, about 17km east. It is, however, a handy base for excursions to beaches and villages around Jervis Bay, north to Berry and inland to Kangaroo Valley and Morton National Park.

Information

The new Shoalhaven Visitor Centre (☎ 1800 024 261) is just south of the bridge over the Shoalhaven River and has copious amounts of information on the district. The post office is on the corner of Junction and Berry Sts in central Nowra. At the civic library (☎ 4429 3709), across the road at 10 Berry St, you can access the Internet for $2 an hour.

There's an NPWS office (☎ 4423 2170) at 55 Graham St.

SOUTH COAST

Things to See & Do

The 6.5-hectare **Nowra Animal Park**
(☎ 4421 3949), on the north bank of the
Shoalhaven River, is a pleasant place to
meet some native animals. It's open 9 am to
5 pm daily ($7/4 for adults/children). Head
north from Nowra, cross the bridge and immediately turn left, then branch left onto
McMahons Rd at the roundabout; turn left
again at Rockhill Rd.

Nowra Museum (☎ 4421 2021), at the
corner of Kinghorne and Plunkett Sts, is
open 1 to 4 pm on weekends ($1). **Meroogal**
(☎ 4421 8150), on the corner of West and

Worrigee Sts, is an historic house containing
the artefacts accumulated by its generations
of owners. It's open 1 to 5 pm on Saturday
and 10 am to 5 pm on Sunday ($6/3).

If you're at all interested in planes and helicopters, the **Australian Naval Aviation Museum** (☎ 4421 1920), 10km south of Nowra
at an operational airfield, has an excellent
display, including a Sopwith Camel WWI
biplane and a Douglas Dakota, which you
can climb into. The museum is open 10 am to
4 pm daily ($6/2). Also here is **Nowra Sky-
dive** (☎ 0500 885 556), where you can make
a tandem jump from over 3000m for $280.

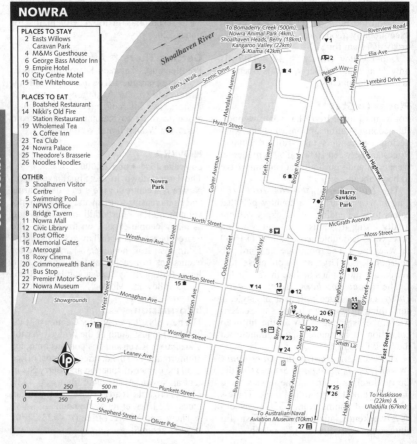

NOWRA

PLACES TO STAY
2 Easts Willows
   Caravan Park
4 M&Ms Guesthouse
6 George Bass Motor Inn
9 Empire Hotel
10 City Centre Motel
15 The Whitehouse

PLACES TO EAT
1 Boatshed Restaurant
14 Nikki's Old Fire
   Station Restaurant
19 Wholemeal Tea
   & Coffee Inn
23 Tea Club
24 Nowra Palace
25 Theodore's Brasserie
26 Noodles Noodles

OTHER
3 Shoalhaven Visitor
   Centre
5 Swimming Pool
7 NPWS Office
8 Bridge Tavern
11 Nowra Mall
12 Civic Library
13 Post Office
16 Memorial Gates
17 Meroogal
18 Roxy Cinema
20 Commonwealth Bank
21 Bus Stop
22 Premier Motor Service
27 Nowra Museum

Walks

The visitors centre produces a handy compilation of walks in the area. The pleasant **Ben's Walk** starts at the bridge near Scenic Dr and follows the south bank of the Shoalhaven River (6km return). North of the river, the 5.5km **Bomaderry Creek Walking Track** runs through sandstone gorges from a trailhead at the end of Narang Rd.

Cruises

Shoalhaven River Cruises (☎ 4447 1978) has tours up this beautiful river on Wednesday and Sunday for $17/8. They leave from the wharf just east of the bridge near the visitor centre.

Horse Riding

Valhalla Trail Rides (☎ 4447 8320) near Falls Creek, 13km south of Nowra, charges $20 for an hour of horse riding and $50 for a day ride. There's also an archery range and rustic but good-value accommodation.

Places to Stay

Camping options include *Easts Willows Caravan Park (☎ 4421 2977)*, off the highway close to the bridge (and thus noisy), but also right on the river. It has sites for $14 and cabins for $41. The *Nowra Animal Park (☎ 4421 3949)* has tent sites in riverside bushland for $5 per person ($9 at peak times).

Nowra has two excellent guesthouses catering to a range of budgets, including backpackers. *M&Ms Guesthouse (☎ 4422 8006, 1a Scenic Dr)* is a wonderfully rustic place in a good location near the river. Singles/doubles in spotless rooms with shared facilities cost $40/45, including a buffet continental breakfast. Backpackers can stay in the equally good bunk rooms for $20, including breakfast. There are common rooms, including a games room with jukebox and pool table, and an outdoor barbecue area.

The Whitehouse (☎ 4421 2084, 30 Junction St) is a beautifully restored guesthouse operated by a friendly family. Rooms with shared facilities in the house are good value at $45/65 with breakfast, and there's a five-bed dorm at the back for $20 per person.

The *Empire Hotel (☎ 4421 2433)* is an ugly cream-brick building on the corner of Kinghorne and North Sts with rooms for $25/35.

The *City Centre Motel (☎ 4421 3455, 16 Kinghorne St)*, next door, is ageing but it's centrally located and a good deal at $42/52. The *George Bass Motor Inn (☎ 4421 6388, 65 Bridge Rd)* is one of many higher standard motels with rooms from $70/75.

Places to Eat

The *Wholemeal Tea & Coffee Inn* is a cosy place in an alley running into Stewart Place from Junction St. It's open during the day on weekdays. You can get snacks, Mexican and Lebanese dishes.

The *Tea Club (46 Berry St)* is a trendy little cafe that's open till 11 pm Tuesday to Saturday. There are informal jam sessions here on Friday nights.

Nikki's Old Fire Station Restaurant (☎ 4423 3433, 55 Junction St) is a good pasta and pizza place in the 1908 fire station not far from The Whitehouse.

The *Nowra Palace (☎ 4422 1067)*, on the corner of Berry and Worrigee Sts, serves Malaysian and Chinese food, with lunch specials for $5. *Noodles Noodles* on Kinghorne St does a pretty good bowl of – what else – noodles; laksa costs $8.

The upmarket *Boatshed Restaurant (☎ 4421 2419)*, overlooking the river just next to the bridge, is the place to go for a meal with a view. It has a bar and a cafe and is open 11 am to 1 am daily. *Theodore's Brasserie (☎ 4421 0300)*, next to Noodles Noodles, is another recommended place.

Getting There & Away

Premier Motor Service's depot is in Stewart Place; it runs bus services north to Sydney ($16, three hours) and south to Melbourne. Greyhound Pioneer runs daily to Sydney and Melbourne, stopping at the Nowra Mall.

Several local bus companies run to various destinations in the area. The visitor centre has timetables.

The train station (☎ 4421 2022) is at Bomaderry. Frequent CityRail trains go to Sydney ($13.40, 2½ hours).

SOUTH COAST

The Princes Hwy runs north to Kiama (42km) and south to Ulladulla (67km), with several turn-offs to Jervis Bay. An interesting and mainly unsealed road runs from Nowra to Braidwood, through Morton National Park and the hamlets of Sassafras and Nerriga. At the south end of Kinghorne St take Albatross Rd, which veers off to the right.

AROUND NOWRA

East of Nowra, the Shoalhaven River meanders through dairy country in a system of estuaries and wetlands, finally reaching the sea at Crookhaven Heads.

Greenwell Point, on the estuary about 15km east of Nowra, is a quiet, pretty, fishing village specialising in fresh oysters. *DJ's*, near the wharf, and *Backgate Seafood* sell oysters (and will also open them) and fish and chips. On the way there from Nowra you'll pass the **Jindyandy Mill**, a convict-built flour mill that is now a craft centre. Farther around the inlet at **Crookhaven Heads** there's a beach and walking tracks leading to a lighthouse.

On the north side of the estuary is **Shoalhaven Heads**, where the river once reached the sea but is now blocked by sandbars. Just north of the beach here is the **Seven Mile Beach National Park** stretching up to Gerroa.

Just before Shoalhaven Heads you pass through **Coolangatta**, the site of the earliest European settlement on the south coast. **Coolangatta Estate** (☎ 4448 7131) is a slick winery with a golf course, a good restaurant and expensive accommodation (from $82/91 for singles/doubles weekdays) in convict-built buildings. You can sample the wines from 10 am to 5 pm daily. The wine is made from grapes grown here but vintaged at Tyrrells in the Hunter Valley.

JERVIS BAY

Despite extensive housing development, this large, sheltered bay retains its clean, white beaches and crystal-clear water (no large rivers flow into it). Dolphins are regularly seen, and whales sometimes drop in when swimming past on their annual migrations from June to October.

In 1995 the Aboriginal community won a land claim in the Wreck Bay area and now jointly administers the Booderee National Park (formerly Jervis Bay National Park – *Booderee* means 'plenty of fish') at the southern end of the bay.

Most development in Jervis Bay is on the south-western shore, around the towns of Huskisson and Vincentia. The northern shore is much less developed and state forest backs onto the beaches at **Callala Bay**. There are caravan parks near here. Despite the close proximity of Callala Beach, south of Callala Bay, to Huskisson, there's no way of crossing Currambene Creek – you have to drive back out to the highway and head south (which is just the way the locals like it). **Beecroft Peninsula** forms the north-eastern side of Jervis Bay. Most of the peninsula is navy land, which is off limits to civilians, but **Currarong**, near Beecroft Head, is a small town with camping at *Currarong Tourist Park* (☎ 4448 3027).

Huskisson
postcode 2540 • pop 3300
With much of this area turning into a sprawl of holiday homes, it's surprising that Huskisson, the oldest town on Jervis Bay, still has the feel of a small fishing port and a sense of community.

The **Lady Denman Heritage Complex** (☎ 4441 5675), by the bay on the Nowra side of Huskisson, includes an interesting maritime museum and the *Lady Denman*, a ferry dating from 1912. Also here is Timbey's Aboriginal Arts & Crafts, which displays and sells work produced on site by the local Koori community. There's also a boardwalk through wetlands. The museum is open 1 to 4 pm Tuesday to Friday and 10 am to 4 pm weekends and holidays ($3/1.50 for adults/children); the rest of the complex is open 9 am to 5 pm daily.

South of Huskisson, **Hyams Beach** is a spectacularly white stretch of reasonably secluded sand.

Cruises Two companies operate dolphin and whale-watching (June to November) cruises. Dolphin Watch Cruises (☎ 1800 246 010) has several trips, starting at $20/10 for two hours. Baywatch Cruises (☎ 1800 444 330) also visits a seal colony ($40/18) and has a three-hour twilight cruise ($36/16). Both have offices on Owen St (the main street).

Diving Jervis Bay is popular with divers and at least two places in Huskisson offer diving and courses. Pro Dive (☎ 4441 5255), 64 Owen St, charges $35 for a boat dive or $65 for two dives, plus equipment hire (about $35 for a full set). You can do a Professional Association of Diving Instructors (PADI) open-water dive course for $250. Sea Sports (☎ 4441 5012), also on Owen St, has similar rates and also runs cruises. There are some good wreck dives in the bay.

Places to Stay The Shoalhaven Council's *Huskisson Beach Tourist Resort (☎ 1800 676 433)* has a great location right on the beach. It's a little way out of Huskisson on the road to Vincentia. There are several other caravan parks in the area. There's quite a lot of guesthouse and motel accommodation in Huskisson and Vincentia (which more or less merge into one), but book ahead on weekends.

The two-storey *Huskisson Beach Motel (☎ 4441 6387, 9 Hawke St)* overlooks the beach and has singles/doubles from $55/60; the rates more than triple in peak periods. The *Husky Pub (☎ 4441 5001)*, on Owen St, has rooms for $30/55 (more during holidays).

Booderee National Park

This national park occupies Jervis Bay's south-eastern spit. It's an interesting park offering good swimming, surfing and diving on bay and ocean beaches. Much of it is heathland, with some forest, including small pockets of rainforest. It's administered by the federal government jointly with the Wreck Bay Aboriginal Community, and it's home to the naval training base HMAS Creswell (☎ 4429 7845). The base is open to visitors for a short 'drive through' on weekends and you may be able to visit its museum.

There's a good visitors centre (☎ 4443 0977) at the park entrance with walking trail maps and information on camping. In-side the park is the **Booderee Botanic Gardens**, open 8.30 am to 5 pm daily, with a number of walks in varying environments.

There are many walking trails around the park and some good secluded beaches. Be careful on the cliff tops as apparently people occasionally fall off. After walking in the park check for ticks, which are common. Although Wreck Bay is a closed community, you can experience some Aboriginal culture with a local guide on Barry's Bush Tucker Tours (☎ 4442 1168). The program of tours varies so call first.

Entry to the park costs $5/2 per car/ motorcycle and is valid for a week (NPWS passes are not valid). There are camp sites at Green Patch ($13 to $16) and Bristol Point, and a more basic camping area at Caves Beach ($8 to $10). You have to book and sites might not be available at peak times.

JERVIS BAY TO ULLADULLA

The southern peninsula of Jervis Bay encircles **St Georges Basin**, a large body of water that has access to the sea through narrow Sussex Inlet. The north shore of the basin has succumbed to housing developments reminiscent of the suburban sprawl on the Central Coast.

Farther along is pretty **Lake Conjola**, with a quiet town of holiday shacks and a couple of caravan parks; the *Lake Conjola Entrance Tourist Park (☎ 4456 1141)* is the closest to the ocean.

Milton, on the highway 6km north of Ulladulla, is this area's original town, built to serve the nearby farming communities. Like so many early towns in this coastal region, Milton was built several kilometres inland – how tastes have changed! There are several cafes and a few antique shops on the main street (the Princes Hwy) and it gets pretty busy here on weekends. *Pilgrim's Wholefood* has healthy lunches and coffee.

ULLADULLA
postcode 2539 • pop 11,300

Ulladulla isn't an especially attractive town but it has excellent beaches and is close to Pigeon House Mountain in the far south of Morton National Park, and to Budawang

SOUTH COAST

National Park. It's also the largest town on the highway between Nowra and Batemans Bay.

Orientation & Information
Ulladulla is on rocky Warden Head, but a short walk north of Ulladulla harbour is Mollymook, a suburb on a lovely surf beach.

Burrill Lake, a few kilometres south of Ulladulla, is a small town on the inlet to the lake of the same name.

Ulladulla's visitors centre (☎ 4455 1269), in the Civic Centre opposite the harbour, is open 9 am to 5 pm weekdays and 10 am to 5 pm weekends. The library, in the same building, has Internet access for $1 per half hour. It's open 10 am to 7 pm weekdays and 9 am to noon on Saturday.

Things to See & Do
The **Coomee Nulunga Cultural Trail** is a walking trail in town, established by the local Aboriginal Land Council. It begins near the Lighthouse Oval (take Deering St east of the highway) and follows the headland through native bush to the beach.

Climbing **Pigeon House Mountain** (720m) in the far south of Morton National Park is an enjoyable challenge. A road runs close to the summit, from where it's a walk of four hours to the top and back. The first hour's walk from the car park is a steady climb, but after that it levels out a little. The main access road to Pigeon House Mountain leaves the highway about 8km south of Ulladulla, then it's 26km to the car park.

Ulladulla Divers Supplies (☎ 4455 5303), on Wason St (the street leading down to the fishing wharf), runs **dive courses** and offers single boat dives for $28 ($70 if you need gear). Shoalhaven Dive Adventures (☎ 4454 1289) has boat dives from $25. Murramarang Wildtrails (☎ 4457 2022), based at Termeil, organises 4WD and mountain biking **tours**. Bike tours start at $35 for three-hours.

There's a good 36-hole **golf course** (☎ 4455 1911) at Mollymook; the beachside nine costs $12 and club hire is $8.

Special Events
At Easter there is a Blessing of the Fleet ceremony and local celebrations. In late August there's a Food & Wine Fair. In nearby Milton, the Settlers Fair is held on the first holiday Monday in early October.

Places to Stay
The **Ulladulla Tourist Park** (☎ 4455 2457) is on the headland a few blocks from the town centre (at the end of South St) but a bit of a walk from the beach. Sites cost from $13 and cabins range from $35 to $120.

South Coast Backpackers (☎/fax 4454 0500, 63 Princes Hwy) is north of the shopping centre. It's a small, clean place with spacious five-bed dorms. Dorm beds cost $17; doubles cost $37. Staff run trips to Murramarang National Park or Pigeon House Mountain for $15, and to Jervis Bay for snorkelling. You can hire bikes for $10.

Hotel Marlin (☎ 4455 1999), on the corner of the highway and Wason St, is central, loud and has standard pub singles/doubles for $20/40.

Ulladulla has plenty of motels. **Top View Motel** (☎ 4455 1514, 72 South St) has a good location overlooking the town and is possibly one of the friendliest motels on the south coast. Rooms start at $45/50 and there are self-contained units (one for backpackers at $20 per person). **Quiet Garden Motel** (☎ 4455 1757, 2 Burrill St), in a quiet spot overlooking the beach and harbour, has rooms for $50/55.

Mollymook, 2km north of Ulladulla, is a nice place to stay thanks to its proximity to a good beach. Most motels are pricey during holiday periods but reasonable at other times. **Seaspray** (☎ 4455 5311, 70 Ocean St), close to the beach, has rooms from $75/85, and there are some cheaper places up on the hill near the highway.

Following the beachfront road north through Mollymook you rise up onto the headland and come to **Bannisters Point Lodge** (☎ 4455 3044, 191 Mitchell Parade), a motel with superb views of the coast and ocean. Rates start at $75 a double ($100 on weekends). It has a licensed restaurant.

Places to Eat
There are plenty of coffee shops and pasta places on Ulladulla's main street and in the

arcades running off it. The *Coffee House*, in Rowen's Arcade, is good for light lunches and cakes. *Tony's Italian*, on Wason St, has pasta and pizza from $6.

You can't beat the *Milton-Ulladulla Bowling Club*, near the tourist office, for value meals – lunches cost as little as $2. *Soba*, in the Pavilion Centre opposite the visitor centre, is a trendy mixed Asian place (including Japanese and Thai) with mains from $8, lunch specials for $6 and sushi on Wednesday.

Down at the harbour, *Fisherman's Wharf Seafood* is the place to buy fresh fish, and across the road on Wason St *Tory's Seafood Restaurant* is a good licensed restaurant.

Harbourside Restaurant (☎ 4455 3377) has nice views overlooking the harbour and some interesting seafood dishes such as mango prawns ($13) and Balinese fish curry ($19.50). It's licensed to serve alcohol or you can bring your own (BYO) wine.

Cookaburra's (☎ 4454 1443, 10 Wason St) is a recommended restaurant with a cosy atmosphere and mains for around $22. It's BYO, but oyster shooters (with vodka) are a speciality at $2.50.

Getting There & Away

Buses stop on the highway outside the Marlin Hotel (northbound) or Traveland (southbound). Ticket agents are Traveland (☎ 4455 1588) and Harvey World Travel (☎ 4455 5122), in Powers Arcade.

Priors Scenic Express (☎ 1800 816 234) is a good bus to catch if you want to get off at the smaller places such as Milton, Burrill Lake, Tabourie Lake or Termeil. It continues on to Narooma.

Getting Around

Ulladulla Bus Lines (☎ 4455 1674) services the local area, mainly between Milton, Mollymook, Ulladulla and Burrill Lake. There are two services each weekday.

Far South Coast

The far south coast is the least developed stretch of coast in the state and it has some of the best beaches and forests. The population triples during holiday times, especially in the Eurobodalla area (from Batemans Bay to Narooma), and prices rise accordingly. As well as the beaches and inlets, with swimming, surfing and fishing, there are good walks in the national parks and whale watching during the migrating season. The Sapphire Coast, stretching from Bermagui to Eden, is a popular holiday area centred on Merimbula.

The visitors centres in Batemans Bay and Narooma sell topographic maps and copies of Graham Barrow's book *Walking on the*

South Coast, which details mainly short walks between Nowra and Eden. There are NPWS offices in Narooma (☎ 4476 2888) and Merimbula (☎ 6495 5000).

The Ulladulla to Narooma and Narooma to the Border maps apply to this section.

MURRAMARANG NATIONAL PARK

This beautiful coastal park begins about 20km south of Ulladulla and extends almost all the way south to Batemans Bay.

Merry, Pebbly and Depot Beaches are all popular with surfers, as is Wasp Head south of Durras. There are numerous walking trails snaking off from these beach areas and a steep but enjoyable walk up Durras Mountain (283m). If you stay overnight you'll have to pay the park entry fee of $7.50 per car plus any camping fees.

Places to Stay

In the Park The NPWS *Pebbly Beach camp site (☎ 4478 6006)* is in a lovely spot. Sites cost $10 a double and are scarce during school holidays, so you should book. *Pebbly Beach Holiday Cabins (☎ 4478 6023)* charges from $60 a night (minimum two nights) and has reasonable weekly rates.

To get to Pebbly Beach, turn off the highway onto North Durras Rd south of East Lynne – avoid Pebbly Beach Rd, which is very rough. Caravans can't be taken on the last section of the road to Pebbly Beach.

The NPWS *Depot Beach camping area (☎ 4478 6582)* has tent sites for $10 and cabins from $50 a night ($90 in peak season). There's a basic bush camping site (free) in the far south of the park at North Head Beach; turn off the highway at Benandarah and follow North Head Rd.

Nearby Settlements There are small towns on the borders of the park and one or two on old leases within the park itself. If camp sites in the park are booked out you could try these places.

Turn off the highway at Termeil to get to **Bawley Point** and **Kioloa**, near the north end of the park. There are caravan parks in these small towns, and just south of Kioloa are

caravan parks at **Merry Beach** and **Pretty Beach**, both privately run. They're reasonable places and the beaches are excellent, but they lack the steep and forested slopes behind the beaches that you'll find farther south.

Take the East Lynne turn-off from the highway to get to **North Durras**, on the inlet to Durras Lake. There's not much here except a lovely beach and six million caravans squeezed into three abutting caravan parks. *Durras Lake North Caravan Park (☎ 4478 6072)* has a cabin or an on-site van set aside for backpackers and charges $10 a bed.

In the south of the park (turn off the highway at Benandarah), **Durras** is a quiet village of substantial holiday houses. At the south end of the town is *Murramarang Resort (☎ 4478 6355)*. It's a big, modern place with pricey tent sites (from $18 to $35), onsite vans (from $44) and cabins (from $62). Prices rise considerably during holidays. It also has lots of activities and even 'floorshow' entertainment!

Getting There & Away

The Princes Hwy runs parallel to Murramarang but it's about 10km from the highway to the beaches or the small settlements in and near the park. There's no public transport into the park but Priors buses stop on the highway at Termeil, East Lynne and Benandarah. Staff at the backpacker hostel in Ulladulla will drive guests to Pebbly Beach for $15.

BATEMANS BAY
postcode 2536 • pop 7500

Batemans Bay is a fishing port that has boomed to become one of the south coast's largest holiday centres, partly because of its good beaches and beautiful estuary and partly because it's the closest coastal town to land-locked Canberra.

Information

The large visitors centre (☎ 1800 802 528) is on the Princes Hwy opposite McDonald's. It's open 9 am to 5 pm daily. Neville's Cafe on Orient St is a convenient place to access the Internet.

Things to See & Do

The **Old Courthouse Museum** (☎ 4472 8993), on Museum Place just off Orient St, has displays relating to local history. It's open 1 to 4 pm Tuesday and Thursday and admission is steep at $5/1 for adults/children. Just behind the museum is the small Water Garden Town Park and a **boardwalk** through wetlands.

On the north side of the estuary just across the bridge (if you're driving you'll have to keep going to the Canberra turn-off and take the first left) there are a couple of **boat hire** places. Oyster Shed Boat Hire

(☎ 4472 6771) hires out runabouts from $40 for two hours. You can hire canoes, surf skis and sail boats from the shed next to Jameson's on the Pier restaurant.

Several boats offer **cruises** up the Clyde River estuary from the ferry wharf just east of the bridge. The standard three-hour cruise stops at Nelligen, costs $18/9 and you can have lunch on board (usually fish and chips). There are also sea cruises, during which you might see penguins at the Tollgate Islands Nature Reserve in the bay.

Birdland Animal Park (☎ 4472 5364), on Beach Rd near Batehaven, is open 9.30 am

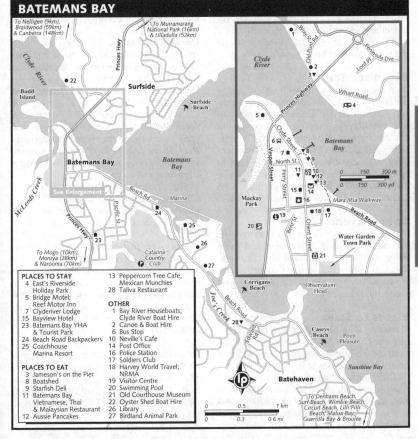

BATEMANS BAY

PLACES TO STAY
4 East's Riverside
   Holiday Park
5 Bridge Motel;
   Reef Motor Inn
7 Clyderiver Lodge
15 Bayview Hotel
23 Batemans Bay YHA
   & Tourist Park
24 Beach Road Backpackers
25 Coachhouse
   Marina Resort

PLACES TO EAT
3 Jameson's on the Pier
8 Boatshed
9 Starfish Deli
11 Batemans Bay
   Vietnamese, Thai
   & Malaysian Restaurant
12 Aussie Pancakes

13 Peppercorn Tree Cafe;
   Mexican Munchies
28 Taliva Restaurant

OTHER
1 Bay River Houseboats;
   Clyde River Boat Hire
2 Canoe & Boat Hire
6 Bus Stop
10 Neville's Cafe
14 Post Office
16 Police Station
17 Soldiers Club
18 Harvey World Travel;
   NRMA
19 Visitor Centre
20 Swimming Pool
21 Old Courthouse Museum
22 Oyster Shed Boat Hire
26 Library
27 Birdland Animal Park

SOUTH COAST

to 4 pm daily ($9/5). It has snake and wombat displays and koala feeding.

Beaches

Corrigans Beach is the closest beach to the town centre. South of Corrigans Beach is a series of small beaches nibbled into the rocky shore. There are longer beaches along the coast north of the bridge, leading into Murramarang National Park.

Surfers flock to Surf Beach, Malua Bay, the small McKenzies Beach (just south of Malua Bay) and Broulee, which has a small wave when everywhere else is flat. For the experienced, the best surfing in the area is at Pink Rocks (near Broulee) when a north swell is running. Locals say the waves are sometimes 6m high. Broulee itself has a wide crescent of sand but there's a strong rip at the northern end.

Organised Tours

Two good guided tours (☎ 1800 802 528) are run by and leave from the visitors centre. The Eco Walk'n'Cruise is on Thursday and Saturday and includes a forest walk and river cruise covering the local oyster-farming industry ($16/9). The Discovery Tour is on Tuesday and includes a visit to Mogo village ($12/6). Oz Trek (☎ 4471 1683) has 4WD tours into the forests and coastal parks for $60/110 a half/full day.

Special Events

The Batemans Bay Festival is held over the second weekend in November, and there are game-fishing tournaments in February and May. Up in Nelligen, a Country Music Festival twangs along during the first weekend in January.

Places to Stay

Camping The big *East's Riverside Holiday Park* (☎ 4472 4048), on Wharf Rd just north of the bridge, has sites from $15 and en suite cabins from $50.

There are several caravan parks along the coast road south of town. *Coachhouse Marina Resort* (☎ 1800 670 715, 49 Beach Rd) is a well-equipped park at the beginning of Corrigans Beach. Sites cost $16, cabins start

at $35 a double and there are some great little Queenslanders (a style of weatherboard home) from $75, plus a range of deluxe cabins. There's also a good bar/restaurant and a pool.

Hostels The friendly *Beach Road Backpackers* (☎ 4472 3644, 92 Beach Rd) is a comfortable hostel in a converted house opposite the marina. Dorm beds cost $16.

Batemans Bay YHA (☎ 4472 4972) is in the Batemans Bay Tourist Park on the Old Princes Hwy just south of the centre. There's a backpacker section with dorm beds for $16, twins for $18 per person, a TV room and kitchen. There are also bikes and canoes for hire. Both hostels organise various tours.

Hotels & Motels The *Bayview Hotel* (☎ 4472 4522, 20 Orient St), in the town centre, has backpacker accommodation. Singles/doubles cost $15/25.

There are many motels. The *Bridge Motel* (☎ 4472 6344, 29 Clyde St) is a good, central mid-range place. Off-season rates are about $65 for a double, or $80 for the balcony rooms facing the river. Next door, the *Reef Motor Inn* (☎ 4477 6000) has rooms from $77/87; prices more than double at Christmas and Easter.

The *Clyderiver Lodge* (☎ 4472 6444, 3 Clyde St), opposite the wharf, is a cheaper place with doubles from $55, or $60 for the sea view rooms.

Rental Accommodation There are many holiday apartments that do good business in summer. Out of season you might be able to rent one for less than a week. Letting agents include The Professionals (☎ 1800 808 054) – they have a Web site at www.bayproperty.com.au – and Ray White Real Estate (☎ 4472 4799).

Houseboats On the north side of the river on Wray St, *Bay River Houseboats* (☎ 4472 5649) hires out eight- and 10-berth houseboats. From May to August (low season) an eight-berth boat costs $520 for four nights (Monday to Friday) and $550 for the weekend, or $800 for a full week. This almost doubles in December and January. Shared between a few people this is good value in the shoulder season, and a great way to get around. *Clyde River Boat Hire (☎ 4472 6369)*, also on Wray St, also hires out houseboats for about the same rates.

Places to Eat

The main shopping area around Orient St and the riverfront has some good cafes and restaurants. The *Boatshed* on the Clyde St fishing wharf sells seafood straight off the boats and fish and chips.

The *Starfish Deli* is a buzzing place with a great outdoor dining area right on the waterfront. You can get gourmet wood-fired pizzas from $13, pasta from $9.50 and mains around $18. If you wander around the corner and along the Mara Mia walkway you'll find interesting waterfront places (also accessible from Orient St). *Aussie Pancakes* has a good early breakfast (from 7 am) for $6.90. Farther along, the *Peppercorn Tree Cafe* is a pleasant spot for coffee or lunch, and *Mexican Munchies (☎ 4472 8746)*, upstairs, has main courses from $12 to $17. It's open from 6 pm and the food and service are pretty good.

Across from the post office, the *Batemans Bay Vietnamese, Thai & Malaysian Restaurant* has lunchtime specials for $5 and main courses for $9.

Jameson's on the Pier (☎ 4472 6405), on Old Punt Rd, is one of Batemans Bay's finest restaurants, although you wouldn't know to look at it. The rickety construction looks like it might collapse into the water at any minute, but it's a superb place for lunch, or dinner on a balmy evening. The emphasis is on fish; a huge whole snapper costs $20.

Taliva Restaurant (☎ 4472 4278, 236 Beach Rd), in Batehaven, is a highly rated French and 'Mod Oz' restaurant. Mains cost from $19.50.

Entertainment

The *Bayview Hotel* gets going on weekends. It should do since it's the only real pub in town. The *Soldiers Club* and the *Catalina Country Club* have music of some sort on weekends.

Getting There & Away

Harvey World Travel (☎ 4472 5086), on Orient St, handles bus bookings and has timetables in the window. The bus stop is outside the newsagent on Clyde St.

Greyhound Pioneer buses stop here on the run between Sydney ($38) and Melbourne. Premier Motor Service runs south to Eden ($26) and north to Sydney ($30) twice a day. Murrays (☎ 13 2251) runs to Narooma ($12) and Canberra ($21.75) at least daily. The Sapphire Coast Express (☎ 1800 812 135) runs between Batemans Bay and Melbourne ($65) twice a week.

As an alternative to the Princes Hwy, you can follow the beachfront road south as far as the north shore of the Deua (Moruya) River and rejoin the highway at Moruya. A scenic road runs inland to Nelligen, Braidwood and Canberra from the highway just north of Batemans Bay.

DEUA NATIONAL PARK

Inland from Moruya, Deua National Park (82,926 hectares) is a mountainous wilderness area with swift-running rivers (good for canoeing) and some challenging walking. There are also many caves. There are simple camping areas off the scenic road running between Araluen and Moruya and off the road between Braidwood and Numeralla, plus a couple more on tracks within the park. On the eastern side of the park, near the Berlang camping area, the Big Hole and Marble Arch are excellent short walks.

Contact the NPWS office (☎ 4476 2888) in Narooma for more information.

BATEMANS BAY TO NAROOMA

This stretch of coast features the **Eurobodalla National Park**, an area of many lakes, bays and inlets backed by spotted-gum forests. Eurobodalla is an Aboriginal word meaning 'place of many waters'.

Mogo

Mogo is a quaint strip of old wooden shops and houses almost entirely devoted to Devonshire teas, crafts and antiques. Just off the highway on James St is **Old Mogo Town**

(☎ 4472 2123), a rambling re-creation of a pioneer village, open from 10 am daily ($12/5 for adults/children). **Mogo Zoo** (☎ 4474 4930), 2km east off the highway, is a small but interesting zoo with exotic wildlife such as Bengal and Sumatran tigers, a Himalayan red panda, snow leopards and jaguars. Feeding time for the tigers is 11 am and 2 pm. It's open 9 am to 5 pm daily ($10/5). About 2km farther down this road is **Mogo Goldfields** (☎ 4471 7381), another small historic park with gold-mine tours on weekends ($9/5). You can also pan for gold and there's a small *caravan park* here.

Moruya

Moruya, 25km south of Batemans Bay and about 5km inland, is on the estuary of the Deua River (also called the Moruya River). The river's banks turn into wetlands as it sprawls down to the sea at **Moruya Heads**, the hamlet on the south head, where there's a good surf beach and views from Taragy Point.

The **Bush Orchestra** (☎ 4474 3554), about 2km west of the highway on Ted Hunt Terrace, is a guided forest walk with the 'music' provided by the abundant birdlife – bellbirds, lorikeets, bowerbirds and cockatoos. There's a popular country **market**, on the south side of Moruya Bridge, every Saturday.

In town there are a couple of motels and a caravan park by the river, but you're better off going to Moruya Heads, 7km east. The large and pleasant *Dolphin Beach Caravan Park* (☎ 4474 2748) charges about $12 for tent sites and from $35 a double for cabins. Prices jump during the Christmas week and at Easter. Priors Scenic Express buses run from Batemans Bay to Moruya and you might be able to get a lift to Moruya Heads on a school bus.

Congo

South of Moruya Heads, Congo, in the national park, is a small cluster of houses on an estuary and a long surf beach. It's very pretty and peaceful. Volunteers are helping to repair damage to the dunes here and they welcome assistance. There's a basic *camping area* where sites cost $5 for two. You'll need to bring in all your food and bring or boil drinking water.

A dirt road to Congo runs off the road between Moruya and Moruya Heads; another partly sealed road leaves the highway about 10km south of Moruya.

NAROOMA
postcode 2546 • pop 5000
Narooma is a seaside holiday town that isn't as developed as Batemans Bay to the north or Merimbula to the south, yet it's one of the more attractive spots on the south coast.

The good visitors centre (☎ 4476 2881), on the highway just south of the bridge, is open 9 am to 5 pm daily. Narooma is an access point for both Deua and Wadbilliga National Parks, and there's a NPWS information office (☎ 4476 2888) on the highway at the corner of Field St.

There's free Internet access at the library (☎ 4476 1164) behind the Narooma Kinema.

Things to See & Do

You can **cruise** inland up the Wagonga River on the *Wagonga Princess*. A three-hour cruise, including a stop for a walk through the bush and some billy tea, costs $18/12 for adults/children. Book at the visitors centre or on ☎ 4476 2665.

There are several boat-hire places along Riverside Dr, so you can go boating on Wagonga Inlet under your own steam. There's a nice **walk** along the inlet and around to the ocean, and safe swimming just inside the heads.

The cliff-top **Narooma Golf Club** (☎ 4476 2453) enjoys perhaps the most spectacular setting of any course on the south coast. It's $25 for 18 holes and club hire costs $18.

A good rainy-day weekend activity is to see a film at the **Narooma Kinema** (☎ 4476 2352), a picture palace that began showing flicks in 1926 and hasn't changed much since.

For **surfing**, Mystery Bay, between Cape Dromedary and Corunna Point, is rocky but good, as is Handkerchief Beach, especially at the north end. Narooma's Bar Beach is best when a south-easterly is blowing. Potato Point is another popular hang-out.

Fishing charters are popular and cost around $70 for five hours including all equipment. The visitors centre has a list of operators.

The small **Lighthouse Museum** is near the visitors centre.

Montague Island

About 10km offshore from Narooma, this small island was once an important source of food for local Aborigines (who called it Barunguba) and is now a nature reserve. **Fairy penguins** nest here and although you'll see some all year round, there are many thousands in late winter and spring. Many other seabirds and hundreds of seals make their homes on the island. There's also an historic **lighthouse**. A 30-minute boat trip to Montague Island and a tour conducted by a NPWS ranger costs $60/45 for adults/children. Take the afternoon trip if you want to see the fairy penguins. Trips should leave daily in summer but are dependent on numbers and weather conditions at other times, so book ahead through the visitor centre or NPWS office.

The clear waters around the island are good for **diving**, especially from February to June; you can snorkel with the seals.

Special Events

The Narooma Festival is held in February and the Surfboat Marathon is in November.

Places to Stay

Narooma Real Estate (☎ 4476 2169), across road from the visitors centre, deals in holiday accommodation.

There are several caravan parks, including two members of the *Easts* chain (☎ 4476 2161, 4476 2046) on the highway near the information centre, and the smaller *Surf Beach Resort* (☎ 4476 2275). Sites at the latter cost $14 and cabins start at $40 a double.

The YHA *Bluewater Lodge* (☎ 4476 4440, 11–13 Riverside Dr) is a well-run, recommended hostel. Dorm beds cost $16; twins and doubles cost $35. You can hire bikes and canoes here for only $6 a day.

There are plenty of motels, most of which charge around $45 a single in the off-

season but much more in summer. Cheaper places include *Vintage Motor Inn* (☎ 4476 2256), on the corner of Tilba St and the highway, with singles/doubles for $40/45. *Whale Motor Inn* (☎ 4476 2411), on Wagonga St, has large, clean rooms for $50/60 and a restaurant.

You can hire an eight-berth *houseboat* (☎ 4476 4654) from $200 a night ($350 over Christmas) or $595 a week ($890 at Christmas).

Places to Eat

Diagonally opposite Lynch's Hotel, *Casey's Cafe* has the best coffee in town and serves well-presented meals and great smoothies.

The licensed clubs are unbeatable for their $5 buffet meals. The *Bowling Club* has one on Thursday and the *Golf Club* on Monday.

Quarterdeck Marina, on Riverside Dr, has a bistro overlooking the lake, and does fresh takeaway seafood. The bistro at *O'Brien's Hotel*, on the highway in town (opposite Narooma Kinema), also has a great outdoor seating area with beach views and counter meals, including $6 lunches. *Rockwell Restaurant* (☎ 4476 2040, 107 Campbell St) is a highly rated licensed restaurant featuring local wines. *Simply Seafood* (☎ 4476 2403), at the marina on Riverside Dr, gets good reports.

Getting There & Away

Bus bookings are handled by Traveland (☎ 4476 2688), near the post office on the hill. Buses stop nearby.

Greyhound Pioneer and Premier Motor Services buses stop here on the run between Sydney and Melbourne; Murrays stops on its daily run between Narooma and Canberra via Batemans Bay.

AROUND NAROOMA
Mystery Bay

Near Cape Dromedary, about 12km south of Narooma, this little settlement of new houses has a fine rocky beach (there are sandy beaches nearby) and a big but basic *camping area* (☎ 4473 7242) in a forest of spotted gums.

Central Tilba & Around

Central Tilba is a tiny town that has remained almost unchanged since last century – except that now the main street is jammed with visitors' cars, especially on summer weekends. There's information, including a town guide, at the Tilba store at the start of the main street. You can visit several working craft shops and the **ABC Cheese Factory** (☎ 4473 7387), producer of some fine cheeses, open 9 am to 5 pm daily.

Not far from Central Tilba towards Batemans Bay are **Tilba Valley Wines** (☎ 4473 7308) and **Brooklands Deer Farm** (☎ 4473 7330).

The Tilba Festival, with lots of music and entertainment, is held at Easter; it's hard to imagine how this small town can cope with the 8000-plus visitors.

Central Tilba perches on the side of **Mt Dromedary** (797m), one of the highest mountains on the south coast. There's lush forest on the mountain, which forms the Gulaga Flora Reserve, and great views from the top. Beginning at Pam's Store in **Tilba Tilba** you can walk up along an old packhorse trail. The return walk of 11km takes about five hours, but don't miss the loop walk at the summit. There is often rain and mist on the mountain, so come prepared.

From Tilba Tilba the highway swings inland to **Cobargo**, another small town that has changed little since it was built, and where there are craft shops, a pub and motels.

Places to Stay & Eat In Central Tilba, the *Dromedary Hotel* (☎ 4473 7223) is a nice old pub with basic singles/doubles for $30/60, including a light breakfast. There are a couple of B&Bs: *Wirrina Guesthouse* (☎ 4473 7279) charges $70/95 and the *Two Storey B&B* (☎ 1800 355 850), next to the Tilba store, charges $75/85.

About 3km on from Central Tilba (continue down Bate St) is *Braeside Farm Cabins* (☎ 4473 7353), a small group of self-contained two-bedroom brick cabins in a secluded spot. At $45 a night or $200 a week in the low season these are a real bargain. Peak season rates are still cheap at $68/450.

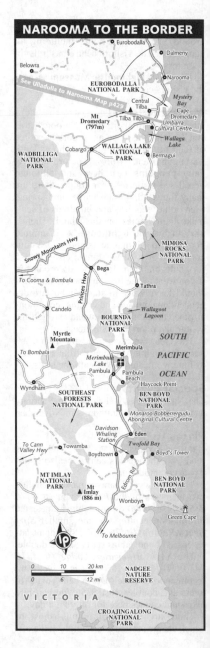

NAROOMA TO THE BORDER

There are plenty of good cafes and teashops on Bate St in Central Tilba. The *Camel Rock Cafe* has an interesting menu and nice views from its back veranda, and the *Rose & Sparrow* does Devonshire teas.

Getting There & Away Premier Motor Service buses come through both Central Tilba and Tilba Tilba on their daily run between Sydney and Melbourne.

If you're heading for Bermagui or if you just want an interesting drive, leave the highway at Tilba Tilba and take the sealed road that follows the coast through Wallaga Lake National Park to Bermagui.

WADBILLIGA NATIONAL PARK
A rugged wilderness area of 79,000 hectares, Wadbilliga offers good walking for experienced bushwalkers. One popular trail is along the 5km Tuross River Gorge to the Tuross Falls. There's a camping area on the north-western side of the park, near the walk to the falls. Access is off the road running from Countegany south to Tuross. Another camping area, in the centre of the park on the Wadbilliga River, is reached via Bourkes Rd from the east.

For more information, contact the NPWS office (☎ 4476 2888) in Narooma.

Brogo Wilderness Canoes (☎ 6492 7328) offers **canoeing** trips through the park for $30 a day.

WALLAGA LAKE NATIONAL PARK
This small park takes in most of the western shore of Wallaga Lake, a beautiful tidal lake at the mouth of several creeks, and has prolific birdlife. There's another chunk of the park off the highway west of here.

There's no road access into the park (and no camping allowed), but the little settlements of **Beauty Point** and **Regatta Point** are on the lake and you can hire boats there. Merriman Island, in the lake off Regatta Point, is off limits because of its significance to the Aboriginal community. Similarly, sites (such as middens, the remains of shellfish feasts) and relics you might come across in the park are protected.

Umbarra Cultural Centre (☎ 4473 7232), run by the Yuin people from Wallaga Lake Koori community, has an excellent tour of the lake and other places of historical and cultural importance ($45). The centre, 3km from the highway on the road to Wallaga Lake, also has a display of local Aboriginal art and culture. It's open 9 am to 5 pm weekdays and till 4 pm on weekends.

Places to Stay
There are several caravan parks in and near Regatta Point and Beauty Point.

The big *Ocean Lake Caravan Park* (☎ 6493 4055) is one of the nicest around with sites for $14, on-site vans from $40 a double and en suite cabins for $70. Closest to the ocean is *Wallaga Lake Park* (☎ 6493 4655), off the main road between Bermagui and Narooma, just south of Beauty Point. Tent sites cost $12 (off peak), vans from $30 and en suite cabins $50.

Hubara Motel (☎ 6493 4037), near Regatta Point, has comfortable log cabins that are reasonably priced at $28/38 a single/double in the low season. There's also a restaurant and a pool here.

BERMAGUI
postcode 2456 • pop 1560
Bermagui is a small fishing community centred on pretty Horseshoe Bay. Many visitors come here, mainly to fish, and there are six big-game tournaments a year. April to May is the busiest season. It's also a handy base for visits to Wallaga Lake, Mimosa Rocks and Wadbilliga National Parks.

US novelist Zane Grey (1872–1939), author of more than 80 books and considered the father of the western literary genre, was a renowned game-fishing enthusiast. He once visited Bermagui and included his experiences in *An American Angler in Australia*.

The information centre (☎ 6493 3054) on Lamont St (the main street) is open 10 am to 4 pm daily.

There are several **walks** around Bermagui. You can wander 6km along the coast north to Camel Rock Beach (a good surfing spot) and a farther 2km around to Wallaga Lake. The route follows Haywards Beach.

Places to Stay & Eat

Overlooking Horseshoe Bay, *Zane Grey Park* (☎ 6493 4382), in the town centre, has sites for $12.50 and cabins from $38 for two. Prices rise considerably at peak times.

Blue Pacific (☎ 6493 4921, 77 Murrah St) has comfortable holiday units with provision for backpackers ($18 per person) in a six-bed self-contained unit. If you want to book out a unit they cost $600/250 a week in high/low season. Overnight stays cost $48 a double all year, although there's unlikely to be a vacancy in the peak season. If you arrive on the Greyhound bus, the owners will pick you up from the highway for a small fee.

There are many other holiday houses and apartments. Letting agents include Bermagui First National (☎ 6493 4255) at 14 Lamont St. It has a Web site at www.bermifirst .com.au.

The *Horseshoe Bay Hotel/Motel* (☎ 6493 4206, 10 Lamont St) has backpacker beds in a bunkhouse for $15, pub singles/doubles for $20/35 and motel units from $55 a double.

Bermagui Fishermen's Cooperative at the wharf has fresh fish and chips and a colony of hungry seagulls outside. Nearby, *Roly's Wharf Restaurant* (☎ 6493 4328) serves seafood in the evenings; mains cost from $12.50 and include a seafood platter ($21.50).

Getting There & Away

Bermagui is off the highway, so not all buses call in here. Bega Valley Coaches (☎ 6492 2418) has a weekday service between Bermagui and Bega, and Premier Motor Service stops here once a day on its Sydney-Melbourne run.

Driving north, the quickest way back to the highway is to go past Wallaga Lake National Park, and this is also a pretty drive. Heading south, the quickest way is to go west and join the highway at Cobargo, but if you have time you could drive south on the unsealed road that runs alongside Mimosa Rocks National Park to Tathra, from where you can rejoin the highway at Bega. Look out for lyrebirds.

MIMOSA ROCKS NATIONAL PARK

Running along 17km of beautiful coastline, Mimosa Rocks (5624 hectares) is a wonderful coastal park with dense and varied bush and great beaches. There are basic *camp sites* at Aragunnu Beach, Picnic Point and Middle Beach, and a camping area with no facilities at Gillards Beach. Camping costs $5 plus the $7.50 park entry fee. These camping areas and the picnic areas are accessible from the road running between Bermagui and Tathra.

Contact the NPWS office in Narooma (☎ 6476 2888) or Merimbula (☎ 6495 5000).

BEGA

postcode 2550 ● pop 4700

Bega is a centre for the rich dairy and cattle country of the southern Monaro Tableland. Most of Canberra's milk and some fine cheddar cheese comes from the valleys around here. After the tourist bustle of the coastal or mountain resorts, you'll find Bega very much a working country town; it's worth a stopover perhaps for that reason alone, and it makes a good base for a number of excursions.

Information

The visitors centre (☎ 6492 2045), in Gipps St near the corner of Carp St, is open 9 am to 5 pm weekdays. It also usually opens on Saturday morning in summer. The library (☎ 6499 2127), on Zingel Place, has Internet access for $3 per half hour.

Things to See & Do

There are a number of mildly interesting old buildings; the visitors centre has a **walking-tour** map.

The **Bega Family Museum** (☎ 6492 1453), Bega St, is open 10.30 am to 4 pm weekdays (and from 10 am to noon Saturday during school holidays). It's an historical museum housed in the former Family Hotel ($2.50/0.50 for adults/children). There's an **art gallery** with changing exhibitions (free) next to the library on Zingel Place. It's open 10 am to 4 pm Wednesday to Sunday.

At the **Bega Cheese Factory & Heritage Centre**, north across the river, you can look down on the factory operations from a viewing area, taste cheese samples until you've made a nice little pile of cocktail sticks, and visit an interesting dairy museum. It's open 9 am to 5 pm weekdays and 10 am to 4 pm on weekends. **Grevillea Estate Winery** is open to visitors 9 am to 5 pm daily for tastings and sales. It's about 2km from the town centre – follow the highway across the river and take the first left after the bridge.

Places to Stay

The *Bega Caravan Park (☎ 6492 2303)*, on the highway south of the centre, has tent sites for $16 and on-site vans from $30. It also has self-contained units for $44 a double (much more in summer).

Bega YHA (☎ 6492 3103), Kirkland Crescent, is a clean, friendly, family run (and owned) hostel in a quiet area just west of town. The mud-brick building is spacious and comfortable, with dorm beds for $13 and a twin room for $34. The owners offer a free tour of the cheese factory and Grevillea Winery, and have inexpensive 4WD trips to Tathra, Bournda and Mimosa Rocks National Parks, a horse stud, Tilba and Mumballa Falls.

The *Hotel Commercial (☎ 6492 1011)*, on the corner of Carp and Gipps Sts, has singles with shared bathroom for $30, or en suite doubles for $45, including continental breakfast. Several other pubs also provide accommodation.

The *Central Private Hotel (☎ 6492 1263)*, Gipps St, is a big, old-style place with a bit of character and some permanent residents. B&B singles/doubles with shared bathroom cost $35/45; there's a motel section costing $45/55. It has good breakfasts and there's an Italian restaurant here.

Northside Motel (☎ 6492 1911), near the cheese factory, is the cheapest of the half dozen motels in town. Rooms cost from

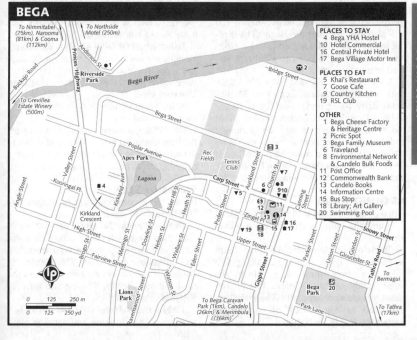

BEGA

PLACES TO STAY
4   Bega YHA Hostel
10 Hotel Commercial
16 Central Private Hotel
17 Bega Village Motor Inn

PLACES TO EAT
5   Khai's Restaurant
7   Goose Cafe
9   Country Kitchen
19 RSL Club

OTHER
1   Bega Cheese Factory & Heritage Centre
2   Picnic Spot
3   Bega Family Museum
6   Traveland
8   Environmental Network & Candelo Bulk Foods
11 Post Office
12 Commonwealth Bank
13 Candelo Books
14 Information Centre
15 Bus Stop
18 Library; Art Gallery
20 Swimming Pool

SOUTH COAST

$45/50. The **Bega Village Motor Inn** (☎ 6492 2466), on Gipps St in the centre of town, has rooms for $65/75.

Places to Eat

There are a couple of good cafes in town. **Country Kitchen**, on Carp St, is open early for breakfast. **Goose Cafe**, in Church St, is a popular little lunch spot with plenty of vegetarian snacks on the menu.

Khai's (☎ 6492 3999, 248 Carp St) is a recommended Asian restaurant with Chinese, Thai and Vietnamese on the menu. The **RSL Club** on Auckland St also has cheap bistro meals.

Grevillea Estate Winery (☎ 6492 3006) has a rustic outdoor restaurant open daily for lunch. Most meals are under $10 so it's good value.

Getting There & Away

Traveland (☎ 6492 3599), 163 Carp St, handles bus bookings. Buses leave from near the tourist office.

Greyhound Pioneer buses stop here on the run between Sydney and Melbourne and will also drop off near the Bega YHA if requested. Premier Motor Service also stops here. Countrylink's Eden to Canberra service passes through Bega.

A local service, Edwards (☎ 6496 1422), runs between Bega and Eden (via Merimbula) daily (the Sunday service is Countrylink). Bega Valley Coaches (☎ 6492 2418) has a weekday service between Bermagui and Bega. On weekdays, buses to Tathra (☎ 6492 1991) leave from the post office at 9.30 am (7.45 am during school holidays), and from Church St at 2 and 3.30 pm.

AROUND BEGA

Off the highway about 5km north of Bega is **Mumballa Falls**, where there's a picnic area.

Candelo is a pleasant old village 26km south-west of Bega. It straggles along both sides of a steep valley and is split by the large, sandy Candelo Creek. The nearby country is cleared, but pretty. There are several craft galleries. West of Candelo is **Kameruka Estate**, a National Trust homestead, open daily, and farther on is the **Bimbaya Moozeum**, in an old butter factory. The **Candelo Hotel** (☎ 6493 2214) has rooms.

About 6km from Candelo, **Tantawanglo Trail Rides** (☎ 6493 2350) has horse rides into the beautiful surrounding national parks and state forests. Half-day rides must be booked and cost only $20 per person.

From Candelo you can drive back to the Princes Hwy via Toothdale, or continue south to the Bombala road. This route takes you over **Myrtle Mountain** where there's a picnic area with good views, and drives in the state forest. The Bombala road leads you west to **Wyndham**, a small village just after the intersection with the Candelo road, or east to Pambula and Merimbula.

TATHRA

postcode 2550 • pop 1680

This small town is popular with people from the Bega area in summer. It starts on a headland, where you'll find the post office and the pub, as well as access to the historic wharf. Down a steep road and to the north, Tathra follows a long beach towards Mimosa Rocks National Park.

Tathra wharf (☎ 6494 4062) is the last remaining coastal steamship wharf in the state and a popular place for fishing. The wharf storehouse now houses a small **Maritime Museum** (open 9 am to 5 pm daily; $1.50/0.50 for adults/children) as well as a tackle shop and small cafe.

Cliff Place, a narrow street that runs off the headland road next to the road down to the wharf, has great views. You can take a path that begins near the surf club.

Places to Stay

Prices for accommodation in Tathra rise considerably in summer.

Tathra Beach Tourist Park (☎ 6494 1302), on the beach in the centre of town, has sites from $10, on-site vans from $30 and en suite cabins from $36. **Seabreeze Holiday Park** (☎ 6494 1350) is across the road and has sites for $14, on-site vans for $30 and cabins for $45.

Tathra Hotel-Motel (☎ 6494 1101) is a popular eating, drinking and dancing place on the headland. Reasonable motel units with sea views cost $35/50 for singles/doubles, rising to $60/75 in the holidays. The pub has entertainment on weekends and in summer it hosts big touring acts.

Tathra Beach Accommodation Service (☎ 6494 1306) is one of the agents handling holiday letting.

Places to Eat

The *Tathra Hotel* has counter meals and a bistro with a good view over the ocean. The *Harbourmaster Restaurant*, on the headland next to the road going down to the beach, is a pleasant place in an old house, with lunch specials for $5.

Sisters by the Sea (☎ 6494 1688), right on the beach next to the surf-lifesaving club, is a good BYO restaurant; it's open Thursday to Monday. There's also a takeaway kiosk open on weekends.

Flick's Cinema Restaurant (☎ 6494 5100), just off the Bega Rd as you enter Tathra, is a wonderful restaurant that combines a great meal with an entertaining night out. In a restored church full of old film memorabilia you can enjoy an a la carte meal while watching classic films from the 1920s to '50s. It's open Wednesday to Saturday for dinner.

Getting There & Away

Buses to Bega depart at 8.20 and 10.30 am and 2.30 pm on weekdays. See the Bega Getting There & Away section earlier in this chapter for more information.

Tathra is 18km from the Princes Hwy at Bega. If you're heading north, consider the unsealed road to Bermagui, which runs through forest and alongside Mimosa Rocks National Park. Heading south to Merimbula you can turn off the Bega road 5km out of Tathra onto Sapphire Coast Dr, which runs past Bournda National Park.

MERIMBULA

postcode 2548 • pop 4250

Merimbula is a holiday and retirement mecca, and motels and apartments have mushroomed on the hill sides surrounding the impressive lake (which is actually an inlet). If this sounds like a recipe for tackiness and claustrophobia you're partly right, but there's still some charm about the town's setting and the lake is big enough to dwarf the development. Nearby Pambula Beach is much quieter.

Information

The tourist information centre (☎ 1800 670 080), on the waterfront at the bottom of Market St, the main shopping street, is open 9 am to 5 pm Monday to Saturday and 10 am to 4 pm Sunday. Next door (in the same building) is a handy booking office (☎ 1800 150 457) for accommodation, tours and activities. You can access the Internet at the library ($3 for half an hour).

There's a useful NPWS office and 'Discovery Centre' (☎ 6495 5000) on the corner of Merimbula and Sapphire Coast Drives.

Things to See & Do

At the wharf on the eastern point is the small **Merimbula Aquarium** (☎ 6495 3227), open 9 am to 5 pm daily ($8/4 for adults/children). There are good views across the lake from near here and the jetty is a popular little fishing spot. The **Old School Museum** (☎ 6495 2114), on Main St almost opposite the Returned & Services League (RSL) club, has local history displays and is open 2 to 4 pm Tuesday, Thursday and Sunday ($2/ free).

Diving is popular, with plenty of fish and several wrecks in the area, including two tugs sunk in 1987. Merimbula Divers Lodge (☎ 1800 651 861) offers basic instruction and one shallow dive for $65. Four-day PADI-certificate courses cost $350. It also does snorkelling trips.

There are **cruises** from the Merimbula marina, opposite the Lakeview Hotel. The Dolphin Cruise costs $25/15.

There are two boat-hire places – at the Merimbula Marina jetty and at Top Lake, on the north shore west of the bridge (follow Lakewood Dr). They have power boats, small yachts, canoes and rowing boats. Cycle 'n' Surf (☎ 6495 2171), on Marine Parade south of the lake, hires out bikes, boogie boards and surf-skis as well as fishing tackle.

Magic Mountain, on Sapphire Coast Dr north of town, is a better-than-average amusement park with lots of kid-friendly activity. An all-inclusive ticket costs $22/18 ($14 for four- to seven-year-olds).

Places to Stay

Camping The *South Haven Caravan Park* (☎ 6495 1304) and the smaller *Tween Waters Tourist Park* (☎/fax 6495 1530) are south of the bridge with access to surf and lake beaches. Both have sites from about $16 and cabins from $45, rising to infinity over Christmas.

Hostels On the Fishpen near the surf beach, *Wandarrah YHA Lodge* (☎ 6495 3503, 8 Marine Parade) is a clean place with dorm beds for $16 and doubles/twins from $35 to $58, including breakfast. It hires out bikes and canoes and offers tours.

Merimbula Divers Lodge (☎ 1800 651 861, 15 Park St) has shared accommodation for backpackers or divers in a spotless, two-bedroom self-contained unit for $20 per person – a bargain. Whole units are also available for $100. To get here from Market St cut through the Centrepoint Mall (really an arcade) then head across the car park to Park St.

Motels & Rental Accommodation

There are hundreds of motels and holiday apartments scattered all around Merimbula. Self-contained apartments are usually let on a weekly basis, particularly in summer. Letting agents for the area include Fisk & Nagle (☎ 6495 1301), in Centrepoint Mall, and LJ Hooker (☎ 6495 1026), nearby at 35 Market St.

In quiet times you can find motel rooms from around $40/50, but in summer prices go through the roof. Your best chance of finding an affordable room is at one of the motels on the highway west of the town centre. *Merimbula Gardens* (☎ 6495 1206, 36

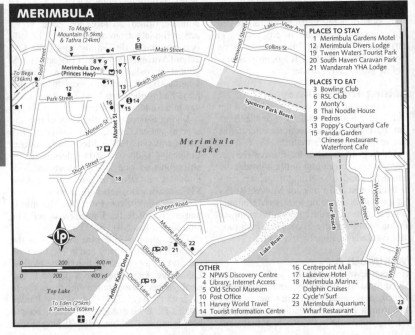

MERIMBULA

PLACES TO STAY
1 Merimbula Gardens Motel
12 Merimbula Divers Lodge
19 Tween Waters Tourist Park
20 South Haven Caravan Park
21 Wandarrah YHA Lodge

PLACES TO EAT
3 Bowling Club
6 RSL Club
7 Monty's
8 Thai Noodle House
9 Pedros
13 Poppy's Courtyard Cafe
15 Panda Garden
  Chinese Restaurant;
  Waterfront Cafe

OTHER
2 NPWS Discovery Centre
4 Library; Internet Access
5 Old School Museum
10 Post Office
11 Harvey World Travel
14 Tourist Information Centre
16 Centrepoint Mall
17 Lakeview Hotel
18 Merimbula Marina;
  Dolphin Cruises
22 Cycle'n'Surf
23 Merimbula Aquarium;
  Wharf Restaurant

Merimbula Lake

Spencer Park Beach

Fishpen Road

Bar Beach

Lake Beach

To Magic Mountain (1.5km) & Tatra (24km)

To Bega (36km)

To Eden (25km) & Pambula (65km)

Top Lake

Merimbula Dr) is one of the cheaper central options, with singles/doubles for $38/45, rising to $70/85 in peak season.

Places to Eat

Merimbula offers quite a wide range of eateries, most of them concentrated in the busy shopping area. The *Waterfront Cafe*, next to the information centre, is a good place to have a coffee or snack while looking out over Merimbula Lake. *Panda Garden Chinese Restaurant*, next door, has good value three-course dinners for $7.80. *Poppy's Courtyard Cafe*, opposite the information centre, is open early for breakfast and has a wide range of sandwiches and snacks.

There's a cluster of restaurants between Main St and Merimbula Dr. *Thai Noodle House (☎ 6495 4410)* has curries and stir-fries for $9.50, while *Pedros (☎ 6495 1546)*, down an alley opposite Harvey World Travel, is a reasonably priced BYO Mexican restaurant. *Monty's (☎ 6495 1343)*, towards the top end of Market St, is a bar and restaurant with a stylish menu. Seafood paella costs $18.50, but most mains are cheaper.

The *Wharf Restaurant (☎ 6495 4446)*, at the aquarium, is a BYO Thai restaurant with some good seafood and vegetarian dishes for $9.50 to $22.50.

Licensed clubs, including the *Bowling Club* and the *RSL Club*, both on Main St, have bistros and restaurants.

Getting There & Away

Travel bookings can be made at Harvey World Travel (☎ 6495 1205), on Merimbula Dr, or Summerland Travel (☎ 6495 1008), 16 Market St.

There are daily flights to Melbourne ($204) with Kendell Airlines and to Sydney ($213) with Hazelton Airlines. The airport is 1km out of town on the road to Pambula.

Buses stop outside the Centrepoint Mall on Market St.

Greyhound Pioneer Australia and Premier Motor Service buses stop here between Sydney and Melbourne. Countrylink stops here between Eden and Canberra.

Edwards (☎ 6496 1422) is a local bus company that runs between Bega and Eden.

AROUND MERIMBULA
Bournda National Park

Taking in most of the coast from Merimbula north to Tathra, Bournda National Park (2378 hectares) has some good beaches and several walking trails, which can get pretty crowded at peak times. *Camping* is permitted at Hobart Beach, on the southern shore of the big Wallagoot Lagoon, where there are toilets and hot showers. During the Christmas and Easter holidays, sites are usually booked out. Contact the NPWS office in Merimbula (☎ 6495 5000) for more information.

Woodbine Park (☎ 6495 9333) borders Bournda and is 1km from the beach. It's a friendly place with six-person self-contained cabins from $60/260 a night/week for a double (extra for more people) in the low season (May to September, other than school holidays), and up to $130/840 in January. Head north from Merimbula on Sapphire Coast Dr and take the signposted turn-off after about 7km.

Pambula
postcode 2551 • pop 700

Just south of Merimbula, Pambula is a small town that has largely avoided the development of its glitzy neighbour. At Pambula Beach, 4km east, there's the *Holiday Hub Tourist Park (☎ 6495 6363)* with tent sites from $15, en suite cabins from $48 and some very friendly marsupials. Keep your food hidden!

Between Pambula and Merimbula, Wheeler's Kiosk (☎ 6495 6089) is run by one of the local oyster farmers (there are many oyster leases on the inlets around Merimbula). There are tours of the small processing factory daily (except Sunday) at 11 am, as well as a video screening and oyster tasting. The cost is $5/2 for adults/children. You can also buy fresh oysters and other seafood here.

EDEN & AROUND
postcode 2551 • pop 3270

Eden is still very much a fishing port, with one of the largest fleets in the state and a busy enclosed harbour. It's also a timber town. The local population doubled when a woodchip mill opened in the 1970s, so you won't meet many people voicing antiwood-chipping sentiments. It's a good place to base yourself, with easy access to the sur-rounding national parks and a more laid-back feel than Merimbula. In summer, Eden's flies can drive you to distraction.

The Eden Visitor Centre (☎ 6496 1953) on Imlay St (the Princes Hwy) is open 9 am to 4 pm weekdays and 9 am to noon on week-ends. The library (☎ 6496 1687), on Bass St, has Internet access for $3 for half an hour.

Things to See & Do

The interesting **Killer Whale Museum** (☎ 6496 2094), at the bottom end of Imlay St, was established in 1931, mainly to pre-serve the skeleton of Old Tom, a killer whale and local legend (see the boxed text 'From Whaling to Whale Watching'). If you've ever read *Moby Dick*, this is your chance to see a real whale boat with all those arcane pieces of equipment described by Melville. The museum is open 9.15 am to 3.45 pm Monday to Saturday and 11.15 am to 3.45 pm Sunday ($4/1 for adults/children).

Cat Balou Cruises (☎ 6496 2027) has **whale-spotting cruises** for $45/30 in Octo-ber and November. At other times of year, dolphins, seals and seabirds can usually be seen during the shorter bay cruise ($22.50). These and other boat and canoe day trips can be booked at the visitor centre.

Monaroo Bobberrergudu (☎ 6496 1922) is a new Aboriginal cultural centre estab-lished at Jigamy Farm, just off the highway about 8km north of Eden. It had not opened when we visited but the concept looked ex-cellent, with a large interpretive centre, a cultural village re-creating traditional Abori-ginal lifestyles, and tours and demonstra-tions given by local Koori guides.

Boydtown, off the highway 10km south of Eden, has relics of Ben Boyd's stillborn empire (see the boxed text 'The Rise & Fall of Benjamin Boyd' later in this chapter). The ruins of a church can be seen, and the impressive Seahorse Inn still operates (see Places to Stay in this section).

Special Events

Eden comes alive in mid-October for the Whale Festival, with the typical carnival, street parade and stalls, and the more bizzare 'blub-ber drag' and harpoon-throwing competition.

From Whaling to Whale Watching

Migrating humpback and southern right whales pass so close to the coast near the fishing port of Eden that whale-watching ex-perts consider this one of the best places in Australia to observe these magnificent crea-tures. Often they can be seen feeding or rest-ing in Twofold Bay during their southern migration back to Antarctic waters.

Around 170 years ago, the whales at-tracted interest for very different reasons. Australia's first shore-based whaling station was set up here in 1828, starting a prosper-ous and lucrative whaling industry that con-tinued until 1929. When a pod of whales was spotted, crews (many of them Aborigines re-cruited from the area) would race out in open whaling boats, but it was a remarkable al-liance between the whalers and the wild killer whales (orca) that made Eden so unique.

The killer whales would gather, locate the migrating whales, then herd them into Twofold Bay for the waiting whalers. They would then assist the whalers in making the kill, preventing the hapless whales from es-caping or diving. Why? It was a matter of convenience. Once the whales had been killed, the orcas would feast on the huge lips and tongue – the only bits they wanted – and the whalers would later take the rest of the carcass for the valuable whale oil.

'Old Tom' was the leader of the most suc-cessful killer whale pack, assisting the whalers in their slaughter for many years until his death in 1930 (around the same time that whaling ceased in Eden). Discovering Old Tom's carcass in the bay, locals decided to save the skeleton and exhibit it for future generations. You can see it at the Killer Whale Museum in Eden. You can also see the ruins of the Davidson Whaling Station on Kiah Inlet in Ben Boyd National Park.

Places to Stay

The *Garden of Eden Caravan Park* (☎ 6496 1172) and the *Fountain Caravan Park* (☎ 6496 1798) are on either side of the highway north of town. *Eden Tourist Park* (☎ 6496 1139), serenely situated on a spit separating Aslings Beach from Lake Curalo, has sites from $12/16 in the low/high season, on-site vans for $26/42 and en suite cabins for $37/60.

The *Hotel Australasia* (☎ 6496 1600), on Imlay St, has backpacker beds for $15, pub singles/doubles for $20/25 and motel-style units for $30/35. The *Centretown Motel* (☎ 6496 1475, 167 Imlay St) is one of the cheaper motels in town with rooms from $38/40, but as with other places, prices rise considerably in summer.

The *Crown & Anchor Inn* (☎ 6496 1017, 239 Imlay St) is the place to stay if you really want to spoil yourself. The historic house (1845) has been beautifully restored and has a lovely view over Twofold Bay from the back patio. Each room is different but all have stylish period furniture (such as four-poster beds and claw-foot baths). B&B starts at $100/120.

At Boydtown, the *Seahorse Inn* (☎ 6496 1361) overlooks Twofold Bay and is a solid old building, built by Ben Boyd as a guesthouse in 1843. Rooms with shared facilities cost $55 per person, and the en suite room is $65 per person; both include cooked breakfast. There are packages that include dinner. There's also a *camping ground* here, with sites for $10.

Places to Eat

On Imlay St near the Killer Whale Museum, *Heritage House Coffee Shop* is a good place for morning or afternoon tea or a light meal.

Down at Snug Cove, Eden's fishing harbour, *Eden Wharf Seafood* has seafood to take away or eat in. For more upmarket seafood try the *Wheelhouse Restaurant* (☎ 6496 3392) around the corner; fish of the day costs $18.50 and the seafood platter is $50 for two.

Bianca's, at Hotel Australasia, is a fine restaurant separated from the noisy bar; there's a cheaper bistro area as well.

Benjamin's Restaurant is at the Seahorse Inn in Boydtown.

Getting There & Away

Bus bookings can be made at Traveland (☎ 6496 1314), on the corner of Bass and Imlay Sts.

BEN BOYD NATIONAL PARK

Protecting some relics of Ben Boyd's operations, this national park (9450 hectares) has dramatic coastline, bush and some walks. The main access road to the park is the sealed Edrom Rd, which leaves the Princes Hwy about 25km south of Eden. Edrom Rd ends at the big woodchip mill on the south shore of Twofold Bay.

Before the mill there's a turn-off to the left that leads to the old **Davidson Whaling Station** on Twofold Bay, now an historic site. There's not much left of the try works, which turned whale blubber into oil from the late 19th century, but interpretive signs tell the story. Farther along Edrom Rd is the turn-off for **Boyd's Tower**, an impressive structure built with sandstone brought from Sydney. It was intended to be a lighthouse but the government wouldn't give Boyd permission to operate it. From the lookout at Redstone Point you can see the forces of nature in the folded rock on the coastline.

Off Edrom Rd closer to the highway is Green Cape Rd, which runs right down to Green Cape, from where there are some good views and a **lighthouse**. Running off Green Cape Rd are smaller roads which lead to **Saltwater Creek** and **Bittangabee Bay**. There are *camp sites* at both places and a 9km walk between the two. You should book sites for Christmas and Easter at the NPWS office in Merimbula (☎ 6495 5000).

The northern section of Ben Boyd National Park runs up the coast from Eden; access is from the Princes Hwy north of the town. From Haycock Point, where there are good views, a walking trail leads to a headland overlooking the Pambula River. Another good walk is to the **Pinnacles**, an eroded formation of layered rock; access is from the car park not too far in from the Princes Hwy.

The Rise & Fall of Benjamin Boyd

Benjamin Boyd was a strange person, part empire builder, part capitalist and part adventurer, mixed with a large dash of incompetence. He never really completed anything he set out to do and he was unsuccessful in a big way.

Boyd was a stockbroker in London who decided that the colony of New South Wales (NSW) offered scope for the large amounts of money he could raise. His plans were vague and included a half-baked idea for a private colony in the South Pacific.

He founded the Royal Bank, which quickly attracted £1,000,000 in investments, then set out for Sydney in his racing yacht *Wanderer*, arriving in 1842. Boyd, who so far had accomplished nothing except the acquisition of a great deal of other people's money, was greeted with much official and public enthusiasm in Sydney.

He began a coastal steamship service, but the boat was damaged and withdrawn in its first year of operation. Boyd nevertheless convinced the governor that he was a fit person to be granted vast landholdings, second only in size to the Crown's.

Boyd decided to set up headquarters at Twofold Bay and an extensive building program began. Money ran short, although the investors were assured that their golden reward was just around the corner, and Boyd issued his own banknotes.

Things went from bad to worse and the Royal Bank (nominally the owner of Boyd's empire) sacked him. By 1849 the bank decided that it was easier simply to collapse than to untangle Boyd's complex financial wheelings and dealings.

The entrepreneur smiled amid the ruins of his speculations, decided NSW wasn't really the right place for his ventures after all and set sail in *Wanderer* for the Californian goldfields.

Things didn't quite work out there either, and in 1851 Boyd sailed back into the Pacific. One morning, while moored at Guadalcanal in the Solomon Islands, he left his yacht to go shooting and disappeared without trace.

NADGEE NATURE RESERVE

Nadgee Nature Reserve continues down the coast from Ben Boyd National Park, but it's much less accessible. Much of it is official Wilderness Area, and vehicle access is allowed as far as the ranger station near the Merrica River, 7km from Newton's Beach.

On Wonboyn Lake at the north end of the reserve, the small settlement of **Wonboyn** has a store selling petrol and basic supplies. Wonboyn is near access roads into Nadgee, including one down to Wonboyn Beach.

Wonboyn Cabins & Caravan Park (☎ 6496 9131) has some friendly rainbow lorikeets. Tent sites cost from $12, on-site vans $32 and cabins $50.

MT IMLAY NATIONAL PARK

This small national park (3808 hectares), 32km south-west of Eden, surrounds **Mt Imlay** (886m). The tough 3km **Mt Imlay Walking Track**, from the car park to the summit, is steep, and the last 500m follows an extremely narrow ridge. There are no facilities in the park.

The road to the start of the track runs westwards from the Princes Hwy just south of the turn-off into Ben Boyd National Park.

Australian Capital Territory

When the separate colonies of Australia were federated in 1901 and became states, the decision to build a national capital was part of the constitution. The site was selected in 1908, diplomatically situated between arch-rivals Sydney and Melbourne, and an international competition to design the city was won by the US architect Walter Burley Griffin. In 1911 the Commonwealth government bought land for the Australian Capital Territory (ACT) and in 1913 decided to call the capital Canberra, believed to be an Aboriginal term for 'meeting place'.

Development of the site was slow, and until 1927, when parliament first convened here, Melbourne was the seat of the national government. The Depression virtually halted development and things really only got under way after WWII. In 1960 the population topped 50,000, reaching 100,000 by 1967. Today the ACT has about 310,000 people, with almost all living in the urban Canberra area, which adjoins Queanbeyan (technically, New South Wales).

The main industry in the ACT is bureaucracy, although there is a growing private sector and in rural areas sheep-grazing is significant. Canberra is also known as the porn capital of Australia.

Canberra

☎ 02 • pop 300,000

Despite its image as a dull, urban centre stuffed with bureaucrats, Canberra is well worth visiting. The first things you'll notice are the generosity of space and the bush – the Canberra Nature Park incorporates at least a dozen large parks throughout Canberra and the city is surrounded by hills and bushwalking country.

Some of the best architecture and exhibitions in Australia can be found here and the whole city is fascinating because it's totally planned and orderly, although you'll soon appreciate that living here without a car

Australian Capital Territory p469

Canberra p456
Civic p458

Canberra Suburbs p450

might not be such fun. If you do have wheels you'll enjoy some of the best urban driving or cycling conditions in Australia.

Canberra is a place of government with few local industries and a unique, stimulating atmosphere that's only to be found in national capitals. It also has the furnishings of a true centre of national life – eg, the exciting National Gallery of Australia (NGA), the splendid new Parliament House and the Australian National Botanic Gardens – and entry

447

AUSTRALIAN CAPITAL TERRITORY

to most of these attractions is free. Canberra has quite a young population, including students, and entertainment is livelier than we're usually led to expect. Finally, this is the only city in Australia where it's possible to bump into kangaroos – they sometimes graze in the grounds of Parliament House.

Orientation

The city is arranged around the natural-looking, but artificial, Lake Burley Griffin. On the north side is Canberra's city centre, known as Civic. Nearby you'll find most of the short-term accommodation, the Australian National University (ANU) and inner-north suburbs.

The huge Vernon Circle on the north side of the lake is the centre of Civic. Surrounding the circle is the hexagonal London Circuit. The mirror-image Sydney (east) and Melbourne (west) Buildings, with their distinctive colonnaded archways, flank the beginning of Northbourne Ave, the main artery north of the lake leading to the suburbs of Braddon, Lyneham, Downer and Dickson. At the Jolimont Centre, in Northbourne Ave, are the long-distance bus station, Countrylink Travel Centre, airline offices and luggage lockers. From Civic, local buses run from the interchange on East Row.

The main shopping and restaurant area is around the Sydney Building and the nearby pedestrian malls – Garema Place, City Walk and Petrie Plaza. The merry-go-round located here began life in 1914 on Melbourne's St Kilda Beach; it now operates daily except Sunday in summer ($2). The big Canberra Centre is the largest shopping centre in Civic and has a good supermarket.

South of Vernon Circle, Northbourne Ave becomes Commonwealth Ave, which runs over Lake Burley Griffin to Capital Circle. Capital Circle surrounds the new Parliament House on Capital Hill and is the apex of Walter Burley Griffin's parliamentary triangle, formed by Commonwealth Ave, Kings Ave and the lake. Many important buildings are located within this triangle, including the National Library of Australia (NLA), the High Court, the NGA and old Parliament House. Bus No 34 runs from Civic to all these places.

The suburbs surrounding Capital Circle are Parkes, Barton, Forrest, Deakin and Yarralumla. South-east of Capital Hill is Kingston, where you'll find the train station, and Manuka, where there is a large shopping centre and plenty of eating places.

Canberra also includes the 'towns' of Belconnen, Woden, Weston Creek, Tuggeranong and Gungahlin, each with its own collection of suburbs.

Maps The National Roads & Motorists Association (NRMA; ☎ 13 2132), at 92 Northbourne Ave, has an excellent map of Canberra. If you plan to do a lot of driving, Gregory's publishes useful street directories.

For topographic maps of the ACT try the visitor centre, the ACT Government Info Shop (☎ 6247 7211), on the corner of Mort and Bunda Sts, or the Environment Centre (☎ 6247 3064), in Kingsley St. Travellers Maps & Guides (☎ 6249 6006), in the Jolimont Centre, has a wide range of maps (and, of course, guides).

Information

Tourist Offices The flash and friendly Canberra Visitor Centre (☎ 1800 026 166) is on Northbourne Ave, near the corner of Morphett St, Dickson, about 2km north of Civic. It's open from 9 am to 5.30 pm weekdays and to 4 pm weekends. There's a free 10-minute video showing at regular intervals in the theatrette, and there's also a cafe (open from 8 am). You can pick up a free copy of the useful booklet *This Week in Canberra*, and book accommodation and tours here.

Post & Communications To receive mail, have it addressed to Poste Restante at the Canberra City Post Office, 53–73 Alinga St, Civic, ACT 2601. The Post Office is open from 8.30 am to 5.30 pm weekdays.

There are pay phones and credit-card phones outside the post office and in the nearby Jolimont Centre (and elsewhere).

Civic Library, on East Row, Civic, is the most convenient place to access the Internet (free). You can also get on-line for $0.20 a minute at Cafe Cactus (☎ 6248 0449), in Garema Place, Civic. The National Library

COLIN BARNES

Early risers in the Snowy Mountains

MANFRED GOTTSCHALK

View of Lake Albina, Kosciuszko National Park

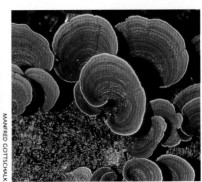

SARA-JANE CLELAND

Fungi, Border Ranges National Park

PAUL SINCLAIR

Murramarang National Park

The view of Parliament House and Mt Anslie (right) from Red Hill, Canberra

Tidbinbilla Tracking Station, south-west of Canberra

Canberra Festival

Early morning mist rolls through the Brindabella valley, near Canberra

has one computer available for Internet and email access (free).

Bookshops Canberra has many good bookshops. The ACT Government Info Shop (☎ 6247 7211), at 10 Mort St, has useful publications, plus some glossy books that make good souvenirs. Smith's Bookshop (☎ 6247 4459), at 76 Alinga St, on the north side of the Melbourne Building, is a good general bookshop.

Electric Shadows (☎ 6249 8352), on City Walk near the cinema of the same name, has books on theatre, films, politics and the arts.

Book Lore (☎ 6247 6450), at 94 Wattle St in the Lyneham shopping centre, is an excellent second-hand bookshop.

Medical Services The Travellers Medical & Vaccination Centre (☎ 6257 7156), 5th floor, 8–10 Hobart Place, west of London Circuit, is open from 9 am to 5 pm weekdays. Treatment is by appointment only (no bulk billing). The Canberra Hospital (☎ 6244 2222) is on Yamba Drive, Garran.

Emergency In the case of emergency, phone ☎ 000 for ambulance, fire and police; ☎ 13 1114 for Lifeline; and ☎ 1800 424 017 for the Rape Crisis Centre. For nonemergency police inquiries, phone the city station on ☎ 11 444.

Lookouts

There are fine views of Canberra from the surrounding hills. West of Civic, **Black Mountain** rises to 812m and is topped by the 195m **Telstra Tower** (☎ 1800 806 718), complete with a revolving restaurant (☎ 6248 6162). The tower also has a display on telecommunications history and is open from 9 am to 10 pm daily ($3/1 for adults/children). There are no buses up to the tower, but you can walk up on a 2km trail through the bush, starting on Frith Rd. Other good bushwalks, accessible from Belconnen Way and Caswell Drive, meander round the back of the hill.

Other lookouts, all with road access, are **Mt Taylor** (855m), **Mt Ainslie** (843m), **Red Hill** (720m) and **Mt Pleasant** (663m). Mt Ainslie is close to the city, on the north-east side, and has particularly fine views down Anzac Parade to Parliament House. From the top you'll also appreciate how full of parks Canberra is. The view is fabulous at night, with the city lights blinking away. There are good walking trails up Mt Ainslie (45 minutes) from behind the Australian War Memorial and on to Mt Majura (888m) 4km away.

Lake Burley Griffin

The lake was named after Canberra's designer, and, although it was part of the city's original design, it was not created until the Molonglo River was dammed in 1963. Swimming in the lake isn't recommended, but you can go boating (beware of strong winds which can blow up suddenly from nowhere). You can hire boats, bikes and inline skates near the Acton Park ferry terminal, on the northern side of the lake. There's also a tiny coal-driven steamboat that chugs across the lake, stopping at the Regatta Point and Library jetties. A short ride costs $3/2 for adults/children.

There are a number of places of interest around the 35km shore. The most visible is the **Captain Cook Memorial Water Jet**, which flings a column of water 147m into the air and gives you a free shower if the wind is blowing from the right direction. The jet, built in 1970 to commemorate the bicentenary of Captain Cook's visit to Australia, operates from 10 am to noon and 2 to 4 pm daily (plus 7 to 9 pm during daylight-saving time). At **Regatta Point**, nearby on the northern shore, is a skeletal globe with Cook's three great Pacific voyages traced on it. Just north of here, beautiful **Commonwealth Park** has a series of paths through flower gardens and pools – a great place for a stroll or picnic.

The **National Capital Exhibition** (☎ 6257 1068), also at Regatta Point, is open from 9 am to 6 pm daily and has displays on the growth of the capital (free). It gives an excellent overview of Canberra's history and layout. Farther east is **Blundell's Cottage** (1860). The simple stone-and-slab cottage, containing period furnishings and fittings, is a reminder of the area's early farming history; it's open from 10 am to 4 pm Tuesday to Sunday ($2/1).

AUSTRALIAN CAPITAL TERRITORY

CANBERRA SUBURBS

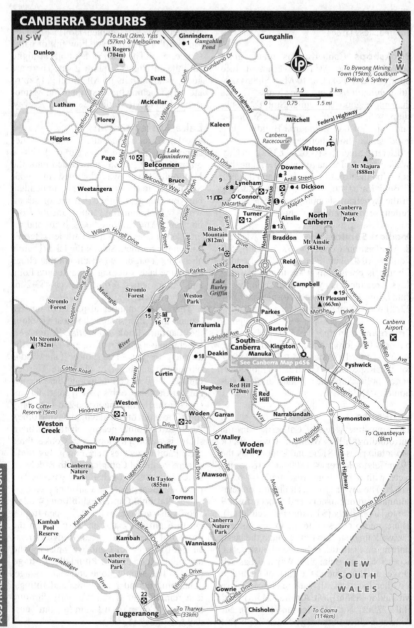

AUSTRALIAN CAPITAL TERRITORY

CANBERRA SUBURBS

1	Ginninderra Village; Federation Square; Cockington Green; National Dinosaur Museum	5	Dickson Shopping Centre	15	National Aquarium & Wildlife Park
2	Canberra Carotel	6	Visitor Centre	16	Scrivener Dam Lookout
3	Blue & White Lodge; Canberran Lodge; Miranda Lodge	7	Lyneham Shopping Centre	17	Government House
		8	Canberra YHA Hostel	18	Royal Australian Mint
		9	Australian Institute of Sport	19	Royal Military College, Duntroon
4	Downer Club (Space Dome & Observatory); Bicycle Museum	10	Belconnen Mall	20	Woden Plaza
		11	Canberra Motor Village	21	Weston Creek Centre
		12	O'Connor Shopping Centre	22	Tuggeranong Hyperdome
		13	Pavilion on Northbourne		
		14	Australian National Botanic Gardens		

At the eastern end of Commonwealth Park is the **carillon**, on Aspen Island. The 53-bell tower was a gift from Britain in 1963 to commemorate Canberra's 50th anniversary. The Carillon was completed in 1970, and the bells weigh from 7kg to six tonnes. There are recitals at 12.45 pm weekdays (Wednesday only in winter) and at 2.45 pm on weekends and public holidays, with an additional recital at 5.45 pm in summer.

Parliament House

South of the lake at the end of Commonwealth Ave, the gleaming four-legged flagpole on top of Capital Hill marks the new Parliament House. Opened in 1988, it cost $1.1 billion and took eight years to build. It replaced old Parliament House down the hill on King George Terrace, which served 11 years longer than its intended 50 years.

The new Parliament House was designed by the US-based Italian Romaldo Giurgola, who won the design competition entered by more than 300 architects. It's built into the hill and the roof has been grassed over to preserve the shape of the original hilltop (you can walk over the roof). The interior design and decoration is splendid. A different combination of Australian timbers is used in each of its principal sections. Seventy new art and craft works were commissioned from Australian artists and a further 3000 were bought.

The building's main axis runs north-east to south-west in a direct line from the old Parliament House, the Australian War Memorial across the lake and Mt Ainslie. On either side of this axis, two high, granite-faced walls curve out from the centre to the corners of the site – on a plan these walls look like back-to-back boomerangs. The House of Representatives is to the east of the walls and the Senate to the west. They're linked to the centre by covered walkways.

Extensive areas of Parliament House are open to the public from 9 am to 5 pm daily. You enter through the white marble **Great Veranda** at the north-end of the main axis, where Nelson Tjakamarra's *Meeting Place* mosaic represents a gathering of Aboriginal tribes. Inside, the grey-green marble columns of the foyer symbolise a forest, while marquetry panels on the walls depict Australian flora. From the 1st floor you look down on the **Great Hall**, with its 20m-long Arthur Boyd tapestry. A public gallery above the Great Hall has a 16m-long embroidery, created by 500 people.

Beyond the Great Hall you reach the gallery above the Members' Hall – the central 'crossroads' of the building – with the flagpole above it and passages to the debating chambers on each side. One of only four existing originals of the **Magna Carta** is on display here. South of the Members Hall are the committee rooms and ministers' offices.

If you want to make sure of a place in the **House of Representatives'** gallery during question time, book by phone (☎ 6277 4889). Some seats are left unbooked but on sitting days you'd have to queue early to get one. Debating starts at 2 pm. Seats in the **Senate** gallery are almost always available. Senate debates are much tamer affairs than those in the House of Representatives, where the prime minister and leader of the opposition slug it out.

AUSTRALIAN CAPITAL TERRITORY

Federal Politics Since 1901

With only around a century of federal government, Australian political history is much more accessible than that of older nations. The virtues, failings and foibles of the 20-odd prime ministers are remembered and form part of the country's popular history.

The Early Years

In the first decade or so, questions of trade (free or protected) dominated the political discussion, and the notorious White Australia policy was established. Pacific Islanders had been brought to the Queensland cane fields as virtual slaves since the late 1800s; many of the labourers had been tricked into coming to Australia, and some were even kidnapped. The new policy was just as blatantly racist, preventing the importing of people from Pacific islands, and deporting those still remaining in 1906.

During WWI the Labor Party won office and in 1915 Billy Hughes ('the little digger') became prime minister. Hughes decided that conscription was necessary to bolster Australia's contribution to the European war, but his party disagreed, as did the Australian people who narrowly rejected conscription in an acrimonious referendum. Hughes was sacked as leader of the Labor Party, but he joined with conservatives to form a new government and remained prime minister. Another referendum on conscription was lost in 1917, but Hughes established himself as a world figure during the post-war peace conferences at Versailles and remained prime minister until 1923.

Stanley Bruce, the epitome of a conservative prime minister, took over from Hughes and led the government until 1929 when Labor won the general election. Internal squabbling saw Joe Lyons leave the party and join the conservatives to form the United Australia Party (UAP), which won government in 1931.

The Menzies Era

In 1939 Robert Menzies became leader of the UAP, and thus prime minister. Like Stanley Bruce, he was very proper and very conservative. The Labor Party ousted Menzies in the 1941 election and John Curtin steered the country through WWII. Curtin died just before the war ended and Ben Chifley, a train driver from Bathurst, became the Labor prime minister.

Chifley's policies of welcoming refugees from Europe, building universities and instituting large projects such as the Snowy Mountains Hydro-electric Scheme shaped post-war Australia.

In 1949 the conservatives won office, again under Robert Menzies, now leader of the new Liberal Party (which is *not* a liberal party, except in the economic sense). He ruled until 1966, when he retired. After a bout of McCarthy-style repression of communists, the Menzies years passed like a long, long dream where old values comfortably enveloped and smothered new ideas.

Menzies was besotted with the British royal family, but saw that alliance with the USA had become essential and he led the country into the Vietnam disaster. After his retirement, subsequent Liberal prime ministers continued conscripting 18-year-olds (who were too young to vote) to fight in Vietnam. 'All the way with LBJ', simpered Prime Minister Harold Holt. Massive protests against the war helped the Labor Party, under Gough Whitlam, to win power in the 1972 election.

On nonsitting days there are free **guided tours** every half-hour from 9 am to 4pm; on sitting days there are talks on the building in the Great Hall gallery every half-hour. Audio guides are available in English, French, German, Mandarin and Japanese ($5).

Bus Nos 34 and 39 run from Civic to Parliament House.

Old Parliament House

On King George Terrace, halfway between the new Parliament House and the lake, old Parliament House was the seat of Australia's federal government from 1927 to 1988. It's a grand old building – all leather chairs and wood panelling – but some of the tiny, cluttered offices show why the back-

Federal Politics Since 1901

Whitlam & the Dismissal

The Whitlam government irrevocably changed Australia. In the government's three hectic years many things now taken for granted were instituted: free health care, free tertiary education (now disappearing), land rights for Aborigines, equal pay for women, no-fault divorce, legal aid and much more.

However, the pace of change stirred up strong opposition and the government became embroiled in a series of scandals. On 11 November 1975, Governor General John Kerr dismissed the government.

The proclamation dismissing Whitlam and installing Liberal leader Malcolm Fraser as prime minister ended with the phrase 'God save the Queen'. Whitlam's fiery response concluded 'Well may you say God save the Queen, because *nothing* will save the Governor General'. Until then most Australians had considered the governor general as a quaint piece of decoration, a hangover from the days when the country was a British colony. To find that the Queen, via the governor general, could dismiss an elected government came as a rude shock, but Whitlam nevertheless lost the subsequent elections.

Malcolm Fraser then spent six years dismantling Whitlam's reforms. It seemed that another Menzies era was beginning, but Bob Hawke, leader of the powerful Council of Trade Unions, was hurried into Parliament and manoeuvred into leadership of the Labor Party in time to win the 1983 election. The Labor leader whom Hawke replaced was Bill Hayden, a left-winger with republican leanings who later became governor general. After the Whitlam debacle the Labor Party decided not to rock the boat, with the result that Hawke's years at the helm seemed comparatively bland.

Politics in the 1990s

In 1991 Hawke was ousted as party leader by his treasurer, Paul Keating, who became prime minister. Keating earned his spurs by winning the apparently unwinnable election of 1993, and, despite a penchant for Italian suits and antique clocks, his rough-house debating style earned him a reputation as a tough Labor leader of the old school.

Keating was a politician who liked to lead from the front, and he pushed for closer ties with Asia and for Australia to become a republic. But in 1996 the conservative Liberal-National Party coalition was returned to power. Liberal Party leader John Howard became prime minister and National Party leader Tim Fischer became his deputy (to be replaced by John Anderson). One of Howard's first acts as prime minister was to hang a picture of the Queen in his office.

Republicans largely blamed the prime minister for the no vote in the 1999 republic referendum. Mr Howard, who opposed cutting ties with the British monarchy and replacing the Queen with a president, insisted on a model that would see a president elected by a two-thirds majority of Parliament (rather than by popular vote). The referendum comprehensively opted for the status quo – the ACT was the only state or territory to vote in favour of replacing the Queen with an Australian head of state.

Tax reform has been one of the Howard government's major policy agendas and the Liberals went into the 1998 election proposing a controversial Goods & Service Tax (GST). Despite a greatly reduced majority, the Liberal-National coalition was returned to power and the GST was introduced in mid-2000.

benchers in particular were so keen to move out.

The end of its parliamentary days was marked in style. As the corridors of power echoed with the defence minister's favourite Rolling Stones records, the prime minister and the leader of the opposition joined together in song, arm-in-arm. Bodies were seen dragging themselves away well after dawn the next morning – and that's just what got into print!

The views from the grounds are good, and inside the building there are displays from the collections of the National Museum. The building is also home to the **National Portrait Gallery** (NPG; ☎ 6273 4723). The gallery's collection features portraits, in various mediums, of prominent Australians – including bushranger Ned Kelly, athlete Cathy Freeman and musician Nick Cave – and it has a program of changing exhibitions. As well as free guided tours (roughly, every 45 minutes from 9.30 am to 3.15 pm) there's an interesting half-hour sound-and-light show in the House of Representatives chamber at noon and 4.15 pm.

Old Parliament House is open from 9 am to 5 pm daily ($2/1 for adults/children). Bus Nos 31, 36 and 39 run here from Civic.

On the lawn in front of Old Parliament House is the **Aboriginal Tent Embassy**, now recognised by the Australian Heritage Commission as a site of cultural significance. The embassy, which first appeared on Australia Day 1972, symbolises the Aboriginal claim for land rights and self-determination.

National Gallery of Australia

This excellent art gallery (☎ 6240 6502) is on Parkes Place, beside the High Court. The Australian collection ranges from traditional Aboriginal art through to 20th-century works by Arthur Boyd, Sidney Nolan and Albert Tucker. Aboriginal works include bark paintings from Arnhem Land, *pukumani* burial poles from the Tiwi people of Melville and Bathurst Islands off Darwin, printed fabrics by the women of Utopia and Ernabella in central Australia, and paintings from Yuendumu, also in central Australia. There are often temporary exhibitions from the Kimberley and other areas where Aboriginal art is flourishing.

In addition to works from the early decades of European settlement and the 19th-century romantics, there are examples of early nationalistic paintings by Charles Conder, Arthur Streeton and Tom Roberts. There are also many international works, such as Jackson Pollock's famous (and controversial) *Blue Poles*. The collection is not confined to paintings; sculptures, prints, drawings, photographs, furniture, ceramics, fashion, textiles and silverware are all on display. The Sculpture Garden, which is always open, has a variety of striking works,

including the unusual *Fog Sculpture* (a fine mist spray that operates from noon to 2 pm daily). The garden is a great place to listen to the carillon recitals.

The gallery is open from 10 am to 5 pm daily. General admission is free, but there's a charge for special exhibitions. There are free tours at 11 am and 2 pm daily. Every Thursday and Sunday the 11 am tour focuses on Aboriginal art. The gallery often provides free lectures relating to its exhibitions, and presents films on Fridays at 12.45 pm. Phone for details or check Saturday's *Canberra Times*. Bus No 34 runs to the gallery from the city centre.

High Court

The High Court building (☎ 6270 6811) is open from 9.45 am to 4.30 pm daily (free). Opened in 1980, its grandiose magnificence caused it to be dubbed 'Gar's Mahal', a reference to Sir Garfield Barwick, Chief Justice during the construction of the building. High Court sittings are open to the public (call to find out the times) and, because of the good acoustics, music is often played in the lobby on weekends.

National Science & Technology Centre – Questacon

This is a 'hands on' science museum (☎ 6270 2800) in the snappy white building on King Edward Terrace between the High Court and the NLA. There are over 200 'devices' in the centre's five main galleries, plus areas where you can use 'props' to get a feeling for a scientific concept and then see it applied to an everyday situation. Displays include the earthquake experience, 12 million volts of caged lightning and plenty of computer 'games'. It might be educational, but it's also great fun.

Questacon is open from 10 am to 5 pm daily ($8/4 for adults/children).

National Library of Australia

On Parkes Place beside the lake is the National Library of Australia (☎ 6262 1111), one of the most elegant buildings in Canberra. The visitor information desk is staffed from 9 am to 5 pm Monday to Friday.

The library has more than six million books, and among its collection are rare books, paintings, early manuscripts and maps, Captain Cook's *Endeavour* journal and a fine model of the ship. The library has ongoing displays and special exhibitions. There are guided tours (☎ 6262 1699) at 2 pm Tuesday to Thursday and free films (☎ 6262 1475) are shown at 7 pm Thursday.

The library is open from 9 am to 9 pm Monday to Thursday and from 9 am to 5 pm Friday to Sunday (the Main Reading Room opens from 1.30 to 5 pm on Sunday).

National Archives

The National Archives (☎ 6212 3600), on Queen Victoria Terrace, behind the Old Parliament House, holds a treasure-trove of national history, with all sorts of files, records and photographs. It's great if you want to do some political or historical research, but also worth seeing for its exhibitions and galleries. It's open from 9 am to 5 pm Monday to Saturday and from noon to 5 pm Sunday (free). Bus Nos 31, 36 and 39 run nearby.

Foreign Embassies

There are about 80 embassies and high commissions in Canberra. A few are worth looking at – the US Embassy is a facsimile of a Virginian mansion; the Thai Embassy is similar to a Bangkok temple; the Indonesian Embassy has a small display centre next door exhibiting examples of Indonesia's colourful culture (open 9.30 am to 12.30 pm and 2 to 4 pm weekdays); and Papua New Guinea's Embassy looks like a *haus tambaran* spirit-house from the Sepik River region of PNG.

Most of the embassies are in Yarralumla, south of the lake. Some have open days; check with the visitor centre to see if any are scheduled. Bus No 31 will get you there.

Embassy-spotting enthusiasts can buy *Canberra's Embassies,* by Graeme Barrow, or see the Facts for the Visitor chapter for a partial list of foreign embassies in Canberra.

Australian War Memorial

The massive War Memorial, north of the lake and at the foot of Mt Ainslie, faces old Parliament House from the end of Anzac Parade. It was conceived in 1925 and finally opened in 1941, not long after WWII broke out in the Pacific. It houses an amazing collection of pictures, dioramas, relics, valour medals and exhibitions, including a fine collection of old aircraft and a lifeboat that carried soldiers ashore at Gallipoli in 1915. A new aircraft hall was due to open at the time of writing. For anyone with an interest in toy soldiers, the miniature battle scenes explaining key offensives from the two World Wars are absorbing. For the less military-minded, the memorial has a superb art collection.

The **Hall of Memory** is the resting place of the Unknown Australian Soldier, whose remains were brought here in 1993 from a WWI battlefield.

The War Memorial is open from 10 am to 5 pm daily (free). Phone ☎ 6243 4211 for (free) tour times. Bus No 33 runs to the memorial from Civic.

Several other memorials line **Anzac Parade**, including the impressive Australia Hellenic memorial and the Vietnam and Korean war memorials.

Royal Australian Mint

The mint (☎ 6202 6819), south of the lake on Denison St in Deakin, produces all Australia's coins. Through plate-glass windows you can see the whole process, from raw materials to finished coins. There's also a collection of rare coins in the **Coin Museum**. You can even mint your own shiny $1 coin but the privilege will cost you $2. The mint is open from 9 am to 4 pm weekdays and from 10 am to 3 pm weekends (free). Bus No 30 runs past it.

Canberra Museum & Gallery

This new gallery (☎ 6207 3968) in Civic Square, at 176 London Circuit, is a contrast to the NGA. Its focus is on contemporary and offbeat exhibitions combining social history and youth culture with visual arts. The result is, according to its literature, 'public art'. It also hosts a program of workshops, recitals and lectures, and is open from 10 am to 5 pm Tuesday to Sunday (to 9 pm on Friday). General entry is free, although there's a charge for some exhibitions and most events.

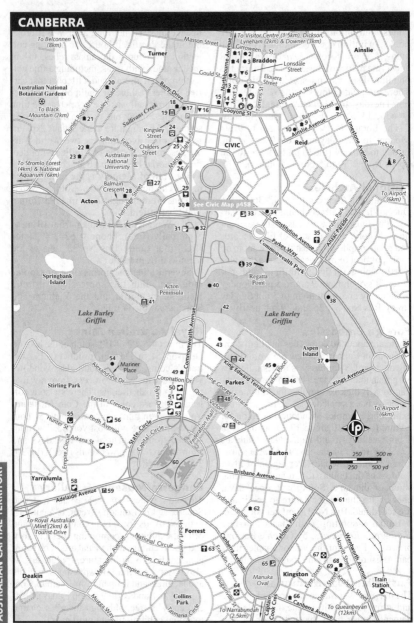

CANBERRA

To Belconnen (8km)

Masson Street

To Visitor Centre (1.5km), Dickson, Lyneham (2km) & Downer (3km)

Turner

Northbourne Avenue

Girraween St

Ainslie

1 ● 2
● 3
4 ● Braddon

Gould St
▼ 5
6 ▼
Lonsdale Street
Elouera Street

Barry Drive

Daley Road

20

Australian National Botanical Gardens

To Black Mountain (2km)

Cunes Ross Street

21

Sullivans Creek

Kingsley Street

15
18 ● 17
19 ●
24
25
Childers Street

Sullivan Fellows Road

22
23

Australian National University

Balmain Crescent
28

26
27

29

30 ■

Acton

Livingede Street

Marcus Clarke St

Gould St
Torrens St

12
13
14 ● 11
10

Cooyong St

Donaldson Street

Batman Street
9

Ainslie Avenue

Limestone Avenue

Reid

Treloar Cres

8

To Airport (6km)

CIVIC

See Civic Map p458

33

Constitution Avenue

35

Anzac Park
Anzac Parade

31
32

Parkes Way

Commonwealth Avenue

39

Commonwealth Park

Regatta Point

Springbank Island

Acton Peninsula

40

41

42

Lake Burley Griffin

Lake Burley Griffin

38

Aspen Island

36

54 Mariner Place

Alexandrina Dr

Coronation Dr

49
50
51
52
53

43

King Edward Terrace
44

Parkes

King George Terrace
48

Queen Victoria Terrace

47

45 Parkes Place
46

37

Kings Avenue

To Airport (6km)

Stirling Park

Forster Crescent

55
Hunter St
56
Perth Avenue

Empire Circuit

Arkana St
57

State Circle

Flynn Drive

Commonwealth Avenue

Federation Mall

60

Capital Circle

Barton

Brisbane Avenue

N

0   250   500 m
0   250   500 yd

LP

Yarralumla

58
Adelaide Avenue

59

To Royal Australian Mint (2km) & Tourist Drive

Deakin

Melbourne Avenue

National Circuit

Dominion Circuit

Empire Circuit

Mugga Way

Collins Park

Tasmania Circle

Sydney Avenue

62

61

Forrest

Hobart Avenue

Canberra Avenue

63

Franklin Street

Bougainville St

64

National Circuit

Telopea Park

65

Manuka Oval

66

Kingston

67
68
69

Eyre Street

Howitt Street

Oawes Street
Kennedy Street

Wentworth Avenue

Train Station

To Narrabundah (2.5km)

Captain Cook Cres

Canberra Avenue

To Queanbeyan (12km)

CANBERRA

PLACES TO STAY
1   Capital Hotel
4   Chifley on Northbourne;
    Kythera Motel
7   Olim's Canberra Hotel
9   Acacia Motor Lodge
13 Quality Inn Downtown
15 Canberra Central Apartments
18 Toad Hall
20 Bruce Hall
21 Burton & Garran Hall
22 Ursula College
23 Burgmann College
28 University House
30 Capital Tower
49 Hyatt Hotel Canberra
62 Macquarie Hotel
66 Kingston Hotel
68 Victor Lodge
69 Motel Monaro

PLACES TO EAT
6   Cornucopia Bakery
14 Mosaics; James Court
    Apartments
16 Fringe Benefits

OTHER
2   Budget Car Rental; Shell
    Service Station

3   Thrifty Car Rental
5   NRMA
8   Australian War Memorial
10 Gorman House Arts Centre
11 Hertz Car Rental
12 Avis Car Rental
17 Environment Centre
19 Drill Hall Gallery
24 Street Theatre
25 Canberra Worker's Club
26 Travellers Medical
    & Vaccination Centre
27 ScreenSound Australia
29 Rydges Canberra Hotel;
    Bobby McGee's
31 Acton Park Ferry Terminal;
    Dobel Boat Hire
32 Mr Spokes Bike Hire
33 Olympic Swimming Pool
34 National Convention Centre
35 Church of St John the Baptist
36 Australian-American
    Memorial
37 Carillon
38 Blundell's Cottage
39 National Capital Exhibition
40 Captain Cook Memorial
    Water Jet
41 Proposed site for National
    Museum

42 Library Jetty
43 National Library of Australia
44 National Science &
    Technology Centre
    (Questacon)
45 High Court
46 National Gallery
    of Australia
47 National Archives
48 Old Parliament House
54 Canberra Yacht Club;
    Southern Cross Cruises
55 Canberra Mosque
59 The Lodge
60 Parliament House
61 Old Bus Depot Market
63 Serbian Orthodox Church
64 Manuka Shopping Centre
65 Manuka Oval &
    Swimming Pool
67 Kingston Shopping Centre

EMBASSIES
50 UK Embassy
51 NZ Embassy
52 Canadian Embassy
53 PNG Embassy
56 Indonesian Embassy
57 US Embassy
58 Thai Embassy

ScreenSound Australia

The revamped and renamed National Film & Sound Archive (☎ 6248 2000) is housed in an Art Deco building on McCoy Circuit, at the south-eastern edge of the Australian National University (ANU). Interesting exhibitions (some interactive) from the archive's collections are on show, as well as old photographs and props from Australian movies. There's also a theatre showing old film. ScreenSound is open from 9 am to 5 pm daily (exhibitions cost $2/1 for adults/children).

Australian National University

The ANU's attractive grounds take up most of the area between Civic and Black Mountain, and they're pleasant to wander around. On Kingsley St near Hutton St, is the **Drill Hall Gallery** (☎ 6249 5832), an offshoot of the NGA, which has changing exhibitions of contemporary art. It's open from noon to 5 pm Wednesday to Sunday (free).

Australian National Botanic Gardens

On the lower slopes of Black Mountain, behind the ANU, the beautiful 50-hectare botanic gardens are devoted to Australia's unique native flora. There are educational walks, including one among plants traditionally used by Aborigines. A highlight is Rainforest Gully, achieved in this dry climate by a 'misting' system. The eucalypt lawn has 600 species of this ubiquitous Australian tree, while the Mallee section displays the typical vegetation of semidesert country.

There are **guided walks** from the visitor centre at 11 am weekdays and at 11 am and 2 pm weekends. The visitor centre (☎ 6250 9540), open from 9.30 am to 4.30 pm daily, has an introductory video about the gardens, and the Botanical Bookshop has an excellent range of books, cards and posters. Near where the walks start and finish is a cafe with a pleasant outdoor section.

AUSTRALIAN CAPITAL TERRITORY

The gardens are open from 9 am to 5 pm daily and are reached from Clunies Ross St.

Australian Institute of Sport

Founded in 1981 as part of an effort to improve Australia's performance at events such as the Olympics, the Australian Institute of Sport (AIS; ☎ 6214 1010) is located on Leverrier Crescent in the north-western suburb of Bruce. It provides training facilities for the country's elite athletes, who lead hour-long **tours** of the institute at 11.30 am and 2.30 pm daily, with additional tours at 10 am and 1 pm on weekends ($10/5 for adults/children).

The tennis courts and swimming pools are open to visitors; phone ☎ 6252 1281 for bookings.

Bus No 80 runs to the AIS from the city centre.

National Aquarium & Wildlife Park

The impressive aquarium (☎ 6287 1211) is about 6km south-west of Civic on Lady Denman Drive, near Scrivener Dam, at the western end of Lake Burley Griffin. It also includes a native wildlife sanctuary. It's open from 9 am to 5.30 pm daily ($10/6 for

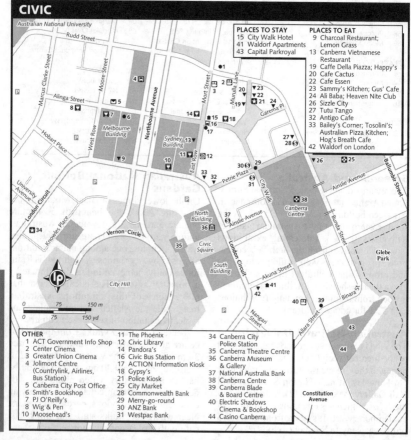

CIVIC

PLACES TO STAY
15 City Walk Hotel
41 Waldorf Apartments
43 Capital Parkroyal

PLACES TO EAT
9 Charcoal Restaurant; Lemon Grass
13 Canberra Vietnamese Restaurant
19 Caffe Della Piazza; Happy's
20 Cafe Cactus
22 Cafe Essen
23 Sammy's Kitchen; Gus' Cafe
24 Ali Baba; Heaven Nite Club
26 Sizzle City
27 Tutu Tango
32 Antigo Cafe
33 Bailey's Corner; Tosolini's; Australian Pizza Kitchen; Hog's Breath Cafe
42 Waldorf on London

OTHER
1 ACT Government Info Shop
2 Center Cinema
3 Greater Union Cinema
4 Jolimont Centre (Countrylink, Airlines, Bus Station)
5 Canberra City Post Office
6 Smith's Bookshop
7 PJ O'Reilly's
8 Wig & Pen
10 Moosehead's
11 The Phoenix
12 Civic Library
14 Pandora's
16 Civic Bus Station
17 ACTION Information Kiosk
18 Gypsy's
21 Police Kiosk
25 City Market
28 Commonwealth Bank
29 Merry-go-round
30 ANZ Bank
31 Westpac Bank
34 Canberra City Police Station
35 Canberra Theatre Centre
36 Canberra Museum & Gallery
37 National Australia Bank
38 Canberra Centre
39 Canberra Blade & Board Centre
40 Electric Shadows Cinema & Bookshop
44 Casino Canberra

AUSTRALIAN CAPITAL TERRITORY

adults/children). There are no buses running here from Civic.

National Museum of Australia

A site for this long-awaited museum, due to open on 1 January 2001, has been set aside on Acton Peninsula, west of the Commonwealth Ave Bridge. The museum, combining displays, hands-on activities and performances with new technologies, will focus on Aboriginal and Torres Strait Islander cultures and histories, and the Australian environment.

Other Attractions

On all but one or two days of the year you can do little more than drive by and peek through the gates of the prime minister's official Canberra residence, **The Lodge**, on Adelaide Ave, Deakin. The Canberra Visitor Centre (☎ 1800 026 166) can give details of annual open days here and at **Government House**, the impressive residence of the governor general, which is on the south-west corner of Lake Burley Griffin. Southern Cross Cruises (☎ 6273 1784) offers garden tours at Government House weekly during summer, and there's a lookout beside Scrivener Dam, at the western end of the lake, giving a good view of the building. The governor general is the representative of the Australian monarch – the Queen of Britain.

The **Australian-American Memorial**, at the eastern end of Kings Ave, is a 79m-high pillar topped by an eagle that commemorates US support of Australia during WWII.

The **Church of St John the Baptist**, in Reid just east of Civic, was built between 1841 and 1845 and thus predates the capital. The stained glass windows show pioneering families of the region. The adjoining **St John's Schoolhouse Museum** (☎ 6249 6839) has some early relics and is open on from 10 am to noon Wednesday and from 2 to 4 pm weekends.

Farther east, the **Royal Military College, Duntroon** was once a homestead, with parts dating from the 1830s. You can drive around the grounds (stay under 40km/h) and have a look.

The free **Bicycle Museum**, in the enterprising Tradesmen's Union Club (☎ 6248

0999) at 2 Badham St in Dickson, has a large collection of 'old and unusual bicycles'.

The club also runs the Downer Club (☎ 6248 5333), nearby on Hawdon Place. It's home to the **Canberra Space Dome & Observatory**. As well as a planetarium (shows at 3, 7 and 8.30 pm), there are astronomy sessions in the observatory at 8.30, 9.30 and 10.30 pm. It's open Tuesday to Saturday ($8/5.50 for adults/children). There's also (oddly enough) an Antarctic igloo display here.

Near the train station on Geijera Place (off Cunningham St) in Kingston, you'll find Australia's oldest steam locomotive at the **Canberra Railway Museum** (☎ 6239 6707). It's open from 1 to 4 pm Saturday and Sunday ($4/2).

Canberra's **mosque** is in Yarralumla, on the corner of Hunter St and Empire Circuit.

Kids might enjoy a visit to **Weston Park**, in Yarralumla beside the lake. There's a maze and a miniature railway, which operate on weekends and during school holidays, as well as treehouses and other distractions.

Activities

Bushwalking Tidbinbilla Nature Reserve has marked trails and the huge Namadgi National Park has many good walks; see the boxed text 'The Bush Capital' later in this chapter. There are shorter and more accessible walks in sections of the Canberra Nature Park, which encompasses large pockets of bush surrounding the city.

The Canberra Bushwalking Club (☎ 6288 7862) organises regular walks. The club can also be contacted through the Environment Centre (☎ 6247 3064), in Kingsley St on the ANU campus. Here you can buy *Above the Cotter* ($16), which details walks and drives in the area. Graeme Barrow's *Walking Canberra's Hills and Rivers* ($14.95) is also useful. The centre is open daily except Monday.

Water Sports Dobel Boat Hire (☎ 6249 6861), at the Acton Park ferry terminal, rents out canoes for $16 an hour and paddleboats for $18 an hour; it also hires out sailboards and surfskis. Private powerboats are not allowed on the lake. Canoeing in the Murrumbidgee River, about 20km west of Canberra city centre at its closest point, is also popular.

Swimming pools around the city include the Olympic Pool, on Allara St, Civic, and the Manuka Swimming Pool, on Currie St, south-east of Parliament House.

River Runners (☎ 6288 5610) offers a 5½-hour white-water rafting trip on the Shoalhaven River, 1½ hours from Canberra, for $115.

Cycling Canberra has great bicycle tracks – probably the best in Australia. See Canberra's Getting Around section for information.

In-Line Skating Several places hire out in-line skates. Canberra Blade & Board Centre (☎ 6257 7233), at 38 Allara St, Civic, charges $15 for the first two hours and $5 for each subsequent hour, or $30 a day. Mr Spokes Bike Hire (☎ 6257 1188), near the Acton Park ferry terminal, charges $10 an hour. Fees at both places include all safety gear.

Canberra on the Web

With so many government and bureaucratic connections, it's hardly surprising that there's a wealth of information on the national capital to be gleaned from the Internet. Most of it's stuffy and boring, but for an interesting (or at least useful) virtual tour, point your browser in the direction of these sites:

Canberra Visitor Centre The first stop if you want tourist information, accommodation, events, entertainment and shopping.
www.canberratourism.com.au

National Gallery of Australia Search the collection of this superb gallery and check out new exhibitions and acquisitions.
www.nga.gov.au

National Library of Australia A good online resource for research.
www.nla.gov.au

Australian War Memorial Take a virtual look at the displays in this awesome museum.
www.awm.gov.au

Action Buses Timetables, fares and everything else you need to know about bussing around Canberra.
www.action.act.gov.au

Australian National University The ANU's coming events, student accommodation and student-oriented information on Canberra.
www.anu.edu.au

Canberra Times The site of Canberra's daily newspaper contains up-to-date news and sport, classified ads, jobs and features.
www.canberratimes.com.au

Canberra Raiders If rugby league is an interest, check out the local NRL club.
raiders.131shop.com.au/index2.htm

Canberra Bushwalking Club Puts you in touch with the local bushwalking enthusiasts and their activities.
www.pcug.org.au/~amikkels/cbc

Canberra Theatre Centre Find out what's going on and coming up at the city's main performing arts venue.
www.canberratheatre.org.au

Canberra Region Restaurant Book The excellent online version of this book, updated annually; not many impartial reviews, but a full listing of Canberra's restaurants and cafes.
www.users.bigpond.com/virtprog

Organised Tours

The visitor centre has details of city and ACT tours. Half-day city tours cost around $30 and there's a variety of day trips to places such as the Snowy Mountains, nature reserves, the satellite tracking station, sheep stations, horse studs and fossicking areas. Murrays (☎ 13 2251) has full-day city tours, including lunch and admission fees ($69/30 for adults/children). Canberra Private Tours (☎ 6295 3822) has half-day city tours, an ACT highlights tour (both $60) and a shopping tour.

Several operators offer cruises on Lake Burley Griffin. Australian Capital Cruises (☎ 6284 7160) has one-hour jaunts from the Acton Park ferry terminal at 10.30 am and 2 pm ($12/6) and a 1½-hour cruise at noon ($15/8). Southern Cross Cruises (☎ 6273 1784) has one-hour cruises from the Canberra Yacht Club on the lake's southern shore ($10/8).

Umbrella Tours (☎ 6285 2605) has 1½-hour walking tours of the city. The Environment Centre on the ANU campus offers nature and ecology tours (prices start at $39); call ☎ 6249 1560 for information and bookings.

Canberra Wineries (☎ 6231 6997) has daily tours of the wineries north of Canberra for $65/49 a full/half day. National Capital Wine Tours (☎ 6287 5218) has day tours for $69 (weekends only).

Taking a flight is a great way of seeing the grand scale of the city's plan. The Canberra Flight Training Centre (☎ 6248 6766), based at the airport, can arrange 30-minute flights for $60.

Better still is floating over the city in a hot-air balloon. Dawn Drifters (☎ 6285 4450) and Balloon Aloft (☎ 6285 1540) are two companies offering dawn flights. Both charge $195 per person on weekends, but weekdays are cheaper.

Special Events

The Canberra Festival takes place over 10 days each March and celebrates the city's birthday with music, food, Mardi Gras, displays, a raft race, a birdman and birdwoman rally, and a parade. Many events are held in Commonwealth Park, which is the site of a carnival. A popular event is the Royal Military College band playing the *1812 Overture,* complete with cannon!

Winter is freezing in the ACT so spring is something to celebrate, and Canberra does it with verve through its Floriade festival in September and October. It concentrates on Canberra's spectacular spring flowers, but there are many related events and activities.

The Street Machine Summernats, basically a big hot-rod show, is held in late December at Exhibition Park in Mitchell.

Places to Stay

Large numbers of public servants arrived in Canberra before residential areas were developed, so the government established hostels to house them. Many of these are now privately run guesthouses, hotels and motels. They can be perfectly all right but some retain a rather institutional feel. The visitor centre has an accommodation list and can make bookings.

Camping In O'Connor 3km north-west of the centre, *Canberra Motor Village (☎ 1800 026 199),* on Kunzea St, has a bush setting and charges $12/20 for tent/powered sites and $69 for en suite cabins (bring your own linen). There's a restaurant, kitchen, tennis court and swimming pool.

Canberra Carotel (☎ 6241 1377), on the Federal Hwy 6km north of Civic in Watson, is a well-equipped place with sites starting at $10/12, on-site vans for $30 for two people and cabins and motel units starting at $55.

Hostels The *City Walk Hotel (☎ 6257 0124, 2 Mort St)* is smack in the middle of Civic, a short stagger from the bus station. It has basic dorm beds for $18 and singles/doubles starting at $40/45; most rooms share bathrooms. It's a reasonable option, with a spacious TV lounge and kitchen facilities, but it can be a bit noisy and, if you have a car, there's no parking.

Canberra YHA Hostel (☎ 6248 9155, 191 Dryandra St, O'Connor) is in a peaceful bushland area, about 6km north-west of Civic. It's purpose-built, well designed and has a pleasant outdoor deck. There's a travel desk (☎ 6248 0177), which handles domestic and international travel. Dorm beds cost $16 to $18, twin rooms with attached bathrooms cost $42, or $46 with en suite ($3 extra for nonmembers). The office is open from 7 am to 10.30 pm, but you can check in until midnight if you let staff know. There's a free pick-up service, otherwise bus No 35 runs from the Civic bus station past the front door. You can hire bicycles at the hostel.

Victor Lodge (☎ 6295 7777, 29 Dawes St, Kingston) is a clean, friendly place a couple of kilometres south-east of Parliament House. A comfy bed in a four-bunk room costs $19, including a continental self-serve breakfast. Rooms with shared bathrooms cost $39/49. It has a barbecue and bikes for rent. Phone ahead for a pick up from the bus station.

Kingston Hotel (☎ 6295 0123, 73 Canberra Ave) is a large, popular pub. It has simple shared accommodation in two- and four-bed dorms for $12, with optional linen hire ($4), cooking facilities and counter meals. Bus No 39 from Civic runs close by.

University Accommodation The ANU is a pleasant place to stay. Several residential colleges rent out rooms during vacations.

Toad Hall (☎ 6267 4999), on Kingsley St near the corner of Barry Drive, is the closest accommodation to Civic. It's good value for visiting students with rooms for $25, but nonstudents pay $45.

Most other colleges are along Daley Rd, at the western end of the campus. *Burgmann College* (☎ 6267 5209) charges students/nonstudents $32/44 with breakfast or $44/52 for full board. *Bruce Hall* (☎ 6267 4333) and *Burton & Garran Hall* (☎ 6267 4333) have rooms for $24/31 a night, or $96/114 a week for students/nonstudents. *Ursula College* (☎ 6279 4300) and *Fenner Hall* (☎ 6279 9000) have rooms at similar rates.

Guesthouses There is a cluster of guesthouses east of Northbourne Ave in Downer. All are clean, homely and comfortable, and most include breakfast in the price. It's 4km or so into Civic, but bus No 50 runs past Downer, and Dickson shopping centre isn't far away.

The *Blue & White Lodge* (☎ 6248 0498, 524 Northbourne Ave) has singles/doubles – some are lovely refurbished en suite rooms with TV and fridge – starting at $75/85, including a cooked breakfast. Some rooms have balconies. The same people run *Canberran Lodge* at No 528, which has the same rates. *Miranda Lodge* (☎ 6249 8038, 534 Northbourne Ave) charges $70/85 for bed and cooked breakfast.

Motels Most standard motels are quite expensive for what you get. You might do better than the prices listed here if you book through the visitor centre, as it often has special rates.

Acacia Motor Lodge (☎ 6249 6955, 65 Ainslie Ave, Braddon) has singles/doubles for $72/78, including a light breakfast. The rooms are fairly small, but it's a friendly enough place.

Quality Inn Downtown (☎ 1800 026 150, 82 Northbourne Ave) is well located and has good double rooms for $85. A little farther out, *Kythera Motel* (☎ 6248 7611, 98 Northbourne Ave) has relatively drab rooms for $77.

Motel Monaro (☎ 6295 2111, 27 Dawes St, Kingston), next to Victor Lodge and run by the same people, has doubles for $89.

Other places are scattered through the suburbs, with a concentration of mid-range motels about 8km south of the city in Narrabundah.

Apartments On the corner of Northbourne Ave and Barry Drive, *Canberra Central Apartments* (☎ 1800 629 700) has rather small motel-style doubles for $60/250 a night/week, and larger self-contained apartments with kitchenette for $70/350.

Canberrawide Budget Apartments (☎ 6257 7637, 8 Ijong St, Braddon) has a range of apartments around the city. These are usually let by the week, starting at $400 for a one-bedroom apartment and $530 for a two-bedroom apartment.

University House (☎ 1800 814 864), in Balmain Crescent on the ANU campus, has one-/two-bedroom apartments for $105/146.

Capital Hotel (☎ 6295 1111, 108 Northbourne Ave) has studio apartments for $135 and larger single-bedroom apartments with spa for $165. *Capital Tower (☎ 6276 3444, 2 Marcus Clarke St)* has serviced apartments from $145 to $190.

Waldorf Apartments (☎ 1800 188 388, ✉ sale@waldorfcanberra.com.au, 2 Akuna St) is Canberra's newest hotel. It's well set up for business travellers. Stylish studio apartments cost $145 and one-bedroom apartments are $165.

Hotels Rates at top-end places can vary: ring around or ask at the visitor centre.

Macquarie Hotel (☎ 6273 2325, 18 National Circuit) is a large, fairly modern place with over 500 rooms, all with shared bathrooms. Singles cost $35 to $45 ($145 to $185 weekly) and doubles are $65 ($265 weekly). Bus No 36 from Civic runs past.

Olim's Canberra Hotel (☎ 6248 5511), on the corner Ainslie and Limestone Aves east of Civic, is a pleasant old-style hotel with a tranquil courtyard garden. Rooms start at $95, or $145 for deluxe.

Northbourne Ave has several similar hotels. The *Chifley on Northbourne (☎ 1800 065 064),* at No 102, has rooms for $159 ($120 for NRMA members) and spa rooms starting at $163. *Pavilion on Northbourne (☎ 1800 026 305),* at No 242 near the corner of Wakefield Ave, has standard rooms for $115, and apartments with spa for $145.

Rates at the *Capital Parkroyal (☎ 6247 8999, 1 Binara St),* near the casino, start at $145 but there are often weekend package deals.

The *Hyatt Hotel Canberra (☎ 6270 1234),* Commonwealth Ave, Yarralumla, is Canberra's only five-star hotel. This is the old Hotel Canberra, a venerable institution. Rooms cost $270 to $320, with suites starting at $520.

Places to Eat

Canberra's fine eating scene is continually changing and improving. There are plenty of choices around Civic, an upmarket selection at Manuka and Kingston, an Asian strip in Dickson and other possibilities in shopping centres scattered around the suburbs – just head for the self-contained shopping areas and take your pick.

Many of the city-centre places offer weekday lunchtime specials to entice office workers. Smoking isn't allowed in Canberra's eateries, which is one reason why so many people sit at outside tables.

Civic There's a *food hall* in the Canberra Centre where you can fill up on burgers, pasta, croissants and snacks from $4. There's a smaller food hall on the ground floor in City Market, Bunda St, where the excellent *Sizzle City* has cheap Japanese lunch packs.

The *Canberra Vietnamese Restaurant (☎ 6247 4840, 21 East Row),* upstairs in the Sydney Building, has main courses for around $10.

Bailey's Corner, on the corner of East Row and London Circuit, has a couple of places with outdoor tables. *Tosolini's (☎ 6247 4317)* is an established Italian bistro that is good for a drink or a meal, including breakfast. Pasta dishes cost around $10. The *Australian Pizza Kitchen (☎ 6257 2727),* downstairs, has wood-fired pizzas for around $13 and lunch-time specials for $7; it also brews its own beer. There's a branch of the *Hog's Breath Cafe,* with filling burgers and steaks, next door. *Antigo Cafe (☎ 6249 8080),* in Petrie Plaza, is a cafe and bar open daily until late. The diverse menu includes pasta for $13 and most mains starting at $16.

Lemon Grass (☎ 6247 2779), on the south side of the Melbourne Building is a recommended Thai restaurant with mains for around $14 and a good vegetarian selection. It's licensed and BYO. The licensed *Charcoal Restaurant (☎ 6248 8015),* two doors down, specialises in big steaks starting at $23. The colossal prime rib costs $33.50! *Waldorf on London (☎ 6262 9623)* is a flash-sounding new restaurant on Akuna St. The menu is diverse and the prices are reasonable (mains start at $14.50).

Fringe Benefits (see Canberra map; ☎ 6247 4042, 54 Marcus Clarke St) is an intimate little brasserie that gets rave reviews and has main courses for around $22.

Mosaics (see Canberra map; ☎ 6257 4788), on the ground floor of the James Court Apartments on Northbourne Ave, is a busy, modern restaurant with great food and service. It has an innovative a la carte menu and does gourmet wood-fired pizzas and mouthwatering desserts. Main courses start at $15.

Garema Place, north-east of London Circuit, is packed with restaurants and cafes with busy outside tables.

Caffe Della Piazza is an excellent choice for pasta and pizza. *Happy's (☎ 6249 7015)*, nearby, is a popular, reasonably priced Chinese restaurant with inexpensive noodle dishes.

Cafe Essen is a great little place for breakfast and coffee – it boasts 34 flavours of coffee ($2) and 23 types of tea ($3 a pot). Main meals cost around $7. *Gus' Cafe*, round the corner on Bunda St, has outdoor tables and is always crowded. *Sammy's Kitchen (☎ 6247 1464)*, farther along, is a hugely popular Chinese/Malaysian place with a good reputation; dishes cost $8 to $13. *Ali Baba*, on the corner of Bunda St and Garema Place's southern arm, does Lebanese takeaways, with shwarmas and felafels for around $5.

Tutu Tango (☎ 6257 7100, 145 Bunda St) is a trendy restaurant and bar with a varied menu; mains cost around $16.50.

Manuka & Kingston South of the lake, not far from Capital Hill, is the Manuka shopping centre, which services the diplomatic corps and well-heeled bureaucrats from surrounding suburbs. There are plenty of cafes and restaurants on Franklin, Furneaux and Bougainville Sts and on Flinders Way.

On Franklin St you'll find *My Cafe*, with bagels and focaccias from $8; nearby is *Caphs*, with main courses for around $16. There's another branch of *Tosolini's (☎ 6232 6600)* on the corner of Furneaux and Franklin Sts; pasta mains cost around $14. Several bar-cum-cafes stay open late. The stylish *La Grange (☎ 6295 8866)* is a bar, brasserie and dance club that has main courses for around $13.

Timmy's Kitchen (☎ 6295 6537), on Furneaux St, is the popular sibling of Sammy's (in Civic) and has a similar menu. You'll probably need to book to get in here.

A short walk away, Kingston also has a collection of good restaurants, cafes and bars clustered around Green Square. The *First Floor Restaurant (☎ 6260 6311)*, above the Holy Grail, is a classy place with mains for around $14 and occasional jazz bands. *Thai Amarin (☎ 6295 9798)*, a few doors down, is a fine Thai restaurant, and the *Harem (☎ 6295 0386)* is a favourite among Canberra's Turkish restaurants.

There's another string of places on Kennedy St. *Portia's Place* is a good Chinese restaurant, with most mains under $10, and at *Cyberchino (☎ 6295 7844)* you can read your emails over a coffee or indulge in some pricey cafe food with netty names – like Yahoo chicken.

Dickson The Dickson shopping area, a few kilometres north of Civic, is a busy restaurant district and is sometimes called Little China because of its many Asian restaurants, most of them on Woolley St.

Dickson Asian Noodle House (☎ 6247 6380, 19 Woolley St) is an excellent cheap Lao and Thai cafe, with dishes for around $9. It's got that authentic Asian character with no-frills decor and a bustling atmosphere. *Sakura (☎ 6247 1455)*, at No 51 opposite the BP petrol station, has a range of Japanese dishes, including teppanyaki and sushi, and lunch specials. The Malaysian *Rasa Sayang (☎ 6249 7284)*, at No 43, is reasonably priced with noodles for under $10 and a good vegetarian selection.

Pho Phu Quoc (☎ 6249 6662, 4–6 Cape St) is another good Vietnamese restaurant. *Belluci's Trattoria (☎ 6257 7788)* does great pizzas.

Other Areas There's cheap food at the ANU student union *Refectory* – enter the campus from the end of University Ave.

At the Lyneham shopping centre, *Tilley's (☎ 6249 1543, 96 Wattle St)* is a classic cafe, bar and restaurant, open all day. The food isn't particularly cheap, but the laid-back atmosphere makes it a great place to spend an afternoon (or morning or evening) over coffee and a light meal.

Cornucopia Bakery (40 Mort St), just north of the city centre in Braddon, is a popular place for Saturday breakfast.

Bernadette's (☎ 6248 5018), in Wakefield Gardens at the Ainslie shops, is a recommended vegetarian and vegan restaurant with salads starting at $7 and a variety of pizzas and focaccias at $8.

Entertainment

Canberra is far more lively than its reputation suggests. Liberal licensing laws allow hotels unlimited opening hours and there are some 24-hour bars. Under-age drinking is strictly policed; if you don't have ID to prove you're over 18, forget it. The 'Times Out' section in Thursday's *Canberra Times* has entertainment listings, while the free monthly *BMA* magazine lists bands and other events.

Also check with foreign cultural organisations, such as the British Council (☎ 6326 2365) and the Goethe Institute (☎ 6247 4472), to find out what's on – see the *Yellow Pages* under 'Clubs, Social & General'.

Pubs & Bars Friday night is the big drinking night in Canberra when everyone winds down after a hard week. Thursday is the big night out (well, one of them) for students.

In Civic, a wander around the Sydney and Melbourne Buildings will reveal quite a few popular pubs and bars. The huge *PJ O'Reilly's*, on Alinga St, takes up a large chunk of the Melbourne Building. It's a heaving, noisy drinking spot with some concessions to Irishness (such as Guinness on tap) and regular live bands. The *Wig & Pen*, farther west, is a smaller, quieter British-style pub serving real ale. In the Sydney Building *Moosehead's (105 London Circuit)* attracts a young crowd. *The Phoenix (21 East Row)* has an earthy character, and it hosts poetry and quiz nights.

Bobby McGee's, at Rydges Canberra Hotel on London Circuit, is a popular dining/drinking/dancing complex with student night (cheap drinks) on Monday.

At the Kingston shopping centre, *Filthy McFadden's* is a popular Irish pub with music most nights. Nearby, the *Durham Castle Arms* occasionally has live jazz and blues bands. At the O'Connor shopping centre, *All Bar Nun* is a good watering hole with regular music and serving meals.

Live Music & Clubs There's live music two or three nights a week during term at the ANU *Uni Bar*, a good place for a drink even when there's no entertainment. Big touring acts often play at the union's *Refectory*, the *Theatre Royal (☎ 6257 4905, 31 Constitution Ave)*, in the National Convention Centre, and *Bruce Outdoor Stadium (☎ 6253 2111)*, Battye St, Bruce, part of the AIS complex.

In Civic, the *Gypsy Bar*, downstairs on the corner of Alinga St and East Row, hosts local and visiting bands and retro nights; entry costs around $5. Not far away, *Pandora's*, on the corner of Alinga and Mort Sts, has a bar downstairs and a dance club upstairs.

Heaven Nite Club (☎ 6257 6180), on Garema Place, is popular with gays.

In Lyneham, *Tilley's (☎ 6249 1543)* has some great live music – a cut above most pub acts – and an intimate atmosphere. There's a cover charge depending on the class of the act.

Other places that occasionally have bands include the *Canberra Workers' Club (☎ 6248 0399)*, Childers St, Civic, and the *Tradesmen's Union Club (☎ 6248 0999, 2 Badham St, Dickson)*.

Gambling The small *Casino Canberra (☎ 6257 7074, 1800 806 833, 21 Binara St)* opens from noon to 6 am daily. It's a fairly casual place: before 7 pm T-shirts, jeans and sports shoes are OK but after 7 pm men have to wear a shirt with a collar and no-one can wear sports shoes. When all else fails, there's a nightclub here.

Cinemas Most of the mainstream cinemas have half-price tickets on Tuesday or Wednesday.

In Civic, *Center Cinema (☎ 6249 7979)*, on Bunda St near Mort St, and *Greater Union (☎ 6247 5522, 6 Mort St)* show

AUSTRALIAN CAPITAL TERRITORY

mainstream films, as does *Capitol Cinema* (☎ 6295 9042), on Franklin St at the Manuka shopping centre. *Electric Shadows* (☎ 6247 5060) is an art-house cinema on City Walk near Akuna St; tickets cost $12 ($5 on Wednesday).

Performing Arts On Civic Square, *Canberra Theatre Centre* (☎ 6257 1077, 1800 802 025 for tickets) has several theatres and offers a varied range of events from rock bands and drama to ballet, opera and classical concerts. The *Street Theatre* (☎ 6247 1519), on the ANU campus (opposite the Canberra Workers' Club) hosts smaller plays and comedy productions.

Spectator Sports

The Canberra Raiders are the much-loved home-town rugby league side and they play regularly at Bruce Outdoor Stadium. Soccer is generating quite a following with the Canberra Cosmos representing the capital in the National Soccer League.

Shopping

The Saturday market at the Gorman House Arts Centre (☎ 6249 7377), on Ainslie Ave, is central and has an interesting range of arts, crafts and stalls. It's on from 10 am to 4 pm. Artwares Gift Gallery, also at the centre, is open from Wednesday to Sunday and sells craftwork by local and interstate artisans.

The Old Bus Depot Market (☎ 6292 8391), on Wentworth Ave in Kingston, is on from 10 am to 4 pm Sunday. It sells food, art and craft. Second-hand Saturday is held from 8 am to 2 pm on the first Saturday of the month.

There's a huge produce and craft market held at the showgrounds in Hall, north-west of the city, on the first Sunday of the month.

Getting There & Away

Air Canberra's isn't an international airport. Sydney is about half an hour away and the standard one-way fare is $163, although Impulse Airlines (☎ 13 1381) charges $119. The flight to Melbourne takes about an hour and costs $232. Direct flights to Adelaide cost $337 and to Brisbane $341. These prices

drop dramatically when you book in advance and other special deals are often available.

Qantas Airways (☎ 13 1313) and Ansett Airlines (☎ 13 1300) both have offices in the Jolimont Centre on Northbourne Ave.

Other smaller airlines fly to NSW country destinations. Air Facilities (☎ 6041 1210, 13 1300) flies daily to Albury ($159).

Bus Several bus companies have their booking offices and also their main terminal at the Jolimont Centre.

Greyhound Pioneer (☎ 13 2030) has the most frequent Sydney service ($28 one way), which takes four to five hours. It also runs to Adelaide ($96) and to Melbourne ($45, or $54 express). Services to Cooma ($25) and Thredbo in the NSW snowfields ($44) run twice daily in winter, once daily in summer.

Murrays (☎ 13 2251) has daily express buses to Sydney (under four hours) and Wollongong ($28), and to the south coast as far as Narooma ($32.95) and Nowra ($39.75) via Batemans Bay ($21.75). Countrylink has a bus to Eden, via Cooma and Bega, three times a week.

McCafferty's (☎ 13 1499) also has buses to Sydney, Melbourne and Adelaide; you can book through the Travellers Maps & Guides (☎ 6249 6006) shop.

Transborder Express (☎ 6226 1378) runs to Yass ($10 one way), and connects with a Fearnes coach to Wagga Wagga ($30). Sid Fogg's (☎ 4928 1088) runs direct to Newcastle on Monday, Wednesday and Friday during school holidays only. T-Trek Tours (☎ 1800 645 977) has a daily bus to Batemans Bay ($29).

Train Canberra's train station (☎ 6239 7039) is south of Lake Burley Griffin, on Wentworth Ave in Kingston. You can make bookings for trains and connecting buses at the Countrylink Travel Centre (☎ 13 2232) in the Jolimont Centre. To Sydney ($45, four hours) there are three trains daily.

There's no direct train to/from Melbourne, but Countrylink has daily train/bus services via Cootamundra ($90 one way, nine hours). The daily V/Line Canberra Link service involves a train between Melbourne and Wodonga and a connecting bus to Canberra ($49, nine hours). A longer, more interesting bus/train service to Melbourne is the V/Line Capital Link. It runs three times weekly via Cooma and the superb mountain forests of Victoria's East Gippsland, then down the Princes Hwy to Sale, from where you catch a train to Melbourne. This takes just over 11 hours and costs $49.

Car & Motorcycle The Hume Hwy, connecting Sydney and Melbourne, passes about 50km to the north of Canberra. The Federal Hwy runs north to the Hume Hwy near Goulburn, while the Barton Hwy from Canberra meets it near Yass. To the south, the Monaro Hwy connects Canberra with Cooma.

Rental Major companies with offices in Civic are:

Avis (☎ 6249 6088) 17 Lonsdale St, Braddon
Budget (☎ 6257 1305, 13 2727) Corner of Mort and Girroween Sts, Braddon
Hertz (☎ 6249 6211, 13 3030) 32 Mort St, Braddon
Thrifty Car Rental (☎ 6247 7422) 29 Lonsdale St, Braddon

These companies also have desks at the airport. Cheaper outfits include Rumbles (☎ 6280 7444), at 157 Gladstone St in Fyshwick, and Rent a Dent (☎ 6257 5947), at 8 Ijong St in Braddon. Expect to pay from $25 to $40 a day (including 100km free), with better deals on longer rentals.

Getting Around
To/from the Airport Canberra airport is 7km south-east of Civic. Bus No 80 goes there from Civic interchange on weekdays.
The taxi fare from the airport to Civic is around $12.

Bus The Australian Capital Territory Internal Omnibus Network (ACTION; ☎ 13 1710) runs a fairly frequent and extensive bus network. The main bus interchange is at the intersection of Alinga St and East Row in Civic. The information kiosk, at the corner of Alinga St and East Row, is open from 7 am

to 6 pm weekdays. You can pick up a free route map and timetables here. The *Sightseeing around Canberra* brochure lists buses and platform numbers for 22 of the most popular destinations. The intertown buses – the 300 series – shuttle regularly between the Tuggeranong, Woden, Civic and Belconnen stations. Finally, there's an hourly Nightrider service from the Civic interchange out to the suburbs, running from about 11.15 pm to 6.45 am.

Single tickets work on a one-hour system. Validate your ticket when you board, then you can ride any bus for an hour. A single trip or one-hour Zone 1 fare is $2, an all-zone trip is $4. Daily tickets are good value, offering unlimited travel in all zones for $7. Students and concession-card holders pay half-price. You can save money with pre-purchase tickets, available from newsagents and elsewhere (but not on buses). A weekly ticket or a book of 10 Faresaver tickets costs $17.

Car & Motorcycle Canberra's wide, relatively uncluttered main roads make driving a joy, although once you enter the maze of curving roads in the residential areas things become more difficult. Get a map and study it before entering the fray. Speeding on the main roads is common (if illegal as well as dangerous), but everyone observes the 40km/h limit in school areas.

You could also spend some time looking for a petrol station. By design, most are off the main roads – look for signs. In Civic try Lonsdale St, two blocks east of Northbourne Ave.

Taxi There's a central taxi rank on the corner of Bunda and Mort Sts, or call Canberra Cabs (☎ 13 2227).

Bicycle Canberra is a cyclist's paradise, with plenty of bike paths. One popular track is a circuit of the lake, or you can use the Commonwealth Avenue bridge and ride around the more interesting eastern half of the lake. There are also peaceful stretches of bushland along some suburban routes. Get a copy of the *Canberra Cycleways* map ($5.95) from bookshops or the visitor centre.

Mr Spokes Bike Hire (☎ 6257 1188), near the Acton Park ferry terminal, charges $8 an hour and $7 for each subsequent hour. Capital Bicycle Hire (☎ 6248 9155), at the Canberra YHA, has bikes for $25/15 a full/half day ($16/10 for hostel guests), including helmet, lock and a basic map of the bike paths.

Around Canberra

The ACT is about 88km from north to south and about 30km wide. There's plenty of unspoiled bush just outside the urban area and a network of paved roads into it. The NRMA's *Canberra & District* map and the visitor centre's *Canberra Sightseeing Guide with Tourist Drives* are helpful.

The plains and isolated hills around Canberra rise to rugged ranges in the south and west of the ACT. The Murrumbidgee River flows across the territory from south-east to north-west. Namadgi National Park in the south covers 40% of the ACT and adjoins Kosciuszko National Park.

If you have a car, many of the following places of interest make good day trips from Canberra.

The Bush Capital

Canberra is an incredibly leafy capital with manicured parks and gardens cloaking the city area, but you only have to venture a short distance out of the suburbs to really be in the bush.

At **Tidbinbilla Nature Reserve**, 45km south-west of the city, in the hills beyond the Canberra Deep Space Communication Complex at Tidbinbilla, you'll come face to face with a wide range of native wildlife and birds. Most of the reserve is criss-crossed with excellent bushwalking tracks and nature trails – some leading to interesting rock formations. In the centre of the reserve are the large wildlife enclosures where you'll see many types of wallabies (including the rare brush-tailed rock wallaby), both grey and red kangaroos, emus and koalas. There's also a bird hide, a wetlands area full of birdlife and platypus ponds. Tidbinbilla is open from 9 am to 6 pm daily (to 8 pm during daylight-saving time) and the new visitor centre (☎ 6205 1233), just before the park entrance, is open from 9 am to 4.30 pm weekdays and from 9 am to 5.30 pm weekends. Entry is $8 per car.

There is no public transport to the reserve. Round About Tours (☎ 6259 5999, 0417 466 862) has informative day trips. The cost is $50 ($40 for YHA/VIP members), which includes some bush tucker and billy tea.

Namadgi National Park, occupying the south-west of the Australian Capital Territory and partly bordering Kosciuszko National Park in New South Wales' Snowy Mountains, has seven peaks over 1600m and offers challenging bushwalking. Good walks include the Square Rock trail (8.5km return), off Corin Rd, and the Yankee Hat trail (6km return) off Old Boboyan Rd. The Yankee Hat trail leads to Aboriginal rock-art sites.

Booroomba Rocks in the park are popular with rockclimbers and there is sometimes enough snow for cross-country skiing.

The partly-surfaced Boboyan Rd crosses the park, going south from Tharwa in the ACT to Adaminaby. The informative park visitor information centre (☎ 6207 2900) is on this road, 2km south of Tharwa. It's open from 9 am to 4 pm daily and hosts exhibitions and lectures on the native environment. You can get also get brochures and maps on Namadgi at the Canberra Visitor Centre.

There are three formal camping areas with basic facilities at Namadgi. These are the Orroral River crossing, off Orroral Rd; the site of the former Honeysuckle tracking station, on Honeysuckle Rd; and at Mt Clear, in the south of the park, just off Boboyan Rd. Camping permits are required and are available from the visitor centre ($6 per night for two people, $5 at Mt Clear); sites should be booked ahead during holiday periods. There are also numerous picnic areas.

Wild Thing Tours (☎ 6254 6303) has trips starting at $70, including visits to the Valley of a Thousand Kangaroos and Aboriginal rock-art sites. Round About Tours (☎ 6259 5999) also has tours.

AUSTRALIAN CAPITAL TERRITORY

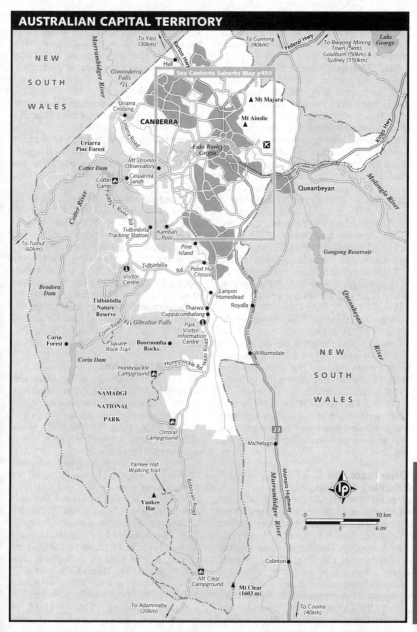

AUSTRALIAN CAPITAL TERRITORY

NEW SOUTH WALES

To Yass (30km)

To Gunning (40km)

Federal Hwy

To Bwyong Mining Town (5km), Goulburn (50km) & Sydney (150km)

Lake George

Murrumbidgee River

Ginninderra Falls

Barton Hwy

Hall

See Canberra Suburbs Map p450

Uriarra Crossing

CANBERRA

Uriarra Road

Mt Majura

Mt Ainslie

Kings Hwy

Uriarra Pine Forest

Cotter Dam

Mt Stromlo Observatory

Lake Burley Griffin

Casuarina Sands

Cotter Camp

Cotter River

Paddy's River Rd

Queanbeyan

Molonglo River

Tidbinbilla Tracking Station

Kambah Pool

Googong Reservoir

To Tumut (60km)

Pine Island

Tidbinbilla Rd

Point Hut Crossing

Bendora Dam

Visitor Centre

Lanyon Homestead

Royalla

Queanbeyan River

Tidbinbilla Nature Reserve

Corin Road

Gibraltar Falls

Tharwa

Cuppacumbalong

Corin Forest

Square Rock Trail

Booroomba Rocks

Park Visitor Information Centre

Naas Road

Williamsdale

NEW SOUTH WALES

Corin Dam

Honeysuckle Campground

Honeysuckle Rd

NAMADGI NATIONAL PARK

Orroral Campground

23

Michelago

Monaro Highway

Yankee Hat Walking trail

Boboyan Road

Murrumbidgee River

Yankee Hat

0   5   10 km

0   3   6 mi

Mt Clear Campground

Mt Clear (1603 m)

Colinton

To Adaminaby (20km)

To Cooma (40km)

Picnic & Walking Areas

Picnic and barbecue spots, many with gas barbecues or with wood supplied, are scattered around Canberra.

Black Mountain, west of the city, is convenient for picnics and there are good swimming spots along the Murrumbidgee and Cotter Rivers. Other riverside areas include **Uriarra Crossing**, 24km north-west of Civic, on the Murrumbidgee near its meeting with the Molonglo River; **Casuarina Sands**, 19km west at the meeting of the Murrumbidgee and Cotter Rivers; **Kambah Pool**, about 14km farther upstream (south) on the Murrumbidgee River; the **Cotter Dam** (☎ 6207 2204), 23km west of town on the Cotter River, which has a camping area ($10); **Pine Island** and **Point Hut Crossing**, on the Murrumbidgee, upstream of Kambah Pool; and **Gibraltar Falls**, 45km south-west of the city, which also has a camping area.

There are good walking tracks along the Murrumbidgee from Kambah Pool to Pine Island (7km), or to Casuarina Sands (about 14km).

The spectacular **Ginninderra Falls** (☎ 6278 4222), at Parkwood, north-west of Canberra across the NSW border, are open daily; there are gorges, a nature trail, canoeing and camping. The reserve is open from 10 am to 8 pm or to 5 pm in winter ($4/2 for adults/children).

At the **Corin Forest** (☎ 6247 2250), south-west of the city, there's a 1km-long metal bobsled that runs on weekends and during school holidays. There's also a flying fox.

Observatories & Tracking Stations

The **Mt Stromlo Observatory** (☎ 6249 0232), 16km south-west of Canberra, has a 188cm telescope plus a visitors' annexe that's open from 9.30 am to 4.30 pm daily. The Astronomy Hall has hands-on exhibits and telescopes ($5/3 for adults/children). There's also a good cafe here, with views over the Brindabella Range.

A joint US-Australian deep-space tracking station, the **Canberra Deep Space Communication Complex** (☎ 6201 7800), also called

the Tidbinbilla Tracking Station, is 40km south-west of Canberra. The visitor centre has displays of spacecraft and tracking technology. It's open from 9 am to 5 pm (to 8 pm during daylight-saving time) daily (free).

Gold Creek

Near the Barton Hwy about 11km north-west of the city, Gold Creek has a little cluster of attractions. Hard to resist is the **National Dinosaur Museum** (☎ 6230 2655). This is a private collection, with replica skeletons of 10 dinosaurs and many real bones and fossils. It's open from 10 am to 5 pm daily ($8/5 for adults/children).

Gininderra Village, on the corner of the Barton Hwy and Gold Creek Rd, is a collection of craft workshops and galleries. There's also a reptile centre and a walk-in aviary. The village is open from 10 am to 5 pm daily (free). Next door, **Cockington Green** (☎ 1800 627 273) is a miniature replica of an English village that is open from 9.30 am to 4.30 pm daily ($8.50/4.25).

Federation Square, with its shops and cafes, is another attraction here. Get to Gold Creek on bus No 50 from the Civic or Belconnen stations.

Other Attractions

About 25km north-east of Canberra, **Bywong Mining Town** (☎ 6236 9183), on Millyn Rd off the Federal Hwy, is a re-creation of a mining settlement. It's open from 9.30 am to 4.30 pm daily ($7.50/4.50 for adults/children). Bring a picnic if you intend to spend a bit of time here.

Beautifully restored, **Lanyon Homestead** (☎ 6237 5136), on Tharwa Drive off the Monaro Hwy near Tharwa, is about 30km south of Canberra's city centre. The early stone cottage on site was built by convicts and the grand homestead was completed in 1859. This National Trust homestead, which represents life in the region before Canberra existed, is open from 10 am to 4 pm Tuesday to Sunday. The **Nolan Gallery** (☎ 6237 5192), containing a collection of Sidney Nolan's paintings, is a major attraction.

Cuppacumbalong (☎ 6237 5116), on Naas Rd near Tharwa, is another old homestead, now a craft studio and gallery that's open from 11 am to 5 pm Wednesday to Sunday.

QUEANBEYAN
pop 27,000
Across the NSW border about 12km south-east of central Canberra, Queanbeyan is virtually a suburb of the capital city it predates. It's obvious that Canberra's planning regulations don't apply here. Most of Queanbeyan's historic buildings date from around 1838 when it was proclaimed a township.

The Queanbeyan Information & Tourist Centre (☎ 1800 026 192) is at 1 Farrer Place.

Across the road from the information centre, the Queanbeyan **Museum** has displays on the town's history. There are good lookouts on **Jerrabomberra Hill** (5km west of the town centre) and **Bungendore Hill** (4km east).

Motel accommodation is slightly cheaper than in Canberra. *Rainbow Motel (☎ 6297 2784, 41 Bungendore Rd)* has singles/doubles starting at $44/48.

Eastern Islands

Lord Howe Island

☎ 02 • postcode 2898 • pop 300

Stunning Lord Howe is a tiny subtropical island 550km east of Port Macquarie and 770km north-east of Sydney. It's the largest of a cluster of 27 islands and outcrops that are the eroded remnants of a huge shield volcano, which emerged from the ocean about seven million years ago. Ball's Pyramid, the spectacular spire sticking up 23km south-east of the island, is the remains of another volcano.

What Lord Howe may lack in island culture it makes up for in natural beauty. Listed on the World Heritage Register, it is dominated by the towering twin peaks of Mt Lidgbird (777m) and Mt Gower (875m), visible from almost 100km out to sea. It boasts some beautiful beaches, a wide lagoon sheltered by a coral reef, and excellent fishing and snorkelling. For many visitors, though, the main attraction is walking in the dense rainforests that cover most of the island. The forests are home to some 70 plant species that occur naturally only on Lord Howe Island. They include the hardy kentia palm *(Howea forsteriana),* prized by gardeners all over the world.

Although tourism is the main industry, the laid-back nature of this remote island is maintained by a restriction on visitor numbers – around 400 at any one time. Lord Howe is really not a budget destination, but it's not an exclusive resort either.

History
The first Europeans to set eyes on Lord Howe Island were the crew of the HMS *Supply,* which sailed past on its way from the newly founded Port Jackson (Sydney) to Norfolk Island on 17 February 1788 under the command of Lieutenant Henry Lidgbird Ball.

From a distance, Ball thought he had discovered two islands. He named the larger one Lord Howe, after the first lord of the admiralty, and the lesser one Lidgbird Is-

Lord Howe Island
• Bushwalking in World-Heritage-listed forests
• Watching the daily fish feeding frenzy at Ned's Beach
• Snorkelling and kayaking in the lagoon

Norfolk Island
• Exploring the historic convict settlement of Kingston
• Experiencing the solitude and fine coastal views at Norfolk Island National Park
• Watching the locals unload goods using lighter boats at the Kingston and Cascade jetties

land, after himself. Upon closer inspection, they turned out to be two mountains rising from the one landmass. Tactfully, he chose to run with Lord Howe's name for the island, while his 'island' became Mt Lidgbird.

The first settlers didn't arrive until 1834, when a whaling supply station was established at Old Settlement Beach. Since then the islanders have dabbled in various activities in search of an income. For a long time

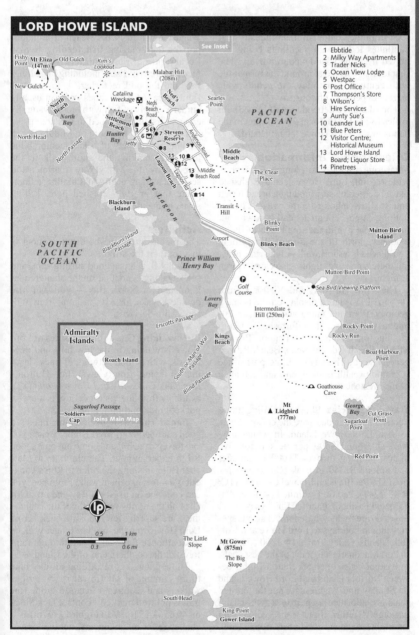

LORD HOWE ISLAND

See Inset

1 Ebbtide
2 Milky Way Apartments
3 Trader Nicks
4 Ocean View Lodge
5 Westpac
6 Post Office
7 Thompson's Store
8 Wilson's
  Hire Services
9 Aunty Sue's
10 Leander Lei
11 Blue Peters
12 Visitor Centre;
   Historical Museum
13 Lord Howe Island
   Board; Liquor Store
14 Pinetrees

Fishy Point
Mt Eliza (147m)
Old Gulch
Kim's Lookout
New Gulch
Malabar Hill (208m)
Catalina Wreckage
Neds Beach
Searles Point
Neds Beach Road
PACIFIC OCEAN
North Beach
North Bay
Old Settlement Beach
Stevens Reserve
Anderson Road
Hunter Bay
Jetty
North Head
North Passage
Middle Beach
The Clear Place
Lagoon Beach
Lagoon Rd
Middle Beach Road
Blackburn Island
Transit Hill
The Lagoon
Blinky Point
Mutton Bird Island
SOUTH PACIFIC OCEAN
Blackburn Island Passage
Airport
Blinky Beach
Prince William Henry Bay
Golf Course
Mutton Bird Point
Sea Bird Viewing Platform
Lovers Bay
Erscotts Passage
Intermediate Hill (250m)
Rocky Point
Rocky Run
Kings Beach
Boat Harbour Point
South or Man of War Passage
Blind Passage
Goathouse Cave
George Bay
Cut Grass Point
Mt Lidgbird (777m)
Sugarloaf Point
Red Point

Admiralty Islands

Roach Island

Sugarloaf Passage

Soldiers Cap

Joins Main Map

0   0.5   1 km
0   0.3   0.6 mi

The Little Slope
Mt Gower (875m)
The Big Slope
South Head
King Point
Gower Island

there was good money to be made selling seed from the kentia palm, an industry that continues today with seedlings being exported from the island's palm nursery. The first tourists arrived at around the turn of the 19th century, and today the economy is largely dependent on tourism.

The island is a dependency of New South Wales (NSW), with local government in the hands of the Lord Howe Island Board.

Orientation & Information

Measuring around 11km long by 3km at its widest point, Lord Howe Island is shaped like a boomerang surrounding a broad beach and shallow lagoon to the west. There's nothing large enough to call a town, but most people live in the small area of flatter land just north of the airport. Everything you'll need is a short walk or bike ride away, but there's no street lighting so carry a torch at night.

The Lord Howe Island Visitor Centre (☎ 6563 2114) has a display on the island's geology, flora and fauna and screens a 20-minute video. It's in the refurbished museum building on the corner of Lagoon Rd and Middle Beach Rd. On Ned's Beach Rd is a general store (Thompson's), the post office (Commonwealth Bank agent) and a branch of the Westpac bank.

Travel Agencies Short of sailing there yourself, package deals are the cheapest way to visit Lord Howe Island. In winter they start at around $599 per person for five nights, jumping to over $1000 in summer and around $1250 in peak (Christmas) period. The Pacific Island Travel Centre (PITC; ☎ 13 2747), Pacific Unlimited (☎ 1800 810 555) and Fastbook Pacific Holidays (☎ 1300 361 153) are Sydney-based travel agents specialising in holidays to Lord Howe and Norfolk islands. Oxley Travel (☎ 1800 671 546) in Port Macquarie has some of the best deals.

Fastbook also operates charter flights between Norfolk Island and Lord Howe Island on Sunday and Wednesday, but the limited seats are allocated as part of a twin-island package. A return flight from Sydney with six nights on each island costs from $1699.

Things to See & Do

Wander down to Ned's Beach at around 4 pm for the amazing **fish feeding** frenzy. Local resident Brian Simpson visits daily to feed hundreds of fish – including huge kingfish and the odd reef shark – just metres from shore. At other times you can usually attract a variety of fish with bread. Naturally enough, fishing is banned in this area.

The historical **museum** on Middle Beach Rd houses a display of island memorabilia. It's worth making the short walk to the slopes above the Milky Way Apartments to see what's left of the **RAAF Catalina**, a floatplane that in 1948 crashed here, killing seven of the nine crew.

Activities

The picturesque nine-hole **golf course** is just south of the airport.

Blinky Beach is a good **surfing** spot, and **sea kayaking** is popular on the sheltered lagoon and in North Bay – you can hire double kayaks for $10 an hour from Wilson's Hire Services.

Bushwalking One of the pleasures of Lord Howe is walking in the low hills and rainforests, with a good network of tracks leading to some fine views. Ian Hutton's *Ramblers Guide to Lord Howe Island* ($7), available from the visitor centre, is a useful pocket guide outlining nine walks.

Transit Hill, with its lookout, makes a good starting point; from Blinky Beach you can traverse the hill and come out on Lagoon Rd in under an hour. The climb up to **Malabar Hill** and along the ridge to **Kim's Lookout** is another excellent walk. From here you can continue on to North Bay and up to **Mt Eliza** on the north-western tip of the island – there are superb views looking back across Lord Howe from the top. The longer walk up to **Goathouse Cave** takes you through rainforest at the southern end of the island.

The arduous but rewarding all-day hike to the summit of **Mt Gower** is for serious walkers and requires a licensed guide (the trail is not well marked); contact Jack Shick on ☎ 6563 2218. **Mt Lidgbird** (777m) is a challenge for mountaineers, not walkers.

Sea Birds of Lord Howe

Visit Lord Howe Island from September to April and you'll be struck by the vast number of sea birds breeding on this tiny oasis.

The island has the world's largest breeding population of flesh-footed shearwaters (also known as mutton birds), the only breeding colony of providence petrels and large numbers of sooty terns and red-tailed tropicbirds. You may also spot the masked booby, white tern and common noddy. Many of these birds can be observed (and certainly heard) at nesting places around the island. The flesh-footed shearwaters can be found among the palm stands behind Ned's Beach or on the trail to The Clear Place, where they nest in burrows. They leave the nest early in the morning and spend the day out at sea, but can usually be seen returning at sunset. One of the best places to see sooty terns is along the track to Mt Eliza, where they lay a single speckled egg on the ground. Red-tailed tropicbirds – famous for their aerial-courtship displays – can be seen from the ridge between Malabar Hill and Kim's Lookout.

The white tern nests near Lagoon Beach, where it lays a speckled egg straight onto the branch of a tree. During winter most of these sea birds fly north to warmer climes, but the rare providence petrel breeds on Lord Howe in winter. This dark grey bird can often be seen around Mt Lidgbird and Mt Gower. The nonmigratory masked booby, white with a distinctive black eye mask, is best seen from the viewing platform at Mutton Bird Point.

Diving & Snorkelling Lord Howe Island claims the world's most southerly coral reef, with excellent snorkelling out from the lagoon and off Ned's Beach. Snorkelling gear, wet suits, body boards and surf skis are available for hire at the shelter on Ned's Beach – all on an honesty system!

There are a couple of scuba diving outfits operating from Lagoon Beach and both offer Professional Association of Diving Instructors (PADI) dive courses. Pro Dive (☎ 6563 2154) charges $350 for an open-water course and $50 for a boat dive.

Organised Tours

Half-day bus tours of the island ($18) and boat tours can be booked at Thompson's Store or Wilson's Hire Services.

Ron's Ramble is an interesting three-hour nature walk covering some of the island's history, while Jim's Walks & Tours includes a guided tour of the palm nursery. Fishing charters and glass-bottom boat trips are also available.

Places to Stay

There's a variety of accommodation in lodges and self-contained apartments, but the best way to get a decent deal is to buy a flight/accommodation package. Some places close in winter while others cut their rates. Camping is prohibited.

Ocean View Lodge (☎ 6563 2041), Lagoon Rd, is one of the cheaper places, charging around $120 for two in a self-contained apartment ($80 in winter). It has a lawn tennis court and a swimming pool.

Leander Lei (☎ 6563 2195, fax 6563 2095), Middle Beach Rd, has clean and spacious self-contained apartments. Studio rooms cost $170 ($140 in winter). One-bedroom units cost $225/160. *Ebbtide* (☎/fax 6563 2023, ℮ ebbtide@watch4you .com), Mutton Bird Dr, has pleasant self-contained units/cottages for $170/190 ($60 in winter).

Pinetrees (☎ 1800 226 142, ℮ info@ pine trees.com.au), Lagoon Rd, is one of the original island guesthouses and offers packages with all meals included. Basic motel-style units cost $390 per night. Winter packages cost from $1200 per person for seven nights, including air fare. *Trader Nick's* (☎ 1800 063 928, ℮ tradernicks@ lordhowe.com.au), Lagoon Rd, is also pricey but its 'jungle-style' rooms are unusual.

Places to Eat

There are several restaurants on the island but eating out is expensive – there's really not much in between a cheap evening barbecue at one of the many picnic areas or a night of fine dining.

In summer, *Blue Peters* on Lagoon Rd has a bistro menu, bar and pleasant outdoor eating area. *Thompson's Store*, Ned's Beach Rd, has takeaway food (noon to 2 pm) and a bakery.

Pinetrees offers a set three-course menu ($30) and on Monday evenings it has an excellent gourmet fish fry ($25). *Aunty Sue's*, on Anderson Rd, has an interesting a la carte menu, with mains for around $18.

Getting There & Away

Eastern Australia Airlines has four flights a week from Sydney for $852 return ($554 with seven-day advance purchase), while Sunstate flies from Brisbane on Sunday only for $808 return ($471 advance purchase). Both are subsidiaries of Qantas Airways (☎ 13 1313). Fastbook Pacific Holidays has charter flights to Lord Howe and Norfolk Islands – see Travel Agents in the Orientation & Information section earlier in this chapter.

Yachties are welcome to harbour off the island but should contact the port operations manager (☎ 6563 2266, VHF channel 16 or 12) prior to arrival; there's a mooring fee of $16 per night and a once-off island service levy of $20 per person.

Getting Around

There are a few rental cars on the island but a bike is all you need. They can be hired from Wilson's Hire Service (☎ 6563 2045) on Lagoon Rd (closed Saturday). Bikes costs $5 per day; a car is $40 a day. There's a 25km/h speed limit throughout the island.

Norfolk Island

☎ 6723 • postcode 2899 • pop 1800

Norfolk Island is a green speck in the vast South Pacific Ocean, 1600km north-east of Sydney and 1000km north-west of Auckland, New Zealand (NZ). It's the largest of a cluster of three islands emerging from the Norfolk Ridge, which stretches from NZ to New Caledonia – the closest landfall, almost 700km to the north.

With its fascinating past and 'country-town' atmosphere, Norfolk is a popular tourist destination, particularly with older Australians and New Zealanders on pack-

age holidays. As well as being tax-free, the island is virtually crime-free and you'll almost certainly spend time mixing with the friendly locals – hardly surprising since tourism accounts for more than 90% of the local economy.

Norfolk is a lush, green island, with the rich volcanic soil and mild subtropical climate providing perfect growing conditions. There are 40-odd plant species that are unique to the island, including the handsome Norfolk Island pine *(Araucaria heterophylla)*, which grows everywhere.

History

Little is known about the island before it was sighted by Captain Cook on 10 October 1774 and named after the wife of the ninth Duke of Norfolk. Fifteen convicts were among the first settlers to reach the island on 6 March 1788 – only weeks after the First Fleet had arrived to settle at Port Jackson. It may have been Cook's description of the tall, straight Norfolk Island pines that prompted the speedy settlement, but it was later found that the timber was too brittle for its intended use as ships' masts and spars. The penal colony founded under Lieutenant Philip Gidley King continued until 1814.

The island was abandoned for 11 years before colonial authorities decided to try again, and Governor Darling planned this second penal settlement as 'a place of the extremest punishment short of death'. Under such notorious sadists as commandant John Giles Price, Norfolk Island became known as 'hell in the Pacific'.

The penal colony lasted until 1854, when the prisoners were shipped off to Port Arthur in Van Diemen's Land (Tasmania). The following year Queen Victoria agreed to hand Norfolk Island over to the descendants of the mutineers from the HMS *Bounty*, who had outgrown their adopted Pitcairn Island. About a third of the present population are descended from these settlers.

Government & Politics

Norfolk Island is a self-governing external territory of Australia, and since 1979 has had its own locally elected legislative

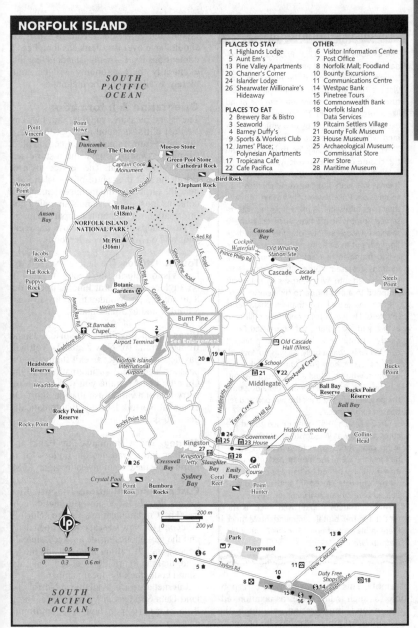

NORFOLK ISLAND

PLACES TO STAY
1 Highlands Lodge
5 Aunt Em's
13 Pine Valley Apartments
20 Channer's Corner
24 Islander Lodge
26 Shearwater Millionaire's Hideaway

PLACES TO EAT
2 Brewery Bar & Bistro
3 Seaworld
4 Barney Duffy's
9 Sports & Workers Club
12 James' Place; Polynesian Apartments
17 Tropicana Cafe
22 Cafe Pacifica

OTHER
6 Visitor Information Centre
7 Post Office
8 Norfolk Mall; Foodland
10 Bounty Excursions
11 Communications Centre
14 Westpac Bank
15 Pinetree Tours
16 Commonwealth Bank
18 Norfolk Island Data Services
19 Pitcairn Settlers Village
21 Bounty Folk Museum
23 House Museum
25 Archaeological Museum; Commissariat Store
27 Pier Store
28 Maritime Museum

SOUTH PACIFIC OCEAN

Point Vincent

Point Howe

Duncombe Bay

The Chord

Moo-oo Stone

Green Pool Stone
Cathedral Rock

Captain Cook Monument

Duncombe Bay Road

Elephant Rock

Bird Rock

Anson Point

Anson Bay

Mt Bates (318m)

NORFOLK ISLAND NATIONAL PARK

Mt Pitt (316m)

Red Rd

Cascade Bay

Cockpit Waterfall

Prince Philip Rd

Old Whaling Station Site

Cascade

Cascade Jetty

Jacobs Rock

Flat Rock

Puppys Rock

Selwyn Pine Road

J.E. Road

Mount Pitt Rd

Grassy Road

Botanic Gardens

Steels Point

Mission Road

St Barnabas Chapel

Anson Bay Rd

Headstone Rd

1

2

Burnt Pine

See Enlargement

Airport Terminal

Headstone Reserve

Headstone

Norfolk Island International Airport

Old Cascade Hall (films)

20 19

School

21 22

Middlegate

Middlegate Road

Stockyard Creek

Ball Bay Reserve

Bucks Point Reserve

Ball Bay

Bucks Point

Rocky Point Reserve

Rocky Point

Rocky Point Rd

Town Creek

Rooty Hill Rd

Historic Cemetery

Collins Head

Kingston

24
25

27
28

Government House

23

Golf Course

26

Cresswell Bay

Kingston Jetty

Slaughter Bay

Emily Bay

Crystal Pool

Point Ross

Bumbora Rocks

Sydney Bay

Coral Reef

Point Hunter

SOUTH PACIFIC OCEAN

0   0.5   1 km
0   0.3   0.6 mi

0   200 m
0   200 yd

Park

Playground

13

7

12

3

4

6

5

Taylors Rd

11

New Cascade Road

Duty Free Shops

18

8

10

9

14

Village Place

15

16 17

John Giles Price – Norfolk's Cruellest Commandant

The exploits of John Giles Price as commandant of Norfolk Island are vividly recorded in Robert Hughes' study of the Australian convict era *The Fatal Shore*. Hughes paints a picture of a demented sadist who ran the island like a torture chamber. The evidence of Price's excesses was provided by two visiting clergymen who were appalled by what they saw. Their reports eventually led to his recall and the closure of the penal colony.

While Price's predecessors had contented themselves with flogging their charges into submission, Price devised new ways to make their lives miserable. A mere flogging was reserved for trivial offences such as losing a shoelace. More serious offenders would be flogged, put in a straitjacket and strapped to a bed frame for a week or two while their wounds festered. Others were reportedly transformed into living corpses by being left strapped to a bed for up to six weeks.

Price was also a larger-than-life character in the flesh. He was a tall, powerfully built man with a withering stare, yet he dressed like a dandy – complete with a monocle in his left eye. While he was a bully, he was no coward. Hughes relates how Price 'once stared down a convict who snatched a pistol from his belt, taunting the man as a coward and a dog until the prisoner handed back the weapon and fell beaten to his knees'.

On 26 March 1857, when Price visited the convict quarry at Williamstown (Melbourne), in his capacity as inspector-general of Victoria's penal system, the men he had treated like animals finally turned on him. His escorts fled as the convicts closed in, and Price disappeared beneath an avalanche of blows.

Author Marcus Clarke used Price as the model for the brutal commandant Maurice Frere in his convict novel *For the Term of His Natural Life*.

veto. The question of who 'owns' Norfolk Island and how much control Australia should have over its affairs has long been a contentious issue – many islanders fear that eventually their autonomy will be completely swallowed by the mainland.

Orientation & Information

The island measures roughly 8km by 5km. Vertical cliffs surround much of the coastline, apart from a small area of coastal plain (formerly swamp) around the historic settlement of Kingston. The service town of Burnt Pine, at the centre of the island and near the airport, is the main settlement and contains most of the island's shopping and information services in a compact strip.

Most shops and services close on weekends and on Wednesday afternoons.

Tourist Offices The helpful Norfolk Island Visitor Information Centre (☎ 22 147), on Taylors Rd in Burnt Pine, is open from 8.30 am to 5 pm Monday to Friday, to 1 pm Saturday and to 3 pm Sunday.

Visas When travelling to Norfolk Island from Australia (or New Zealand), you will pay departure tax, get an exit stamp in your passport and board an international flight. On return to Australia you will need a re-entry visa or a valid Australian passport. On arrival at Norfolk Island you automatically get a 30-day visa.

Money The Commonwealth Bank and Westpac have branches on Taylors Rd in Burnt Pine; the Commonwealth has an ATM.

Post & Communications The post office is next door to the visitor information centre. The Communications Centre (Norfolk Telecom) on New Cascade Rd is open daily and the pay phones inside are accessible 24 hours a day. If calling from outside the island, dial the international access code, the island code, then the local number.

Internet access is available at Norfolk Island Data Services in Village Place, Burnt Pine, for $10 per hour ($5 minimum charge).

assembly. This local government is responsible for such major issues as taxation, education and immigration, although the Australian Administrator has the power of

Kingston

The historic settlement of Kingston, built by convicts of the second penal colony, is the island's main attraction. Most of the buildings have been restored and the finest of these, along **Quality Row**, still house the island's administrators, including the Magistrates Court. Four of the buildings have been turned into small but excellent **museums**: the Pier Store; the Maritime Museum (with the salvaged anchor of the ill-fated HMS *Sirius*, a First Fleet ship wrecked off Norfolk Island in 1790); the House Museum; and the Archaeological Museum. Entry costs $6 to each or $18 for a combined ticket to all four; they open from 11 am to 3 pm daily. The sandstone used for the buildings was quarried from nearby Nepean Island.

The **cemetery**, at the eastern end of Quality Row, was established soon after the second settlement. It has some very poignant epitaphs on the headstones, such as that of James Saye, a convict who was killed in 1842 during an abortive mutiny:

> Stop Christian, stop and meditate
> On this man's sad and awful fate
> On earth no more he breathes again
> He lived in hope but died in pain.

Between the cemetery and Government House is the small, undulating **golf course**, which has 18 tees but only nine greens.

Norfolk Island National Park

There are various walking tracks in this lush 460-hectare national park, and good views from Mt Pitt (316m) and Mt Bates (318m). Mt Pitt was the higher of the two before the top was levelled to build a radio transmitter. The park can be entered from the south along Mt Pitt Rd or Selwyn Pine Rd, or you can drive to the Captain Cook monument at the end of Duncombe Bay Rd and walk the Bridle and Bird Rock Tracks for good coastal views.

Other Attractions

Just south of Kingston is **Emily Bay**, a good sheltered beach and picnic area; from here you can take a glass-bottom boat ($12/6 for adults/children) to view the corals in the bay.

The impressive **St Barnabas Chapel**, west of Burnt Pine along Douglas Dr, was built by the (Anglican) Melanesian Mission, which was based on the island from 1866 to 1920. It features a beautiful rose window designed by William Morris, and inward-facing pews.

You could spend hours poking around the **Bounty Folk Museum** on Middlegate Rd. Crammed with a motley display of historical memorabilia relating to the convict era, the *Bounty* mutineers and the island's early development as a free settlement, it's open from 10 am to 4 pm daily ($5/1).

If you don't make it into the national park, the 0.6ha **botanic gardens** offer a pleasant forest walk. The main entrance is on Mission Rd, where you'll also find an aviary housing the endangered Norfolk Island green parrot.

There's good **snorkelling** in Emily Bay, or you can go **diving** – the wreck of the HMS *Sirius* makes an interesting trip. Bounty Divers (☎ 22 751) has an excellent Web site at users.nf/bountydivers.

Organised Tours

Pinetree Tours (☎ 22 424), on Taylors Rd in Burnt Pine, has half-day introductory tours ($18) taking in all the major points of interest. Other tours include the Sound at Light Show ($18), which brings the convict settlement at Kingston to life, and the Island

---

Island Supplies

Norfolk Island has no real port, so the job of transporting goods from cargo freighters to the island falls on 'lighter boats', which are basically big wooden dinghies.

They transport everything from the freighters – from toilet paper to beer and even cars and buses. For large items, such as a bus, two lighter boats are tied together and the goods laid across them.

All this goes on at the Kingston or Cascade jetties, depending on the weather and tides, and it's fascinating to watch – but you'll need to adopt the island pace. With a crane the most modern technology in use, unloading one freighter can take several days.

Talking Norfolk

Visiting Norfolk Island can seem like a step back in time, and hearing the islanders engage in the curious native language only enhances this feeling. Brought by the Pitcairners in 1856 and still spoken among the descendants of the *Bounty* mutineers, the dialect is a mix of old north-country English and Polynesian, with a touch of Scottish thrown in (*ucklun*, meaning 'us', is derived from 'our clan').

Many of the words and phrases are easily recognisable as being a simplified, or pidgin, English, but when a local launches into Norfolk at full pace, you can forget about following it! Most of the time you'll hear plain English spoken, but some phrases you might hear include: *watawieh you?* (how are you)?; *kushu* (fine); *webout you gwen?* (where are you going?); *wha* (I beg your pardon); and *dars gude* (that's good).

Culture tour ($18). Bounty Excursions (☎ 23 693) offers similar tours in smaller groups.

Pitcairn Settlers Village (☎ 22 420), just off Queen Elizabeth Ave, offers three-hour tours ($15) through one of the island's early properties, established in 1877 by Pitcairner Emily Christian and her husband George Bailey.

Other options include around-island cruises and fishing charters, 4WD jaunts and a bewildering array of speciality tours – the visitor information centre has details.

Special Events

Bounty Day, on 8 June, is the island's major annual festival, celebrating the day the 194 Pitcairners arrived to settle on Norfolk in 1856. Locals dress up in period costume and re-enact the event at Kingston jetty. Foundation Day, on 6 March, marks the day Norfolk Island was first colonised in 1788.

Places to Stay

Accommodation is generally expensive, but most visitors come on package deals anyway and you must have a booking before arriving on the island. There are lots of places to choose from, ranging from guest-houses to large motel-style resorts. Basic but comfortable self-contained apartments such as *Pine Valley* and *Polynesian*, both on New Cascade Rd, are among the cheapest places; doubles cost from around $85.

Channer's Corner (☎ 22 532), Taylors Rd, has stylish apartments for $95 for two people.

Aunt Em's (☎ 22 373), Taylors Rd, is an old-style guesthouse with real character (the home was built in 1914) and it's right in the middle of Burnt Pine. B&B costs $65/110 for a single/double.

Islander Lodge (☎ 22 114, fax 23 014), Middlegate Rd, enjoys great views. Perched on a hillside, the five self-contained apartments have large front windows overlooking Kingston, and Emily and Slaughter Bays. The cost is $140 a night for two people.

Highlands Lodge (☎ 22 741), Selwyn Pine Rd, is a good place nestled on the hillside below the national park. Doubles start at $148.

Shearwater Millionaire's Hideaway (☎ 22539, fax 23359), at Point Ross, has comfortable cottages and a great location. Despite the name, you only need to come up with $220 a night for two people, or $100 for the studio apartment.

Places to Eat

There are dozens of restaurants and cafes offering everything from humble fish and chips to upmarket a la carte. Events such as the progressive dinner – a four-course meal with each course taken at the home of a local resident ($36) – and the island fish fry on the coast near Anson Bay ($24) are popular and worth doing. They can be booked through tour operators (see Organised Tours earlier in the Norfolk Island section for details of tour operators).

Tropicana Cafe, in Burnt Pine, opens for breakfast and does a good range of sandwiches, pies, milk shakes and hot drinks for lunch. *Cafe Pacifica*, in a plant nursery on Cutters Corn Rd, is a more upmarket place, with light lunches and salads.

The *Sports & Workers Club* on Taylors Rd has bistro meals for under $10, while the *Brewery Bar & Bistro*, on Douglas Dr

Lord Howe Island offers excellent bushwalking

Lagoon Beach below Mts Lidgbird and Gower

Fish feeding at Ned's Beach

Cycling near Mt Gower, Lord Howe Island

Surf's up at Blinky Beach

Norfolk Island pines

Convict buildings that housed prisoners during the 18th century

St Barnabas Chapel, built by the Melanesian Mission

Kingston cemetery

Anson Bay on Norfolk Island's rugged north coast

opposite the airport, has cheap counter meals (around $6) and brews its own beer. There are tours of the brewery at 2 pm on Thursday ($10).

Barney Duffy's, in Burnt Pine, is a popular steakhouse noted for its smoked spare ribs, while *Seaworld* nearby has good specials; try the $10 fish fry on Sunday night.

The unassuming *James' Place*, on New Cascade Rd, is one of the island's top little restaurants. Main courses on the innovative a la carte menu cost $16 to $20.

Entertainment

Tourism is inextricably linked with the island's history and the locals have capitalised on this – usually to good effect. Much of the evening entertainment consists of shows and cabarets such as the *Mutiny on the Bounty* show, staged in a purpose-built amphitheatre with replica ship (Tuesday and Thursday; $20). The *Trial of the Fifteen* is a clever play that traces the island's history by putting 15 characters on the courtroom stand. It's held in the Pier Store, Kingston, every Wednesday ($15).

Check with the visitor information centre or tour operators about other dinner tours and cultural nights.

Shopping

The tourist brochures rave about Norfolk Island's duty-free shopping and Burnt Pine boasts a string of well-stocked shops.

Everything is tax-free but nothing much is cheap – unless you're after an Armani figurine or a pair of Italian shoes you may be a little disappointed. Still, jewellery, perfume, designer clothes and toys can all be picked up cheaper than on the mainland.

Getting There & Away

Flightwest (☎ 1300 130 092) flies four times a week from Sydney ($1070 return, or $750 for a 14-day advance purchase) and Brisbane ($1050/736). Norfolk Jet Express (☎ 07 3221 6677) has three flights a week from Sydney, and a Saturday flight from Brisbane for the same fares.

Air New Zealand flies twice a week from Auckland (from NZ$629 return). Five-night packages (flight and accommodation) to Norfolk Island start at around $740 in winter and $900 in summer, but you'll need to shop around for these prices; see Travel Agencies in the Lord Howe Island section for contact details.

There's a departure tax of $25, payable at the airport.

Getting Around

You can hire a car at the airport for as little as $20 a day, plus insurance ($5). Petrol is expensive (just over $1 a litre), but you'll struggle to use much. Roaming cows have right of way on the island's roads, and there's a $300 fine for hitting one. The speed limit around most of the island is 50km/h.

LONELY PLANET

Guides by Region

onely Planet is known worldwide for publishing practical, reliable and no-nonsense travel information in our guides and on our Web site. The Lonely Planet list covers just about every accessible part of the world. Currently there are 15 series: travel guides, Shoestring guides, Condensed guides, Phrasebooks, Read This First, Healthy Travel, Walking guides, Cycling guides, Pisces Diving & Snorkeling guides, City Maps, Travel Atlases, Out to Eat, World Food, Journeys travel literature and Pictorials.

AFRICA Africa on a shoestring • Africa – the South • Arabic (Egyptian) phrasebook • Arabic (Moroccan) phrasebook • Cairo • Cape Town • Cape Town city map • Central Africa • East Africa • Egypt • Egypt travel atlas • Ethiopian (Amharic) phrasebook • The Gambia & Senegal • Healthy Travel Africa • Kenya • Kenya travel atlas • Malawi, Mozambique & Zambia • Morocco • North Africa • Read This First Africa • South Africa, Lesotho & Swaziland • South Africa, Lesotho & Swaziland travel atlas • Swahili phrasebook • Tanzania, Zanzibar & Pemba • Trekking in East Africa • Tunisia • West Africa • Zimbabwe, Botswana & Namibia • Zimbabwe, Botswana & Nambia Travel Atlas • World Food Morocco
Travel Literature: The Rainbird: A Central African Journey • Songs to an African Sunset: A Zimbabwean Story • Mali Blues: Traveling to an African Beat

AUSTRALIA & THE PACIFIC Auckland • Australia • Australian phrasebook • Bushwalking in Australia • Bushwalking in Papua New Guinea • Fiji • Fijian phrasebook • Healthy Travel Australia, NZ and the Pacific • Islands of Australia's Great Barrier Reef • Melbourne • Melbourne city map • Micronesia • New Caledonia • New South Wales & the ACT • New Zealand • Northern Territory • Outback Australia • Out to Eat – Melbourne • Out to Eat – Sydney • Papua New Guinea • Pidgin phrasebook • Queensland • Rarotonga & the Cook Islands • Samoa • Solomon Islands • South Australia • South Pacific • South Pacific Languages phrasebook • Sydney • Sydney city map • Sydney Condensed • Tahiti & French Polynesia • Tasmania • Tonga • Tramping in New Zealand • Vanuatu • Victoria • Western Australia
Travel Literature: Islands in the Clouds • Kiwi Tracks: A New Zealand Journey • Sean & David's Long Drive

CENTRAL AMERICA & THE CARIBBEAN Bahamas, Turks & Caicos • Bermuda • Central America on a shoestring • Costa Rica • Cuba • Dominican Republic & Haiti • Eastern Caribbean • Guatemala, Belize & Yucatán: La Ruta Maya • Jamaica • Mexico • Mexico City • Panama • Puerto Rico • Read This First Central & South America • World Food Mexico
Travel Literature: Green Dreams: Travels in Central America

EUROPE Amsterdam • Amsterdam city map • Andalucía • Austria • Baltic States phrasebook • Barcelona • Berlin • Berlin city map • Britain • British phrasebook • Brussels, Bruges & Antwerp • Budapest city map • Canary Islands • Central Europe • Central Europe phrasebook • Corfu & Ionians • Corsica • Crete • Crete Condensed • Croatia • Cyprus • Czech & Slovak Republics • Denmark • Dublin • Eastern Europe • Eastern Europe phrasebook • Edinburgh • Estonia, Latvia & Lithuania • Europe on a shoestring • Finland • Florence • France • French phrasebook • Germany • German phrasebook • Greece • Greek Islands • Greek phrasebook • Hungary • Iceland, Greenland & the Faroe Islands • Ireland • Italian phrasebook • Italy • Krakow • Lisbon • The Loire • London • London city map • London Condensed • Mediterranean Europe • Mediterranean Europe phrasebook • Munich • Norway • Paris • Paris city map • Paris Condensed • Poland • Portugal • Portugese phrasebook • Portugal travel atlas • Prague • Prague city map • Provence & the Côte d'Azur • Read This First Europe • Romania & Moldova • Rome • Russia, Ukraine & Belarus • Russian phrasebook • Scandinavian & Baltic Europe • Scandinavian Europe phrasebook • Scotland • Slovenia • Spain • Spanish phrasebook • St Petersburg • Sweden • Switzerland • Trekking in Spain • Tuscany • Ukrainian phrasebook • Venice • Vienna • Walking in Britain • Walking in Ireland • Walking in Italy • Walking in Spain • Walking in Switzerland • Western Europe • Western Europe phrasebook • World Food Ireland • World Food Italy • World Food Spain
Travel Literature: The Olive Grove: Travels in Greece

INDIAN SUBCONTINENT Bangladesh • Bengali phrasebook • Bhutan • Delhi • Goa • Hindi & Urdu phrasebook • India • India & Bangladesh travel atlas • Indian Himalaya • Karakoram Highway • Kerala • Mumbai (Bombay) • Nepal • Nepali phrasebook • Pakistan • Rajasthan • Read This First: Asia & India • South India • Sri Lanka • Sri Lanka phrasebook • Tibet • Tibetan phrasebook • Trekking in the Indian Himalaya • Trekking in the Karakoram & Hindukush • Trekking in the Nepal Himalaya
Travel Literature: In Rajasthan • Shopping for Buddhas • The Age Of Kali

LONELY PLANET

Mail Order

Lonely Planet products are distributed worldwide.They are also available by mail order from Lonely Planet, so if you have difficulty finding a title please write to us. North and South American residents should write to 150 Linden St, Oakland CA 94607, USA; European and African residents should write to 10a Spring Place, London, NW5 3BH, UK; and residents of other countries to Locked Bag 1, Footscray, Victoria 3011, Australia.

ISLANDS OF THE INDIAN OCEAN Madagascar & Comoros • Maldives • Mauritius, Réunion & Seychelles

MIDDLE EAST & CENTRAL ASIA Bahrain, Kuwait & Qatar • Central Asia • Central Asia phrasebook • Dubai • Hebrew phrasebook • Iran • Israel & the Palestinian Territories • Israel & the Palestinian Territories travel atlas • Istanbul • Istanbul City Map • Istanbul to Cairo on a shoestring • Jerusalem • Jerusalem City Map • Jordan • Jordan, Syria & Lebanon travel atlas • Lebanon • Middle East • Oman & the United Arab Emirates • Syria • Turkey • Turkey travel atlas • Turkish phrasebook • World Food Turkey • Yemen
Travel Literature: The Gates of Damascus • Kingdom of the Film Stars: Journey into Jordan • Black on Black: Iran Revisited

NORTH AMERICA Alaska • Backpacking in Alaska • Baja California • California & Nevada • California Condensed • Canada • Chicago • Chicago city map • Deep South • Florida • Hawaii • Honolulu • Las Vegas • Los Angeles • Miami • New England • New Orleans • New York City • New York city map • New York Condensed • New York, New Jersey & Pennsylvania • Oahu • Pacific Northwest USA • Puerto Rico • Rocky Mountain • San Francisco • San Francisco city map • Seattle • Southwest USA • Texas • USA • USA phrasebook • Vancouver • Washington, DC & the Capital Region • Washington DC city map
Travel Literature: Drive Thru America

NORTH-EAST ASIA Beijing • Cantonese phrasebook • China • Hong Kong • Hong Kong city map • Hong Kong, Macau & Guangzhou • Japan • Japanese phrasebook • Japanese audio pack • Korea • Korean phrasebook • Kyoto • Mandarin phrasebook • Mongolia • Mongolian phrasebook • Seoul • South-West China • Taiwan • Tokyo
Travel Literature: Lost Japan • In Xanadu

SOUTH AMERICA Argentina, Uruguay & Paraguay • Bolivia • Brazil • Brazilian phrasebook • Buenos Aires • Chile & Easter Island • Chile & Easter Island travel atlas • Colombia • Ecuador & the Galapagos Islands • Healthy Travel Central & South America • Latin American Spanish phrasebook • Peru • Quechua phrasebook • Rio de Janeiro • Rio de Janeiro city map • South America on a shoestring • Trekking in the Patagonian Andes • Venezuela
Travel Literature: Full Circle: A South American Journey

SOUTH-EAST ASIA Bali & Lombok • Bangkok • Bangkok city map • Burmese phrasebook • Cambodia • Hanoi • Healthy Travel Asia & India • Hill Tribes phrasebook • Ho Chi Minh City • Indonesia • Indonesia's Eastern Islands • Indonesian phrasebook • Indonesian audio pack • Jakarta • Java • Laos • Lao phrasebook • Laos travel atlas • Malay phrasebook • Malaysia, Singapore & Brunei • Myanmar (Burma) • Philippines • Pilipino (Tagalog) phrasebook • Read This First Asia & India • Singapore • South-East Asia on a shoestring • South-East Asia phrasebook • Thailand • Thailand's Islands & Beaches • Thailand travel atlas • Thai phrasebook • Thai audio pack • Vietnam • Vietnamese phrasebook • Vietnam travel atlas • World Food Thailand • World Food Vietnam

---

ALSO AVAILABLE: Antarctica • The Arctic • Brief Encounters: Stories of Love, Sex & Travel • Chasing Rickshaws • Lonely Planet Unpacked • Not the Only Planet: Travel Stories from Science Fiction • Sacred India • Travel with Children • Traveller's Tales

LONELY PLANET

You already know that Lonely Planet produces more than this one guidebook, but you might not be aware of the other products we have on this region. Here is a selection of titles that you may want to check out as well:

Australia
ISBN 1 86450 068 9
US$24.95 • UK£14.99 • 180FF

Australian phrasebook
ISBN 0 86442 576 7
US$5.95 • UK£3.99 • 40FF

Outback Australia
ISBN 0 86442 504 X
US$21.95 • UK£13.99 • 170FF

Sydney
ISBN 0 86442 724 7
US$15.95 • UK£9.99 • 120FF

Out to Eat - Sydney
ISBN 1 86450 141 3
US$14.99 • UK£9.99 • 99FF

Cycling Australia
ISBN 1 86450 166 9
US$21.99 • UK£13.99 • 169FF

Healthy Travel Australia, NZ & the Pacific
ISBN 1 86450 052 2
US$5.95 • UK£3.99 • 39FF

Sydney City Map
ISBN 1 86450 015 8
US$5.95 • UK£3.99 • 39FF

Australia Road Atlas
ISBN 1 86450 065 4
US$14.99 • UK£8.99 • 109FF

Sydney Condensed
ISBN 1 86450 045 X
US$9.95 • UK£5.99 • 59FF

Walking in Australia
ISBN 0 86442 669 0
US$21.99 • UK£13.99 • 169FF

Available wherever books are sold

Index

Text

Bold indicates maps.

Bold indicates maps.

Bold indicates maps.

Bold indicates maps.

Boxed Text

MAP LEGEND

CITY ROUTES

Freeway .... Freeway	= = = = ... Unsealed Road
Highway ...... Primary Road	===== :.... One-Way Street
Road ...... Secondary Road	.... Pedestrian Street
Street .... Street	⊏⊐⊏⊐⊏⊐ ...... Stepped Street
Lane .... Lane	⟩= = = ... Tunnel
.... On/Off Ramp	.... Footbridge

HYDROGRAPHY

.... River; Creek
.... Lake
.... Dry Lake; Salt Lake
...... Spring; Rapids
.... Waterfalls

AREA FEATURES

.... Building
⊕ .... Park; Garden
.... Market
.... Sports Ground
.... Beach
+ + + ... Cemetery

TRANSPORT ROUTES & STATIONS

⊢—⊦—●— .... Train	– – – – – ...... Walking Trail
⊢ + + + -. Underground Train	• • • • • ...... Walking Tour
⊩—⊩—⊩—⊩. Cable Car; Chairlift	.... Path
– – – – –◻ .... Ferry	.... Pier; Jetty

BOUNDARIES

▬ ▬ ▬ .... International
▬ ▬ ▬ ▬ .... State

REGIONAL ROUTES

.... Tollway; Freeway
.... Primary Road
.... Secondary Road
.... Minor Road

POPULATION SYMBOLS

✪ **CAPITAL** .... National Capital	● **CITY** .... City	● Village .... Village
◉ **CAPITAL** .... State Capital	● Town .... Town	.... Urban Area

MAP SYMBOLS

▮ .... Place to Stay	▼ .... Place to Eat	● .... Point of Interest

⊞ .... Airfield	⌂ .... Cave	⚰ .... Monument	⚐ .... Ski Field
⊠ .... Airport	⊞ .... Cinema	▲ .... Mountain	⊠ ...... Swimming Pool
⊝ .... Bank	⊗ .... Cycling Path	⎕ .... Museum; Gallery	⚓ .... Surf
➚ .... Beach	⊡ .... Embassy	⊡ ...... National Park	⊡ .... Taxi
⊡ .... Bus Station	⊕ .... Golf Course	⎕ .... Parking	⊡ .... Telephone
⊟ .... Bus Stop	⊕ .... Hospital	⊗ .... Picnic	⊟ .... Theatre
⊠ .... Camping Ground	⊡ .... Internet Cafe	⊡ ...... Police Station	⊙ .... Toilet
⊡ .... Caravan Park	⚘ .... Lighthouse	⊡ .... Post Office	⊙ .. Tourist Information
⊡ ⊡ .. Cathedral; Church	※ .... Lookout	⊡ .. Pub; Bar; Nightclub	⊞ .... Winery
		⊗ ..... Shopping Centre	⊡ .... Zoo

Note: Not all symbols displayed above appear in this book

LONELY PLANET OFFICES

Australia
Locked Bag 1, Footscray, Victoria 3011
☎ 03 9689 4666 fax 03 9689 6833
email: talk2us@lonelyplanet.com.au

UK
10a Spring Place, London NW5 3BH
☎ 020 7428 4800 fax 020 7428 4828
email: go@lonelyplanet.co.uk

USA
150 Linden St, Oakland, CA 94607
☎ 510 893 8555 TOLL FREE: 800 275 8555
fax 510 893 8572
email: info@lonelyplanet.com

France
1 rue du Dahomey, 75011 Paris
☎ 01 55 25 33 00 fax 01 55 25 33 01
email: bip@lonelyplanet.fr
www.lonelyplanet.fr

World Wide Web: www.lonelyplanet.com *or* AOL keyword: lp
Lonely Planet Images: lpi@lonelyplanet.com.au